De Gruyter Handbook of Responsible Project Management

De Gruyter Handbooks in Business, Economics and Finance

—

De Gruyter Handbook of Responsible Project Management

Edited by
Beverly Pasian and Nigel Williams

DE GRUYTER

ISBN 978-3-11-161991-0
e-ISBN (PDF) 978-3-11-072478-3
e-ISBN (EPUB) 978-3-11-072482-0
ISSN 2748-016X
e-ISSN 2748-0178

Library of Congress Control Number: 2022938348

Bibliographic information published by the Deutsche Nationalbibliothek
The Deutsche Nationalbibliothek lists this publication in the Deutsche Nationalbibliografie;
detailed bibliographic data are available on the internet at http://dnb.dnb.de.

www.degruyter.com

De Gruyter Handbooks in Business, Economics and Finance

De Gruyter Handbook of Personal Finance
 Edited by: John E. Grable and Swarn Chatterjee

De Gruyter Handbook of Entrepreneurial Finance
 Edited by: David Lingelbach

De Gruyter Handbook of Organizational Conflict Management
 Edited by: LaVena Wilkin and Yashwant Pathak

De Gruyter Handbook of Sustainable Development and Finance
 Edited by: Timothy Cadman and Tapan Sarker

For more information, scan QR code below or visit https://www.degruyter.com/serial/dghbef-b/html

Contents

Herbert Daly, Nicole Ferdinand, Karen Thompson, and Nigel Williams

Contributors

Loredana Abramo is a global citizen, who has lived and worked in several locations, across four continents. After receiving her doctorate in electrical engineering, she started her career developing and delivering large national telecommunications networks in Europe, Asia, and Australia, alternating customer delivery leadership roles, business development, service readiness, and program management in the corporate program office with AT&T Bell Labs, Lucent Technologies, Alcatel-Lucent, and Nokia. Loredana is an adjunct professor at Boston University Metropolitan College, where she focuses on project, program, and portfolio management courses and maintains multiple memberships in professional societies.

Ghasan Hamed Almaamari has a PhD in project management from Bournemouth University. Ghasan is the founder of Zawad Development and Consultancy and specializes in PM and tourism development in Oman. His research interests are in project management, sustainable tourism, and tourism's impact on culture.

Darren Dalcher is a professor in strategic project management at Lancaster University Management School, and Visiting International Scholar at InnoLab, University of Vaasa. He is the founder and director of the National Centre for Project Management, an interdisciplinary center of excellence operating in collaboration with industry, government, academia, third-sector organizations, and the learned societies. He is editor-in-chief of the *Journal of Software: Evolution and Process*, published by Wiley and editor of the *Routledge Frontiers in Project Management* series of research books. His research focuses on rethinking project success and repositioning the concept of agility, especially in the context of strategy, sustainability, and innovation, as well as engaging with the impact of morality, complexity, and reflective practice.

Herbert Daly is a senior lecturer in the Department of Computer Science at the University of Wolverhampton. He holds a Bachelor of Science in computer science, a Master of Science in software engineering, and is a Doctor of Philosophy in multi-method modeling. His research interests include enterprise systems, digital transformation, and project management for emerging technologies such as AI and quantum computing.

Ganesh Devkar is an associate professor at the CEPT University, Ahmedabad, India. He holds a doctorate in construction management from Indian Institute of Technology Madras (IIT Madras). His doctoral work focuses on competencies in urban local bodies for implementing water, sanitation, and solid waste management public private partnership (PPP) projects in India. Ganesh teaches construction quality and safety management, project appraisal, lean construction, and public private partnerships. He has been researching in the areas of public private partnerships, lean construction, and megaprojects. He has participated in four systematic reviews focusing on delivery of infrastructure like water supply, sanitation, hygiene, telecom, electricity, and transport. He received the "Young Research Scholar Award" from Project Management Institute, India.

Nicole Ferdinand is program lead, post-graduate programs at the Oxford School of Hospitality Management, Oxford Brookes University. She regularly publishes in the areas of tourism, culture, events, and project management. She holds a PhD in culture, media, and creative industries from King's College, London, as well as an MSc in marketing and BA in English from the University of the West Indies, St. Augustine.

https://doi.org/10.1515/9783110724783-203

Leticia Fuentes-Ardeo is a telecommunication engineer (2006) from the University of Deusto (UD); she has complementary formation as project management master, innovation and knowledge management master, and information technology master, and is a PhD student at the University of the Basque Country. She is a project manager with more than 15 years of experience coordinating innovative and multimedia projects and she has worked on European projects leading different work packages. Leticia is developing her PhD student career focused on the integration of sustainability in project management.

Bandara Gamlath is a senior lecturer in the Department of Finance and Accountancy, Faculty of Business Studies, University of Vavuniya, Sri Lanka. He received his MPhil degree in management (finance) from the University of Jaffna, Sri Lanka, a postgraduate diploma in industrial and business management from the University of Kelaniya and his BSc special degree in financial management from the Sabaragamuwa University of Sri Lanka. His research includes capital market development, capital structure, development finance, entrepreneurship, financial management, human resource management, project governance, and tourism management. He has published research papers in ACADEMICIA – the *International Multidisciplinary Research Journal*, *Journal of Business Studies*, *Journal of Management Matters*, *Journal of Management and Tourism Research*, *Sabaragamuwa University Journal*, *Sri Lankan Journal of Banking and Finance*, and *SJCC Management Review*. He is a fellow member of the Association of Public Finance Accountants of Sri Lanka (APFASL), the public sector wing of the Institute of Chartered Accountants of Sri Lanka, and an academic member of the Sri Lanka Finance Association.

John Lannon has been a consultant and researcher with a range of international development and human rights organizations, primarily in the area of information management and technology use. Prior to becoming Doras CEO, he worked at the Kemmy Business School at the University of Limerick, where his primary areas of interest were project and program management, organized responses to social inequality, and using social media to achieve social good. He has been a human rights activist and campaigner for over 20 years, and has been involved in a range of social justice campaigns during that time. He has also previously served as chairperson of the Board of Doras. John holds a bachelor's degree in engineering, an MA in peace and development studies, and a PhD in the area of human rights information management.

José Ricardo López-Robles received a bachelor's degree in industrial engineering from the Monterrey Institute of Technology and Higher Education (Mexico, 2007), master's degree in project management from the University of the Basque Country (Spain, 2010), master's degree in business administration from the ENEB Business School (Spain, 2017) and PhD in engineering from the University of the Basque Country. He is the recipient of the Ibero-American Award "Veta de Plata 2016" in the category "Science and Technology" and he has published over 15 scientific articles in journals and books. Finally, he is collaborating professor of the unit accounting and management at the Autonomous University of Zacatecas (Mexico).

Rich Maltzman, PMP, is master lecturer at Boston University. He is an author, consultant, and speaker, focused on a suite of courses, laboratories, and workshops on project leadership. Rich has four decades of experience in technical project management. He has been a researcher and international speaker on the intersection of project management and sustainability, coauthoring several books (including *Green Project Management*, a PMI Cleland Award-winner) with an objective to integrate long-term thinking into the mindset of project leaders. As a member of the editorial board for the new *PMBOK® Guide*, seventh edition and *Standard for Project Management*, Rich and others have successfully built these principles into project management standards and practices, although there is much more to be done.

Luigi Morsa has a PhD in Aerospace Engineering and is a project manager working for the consultant company SII Germany Engineering and IT. Luigi's passion for project management has led to several publications including three books by Dr. Harold Kerzner, the pioneer and globally recognized expert in project management. Luigi wrote three case studies about the aircraft industry for *Project Management Case Studies*, fifth and sixth editions (Wiley, 2017, 2022), and two sections and the chapter "Innovation Management Software" for *Innovation Project Management* (Wiley, 2019). As a frequent international speaker, his focus is on the complexity of the aircraft industry market, with particular emphasis on the relationship between product and customer needs. He is also contributor for the blog of the International Institute of Learning based in NY.

Alexia Nalewaik has over 30 years of experience in project audit, estimating, cost/risk management, and governance. She is a fellow of RICS Americas, AACE International, the Guild of Project Controls, and ICEC. Alexia is a member of the governing council for the RICS, representing the US Market Seat, and is also a past president of AACE International, and past chair of the International Cost Engineering Council. She has published two books, on performance audit and reporting.

Yogarajah Nanthagopan is the present dean and senior academic in project management at the Faculty of Business Studies, University of Vavuniya, Sri Lanka. Nanthagopan is the founder and the first coordinator of the project management (PM) degree program at the Faculty of Business Studies. Nanthagopan has 18 years of experience in teaching and consulting in Business and Project Management. His research interests include project management, organizational development, and strategic management.

Vladimir Obradović is a professor at University of Belgrade and visiting professor of two other universities. He is editor in chief of *European Project Management Journal*, and editorial board member of several top-tier international scientific journals. Vladimir is an author and the editor of many publications in the field of project management, with a special research interest in sustainability, project society, and resilience. He is a member of several research bodies at International Project Management Association.

José Ramón Otegi-Olaso is an industrial engineer and doctor in project management (2005) from the University of the Basque Country. Since 2001, he has been teaching project management at the Bilbao Faculty of Engineering. He is responsible for the master's degree in project management at the same university. He combines teaching with consultancy projects in project management. He frequently acts as an external expert in public programs for the evaluation of research and technological development projects. His current lines of research focus on project management and sustainability.

Beverly Pasian studies how projects contribute to quality-of-life in 'smart' cities. One of the best decisions of her professional life was to complete a second PhD and redirect her project management research career toward one with greater social impact. And using her decades of teaching, education and publications experience, she is eager to work with companies and universities to navigate the opportunities for projects and project managers in future urban planning. Despite the certainty of future environmental challenges, planners of smart cities use projects for social innovation that could maximise our chances of overcoming them. What is more responsible than that?

Shankar Sankaran is a professor of organizational project management at the University of Technology, Sydney, Australia. He has published books, book chapters, and journal articles on project leadership. He also led projects and operations in industry as a project director and technical director. He has edited books and written book chapters including *Megaproject Leaders: Reflections on Personal Life Stories* and *Balanced Leadership: Making the Best Use of Personal and Team Leadership in Projects* and won an IPMA award for research excellence conducting research on project leadership.

Shirley Thompson is a member of the Responsible Project Management team. She pursues the idea of responsible conversation which seeks to establish shared intentions and boundaries ahead of conversation. As a professional coach and coach supervisor, Shirley seeks to help technical leaders and coaches to develop their skills. Her research interest is in empowerment for the individual and in relation to the intentions for relationships. She received her doctorate in coaching and mentoring from Oxford Brookes University in 2019 which supported her desire to introduce project managers to the art of soft skills after being a project manager in software development at IBM until 2005. She now runs a small coaching practice and is an active volunteer.

Karen Thompson is a senior academic and member of the Environment and Threats Strategic Research Group at Bournemouth University and a fellow of Advance HE. She designed and now leads the MSc organizational project management program. Her research has examined stakeholder engagement and use of social media for project communication using organizational development and sustainable development concepts. Her early career was in information systems and technology, leading projects and strategy development in local government, financial services, and the voluntary sector.

Marija Todorović is a professor at the faculty of organizational sciences, University of Belgrade. Team leader of the research management team within International Project Management Association, Marija has published a number of papers in the field of project management. Her research interest is oriented to strategy and project diversity. Marija is editorial board member of several scientific journals, and member of several professional associations.

Rodney Turner is now retired. He is a visiting professor at the University of Leeds and an honorary professor at the University of Warwick. Most recently, he was a professor of project management at SKEMA Business School in Lille, France. He was scientific director for the PhD in project and program management, SAIPEM professor of Project Management at the Politecnico di Milano, and professor and high-end foreign expert at Shanghai University. Rodney is the author or editor of 18 books, including *The Handbook of Project-based Management*, the best-selling book published by McGraw-Hill, and the *Gower Handbook of Project Management*. He was editor of *The International Journal of Project Management* for 25 years until 2017. His current research interests cover the relationship between governance and decision making on projects, stakeholders and customer experience, and the relationship between megaprojects and post-modernism. Rodney is vice president, honorary fellow and former chairman of the UK's Association for Project Management, and honorary fellow and former president and chairman of the International Project Management Association. In 2004, he received a lifetime research achievement award from the Project Management Institute, and in 2012, from the International Project Management Association.

Greg Usher is the executive general manager for RPS Buildings and Property. He has almost 20 years' experience in construction and project management. He has published a number of peer-reviewed articles, presented his research Internationally, and recently published his latest book

Project Management in the 21st Century: What You Need to Know About the Elephant, Eco-system and Experience which challenges the foundations and traditional methods of project management. He is an adjunct research fellow at University of Southern Queensland, a fellow of Australian Institute of Project Management, chair of the AIPM Industry Leaders Group and holds board positions with Housing All Australians. He is passionate about the role project management can play in delivering social, economic, and environmental value for the global community.

Ramesh Vahidi is a senior academic at Southampton Business School, leading the MSc in project management (PM) she designed in 2012. She studied industrial engineering (BEng and MEng) and project management (MSc and PhD) in Iran, Sweden, and the UK. She has held senior analyst, consultant, and project manager roles in national programs within IT, power generation, management systems design companies. Working closely with PM professional bodies, she has been contributing as branch committee member, CDP trainer, and judge. She has widely presented in conferences on responsible PM education and decision making/tradeoffs. Ramesh was the coinvestigator and coauthor of the book *Responsible Leadership in Projects: Insights into Ethical Decision Making* (sponsored and published by PMI).

Krishanthi Vithana (Krish) is an associate professor in accounting in the School of Business at the University of Southampton. Her main research focuses on accounting for human capital resource in organizational context. She has published her research in reputed academic journals including, *Journal of Business Ethics*, *Accounting Forum*, and *The International Journal of Human Resource Management*. Krish has been the principal investigator for several ESRC IAA funded research projects and has actively engaged with industry partners including the Global Responsible Investment team of Aviva Investors, Living Wage Foundation, and Platform Living Wage Financials.

Reinhard Wagner has more than 35 years of project and leadership experience in business, public service, and non-profit organizations. Based on this experience, he supports as managing director of Tiba Managementberatung GmbH and, in volunteer roles, numerous organizations in professionalizing their project management. He has published more than 40 textbooks and successfully completed his doctoral thesis on the projectification of society at the Alma Mater Europaea in Maribor.

Nigel Williams is cofounder of Responsible Project Management, PMP, reader in Project Management, and research lead in the Organizations and Systems Management Subject Group at the University of Portsmouth. His PhD is in engineering from the University of Cambridge. Nigel's research has examined stakeholder interactions using social network analysis, project capacity of organizations in post conflict countries, responsibility in project research, and the evolution of project capabilities in organizations. Before joining academia, he worked as a manager and business consultant for enterprises in the Caribbean.

Beverly Pasian and Nigel Williams

Introduction

More than 30 years ago, the idea of responsible project management was introduced by Laszlo (1991), who commented on the "unique role and great responsibility" that project managers have to help organizations meet global problems. Peter
Morris, years later, made multiple entreaties as he tried to raise our awareness to
the scales and complexities of the twenty-first century (Morris, 2012). He challenged
us to move beyond scope, budget, and timeliness and focus on the impact of our
work as humankind faces the inevitable threat of climate change. Of course, those
urgent challenges can also be unexpected as we have all seen during the Covid pandemic and upheaval in Ukraine.

While progress has been slow, project managers are increasingly embracing
their responsibility beyond value creation for their project stakeholders. These arguments can be seen with the earlier agile movement that popularized customer value
concepts in project management and is now being extended to examine societal
value (Nalewaik & Williams, 2021). For project managers, responsibility also requires direct engagement with systems that exhibit multidimensional complexity
and nonlinearity. These issues are not easily reducible to a unitary objective function such as cost, time, or quality that can then be managed using numerical metrics (Schaltegger et al., 2019).

This perspective is advanced in other professions, and the debate about the nature
and extent of the responsibility of organizational managers, shareholders, and stakeholders has been a prominent subject in management research for some time. From an
organizational perspective, responsibility has been defined as the strategies and processes employed by organizations to address obligations to society and stakeholders.
In this definition, improving responsibility requires the reduction of information asymmetries via approaches such as life cycle assessment or GRI (Global Reporting Initiative) accounting tools along with philosophies such as the triple bottom line (Hasan
et al., 2019). Organizational responsibility can also be considered an intuitional character evidenced by a visible institutional commitment to humanistic values beyond financial performance (Adler & Laasch, 2020).

Responsible management extends these discussions by shifting the focus from
the organization to managers' beliefs, behaviors, and practices (Carroll et al., 2020).
Responsible management seeks to explicitly address various stakeholders' different
types of responsibilities by modeling managers as active participants embedded in
organizational, community, and country contexts. Integrating these definitions implies a perspective of managers who take ownership of environmental sustainability and social responsibility and enact them in their daily practice (Laasch &
Conaway, 2014). This perspective raises questions of managerial agency (what is
our role and scope of action), the nature of responsibility managed (when should

https://doi.org/10.1515/9783110724783-001

we act?), and the extent of managerial responsibility (to whom are we responsible/ where are we responsible) (Laasch, 2018).

In this way, responsible management is differentiated from corporate social responsibility (CSR), which is focused on organizational level representations and processes of enacting societal and community responsibility. This scenario has implicit tension as organizational conceptualizations, and delegated agency may clash with individuals' perceptions of responsibility. In addition to the shift in the level of analysis, responsible management examines the actions of managers (e.g., project managers) who may not have formally delegated organizational accountability and authority for CSR and ethics as part of their roles.

In project management, researchers and professional associations have debated the nature of the responsibility of project managers. The Association for Project Management(apm.org.uk) identified political responsibility (understanding of the environment or context of the project), intellectual responsibility (understanding and adapting practice), and moral responsibility (understanding the difference between right and wrong). Others have differentiated between responsibility and accountability. In one conceptualization, responsibility is an obligation to perform a task (McGrath & Whitty, 2018) which becomes accountability when subject to sanctions. Others have gone more broadly to define responsibility as all obligations, tasks, and others that may or may not be subjected to rewards or penalties (Zwikael & Meredith, 2018). While implicit in these definitions is that PMs may seek to redefine their roles to incorporate responsible management dimensions independent of the organizational context, this area has not been explored in PM (project management).

Several well-publicized organizational scandals renewed interest in the actions and roles of managers (Mena et al., 2016). Organizations and institutions created frameworks that sought to prevent these scandals. These principle-based initiatives identify values that stakeholders can use to initiate responsible management actions (Rasche & Waddock, 2017). They include reporting initiatives such as GRI (2002), disclosure schemes around issues such as modern slavery, and the UN's *Sustainable Development Goals* (SDGs). Organizations can also express topical issues like climate change, such as *Project Managers Declare* (UK. Projectmanagersdeclare.com).

Managers may have distinct roles in ethics, sustainability, and social responsibility that their host organization has formally ascribed to them. Managers may also integrate these dimensions into their conventional roles, say, project managers (Carollo & Guerci, 2018). Managers are also embedded in group and team settings which may be ascribed dimensions of responsibility to enact (e.g., sustainability improvement) or co-construct agency for responsible actions.

Organizations may be both enablers and constraints to responsible actions. As expressed by norms, communications, affiliations, and visible commitment to frameworks such as the SDGs, organization values can frame team and individual action. This is not a one-way relationship, as managers can encourage adopting innovative practices and frameworks that can include sustainability (Ernst et al., 2016). Individual practices can, directly and indirectly, influence group activities and encourage the adoption of responsibility at the societal level. The reverse can also occur as changing societal norms can encourage professional and organizational changes that influence daily practices.

Beyond the organization, the profession determines the types of activities that are considered to be within a given manager's scope of action and responsibility. The profession can respond to changing societal expectations of value which is an emergent property from the interaction between societal stakeholders, project processes, and project outputs. This is a multidimensional outcome that combines subjective (perceptions and experiences of stakeholders) and objective aspects (measurable project outputs) (Hall, 1961). In this view, PMs can create and destroy value by prioritizing one group of stakeholders (e.g., sponsors) over another (the community). Value can be destroyed by adopting wasteful project practices or created by generating social and economic benefits for communities.

In this book, our authors explore these perspectives using various country contexts, including the global south, industries, and project types, including emerging domains such as blockchain and non-fungible tokens.

While responsible management focuses on the individual, there is a need to acknowledge the domains and dimensions of interactions of the manager that influence the scope of action and managerial agency (Laasch et al., 2020). The former incorporates a range of scales that may begin with the individual daily practice domain of the manager, the professional practice domain, and finally, society. For dimensions,

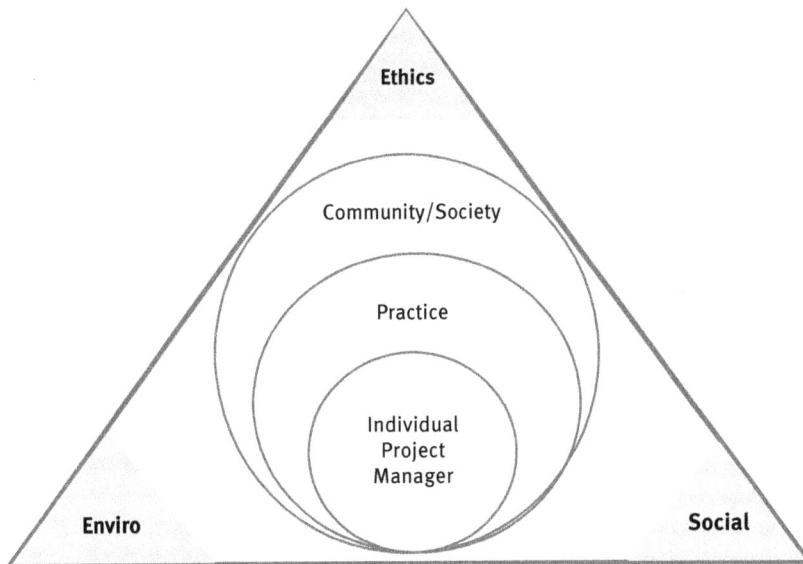

Figure 1: Dimensions affecting project manager roles.

responsible management research examines manager norms and practices in environmental sustainability, ethics, and social responsibility (Laasch & Conaway, 2014). These dimensions and domains influence managers' roles (Figure 1) and, ultimately, the impact of their work on meeting the challenges communities face worldwide. This book is one step in providing insight and guidance on how that is possible.

References and Further Reading

Abrams, F. W. (1951). Management's responsibilities in a complex world. *Harvard Business Review, 29*(3), 29–34.

Adler, N. J., & Laasch, O. (2020). Responsible leadership and management: Key distinctions and shared concerns. In *Research Handbook of Responsible Management*. Edward Elgar Publishing.

Carollo, L., & Guerci, M. (2018). 'Activists in a suit': Paradoxes and metaphors in sustainability managers' identity work. *Journal of Business Ethics, 148*(2), 249–268.

Carroll, A. B., Adler, N. J., Mintzberg, H., Cooren, F., Suddaby, R., Freeman, R. E., & Laasch, O. (2020). What is responsible management? A conceptual potluck. In *Research Handbook of Responsible Management*. https://www.e-elgar.com/shop/usd/research-handbook-of-responsible-management-9781788971959.html

Dam, L., & Petkova, B. N. (2014). The impact of environmental supply chain sustainability programs on shareholder wealth. *International Journal of Operations and Production Management, 34*(5), 586–609. https://doi.org/10.1108/IJOPM-10-2012-0482

Ernst, L., de Graaf-Van Dinther, R. E., Peek, G. J., & Loorbach, D. A. (2016). Sustainable urban transformation and sustainability transitions; conceptual framework and case study. *Journal of Cleaner Production, 112*, 2988–2999.

Friedman, M. (1970). A Friedman doctrine: The social responsibility of business is to increase its profits. *The New York Times Magazine, 13*(1970), 32–33.

GRI, G. R. I. (2002). Global reporting initiative. *Sustainability Reporting Guidelines*. https://www.r3-0.org/wp-content/uploads/2020/03/GRIguidelines.pdf

Hall, E. W. (1961). *Our Knowledge of Fact and Value*. Everett W. Hall Chapel Hill, University of North Carolina Press (1961)

Hasan, U., Whyte, A., & Al Jassmi, H. (2019). Critical review and methodological issues in integrated life-cycle analysis on road networks. *Journal of Cleaner Production, 206*, 541–558. https://doi.org/10.1016/j.jclepro.2018.09.148

Karakhan, A. A., Gambatese, J., & Simmons, D. R. (2020). Development of assessment tool for workforce sustainability. *Journal of Construction Engineering and Management, 146*(4), 04020017.

Laasch, O. (2018). Just old wine in new bottles? Conceptual shifts in the emerging field of responsible management. *Centre for Responsible Management Education Working Papers, 4*(1).

Laasch, O., & Conaway, R. (2014). *Principles of Responsible Management: Glocal Sustainability, Responsibility, and Ethics*. Nelson Education. Cengage.

Laasch, O., Suddaby, R., Freeman, R. E., & Jamali, D. (2020). Mapping the emerging field of responsible management: Domains, spheres, themes, and future research. In O. Laasch, R., Suddaby, Freeman, R. E. & D. Jamali (Eds.), *The Research Handbook of Responsible Management*. Cheltenham: Edward Elgar

Laszlo, E. (1991). Responsible (project) management in an unstable world. *International Journal of Project Management, 9*(2), 68–70. https://doi.org/10.1016/0263-7863(91)90061-Y

McGrath, S. K., & Whitty, S. J. (2018). Accountability and responsibility defined. *International Journal of Managing Projects in Business*, 11 (3). pp. 687–707. ISSN 1753-8378

Mena, S., Rintamäki, J., Fleming, P., & Spicer, A. (2016). On the forgetting of corporate irresponsibility. *Academy of Management Review, 41*(4), 720–738.

Morris, P. W. G. (2012). Cleland and king: Project management and the systems approach. *International Journal of Managing Projects in Business, 5*(4), 634–642. https://doi.org/10. 1108/17538371211268951

Morris, P. W. G. (2013). Reconstructing project management reprised: A knowledge perspective. *Project Management Journal, 44*(5), 6–23. https://doi.org/10.1002/pmj.21369

Nalewaik, A., & Williams, N. (2021, March). Emergent and unexpected sources of value from radio astronomy projects. In 2021 IEEE European Technology and Engineering Management Summit (E-TEMS) (pp. 59–64). IEEE.

Rasche, A., & Waddock, S. (2017). Standards for CSR: Legitimacy, impact and critique. In A. Rasche, M. Morsing, & J. Moon (Eds.), *In Corporate Social Responsibility: Strategy, Communication, Governance* (pp. 163–187). Cambridge University Press.

Schaltegger, S., Hörisch, J., & Freeman, R. E. (2019). Business cases for sustainability: A stakeholder theory perspective. *Organization & Environment, 32*(3), 191–212.

Zwikael, O., & Meredith, J. R. (2018). Who's who in the project zoo? The ten core project roles. *International Journal of Operations & Production Management*. 38. 10.1108/IJOPM-05-2017-0274. https://www.researchgate.net/publication/322777375_Who%27s_who_in_the_project_zoo_The_ten_core_project_roles

Section 1: **Responsible Individuals**

The term "responsible project management" was first used more than 3 decades ago (Laszlo, 1991), and in the following decades, authors have examined the need for project management to create societal value ethically. Subsequent authors have examined the direct environmental impact of carbon emissions and material waste generated. Project management researchers have also examined the social impacts of projects by creating new systems and processes that change community interactions.

The debate about the nature and extent of the responsibility of professionals has been long established in the organizational academic literature (Laasch, 2018). Most of this work focuses on *Corporate Social Responsibility* as enterprises seek to meet their changing obligations to shareholders and stakeholders. As part of this process, organizations will develop roles in social sustainability, environmental sustainability, and ethics to realize these responsibilities. More recently, an individual's perspective on responsibility examines the activities of nonspecialized managers who take ownership of environmental sustainability and social responsibility and enact them in their daily practice (Laasch & Conaway, 2015).

This section begins this book because we wanted to differentiate the work of our contributors from the other types of published PM research. PM rarely spends time in introspection to examine the deeper motivations for actions. The leading chapter "Morality and Spirituality" is perhaps the most challenging contribution in the book. Darren asks us to examine ourselves with difficult questions about the nature and extent of responsibility for project managers. This issue requires project managers to reflect on morality and consider the principles that would be encompassed within these spaces with multiple stakeholders with different perspectives.

Loredana Abramo provides a person-centered narrative that looks at the gap between rhetoric and the reality of inclusion in project teams. The chapter illustrates how emerging research into the nature of diverse teams can be used to develop a fairer version of project management for the people delivering projects.

Krish Virsana extends this perspective in her chapter to discuss how decent work can be secured for the individuals working in project management. The chapter looks at the human capital challenges from decent work rather than the perspective of merely resources. This chapter is an essential early contribution on how project employees should be treated in a project context. Its ethos and approach can benefit project management in the long term.

https://doi.org/10.1515/9783110724783-002

References

Laasch, O. (2018). Just old wine in new bottles? Conceptual shifts in the emerging field of responsible management. *Centre for Responsible Management Education Working Papers, 4*(1), 135–147.

Laasch, O., & Conaway, R. (2015). *Principles of responsible management: Glocal sustainability, responsibility, and ethics*. Mason: Cengage.

Laszlo, E. (1991). Responsible (project) management in an unstable world. *International Journal of Project Management, 9*(2), 68–70.

Darren Dalcher

1 Morality and Spirituality: Essential to Responsible Project Management

Context: This chapter examines the complexities of defining and embedding morality in the decision-making process of project managers

Characters and entities: The individual mindsets and perspectives of project managers

Locations: Examples are drawn from Italy and France of individual actions that can lead to collective harms

Research gaps: The chapter encourages project managers to reflect on the nature of their responsibilities to stakeholders and communities and how morality shapes their actions

Challenge/conflict/tensions: Morality requires project managers to negotiate individual values and collective needs to become stewards that serve shared interests

Keywords: morality, spirituality, pragmatism, consequentialism, freedom

1.1 Introduction

Having agreed to author this chapter, the scale of the undertaking gradually dawned on me. Grappling with morality and spirituality is never a simple task; writing about it in an engaging way that incorporates philosophy and pragmatism into a coherent and sensible new arena of action for responsible project managers seems even more demanding as it brings together multiple disciplines and concerns. And yet the topic raises many fascinating questions: Why do we need to act morally? What is morally responsible project management? What principles and areas does it encompass? More crucially, whose morality are we endeavoring to invoke, support, and enable? Are we conceding primacy to the perspective of the project? Is it to do with people and stakeholder needs? Who supports citizens and communities? Should we consider the more comprehensive and lasting impacts of our actions? And what about the moral and environmental legacy that projects leave for our grandchildren and future generations? Morals, duties, and responsibilities seem to be intricately interlinked and indelibly intertwined. This chapter tries to rise to the challenge and open up a much-needed and long-overdue conversation around these questions.

https://doi.org/10.1515/9783110724783-003

1.2 The Moral Imperative

In a landmark review of the role of management, Peter Drucker remarked that "rarely in human history has any institution emerged as fast as management or had as great an impact as quickly. In less than 150 years, management has transformed the social and economic fabric of the world's developed countries. It has created a global economy and set new rules for participating countries as equals. And it has itself been transformed" (Drucker, 1988: p. 65). And yet, the moral and ethical fabric and nature of management activity have been questioned and challenged, often showing to be wanting, leading Drucker to conclude: "So we must think through what management should be accountable for; and how and through whom this accountability can be discharged. The stockholder's short- and long-term interest is one of the areas to be sure of. But it is only one" (p. 74). Indeed, the interests of shareholders are rarely compatible with the needs of the economy, society, or the environment or with the legacy that our present actions leave for future generations.

Recognizing the moral obligations of management activity has long permeated management thinking and philosophy. Chester Barnard positioned the functions of the executive in terms of the need to maintain communication channels, ensure individual contributions, and formulate organizational goals. However, he astutely observed that the executive process "is not intellectual; it is aesthetic and moral, involving a sense of fitness, appropriateness, responsibility" (Barnard, 1938, p. 257). The role and position of the executive, in his view, was to "inspire cooperative personal decisions by creating faith in common understanding, faith in the probability of success, faith in the ultimate satisfaction of personal motives and faith in the integrity of common purpose" (259). Simon (1947) and Learned et al. (1965) similarly emphasized the moral component of choice residing in administrative and management decisions and its impact on the public good.

However, the engagement with the integrity of common purpose and public good predates the relatively modern preoccupation with morality in management. Since the dawn of early civilization, Gardner (2011b) maintains that humanity has struggled to define the relatively subjective and situated concepts of truth, beauty, and goodness. Indeed, every society appears to have grappled with and endeavored to develop its interpretations of these timeless virtues, thereby confronting some of humanity's most perplexing challenges and most enduring dilemmas in their unique ways. Goodness, in particular, makes for a complex conundrum. The tussle between good and evil, right and wrong, has been intensely challenging for many civilizations, generating deep reflections on morality and its role in guiding, informing, and dictating action. As the nature of knowledge (and truth) shifts, many dilemmas become more perplexing. According to Gardner (2011a, p. xvii), the challenge to fundamental truth as a virtue emanates from three complementary sources:
- Increased knowledge about the wide range of cultures around the globe, many of which hold incompatible views of the world

- The postmodern critique of such traditional notions of truth, where claims to truth are often conceived as assertions of power
- The human tendency, particularly during adolescence to early adulthood, to adopt relativistic stances (often invoked through the argument for entitlement: You have got the right to your opinion, just like I have the right to mine)

Making informed moral judgments becomes increasingly more arduous when additional perspectives, views, and ideas emerge, and a single simplistic truth is replaced by the multiplicity of values, preferences, and objectives held by different parties. Traditional resolution methods related to difficult decisions and moral judgments often transmute into abrogation of power to more powerful, better positioned, and capable agencies. Yet, outsourcing morality to markets or governments presents a modern culture shift; neither position has proved itself capable of bearing the moral weight required to guide behavior for the common good (Sacks, 2020). Therefore, investigating the role of morality in projects, society, and decision-making requires a fundamental understanding of morality, morals, values, and the responsibility for taking moral actions.

1.3 Starting with Morality

Morality relates to principles or guidelines concerning the distinction between right and wrong or good and bad behavior. The *Cambridge English Dictionary* positions morality as "a set of personal or social standards for good or bad behaviour." The rules or behaviors enable individuals to function cooperatively in groups, enabling the creation of a broader society. Morality emphasizes the distinction between proper and improper intentions, decisions, and actions (Long & Sadley, 1987, pp. 366–7). It, therefore, focuses on the essential virtue of goodness (Gardner, 2011b), or the "rightness" or "wrongness" of a particular behavior rather than how we feel about that specific behavior (Gentile, 2010). Morality implies that at some level, there is a belief that some behavior is appropriate, fitting, and acceptable, while other behavior is wrong, unfair, or improper and could not be tolerated by the group or collective. The *Stanford Encyclopedia of Philosophy* (SEP, 2020) invokes a further distinction between morality in a descriptive sense that refers to specific more concrete codes of conduct enacted by a society, group, or culture or that are accepted by an individual for their behavior and morality in a normative sense as a universal set of codes that might be applied collectively to every person.

Moral principles extend beyond legal boundaries. Laws evolve over centuries and often reflect, express, or encompass the political and moral judgments and preferences of society (Badracco, 1997). Yet the positioning and framing are different. Laws and legal procedures delineate prohibited and excluded behaviors. They are often specified in explicit rules that carry established penalties and incorporate systems, infrastructure, and representative officials required to identify explicit breaches, interpret the laws, determine responsibility and blame, and apply the penalties. Business law codifies the duties of managers and leaders as developed and enshrined through legally binding protocols. Consequently, the law is mandatory, offering a framework for determining what is acceptable so that one is obliged to obey the principles enshrined in legal definitions.

Note, however, that even in a legal context, differing interpretations and precedents can sometimes redefine right and wrong. On the other hand, ethics and morality extend beyond the mandatory dictates of the legal system into the discretionary world of choice. The basis for morality focuses on values held by different individuals and groups and reconciling different sets of subjective values and expectations. Therefore, the legal position defines *what* must be done, while the moral stance determines *how* things should be done. There is one further important distinction: Just because a procedure or an action is legal at a certain point in time, it does not make it morally acceptable (e.g., when considering torture, child labor, or slavery – see Driver (2010)) – morality considerations should therefore be applied to critical decisions and problems irrespective of their legal status.

Moral theories and perspectives encompass different principles and value systems and can be generally classified into four distinct reasoning systems (see Figure 1.1).

Consequentialist moral reasoning: Consequentialists focus on the results of an action to determine whether it is right or wrong, implying a need to maximize goodness – or "less bad" – results. The correct action depends solely on the goodness of the result of the consequences (Driver, 2011). This position locates morality in future consequences, as this provides the ultimate basis for judging the appropriateness of action on the greater balance of generating "good" over "evil." Consequentialist or teleological reasoning aims to maximize a value for a maximized number of people (Baron, 2016, p. 9). Put simply, the only thing that matters is the outcome of a decision (Portmore, 2020): What is best, or right, is whatever makes the world best in the future (SEP, 2019) by producing the best overall outcome as judged from an impersonal viewpoint (Scheffler, 1988) or by ranking outcomes relative to the alternatives (Portmore, 2011).

Categorical moral reasoning: Categorical or deontological moralists take issue with each act, investigating its appropriateness, arguing that some actions, such as murder, are categorically wrong or morally forbidden regardless of the attractiveness of the effects. Categorical reasoning takes issue with the act itself, thereby locating morality in specific duties and rights and being guided by rules and absolutes. It is, therefore, not the consequences that make an action right or wrong, but the conformity with moral norms. The right does not necessarily maximize the good (Holyoak & Powell, 2016), as duties and prohibitions binding upon the agent apply irrespective of the consequences (Tännsjö, 2013). Therefore, the morality of an action is contingent on the intrinsic nature of the action (Conway & Gawronsky, 2013).

Virtue moral reasoning: Virtue moralists seek and emphasize moral virtue over vice. Virtues are character traits that make the possessor a good person, while vice makes them "bad." Virtue ethics considers how we ought to be. Virtuous acts in the Aristotelian tradition result from deliberation and choice, seeking habitual development of sound character traits. Resolving dilemmas may imply invoking someone admired such as Gandhi, Mandela, Martin Luther King, or Mother Theresa and considering how this virtuous person would have behaved under a similar situation (Driver, 2010), thereby constructing a model for making moral judgments based on cherished virtues or character traits (Van Zyl, 2018), while seemingly avoiding the threat of vices. The virtuous agent thus chooses virtue and proceeds to perform the virtuous action. Therefore, the most fundamental question is not what we ought to do but what kind of person we ought to be (Tännsjö, 2013).

Pragmatic moral reasoning: Pragmatic moralists employ pragmatism as they recognize that society can progress morally through experimentation and learning (Lekan, 2003). Pragmatic moralism offers a more descriptive approach to the gradual evolution of norms, principles, and moral criteria in a society or group over time rather than focusing on a specific action. The perspective encourages continuous improvement of ethical conduct.

The moral stance, theory, and perspective that we select may impact the solutions that seem feasible or moral and the choices and resulting actions (see Figure 1.1).

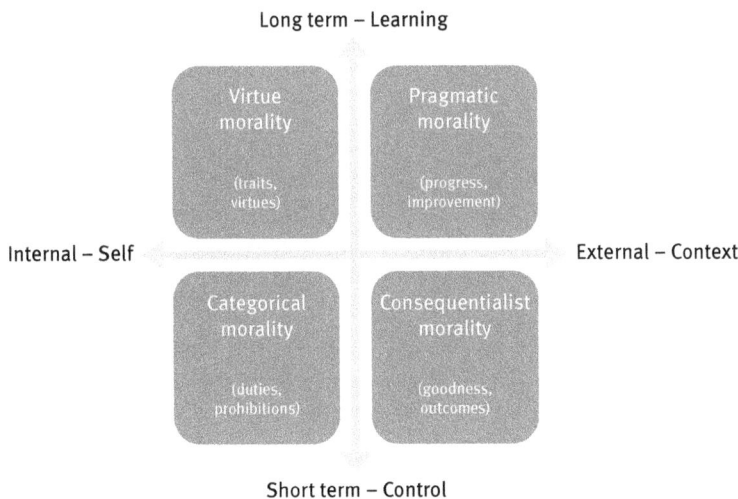

Long term – Learning

| Virtue morality | Pragmatic morality |
| (traits, virtues) | (progress, improvement) |

Internal – Self   External – Context

| Categorical morality | Consequentialist morality |
| (duties, prohibitions) | (goodness, outcomes) |

Short term – Control

Figure 1.1: Moral reasoning systems and their focus.

When discussing morals, the consequentialist and categorical traditions are often contrasted (see, e.g., Tanner et al., 2008; Crockett, 2013; Tännsjö, 2013; Gawronski & Beer, 2017) as they both focus on short-term actions by agents. The former uses the balance of consequence to justify actions purposefully (e.g., committing a minor transgression such as stealing or lying) to save a life recognizing that the ultimate rightness or wrongness depends on the result. The latter is guided by the absolute correctness and appropriateness of each act we commit so that right takes distinct priority over good. The contrast can also be depicted as a choice between theories seeking better value, thereby emphasizing end, purpose, and goal, and those concerned with right action, duty, obligation, and correct function (SEP, 2021).

In comparison, virtue ethics offers a metaethical, or improvement, perspective, maintaining that the sound, balanced character, motivation, and intention of an individual are more important than the person's actual conduct and its consequences (Petrick & Quinn, 1997), while pragmatic morality encourages a learning or evolutionary approach over extended time horizons in response to external stimuli. Other perspectives and strands emphasizing rights, egotism, or alternative external factors may also be considered and are likely to lead to different oral formulations, prioritization systems, and selected option combinations.

1.4 Morality in Harm's Way

Moral dilemmas are often difficult, complex, entangled, or messy as they entail harms caused or brought on to others, often without their explicit approval or consent (Hosmer, 1994). Indeed, such harm to specific individuals or groups in ways outside their control has been pronounced as the focal point of moral problems (ibid., pp. 19–20). Crockett et al. (2014, pp. 17320) similarly maintain that the concern for the suffering of others is central to moral decision-making, especially given that moral decisions often require sacrificing personal benefits to prevent or alleviate the suffering of others. Put simply, harm to others outweighs the harm to self.

The fixation on avoiding harm emphasizes the importance of morality in resolving dilemmas and concerns framed in terms of bad impacts and consequences. Many fields, such as construction and engineering, have attempted to legislate against negative consequences in structures, projects, and actions. Ancient societies and civilizations have practiced various approaches to introducing such principles. Hammurabi provided the earliest known example, King of Babylon, who recognized the perils of construction and management some 3,775 years ago and enacted a building code that clarified the ultimate "responsibilities" of designers and builders: "If a builder has built a house for a man and his work is not strong, and if the house he has built falls and kills the householder, that builder shall be slain" – Code of Hammurabi, 1755 BC.

Hammurabi's decree recognizes the impacts of the actions taken by designers and builders. Similar sentiment concerned with the obviation of consequential harm prevailed in other cultures. Cicero's Creed, widely acknowledged as engineering's oldest ethic, simply states, "Salus Populi suprema est lex," translated as "the public's safety shall be the highest law." This is habitually interpreted as a categorical imperative to avoid harm to others (Miller & Voas, 2008), comparable in stature to Hippocrates's medical maxim "primum non nocere," which is widely understood as "first, not harm." Marcus Tullius Cicero (106–43 BC), considered Rome's greatest orator, was concerned with obligating the engineer to ensure the public's safety. Cicero's Creed seems to have informed all of the significant engineering professional organization codes (Martin & Schinzinger, 2004) and has also been institutionalized in many technology areas (Pinkus et al., 1997). Indeed, Davis (1998) concludes that thinking like an engineer must be primarily focused on ensuring the safety of others. The perspective encourages scrutiny of potential harm operationalized through assessments of safety, risk, and the potential for failure. The explicit focus on the bad primarily emphasizes the sabotage of harms (Sparrow, 2008) to ensure a net reduction in the risk that humans, and broader society, are exposed to.

The moral idea of avoiding harm to the public re-emerges in the writing of English Philosopher John Stuart Mill in 1859, in the guise of the harm principle, which states that "the only purpose for which power can be rightfully exercised over any member of a civilised community, against his will, is to prevent harm to others" (Mill, 2015, p. 13). Therefore, the main limitation to the freedom and sovereignty of individuals comes from a distinct and categorical prohibition on causing harm to others. Linklater (2006) reframes the harm principle as the obligation not to cause serious bodily or mental harm to members of society or other social groups. The principle is not intended to guide individuals' actions or restrict their freedom but to set a boundary and justify external intervention when the actions of an individual may harm others. This is often explained through the idea that the limitation of one's ability to exercise their freedom or the movement of their hand stops at the contours of the face of the following individual.

A somewhat similar philosophical stance is demonstrated through the precautionary principle, an epistemological, moral, and legal approach urging for erring on the side of caution, particularly with new technologies and endeavors. The precautionary principle represents a categorical prohibition on endangering others by imposing the burden of proof on those who seek and create potential risks, requiring strict regulation of activities even if it cannot be shown that these activities are likely to produce significant harm to others (Sunstein, 2003, p. 1003). This is particularly applicable when the cause and effect relationships are not fully established scientifically and when there is a lack of inconclusive evidence, as is often the case for immature or novel technologies and innovative projects and initiatives. The principle has become enshrined in international law and has even been applied as a critical guideline in European and international environmental legislation (Foster et al., 2000; Kriebel et al., 2001) and in sustainable development, trade, and food safety.

Drucker (2007) asserts that no professional, be they a doctor, lawyer, or manager, can promise to do good for their client; the best they can do is try, but they can and should all avow to not knowingly do any harm (2007, p. 48). Campbell and Kitson (2008, p. 8) extend the principle to corporate moral excellence, asserting that organizations can likewise be required not to harm. The notions of harm suppression, elimination, and reduction have featured in many areas of human endeavor, including health, drugs, and social and public policies (Roe, 2005; Rhodes & Herich, 2010). They have developed a tradition of safety margins, tolerances, and thresholds in many engineering disciplines (Adams, 1991; Pinkus et al., 1997; Davis, 1998; RAE, 2011), and new techniques focused on the aversion and mitigation of risk. Risk management, a commonly used approach to prioritizing and managing potential threats, is similarly predicated on identifying, evaluating, tracking, and mitigating prospective harms (Finkelstein, 2002; Rhodes, 2002). Yet, the methods of risk management and the application of the precautionary principle introduce their complications and risks, opening the potential for deeper moral discourse around knowledge, uncertainty, and the mass reduction of potential harm (Postrel, 1998; Morris, 2000; Power, 2007; Hubbard, 2020; Sunstein, 2021).

Moral deliberations in the face of emerging technologies and initiatives have been not limited to philosophical ruminations. The story of Prometheus has been adapted from Greek mythology, retold and reworked countless times to emphasize the risk of an inventor or innovator overreaching with a proposed new technology and endangering the future of the human race, often leading to tragedy. Mary Shelley's Frankenstein, often used as an allegory for the folly of scientific experimentation, actually tells the story of an "assembled" powerful creature – capable of extreme and destructive violence but who also learns to speak, secretly cares for a low-income family, reads literature, and yearns for a soul mate – and his struggle to reconcile power, autonomy, and feelings (Shelley, 1818). It can also be read as a commentary on an irresponsible creator who fails to recognize and embrace his responsibilities to his creation and society.

Isaac Asimov (1950) formulated the Three Laws of Robotics with a foundational requirement that "a robot may not injure a human being or, through inaction, allow a human being to come to harm." This first law implies both the categorical prohibition on doing harm and consequentialist assessment of the implication of taking no action. His second law requires robots to obey all instructions given by humans, except for when such orders would conflict with the first law, demanding further scrutiny of consequences. Asimov's writing is concerned with the safe behavior of autonomous robotic machines and their greater impact on individuals and society. His fictional stories explore the dilemmas of unexpected events, counterintuitive behaviors, unexplored boundary conditions, and the unintended consequences of applying such laws. The range of literary contributions builds upon and reemphasizes the importance of morality in making sense of threats while stressing the responsibility of agents and proponents in considering the different priorities and expectations and the unintended consequences of potential harms associated with new initiatives and technologies.

1.5 Taking Responsibility Seriously

Not surprisingly, the notion of causing or inflicting harm to others has often featured in moral discourse. Kamm (2008) distinguishes between harming and not aiding, thereby separating active causation from a more passive decision not to engage. This may become particularly pertinent if there is a strict categorical moral prohibition to "do no harm unto others" and prioritize those obligations above all others. However, observers who may perceive a potential for harm cannot be certain of the consequences of any action or interference and may opt to stall or delay action until some of the unknown and uncertain factors are clarified or the potential for harm is proven. The context described above further invokes a similar differentiation between intending harm and foreseeing harm, thus leading to direct questions about intention, the agent's level of involvement, and the moral reasoning system they choose to adopt and apply.

Adopting a moral system implies a responsibility for dealing with harms (or ignoring them). Mill's harm principle specifies that for actions that are "prejudicial to the interests of others, the individual is accountable, and may be subjected to social or legal punishments" (2015, p. 91). The precautionary principle locates the responsibility to anticipate potential harm to others – requiring decision-makers, engineers, and managers to develop credible proof that new endeavors will not endanger other individuals or the environment. Cicero's Creed obligates engineers to "ensure the public's safety" (Pinkus et al., 1997, p. 39). This is particularly important considering the experimental nature of every project and undertaking, the residual uncertainty that accompanies them, and the inability to predict and forecast all potential side effects and consequences (Martin & Schinzinger, 2010). Frankenstein's monster and Asimov's laws of robotics similarly represent early literary attempts to come to terms with the morality of deploying robots, inventions, and other uncertain projects, recognizing the agency of humans and their ability to anticipate consequences and intervene in moral dilemmas. The new uncertainties that come with the use of innovative technologies and projects require paying more attention to the responsibility of designers for their creations and innovations.

Given that the responsibility for deploying projects and overseeing their outcomes resides with project managers and project sponsors, their ability to act independently and make decisions and their professional responsibility is crucial to understanding the role and impact of morality and ethics in this area. The *Oxford*

Dictionary defines "responsible" as either "liable to be called to account" or "morally accountable for one's actions," thus encompassing two rather different interpretations. Nonetheless, the increasing focus on the certification of project managers and the development of a chartered status standard for the profession in the UK carry significant implications in terms of assumed responsibility. Much like in the days of Hammurabi, employing a professional represents the transfer of risk and decision-making obligations to a better-qualified agency, also known as transcendent responsibility. It carries within it the implicit assumptions of:

– trust in their ability;
– security in the knowledge that a qualified expert is employed; and
– the comfort and peace of mind that comes from this knowledge.

The expert is expected to deliberate, justify, and make professional decisions for sound moral reasons, thereby displaying *antecedent responsibility* assuming their predictable outcomes and thus discharging their *consequent responsibility*. In essence, employing a professional expert is akin to buying additional insurance (through a risk transfer). In return for the **trust** exhibited by the client, the professional project manager takes **responsibility** for the deployment of the agreed function, capability, or quality for the process and the product itself. This aspect of responsibility is subject to professionalism, morality, and ethics.

Responsibility typically extends beyond direct action. The *Kew Gardens Principle*, which is often used to determine the level of responsibility for intervention, arose out of a tragic case of an attack on a woman in New York City, when multiple individuals assumed that others would intervene, act, or alert the relevant authorities, leaving the woman to die. The set of principles asserts that under specific circumstances, agents, individuals, communities, and institutions have positive duties, a specific responsibility to intervene and help remedy harms they did not cause. *The Kew Gardens Principle* (Simon et al., 1972) determines the level of responsibility for intervention based on four distinct factors:

Need: Based on criticality, the greater the need, the greater the obligation.

Proximity: Extends beyond mere closeness to the harm to encompass awareness of it happening.

Capability: Ability to act to counter or resist the wrong.

Last resort: Responsibility to act increases if only a few or no others can do so.

The *Kew Gardens Principle* extends responsibility beyond the commission of harmful acts to include omission, procrastination, and willful lack of action. Professionals, and indeed most agents, are therefore expected to act when proposals, plans, and projections indicate a potential for harm. It is used in cases related to the welfare of refugees, infants, experiment subjects, and other vulnerable individuals (see, e.g., Hollenbach, 2016). It can be extended to include societal and environmental implications. While responsibility entails owning up to acts, effects, and consequences, one can identify distinctly different types of responsibility (Dalcher, 2007; see Table 1.1).

Table 1.1: Different types of responsibility.

Causal responsibility	Associated with bringing something about directly or indirectly (e.g., ordering someone else)
Legal responsibility	Associated with fulfilling the requirements for accountability under the law
Moral responsibility	Associated with having a moral obligation or fulfilling the criteria for deserving blame or praise for a morally significant act or omission and the resulting consequences
Role responsibility	Associated with performing duties attached to particular professional, societal (or even biological), roles. Failure to fulfill such duties can expose the role-holder to censure, moral, legal, or constitutional.

Moral responsibility implies being answerable for one's actions and decisions and normally assumes causal responsibility. Therefore, a professional can also be held morally responsible for failing to act (i.e., resetting the focus and scope of responsibility from harming to not aiding). Guilds, associations, and professional bodies often look after the role responsibility aspect, thereby helping to enforce a more professional practice. Professional codes, introduced by such bodies, allow us to appreciate the standard, evaluate what could be expected from a member of the profession, and provide an implicit definition, at the very least, of acceptable professional behavior.

Pinkus et al. (1997, p. 22) progress a normative framework for addressing moral and ethical conflicts and dilemmas, informed by lessons derived from their research into recognized failure cases. Their framework is themed into three core concepts that underpin performance: competence, responsibility, safety, and repositioning as an update to Cicero's Creed. Competence establishes the engineer as the domain expert; responsibility acknowledges the power of knowledge and the imperative to use it wisely; while safety recognizes that engineers must strive to avoid the potential for harm. Martin and Schinzinger (2010, pp. 85–6) position engineers as responsible experimenters participating in social experiments conducted through projects, requiring: a conscientious commitment to live by moral values, a comprehensive perspective, autonomy, and accountability. In practice, being responsible while working in an experimental context implies:

1. A primary obligation to protect the safety of human subjects and respect their right of consent;
2. Constant awareness of the experimental nature of any project, imaginative forecasting of its possible side effects, and a reasonable effort to monitor them;
3. Autonomous, personal involvement in all steps of a project;
4. Accepting accountability for the results of a project. (ibid., p. 86)

Developing a code for resolving dilemmas and making moral decisions by building on the preceding discussion would therefore place several essential requirements on professional engineers and project managers, including:
– an obligation to technical, managerial, leadership, and moral competence, which may also entail personal and organizational recognition of gaps, shortfalls, limitations, and lack of expertise, knowledge, capability, or experience;
– an obligation to voice concerns and speak truth to power in moral dilemmas;
– an acceptance of responsibility (causal, legal, and moral) for actions, impacts, and consequences;
– an obligation to limit the harms and ensure the safety of products, systems, and outcomes; and
– an obligation to guard the interests of multiple participants and stakeholder groups.

Responsibility thus encompasses constant awareness, total autonomy, and explicit accountability. The focus on accountability for consequences and outcomes of actions (or lack thereof) is particularly important in projects, programs, portfolios, and initiatives and can point to the potential for severe impact following deployment, during usage, and beyond, extending into decommissioning and disposal. It also recognizes the impacts on others, including human, societal, and environmental effects.

It is worth noting that the discussion thus far has focused on the ability of individual agents and project managers to make morally sound judgments; however, individuals do not operate in a void. Competence, responsibility, and safety apply to teams and the wider organization. However, this raises important questions surrounding moral autonomy and the ultimate allocation of responsibility between individual agents and the organizations they represent, serve, and belong to. Nonetheless, various authors (Pinkus et al., 1997; Verkerk et al., 2001) identify a need to address responsibility at an organizational or an enterprise level and the personal level, given that individual knowledge experts work within an organizational arrangement. Indeed, if we extrapolate it to temporary settings, projects and initiatives occur in larger settings influenced by organizational concerns, systems, structures, dynamics, and politics irrespective of an individual manager's skill, capability, and responsibility. Consequently, complex interactions between individuals, groups, and diverse priorities and interests are likely to feature in any deliberations related to morality and action. The relationship between the individual and the collective therefore demands further attention.

1.6 Repositioning Freedom Beyond Individual Actions

Individuals seem to be overly preoccupied with their interests, preferences, priorities, issues, concerns, and tribulations to observe the wider implications and effects beyond their immediate context. It is often said that free will is a matter of free will. Yet, it increasingly appears that our small private arrangements and engagements can encroach on the wider world beyond our immediate and obvious concerns – this carries direct implications for how we perceive and discharge our moral responsibility. As the case below demonstrates, the individual's desires can overwhelm the interests of the collective.

What can be more innocent than a public declaration of love? Lovelocks are padlocks attached to bridges, fences, gates, posts, or monuments to symbolize everlasting love. Couples typically inscribe their names or initials onto the lock before affixing it to a public monument or gateway and throwing away the key into a river or waterway to symbolize an unbreakable bond. Lovelocks are a harmless phenomenon demonstrating an aspiration for an enduring partnership for the individuals involved. Indeed, one could argue that lovelocks are significantly less intrusive than carving, daubing, or plastering the names onto a bridge, monument, ancient wall, prehistoric ruin, subterranean cave, or a natural beauty spot.

Lovelocks have proliferated in many countries and regions since the early 2000s, particularly adorning bridges in the center of main cities. In Rome, the attaching of lovelocks to the Ponte Milvio bridge was documented in a popular book, *I Want You* by Federico Moccia, published in 2006 and further immortalized when adapted into a film in 2007.

Nonetheless, many people associate lovelocks with the Pont des Arts bridge in the center of Paris. Pont des Arts, also known as Passerelle des Arts, is a popular pedestrian bridge that crosses the River Seine, connecting the Institut de France to the central square of the Palais Du Louvre. It was the first iron bridge built in France, which opened in 1804 as a toll footbridge. In 1991, UNESCO listed the entire Parisian riverfront between the Eiffel Tower and the Ile Saint Louis, including the Pont des Arts, as a World Heritage Site. Since 2008 lovelocks have been appearing on the Pont des Arts bridge. By 2012, the number of locks covering the bridge had become overwhelming, with locks being placed upon other locks. In February 2014, Le Monde estimated over 700,000 locks on the bridge. With little free space remaining on the bridge, lovelocks have since spread to at least 11 other Seine bridges, the footbridges on the Canal St Martin, and more recently, to fences and posts in parks and public monuments all over the city, including the site of the Eiffel Tower.

Where is the harm in publicly sharing a couple's commitment? It would appear that many little gestures can be magnified into significant unintended consequences. As a result of the continuous addition of individual locks, the historic bridge at Pont des Arts started experiencing new problems. Paris would later remove 1 million locks attached to the Pont des Arts, with a total weight above 45 tons. In May 2014, the Paris Mayoress, Anne Hidalgo, concerned about the safety of the historic bridge and the wider impact on the city, had tasked her First Deputy Mayor with finding alternatives to lovelocks in Paris. A month later, in June 2014, the parapet on the bridge collapsed under the combined weight of the lovelocks (BBC, 2014). Under the added weight, one side of the railing crumpled into the water. The railing was replaced, and notices were left requesting that people stop the lovelock habit. Still, the love tokens started reappearing, ultimately forcing the city to replace the railings with protective glass panels in search of an alternative material to which lovelocks could not be attached.

The original bridge featured in many films and TV shows and has been enjoyed by millions of tourists and locals. It had survived aerial bombardments during World War I and World War II as well as multiple collisions with boats (although it had been replaced after a barge crashed into it in 1977); however, over 1 million individual acts of demonstrative love overwhelmed the structure and its built-in safety margins and tolerances, causing the side to collapse.

The Paris City Council reports two main concerns for the city resulting from the trend of leaving lovelocks on bridges: degradation of property heritage and a risk to the safety of visitors and locals. Locals also complain about the resulting graffiti, pickpockets, and vendors selling cheap padlocks, turning former heritage areas into unpleasant no-go zones. Some would even argue that the lovelock phenomena endangered the entire UNESCO World Heritage designation. Furthermore, the rust from the locks (and the rust and pollution caused by keys discarded into river beds) has also been cited as problematic.

Throughout Paris, workers have been regularly removing lovelocks from bridges. Chicago has been removing lovelocks from the city's movable bridges raised for boat traffic out of fear of damaging boats and hurting people on them. Paris and other cities have been experimenting with legislation to ban the practice. In Berlin, affixing a lovelock to a bridge is a misdemeanor and can generate fines of 35 Euros. Venice has introduced a 3,000 Euro fine for the same offence. Moscow offers a different and more creative approach by installing metal trees for lovers to hang their locks from while creating a dynamic new form of street art. Meanwhile, while it is now possible to preorder and customize engraved physical love padlocks online, eco-entrepreneurs offer lasting virtual lovelock-free alternatives to replace the physical artifacts.

From a moral perspective, freedom often comes with a price. Individuals appear to be focused on their actions, needs, and motivations, often ignoring the wider consequences not framed within their direct and immediate context. This enables consequences of actions to escape closer scrutiny as they reside in a different time frame that persists beyond the action space and therefore defies attention and consideration. Perhaps a key lesson is that we need to become more mindful of our actions and their impacts, however, well-intentioned. If a relatively inconsequential padlock can multiply and lead to collapsing bridges, boat accidents, deterioration of neighborhoods, and destruction of recognized international monuments, perhaps it is also time to consider the longer term implications of more significant and preplanned undertakings, such as projects, programs, and strategic, societal, and environmental change initiatives.

Individuals, nations, and societies continuously crave greater freedom. Indeed, notions such as freedom are predicated on greater power (Oppenheim, 1961; Parkinson, 1971; Hamilton, 2014; Baum, 2016; Benkler, 2016) or the liberty to act freely on our terms (Pettit, 1996) and beyond any limitations (Bauman, 1988). In a Kantian sense, freedom and responsibility are intertwined as morality and responsibility are largely invoked and enacted by recognizing agency and control in a particular context (Nelkin, 2011), enabling free choice. Yet, freedom requires more than just being left alone (Pettit, 2014), especially given the increased potential for causing harm to others and the obligation to competence in terms of choice making. Grappling with the modern condition and its residual impact on society, individuals, and the environment, Sacks (2020, p. 21) concludes that "there is no liberty without morality and no freedom without responsibility."

A similar theme is explored by Viktor Frankl, a world-renowned Viennese psychiatrist before World War II, who was uniquely able to observe how he and others imprisoned in Auschwitz coped with the harrowing experience of the holocaust. His reflection on Man's search for meaning (1992) is positioned as a tribute to hope, even in the most challenging times. It chronicles his experience in Nazi concentration camps and has sold over 16 million copies and been translated into 24 languages. Frankl cautions that freedom threatens to degenerate into mere license and arbitrariness unless it is lived responsibly:

> Freedom is not the last word. Freedom is only part of the story and half of the truth. Freedom is the negative aspect of the phenomenon, whose positive aspect is responsibility. Freedom is in danger of degenerating into mere arbitrariness unless it is lived in terms of responsibility. I recommend that the Statue of Liberty on the East Coast be supplemented by a Statue of Responsibility on the West Coast. (p. 134)

Frankl's experience and observations have taught him that freedom without responsibility is an oxymoron as the two aspects need to be balanced. The singularity of a statue on one side of a continent celebrating liberty and freedom thus necessitates a counterbalance in the form of an inspiring and enduring symbol on the opposite coast. The statue of responsibility is offered as a standalone monument celebrating the virtue of responsibility. The purpose of the monument is to encourage individuals, groups, communities, businesses, and governments worldwide to embrace responsibility as an important virtue and balance it with liberty and freedom. Frankl's vision is being realized on the west coast of the USA with the proposed erection of a 305-foot statue designed to celebrate and promote responsibility in society (SOR, 2021). The statue by Gary Lee Price will consist of a pair of clasped hands oriented vertically, representing the amalgamation of liberty and responsibility. Visiting the new statue, exhibition, and responsibility center will allow international visitors to have a meaningful "responsibility experience," gaining deeper insights into the need for responsible thinking and reasoning as the all-important counterbalance to freedom.

1.7 The Individual and the Collective – My Freedom or Yours?

Freedom can denote the absence of domination, restraint, or interference (Pettit, 2014, p. 13). But does freedom scale up? The notion of freedom is typically applied to the self rather than to a collective. The continuous tension between the wishes of an individual and the wider community's needs, made up as it is of a collective of individuals with their priorities and preferences, has long been recognized. Indeed, if only one individual was to deposit a padlock on a single bridge, the overall impact of a relatively harmless action would be negligible. However, it is no longer harmless if everyone behaves similarly, impacting overall resources or common assets. Ecologists, economists, and social scientists refer to this effect as the tragedy of the commons (Lloyd, 1833; Hardin, 1968), when a shared resource, such as the common land traditionally used by all inhabitants for grazing their flocks, is destroyed as a result of mass action and exploitation by many individuals all acting independently according to their self-interest. The combined effect of many such individual actions is to erode, deplete, spoil, and destroy the common resource. In this context, the commons is taken to mean any shared and unregulated resource ranging from the natural atmosphere, beauty spots, open space, rivers, oceans, lakes, energy, trees, oil, coal and animals, bird and fish stock, to the artificial, man-made artifacts including roads, highways, bridges, parks, and monuments.

Sometimes, the greater good is not your good. The tragedy of the commons refers to the situation where individuals, acting independently in their own best self-interest, combine to abuse the common resource they hold in trust. For example, as each commoner increases the size of their herds, fewer and fewer grazing areas remain available to others whose herds are also growing, leading to overgrazing and the destruction of the common resource. While the action of each individual taken in isolation may seem rational and in their interest, the pressure resulting from the combination of individual acts overwhelms the shared asset, ultimately endangering the sustainability of the entire community.

Morality provides a blueprint and a unifying universal approach for addressing and balancing the mismatch between individual autonomy and collective interdependence. Morality can thus offer a naturalist and pragmatic moral stance to facilitate cooperation. For instance, this leads Greene (2013, p. 23) to observe that "morality is a set of psychological adaptations that allow otherwise selfish individuals to reap the benefits of cooperation." From an evolutionary perspective, morality offers a form of cooperation, which requires individuals either to suppress their self-interest or equate it with others (Tomasello & Vaish, 2013). The theory of morality-as-cooperation contends that morality consists of a collection of biological and cultural solutions to the problems of coexistence, cooperation, and conflict recurrent in human social life (Curry, 2016; Curry et al., 2019). Haidt similarly asserts that "moral systems are interlocking sets of values, virtues, norms, practices, identities, institutions, technologies, and evolved psychological mechanisms that suppress or regulate self-interest and make cooperative societies possible" (2011, p. 270).

The tragedy of the commons demonstrates what happens when each participant maximizes their self-interest, ignoring the overall impacts on the whole system. Common pool resources yield finite flows of benefits, encouraging rational utility maximizing individuals to overdraw rather than conserve benefits for the common good (Ostrom, 2008). The actions that are taken further inflate the stakes, resulting in destructive dynamics which ultimately descend toward an inevitable disastrous outcome, leading Hardin to conclude that freedom in a commons brings ruin to all (Hardin, 1968, p. 1245). Common resource systems can thus collapse due to overuse by the wider community unless an effort is made to regulate or govern use (Ostrom, 1990; Ostrom et al., 2002). Such regulation could be done by the wider community or group or emerge from cognizant individuals' responsible or moral actions.

Traditional economic modes of thinking and technologies devised around them appear inadequate for resolving tragedy of the commons dilemmas without resorting to a more fundamental reevaluation of moral, behavioral, and ethical systems. Hardin reflects that "Individualism is cherished because it produces freedom, but the gift is conditional: The more the population exceeds the carrying capacity of the environment, the more freedoms must be given up" (Hardin, 1998, p. 683).

Various authors contend that users may be able to self-restrict access to a resource or establish rules for its sustainable use (see, e.g., Berkes, 1985; Feeny et al., 1990; Feeny et al., 1996). Elinor Ostrom (1990, 2008, 2012) argues that neither state control nor privatization of resources offers a sustainable and satisfactory solution, advocating instead for voluntary organizations that can take democratic control of common pool problems. Ostrom's thesis, for which she won the Nobel Prize in Economic Sciences in 2009, maintains that users can find fruitful ways to communicate and organize themselves to limit overuse and conserve resources. In particular, Ostrom (2008, p. 2) contends that common pool users will:

- expend considerable time and energy devising workable institutions for governing and managing common pool resources;
- follow costly rules so long as they believe that others also follow these rules;
- monitor each other's conformity with these rules; and
- impose sanctions on each other at a cost to themselves.

Finding a shared purpose may hold the key to amicably resolving common resource dilemmas and establishing cultural expectations, controls, and norms to replace the allure of immediate returns. Collectively agreed arrangements operate without the need for governmental coercion, externally imposed solutions, or regulated central planning, emphasizing instead the responsibility of individual actors and their willingness to continue to obey commonly agreed rules. An initial requirement is that relevant beneficiaries and stakeholder communities be established. Beneficiaries can be expected to have a stake in maintaining the common resource so that all commoners can agree upon a set of permissible activities and forbidden actions. Suppose most agents can identify and embrace a common purpose. In that case, it can form the basis for negotiation and agreement that endeavor to support the long-term flourishing of the community, as opposed to satisfying the immediate selfish preferences of individuals. Critically, it can also provide the common basis needed for resolving moral challenges and assuring the integrity of the common purpose while balancing the interests of the individual with the enduring priorities of the wider community.

1.8 Finding Your True North

Identifying and agreeing on a common purpose or an aspiration for what can be is never simple. "Purpose" is a commonly used term that carries many different meanings and interpretations. It is also patently missing from the project management bodies of knowledge, approaches, methodologies and standards, and general management's cannons. The *Cambridge English Dictionary* refers to "an intention or aim; a reason for doing something or allowing something to happen." For Fisk (2021), purpose defines the potential contribution to the world or why the world would be a lesser place if the business did not exist. It creates an enduring cause that the business is willing to fight for and engenders a richer sense of meaning. Collins and Porras position core purpose as the organization's fundamental reason for being, reflecting people's idealistic motivations, and ultimately capturing the soul of the organization:

"Whereas you might achieve a goal or complete a strategy, you cannot fulfil a purpose; it is like a guiding star on the horizon – forever pursued but never reached. Yet, although purpose itself does not change, it does inspire change. The fact that purpose cannot be fully realised means that an organisation can never stimulate change and progress" (Collins & Porras, 1996, p. 69).

Sound leadership is driven by a shared purpose, a common cause. Mourkogiannis (2006, p. 16) positions purpose as preparation for doing right and worthwhile. Instead of being an obligation, it provides a way of knowing what can. It cannot be done by offering confidence, commitment, and the potential for interpretation and engagement by individuals pursuing what is right and worthwhile. Frankl (1992) locates purpose and meaning at the core of people's behavior and motivation as part of *man's search for meaning*. Mauri (2020, pp. 119–20) maintains that purpose offers three motivations: giving meaning, clarifying, and simplifying. Kempster et al. (2011, p. 321) situate purpose as an aim that guides action in a broader societal realm – achieving a goal in a particular context, while Craig and Snook (2014, p. 107) note that "Purpose is increasingly being touted as the key to navigating the complex, volatile, ambiguous world we face today, where strategy is ever-changing, and few decisions are right or wrong."

Moral awareness incorporates both purpose and values. Moral values can be defined as the inherent worth and quality of a thing or an idea with a moral or ethical aspect (Gentile, 2010, p. 28). Values draw on shared beliefs across cultures and support the purpose of an organization or society, thereby enabling decisions that extend beyond codes. Values are contextualized and approached from a self-motivated, aspirational stance – they often underpin value judgments that sit alongside moral arguments. In that sense, values play a key part in helping to answer the key question in morality: Are we getting better or worse?

Values are fundamental; they point to significant aspects, including what we stand for, what we value, and which aspects we would be willing to fight for or even die for. Well-articulated and lived values bind people to a common cause. Defining the core moral values is therefore essential for resolving right-versus-wrong manifestations of moral questions, especially where moral temptations may lure us away from the safety of our moral compass. It is also important in resolving and balancing competing priorities when multiple values clash or when different groups have valid claims to rights and protection in a right-versus-right moral quandary. While the former relates to immoral enticements, the latter presents real moral dilemmas in situations where conflicting values may be contending for sympathy and support. Using a moral compass informed by the relevant moral values can help chart a moral course through choppy waters by eliminating immoral temptations and illuminating moral predicaments.

The metaphor of the moral compass refers to the inner sense of right and wrong that allows one to stay on track; Moore and Gino (2013, p. 54) refer to it as the internal voice that tells individuals what they should and should not do. However, sociopsychological processes can facilitate moral neglect, moral justification, and immoral action, undermining moral behavior, thus explaining unethical conduct (ibid.). The moral failings cause the moral compass to deviate from the true north. Personal psychological biases have been known to play a role and impact individuals and their choices; however, the impact of interpersonal social processes on moral judgments remains largely unexplored. Indeed, social science has proved better at identifying causes of unethical behavior than identifying potential approaches for correcting it (Margolis, 2009). Interventions that disempower the social triggers of unethical behaviors include the promotion of moral exemplars (Moore & Gino, 2013, p. 68) – for example, choosing role models that emphasize specific virtues and behaviors. Careful and cognizant goal setting also plays a key part (p. 69). Projects and initiatives often establish overly ambitious goals that blind individuals to other important objectives (Staw & Boettger, 1990). Additionally, overcommitment to goals motivates individuals to do whatever it takes to reach them (Moore & Gino, 2013, p. 69). Increasing self-awareness, enhancing sensitivity to moral emotions, and expanding one's circle of moral regard can further influence intrapersonal processes to regain control of one's moral compass (ibid., pp. 69–70).

Psychological and social processes can play an important part in supporting moral behavior. A common purpose helps to bring a community together. True north provides an orienting point. In a simple sense, as long as the true moral north can be fixed and the other core values repositioned, our moral location can be charted. But many key questions remain: Whose values should we adopt and consider? Which single aspect do we anchor as our true north?

Moreover, what happens when we are obliged to work with multiple stakeholders, contested priorities, and conflicting interests? Kaplan (2020, p. 3) observes that purpose is important for many competing stakeholder groups. In organizational settings and project situations, this results in intense pressure to address stakeholder demands from all directions. Consumers demand socially responsible products, employees seek meaningful work, and investors screen on environmental, social, and governance criteria, while various interest groups create social media storms over missteps. Progressing in such a contested terrain requires the establishment of common ground around both values and purpose to enable the exploration to focus and feature a unifying common cause.

1.9 Goodness as a Virtue

One way of approaching the different priorities and needs of diverse stakeholders and communities is to focus on the common good. The notion of the common good can be traced through the writing of Plato, Aristotle, Cicero, Saint Thomas Aquinas, John Locke, David Hume, Jean-Jacques Rousseau, and more modern political scientists. Etzioni (2014) maintains that no society can flourish without a shared obligation to the common good, which connotes to the goods and institutions that serve all of us (2014, p. 1). The common good is more than the aggregation of all personal goods and encompasses aspects that serve the entire community. Investment in the common good is not for personal reasons but is considered the right thing to do (ibid.). Gardner (2011b) refers to the major virtue of goodness, while Kotler (2019) emphasizes wellness, and Singer (2015) singles out effective altruism as the basis for making the most good we possibly can do while also giving meaning to our own lives, all reflecting a common good core objective resonating with John Stuart Mill's goal to "defend and promote the general welfare" (Kottler, 2019, p. 5).

The *common good* represents a specific and timely context of society, not least because of balancing individual rights and the common good (Etzioni, 2017), especially in the prevailing political climate reflecting current beliefs and values. According to Kottler (2019, p. 3), if citizens were asked to identify the values that underpin the *common good*, they would mention freedom, equality, fraternity, opportunity, justice, and security; all "goods" as opposed to "bad." This contrasts directly with preventive morality focused on eliminating all forms of harm.

Advancing wellness globally can be achieved in a multitude of ways. The common good approach encourages consideration of interventions as dealing with a community of persons within society rather than as a system of competing and conflicting stakeholder interests (Melé, 2011, p. 112). The community's common good, or society, can thus become a focus for governance and management, particularly moral considerations, while allowing a higher perspective than the traditional stakeholder-centric approach. Sociability, as a key feature of a community, entails a willingness to live together under an expectation of cooperation to advance the common good and avoid the dynamics exhibited in the tragedy of the commons. Indeed, sociability "leads to assuming social responsibility for the impact of one's actions – or business activity – on others or society" (ibid., p. 113). The advantage of seeking the common good is that it allows individuals to maintain their autonomous status while joining forces around a common interest and collaborating to share and preserve that common interest for the greater good.

The *common good* perspective extends beyond immediate financial and economic dimensions and concerns (Porter & Kramer, 2011; Tata et al., 2013; Birkinshaw et al., 2014), to offer meaningful and sustainable long-term performance. Given that the role of the organizations and the projects that support and underpin them is to create value, what kinds and types of sustainable value should we cherish? Kempster et al. (2019) attempt to focus on the broader responsibilities of organizations and groups, including human, social, reputational, and environmental impacts. Defining a broader purpose or intent makes it possible to embrace more purposeful arrangements, thereby linking the organization, its participants, and stakeholders to realize a more sustainable and enduring value. Suppose that the *tragedy of the commons* occurs when individuals focus on limited, immediate short-term gratification. In that case, the wider focus provides a communal basis for harnessing interpersonal trust and addressing and engaging in the more sophisticated discourse around longer term aims, overarching purpose and aspirational intent. With a wider perspective on an increasing range of stakes and stakeholders, it becomes possible to engage with communities and participants and consider new ways of developing governance and oversight of shared resources while identifying enlightened ways of replenishing, sustaining resources, and thriving as communities or thriving firms.

Realizing value from all capitals, including financial, manufactured, intellectual, human, social and relational, and natural (IIRC, 2013), can develop more powerful and purposeful synergies and value propositions and identify opportunities for prosperity and development within a system. Indeed, as seen earlier, harnessing social and relational capital underpins the resolution of common resource challenges. Kempster et al.

(2019, p. 22) duly seek to utilize all six capitals to realize the six good dividends – financial, human, social, brand, operational, and one-planet returns– and subsequently generate good growth and sustainably replenish the capitals. Good dividends are drawn from the use of capital (p. 4), offering a wider notion and share of ownership. Many businesses and groups rely on intangible factors, such as their people, capabilities, links, reputation, and brand. The intangibles are often critical to realizing the value and engendering growth and sustainable improvement. By offering a wider perspective, emphasizing purpose, and recognizing the connections between good dividends and the various capitals, it becomes possible to find novel ways to engage with some of the challenges encountered in contemporary contexts. The lens of responsible and purposeful leadership thus focuses on realizing value for an expanding range of constituencies, thereby addressing and accommodating multiple concerns and needs while embracing the relationships between leaders, groups, and stakeholder communities.

The notions of the *common good*, wellness, and good dividends distributed across a community or a group can be shown to support a balanced focus on *goodness* as an overall virtue that extends beyond the obligation to avoid all forms of *harm*. Wellness can also underpin various concerns, considerations, and interested stakes while accommodating different time frames and scopes. It enables, for example, a communal interest that seeks to increase the balance of benefits over harm to serve the needs of the greatest number of community members and stakeholders without violating the rights of the individual, minorities, and the most defenseless. It does this while also seeking to maintain the long-term prosperity and sustainability of the community and guarding its future resources and potential options and dividends, which may be required for consequent development and improvement. It thereby focuses on a more meaningful and responsible relationship with our cherished common resources by enacting the concept of stewardship.

1.10 The Case for Stewardship

An alternative to imposed governance and top-down regulation can come from informed stewardship where interested and engaged local members with a strong sense of purpose cooperate and coordinate their actions to avoid the collapse of common resources and sustain the common good. This can build on the notion of stewardship which embodies responsibility, added consideration, and a focus on sustaining the common interest. The *Oxford Dictionary* describes stewardship as "the act of taking care of or managing something, for example, property, an organisation, money or valuable objects." The *Merriam-Webster Dictionary* defines stewardship as "the conducting, supervising or managing of something, especially the careful and responsible management of something entrusted to one's care," offering a specific example of stewardship of natural resources. Stewardship thus seems to refer to the way we protect, utilize, share, and manage special resources or a specific capability or value. In theological discourse, it is often referred to as the theological belief that humans are responsible for the world or the universe and should cherish and take care of it across multiple religions.

Peter Block's book *Stewardship* popularized the term: *Choosing Service Over Self-Interest*, published in 1993 to great acclaim. Block (2013, p. xxiv) defines stewardship as "the choice to preside over the orderly distribution of power." This entails giving people at the bottom and the boundaries of an organization or society choice over how to serve a customer, citizen, or community while recognizing that they are operating in service rather than in control. In a nutshell, stewardship is accountability without control or compliance (ibid.). This is done by deepening the commitment to service and supporting the wider community with a special emphasis on considering the long-term and those with limited power.

Block views stewardship as an intention to distribute power more widely, especially to the marginalized groups, thereby emphasizing the common good for the communities. The starting point is the willingness to be accountable for some larger body than ourselves: a team, an organization, or a community through the notions of service and commitment.

> Stewardship is the set of principles and practices that have the potential to make dramatic changes in the governance of our institutions. It is concerned with creating a way of governing ourselves that creates a strong sense of ownership and responsibility for outcomes at every level of the organisation. It is a buck that stops everywhere. It means having more partnerships with customers and creating self-reliance on all the institution touches. The answer to economic problems is not reduced costs or better funding; it focuses first on relationships, reciprocity, and participation. These are the elements that produce the service we seek. This is what will put us closer to our employees and our marketplace. Stewardship is creating a sustainable connection with the people in our playing field that is the answer to our concerns about economics.
> (Block, 2013, p. 15)

Block argues compellingly for a move away from typical patriarchy and hierarchy as the core forms of governance. The shift aims to liberate initiative and spirit within organizations and their employees by fostering empowerment, ownership, and responsibility. The position distinguishes the capacity to decide and the responsibility for our thoughts and actions. The change in attitude and approach requires several fundamental adjustments and intentional choices, which Block poses as:

- Replacing leadership with stewardship
- Choosing partnership over patriarchy
- Choosing adventure over safety
- Choosing service over self-interest

Davis et al. (1997) position stewardship as an alternative to agency theory, thereby eschewing an economic basis for governance considerations, focusing on sociological and psychological approaches and considerations. Individuals can thus be viewed as collectivists, pro-organizational and trustworthy (p. 20). Hernandez (2012, p. 174) defines stewardship as "the extent to which an individual willingly subjugates his or her interests to act in protection of others' long-term welfare."

Stewardship does not require a formal position, power, or authority; stewardship behaviors, much like morality, can be enacted across all levels of an organization. The underlying assumption is that managers and workers will act as responsible stewards of assets and resources at their disposal, preferring pro-organizational behavior to self-serving individualism. Stewards typically pursue a more responsible, long-term, and trustworthy agenda. The concept of stewardship has been applied to many different aspects, including nature, the environment, resources, economics, health, and data.

The notion of stewardship, framed as a move from self-interest toward service, makes an important addition to the discourse around responsibility, particularly in the commitment to future generations, conservation and sustained communities. Adopting the lens of stewardship enables, facilitates, and encourages important development in considering the wider implications of actions extending beyond individuals' self-interest and selfish acts. Stewardship is tasked with protecting and cherishing the public interest. This can be done by adopting the commons imperative and considering the greater good, which adds a social dimension to the environmental considerations. Stewardship extends beyond prohibition and regulation to develop a more systemic and comprehensive mindset that allows ownership and empowerment of all participants. Stewardship is thus entrusted to individuals who can consider the wider implications of their actions and safeguard global resources for the common good.

Developing stewards requires new ways of planning projects, building organizations, making decisions, prioritizing, and managing. By encouraging individuals to consider the implications of potential actions, the collective can become more responsible and better accountable for shared resources ranging from bridges and beauty spots to water, livestock, and the environment. It can also offer social and societal empowerment needed to underpin wider considerations. Collaborating for the greater good is essential to include and support ever-growing communities. Sir Michael Barber (2015, 2021) aptly observes that stewardship is about leaving a system better than you found it. Our key to the prosperity of future communities may well be fostering stewardship skills and capabilities in all aspiring members as we begin to collaborate toward creating and facilitating a better common future.

1.11 Spirituality as a Moral Compass

Stewardship distinguishes a resource or community entrusted into our care and sphere of responsibility. It also chimes with a growing need to focus on societal and environmental concerns. Indeed, Hamel (2012, p. 3) concludes that any leader within any type of organization is a steward – of careers, capabilities, the environment, and organizational values. In increasingly demanding and challenging times, we can discern a greater and more urgent need for management in general and managers, in particular, to embrace the responsibility and duties of stewardship to safeguard the future and the various resources, capabilities, capitals, and dividends that can sustain communities, organizations, and society.

The publication of the book *Man's Responsibility for Nature* (Passmore, 1974) challenged the majority view of a human-centered world, invoking two minority traditions that human beings are trustees of the world of nature, entrusted with its care; or that the role of humans is to improve the world by bringing out its potential. The scope of moral standing has long been challenged to determine if animals and nature should also be considered. Environmental or ecological ethics counters that humans have moral status and nature itself, resulting in duties incumbent upon us to preserve nature (Tännsjö, 2013, p. 132) and protect different aspects, including animals, plants, and the ecology. The idea fits Moore's moral imperative to protect a beautiful world (Moore, 1903, pp. 33–4). It also provides the intellectual underpinning for environmental pragmatism, which contends that theoretical debates are hindering the ability of the environmental movement to progress initiatives, agitating instead for a dose of pragmatism needed to galvanize action focused on solving practical problems (Light & Katz, 1996, p. 2).

Jonas (1985) makes a compelling case for rethinking and repositioning morality. He contends that ethical discourse has taken the survival of mankind and the continued existence of the world for granted. Still, the potential harm generated by new technology and human capability seriously challenges the viability of that proposition. This changed condition places the species' continued survival and the world as the highest and most urgent priority. The stance demands a new level of "duty" featuring stewardship and responsibility capable of accommodating deeper consideration of the moral standing of future generations, as well as the conservation and care related to ecological preservation and confronting diversity and sustainability issues.

Spirituality offers a way of developing a more holistic and long-lasting approach to addressing universal intergenerational justice concerns and defending cherished commodities, capabilities, and values entrusted to us. The particular advantage is that spirituality offers a way of looking at organic aspects and recognizing that the organic whole has a spirit (Tännsjö, 2013, p. 127), a value, and an overarching purpose greater than oneself. Contemporary (nonreligious) definitions of spirituality often view it as either an integrating factor concerned with the whole or an evocative search for meaning (Sheldrake, 2012, p. 5). Neal and Harpham (2012, p. 13) position spirituality as an innate human attribute: "Spirituality is a state or experience that can provide individuals with direction or meaning, or provide feelings of understanding, support, inner wholeness or connectedness. Connectedness can be to themselves, other people, nature, the universe, a god or other supernatural power."

Spirituality denotes a basic desire to find ultimate meaning and purpose in one's life and live an integrated life (Mitroff & Denton, 1999, p. xv). Neal and Harpham identify a vertical component in spirituality concerned with the desire to transcend the individual ego or the personal self. A horizontal component represents the desire to be of service to others and the planet (2012, p. 14). Drawing on both components allows individuals and organizations to contribute in more meaningful ways while operating as caring, compassionate, and supportive stewards pursuing a more fulfilling purpose. Moreover, spirituality provides a unifying element that encourages individuals to express more of themselves in the workplace (Mitroff & Denton, 1999, p. 7), making a purposeful difference.

Spirituality has been proposed as the missing focus needed to solve the ethical deficit exhibited in business (Bouckaert & Zsolnai, 2011, p. 4). Spirituality fits the bill because the inner experience of interconnectedness with all living things opens a space of distance from the normal pressures of business, a necessary precondition for developing innovative, ethical ideas and concepts (p. 5). The rationale for embracing spirituality is given by Bennis (1999, p. xii): "Individuals and organisations that see themselves as 'more spiritual' do better. They are more productive, creative and adaptive. These organisations are more energised and productive because they aren't solely about stock options, vacations and coffee breaks. Spiritual organisations are animated by meaning, by wholeness, and by seeing their work connected to events and people beyond themselves."

Therefore, a new form of spiritual capital can be recognized as a vision and a model for organizational and cultural sustainability within a wider framework of community and global interests that are amassed through serving the deeper concerns of humanity and the planet (Zohar & Marshall, 2004, p. 4). The capital reflects shared meanings, values, purposes, and motivations that can inform judgments and decisions. Spirituality is normally positioned at the highest level of Maslow's hierarchy of needs in the realm of self-actualization, as represented by morality, creativity, problem-solving, and lack of prejudice (Sheldrake, 2012, p. 62), although Maslow (1971) himself ultimately situated self-transcendence as a higher level of human need, and Barrett (2006) has subsequently constructed three additional levels of spiritual needs, respectively, encompassing, in ascending order, a focus on internal cohesion, making a difference and service. Leveraging the spiritual capital requires new apparatus to underpin new capabilities and enable informed judgment. Research in psychology and economics has therefore focused on spiritual intelligence as a tendency to inspire novel creativity or innovation (Neubert et al.,

2017) and encourage moral, ethical, and responsible behavior as an adjunct to intellectual and emotional intelligence (Dalcher, 2014, p. 9).

> Spiritual intelligence is our moral intelligence, giving us an innate ability to distinguish right from wrong. It is the intelligence with which we exercise goodness, truth, beauty, and compassion in our lives. If you like, the soul's intelligence if you think of the soul as that channelling capacity in human beings that brings things up from the deeper and richer dimensions of imagination and spirit into our daily lives, families, organisations and institutions.
>
> (Zohar & Marshall, 2004, pp. 4–5)

Spiritual intelligence can be depicted as the ability to think about the world and oneself and to spend one's life accordingly in the form of a lived experience that directs and influences according to spiritual meaning (Ronel, 2008). Spiritual intelligence draws on spiritual capital, accessing the most fundamental purpose, values, beliefs, and meaning. Spiritual capital, therefore, underpins moral judgment. It can also be understood as a multilevel form of organizational value, operating at the individual level as the disposition to serve, and subsequently at the organizational level as the values, systems, norms, and culture that enable and facilitate it (Middlebrooks & Noghiu, 2010). Zoher and Marshall (2004, p. 6) ultimately resolve that spiritual capital makes people, organizations, and cultures more sustainable because it enables decisions informed by values, global concerns, compassion, long-term thinking, and spontaneity.

Spirituality brings a personal and individualistic connection to morality's internal tailoring and processing and its associated duties, virtues, and expectations. Spirituality then is our moral compass: A spiritual sense can help to refine and guide our moral compass by developing and empowering a personal view of goodness and honing an internal determination of right and wrong that serves to reset and recast our ongoing focus on true north and our inclination to become the stewards of treasured values and irreplaceable resources. While spirituality enables us to live a purposeful, more fulfilled, and virtuous life, it also forms the basis for guiding an active pursuit of our true north over an extended time horizon. Therefore, its core significance is in informing, facilitating, and supporting our ability to solve moral problems and make difficult choices.

1.12 Making Moral Choices

Managing often implies multifaceted prioritization and tricky trade-offs between different priorities, expectations, stakeholder groups, and communities. Hosmer (1994, p. 20) reasons that moral problems in corporate management are particularly complex because the potential harms for some individuals and groups are inevitably associated with benefits to other individuals and groups, including suppliers, distributors, creditors, managers, teams, and customers, owners, and workers. Nonetheless, managerial actions are still required across most projects, initiatives, and undertakings despite their tendency to distil, distribute, and dispense harms to some and benefits to others. Trade-offs between benefits and harms become more complicated as additional participants and stakeholder groups are added and considered.

Resolving moral problems requires *moral competence* – the ability to recognize, react, and respond to the nuances of moral deliberations. But how do people make such moral choices? Where do the strategies come from? How do we conduct moral trade-offs? This section will turn to psychology to identify some of the key aspects of moral decisions. Human reason arises from the nature of our brains, bodies, and bodily experience (Lakoff & Johnson, 1999, p. 4), implying that moral deliberation and judgment are rooted in embodied processes and embodied manifestations of value (Tillman, 2016:16). Yet, morality is known to develop over a lifetime (Piaget, 1928, 1932), conditioned by experiences, social interactions, and a growing sense of right and wrong (Kohlberg, 1963, 1973, 1981). Michener et al. (1990, p. 72) discovered that children intuitively use three principles when making difficult moral decisions:
- Amount of harm/benefit
- Actor's intentions
- The application of agreed-upon rules or norms

These principles offer the foundation for the more complex strategies applied by professionals. Moral deliberation requires the ability to make a judgmental determination regarding the context and the situation. Individuals are better equipped to make moral decisions when they are aware of the relevant moral values and the consequences of the decisions that they are facing (Moore & Gino, 2013, p. 60). Improvement and developmental transitions occur through constant interaction with the environment over time (Dahl, 2019). James Rest (1986) posits that *moral behavior* is determined by four interrelated psychological components which enable moral decision-making and contribute to moral behavior. For an individual to be able to deal with moral situations correctly and become morally mature, the following components must be developed:

Moral sensibility: Awareness of the moral dimensions of a decision or situation or the moral issues implied in a proposal (or business case). Encompasses recognition of the relevant moral principles, norms, and guidelines and understanding of the potential impact of a decision or action on the well-being of actors, participants, stakeholders, or other concerns.

Moral judgment: Ability to evaluate whether a proposed action or decision is morally right or wrong and determine its acceptability. Relies on the foundation of moral sensibility.

Moral motivation: The driving force for acting, or not acting, for moral reasons based on judgment. May conflict with motivations based on other rewards, such as financial, role, status, power, and prestige.

Moral character: Shaped and informed by moral virtues; this is developed by acting with moral motivation and doing good. It is particularly useful when moral motivation conflicts with other aspects as it provides strength and support for taking the "right" course of action.

Further psychological research offers new insights into the nature of moral judgment. Schaich Borg et al. (2011, p. 398) introduce a neurally inspired distinction between **moral deliberation**, defined as the detection, filtering, and weighing of relevant moral principles, heuristics, or concepts, leading to the creation of a moral context and the ultimate **moral verdict** as the valenced opinions or commitments to what may be wrong, or what actions it may merit. Damon and Bronk (2007, p. 24) identify a strong link to **moral identity** and purpose. Identity is often offered as a source of moral motivation. Moral identity is a newer construct at the intersection of moral development and identity formation, representing how being a moral person is important to a person's identity (Hardy & Carlo, 2005, 2011). Moral identity can be viewed as the source of moral motivation combined with moral judgment to shape moral behavior (Reynolds & Ceranic, 2007). Therefore, a stronger sense of moral identity is associated with knowing what is right and acting morally in a sustained fashion. According to Damon and Bronk, "(we have found that) moral identity is the best predictor of a person's commitment to moral action because it determines not merely what a person considers to be the right course of action but also why the person would decide that" (2007, p. 25).

Moral identity engenders a sense of personal responsibility for taking moral action (ibid.). Therefore, action can originate from a highly articulated sense of moral identity, reflecting the sense of purpose at the core of that moral identity (p. 24). In a professional context, this may imply defining the self that includes work-related skills, capabilities, and interests, the purpose for one's work, the personal sense of ethical restrictions, and the responsibility to one's community (p. 25). A strong moral identity can thus foster personal responsibility that underpins moral judgment and enables moral behavior.

While the psychological mechanisms related to making moral decisions have been covered, there appears to be a potential disconnect in putting moral precepts into practice as exhibited behavior often contradicts moral expectations, predictions, and assertions. For instance, moral choices experienced in real life frequently contrast the fundamental of not harming others (Greene et al., 2001) with evidence of self-benefit and exploitation of the opportunity to maximize self-gain (Haidt, 2007). Indeed, many organizational failures indicate a similar mismatch between moral intention and action. Psychologists recognize that the difference between what we espouse and what we do can be rather significant as moral beliefs appear to have a weaker impact when significant self-gain is present, tempting individuals and organizations into making highly self-serving choices (Feldman Hall et al., 2012, p. 998). Hendry (2004) asserts that we live in a bimoral society where lives are governed by two contrasting sets of principles, emphasizing traditional morality, particularly in terms of duties and obligations to others, and a rather competitive entrepreneurial self-interest. More flexible forms of organizing can release people's creative spirit and enhance the potential for imaginative capability, benefiting society. However, the pursuit of new entrepreneurial spaces and blue ocean possibilities through strategic initiatives and projects can lead to questions related to the appetite and morality of seeking innovation and pursuing opportunity and tempting prospects for personal or organizational gain. Indeed, scaling morality to the organizational level can lead to oversight and governance challenges as values, duties, responsibilities, priorities, and opportunities continue to emerge, interact, and clash. Yet, balancing and resolving moral conflicts merits further consideration regardless of scale.

1.13 Moral Dilemmas – Dimensions of Choice

Moral judgment relies on moral deliberation and a resulting moral verdict, informed by moral sensibility, identity, motivation, and character. However, some choices present particularly vexing moral dilemmas at a practical level. Dilemmas are difficult situations requiring a choice between contending alternative positions. Cameron and Quinn (1988, p. 2) clarify that dilemmas require an either–or choice where one alternative has to be selected. A dilemma further implies that neither of the propositions is unambiguously and universally preferable, mandating a new capability for dealing with competing and even opposing moral positions, rules, and criteria.

Not all things packaged as moral dilemmas are moral choices in the strict sense. Morality pertains to the right behavior. Choosing between moral and immoral options is relatively simple, as it implies a straightforward moral choice between right and wrong – although it may still require a need to recognize the moral contours of a situation or context or to identify moral lapses in the framing or potential behavior (see O'Boyle, 2011; Dalcher, 2020). An extension of this scenario requires choosing between a moral duty, typically framed as a moral prohibition, and obeying orders from superiors, which may require one to ignore a moral prohibition. It is worth noting that obeying orders is neither an acceptable legal nor moral defense for immoral actions. A similar situation may arise when professionals are forced to choose between a moral prohibition and the economic implications of selecting a moral option that would not be in the organization's best interest. Innovators and project leaders may similarly choose between traditional morality and potential prohibitions, and entrepreneurial self-interest, especially with new, unproven, or impactful new technologies. While these may be framed as business dilemmas, they are relatively simple to resolve from a moral perspective.

On the other hand, moral dilemmas are problematic because they represent a clash between right and right (or even between wrong and wrong), implying a direct conflict between competing moral requirements. For instance, how do we choose between being a good parent and a good employee? The existence of moral pluralism is problematic precisely because it eliminates the judgment between right and wrong as the deciding criterion, introducing a need for demarcating different shades of goodness, developing grading structures for determining preferential or better fits, or determining who should suffer more and over what time. Moreover, eschewing the dialectical dance between right and wrong implies a deeper moral uncertainty that stems from moral, judgmental, or evaluative difficulties (Lockhart, 2000; MacAskill et al., 2020). Resolving moral ambiguities may be exacerbated by competing claims for scarce resources by different stakeholders, potentially leading to moral stress (Reynolds et al., 2012). Moral challenges and ambiguities have featured in philosophical works of most cultures because they pose intriguing conflicts that question foundational values and moral principles and can provide ideal reflection, learning, and discussion points. Indeed, trading off one set of rights, harms, or benefits against another, especially between and across groups, goes to the core of how we address moral decisions in real life.

Dilemmas are becoming an increasing feature of the business context. Johansen (2012) maintains that listening to an increasingly uncertain and volatile future will require dilemma flipping skills, the ability to hold two opposing ideas, and turn them into an advantage or opportunity. Future dilemmas will be unsolvable, recurrent, complex, messy, threatening, confusing, and puzzling (p. 59). Moral dilemmas are controversial because they can lead to contrasting conclusions between different moral systems and deeply held values. They may depict the interests of future generations against the current generation or force us to weigh the priorities of distant strangers against our compatriots (MacAskill et al., 2020). Reflecting on the opposing ideas, values, or duties and using different lenses to consider their implications before identifying a moral way forward will remain an essential capability in a morally challenging world. Indeed, invoking dualisms draws on the long Socratic tradition of exploring and arguing publicly. As we move toward concluding this chapter, it may be useful to reflect on the journey thus far and pick out seven (plus one) of the essential and most common types of moral dilemmas and contradictions as a way of reexamining the different dimensions of moral and spiritual choice competing for our attention:

Harm versus benefit: When positive and negative moral duties collide, the negative duty, presented as a prohibition, or a minimum requirement, normally takes precedence. For instance, non-malfeasance, the requirement to "not harm," is typically prioritized above beneficence, the requirement to "do good." The direct implication is that the elimination of harm and risk must take precedence over the pursuit of benefit – a direct contradiction to the spirit of exploration, innovation, and the novelty and discovery that feature in project work. Nonetheless, positioning can play a key part in framing moral dilemmas.

Categorical versus consequential reasoning: Earlier discussion emphasized the different reasoning systems related to proposed actions. Categorical morality would demand that practitioners avoid inflicting any form of harm and, therefore, necessitate the removal of harm-causing actions, alternatives, and options as a primary obligation. A consequentialist would require professionals to consider both the amount, type, and potential recipients of benefits and the amount and recipients of harm associated with each potential option or proposed course of action and come to judgment based on the best set of consequences or the level of utility associated with the action.

It is worth noting that other moral systems can enrich the position: Virtue morality would seek to emphasize features associated with goodness but would inevitably depend on its definition. Defining goodness as a combination of non-malfeasance and beneficence may allow professionals to avoid harm while aiming to produce as many benefits as possible to as many stakeholders as plausible. Pursuing important qualities or emphasizing desirable virtues can deemphasize the inherent focus on actions.

Pragmatists might advance the discussion further by asking if the action causing harm is the only way to satisfy the objectives or work toward the purpose; alternatively, to consider whether the same benefits may be achieved in some other way or through a different project or initiative. Pragmatists may reason that it may be impossible to avoid all harm to all people, all of the time, and therefore legitimately redefine their obligation as a requirement not to cause unnecessary and gratuitous harm. From a professional practice perspective, this could also be reframed as a new requirement to seek the best common good result for participants, clients, humanity, and nature.

Liberty versus responsibility: This contradiction depicts freedom and the pursuit of free will as new powers, positioned against the responsibility required to regulate, control, govern, and contain new powers and limit the potential harm to others. Morality is ultimately essential to enabling freedom: If freedom is a power, it must be accompanied by a sense of responsibility. Moreover, the greater choice must come greater responsibility – especially if we seek to jettison surveillance or imposed controls. The proposed statue of responsibility may serve as a reminder of the power of responsibility and the underlying need for morality, thereby acting as the much-needed enabler and counterbalance to freedom, liberty, and the yearning for free choice

Justice versus mercy: This dichotomy depicts fairness, equitable adherence to standards, norms and social controls, and systematic consistency of application against compassion and caring for individuals (Kidder & Bloom, 2001, p. 65). The dignity and needs of a suffering or underperforming individual may trigger our attention, encouraging compassion or relaxation of the rules, with little concern for precedent or appearance (ibid.).

Individual versus community: The personal needs and wishes of the individual may often clash with the priorities and expectations of the community. This can be depicted as the difference between "I" and "we" from a personal perspective. From a technological perspective, it can help emphasize the value and power of collaboration. From a moral perspective, especially when benefits and harms are redistributed and shared and goodness is defined with a nod to the communal common good, it can have significant ramifications on how initiatives are proposed, cases are written, and decisions and trade-offs are deliberated and positioned. The experience of the Covid pandemic reemphasizes the power of the community to support individuals and make significant and meaningful change possible, even during terrible times, while also recognizing that a community is stronger and more resilient when it is compassionate and cares for its weakest. This grouping can also encompass the balance between prioritizing shareholder returns and stakeholder interests (Freeman, 1984; Goodpaster, 1991; Dalcher, 2020) or even embracing a potential focus on the common good through a new societal arrangement as we reposition to support and sustain a burgeoning community rather than consume a scarce commodity.

Economic versus social versus environmental: A lot has been written about the triple bottom line encompassing profit, people, and planet. While the distinctions are not always useful, as they may distract from developing more integrated and all-encompassing solutions by grouping and classifying activities and impacts, the three elements serve as a reminder that priorities and trade-offs encompass multiple sets of concerns. Dividing and prioritizing among the groups and the needs of different stakeholders and communities can lead to moral challenges and dilemmas regarding priorities, resources, funding, potential returns, and impacts. It is worth stressing that focusing on economic returns emphasizes outcomes rather than means, processes, or the action's appropriateness or morality of the action. Spiritual approaches may play a part in integrating and balancing the various perspectives and seeking more comprehensive and purposeful solutions. Indeed, wider stakeholder communities informed by shared values can encompass a wide constituency of interests, internal and external, current and future, human and environmental (Mitroff & Denton, 1999), and play a part in preserving culture and tradition while pursuing good dividends and the common good.

Short term versus long term: The contrast between immediate or short-term gains and priorities and the sustainable or long-term impacts and needs presents another morally charged dimension of contention. Preference for the immediate often neglects residual impacts and long-term consequences. This charge can be levied against many projects and initiatives that are rushed through by prioritizing a financial business case with immediate returns. The consideration of harm, benefit, and success is often normalized through the lens of near-instant gratification. Bringing future generations, nature, the environment, or the stewardship and preservation of a nation, culture, tradition, or common resources held in trust into the conversation opens up a longer term assessment of opportunities, impacts, and the irreversibility of some actions and behaviors.

Figure 1.2 offers a pictorial representation of some of the main ideas and tensions embedded within the realm of moral behavior. The dimensions depict the shift from practical needs to consideration of a higher purpose and from a focus on the short term to a consideration of longer term impacts. The figure captures the resulting shift in perspective from me (and my immediate needs) toward a community represented as "we." The transition from *me to we* also reflects a similar move from considering the immediate *here and now* toward a longer term interest in cooperation and collaboration over an extended time horizon, shown as *together and forever,* which can offer enduring benefits. Responsibility extends beyond the individual agent, represented pictorially as an expanding *cone of responsibility*, depicting the growing scope of responsibility extending into longer term and higher purpose territory. This is where responsible behavior and stewardship can make a lasting difference. The diagram also identifies the zone of *the common good*, where the community's interests begin to take precedence, coinciding with the shift from *me to* us and from my immediate interests and concerns toward the long-term and collective considerations regarding prosperity and sustainability. It is important to note that responsibility and stewardship thus encroach on, interrelate to, and are indelibly embedded within our place in the wider community and the extended longer term considerations.

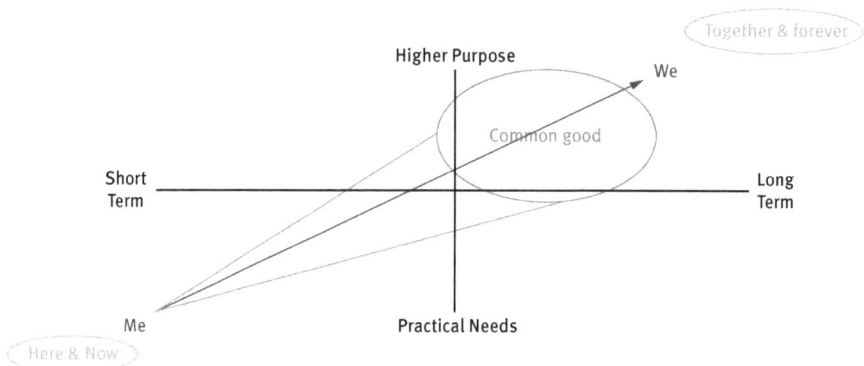

Figure 1.2: Summary of morality concepts and dimensions.

Individual versus organization: Perhaps another conflicting dimension of tension that bubbles under the surface and merits further attention is the contrast between the individual and the broader organization, especially institutional agency. Indeed, can organizations and society at large act morally other than through the action of individual members? Individual agents employ a situational way of looking at value problems (Fletcher, 1966), which is further conditioned by their sense of purpose (Frankl, 1992). Responsibility and morality relate to how individuals discharge their duties, use their knowledge, and interact with others, but they also require a supportive organization's scope, context, and setting. There is further a mismatch between individual responsibility and the parent organization. Responsibility is often accounted against and allocated to an individual name, but an agency can sometimes extend to groups, organizations, and institutions (Levy, 2018). Ultimately, organizations need individuals to act morally but give their employees space, power, and liberty. Yet, in providing such support, there can be an implication of (assumed) agency and an occasional inducement to conform to institutional priorities, politics, influences, and preferences. To overcome such tensions, sustained corporate moral excellence may require building institutions that are more resilient to moral failures. This is where spirituality may provide a holistic setting for enabling and empowering purposeful, meaningful, and even more passionate action from individuals seeking to shape, contribute, make a difference, and serve. Stewardship models can thus compete with traditional management and control structures as organizations learn to embrace new forms of creative engagement and deliver purposeful and considered actions.

1.14 Asking the Right Questions

You may have noticed the proliferation of open questions presented throughout this chapter to stimulate reflection and deeper discussion. Moral dilemmas ultimately require that we live with uncertainty, ambiguity, and contradiction as we seek to recalibrate our moral compass. However, the clashes between the different dimensions of morality often create confounding moral mazes requiring us to accommodate incommensurate positions. Morality does not provide guaranteed clarity, prescription, or magic solutions but rather an incessant system of posing, asking, questioning, and seeking sense. Verducci (2007, p. 43) is interested in the *response-ability* part of the responsibility, the ability to respond to needs by understanding what is required and identifying appropriate moral action. Gibbs (2012, p. 3) positions philosophical morality as the unremitting questioning between people while similarly placing a greater emphasis on the ability to answer, reflect, and engender a *response*. Gibbs' philosophy is predicated on the practice of questioning and responding to the questions of others, perhaps through posing additional questions in the form of common deliberation. Ethical thinking is often honed through continuously engaging with problems and questions. Grappling with questions seems an essential part of engaging with, making sense of, and sustaining our moral stance, thereby embedding morality as a process and a living and evolving (responsible) practice. We, therefore, conclude this chapter in that same tradition by posing a series of question clusters that will encourage the incessant search and adjustment needed for refreshing and retaining our true north moral focus while recognizing the situated nature of our morality:

- What is keeping me awake at night? Why has it not been resolved?
- What does success look like? Is it financial/economic, or does it encompass any dimension of engaging, stewardship, doing good, or giving back? Is it balanced?
- Is it harmful? To whom? How do we take risks entailing potential harm in situations of uncertainty? Is our role in avoiding risks or sharing the goods?
- Who is responsible? Are we responsible for outcomes extending beyond the life of a project? Can we justify our project choices based on actual consequences and outcomes? If so, how do we choose which action to undertake in situations of uncertainty? Are we considering long-term impacts? Where do usage, future upgrades, future-proofing, disposal, and decommissioning figure in our plans?
- In whose interest? Which stakeholders do we serve? Whose arguments count? How would I act if I cared about all involved? Who is representing our grand-children? Who is defending tradition, history, culture, and shared purpose and value for communities? Who will look after nature?
- How do we disentangle competing roles and duties? Whose moral norms are we applying? Am I forced to consider (or reconsider) where my obligations and duties lie? Is it more important to be a good employee or a good citizen?
- What is my purpose? What are my duties and obligations to the community and society? Am I doing enough? Am I a steward? Can I become a steward of a product, process, or resource? What resources should be cherished?
- Am I acting with fairness? Is this how I would like to be treated?
- Are there any warning signs? Am I being pressured to compromise or take a particular action? Is there any pressure on me to do "what is right"? Am I being reminded to look at the bigger picture? Am I being told that everyone does it or that no one will ever know?
- Does this feel right? Is this the right moral stance? How will it make me feel about myself? What actions will make me feel better about myself? And most importantly, will I still be able to look at myself in the mirror or sleep at night?

References

Adams, J. L. (1991). *Flying buttresses, entropy and o-rings: The world of an engineer*. Boston: Harvard University Press.
Asimov, I. (1950). *I, robot*. New York: Gnome Press.

Badaracco, L. (1997). *Defining moments: When managers must choose between right and right*. Boston: Harvard Business Press.

Barber, M. (2015). *How to run a government so that citizens benefit and taxpayers don't go crazy*. London: Allen Lane.

Barber, M. (2021). *Accomplishment: How to achieve ambitious and challenging things*. London: Allen Lane.

Barnard, C. I. (1938). *The functions of the executive*. Cambridge: Harvard university press.

Baron, P. (2016). *Utilitarianism & situation ethics*. Independently published: Active Education.

Barrett, R. (2006). *Building a values-driven organization*. Oxford: Butterworth-Heinemann.

Baum, B. (2016). *Rereading power and freedom in JS mill*. Toronto: University of Toronto Press.

Bauman, Z. (1988). *Freedom*. Milton Keynes: Open University Press.

BBC. (2014). 'Lovelocks' collapse Paris bridge rail. https://www.bbc.co.uk/news/av/world-europe -27758940/lovelocks-collapse-paris-bridge-rail(accessed July 2021).

Benkler, Y. (2016). Degrees of freedom, dimensions of power. *Daedalus, 145*(1), 18–32.

Bennis, W. (1999). Foreword. In Mitroff, I. I., & Denton, E. A. (Eds.), *A spiritual audit of corporate America: A hard look at spirituality, religion, and values in the workplace*. San Francisco: Jossey-Bass.

Berkes, F. (1985). Fishermen and 'the tragedy of the commons'. *Environmental Conservation, 12*(3), 199–206.

Birkinshaw, J., Foss, N. J., & Lindenberg, S. (2014). Combining purpose with profits. *MIT Sloan Management Review, 55*(3), 49.

Block, P. (1993/2013). *Stewardship: Choosing service over self-interest*. San Francisco: Berrett-Koehler Publishers.

Bouckaert, L., & Zsolnai, L. (2011). Spirituality and business. In Bouckaert, L., & Zsolnai, L. (Eds.) *Handbook of spirituality and business* (pp. 3–8). London: Palgrave Macmillan.

Cameron, K. S., & Quinn, R. E. (1988). Organizational paradox and transformation. In Quinn, R. E., & Cameron, K. S. (Eds.), *Paradox and transformation: Toward a theory of change in organization and management* (pp. 1–18). Cambridge, Mass.: Ballinger Publishing Co.

Campbell, R., & Kitson, A. (2008). *The ethical organisation*. London: Palgrave.

Collins, J. C., & Porras, J. I. (1996). Building your company's vision. *Harvard Business Review, 74*(5), 65–77.

Conway, P., & Gawronski, B. (2013). Deontological and utilitarian inclinations in moral decision making: A process dissociation approach. *Journal of Personality and Social Psychology, 104* (2), 216.

Craig, N., & Snook, S. (2014). From purpose to impact. *Harvard Business Review, 92*(5), 104–111.

Crockett, M. J. (2013). Models of morality. *Trends in Cognitive Sciences, 17*(8), 363–366.

Crockett, M. J., Kurth-Nelson, Z., Siegel, J. Z., Dayan, P., & Dolan, R. J. (2014). Harm to others outweighs the harm to self in moral decision making. *Proceedings of the National Academy of Sciences, 111*(48), 17320–17325.

Curry, O. S. (2016). Morality as cooperation: A problem-centred approach. In Shackelford, T. K., & Hansen, R. D. (Eds.), *The evolution of morality* (pp. 27–51). Cham: Springer.

Curry, O. S., Mullins, D. A., & Whitehouse, H. (2019). Is it good to cooperate? Testing the theory of morality-as-cooperation in 60 societies. *Current Anthropology, 60*(1), 47–69.

Dahl, A. (2019). The science of early moral development: On defining, constructing, and studying morality from birth. *Advances in Child Development and Behavior, 56*, 1–35.

Dalcher, D. (2007). Why the pilot cannot be blamed: A cautionary note about excessive reliance on technology. *International Journal of Risk Assessment and Management, 7*(3), 350–366.

Dalcher, D. (2014). Spiritual inspiration. In Dalcher, D. (Ed.), *Advances in project management: Narrated journeys in uncharted territory* (pp. 97–98). Farnham: Gower.

Dalcher, D. (2020). In whose interest? Repositioning the stakeholder paradox. *PM World Journal, 9* (9), 1–9.

Damon, W., & Bronk, K. C. (2007). Taking ultimate responsibility. In Gardner, H. (Ed.), *Responsibility at work: How leading professionals act (Or Don't Act) responsibly* (pp. 21–42). San Francisco: Jossey-Bass.

Davis, J. H., Schoorman, F. D., & Donaldson, L. (1997). Toward a stewardship theory of management. *Academy of Management Review, 22*(1), 20–47.

Davis, M. (1998). *Thinking like an engineer: Studies in the ethics of a profession*. Oxford: Oxford University Press.

Driver, J. (2010). *Ethics: The fundamentals*. Oxford: Blackwell.

Driver, J. (2011). *Consequentialism*. Abingdon: Routledge.

Drucker, P. F. (1988). Management and the world's work. *Harvard Business Review, 66*(5), 65–76.

Drucker, P. F. (2007). *The Essential Drucker*. Oxford: Elsevier.

Etzioni, A. (2014). *The common good*. Cambridge: Polity Press.

Etzioni, A. (2017). *The new normal: Finding a balance between individual rights and the common good*. New York: Routledge.

Feeny, D., Berkes, F., McCay, B. J., & Acheson, J. M. (1990). The tragedy of the commons: Twenty-two years later. *Human Ecology, 18*(1), 1–19.

Feeny, D., Hanna, S., & McEvoy, A. F. (1996). Questioning the assumptions of the" tragedy of the commons" model of fisheries. *Land Economics, 72*(2), 187–205.

FeldmanHall, O., Mobbs, D., Evans, D., Hiscox, L., Navrady, L., & Dalgleish, T. (2012). What we say and what we do: The relationship between real and hypothetical moral choices. *Cognition, 123* (3), 434–441.

Finkelstein, C. (2002). Is risk a harm?. *University of Pennsylvania Law Review, 151*, 963–1001.

Fisk, P. (2021). *Business recoded*. Chichester: John Wiley & Sons.

Fletcher, J. F. (1966). *Situation ethics: The new morality*. Louisville, KY: Westminster John Knox Press.

Foster, K. R., Vecchia, P., & Repacholi, M. H. (2000). Science and the precautionary principle. *Science, 288*(5468), 979–981.

Frankl, V. E. (1992). *Man's search for meaning*. London: Rider.

Freeman, R. E. (1984). *Strategic management: A stakeholder approach*. New York: Cambridge University Press.

Gardner, H. E. (2011a). *Leading minds: An anatomy of leadership*. New York: Basic Books.

Gardner, H. E. (2011b). *Truth, beauty, and goodness reframed: Educating for the virtues in the twenty-first century*. New York: Basic Books.

Gawronski, B. & Beer, J. S. (2017). What makes moral dilemma judgments "utilitarian" or "deontological"? *Social Neuroscience, 12*(6), 626–632.

Gentile, M. C. (2010). *Giving voice to values: How to speak your mind when you know what's right*. London: Yale University Press.

Gibbs, R. (2012). *Why ethics?: Signs of responsibilities*. Princeton: Princeton University Press.

Goodpaster, K. E. (1991). Business ethics and stakeholder analysis. *Business Ethics Quarterly*, 1(1), 53–73.

Greene, J. (2013). *Moral tribes: Emotion, reason, and the gap between us and them*. New York: Penguin.

Greene, J. D., Sommerville, R. B., Nystrom, L. E., Darley, J. M., & Cohen, J. D. (2001). An fMRI investigation of emotional engagement in moral judgment. *Science, 293*(5537), 2105–2108.

Haidt, J. (2007). The new synthesis in moral psychology. *science, 316*(5827), 998–1002.

Haidt, J. (2011). *The righteous mind: Why Good people are divided by politics and religion*. New York: Pantheon.

Hamel, G. (2012). *What matters Now*. San Francisco: Jossey-Bass.

Hamilton, L. (2014). *Freedom is power: Liberty through political representation*. Cambridge: Cambridge University Press.

Hardin, G. (1968). The tragedy of the commons. *Science, 162*(3859), 1243–1248.

Hardin, G. (1998). Extensions of "the tragedy of the commons". *Science, 280*(5364), 682–683.

Hardy, S. A., & Carlo, G. (2005). Identity as a source of moral motivation. *Human Development, 48* (4), 232–256.

Hardy, S. A., & Carlo, G. (2011). Moral identity: What is it, how does it develop, and is it linked to moral action? *Child Development Perspectives, 5*(3), 212–218.

Hendry, J. (2004). *Between enterprise and ethics: Business and management in a bimoral society*. Oxford: Oxford University Press.

Hernandez, M. (2012). Toward an understanding of the psychology of stewardship. *Academy of Management Review, 37*(2), 172–193.

Hollenbach, D. S. (2016). Borders and duties to the displaced: Ethical perspectives on the refugee protection system. *Journal on Migration and Human Security, 4*(3), 148–165.

Holyoak, K. J., & Powell, D. (2016). Deontological coherence: A framework for commonsense moral reasoning. *Psychological Bulletin, 142*(11), 1179.

Hosmer, L. T. (1994). Strategic planning as if ethics mattered. *Strategic Management Journal, 15* (S2), 17–34.

Hubbard, D. W. (2020). *The failure of risk management: Why it's broken and how to fix it*. Hoboken, New Jersey: John Wiley & Sons.

IIRC. (2013). *The international <IR> framework*. London: Author.

Johansen, R. (2012). *Leaders make the future: Ten new leadership skills for an uncertain world*. San Francisco: Berrett-Koehler Publishers.

Jonas, H. (1985). *The imperative of responsibility: In search of an ethics for the technological age*. Chicago: University of Chicago press.

Kamm, F. M. (2008). *Intricate ethics: Rights, responsibilities, and permissable harm*. New York: Oxford University Press.

Kaplan, S. (2020). *The 360° corporation*. Stanford: Stanford University Press.

Kempster, S., Jackson, B., & Conroy, M. (2011). Leadership as purpose: Exploring the role of purpose in leadership practice. *Leadership, 7*(3), 317–334.

Kempster, S., Maak, T., & Parry, K. (Eds.). (2019). *Good dividends: Responsible leadership of business purpose*. Abingdon: Routledge.

Kidder, R., & Bloom, S. (2001). Ethical fitness in today's business environment. In Moon, C., & Bonny, C. (Eds.), *Business ethics – facing up to the issues* (pp. 57–73). London: The Economist Books.

Kohlberg, L. (1963). The development of children's orientations toward a moral order I. Sequence in the development of moral thought. *Vita Humana, 6*(1–2), 11–33.

Kohlberg, L. (1973). The claim to moral adequacy of a highest stage of moral judgment. *Journal of Philosophy, 70*(18), 630–646.

Kohlberg, L. (1981). *Essays on moral development, vol. I: The philosophy of moral development*. San Francisco, CA: Harper & Row.

Kotler, P. (2019). *Advancing the Common Good: Strategies for Businesses, Governments, and Nonprofits*. Santa Barbara: Praeger.

Kriebel, D., Tickner, J., Epstein, P., Lemons, J., Levins, R., Loechler, E. L., . . . Stoto, M. (2001). The precautionary principle in environmental science. *Environmental Health Perspectives, 109*(9), 871–876.

Lakoff, G., & Johnson, M. (1999). *Philosophy in the flesh: The embodied mind and its challenge to western thought* (Vol. 640). New York: Basic books.

Learned, E. P., Christensen, C. R., Andrews, K. R., & Guth, W. D. (1965). *Business policy: Text and cases*. Homewood, Ill.: Irwin.

Lekan, T. (2003). *Making morality: Pragmatist reconstruction in ethical theory*. Nashville: Vanderbilt University Press.

Levy, N. (2018). Socializing responsibility. In Hutchison, K., Mackenzie, C., & Oshana, M. (eds.), *Social dimensions of moral responsibility* (pp. 2018). New York: Oxford University Press.

Light, A., & Katz, E. (1996). *Environmental pragmatism*. New York: Routledge.

Linklater, A. (2006). The harm principle and global ethics. *Global Society, 20*(3), 329–343.

Lockhart, T. (2000). *Moral uncertainty and its consequences*. New York: Oxford University Press.

Long, A. A., & Sedley, D. N. (1987). *The hellenistic philosophers: Volume 1, translations of the principal sources with philosophical commentary*. Cambridge: Cambridge University Press.

Lloyd, W. F. (1833). *Two lectures on the checks to population*. Oxford: Oxford University Press.

MacAskill, M., Bykvist, K., & Ord, T. (2020). *Moral uncertainty*. Oxford: Oxford University Press.

Margolis, J. D. (2009). The responsibility gap. *The Hedgehog Review, 11*(2), 41–54.

Martin, M. W., & Schinzinger, R. (2004). *Ethics in engineering* (4th ed.). New York: McGraw-Hill.

Martin, M. W., & Schinzinger, R. (2010). *Introduction to engineering ethics* (2nd ed.). New York: McGraw-Hill.

Maslow, A. H. (1971). *The farther reaches of human nature*. New York: Viking Press.

Mauri, T. (2020). *The 3D leader*. Harlow: Pearson UK.

Melé, D. (2011). *Management ethics: Placing ethics at the core of good management*. London: Palgrave Macmillan.

Michener, A., DeLamanter, J., Schwartz, S., & Merton, R. (1990). *Social psychology*. New York: Harcourt Brace Jovanovich.

Middlebrooks, A., & Noghiu, A. (2010). Leadership and spiritual capital: Exploring the link between individual service disposition and organizational value. *International Journal of Leadership Studies, 6*(1), 67–85.

Mill, J. S. (2015). *On liberty, utilitarianism, and other essays*. Oxford: Oxford University Press.

Miller, K. W., & Voas, J. (2008). IT as a profession: Is competent creation the primary goal?. *IT Professional, 10*(6), 15–17.

Mitroff, I. I., & Denton, E. A. (1999). *A spiritual audit of corporate America: A hard look at spirituality, religion, and values in the workplace*. San Francisco: Jossey-Bass.

Moore, C., & Gino, F. (2013). Ethically adrift: How others pull our moral compass from true North, and how we can fix it. *Research in Organizational Behavior, 33*, 53–77.

Moore, G. E. (1903). *Principia ethica*. Cambridge: Cambridge University Press.

Morris, J. (Ed.). (2000). *Rethinking risk and the precautionary principle*. Oxford: Butterworth-Heinemann.

Mourkogiannis, N. (2006). *Purpose: The Starting point of great companies*. New York: St. Martin's Press.

Neal, J., & Harpham, A. (2012). *The spirit of project management*. Farnham: Gower.

Nelkin, D. K. (2011). *Making sense of freedom and responsibility*. New York: Oxford University Press.

Neubert, M. J., Bradley, S. W., Ardianti, R., & Simiyu, E. M. (2017). The role of spiritual capital in innovation and performance: Evidence from developing economies. *Entrepreneurship Theory and Practice, 41*(4), 621–640.

O'Boyle, T. F. (2011). *At any cost: Jack Welch, general electric, and the pursuit of profit*. New York: Vintage.

Oppenheim, F. E. (1961). *Dimensions of freedom: An analysis*. New York: St. Martin's Press.

Ostrom, E. (1990). *Governing the commons: The evolution of institutions for collective action*. Cambridge: Cambridge university press.

Ostrom, E. (2008). Tragedy of the commons. In Durlauf, S. N., & Blume, L. E. (Eds.), *The new Palgrave dictionary of economics* (2nd ed., pp. 360–363). New York: Palgrave Macmillan.

Ostrom, E. (2012). *The future of the commons-beyond market failure and government regulation.* London: Institute of Economic Affairs Monographs.

Ostrom, E. E., Dietz, T. E., Dolšak, N. E., Stern, P. C., Stonich, S. E., & Weber, E. U. (2002). *The drama of the commons.* Washington, DC: National Academy Press.

Parkinson, G. H. R. (1971). Spinoza on the power and freedom of man. *The Monist, 55*(4), 527–553.

Passmore, J. A. (1974). *Man's responsibility for nature: Ecological problems and western traditions.* London: Duckworth.

Petrick, J. A., & Quinn, J. F. (1997). *Management ethics: Integrity at work.* London: Sage.

Pettit, P. (1996). Freedom as antipower. *Ethics, 106*(3), 576–604.

Pettit, P. (2014). *Just freedom: A moral compass for a complex world (Norton global ethics series).* New York: WW Norton & Company.

Piaget, J. (1928). *The child's conception of the world.* London: Routledge & Kegan Paul.

Piaget, J. (1932). *The moral judgment of the child.* London: Routledge & Kegan Paul.

Pinkus, R. L., Shuman, L. J., Hummon, N. P., & Wolfe, H. (1997). *Engineering ethics: Balancing cost, schedule, and risk-lessons learned from the space shuttle.* New York: Cambridge University Press.

Porter, M. E., & Kramer, M. R. (2011). Creating shared value. *Harvard Business Review, 89*(1), 62–77.

Portmore, D. W. (2011). *Commonsense consequentialism: Wherein morality meets rationality.* New York: Oxford University Press.

Postrel, V. (1998). *The future and its enemies: The growing conflict over creativity, enterprise.* New York: Simon and Schuster.

Portmore, D. W. (Ed.). (2020). *The oxford handbook of consequentialism.* New York: Oxford University Press.

Power, M. (2007). *Organized uncertainty: Designing a world of risk management.* Oxford: Oxford University Press.

RAE. (2011). *Engineering ethics in practice: A guide for engineers.* London: The Royal Academy of Engineering.

Rest, J. R. (1986). *Moral development: Advances in research and theory.* New York: Praeger.

Reynolds, S. J., & Ceranic, T. L. (2007). The effects of moral judgment and moral identity on moral behavior: An empirical examination of the moral individual. *Journal of Applied Psychology, 92* (6), 1610–1624.

Reynolds, S. J., Owens, B. P., & Rubenstein, A. L. (2012). Moral stress: Considering the nature and effects of managerial moral uncertainty. *Journal of Business Ethics, 106*(4), 491–502.

Rhodes, T. (2002). The 'risk environment': A framework for understanding and reducing drug-related harm. *International Journal of Drug Policy, 13*(2), 85–94.

Rhodes, T., & Hedrich, D. (2010). *Harm reduction: Evidence, impacts and challenges.* Luxembourg: Office for Official Publications of the European Communities.

Roe, G. (2005). Harm reduction as paradigm: Is better than bad good enough? The origins of harm reduction. *Critical Public Health, 15*(3), 243–250.

Ronel, N. (2008). The experience of spiritual intelligence. *Journal of Transpersonal Psychology, 40* (1), 100–119.

Sacks, J. (2020). *Morality: Restoring the common good in divided times.* New York: Basic Books.

Schaich Borg, J., Sinnott-Armstrong, W., Calhoun, V. D., & Kiehl, K. A. (2011). Neural basis of moral verdict and moral deliberation. *Social Neuroscience, 6*(4), 398–413.

Scheffler, S. (Ed.). (1988). *Consequentialism and its critics.* Oxford: Oxford University Press.

Sheldrake, P. (2012). *Spirituality: A very short introduction.* Oxford: Oxford University Press.

Shelley, M. W. (1818). *Frankenstein; or the modern Prometheus*. London: Lackington, Hughes, Harding, Mavor, & Jones.

Simon, H. A. (1947). *Administrative behavior*; A study of of decision making processes in adminstrative organization. New York: Macmillan.

Simon, J., Powers, C. W., & Gunnemann, J. P. (1972). *The ethical investor: Universities and corporate responsibility*. New Haven: Yale University Press.

SEP. (2019). Consequentialism. Stanford Encyclopedia of Philosophy. Accessed: June 2021, https://plato.stanford.edu/entries/consequentialism/?utm_campaign=Matt%27s%20Thoughts%20In%20Between&utm_medium=email&utm_source=Revue%20newsletter

SEP. (2020). The Definition of Morality. Stanford Encyclopedia of Philosophy. Accessed: June 2021, https://plato.stanford.edu/entries/morality-definition/

SEP. (2021). Value theory. Stanford Encyclopedia of Philosophy. Accessed: June 2021, https://plato.stanford.edu/entries/value-theory/#Tel

Singer, P. (2015). *The most good you can do*. New Haven: Yale University Press.

SOR. (2021). Statue of responsibility. Accessed July 2021. https://statueofresponsibility.com

Sparrow, M. K. (2008). *The character of harms: Operational challenges in control*. New York: Cambridge University Press.

Staw, B. M., & Boettger, R. D. (1990). Task revision: A neglected form of work performance. *Academy of Management Journal, 33*(3), 534–559.

Sunstein, C. R. (2003). Beyond the precautionary principle. *University of Pennsylvania Law Review, 151*(3), 1003–1058.

Sunstein, C. R. (2021). *Averting catastrophe: Decision theory for covid-19, climate change, and potential disasters of all kinds*. New York: New York University Press.

Tanner, C., Medin, D. L., & Iliev, R. (2008). Influence of deontological versus consequentialist orientations on act choices and framing effects: When principles are more important than consequences. *European Journal of Social Psychology, 38*(5), 757–769.

Tännsjö, T. (2013). *Understanding ethics: An introduction to moral theory*. Edinburgh: Edinburgh University Press.

Tata, R., Hart, S. L., Sharma, A., & Sarkar, C. (2013). Why making money is not enough. *MIT Sloan Management Review, 54*(4), 95–96. summer 2013

Tillman, J. J. (2016). *An integrative model of moral deliberation*. London: Palgrave Macmillan.

Tomasello, M., & Vaish, A. (2013). Origins of human cooperation and morality. *Annual Review of Psychology, 64*, 231–255.

Van Zyl, L. (2018). *Virtue ethics: A contemporary introduction*. London: Routledge.

Verducci, S. (2007). The ability to respond. In Gardner, H. (Ed.), *Responsibility at work: How leading professionals act (or don't act) responsibly* (pp. 21–42). San Francisco: Jossey-Bass.

Verkerk, M. J., De Leede, J., & Nijhof, A. H. (2001). From responsible management to responsible organizations: The democratic principle for managing organizational ethics. *Business and Society Review, 106*(4), 353–378.

Zohar, D., & Marshall, I. (2004). *Spiritual capital: Wealth we can live by*. San Francisco: Berrett-Koehler Publishers.

Loredana Abramo
2 Walking the Road to a Diverse and Inclusive Project Team

Context: This chapter examines the issues that project managers, leaders, and teams face when attempting to create an inclusive working environment that embraces diversity.

Characters: The focus of this chapter is on senior management and leaders in project organizations.

Locations: Examples are drawn from project organisations **all over the world**.

Challenges/conflict/tension: This chapter examines the gap between the rhetoric and reality of diversity and inclusion in projects.

Research gaps: What is the story told by data (or lack thereof) from organizations, and how do organizations go forward to implement a new equilibrium? A dynamic vision for a diverse, inclusive, and adaptable team.

Keywords: diversity, inclusivity, teamwork, candidates, internationalization

2.1 Introduction

I have worked on geographically, culturally, and organizationally diverse projects for my entire 30+ years career. As a young woman expatriate, first in the USA, then in Japan and Singapore, I have been the "different one" in most of my projects, so I have been able to experience, learn, and leverage the sense of "not fitting" most of my teams' cultural and behavioral molds. Having experienced the struggles, the rewards, the setbacks, and the successes tied to a work environment ever challenging, I offer my reflections on this aspect of responsible project management. Beyond my own experience, I include the outcomes of interviews with a young entrepreneur, cofounder of a very successful start-up company, and a senior partner at a large consulting corporation who has placed diversity and inclusion as a global priority.

While most organizations pay lip service to the importance of diversity, 23% of project professionals still do not feel their voice is represented in their organization. Most organizations do not have culturally diverse senior leadership (PMI, June 2019). Even when recruitment efforts are in place to widen the organizational landscape, minority individuals feel "un-heard" and disengaged (Moore et al., 2020).

Consider how problematic it is to stubbornly continue down the same path even when faced with evidence that what you are doing is not working. This unhelpful

https://doi.org/10.1515/9783110724783-004

approach is called *escalation of commitment*, a term coined by Berkley psychologist Barry Staw (Guillen, 2020). We need to change the approach used so far by slowly introducing changes to accommodate reality rather than our models or expectations.

What can responsible project managers and sponsors do in practice to foster and empower diversity and inclusion among teams? An essential element on this path is to acknowledge and identify inevitable bias (Lewis, 2016) that prevents accessing the full potential of all individuals in the project.

As responsible project managers, we can leverage an evidence-based approach to focus on engagement and stewardship (RPM Manifesto, 2020) and make sure we use "slow thinking" (Kahneman, 2013) to assess potential and opportunities for each individual in our project teams and the organization.

2.2 Problem Statements

We know from numerous studies and practical experience that "a truly diverse team can deliver better results, tap into a deeper talent pool and bring fresh perspectives to everything we do" (APM.org.uk, 2019). Those in positions of power acknowledge this fact as well. Over 80% of project leaders agree that culturally and geographically diverse teams increase project value (PMI, June 2019). More than 900 CEOs of top companies pledge their commitment to "cultivate a trusting environment where all ideas are welcomed, and employees feel comfortable and empowered to have discussions about diversity and inclusion" (CEOaction, 2020). Yet women, for example, currently hold only about 6.0% of CEO positions at S&P 500 companies (Catalyst, 2020).

There is a mismatch between stated goals and reality.

We have seen it and experienced it first-hand. When our executives choose a "mate from University" over a competent and experienced alternative, when careers thrive only for individuals of a specific background/race/gender, we know that there is no real commitment to a diverse and inclusive working environment. This "escalation of commitment" (Guillen, 2020) leads to monochromatic teams, too narrow-focused opportunities for select individuals and dysfunctional organizations in the long term.

This is the first problem statement:

We perpetuate behaviors that constrain the level of diversity in our project teams.

Why does senior leadership in many organizations continue to blissfully prolong these unhelpful hiring and career growth choices, despite all proof to support the importance of diverse teams?

The alternative requires *slow thinking*, which takes time and effort (Kahneman, 2013). One has to attempt to detach oneself from the easy way out of seemingly mundane decisions. Instead of proposing a one-size-fits-all career development program to all in the project team, we should look at what makes sense for individuals with different backgrounds and cultural traits. Instead of hiring someone who has familiar behaviors, we should choose someone who fits the project's needs and brings a different point of view. Instead of expecting the same contributions from each person, we should *enable* all individuals to deliver by fulfilling their potential.

The second problem statement:

Decision-makers typically "trust their instincts"; they "know best" even when faced with incontrovertible data to the contrary.

Let us consider a concrete case. In a large multinational corporation, the Global PMO had launched a large transformation project, impacting how all 3,500 customer delivery project managers operated, adopting a new process and a global tool enabling seamless cross-functional collaboration, project delivery, and reporting. The project team included a global leader, functioning as the overall general project manager, and regional leaders, who would represent and champion each geographical region in the company. Each regional leader and the overall global leader were senior project managers who had years of experience in managing international customer projects – they had the relationships, credibility, and knowledge to work with the community of project managers impacted by the transformation project. When the global leader moved to a different project and had to be replaced, two regional leaders applied for the position. Instead, the hiring manager chose a candidate well known to him, even if he did not have any project delivery experience or a first-hand understanding of the community's challenges targeted by the transformation project. The project was heavily impacted by the resulting loss of momentum, laborious building of knowledge and relationships, and overall lack of common ground with the target audience for the organizational transformation.

Sound familiar? In this case, ease of interaction (sitting on the same floor in the exact location) was chosen over objective analysis of the candidates' experience and qualifications. The effort required to overcome the initial communications inertia with one of the (better qualified) candidates was more than the hiring manager was willing to make. The research into the candidates' experience and personal traits required an investment in time that was not considered necessary. As a result, the project team, and ultimately the project, had a negative diversity and success bottom line.

Kahneman describes this as a "Lazy System 2" (Kahneman, 2013), where System 2 is the "slow thinking" effortful system, as opposed to "System 1," which is the "fast thinking," intuitive flight-or-fight decision-making that impacts many of our daily choices (Kahneman, 2011). This inherent "intellectual sloth" (Kahneman, 2011) prevents a more deliberative analysis of the facts, which would lead to a more accurate, evidence-based decision. According to Lewis, "Remove their gut feelings, and their judgments improved" (Lewis, 2016) – by consciously taking the time and effort to analyze facts, we can reach more effective decisions.

Bias is present in most project decisions simply because it takes less effort to use our intuition than it would take to gather and analyze the data needed for a fact-based choice. These could be personal, organizational, or cultural biases, they could be evident or implicit, and they might impact us at a different degree of consciousness. We all use heuristics, or "mental shortcuts," to expedite decision-making every day: we rely on what has worked in the past to act quickly (Dale, 2018).

Choosing predictable and familiar patterns instead of embarking on a less familiar and time-consuming analysis of the data, coupled with the inevitable stress of decision-making, are often why we make bad choices as we manage our teams.

As stated by Bazerman, "These biases are created by the tendency to short-circuit a rational decision process by relying on several simplifying strategies, or rules of thumb, known as heuristics. Heuristics allow us to cope with the complex environment surrounding our decisions. Unfortunately, they also lead to systematic and predictable biases" (Bazerman, 2021).

It is something that pervades all domains of human life. As Lewis describes in *The Undoing Project* (Lewis, 2017), even those doctors who helped frame fact-based medical parameters for early cancer diagnostics fail to use these criteria themselves and incorrectly misinterpret symptoms.

The first step in addressing these issues must be tied to acknowledging our own biases, as individuals, as a team, and as an organization.

2.3 Measurement Issues: The Stories Told by Data (or Lack Thereof)

A couple of years ago, a senior project manager saw an enthusiastic blog about International Women's Day from an executive in the senior leadership team of the large corporation she worked for on her corporate social media. When she asked what quantitative measures were in place to track gender equality progress (there was less than 10% female presence both in the senior leadership team and on the board of directors), there was a circuitous answer about privacy and how data could not be shared. When she proposed to track percentages of high-performing women who were coached and offered career opportunities, there was silence.

Transparency of established measurements has a critical role in improving diversity and inclusion.

How can we improve what we do not measure? No plan can be successful without tracking progress from where we are to where we need to be. This means we must take responsibility for implementing any initiatives to increase diversity and inclusion in our teams. How can there be "equal opportunity" without accountability?

Despite achieving diversity recruitment goals, many companies struggle with providing the ability for each individual to leverage their assets and work effectively in the organization. Moore et al. (2020) highlight one more aspect: team "members from diverse backgrounds might participate in multiple levels but might not feel able to contribute fully, or influence processes, or might feel tokenised or unwelcome, potentially contributing to disengagement."

I have discussed this issue with David Simnick, SoapBox CEO and Co-founder. Simnick started a successful company from his apartment right out of college (soapboxsoaps.com, 2020) – predicting a substantial engagement with the community as a key to the value proposition of their soaps and personal care products. According to Simnick, a diverse team has always been a consumer imperative for his company because it fulfills a broad spectrum of personal care needs. As a result, SoapBox has women in 50% of senior leadership positions and employees with a background from six countries over three continents. Given the approach taken by its founders, everyone contributes significantly *because* they come from different backgrounds and have diverse needs and ideas that impact the company's ability to reach a broader consumer base. The variety in skin types and hair texture, the different preferences in skin hydration – these all require decision-makers to pay attention, and to listen to diverse voices around the table. In this case, a diverse and inclusive team is a business imperative. When asked how he managed bias and inclusion, Simnick commented with an insightful point: we all listen to our implicit biases and prejudices more than we listen to reason, and this awareness of our gaps in understanding should drive us to work diligently with our teams, by holding deliberate conversations and enabling everyone's voice.

In general, we have an abundance of data available to us from a large variety of sources: we even must come up with new terms to measure all the data available in the data warehouses. Nevertheless, organizational diversity information is not collected nor analyzed. It is shrouded in mystery, with a few exceptions.

Why? Maybe we do not know *what* we need to measure at the organizational level to assess where we stand and need to be. The inherent difficulty in identifying appropriate measures of team diversity could be a key contributor to the lack of quantitative indicators for diversification.

April and Blass (2010) describe an Inclusion Index™ to help organizations develop insights; this index is based on a 10-dimensional measurement framework:
– senior managers
– immediate manager
– values
– recruitment
– promotion/progression and development
– fitting in
– bullying/harassment
– dialogue
– organizational belonging
– emotional well-being

The use of a dedicated index can support both diversity and inclusion objectives. We can develop such an index based on the specific organizational situation, tailor it to the organization, and make sure it evolves (see Table 2.1).

Table 2.1: Examples of diversity and inclusion indicators (author).

What	Why
Recruitment statistics	Do they reflect the gender/racial/cultural mix of the community we operate in?
Attrition and retention statistics	are some groups more likely to "slow down" their careers or even move on to a different job?
From mid-level and senior positions to executive roles, including the advancement	Do leadership positions statistics reflect the community in which we are working?
Employee engagement (only if using strictly anonymous surveys)	Does everyone feel "heard"?

We can use a weighted matrix, or MESA – Matrix for the Evaluation of Strategic Alternatives (Thiry, 2003), to prioritize and track the areas of improvement we are targeting.

A baseline snapshot and related analysis can trigger actions to identify the root cause (are we recruiting from the same universities, year over year? Are we using the same criteria to assess productivity?) and possible action plans.

Some organizations have invested heavily in tracking progress to implement steps to increase diversity and inclusion at the leadership level. C-level support and championing of these initiatives has been an essential element of success, as is the transparency of diversity and inclusion (DNI) measures and initiatives.

We can measure evolution to a more responsible attitude to team management within our project teams by working from the ground up. What does the team look like? How many cultural, organizational, and geographical examples are there? And – more importantly – what can we do to improve?

2.4 Analyzing Evidence to Diversify and Include Actively

When we examine the type of data we have painstakingly collected, there is tremendous inertia that will induce us to procrastinate, avoid, and even transfer the tasks related to data analysis. It is the "Lazy System 2" we discussed earlier (Kahneman, 2011). Often, our management will direct us to be fast and use our instincts. While experiential instincts are essential in many areas (athletes, musicians, and skilled workers must rely on what they have learned over the years to respond to stimuli), heuristic judgment is often based on likes and dislikes, not supported by reasoning (Kahneman, 2011).

In one of my more complex projects, we needed several team members. Our recruiter had already used standard Applicant Tracking Systems to parse through the candidates' CVs, but we wanted additional screening before starting the interviews. We

Table 2.2: Proficiency requirements (author).

Position: Senior engineer		
Skillset	**Required proficiency***	**Candidate assessment**
IT background	5	
Sales experience	2	
Customer mindset	6	
Cultural intelligence	5	
Project-specific technical knowledge	7	
Communication skills	6	
Ability to adapt to change	6	

*Proficiency 1–7: 1 = low, 7 = expert.

prepared a spreadsheet with the characteristics we needed to include in the project team. I brainstormed with my lead engineers what organizational and technical background we needed *in an abstract* to deliver the project without names or specific individuals in mind. So we set up *proficiency requirements for each position* (Table 2.2). Then we asked a colleague not involved with the project to redact incoming CVs, to remove all information that could trigger unconscious biases, such as:
–   Name/photo: use a number to identify the candidate
–   Place/date of birth and age
–   Any personal data (email, phone number, address)

- University attendance years
- Swap specific dates with durations (years of experience)

We used redacted versions of the candidates' CVs to map individuals to people's requirements and built a candidate's shortlist from the ground up without knowing the candidates' names. While we did get an initial pushback ("yes, I do need to take the time now to do this, rather than make changes in the team in the middle of delivery"), we were able to tailor our interviews to verify our assumptions, adjust the list of final candidates, and eventually obtain a refreshingly diverse team. See details below for an example of redaction (in reality, we used a marker so that no information would be visible) – only information pertinent to the candidate's experience has been extracted. Redactor's notes (in bold) provide the required information.

Candidate #5

- Home Phone **on file**
- Mobile Phone **on file**
- Email **on file**
- Objective: Senior engineer management role in mid-size telecommunications equipment manufacturer
- Key Skills and Expertise: Problem Solving, Process Definition, Customer Relations, Project Management, Customer Presentation, Team Management
- Work Experience:
- Midwest Engineering Manager: *Big Telecommunications Systems, Inc. ~~from 2017 to Present~~* **5 yrs**
- Technical Support Team Leader: *Big Telecommunications Systems, Inc. ~~from 2012 to 2016~~* **4 yrs**
- Deployment Team Technician: *Big Telecommunications Systems, Inc. ~~from 2009 to 2011~~* **3 yrs**
- System Tester: *East Coast Telecommunications Services, Inc. ~~from 2002 to 2006~~* **5 yrs**
- Education:
- Master of Business Administration *~~Private Midwest University 2008~~*
- Bachelor of Science Information Technology *~~Beijing University 2001~~*

The type of redaction and the skill sets required for the positions need to be adjusted for the role, the project, and the overall organizational targets. Having learned firsthand the consequences of rushing through the interviews and recruitment phase, I was confident enough to fight back the inevitable management requests to expedite and ensure we would be diligent in this process. One more step is to rely on data and mitigate unconscious biases. There must be a top-down strategy at the organizational level, cascaded and demonstrated in and by the leadership team.

I talked to Karl Alleman, US Managing Director for Egon Zehnder, a global company with a strong commitment to diversity and inclusion (Egon Zehnder and out leadership announce partnership 2020), to understand how he approaches recruitment retention engagement in his teams. Alleman, who has authored several articles about this topic (Alleman et al., 2019, 2021), has highlighted some critical aspects.

> First, if our recruitment is based on our professional network, chances are we will be looking at individuals who have much in common with us: similar background, education, and cultural identity. We should "widen the bar", according to Alleman, tapping into a wider talent pool from a variety of colleges, backgrounds and professional organisations. Quotas will not work long term: excluding candidates because of their non-minority background would weaken our credibility as an equal opportunity employer and is even illegal in many countries. However, expanding our search to include a wider variety of candidates will provide a way forward to a diverse talent pool.

Retention of a diverse employee population is often an issue, and it is tied to many factors, such as organizational inclusion, appropriate coaching, and focused leadership development. That is why an executive prioritization of these initiatives can be successful if coupled with a grassroots engagement in finding what works for the individuals in the organization and the specific community in which it operates.

Listening, engaging diligently, and demonstrating commitment have been, in Alleman's experience, the most effective leadership tools on the path to tangible, measurable results: he set up a cross-organizational committee of individuals who could reach out and engage employees to determine the most effective course of action, which was then reviewed and implemented with senior management's complete oversight and support.

For example, if we observe high attrition in some job types, we might find out that those are the jobs with the least options for a "career" in the organization. Providing focused attention and options, such as a dual ladder management choice, might address this issue.

Coaching high-performing individuals and ensuring they are offered growth opportunities is important, but the "type" of coaching and the "type" of opportunities are essential. For example, coaching a woman to behave "like one of the boys" will not improve the likelihood of success of that individual. Similarly, proposing a new job opportunity that requires relocation to a much more expensive location might be ineffective without adjusting for the cost-of-living differential.

As project leaders, one of our top requirements is to be humble. Why humility? Because it "is the integration of self-awareness, teachability, and an appreciation of the capabilities of others. These traits allow for inclusive teams and continuous learning that are foundational for creating innovative cultures." (Alleman et al., 2019) And we need humility to make sound decisions, coach our teams, and enable the internal pipeline in our projects and organizations. This aligns with the concept of Servant Leadership (Greenleaf, 1977) and its impact on the organizational culture (Kim et al., 2020).

Inclusion can be an elusive target. Earlier I mentioned engagement surveys. These are helpful only if they are conducted with guarantees of anonymity. I want to state very clearly the importance of maintaining data privacy. When surveying employees, by surveying employees, we must protect personal information and tread carefully as we assess gaps in our engagement surveys.

Through engagement surveys, we can understand who is feeling "left out," even by looking at the participation rates and comparing them to the overall organizational landscape. Are all genders, racial groups, cultures, and geographical represented among the respondents reflecting a balanced subset of the organization? If they are not, then we already have an indicator of who is already disengaged. By examining the results of a well-prepared survey, "listening" to our teams, we can start to understand the symptoms of our inclusion gap.

Let us discuss now something I have called, in the privacy of my thoughts, the "chameleon" behavior, or as it is broadly known "code-switching." Individuals change their speech, looks, and behavior to adapt to their environment to improve the likelihood of "fitting in." Just like an individual bilingual switches between two languages depending on whom they are talking to or what they are discussing, a person can adapt to a different speech style, dress code, or behavior at work. I have done that several times, both linguistically and behaviorally.

"While it is frequently seen as crucial for professional advancement, code-switching often comes at a great psychological cost. Suppose leaders are truly seeking to promote inclusion and address social inequality. In that case, they must begin by understanding why a segment of their workforce believes that they cannot truly be themselves in the office" (McCluney et al., 2019). Some aspects of code-switching are related to objective workspace realities (e.g., we **all** have to abide by a dress code when meeting customers and keep a moderate tone of voice when discussing a topic). There are many situations where a need to fit racial/gender/cultural norms drives individuals to act "a conforming part continually." While this behavior might be necessary and acceptable in some circumstances, it will severely impact, in the long term, any sense of inclusion for those who feel compelled to act this way.

To mitigate the perceived "need" to code-switch, the organizational leadership (or the project leader if all else fails) has to send an unequivocal message that personal preferences are respected. The US Army (just) announced a series of new grooming policies that will allow soldiers to wear ponytails, locks, lipstick, and even earrings (Mizelle, 2021). This step will not immediately resolve all issues related to inclusiveness in the military. However, it is a move in the right direction, a way to show a willingness to "listen" to different grooming preferences.

Code-switching could manifest, for example, by accepting that our peers mispronounce or even outright refuse to pronounce our name. For years, the first question I was asked when joining a new team was: "do you have a nickname?" For years, my answer has been: "no." As asserted by Nathoo, habitually mispronouncing or refusing to learn how to pronounce an unfamiliar name is "a form of implicit discrimination" (Nathoo, 2021): it is like saying to an individual that they are not important enough to make an effort to learn their name. When we lead by example in our projects and take the time to pronounce (and get corrected and try until we get it right) the names of our team members, we send a powerful message: each individual is accepted and deserving of attention. It might seem like a small step, but it will demonstrate respect and acceptance to all team members.

Age discrimination is a pervasive issue that can impact the engagement of our teams: the "generational aspect of the environment, upbringing, values and technology that characterise groups of individuals" (Abramo, 2017). When I worked with some millennial, I found it helpful to text, to have informal chats in a coffee shop, and to ensure our community engagement and corporate outreach programs were visible and accessible. When working with Boomers or Gen X individuals, the courtesy of a phone call has often been well received. This should not be interpreted as a generalization: just by assessing someone's age group, we cannot make assumptions about their preferences in communication methods. All I am saying is that I have found that paying attention to each person's preferences, a relatively small investment in time and effort, has paid off over time by improving the effectiveness of my communication with the team.

Is this a "reverse chameleon"? Indeed, it might well be, and it is a welcome tactic if it helps us reach out and engage our teams so individual contributors feel respected, appreciated, and accepted as they are. Our job as responsible project managers and leaders is to treat everyone as an "Individual Deserving Of Our Attention" without assumptions or constraints, so we can enable them to work effectively. There are also multiple other avenues to promote and leverage diversity beyond recruiting, retention, and inclusion.

For example, vendors and contractors are part of our extended project teams. How do we choose them? By selecting a location for a new depot assessing social and environmental impact for our project. In other words, many of the choices we make as we manage responsibly must consider our overall diversity and inclusion strategy. Some organizations have set up supply chain parameters to include minority-owned vendors.

2.5 Implementation: A Dynamic Vision for Diversity, Inclusivity, and Adaptability

There is no silver bullet or label that can cover all circumstances. It would be unwise to expect a single, universal answer to implement diversity and inclusion in our projects.

Labels and classifications are ever-present traps that can sabotage our best intentions to improve our projects and organizations' diversity and inclusion landscape. Once again, heuristic approaches often introduce error-biased judgments (Dale, 2018). What works today will be obsolete as our team and our projects evolve. A sustainable approach needs to account for inevitable changes in the fabric of the project team: key elements, such as periodic reviews, attrition tracking, and anonymous engagement surveys, can support close monitoring of our progress.

As project leaders, we need to stop and listen. We all have heard that project managers must spend the bulk of their time communicating: I assert that project communication should have a prevalence of listening rather than speaking: it is about gaining as broad a perspective as possible. To quote Greenleaf, "Are we listening? Are we listening to the one with whom we want to communicate? Is our basic attitude, as we approach the confrontation, one of wanting to understand?" (Greenleaf, 1997). When we *listen* to the individuals in our teams or the organization, we can identify and resolve (or at least start to address) the root cause for many of the gaps we observe.

On one of my projects, the project coordinator started suddenly missing workdays, and her performance was rapidly declining. With stringent project deadlines, we could not afford inefficiency. When I brought this issue to her attention, she was initially defensive. However, eventually, we talked candidly about this during a simple one-on-one conversation where both of us were determined to find a solution. She was a single mother with a special needs child who had developed a condition that required her to leave work for unplanned pick-ups from school on any given day. Hence the sudden vacation days and near-miss deliverables. We decided to have a system of notification (a simple, private text message) to know she had to leave and a remote workspace in her apartment to follow up and complete her tasks from home. Her mobile phone would continue to be accessible to other team members, who would not need to know the particulars of her situation. Some team members, managers, and even customers were skeptical about my decision to continue supporting her and her ability to keep up the frantic pace of the project. Facts demonstrated that all her tasks were completed with the highest quality and on time, even if delivered in the wee hours of the morning, by supporting and engaging a different delivery approach for project tasks.

When we invest in making uncomfortable issues clear to all, we help our teams address perceived barriers to understanding and including their peers. Several years ago, the company I worked for hosted a series of talks from transgender and bisexual individuals, who explained how to refer to "they/them," what it means to identify oneself as nonbinary, and the challenges of "coming out." It might seem obvious, but breaking down verbal barriers to understanding each other is necessary for improving engagement and inclusion in our teams. From a management perspective, setting up workshops and informal talks about "uncomfortable" topics sends a clear message: the organization is willing to spend money (our time and the presenters) to help us navigate the turbulent waters of diffidence and ignorance.

While project delivery continues to be a priority, responsible project management must seek a balance between the needs of people, the planet, and profit (RPM, 2020). Have we considered the impact of our project (and our recruitment and choice of suppliers) in the community in which we operate? Even with the most stringent project timelines, we must ask ourselves how we fit in the "bigger picture" – our planet.

According to Raworth,

> Humanity's 21st-century challenge is to meet the needs of all within the means of the planet. In other words, to ensure that no one falls short on life's essentials (from food and housing to healthcare and political voice) while ensuring that collectively we do not overshoot our pressure on Earth's life-supporting systems, on which we fundamentally depend – such as a stable climate, fertile soils, and a protective ozone layer. The Doughnut of social and planetary boundaries is a playfully serious approach to framing that challenge, and it acts as a compass for human progress this century. (Raworth, 2021)

We need to achieve an interdependent, socially adaptable model for team management and growth to move beyond the traditional, GDP-centered economic approach toward a regenerative and distributive economy (Raworth, 2017). This model must adapt and dynamically support nurturing and development of each team member, as Raworth explains because we are social beings, interdependent and essential to support the regenerative balance of a Doughnut economy. It is a responsibility that we need to embrace to continue to deliver projects sustainably over time.

Participation, belonging, and meaning are critical for our teams to be successful (Raworth, 2021), so our steps on the path to diversity and inclusion impact well beyond a single project.

We have seen how we need to raise awareness of unconscious and implicit biases when managing our project teams and organizations. We have also discussed why we need to leverage evidence-based project management: using data to assess diversity, inclusion, risk, estimation (cost/schedule), assumptions, and overall decision-making (Huff, 2016). A simplistic approach, based on labels and the infamous (in my opinion) "low hanging fruit" could lead to disappointment and potentially could prove to be more harmful in the long term: a thoughtful and tailored approach, adjusted dynamically as we analyze the results, delivers trust, and tangible improvement.

Once we determine a strategy based on the highest priority gaps we have measured in our teams, we can start planning how to proceed, taking the time to implement our plan while continuing to track progress and compare it to the plan, assessing the outcomes, adjusting course and plans, and so forth. Good old-fashioned plan–do–check–act is effective because it relies on small steps (Shewhart) and adapts to their outcomes.

We – each of us – have now gained some tools to help us along the path to a diverse and inclusive team, and we need to commit, as responsible project managers, to work tirelessly and continuously to improve diversification, understanding, and inclusion across teams, decisions, and elements of project delivery.

2.6 Reflections

We have discussed steps to take when we actively pursue diversity and inclusion in our project teams.

1. Acknowledge the personal and organizational biases and heuristics that tinge our decisions, starting from our leadership and continuing throughout the fabric of the organization.
2. Identify and gather the facts and data needed to make less-biased project decisions: a baseline and stated goals.
3. Use this data to decide on the best course of action for our project, adapting dynamically and leveraging grassroots initiatives backed by senior leadership.

We are now ready to initiate and plan the approach that makes the most sense in our projects and organizations.

References

A manifesto for responsible project management. Retrieved December 1, 2020, from https://responsiblepm.com/the-manifesto

Abramo, L., & Maltzman, R. (2017). *Bridging the PM competency gap.* J. Ross Publishing. Plantation, FL.

Alleman, K., & Kalt, J. (2019, June 3). *We need more humble leaders. Here is how to get them.* Retrieved January 15, 2021, from https://www.fastcompany.com/90351437/we-need-more-humble-leaders-heres-how-to-get-them

Alleman, K., & Garza, A. *Coming out together: Creating CEO Allyship for LGBTQ+ Inclusion.* Retrieved January 15, 2021, from https://www.egonzehnder.com/ceo-insights/volume-18-ceo-allyship-lgbtq-inclusion

April, K., & Blass, E. (2010, June). *Measuring diversity practice and developing inclusion.* Ashridge Business School. Berkhamsted, United Kingdom.

Bazerman, M. H. (2021). Judgment and decision making. In R. Biswas-Diener & E. Diener (Eds), Noba textbook series: Psychology. Champaign, IL: DEF publishers. Retrieved from http://noba.to/9xjyvc3a

CEO pledge. Retrieved December 1, 2020, from https://www.ceoaction.com/pledge/ceo-pledge

Dale, S. (2018) *Heuristics and biases – the science of decision making.* Retrieved February 2021 from https://www.stephendale.com/2018/07/29/heuristics-and-biases-the-science-of-decision-making/

Egon Zehnder and out leadership announce partnership. Egon Zehnder and Out Leadership Announce Partnership - Egon Zehnder. (2020, November 18). Retrieved December 2, 2020, from https://www.egonzehnder.com/what-we-do/diversity-equity-inclusion/press-releases/egon-zehnder-and-out-leadership-announce-partnership

Ely, R. J., & Thomas, D. A. (2001). Cultural diversity at work: The effects of diversity on workgroup processes and outcomes. *Administrative Science Quarterly*, *46*(2), 229–273.

Greenleaf, R. (1977). *Servant leadership: A journey into the nature of legitimate power and greatness*. Paulist Press. Mahwah, NJ.

Guillen, M. (2020). *2030: How today's biggest trends will collide and reshape the future of everything*. St. Martin's Press. New York.

Huff, A. (2016). *Project innovation: Evidence-informed, open effectual, and subjective*. Retrieved January 12, 2021, from https://www.pmi.org/-/media/pmi/documents/public/pdf/kas/201604_huff_project_innovation.pd

Kahneman, D. (2013). *Thinking, fast and slow*. Farrar: Straus and Giroux.

Kim, T., You, Y., & Hong, J. (2020). A study on effect of servant leadership and perceived organizational support on characteristics of agile organizational culture. *Research in World Economy*, *11*(2).

Lewis, M. (2016). *The undoing project*. W.W. Norton & Company. New York.

McCluney, C. L., Robotham, K., Lee, S., Smith, R., & Durkee, M. (2019, November). The cost of code switching. *Harvard Business Review*. Retrieved January 26, 2021, from https://hbr.org/2019/11/the-costs-of-codeswitching

Mizelle, S. (2021). *US Army announces a new grooming policy in a push for inclusion*. CNN. Retrieved on January 29, 2021, from https://www.cnn.com/2021/01/28/politics/army-grooming-policy/index.html

Moore, K., Xiong, S., Bhattacharya, M., Bustamante, G., & Calvert, C. (2020, October). Beyond diversity: Focusing on and enhancing inclusion in the society for epidemiologic research. *American Journal of Epidemiology*, *189*(10), 1042–1046.

Nathoo, Z. (2021, January 8). *Why Getting a name right matters*. BBC Worklife. Retrieved January 12, 2021, from https://www.bbc.com/worklife/article/20210108-the-signals-we-send-when-we-get-names-wrong

PMI. (2019, June 8). *A case for diversity*. Retrieved December 1, 2020, from https://www.pmi.org/learning/library/case-diversity-teams-11998

Raworth, K. (2017). *Doughnut economics*. Chelsea Green Publishing.

Raworth, K. *What on Earth is the Doughnut? . . .* Retrieved January 20, 2021, from https://www.kateraworth.com/doughnut/

Rowland, M. (2019, September 27). *The value of diversity in project management*. https://www.apm.org.uk/blog/the-value-of-diversity-in-project-management/.

Soapbox Mission. Retrieved December 1, 2020, from https://www.soapboxsoaps.com/pages/ourmission

Thiry, M. (2003). Select and prioritise project with the MESA® (Matrix for the Evaluation of Strategic Alternatives). Paper presented at PMI® Global Congress 2003 – North America, Baltimore, MD. Newtown Square, PA: Project Management Institute.

Women CEOs of the S&P 500. (2020, December 2). https://www.catalyst.org/research/women-ceos-of-the-sp-500/#:~:text=*%20Women%20currently%20hold%2030%20(6.0,at%20those%20S%26P%20500%20companies

Krishanthi Vithana

3 Decent Work and Sustainable Human Capital Management in Responsible Project Management

Context: This chapter discusses responsible human capital management in a project context focusing on promoting decent work to achieve inclusive economic growth and sustainable development.

Characters/entities: The chapter considers examples worldwide of responsible human capital management in a project context, including the human capital-related issues in the Qatar world cup construction project.

Locations: The overall discussion in the chapter takes an international perspective. However, some of the project's human capital management-related issues are being discussed, taking regional and organizational contexts into account. For example, the significance of human capital management issues related to one of the large-scale projects – construction of the Qatar world cup stadiums – and associated labor management and welfare issues in the country since the hosting status was granted have been discussed.

Research gaps: Extent literature covers little or no evidence positioning employees as key stakeholders in a project management context. In a responsible project management context, it is imperative to address this issue and explore further how responsible human capital management can benefit project management in the longer term. We contribute to this gap in literature via the current chapter highlighting human capital management challenges in the project management context with recommendations on how to address and overcome these challenges.

Challenges/conflicts/tensions: Focus on decent work in project human capital management appears to solve existing tensions and challenges project-based and temporary organizations currently face, especially in achieving inclusive economic growth and sustainable development.

Keywords: decent work, sustainable capital, project value, projectification

3.1 Introduction

An increasing trend toward projectification and the changes in structural arrangement toward the temporary organizations can add to the prevailing strains on sustainable human capital management and decent work in organizational contexts.

https://doi.org/10.1515/9783110724783-005

The primary concerns of project-based and temporary organizational arrangements have mostly been the efficient delivery of outputs, efficient use of organizational resources, minimization of the overheads, including human resource expenditure (Zwikael & Smyrk, 2019). However, in the quest for achieving sustainable and inclusive economic growth, decent work and sustainable human capital management practices can no longer be a seldom-discussed topic in a responsible project management context.

Against this backdrop, this chapter focuses on sustainable human capital management practices and decent work in project management, particularly in a responsible project management context. This chapter also helps redefine critical stakeholders in project stakeholder management practices. The key aspects discussed in the chapter include understanding and defining decent work, HRM issues, and challenges and opportunities in project and temporary organization context; recognizing the dimensions of decent work; the role and the importance of decent work; and sustainable human capital management in project and temporary organization context. The chapter concludes by focusing on how decent work becomes a solution for human capital management in a responsible project management context in achieving inclusive economic growth and sustainable development.

3.2 Decent Work

Seven forms of security pursued in the twelfth century, which account for labor market security, employment security, job security, work security, skill reproduction security, income security, and representation security, provide an early framework adopted in developing indices for decent work (Bonnet et al., 2003). Some of these security indicators, such as income security and representation security, have taken priority over the others both in conceptual and empirical analysis, and they are discussed in the academic literature on project settings (Bonnet et al., 2003; Prouska & Kapsali, 2020). However, this would not necessarily imply that the other indices are irrelevant in a project and temporary organizational context. Therefore, the field's scant conceptual and empirical literature can be recognized as a gap for further studies (Blustein et al., 2020). Decent work, which is considered a fundamental human right by the International Labour Organization (2013), plays a crucial role in achieving equitable and inclusive development in society and ascertaining sustainable economic growth. Decent work has become an essential aspect of sustainable development goals, the United Nations agenda for sustainable and inclusive economic growth, and International Labour Organization (ILO) indicators (Department of Economic and Social Affairs, 2012; Di Fabio & Kenny, 2019; Dodd et al., 2019; International Labor Organization, 2016; Torres, 2008). Recent developments tend to consider decent work a fundamental human right (Duffy et al., 2020;

International Labor Organization, 2016; Nam & Kim, 2019) rather than a goal to be aspired toward.

Actors and institutions in the public sector, including international, national, and local authorities, on the one hand, have a significant role to play in bringing this agenda forward (Lawrence et al., 2008). On the other hand, the responsibility to assure decent work for the employees appears to be in the hands of actors and enterprises in the private sector in their persuasion toward responsible management, ethical practices, social values, and sustainability agenda. Additionally, pursuing decent work, particularly as a part of responsible project management, is also within the mandate of relevant professional organizations such as the chartered institute of personal and development, an association for project management, and a project management institute. Conditions for decent work at the institutional or institutional field level require an institutional commitment to decent work, institutional effort toward their commitment, and ascertaining the outcomes that correspond to the expectations about the institutional commitments and the institutional efforts (Bonnet et al., 2003). Therefore, securing decent work for people considering the multidimensional concept of decent work requires a well-coordinated and concerted effort by global, national, and organizational players.

Decent work has been defined in several ways in different contexts. According to the International Labor Organization (1999) goals, securing decent work for people everywhere considers the conditions of freedom, equity, security, and human dignity. It has been the focus of their strategic objectives: promotion of rights at work, employment, social protection, and social dialogue (International Labor Organization, 1999, 2004). These conditions have subsequently been operationalized into 10 substantive elements: employment opportunities; adequate earnings and productive work; decent working time; combining work, family, and personal life; work that should be abolished; stability and security of work; equal opportunity and treatment in employment; safe work environment; social security; and social dialogue, employers, and workers representation (International Labour Organization, 2013, p. 12). In promoting decent work or work of acceptable quality, several aspects of work such as forms of work, conditions of work, and the feeling of value and satisfaction have been taken into account as they are in line with the social needs such as physical and survival needs, connection needs, and self-determination needs (Duffy et al., 2019). Thus, it extends beyond simply the employment that meets the minimum acceptable standards for a good life (Dodd et al., 2019). Thus, the International Labor Organization (2016) definition of decent work involves "opportunities for work that is productive and delivers a fair income, security in the workplace and social protection for families. It offers better prospects for personal development and social integration, freedom for people to express their concerns, organise and participate in the decisions that affect their lives and equality of opportunity and treatment for all women and men," which would lead economies toward sustainable and inclusive growth.

Considering the psychology of the working theory approach, Duffy et al. (2017) proposed the *Decent Work Scale (DWS)*. Shedding more light on ILO definition, the psychological approach to working recognizes the DWS, which takes into account five dimensions in characterizing decent work, namely physical and interpersonal safe working conditions; hours that allow for free time and adequate rest; organizational values that complement family and social values; adequate compensation; and access to adequate healthcare (Duffy et al., 2016). DWS has later been tested in a variety of geographical contexts, including the UK, France, South Korea, Brazil, Turkey, Portugal, and Italy (Buyukgoze-Kavas & Autin, 2019; Di Fabio & Kenny, 2019; Dodd et al., 2019; Ferreira et al., 2019; Masdonati et al., 2019; Nam & Kim, 2019; Ribeiro et al., 2019). However, such a framework is yet to be empirically studied, considering precarious employment conditions such as temporary and project-type organizational structures. Thus, this chapter later focuses on developing the dimensions of decent work applicable for sustainable human capital management practices in project management and temporary organizational context.

In a nutshell, decent work leads to satisfying different human needs, including physical and survival needs, social connection needs, and self-determination needs around the form of work, conditions of work, and feeling of value and satisfaction. While decent work theories, frameworks, and scales have mostly been tested to ascertain the relationship decent work has with organizational functions and performance aspects in a specific organizational context, this has been studied in the project management context (Blustein et al., 2020; Lawrence et al., 2008). Therefore, the demand for sustainable human capital management practices in temporary organization and project-type organizational structure contexts would require a hybrid framework, which can elaborate the dimensions of decent work in sustainable project human capital management context for future applications. Therefore, the following section discusses sustainable human capital management opportunities in a project management context.

3.3 Sustainable Human Capital Management Opportunities

There are several opportunities concerning sustainable human capital management in project management and temporary organization context. These include but are not limited to increased labor market participation due to the unique employment structure; motivation, and inspiration linked with frequent project success; the breadth of experience leading to human capital development and increased employability in the competitive market; the opportunity to focus on the social values, ethics, and sustainability via responsible project management; and increasing gap between demand and supply for project management professionals leading to competitive pay structures among several others.

The unique employment structure of a project and temporary organizations provides an opportunity for a group of labor market participants who would otherwise be unemployed to participate in economic activities. The flexible working arrangement, the ability to discontinue taking part in economic activities, and the increasing ability to adjust the work–life balance are among others. There are several benefits of the project and temporary-type organizational arrangements facilitating some labor market participants who otherwise would not participate in economic activities. This can help invigorate inclusive economic growth and sustainable development.

Clear goals in project-type organizational arrangements result in enhanced employee motivation. The high motivation and inspiration linked with individual project success could also result in a highly motivated and talented pool of labor market participants willing to embark on another unique experience. However, it is also reported that the pressure due to loss of resources, changing preferences or priorities, or project closure may create unnecessary stress (Gällstedt, 2003), leading to mixed outcomes.

The breadth of experience project employees gain by engaging in various projects will make some employees working in a project-based and temporary organizational context more adaptable to future work and career opportunities. From the psychology of working theory point of view, work volition and career adaptability will then be thought to shape their access to decent work (Duffy et al., 2016). Therefore, increasing opportunities to work on project-based or temporary organizations with flexible arrangements and responsible project management appear to help strengthen the overall perception of ethics, social value, and decent work in project-based and temporary organization contexts (Islam & Greenwood, 2021).

Project management professionals report the gap in demand and supply (Project Management Institute, 2017). This has resulted in an increasing number of project management and leadership-related employment opportunities and competitive pay. However, limited or no evidence is reported on the employment statistics about demand and supply of labor concerning the nonmanagerial and nonprofessional employment opportunities in the project sectors. There appears to be a clear research gap to address, especially the precarious type of project-related employment opportunities across the globe.

Agility in a project management setting characterized by innovative and self-managing teams, a learning organization environment, and a customer-driven process provides a unique opportunity for sustainable and flexible human capital management practices in project-based and temporary organizations (Bhatta & Thite, 2018). Additionally, agile and flexible working arrangements in project management, in some ways, could streamline the human capital management function and the administrative cost, because of which employees might be able to enjoy better employment benefits as well.

Investment in people is the way for increased firm value, greater equity, social development, sustainability, and inclusive economic growth (Vithana et al., 2018; Vithana Jayasekera et al.,2021). The opportunity to focus on social values, ethics, and sustainability via decent work in responsible project management will have a spillover effect on the overall human capital management and employee relations practices, inclusive economic growth, and sustainable development (Islam & Greenwood, 2021; Vithana, Soobaroyen et al., 2021). While there are many opportunities for sustainable human capital management in a responsible project management context, the unique nature of project-based and temporary organizations may also lead to several challenges. The following section focused on the sustainable human capital management-related challenges unique to the project management context.

3.4 Human Capital Management Challenges in Project Management

A project can be defined as a relatively temporally and "non-repeated planned work Intended to enhance organisational performance" (Zwikael & Smyrk, 2019, p. 3), which may even act as a separate mini-organizational structure. Projects have the tendency to be considered more as technical systems rather than behavioral systems, in which case there is a tendency to use a mechanistic approach focusing extensively on results, attaining regret dates, financial plans, and controlling the quality of final output. However, behavioral factors such as perception of various stakeholders, including clients, management, customers, and employees and stakeholder engagement and satisfaction, should also be considered key factors for project success. Therefore, these factors were reported as measures to evaluate the project's success (Barker et al., 1988).

Due to the inherent nature of the project and temporary-type organizational structures, sustainable human capital management in this setting has been challenging. Thus, several issues and significant concerns have emerged over the period. These include but are not limited to challenges and issues such as potential discontinuity in organizational arrangements; employment, unemployment, and underemployment measures; increasing emphasis on the project managers role in academic and professional literature as opposed to the overall project human capital; human resource development and learning-related issues (particularly in discontinued project setting); issues related to the compensation for the project employees and industrial relations, employee representation, and the voice of project employees. It is vital to analyze these issues to understand how decent work principles can be applied, taking a solution-oriented approach in project management.

Project human capital resources can be distinguished considerably from project finance and physical resources due to the possibility of expanding their contribution tremendously under appropriate conditions (Murdick & Schuster, 1976). Depending on the type of the organization, industry, the task at hand, the project-based organizations may have temporary, semipermanent or, in certain instances, permanent organizational structures providing different modes of employment opportunities such as permanent or temporary employment contracts, open-ended or fixed-term contracts, and full-time or part-time contracts to their employees. According to the circumstances, either the centrally planned HRM divisions or the project managers themselves – decentralized – become responsible for project human capital management. Under temporary project-based organizational structures, project employees appear to be placed under the supervision of assessment processes of their project-based organizational employers. In certain instances, they may enjoy a subset of the benefits of regular employees. They may or may not be employed continuously by their employers on another project. Therefore, all forms of security aspects related to decent work, such as labor market security, employment security, job security, work security, skills reproduction security, income security, and representational security, are contingent upon many factors such as the country of operation, economic environment, regulatory environment, labor standards and legal frameworks, industry, type of work, and scarcity of talents (Bredin & Söderlund, 2011; Samimi & Sydow, 2021).

As opposed to the HRM professional in a standard organizational setting, the project tasks' relatively temporary and unique nature makes it also challenging to transfer employment-related learning from one project to the other. This also raises the question of how the project learning and employee development would be transferred across different projects and how project workers' learning and human capital development are considered in the project's compensation mechanisms. Additionally, the inherent lack of social capital in project and temporary organization settings also hinders networking and cultural knowledge, affecting the potential for decent work and stable work (Blustein et al., 2020).

As project employees appear to enjoy a subset of benefits of regular employees, the project employees are likely missing out on their rights in industrial relations, in getting their voice heard, and in gaining representation security as opposed to non-project employees (Bonnet et al., 2003; Prouska & Kapsali, 2020). This is particularly the case in temporary organization context as opposed to permanent or relatively permanent project organizational structures. Project employees may encounter several other challenges concerning the industrial relation aspect of project human capital management due to the irrelevance of some practices such as union involvements, negotiation, and tripartism, which can provide a competitive advantage with human capital management processes. However, temporary-type project organizations are less likely to enjoy the said competitive advantage due to the less structured industrial relations structure and institutional framework (Lawrence et al., 2008).

In exploring the literature on project management and employment-related aspects such as decent work, it is evident that there is a general lack of detailed studies on decent work in both project management and temporary organization context (Blustein et al., 2020; Kim et al., 2021). Additionally, limited academic literature and professional publications that are currently available are more skewed toward the project managers than the overall project human capital, employees, employment conditions, and decent work (Project Management Institute, 2017). As an example, in discussing the labor market security, which considers a high level of access to reasonable income-earning activities, a recent report published by Project Management Institute suggests that there is a clear gap between the project management professionals required and the supply of the project management professionals in the market (Project Management Institute, 2017). The report further suggests that skilled project management professionals attracted 82% premium wage in projectized industries in the USA because of the project management talent shortage. The demand–supply gap could even lead to a substantial loss in gross domestic product. However, such analyses on project employees or overall human capital are yet to be commissioned despite the significance of human capital resources on overall project success and outcomes.

Recognizing project-type employment via conventional employment measures such as employment, unemployment, and underemployment will be difficult due to apparent discontinuity in employment structures, especially in countries with fewer regulatory frameworks. This incomplete information on employment statistics could also have a policy-level impact on establishing social and welfare systems. This is recognized as an issue in both developing and developed economies. Moreover, it is also reported that talent retention in project-based and temporary organizations is highly challenging because of the limited opportunities project employees enjoy in expressing their career needs (Ekrot et al., 2016).

Project employment, in certain instances, may have some overlapping characteristics of precarious work (Blustein et al., 2020). Precarious works refer to the work that is temporary, insecure, part-time, often poorly paid, typically without benefits and with minimum social and legal protections (Kalleberg & Vallas, 2017). This was the case for even some significant projects, such as the Qatar World Cup 2022 stadium venues, which draw global attention to labor standards, employee welfare, and health and safety concerns of the immigrant workforce. Figure 3.1 illustrates some of the common characteristics that project-based or temporary organizations share with precarious work: vulnerability, inadequate wages, inadequate rights, and inability to exercise. These employment precarities will significantly adversely impact various decent work dimensions mentioned above.

Additionally, the discontinuity of the operational activities in project-based and temporary organization context has limitations over the organizational learning process, be it at individual, team, project, and organizational levels, which involve changes in both cognition and practices (Bakker et al., 2011). Each project generates a steep learning curve for the project professionals and the employees at individual, team, project, and organizational levels. However, the transferability of learning

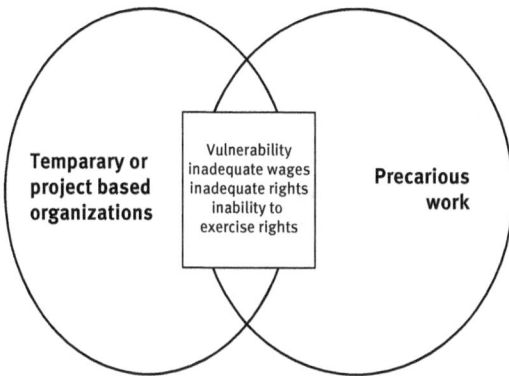

Figure 3.1: Overlapping nature of temporary or project-based organizations and precarious work.

from one project to another via different levels of learning mentioned above depends on several factors such as the nature of the project and repetition of tasks and responsibilities, project context, and project manager leadership characteristics (Berends & Lammers, 2010), and thus will remain challenging in many project settings (Wiewiora et al., 2019, 2020).

Despite the human capital management challenges unique to the project-based and temporary organization-type businesses, policies and practices related to decent work such as employment conditions, social security, employment rights, and social dialogue in the project context can neither be disregarded nor should be isolated from the national, employment, or business policies. Therefore, the following section pays attention to understanding the dimensions of decent work and sustainable human capital management practices, particularly considering the applications in a project and temporary organization context.

3.5 Dimensions of Decent Work and Sustainable Human Capital Management Practices in a Project Setting

Decent work is believed to be the means for achieving equitable, inclusive, and sustainable development across the globe (International Labour Organization, 2013). As explained earlier, the concept of decent work is complex and multidimensional (Lawrence et al., 2008), making it hard to justify in terms of application unless there is a cross-sector-level collaboration addressing different dimensions. Several frameworks have emerged over time, considering broader aspects of decent work and specific indicators elaborating how the agenda is achieved through initiatives such as the ILO agenda for decent work. To align the decent work agenda with human capital resource management in project-based and temporary organization contexts, it is essential to discuss the key pillars of the decent work agenda with the specific indicators and their applicability in the project-based and temporary organization context. To integrate decent work with project human capital resource management, we have considered the critical dimensions of decent work as a form of work, conditions of work, and feeling of value and satisfaction. They have been further elaborated on in the following section.

3.5.1 Forms of Work

As discussed in the previous section, projects provide employment opportunities globally, fulfilling the workforce's physical and survival needs. The increasing trend toward projectification has driven the economies to rely extensively on project-related employment as a part of their national production. While projects can provide employment opportunities, stability, and security of work, leading to full and productive employment, ILO indicators on decent work rule out works that should be abolished, such as child labor and forced labor. Full and productive employment is one of the four strategic pillars of ILO's decent work agenda (International Labour Organization, 2013). Employee opportunities in project and temporary organizational contexts contribute increasingly to the national production of the global economies. For some migrant labor, perhaps project employment could also be a once-in-a-lifetime opportunity in their struggles to come out of poverty.

Project employment as a form of work can contribute toward achievements in labor market security and income security out of the seven forms of security proposed by previous researchers (Bonnet et al., 2003). Labor market security refers to high access to reasonable income-earning activities. In contrast, income security indicates that employment opportunities assure adequate income, which can be the key to freedom of choice, opportunity, and other forms of security. Indicators we discussed under the form of work arguably come under the physical and survival needs of the social needs analysis. In pursuing the agenda for decent work via project and temporary organization employment, due to the significant variations in the labor laws, employment standards, and practices across the globe, issues such as living wage, forced labor, child labor, and the work that should be abolished need to be considered in assessing project human capital management practices in an international context.

3.5.2 Conditions of Work

The second dimension of decent work considers the work atmosphere, leading to fulfilling and productive employment. ILO decent work indicators related to the condition of work include adequate earning and productive work, decent working time, combination work, family and personal life, and a safe working environment (International Labour Organization, 2013). Decent work opportunities in project and temporary organizational contexts should extend the achievements further toward achieving employment security (i.e., whether there is protection against unfair and arbitrary dismissal and whether workers can redress if they are subject to unfair dismissal) and work security (i.e., whether the employment opportunity provides a safe and healthy working condition), out of the seven forms of security proposed by previous researchers (Bonnet et al., 2003). This is despite the unique challenges in the project and temporary organization settings such as discontinuity in operation, precarious nature of work, and the drive toward tangible project outcomes with relatively less regard for the behavioral aspects of the project human capital management as witnessed through some issues discussed in the Qatar World Cup 2022 venue construction (International Labour Organization, 2021). In that sense, project employment may provide the form of work but not necessarily the decent work standards associated with the condition of work. Projects provide employment opportunities and security, yet it is possible to argue that they may not necessarily provide the work security discussed above.

3.5.3 The Feeling of Value and Satisfaction

Feeling of value and satisfaction as the third dimension of decent work is in line with the self-determination or self-actualization needs of the project employees. It refers to the recognition of project employees/employment in economic and social settings. They come under the motivational factors focusing on the employees' recognition, achievement, and growth potential. The form of security that comes under this dimension includes job security, skill reproduction security, and representation security. Job security refers to the possession of a niche at work, allowing some sort of control over the content of the job and the opportunity for building a career. The leading ILO indicators categorized under the third dimension include equal opportunity and treatment in employment, social security, social dialogue, and employers and worker representation. It is reported that newly appointed and experienced project managers themselves find it difficult to find their niche within an organization (Baker, 2020), let alone the rest of the project employees.

Skill reproduction security refers to a wide range of opportunities for training, apprenticeship, and education for project employees to acquire and refine their knowledge and skills. Representation security refers to the individual and the collective representation or the extent to which the voice of the project workers is heard in a project employment context. Research also suggests that project-based and temporary-type organizations face challenges in integrating coordinating systems facilitating employee voice and representation (Prouska & Kapsali, 2020). While adequate earning or income security is taken under the first pillar in this discussion, assurance of adequate income equal to or above the living wage would be the key to freedom of choice, opportunity, and other forms of securities discussed under the third pillar. In a nutshell, considering the nature and the characteristics of the project and temporary-type organizational structures, particularly the ones of precarious nature, the third dimension appears to be the hardest to achieve in the quest for securing decent work in a responsible project management context.

3.5.4 Decent Work Framework for Project Management

Three dimensions of decent work discussed above can be combined with the institutional support for decent work at various levels, including but not limited to global, national, organizational, and professional body levels, to develop a decent work framework in project management, as illustrated in Figure 3.2. Under each level, it is essential to consider the commitment toward decent work, efforts leading to expectations, and outcomes corresponding to the expectations.

The framework suggested through the above review and analysis of literature includes integration of institutional support for decent work at each level with sustainable human capital management, considering the three dimensions form of decent work – forms of work, conditions of work, and feeling of value and satisfaction – as illustrated in Figure 3.2.

3.6 Recommendations to Promote Decent Work in Project-Based and Temporary Organizations

Critical literature evaluation suggests that renewed perception of decent work can solve project human capital management issues. Therefore, relying on prior academic literature and professional publications on project human capital management and the perception of decent work following recommendations are suggested to help promote decent work as a solution for sustainable human capital in a project context.

– It is vital to consider the decent work framework discussed above in project-based and temporary organizations' human capital management decisions. In that case, rather than limiting decent work to be a general discourse, practical

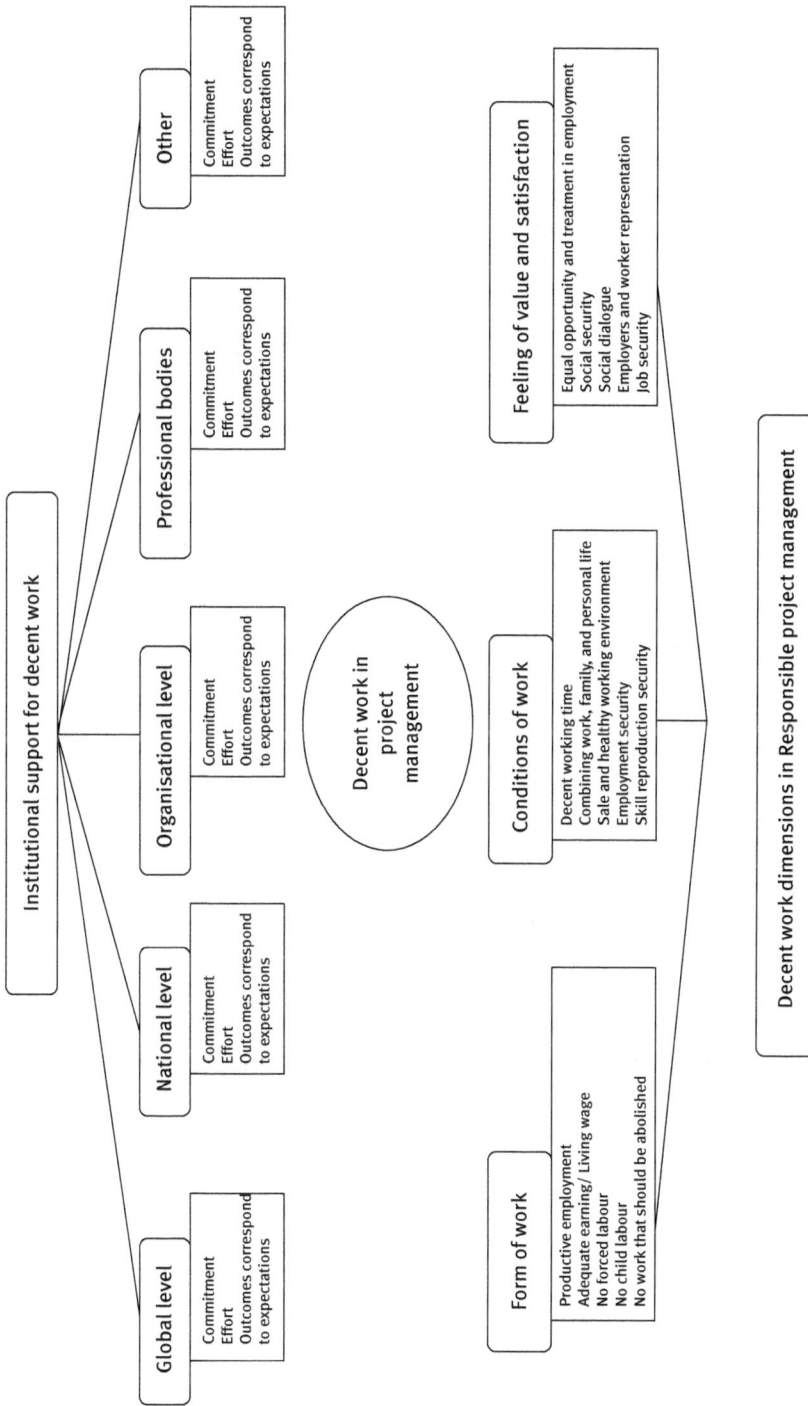

Figure 3.2: Decent work framework (author).

implementation of decent work through a collaborative approach would help take the agenda forward.

- It is advisable to recognize decent work as a contractual obligation in entering third-party contracts. As suggested by previous researchers (International Labour Organization, 2004; Lawrence et al., 2008), the possibility of including additional criteria about decent work in the tendering and procurement mechanism will ensure that decent work is honored throughout as well. This has been a particularly effective technique in implementing public infrastructure projects in economically deprived areas, in which case decent work is promoted locally for infrastructure development and to create decent employment opportunities for the local communities (Watermeyer, 2006).
- Additionally, advocating the perception of decent work among the project-based and temporary organizations and other institutional actors such as local government, policymakers, professional bodies, and nongovernmental and community-based organizations will be instrumental in bringing the agenda forward.
- Welcoming and, most importantly, encouraging alliance between project-based and temporary organization sector and labor unions to create a constructive debate around promoting the decent work agenda will help address issues related to some dimensions of decent work such as a feeling of value and satisfaction in employment. This also involves strengthening urban social dialogues.
- Local authorities need to promote decent work throughout, whether a project-based or a temporary organization. Additionally, encouraging communities to advocate decent work and become actors in promoting decent work through community contracting may help promote the course (International Labour Organization, 2004).
- Participatory planning via the engagement between business organizations, local governments, and civil society can also ensure that a decent work agenda is encouraged through project-based and temporary organization employment (International Labour Organization, 2004).
- Measuring the progress over time toward decent work implementation and achievement of a target could be another key to success in this quest (Lawrence et al., 2008). This involves the continuous collection of data system infrastructure to facilitate collaboration among different actors involved.
- Continuous monitoring of resources required to promote decent work in a project setting and identifying the benefits associated with decent work in a project and temporary organization context could also be instrumental in seeing progress.
- Enforcement of the labor standards could play a vital role in the project and temporary organization context. This is particularly the case due to employment instability because of an inherent problem in project-based and temporary organization contexts. As a result, even though national and local legislation and standards, legal and administrative measures are necessary for monitoring and surveillance.

Moreover, sanctions are to be enforced when the legislation is not respected (Lawrence et al., 2008).

– The support network as a part of overall employment infrastructure through the involvement of national and local government agencies on aspects such as universal living wage, employee welfare, and living and working standards will provide a sense of security to employees in project-based or temporary organizations. Achievements in employment security, work security, and income security will also help the human capital development and reskilling by providing more opportunities to invest in training and development to gain the breadth of skills employees require in a project and temporary organization context.

It is important to note that these recommendations are applicable at different levels, including project or organizational levels, local or national government level or global level, for the efforts to be more concerted.

3.7 Discussion and Conclusion

Much research is being carried out on decent work as a part of human capital management in an organizational context (Barker et al., 1988; Geraldi & Söderlund, 2018; Prouska & Kapsali, 2020; Samimi & Sydow, 2021; Zwikael & Smyrk, 2019). These include theoretical research, the development of conceptual frameworks, and testing the conceptual frameworks in various empirical contexts, nationally and globally. However, theoretical, conceptual, or empirical analysis of decent work as a part of project human capital management rarely exists in the current literature except for some isolated studies on different aspects related to decent work and project human capital management (Prouska & Kapsali, 2020; Samimi & Sydow, 2021). Therefore, the gap in the literature calls for further development of a conceptual framework addressing decent work in a project management context, considering different dimensions of decent work and their applicability in the project management context supported by institutional arrangements. Therefore, this chapter focuses on human capital management issues, challenges, and opportunities in the project management context. Considering the issues, challenges, and opportunities identified, a framework for project human capital management is developed by integrating the dimensions of decent work with the institutional infrastructure, helping achieve the decent work indicators proposed under each dimension. Finally, further recommendations are given to promote decent work in project-based and temporary organizational contexts.

The inherent discontinuity nature of the project-based and temporary organization structures, and their heavy focus on efficient delivery of outputs, minimization of personal and overhead costs, and profit maximization (Burke & Morley, 2016;

Zwikael & Smyrk, 2019) make it challenging, particularly in managing the project human capital resources and attaining responsible human capital management standards. However, due to the increasing trend toward projectification as well as the benefits it offers, such as increasing contribution to national production, cost-effectiveness, resource transferability, flexibility, and effectiveness in terms of innovation and agility (Burke & Morley, 2016; Prouska & Kapsali, 2020), the need to address sustainability-related issues in project management setting has been identified as a way forward in project research (Geraldi & Söderlund, 2018). As project management professionals and academics, it is essential to pay attention to the issue, such as how project-based organizations project funding institutions and policymakers rank responsible human capital management practices and decent work as essential factors. This is in addition to their heavy reliance on the targeted outcomes, cost efficiency, and profit maximization (Zwikael & Smyrk, 2019). Our academic and professional literature analysis shows that decent work remains a marginal concept yet to be applied globally in project management contexts.

Local authorities could be considered catalysts for promoting decent work that guarantees income, equity, security, and dignity of the members of the local communities (Watermeyer, 2006). However, much needs to be done to incorporate several other aspects of decent work such as labor market security, employment security, and representations security to bring the wholistic view on decent work forward through project-based and temporary organizations. One question project managers and leaders can ask themselves in assessing project human capital management is where in the continuums of decent to indecent and precarious to stable (Duffy et al., 2017) the related project employment stands currently. That will help project managers decide recommendations to promote decent work to be implemented in future projects.

References

Baker, B. (2020). Power, leadership and culture as drivers of project management. *American Journal of Management, 20*(1), 9–30.

Bakker, R. M., Cambré, B., Korlaar, L., & Raab, J. (2011). Managing the project learning paradox: A set-theoretic approach toward project knowledge transfer. *International Journal of Project Management, 29*(5), 494–503.

Barker, J., Tjosvold, D., & Andrews, I. R. (1988). Conflict approaches of effective and ineffective project managers: A field study in a matrix organization [1]. *Journal of Management Studies, 25*(2), 167–178.

Berends, H., & Lammers, I. (2010). Explaining discontinuity in organisational learning: A process analysis. *Organisation Studies, 31*(8), 1045–1068.

Bhatta, N., & Thite, M. (2018). Agile approach to e-HRM project management. In *e-HRM* (pp. 57–72). Routledge.

Blustein, D. L., Perera, H. N., Diamonti, A., Gutowski, E., Meerkins, T., Davila, A., . . . Konowitz, L. (2020). The uncertain state of work in the US: Profiles of decent work and precarious work. *Journal of Vocational Behavior, 122*, 103481.

Bonnet, F., Figueiredo, J. B., & Standing, G. (2003). A family of decent work indexes. *International Labour Review, 142*, 213.

Bredin, K., & Söderlund, J. (2011). *Human resource management in project-based organisations: The HR quadriad framework*. Springer.

Burke, C. M., & Morley, M. J. (2016). On temporary organisations: A review, synthesis and research agenda. *Human Relations, 69*(6), 1235–1258.

Buyukgoze-Kavas, A., & Autin, K. L. (2019). Decent work in Turkey: Context, conceptualisation, and assessment. *Journal of Vocational Behavior, 112*, 64–76. https://doi.org/10.1016/j.jvb.2019.01.006

Department of Economic and Social Affairs. (2012). *Back to our common future: Sustainable development in the 21st century (SD21) project summary for policymakers*. Retrieved from https://sustainabledevelopment.un.org/content/documents/UN-DESA_Back_Common_Future_En.pdf

Di Fabio, A., & Kenny, M. E. (2019). Decent work in Italy: Context, conceptualisation, and assessment. *Journal of Vocational Behavior, 110*, 131–143. https://doi.org/10.1016/j.jvb.2018.10.014

Dodd, V., Hooley, T., & Burke, C. (2019). Decent work in the UK: Context, conceptualisation, and assessment. *Journal of Vocational Behavior, 112*, 270–281. https://doi.org/10.1016/j.jvb.2019.04.002

Duffy, R. D., Allan, B. A., England, J. W., Blustein, D. L., Autin, K. L., Douglass, R. P., . . . Santos, E. J. (2017). The development and initial validation of the decent work scale. *Journal of Counseling Psychology, 64*(2), 206.

Duffy, R. D., Blustein, D. L., Allan, B. A., Diemer, M. A., & Cinamon, R. G. (2020). Introduction to the special issue: A cross-cultural exploration of decent work. *Journal of Vocational Behavior, 116*, 103351. https://doi.org/10.1016/j.jvb.2019.103351

Duffy, R. D., Blustein, D. L., Diemer, M. A., & Autin, K. L. (2016). The psychology of working theory. *Journal of Counseling Psychology, 63*(2), 127.

Duffy, R. D., Kim, H. J., Gensmer, N. P., Raque-Bogdan, T. L., Douglass, R. P., England, J. W., & Buyukgoze-Kavas, A. (2019). Linking decent work with physical and mental health: A psychology of working perspective. *Journal of Vocational Behavior, 112*, 384–395.

Ekrot, B., Kock, A., & Gemünden, H. G. (2016). Retaining project management competence—Antecedents and consequences. *International Journal of Project Management, 34(2)*, 145–157.

Ferreira, J. A., Haase, R. F., Santos, E. R., Rabaça, J. A., Figueiredo, L., Hemami, H. G., & Almeida, L. M. (2019). Decent work in Portugal: Context, conceptualization, and assessment. *Journal of Vocational Behavior, 112*, 77–91. https://doi.org/10.1016/j.jvb.2019.01.009

Gällstedt, M. (2003). Working conditions in projects: Perceptions of stress and motivation among project team members and project managers. *International Journal of Project Management, 21*(6), 449–455.

Geraldi, J., & Söderlund, J. (2018). Project studies: What it is, where it is going. *International Journal of Project Management, 36*(1), 55–70.

International Labor Organization. (1999). *Report of the Director-General: Decent Work*. Retrieved from Geneva, Switzerland: https://www.ilo.org/public/english/standards/relm/ilc/ilc87/rep-i.htm

International Labor Organization. (2016). *Decent work agenda*. Retrieved from Geneva, Switzerland.

International Labour Organization. (2004). *Cities at work: Employment promotion to fight urban poverty*. Retrieved from Geneva: https://www.ilo.org/wcmsp5/groups/public/—ed_emp/—emp_policy/—invest/documents/publication/wcms_asist_8109.pdf

International Labour Organization. (2013). *Decent work indicators: Guidelines for procedures and users of statistical and legal framework indicators*, 2nd ed. Retrieved from Geneva, Switzerland: https://www.ilo.org/wcmsp5/groups/public/—dgreports/—stat/documents/publication/wcms_223121.pdf

International Labour Organization. (2021). *One is too many: Collecting and analysing data on occupational injuries in Qatar*. Retrieved from https://www.ilo.org/wcmsp5/groups/public/—arabstates/—ro-beirut/—ilo-qatar/documents/publication/wcms_828395.pdf

Islam, G., & Greenwood, M. (2021). *Reconnecting to the social in business ethics*. Springer.

Kalleberg, A. L., & Vallas, S. P. (2017). *Precarious work*. Emerald Group Publishing.

Kim, H. J., Duffy, R. D., & Allan, B. A. (2021). Profiles of decent work: General trends and group differences. *Journal of Counseling Psychology, 68*(1), 54.

Lawrence, R. J., Gil, M. P., Flückiger, Y., Lambert, C., & Werna, E. (2008). Promoting decent work in the construction sector: The role of local authorities. *Habitat International, 32*(2), 160–171.

Masdonati, J., Schreiber, M., Marcionetti, J., & Rossier, J. (2019). Decent work in Switzerland: Context, conceptualisation, and assessment. *Journal of Vocational Behavior, 110*, 12–27. https://doi.org/10.1016/j.jvb.2018.11.004

Murdick, R., & Schuster, F. E. (1976). *Managing human resources in project management*.

Nam, J. S., & Kim, S. Y. (2019). Decent work in South Korea: Context, conceptualisation, and assessment. *Journal of Vocational Behavior, 115*, 103309. https://doi.org/10.1016/j.jvb.2019.05.006

Project Management Institute. (2017). *Project management job growth and talent gap 2017–2027*. Author.

Prouska, R., & Kapsali, M. (2020). The determinants of project worker voice in project-based organisations: An initial conceptualisation and research agenda. *Human Resource Management Journal*.

Ribeiro, M. A., Teixeira, M. A. P., & Ambiel, R. A. M. (2019). Decent work in Brazil: Context, conceptualisation, and assessment. *Journal of Vocational Behavior, 112*, 229–240. https://doi.org/10.1016/j.jvb.2019.03.006

Samimi, E., & Sydow, J. (2021). Human resource management in project-based organisations: Revisiting the permanency assumption. *The International Journal of Human Resource Management, 32*(1), 49–83.

Torres, R. (2008). *World of work report 2008: Income inequalities in the age of financial globalisation*. International Labour Organisation.

Vithana, K., Jayasekera, R., Choudhry, T., & Baruch, Y. (2018). *HR as cost or investment: The distinction between short-vs. long-term focus of firm valuation*. Paper presented at the Academy of Management Proceedings.

Vithana, K., Jayasekera, R., Choudhry, T., & Baruch, Y. (2021). Human capital resource as cost or investment: A market-based analysis. *The International Journal of Human Resource Management*, 1–32.

Vithana, K., Soobaroyen, T., & Ntim, C. G. (2021). Human resource disclosures in UK corporate annual reports: To what extent do these reflect organisational priorities towards labour? *Journal of Business Ethics, 169*(3), 475–497.

Watermeyer, R. (2006). Evening meeting-poverty reduction responses to the Millennium development goals. *Structural Engineer, 84*(9), 27–36.

Wiewiora, A., Chang, A., & Smidt, M. (2020). Individual, project and organisational learning flows within a global project-based organisation: Exploring what, how and who. *International Journal of Project Management, 38*(4), 201–214.

Wiewiora, A., Smidt, M., & Chang, A. (2019). The 'how'of multilevel learning dynamics: A systematic literature review exploring how mechanisms bridge learning between individuals, teams/projects and the organisation. *European Management Review, 16*(1), 93–115.

Zwikael, O., & Smyrk, J. R. (2019). *Project management: A benefits realisation approach*. Springer.

Section 2: **Responsible Project Practice**

While projects involve people and are inherently political, little work in this area examines these perspectives. The term "politics" has been defined from two perspectives (Goldfarb, 2005). Firstly, "small p" politics examines the everyday interactions among individual, organizational, and place-based identities in the workplace and other settings. Secondly, "big P" politics examines the interactions of government and intergovernmental interactions such as supranational bodies like the European Union. The two are linked, as micro-political interactions can shape international politics and vice versa. In addition to scale, politics in projects are a dynamic process. They can be seen as a political market square in which stakeholders, including governments, industry, community members, and others, interact based on their core interests, demonstrate, develop, and deploy power and engage in conflict (Larson, 2000). The context in which these interactions occur can be permeable, and positions may change over time. Competitors can become collaborators and vice versa. Therefore, project managers (PM) must engage in governance practices that can adapt to these dynamics and are perceived as legitimate by stakeholders and hence trusted.

Projects are a means to realize organizational aspirations, community development, and regeneration. At the national level, they realize sociotechnical imaginaries, creating desirable futures for residents (Jasanoff & Kim, 2009). However, the PM discourse is dominated by the minutiae of project's processes, tools, and techniques. Research that examines the domains of projects and policy identified policy characteristics (ambiguity and conflict), the drivers of projectification, and challenges for PM as policy implementers (Jensen et al., 2018). It is interesting to note that the categorization by these authors in 2018 identified a vaccination program as a low ambiguity and conflict area requiring top-down project management. Recent experiences in Western Europe, the Americas, and parts of Africa have demonstrated that positions can change dramatically over time, underscoring the scale of the challenges in project practice. The chapters in this section have all provided distinct perspectives on how the social systems that underpin project realization influence processes and outcomes.

The first chapter focuses on governance, policy, and politics, as Rodney Turner illustrates the relationship between *small p* politics of community identity and *big P* politics of government. The chapter investigates the role of policy and politics in the realization of projects and the responsibility of PMs. Using illustrative cases drawn from Northern Europe and Australia, the chapter examines how community identity and political stances can impact project delivery.

The chapter from Reinhard Wagner examines the roles of professional bodies in advancing the movement toward responsibility in the project management profession. To date, professional bodies have focused on developing standards that provide best practices, processes, and methods and encourage adopting standards via relationships with industry, qualification, and certification programs. Reinhart argues that professional bodies are ideally positioned to mediate between the various stakeholders in

https://doi.org/10.1515/9783110724783-006

project management and develop a consensus on how the profession can benefit society.

Responsible reporting directs the focus to the content of stakeholder interactions. Reports can allow stakeholders to exchange information and meet governance requirements. Reports may also form part of the accumulated learning from the project and support future activities. Alexia Nalewaik examines how reporting processes can support the development of legitimacy via transparent communication of project status information. Both Reinhardt and Alexia challenge the implicit assumption of rationality that underpins PM's approach to developing responsibility. Professional bodies take an informational approach in which the "right" information will produce the desired outcomes.

Similarly, project teams assume that the provision of comprehensive reports would improve decision-making. These chapters indicate the need to engage stakeholder perceptions of value and responsibility and not merely an imposed idealized state. No discussion on responsibility in project practice is complete without discussing irresponsibility. Richard Maltzman and Luigi Morsa explore the challenges of managing project-based crises using two high profile cases. It identifies lessons learnt for PMs about transparency, including reporting and public engagement.

The following chapter on "Responsible Project Organizing" reviews the activity, temporal, and relational characteristics that distinguish projects from other types of organizing activity. Using examples from the emerging blockchain and non-fungible token projects, the chapter explores the challenges of reconciling multiple perspectives of organizing and value. Drs Obradović and Todorović reinforce the notion of the project value as a multifaceted outcome. It presents a model of a responsible value chain that bridges micro- and macro-perspectives, linking activities in organizational, local, national, or international contexts. These project developments are especially pertinent as stakeholders are increasingly networked, and PMs need to understand the structure of these connections' structure to create value.

While healthcare is an essential domain for well-being and productivity, research in project management has not paid significant attention. This oversight is somewhat surprising as PMs in healthcare systems must negotiate complex adaptive systems composed of human (patients, practitioners, and policymakers) and non-human (technology) elements. These systems are required to meet immediate emergent challenges such as a pandemic and longer term challenges such as responding to the requirements of aging populations. In the domain of technology and project practice, the chapter on "Artificial Intelligence" (Usher, 2022) provides a background to these technologies and current applications. The chapter then explores how widespread adoption across project networks may influence the nature of responsibility of PMs.

Shirley Thompson addresses leadership and changes the focus to the micro-interactions among project participants. Using her personal and professional perspective, she explores the development of responsible leadership by PMs. The chapter discusses how PMs can engage in responsible stakeholder conversations that provide a space to unpack identity-based perspectives and establish shared intentions that support collaboration. Responsible leadership is also examined in the context of megaprojects. These large-scale initiatives consume large amounts of resources to realize national and international aspirations. To ensure these benefits are realized, the chapter discusses the four framework levels for responsible leadership in megaprojects: stakeholder relations, operational roles, leadership roles, and character.

References

Goldfarb, J. C. (2005). The politics of small things. *The Communication Review, 8*(2), 159–183.

Jasanoff, S., & Kim, S. H. (2009). Containing the atom: Sociotechnical imaginaries and nuclear power in the United States and South Korea. *Minerva, 47*(2), 119–146.

Jensen, C., Johansson, S., & Löfström, M. (2018). Policy implementation in the era of accelerating projectification: Synthesizing Matland's conflict–ambiguity model and research on temporary organizations. *Public Policy and Administration, 33*(4), 447–465.

Larson, M. (2000). Interaction in the political market square: Organizing marketing of events. *Projects as business constituents and guiding motives* (pp. 167–180). Boston, MA: Springer.

Rodney Turner

4 Governance, Policy, and Politics

Context: This chapter discusses the role of policy and politics in Responsible Project Management

Characters/entities: The chapter considers policy and politics in public and private sector projects

Locations: The chapter takes an international perspective and provides seven project examples located in different countries. The first is an intercountry project linking a Danish Island to the Swedish Mainland, the second is the Sydney Storm Water Tunnel located in Australia, the West Coast Mainline upgrade and High-Speed Rail 2, both located in the UK, the Gotthard Base Tunnel in Switzerland, a Customer Relationship Management project in France and an organizational change project in Austria.

Research gaps: The chapter identifies how community identity and political identity can impact project delivery and benefits realization.

Challenges/conflict/tensions: Governance choices require Project Managers to make policy and in some cases, political decisions. This can be at odds with the stakeholder school of governance as Project Managers will be required to negotiate between organizational and community demands.

Keywords: Politics, Policy, Governance, Stakeholders, Resistance

4.1 Introduction

In this chapter, I discuss the role of policy and politics in responsible project management. Policy is about making governance choices, and politics is about the exercise of authority in governance. So we start with a description of governance, and its many elements. We then consider policy, and how responsible project management will influence governance choices. There are several ways of viewing politics. In public sector projects, government will make many of the decisions, and so politics will influence the project directly. On private sector projects, authority will have an impact on decisions affecting responsible project management. We close with a description of several projects from both the public and private sectors, and a consideration of the decisions they faced.

https://doi.org/10.1515/9783110724783-007

4.2 Governance

Governance is a strategic-level activity which steers the organization. Governance is the systems, processes, and procedures, which
- provide direction to the organization, defining and balancing goals,
- define how work will be monitored and controlled, and
- define the roles, responsibilities, and rights of and relationships between stakeholders.

Drouin and Turner (2022) give a definition of organizational governance derived from the OECD's (2015) definition of corporate governance:

> The governance of an organization provides the structure through which the objectives of the organization are set, and the means of attaining those objectives and of monitoring performance are determined.

Following the OECD, Drouin and Turner also suggest that governance defines the roles, responsibilities, and rights of and relationships between the organization's stakeholders. The stakeholders include the management, owners, employees, suppliers, customers, and local community. Management, owners, employees, and suppliers are internal stakeholders. Customers and local community are external stakeholders. Drouin and Turner (2022) suggest that there are four levels of governance in project-based organizations (Figure 4.1):
- the governance of individual projects, which they call project governance;
- the governance of the context within which projects take place, which includes the governance of programs, portfolios, and networks of projects, which they call governance of projects;
- governance at the board level of the project-based organization; and
- governmentality, which defines how those in governance roles interact with those they govern (politics), and is the level at which the policy is set.

Strictly, governmentality is a human agency activity, whereas the other three levels are structural. However, Dean (2010) suggests that governmentality is the overarching mechanism from which governance flows. Governmentality is the level at which policy and politics occurs, as illustrated in Figure 4.1. Figure 4.1 shows that policy decisions flow through the other three levels.

The OECD also defines four principles of good governance (Millstein et al., 1998):
1. *Transparency*: This relates to the trust investors and other stakeholders have in the operation of the organization, which relies on information being timely and accurate. Also, people need to do what they say. The principal needs to trust the decisions and action of their agent or steward. People need to act in a way that is consistent with the school of governance adopted.

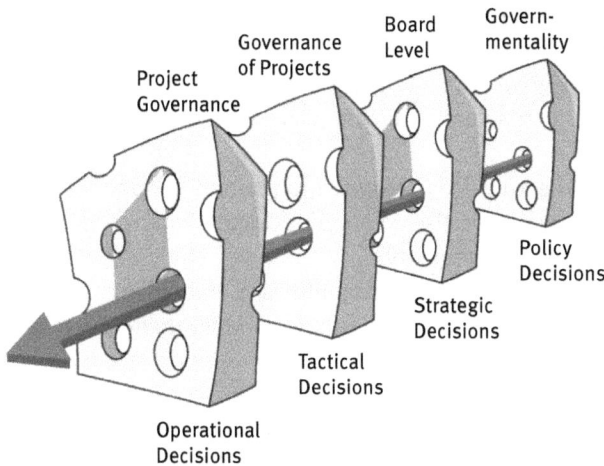

Figure 4.1: Four levels of governance.

2. *Accountability*: This is concerned with the clarity of roles, responsibilities, and rights of the major participants.
3. *Responsibility*: This is about maintaining professional standards and adhering to the law of the society of which the project is a part.
4. *Fairness*: This is about ensuring equal and fair treatment of all the stakeholders, both internal and external. It also relates to the maintenance of ethical standards (Derakhshan et al., 2019a; Müller et al., 2014).

Following Dean (2010) and Barthes (2013), Müller (2019) defined governmentality as the way those in governance roles interact with those they govern. It reflects their mentalities and rationalities toward those they govern during the implementation, maintenance, and modification of the governance structures. Dean (2010) defines three approaches to governmentality:
- *Authoritarian*: Governors clearly articulate to the internal stakeholders the means and ends of achieving the project objectives. The governors control by defining desired behaviors (Ouchi & Maguire, 1975).
- *Liberal*: Governors draw on the rationality and economic thinking of those they govern, by using incentives. The governors control by defining desired outputs (Ouchi & Maguire, 1975).
- *Neoliberal*: Governors build on the self-governance of individuals by setting the values of the organization and encouraging managers to steer themselves in the desired direction. This approach builds on the manager's collective interest and willingness to consent. By setting the contextual framework, managers' behaviors are shaped but not determined. The governors control by defining desired values.

Dean (2010) also suggested four dimensions of governmentality:
1. *Visibility*: This is related to the abovementioned transparency.
2. *Techne*: This defines how governance is performed. It is the means, mechanisms, procedures, instruments, tactics, techniques, technologies, and vocabularies used.
3. *Episteme*: This identifies the knowledge required to perform governance. It relates to thoughts, knowledge, expertise, strategies, calculation, and rationalities. It is closely related to governmentality.
4. *Identity*: This relates to the roles and responsibilities of individuals and how they relate to the collective. It is about how people conduct themselves, their duties, and their rights.

We mentioned earlier that that governance should define the roles, responsibilities, and rights of and relationships between the project's stakeholders. Derakhshan et al. (2019b) investigated how governance builds relationships with the project's stakeholders. They identified three key issues in the project's relationships with its stakeholders:
- Achieving success and project performance, and creating value for all stakeholders, internal and external
- Behaving ethically, creating transparency, and defining accountability as suggested by Millstein et al. (1998)
- Defining the rights and responsibilities of stakeholders, with stakeholders as decision-makers and as creators and targets of value

Using institution theory and attribution theory, Derakhshan et al. (2019a) investigated how external stakeholders assess the legitimacy of the project and its parent organization. They found that:
- The assessment of the legitimacy of the local or national government can influence stakeholder's assessment of legitimacy of project organization and project.
- People's previous experience can influence their assessment of legitimacy. People are lazy, and so they will not change their assessment unless they are encouraged to do so.
- Communities' assessment of legitimacy can influence their assessment of organizational behavior.

4.3 Case Studies

When discussing policy and politics in the next two sections, I will give examples from several case studies. I will provide a brief overview of those projects in this section.

4.3.1 The Øresund Link

The Øresund Link is a fixed link between the Danish Island of Zealand and the Swedish mainland (Hertogh et al., 2008; Russel, 2000). It connects Copenhagen Airport with the Swedish city of Malmö. It consists of a 4 km tunnel from Copenhagen Airport to an artificial island. The artificial island is 4 km long. Then there is an 8 km bridge from the island to Malmö. The total length is 16 km, excluding connecting roads and rail at either end. There is a tunnel at the Danish end because a bridge would interfere with planes landing at Copenhagen Airport. The purpose of the project was clearly to speed up the journey time between Sweden and Denmark. The project has had a substantial impact on the surrounding economy. As house prices are cheaper in Malmö, many people live there and work in Copenhagen. The increase in GDP of the local Swedish region, Skåne, has been higher than anywhere else in Sweden. Copenhagen Airport is closer (20 km) to Malmö than Malmö Airport, which is 30 km. Ralf Müller lives in Malmö and I have been to visit him several times. I fly from London to Copenhagen, and then it is 20 min by train. In June 2018, we were at the EURAM conference in Reykjavik. Another delegate had had a meeting in Malmö immediately before the conference. He had flown from Malmö Airport to Stockholm, and had had a long wait in Stockholm. We had a little giggle; he could have gone to Copenhagen more quickly and flown directly. (Malmö Airport is still useful for flying to other Swedish regional airports, and in fact flying to Stockholm it will give quicker and easier check-in.) A treaty between the Danish and Swedish governments was signed in 1991. Work started in 1993, and the link opened in the summer of 2000.

4.3.2 Sydney Storm Water Tunnel

Between May 1997 and July 2000, Sydney built a stormwater drainage tunnel as part of a program to clean up Sydney's rivers, beaches, and waterways in advance of the Sydney Olympics in 2000 (Pitsis et al., 2019). When it rains in Sydney, it can rain hard; previously, sewage and detritus from the streets would end up in the harbor. The aim was to collect stormwater and divert it from the harbor. The project consisted of 20 km of tunnels in sandstone in the very affluent areas north of Sydney harbor. The owner (principal) was Sydney Water. This project entailed high uncertainty on the design and in the work methods. The geotechnics of the site were not well known, what was sandstone and what was other materials. The tunnel drilling machine had to be ordered before the site was properly surveyed, and adjusted in situ to meet the requirements. The project was a major piece of infrastructure to be built in advance of the Sydney Olympics, using innovative public–private partnership approaches. Further, as with the Gotthard and Lötschberg base tunnels (Hertogh et al., 2008), the geotechnics were poorly known. It was therefore not possible to do a front-end design in advance of inviting contractors to join the project. When contractors were invited to join, the specification was just 28 pages, rather than the normal hundreds of pages, effectively making it a cardinal point procurement (Turner, 2003). The contractors were told the end objectives but had to design how they would be achieved. The owner therefore decided to adopt partnering and alliancing as the contract method.

4.3.3 The West Coast Mainline Upgrade

During the mid-2000s, a major upgrade was done to the West Coast Mainline in the UK (Hertogh et al., 2008; Hertogh & Westerweld, 2010). The West Coast Mainline is the railway line that runs up the west coast, from London, to Birmingham, Manchester, and Glasgow. The West Coast Mainline is the UK's busiest railway line, with a mixture of passenger services and freight. The passenger lines consist of a mixture of intercity, regional, and short-distance commuter lines. The purpose of the project was to provide capacity for growth anticipated over the next 20–30 years; to provide fast and competitive journey times; to provide improved levels of performance, safety, and reliability; to improve the competitiveness of rail and its role in the economy; to overcome a backlog of maintenance and renewals; and to establish cost-effective maintenance regimes. Side effect will be environmental improvements by encouraging a shift in freight from road to rail, and encouraging people to use the rail rather than air. It was meant to solve capacity problems for the next 30 years, but already increased capacity is required, resulting in the new line called HS2 (High Speed 2). (The purpose of HS2 is to increase capacity, but unfortunately its name makes people think its purpose is to reduce journey times.)

4.3.4 Gotthard Base Tunnel

The Gotthard is a railway tunnel of 57 km through the Gotthard Pass in Switzerland (Hertogh et al., 2008; Hertogh & Westerweld, 2010). It is the longest and deepest rail tunnel in the world, being 2,500 m deep at its deepest point. There is a tunnel in both directions, giving 104 km of rail tunnel. But with ventilation, emergency, and other tunnels, there is a total of 153 km of tunnel (Figure 4.2). The purpose of the project is to integrate Switzerland into the European high-speed train network, moving trains to shallower inclines, to reduce journey times for passengers and freight, and to shift freight from road to rail. The maximum incline is 12.5% and the minimum radius of curve is 4,000 m. Since the thirteenth century, the Gotthard Valley has been an important trade route connecting Northern and Southern Europe, connecting the Rhone and Po Rivers. It is suggested that the Swiss Confederation can be formed to manage the route. The Gotthard Rail Tunnel opened in 1882, considerably reducing journey times. That railway line has many curves and switchbacks, and rises to 1,500 m above sea level. You can see the original tunnel in Figure 4.2. The Gotthard Tunnel is 550 m above sea level at its highest point. After electrification in 1922, cars started traveling on trains. But a road was also opened, and a motorway was built with the Gotthard Road Tunnel in 1977. The Gotthard Base Tunnel was first proposed in 1947 as a flight of fancy. But with the adoption of the NEAT (New Rail Links through the Alps) concept, the Swiss Government proposed building much shallower, flatter railways. This involved four tunnels. The Gotthard, Lötschberg, and Ceneri Base Tunnels are now in operation. A fourth tunnel, the Zimmerberg Base Tunnel, just South of Zurich, was only half built, the return line being postponed for environmental reasons. The Gotthard Base Tunnel reduced journey times between Zürich and Milan by half an hour. Passenger trains have a maximum speed of 250 km/h, but will travel at 200 km/h. It is also expected that there will be 210 freight trains a day, and the shallower incline freight trains will be able to carry 4,000 tons rather than 2,000 tons, taking a substantial number of freight lorries off the road. The NEAT concept was created in 1992, and a referendum was held, which passed. In 1993, some exploratory borings were done to begin to establish the geological conditions. Drilling started in 1999. Construction started properly in 2002. The tunnel was opened in 2016.

4.3.5 High Speed 2, HS2

In spite of the upgrade, the West Coast Mainline is already predicted to suffer capacity problems. More intercity, regional, short distance, and freight trains are required. During the upgrade, two tracks were built in both directions along it entire length. It is not possible to have four tracks. The only way to increase capacity is to build a new line, and if you are building a new line, you might as well make it high speed. Unfortunately, because it is called HS2, people assume that the purpose is to reduce journey times, and quite rightly say there is no need to reduce journey times. The purpose is to increase capacity. There are many financial and nonfinancial benefits. Financial benefits include:
- Increased capacity of West Coast Main Line
- Connecting northern power house to Midlands and both to London
- Reduced transaction costs to encourage business to locate in north where costs are less expensive
- Improved access to Heathrow, Birmingham International, and Manchester Airports
- Improved Britain's productivity
- Improved supply chains
- Improved business start-up
- Critical mass of skills and talent pool
- Attract graduates to northern towns

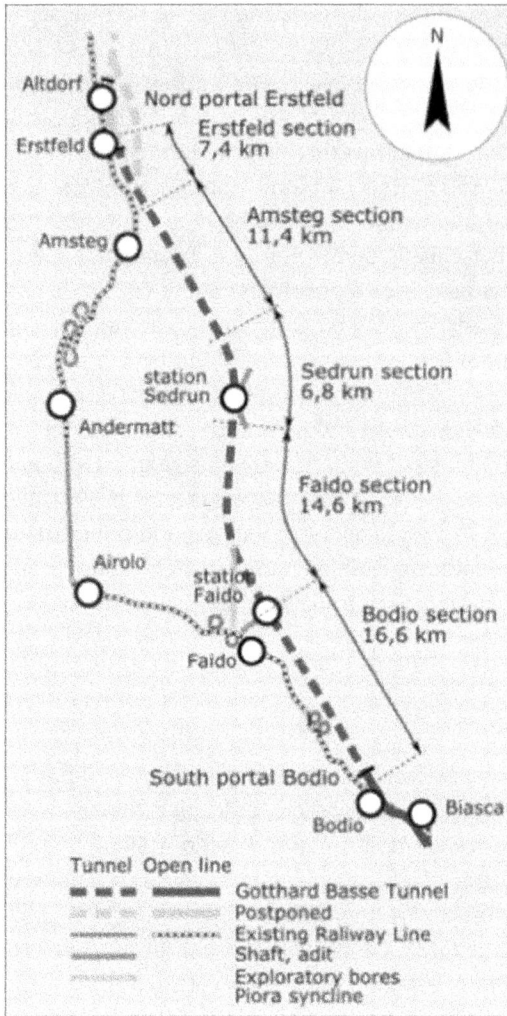

Figure 4.2: Route of the Gotthard Base Tunnel.

Nonfinancial benefits include:
- Pleasant travel experiences on high-speed trains
- Reduced overcrowding, giving more pleasant travel, and meaning Jeremy Corbyn can get a seat between Watford and London
- Reduced journey times
- Reduced congestion on roads
- Reduced air travel
- Improved safety, with a switch from road to rail

- Environmental improvements from the above
- People better able to visit family and friends, go shopping, have a day out, and travel to work

The last two projects are change projects in the private sector.

4.3.6 Customer Requirements Management

A French telecommunications company implemented a customer requirements management (CRM) system (Beldi et al., 2010). The purpose of the project was to:
- Improve interaction and relationships with customers, being better able to provide personalized and customized products and services, and satisfy their needs
- Improve revenue and reduce marketing costs

The company recognized the project as an organizational change project, requiring changes to organizational structure and business processes, as well as implementation of the computer system. The project was implemented in three phases:
1. Planning: The functional architecture was defined, and the CRM modules to be implemented were chosen. Required changes to business processes and organizational structure were also identified.
2. Piloting: Communication with the users was important to implement a user-friendly system. Evolution of employee behavior was tracked, and training implemented.
3. Rollout: The governance structure changed from neoliberal to liberal because it was thought that stricter control was required during rollout. Perhaps an authoritarian governance structure was required, but there was a balance between control and motivation. The training was changed to focus more on the revision to business processes, and less on the technology.

4.3.7 Change of Brand After Acquisition by New Owners

The second organizational change project is another telecommunication company in Austria, which changed its brand from One to Orange on acquisition by new owners (Fiedler, 2010). The company "One" was a stand-alone mobile operator with a 20% market share. However, it was acquired by new owners and became part of the Orange brand.

There were several steps to the change program:
1. Acquisition by new shareholders
2. New management
3. New strategy

4. New organization
5. New processes
6. Change of brand

This is the order in which they happened. The change program led to considerable resistance, and managing that resistance was a significant part of the change program, which we will discuss later under politics.

4.4 Policy

The *Oxford English Dictionary* defines policy as:

> A course or principle of action adopted or proposed by a government, business or individual.

And suggests that it reflects prudent conduct. The *Chambers Dictionary*, also under the definition of policy, suggests that it includes the art of government and statecraft, which is beginning to encompass politics.

Under policy, the organization needs to make governance choices. The project manager, project organization, and investing organization need to make choices about:

– The objectives of the project and creating value for all stakeholders
– The method of achieving those objectives
– The means of monitoring progress
– The roles, responsibilities, and rights of and relationships with the internal and external stakeholders
– Transparency, accountability, responsibility, and fairness
– Whether to adopt authoritarian, liberal, or neoliberal governmentality
– Visibility, techne, episteme, and identity
– Behaving ethically
– Creating legitimacy

4.4.1 Objectives

Defining the objectives is the first stated element of governance, and an early decision is for whom the project should provide value: just the investing organization; other internal stakeholders; or also external stakeholders (Derakhshan et al., 2019a). The shareholder school of governance (Müller, 2009) suggests that the sole responsibility of the organization, and the projects it does, is to make profits for the owners. In the extreme, it is suggested that if providing a value for other stakeholders reduces profits for owners, you should not provide value for the other stakeholders. However, there is substantial evidence that providing value for other stakeholders increases performance in longer term, and this is the stakeholder school of governance (Müller, 2009), but then which stakeholders to provide value for, internal or external.

Providing value for other internal stakeholders means allowing contractors, subcontractors, and suppliers make a reasonable profit. Investors wedded to the shareholder school of governance, especially those who fallaciously think they are tough negotiators, will want their contractors and suppliers to make as little profit as possible. They also think that a contractual relationship based on a principal–agent approach will put them in control (Müller, 2017). But more enlightened investors recognize that if their contractors share their objectives, it will lead to better project outcomes (Turner, 2014). Drouin and Turner (2022) show that investors who chose the cheapest contractor with a principal–agent approach should plan to fail. Choosing the economically most advantageous contractor with a principal–steward approach leads to better outcomes. In choosing the economically most advantageous bid, the investor can also make allowances for other issues, such as environmental performance and benefits to external stakeholders (see later). That is what was done on the Øresund Link (Russel, 2000). They put considerable effort into choosing the economically most advantageous contractor for the three main contracts, the tunnels, island and bridge, and adopted a collaborative form of contracting based on partnership: trust, openness, and cooperation. The investors' project organization, Øresunds Konsortiet (ØSK), also believed strongly that they should command the process, but not exercise detailed control. They should leave that to the contractors. The Sydney Storm Water tunnel had a similar working relationship with its contractors, where the slogan was to do "What is best for the project."

A related issue for a contractor bidding for work is to make the cheapest possible bid, or an economically advantageous bid. That depends of course on how they expect the client to assess the bid. If their client is an unenlightened organization who thinks they are tough, Donald Trump-style negotiators, who are going to screw everybody in sight, they will need to make the bid as cheap as possible. If, on the other hand, their client is an enlightened organization, who is going to judge the bid based on lifetime value and environmental impact, they can make an economically advantageous bid.

Then there is a value for external stakeholders. Both the West Coast Mainline upgrade and the HS2 have identified a long list of nonfinancial benefits, which provide a value to the users of the line, or are environmental benefits which benefit society as a whole. Included in the environmental benefits are safety improvements, which means users will suffer fewer accidents but will also reduce load on the health service. With the West Coast Mainline upgrade, the cost–benefit ratio of the project based purely on ticket sales was 0.85. You will not do that project. However, as with HS2, they identified other financial benefits, and they were able to assess quasifinancial benefit for the nonfinancial benefits by accounting for those who raised the cost–benefit ratio to almost 3.0. The project was now very worthwhile.

However, if you look at the list of financial and nonfinancial benefits for HS2, you will see that many of these accrue to the government, or the country's population at large, and not the investor. That was also the case with the West Coast Mainline upgrade. But in both cases the government owns the train company, and so the benefits accrue to the ultimate owner. That was also the case with the Øresund Link. The governments, who were the ultimate investors, benefited from the increased economic activity (but not increased house prices in Malmö). It was not the case with the channel tunnel link. The investors building the tunnel did not share in the economic benefits accruing to the British and French governments, which made them less able to make a profit. Mrs. Thatcher said the government should not share the risk, but the British government got substantial benefits.

Other external stakeholders are the local community (Di Maddaloni & Davis, 2017, 2018). Often the local community is not treated with respect (Derakhshan et al., 2019a), reducing their assessment of the legitimacy of the project and the investor. Di Maddaloni and Davis give examples (from HS2) of people who own a local shop and live in the flat above it. The building is demolished to make way for the project. They lose their house and their business. The psychology literature has recognized for a long time the importance of possession to people (Johnson & Henley, 1990). Destroying their home and business can leave people feeling denuded (Sayre, 1994). There may be no alternative to demolishing the building, but people need counseling and to be properly compensated. The French are much better at compensating people than the British.

Project managers face lots of choices. The Gotthard Base Tunnel said the maximum incline of the rail should be 12.5% and the minimum radius of curvature should be 4,000 m. In fact, it was preferred that the minimum radius of curvature should be 5,000 m, but at one point it had to be reduced to 4,000 m. The incline was such that the weight that could be carried by freight trains could be increased from 2,000 to 4,000 tons. The curvature was to increase the maximum speed of the trains to reduce journey times and increase the number of trains that could travel on the track. Substantial amounts of freight could then be transferred from road to rail, delivering substantial environmental improvement. If you look at the nonfinancial benefit of HS2, you will see that this delivers many of those benefits. The Swiss government does not own the train company, but is a substantially interested stakeholder.

The Øresund Link had to do dredging to maintain water flows in the Barents Sea. The Swedish environmental courts said currents should not be affected by more than 5%. They managed to do sufficient dredging so that currents were maintained at their original strength. The island was created from the dredging. Originally it was planned that there should be two islands, but a change after work had started to make it one island because of the strength of the soil. The collaborative working meant that change could take place with minimum disruption.

The Sydney Storm Water tunnel required an air vent at a certain point. Originally, it was going to be two vents, but it was redesigned to one vent. It was designed so that the escaping air would be scrubbed and 95% of the water vapor removed. However, the local community objected to the design. There was a conspiracy theory that the escaping air would contain *Legionella* bacteria. They tried to have the vent removed but was impossible. They proposed alternative designs which would have delayed the project beyond the Sydney Olympics. The science suggested that the alternative designs would offer no improvement, but would be more expensive and take longer to build. We will return to this in the next section, but in the end the New South Wales government had to tell the local community to shut up for the sake of the Sydney Olympics. The conservative party was in power in the NSW government, but the local community had voted labor at the recent election.

The CRM system had to make decision about which packages to include in the implementation, to provide customers with the services they desired, and to enable the user to be better able to serve customers. It was though initially that the implementation would not involve much organizational change. However, new business processes were required. The new business processes moved boundaries between departments and changed interdepartmental communication. It was also identified that training was required to enable the sales people to operate the new business processes.

The second step of governance is to decide how the project is to be delivered. The creation of the Gotthard Base Tunnel involved considerable risk and uncertainty. The geology was uncertain. The rock types could be measured at the surface, but it could only be guessed the width of the different rock types at depth. Also water in the rocks would create problems. Trial drilling was done. At one point, a few hundred meters above the tunnel, there was water in the rock, but luckily at the level of the tunnel it was dry. As shown in Figure 4.2, the tunnel was bored in five sections. In the Estfeld and Bodio sections, the drilling machine could start at the tunnel portal. In the Amsteg and Faldo sections, the drilling machine could enter from the side, as shown for the Faldo section. With the Sedrun section, the boring had to be done by blasting, and the equipment had to be taken down vertical shafts. This created considerable safety problems, including how to evacuate staff in the event of an accident. Because the rock was not as expected, boring south in the Sedrun section was quicker than expected, whereas drilling north on the Faldo section was slower than expected, so the breakthrough was further south than originally planned. At its greatest depth, the tunnel was 2,500 m below the highest peak, which created considerable pressure in the rock, which also created safety issue. Also at another point, a new piece of equipment had to be created to do the drilling. There was similar uncertainty about the nature of the geology and the location of the rock with the Sydney Strom Water tunnel. At one point, the tunnel had to be higher than originally planned, creating the need for the vent discussed earlier.

The CRM system was executed in three stages. In the first stage, the system was planned and designed. It was here that decisions were made about which packages to implement to meet the client desires and the user requirements, and to achieve the projects' objectives. The system was then piloted in one department. It was at this stage that the needs for business process reengineering and organizational change were identified, and also the need to provide user training. The system was then rolled out to other departments. During the rollout the project team delegated to the users to implement the system. The users were given guidance and training, but they were responsible for implementation. There had to be a change in governance. During planning and piloting, a neoliberal governance approach was used. Perhaps during rollout it needs to be authoritarian. Users have to be told what to do. But it was thought that would be demotivating, so a liberal governance approach was used.

The third set of governance decisions to be made is how to control progress. On the Øresund Link, it was decided to delegate the monitoring of progress to the contractors. The contractors would gather progress data and report to the client's project organizations, ØSK. The client defined what they would and would not do. They would:
- approve the basic design assumptions, the project quality program documentation, and the basic planning for the works;
- visit, observe, discuss, witness, review quality records, and carry out random sampling;
- review and if required comment and approve site questions;
- review and approve nonconformity reports;
- approve the physical work at payment milestones.

They would not:
- get involved in day-to-day supervision, inspection, and approval of construction;
- inspect setting out;
- inspect construction joints, rebars, formwork, etc.;
- inspect every radiograph of welds;
- watch every batch of concrete being poured;
- be present all day, every day at each construction site;
- produce quality records.

Some of these are a bit amusing, but the client is firmly saying we will not interfere, unlike many clients. ØSK said they were in command of the process, but did not exercise detailed control. That was given to the contractors. ØSK said they assigned responsibility where competence lay with consultants and contractors (Lundhus, 2001). The contractors were responsible for their own quality control. Often clients will employ an army of quality control checkers. ØSK required the contractors to check their quality. They did do a small number of random checks. But ØSK trusted the contractors and their trust was rewarded.

Two sources of uncertainty were information asymmetry and moral hazard (Müller, 2017; Turner, 2014; Winch, 2010). Because the contractors did their own quality control checks, there was asymmetry of information between the client and the contractors and the client, though the random checks reduced that. However, there was no asymmetry of information where it mattered, between the contractors and themselves; they needed to know that the work was being done to good quality. There was a moral hazard risk that the contractors might lie about their quality control checks, but the random checks reduced that. Also the tender evaluation process meant that the most reliable contractors were chosen rather than the cheapest. If you work with the cheapest contractor, you are liable to find yourself working under a principal–agency relationship, and not a stewardship relationship (Müller, 2017). Drouin and Turner (2022) say a principal–agency relationship will not work under radical uncertainty, but it is more likely not to work if you have chosen the cheapest contractor, as the contractor cuts corners to increase their profit. Also, on the Øresund Link, the contractors were properly rewarded for their work, illustrating distributive fairness (Greenberg & Colquitt, 2005), reducing the likelihood of moral hazard.

As I have just said, the CRM system had to base control during the rollout on a liberal form of governance, rather than authoritarian to maintain motivation.

The fourth and final set of governance decisions I am going to discuss is about transparency, accountability, responsibility, and fairness. Transparency is related to trust and legitimacy. Trust flows from transparency; trust will not arise if an organization does not adopt a transparent approach to its stakeholders (Rawlins, 2008). Schneckenburger and Tomlinson (2016, p. 1788) defined transparency as "the perceived quality of intentionally shared information from a sender." Transparency is about an organization's knowledge or information being intentionally shared with the stakeholders. It must be perceived by the stakeholders and thus has a subjective nature, and the level of perceived transparency varies according to the quality of the information shared with the stakeholders. Organizations have the power to manage stakeholder perceptions, thus influencing their assessment of legitimacy (Derakhshan et al., 2019a). Müller et al. (2014) explored trust building through governance, and identified that governance structures based on the stakeholder school lead to greater trust among the stakeholders. Stakeholders need to trust the project organization's ability to solve problems. Both the Gotthard Base Tunnel and Øresund Link had high levels of transparency. That is partially due to the Swiss, Swedish, and Danish cultures. But as we will explore in the next section, the Gotthard Base Tunnel was subject to four referenda, and so the Swiss government and Swiss rail had to be totally open and honest. The Øresund Link had to convince the Swedish environmental courts that they were meeting the constraints they imposed, and so again had to be very transparent. HS2 is perhaps suffering a negative press because they are being less transparent. They should do more marketing, telling the population about what they are doing.

Justice and fairness are topics receiving attention in the literature (Greenberg & Colquitt, 2005). The literature identifies three types of fairness: distributive fairness, procedural fairness, and interactional fairness. Interactional fairness relates more to the treatment of employees and so is less important in the relationship with stakeholders. Distributional fairness is the distribution of benefits, harms, rewards, and costs that affect the well-being of members of a group or community. Distributional fairness can foster effective cooperation and commitment. At an organizational level, it is the extent to which an organization is moral in nature, and the sharing of regards is fair in view of each party's contribution, commitment, and assumption of responsibility. The Øresund Link's actions illustrated moral behavior. The contractors were fairly rewarded for their work, and the client's project organizations, ØSK, assumed responsibility for the geotechnical, weather, and currency risks. Responsibility was assigned where competence lay. The contractors did their own quality control checks, with ØSK's conducting infrequent audits. Procedural fairness is the perception of whether the procedures and decision-making behind the distribution of outcomes are fair. Are the decisions and their execution transparent, unbiased, and correctable? ØSK worked at procedural fairness, and the growing commitment of the contractors showed it was achieving the desired outcomes. The Sydney Storm Water tunnel adopted an alliance form of contracting. They identified four key performance indicators (KPIs) such as time, cost, environmental performance, and external stakeholders, and shared the savings from the project based on performance against the four KPIs. The only one they did not perform well on was external stakeholders because of the contretemps over the vent. But as we said earlier, the slogan for the project was to do "What is best for the project." There is a clear idea that the project performs best if everyone is pulling together rather than ploughing their own furrow (Turner 2014). So we finished the policy where we started, and determined how to share the benefits from the project between the stakeholders.

4.5 Politics

The *Oxford English Dictionary* defines politics as:

> The art and science of government
> The exercise of authority
> Making decisions based on status and authority rather than principle

The *Chambers Dictionary* also suggests that the definition includes policy-making. So the *Chambers Dictionary* takes us backward and forward between policy and politics. The case studies were all subjected to different types of political pressures.

4.5.1 Gotthard Base Tunnel

The Swiss love their referenda, and the tunnel was the subject of four. The Swiss government adopted a concept called NEAT, with the aim of building flatter railways. This involved the construction of four tunnels such as the Gotthard, Lötschberg, Ceneri, and Zimmerberg Base Tunnels, which are now in operation. The Ceneri Base Tunnel is just south of Biasca, as shown in Figure 4.2. The Zimmerberg Base Tunnel is on the same line as the Gotthard Tunnel, but well to the north, just outside Zurich. It is the only one of the four not to have been completed. The Lötschberg is on another line to the west. The NEAT concept was the subject of the first referendum in 1987. It was approved. The second referendum in 1992 arose because the Green Party made an environmental challenge. The project was approved. The European Union said they would prefer road to rail, and so the 1994 and 1998 referenda were about making a choice between road and rail. Rail won. Part of the idea of the tunnel is to move traffic from road to rail.

The ultimate client for the project was the Swiss parliament. The principal was the Department of Environment, Transport, Energy and Communication (UVEK), who delegated responsibility to the Federal Office of Transport (BAV). Swiss rail created a department called AlpTransit Gotthard Limited (ATG), which was the managing contractor for the project. The relationship between ATG, BAV, and UVEK is based on a principal–steward arrangement.

Following the referendum in 1987, in 1988 the Minister of Transport started planning the Gotthard and Lötschberg Base Tunnels. In May 1990, UVEK presented a plan to parliament, and NEAT was approved in 1991. The Green Party made their challenge resulting in the referendum of 1992. Between September 1993 and October 2001, UVEK, BAV, and ATG planned the project. This involved geological surveys, negotiation with cantons, and discussions in parliament. In February 1999, UVEK approved the Gotthard Base Tunnel. In November 1999, the first access tunneling began; in July 2000, the first main tunneling began; and in October 2001, the first main contract was assigned. The project was completed in July 2016, and opened in December 2016.

The project goes through three cantons: Uri, Graubünden, and Ticino. Graubünden and Ticino were always in favor of the project, but Uri, at the north end, became the biggest opponent. Line choice and design of the open track raised hackles. Citizens demanded that more open track be put in tunnels, and as you can see in Figure 4.2, some new open track was not built. A significant problem for the project was the disagreement between the communities within Uri. Some people suggest that Uri achieved a worse outcome than if they had worked more positively with the project.

4.5.2 The Øresund Link

The project required a treaty between the Swedish and Danish governments. Swedish and Danish laws are quite different and so this required some work. One way Swedish and Danish laws are different is in terms of environmental consent. In Denmark, consent is given by the parliament. Since it is their project, they were quite amenable. But consent in Sweden is given by environmental courts independent of parliament. The courts take their responsibility very seriously; hence, environmental consent was not guaranteed. The project had to work hard. That led to much greater transparency, as I said earlier. In the event, the project was able to exceed the environmental standards set and so obtained the consent.

4.5.3 The Sydney Storm Water Tunnel

The project was about cleaning up Sydney's waterways, including Sydney harbor, in advance of the Sydney Olympics in 2000. When it rains in Sydney, it can rain hard, and previously that would wash a lot of detritus into the harbor. The aim of the project was to collect the stormwater and stop that from happening. Everybody wanted it because they wanted to make a good impression to the world, with a nice, clean, shining harbor.

A partnering approach was adopted for the project (Turner, 2006). Clegg et al. (2002) suggest there are several competitive advantages of alliance contracts:
- The parties can invest in tools and equipment specific to the alliance
- There are opportunities for substantial knowledge sharing and exchange
- There are opportunities to combine complimentary but scarce capabilities, resulting in substantial innovation
- There are lower transaction costs with more effective governance mechanisms, as we saw on Øresund Link in Chapter 3. There is reduced inspection based on trust
- An alliance contract acknowledges uncertainty and complexity, rather than using a principal–agent relation to try to pretend that it does not exist.

Three contractors were invited to join the alliance based on the 28-page specification. Before the project started, there was one fixed objective: the project had to be finished by July 2000, before the Sydney Olympics. Pitsis et al. (2003) and Clegg (2019) said the alliance was based on 10 cultural commitments:
1. Build and maintain a champion team with champion leadership, which will be integrated across all disciplines and organizations
2. Commit corporately and individually to openness, integrity, trust, cooperation, mutual support and respect, flexibility, honesty, and loyalty to the project
3. Honor our commitments to one another

4. Commit to a no-blame culture
5. Use breakthroughs and the free flow of ideas to achieve exceptional results in all project objectives
6. Outstanding results provide outstanding rewards
7. Deal with and resolve all issues from within the alliance
8. Act in a way that is best for the project
9. Encourage challenging business as usual behaviors
10. Spread the alliance culture to all stakeholders

The 10 cultural elements were designed by the alliance members for themselves as a point of reference and became a lived experience. The commitments were explicitly oriented toward aligning business objectives, generating mutual incentives, sharing risks, pooling strengths, and building trust. They were extended down to subcontractors and even the trade unions. The trade unions wanted the project to be a success and so bought into them. The commitments created common sense-making frame, where participants could voluntarily agree to be governed by these commitments. Adhering to them is justified in terms of collective interest. If people adhered to the commitments, they would benefit individually and organizationally. Also members of the alliance began to identify with alliance rather than with their parent organizations. The slogan for the project was to do what is "best for the project," rather than yourself (Turner, 2014).

There was some misinterpretation of the commitments. For instance, did the no-blame culture mean you could not complain if someone turned up an hour late to a meeting? No, blame culture meant if there was a problem you should work to solve it, not apportioning blame, and that led to greater innovation.

So when some left-wing trouble makers created problems by questioning the vents, potentially delaying the project beyond the Olympics, the population at large is not happy. The local population had a point. It was important that the air leaving the vent should be properly scrubbed of water vapor and other pollutants. It is impossible to remove all the water vapor, but the proposal was to scrub 95%. The vents were in fact very close to a primary school, so if the conspiracy theory was correct and the vented air was going to contain *Legionella* bacteria, it would not be good. The science said there was no likelihood of *Legionella* bacteria, but once these theories are in Twitter and Facebook, some people do not believe the science anymore. The community proposed alternative designs, but the science said they would make no improvement, but they would be more expensive and take the project beyond the Sydney Olympics. To describe the local community as left-wing troublemakers is probably unfair, but that is how they were perceived. There was an election to the New South Wales parliament. That community returned a Labor member, but the Liberal (conservative) Party won the election. They just told this local community to shut up.

The one KPI the project scored badly was its relationship with external stakeholders.

4.5.4 Change of Brand, One to Orange

The project generated considerable resistance. The early stages of the change, new management, new strategy, new organization, and new processes built up negative impressions that then made employees resistant to the change of brand. The rebranding was conducted as a program and involved a project of internal communications, cultural development, and training. Key elements of this were:
– Building trust between management and employees (which our earlier discussions suggest that it requires transparency)
– Communication between management and employees, (which should entail transparency)
– Involving employees in creating the new brand and letting go the old brand
– Creating the Orange culture
– Improving employee satisfaction and trying to retain existing staff

There were five stages for managing resistance:
– Identify and evaluate potential resistance
– Plan response
– Preparation for resistance
– Resolution of resistance
– Controlling measures and potentials

This is a mixture of risk management and stakeholder management. I am afraid that I have run out of words and have no space to describe this in greater detail. Please refer to Fiedler (2010) for details.

4.6 Summary

Making governance choices involves project managers in making policy and political decisions. The responsible project manager, following the stakeholder school of governance, will make decisions in the best interest of the largest number of stakeholders. Unfortunately, he or she will often do what the organization tells him or her to do, and that was the case with many of the case studies discussed here.

References

Barthes, R. (2013). *Mythologies: The complete edition*. NY: Hill and Wang.

Beldi, A., Cheffii, W., & Dey, P. K. (2010). Managing customer relationship management projects: The case of a large French telecommunications company. *International Journal of Project Management, 28*, 339–351.

Carlsen, A., & Pitsis, T. S. (2020). We are projects: Narrative capital and meaning making in projects. *Project Management Journal, 51*(4), 357–366. https://doi.org/10.1177/8756972820929479

Clegg, S. R. (2019). Govrnmentaility. *Project Management Journal, 50*(3), 266–270.

Clegg, S. R., Pitsis, T. S., Rura-Polley, T., & Marosszeky, M. (2002). Governmentality matters: Designing an alliance culture of inter-organizational collaboration for project management. *Organization Studies, 23*, 317–336.

Dean, M. (2010). *Governmentality: Power and rule in modern society*. Thousand Oaks, CA: Sage.

Derakhshan, R., Mancini, M., & Turner, J. R. (2019a). Community's evaluation of organizational legitimacy: Formation and reconsideration. *International Journal of Project Management, 37*(1), 73–86.

Derakhshan, R., Turner, J. R., & Mancini, M. (2019b). Project governance and stakeholders: A literature review. *International Journal of Project Management, 37*, 98–116.

Di Maddaloni, F., & Davis, K. (2017). The influence of local community stakeholders in megaprojects: Rethinking their inclusiveness to improve project performance. *International Journal of Project Management, 35*, 1537–1556.

Di Maddaloni, F., & Davis, K. (2018). Project Manager's perception of the local communities' stakeholder in megaprojects. An empirical investigation in the UK. *International Journal of Project Management, 36*, 542–565.

Drouin, N., & Turner, J. R. (2022). *The Elgar advanced introduction to megaprojects*. Cheltenham, UK/Northampton, MA: Edward Elgar.

Fiedler, S. (2010). Managing resistance in an organizational transformation. A case study from a mobile operator company. *International Journal of Project Management, 28*, 370–383.

Greenberg, J., & Colquitt, J. (Eds.). (2005). *Handbook of organizational justice*. Mahwah, NJ: Lawrence Erlbaum Associates.

Hertogh, M., Baker, S., Staal-Ong, P. L., & Westerveld, E. (2008). *Managing large infrastructure projects: Research on best practices and lessons learnt in large infrastructure projects in Europe*. Utrecht: AT Osborne BV.

Hertogh, M., & Westerveld, E. (2010). *Playing with complexity: Management and organization of large infrastructure projects* [PhD thesis, Erasmus University Rotterdam].

Johnson, G., & Henley, T. B. (1990). *Reflections on the principles of psychology. William James After a century* (1st ed.). New York: Psychology Press, 344pp. ISBN9780203761656. DOI: https://doi.org/10.4324/9780203761656.

Lundhus, P. (2001). The Owner's organization and management principles. In N. J. Gimsing (Ed.), *The Øresund technical publications: The bridge* (pp. 18–33). Copenhagen: Øresundsbro Konsortiet.

Müller, R. (2009). *Project governance*. Aldershot, UK: Gower.

Müller, R. (Ed.). (2017). *Governance and governmentality for projects: Enablers, practices and consequences*. New York and London: Routledge.

Müller, R., Turner, R., Andersen, E. S., Shao, J., & Kvalnes, Ø. (2014). Ethics, trust, and governance in temporary organizations. *Project Management Journal, 45*(4), 39–54.

Müller, R. (2019). Governance, governmentality and project performance: The role of sovereignty. *International Journal of Information Systems and Project Management, 7*(2), 5–17.

Millstein, I. M., Albert, M., Cadbury, A., Feddersen, D., & Tateisi, N. (1998). *Improving competitiveness and access to capital in global markets*. Paris, France: OECD Publications.

Olchi, W. G. (1978). The transmission of control through organizational hierarchy. *Academy of management Journal, 21*(2), 173–192.

OECD. (2015). *G20/OECD principles of corporate governance*. Paris: Author.

Rawlins, B. R. (2008). Measuring the relationship between organizational transparency and employee trust, Faculty Publications. 885.

Russel, H. (2000). *Partnership pays: Project management the Øresund way*. Swanley, UK: Route One Publishing.

Sayre, S. (1994). Possessions and identity in crisis: Meaning and change for victims of the Oakland firestorm. *Advances in Consumer Research, 21*, 109–114.

Schnackenberg, A. K., & Tomlinson, E. C. (2016). Organizational transparency: A new perspective on managing trust in organization-stakeholder relationships. *Journal of Management, 42*(7), 1784–1810.

Turner, J. R. (2003). Farsighted project contract management. In J. R. Turner (Ed.), *Contracting for project management* (chapter 3, pp. 33–57.). Aldershot: Gower.

Turner, J. R. (2006). Towards a theory of project management: The nature of the project governance and project management. *International Journal of Project Management, 2*(24), 93–95.

Turner, J. R. (2014). *The handbook of project-based management: Leading strategic change in organizations* (4th ed.). New York: McGraw-Hill.

Winch, G. M. (2010). *Managing construction projects* (2nd ed.). Oxford: Blackwell Science.

Shirley Thompson
5 Leadership Development Through Responsible Conversations

Context: This exploration of the requirements for responsible leadership development is based on individual project managers in the UK but concerns the intentions of any project leader. The requirements and suggestions apply to any project management situation.

Characters/entities: Relevant soft skills of experienced project managers are related to my research and volunteer experience within the PMI UK mentoring program, with some empowerment experiences from personal information technology contacts, alongside reflection from my journey as a project manager, a professional coach, and a responsible project management team member.

Locations: Project managers in the UK

Research gap: A pragmatic approach shows a practical means to guide project managers' development, inevitably an evolutionary, ongoing journey requiring regular reflection. It is argued that any stakeholder conversations are project interactions that can affect how responsible a project is perceived.

Challenges: A challenge is the lack of formal guidance and accredited learning that can support project managers in developing responsible stakeholder conversations.

Keywords: leadership, reflection, social responsibility

5.1 Introduction

If all the thoughts of responsible leaders about leadership development had been collected throughout history, what intentions might they recommend that responsible leaders ideally hold? Adams (2019) defines intention as a "deep, sincere desire coupled with the belief that it is possible" and quotes Mahatma Gandhi to link beliefs, thoughts, words, actions, habits, and values that lead to one's actions. The aim here is to consider how project managers' desires and beliefs can encompass responsible project management (RPM) principles, leading to desired outcomes. Because a leader is always responsible for leadership, even for shared leadership (Scouller, 2014), we want leaders to encourage and even ensure that followers adopt such desires and beliefs. In projects, this means exploring the collaborative intentions between project managers and stakeholders since those intentions lead to actions that reflect resultant project leadership in practice.

https://doi.org/10.1515/9783110724783-008

Leadership definition and theory are elusive; the unpredictability of one human being and leadership being a "social, collective, and interactive activity" (Kempster & Carroll, 2016, p. 16) may mean this will inevitably long be so. McCauley et al. (1998) suggest development as "the expansion of a person's capacity to be effective in leadership roles and processes." However, the human relationship element can view leadership as an art form (De Pree, 2004). The idea of responsible leadership exists, but the theory lacks coverage beyond individuals and organizations toward broader societal concerns (Kempster & Carroll, 2016). Clarke et al. (2018, p. 27) write that the idea makes "a useful lens to decipher ethics and the practice of project management." Leaders and followers work together to achieve a goal, and both may need to question the responsibility of the goal, how the goal is achieved, and the ramifications of the project activity and its goals. The additional idea of irresponsible leadership is considered essential to improve the understanding and teaching of responsible leadership because it supports the discussion of scenarios where leaders fail to act responsibly (Martins & Lazzarin, 2019). Considering that project management involves shared leadership and stakeholder engagement, there is a need to prepare project managers to focus on relationship building for responsible decision-making (Clarke et al., 2018).

That professional project managers need leadership skills is well accepted. Leadership, strategy, and business formed the new talent triangle at PMI (2017). The second edition of the APM competency framework (APM, 2016) streamlined their technical, behavioral, and contextual skills into 27 competencies: leadership and teamwork. The scope for leadership development is broad; there is a lack of attention to responsible leadership on projects. Clarke et al. (2018) claim to be the first study to investigate how relationships among a project manager, team members, and stakeholders contribute to ethical decision-making and social responsibility. Once considered a conscience of an organization, HR may have increasingly become a support function that focuses on performance rather than responsibility (Gustafsson & Hailey, 2016).

Corporate social responsibility may now be becoming a performance issue. However, Coleman and MacNicol (2015) suggest that traditional project leadership development programs fail on even performance grounds due to a lack of consideration of context, required mindsets, connecting leader development with organizational intentions, and checking that development programs work. Responsible project leadership extends the breadth of expectations to embrace systems beyond the project and the organization.

There are ideas about developing responsible leaders in the pedagogical world of higher education (Lozano et al., 2017), but an assessment of outcomes is not positive (Lozano et al., 2019). Soft skills development is typically challenged by the need for meaningful contexts found in actual practice (Levasseur, 2013). Beyond higher education, coaching is a recognized management development tool for leadership skills (CIPD, 2021), providing ongoing support at work. In addition, managers are expected to learn coaching skills. Coaching aligns with andragogy, emphasizing self-determined, continual learning, making the individual more responsible for their development.

Rather than debate alternate philosophies of development, attention is drawn to consider how leadership is achieved in practice because it is in practice where responsible leadership happens.

There is a need to take responsibility to foster societal change. The experience of the United Nations Principles for Responsible Management Education (PRME) showed that curricula had to change in business schools and that, faculty members must also engage with the principles involved (Burchell et al., 2019; de Paula et al., 2020). The latter is challenging due to schools' intellectual underpinnings (Cornuel & Hommel, 2015). Embedding new principles and challenging the status quo will be relevant for responsible project managers. Doherty et al. (2014) suggest that some business schools' stakeholders justify systemic change and improve university performance. Project managers will likely need to engage with sponsors and other stakeholders in challenging conversations.

The scope of responsible leadership development extends beyond individual development and must support project managers to translate learning into responsible practice. Just as corporate social responsibility must be embedded in good governance across an organization (Amaladoss & Manohar, 2013), responsible project leadership development must result in responsible governance of projects. People make projects happen; collaboration happens through agreement and thus conversation. A pragmatic perspective recognizes that perceptions of the responsibility of project leadership can change before, at, and beyond project delivery. Nevertheless, project managers can only act in the present. The emphasis is on the intentions project managers hold in the moment, such as the desire and belief to discuss with stakeholders the shared perceptions of project responsibility now and in the future.

Four sections follow. Firstly, the increased need for shared intention is explored. Secondly, coaching philosophy and skills are shown to be one-way project managers can set the intention to discuss responsibility. Thirdly, the idea of responsible conversation is introduced, with coaching, mentoring, and empowering shown as examples of responsible conversation, where expectations and boundaries are established. The rationale is that responsible project managers must have similar conversations and discuss responsibilities and societal perspectives, with responsible project leadership the result. Finally, the leadership development section summarizes the educational topics and practices needed to provide practical learning about sharing societal responsibilities.

5.2 Leadership Development: From Individual to Shared Intention

Clarke et al. (2018) suggest that an intention for shared or collective leadership may be required for responsible project outcomes. Systems thinking with intentions for all affected by the project to act collaboratively is also encouraged (Dymitrow & Ingel-hag, 2020). Encouragingly collaborating with stakeholders has long been an essential focus for projects, with their engagement and participation expected (Eskerod et al., 2015). Whereas project management standards bodies have focused on the risk to projects from stakeholders (Eskerod & Huemann, 2013), societal responsibility suggests that stakeholder relationships provide the basis for shared value and ethical behavior (Freeman & Phillips, 2002; Uribe et al., 2018).

McCauley et al. (1998) reinforce the individual focus in traditional leadership development, yet recognize that although the developmental intentions are for the individual leader, other people participate in the subsequent use of behaviors. Indeed, they suggest that such people may assess leaders' learning, which means others can appreciate what is expected of leaders. Pichler and Beenen (2014) distill leadership skills into supporting others, motivating people, and resolving conflict, assuming that communication and relationship-building skills are present. All interpersonal skills are dependent on these, alongside personal skills and characteristics (Klein et al., 2006), so some self-development is expected. However, the relationship with followers and the skills and characteristics that followers are expected to have could focus more.

Leadership effectiveness is often focused on organizational performance, which implies the performance of everyone involved. The reliance on developing just leaders rather than including those who are not yet leaders may be questionable. This concern is potentially ignored because it is considered that behavior, decisions, and attitudes associated with those in leadership positions make leadership irresponsible, resulting in harm to others (Martins & Lazzarin, 2019). Traditional training may cover processes of supporting, motivating, and resolving conflict but lacks depth in practical scenarios and philosophy to understand relationships and other people in different contexts. It could also imply an assumption of influence and power in leaders over followers, which may not be desirable in shared leadership situations or discussion of responsible outcomes.

Leadership theories show a range of perspectives that relate to the individual leader, the follower, the relationships with followers, and the organization (Khan et al., 2016). Choosing one theory for a development program may be too limited a focus; for example, according to Pless and Maak (2011), servant leadership emphasizes the needs of followers rather than the need to "mobilise others to serve, engage in, and support objectives tied to a mutually desirable social purpose" (p. 7). Situational leadership (Blanchard et al., 1993) has a performance outcome and concern for understanding the development level of followers. Perhaps, a more helpful observation is that leadership types or styles affect the dynamic capabilities of organizations differently (Akkaya, 2020). Rather than analyzing potentially complicated and overlapping styles and proliferating research that can look at one outcome from one style at a time (Khajeh, 2018; Al-Malki & Juan, 2018), perhaps it would be better to focus on desired intentions. Deliberately airing such intentions potentially opens discussion and leadership-style choices, avoiding the one-sided consideration of only the leader. Negotiation on what is essential for the situation may allow shared intention to emerge and increase collaborative efforts.

While organizations have been increasingly adopting a project approach, the classical project mindset that emphasizes task and execution has given way to a more holistic conceptualization. The rethinking project management movement (Svejvig & Andersen, 2015) recognizes broader issues, including achieving projects through people. How things are done emerges: for example, communicating is vital, not just having a communication plan. This emphasizes an individual's relationships with others and the communication to get things done.

The discipline of project management embeds at least a partial assumption of shared intention since projects' aims, processes, and plans are meant to be communicated clearly for agreement. Project managers' skills of anticipatory thinking and risk management involve stakeholders in considering value from outcomes to be delivered and the risks associated with achieving those outcomes. The Agile movement focuses on people and their interactions, providing a manifesto of principles for everyone to work with (Agile, 2021). Similarly, RPM seeks to establish principles, including that many people can and should have the power to influence and contribute to how responsible value is best achieved. Spillane (2006) describes distributed leadership practice in education "as a product of the joint interactions of school leaders, followers, and aspects of their situation such as tools and routines" (p. 3). He relates the dominant heroic paradigm needing to give way to distributed leadership more than shared leadership due to the "collective interactions in many situations"; such interactions are prevalent in Agile and occur in most project management contexts. Therefore, responsible leadership development must be concerned with such interactions and how these lead to desired outcomes; intentions toward societal responsibility are relevant in interactions and project outcomes.

The PRME literature shows that business schools must broadly collaborate with stakeholders (Alcaraz et al., 2011; Abdelgaffar, 2021). This suggests that project managers' negotiations with project stakeholders must be similar. Millar and Koning (2018) give the example of inclusive development, which, though desirable, may be challenging to the current economic principles of business schools. Molthan-Hill et al. (2020) cite the issue of reducing carbon emissions to show that change is influenced at multiple levels, including individuals. Intentions are usually clear in projects regarding outcomes and how they can and will be achieved. Development must then support project managers to engage in broader conversations, consider their own views, and be prepared to discuss these wider concerns with potential conflicts. This may include how team members treat each other for well-being or how stakeholders can engage in respectful discussion of project requirements that meet societal expectations in their communities.

The implication is a policy of airing intention to find shared ground that can help establish a responsible culture that is important when various people may be deemed accountable for project governance after a disaster such as Grenfell Tower

(Khan & Haynes, 2021). Setting ongoing expectations, even for long-term intentions for the lifecycle of project outcomes, sets a thinking record that can be reviewed and renegotiated as circumstances allow and embed a learning cycle.

So far, the ideas for responsible leadership development are to support an individual's development as a leader, have effective relationships with all stakeholders, and recognize the value of shared intention in embracing a responsible project culture. Two points are additionally noted: firstly, some of these skills development could be useful to anyone in a project, not just the leaders, and secondly, managers can be encouraged to create a coaching culture among all employees (Garvey et al., 2014). Experience of responsible management education suggests that responsible cultures are created by managers (Laasch, 2018a), rather similarly to coaching culture. This section has emphasized intention beyond just a leader's perspective to the shared intentions of all project stakeholders.

5.3 Coaching: A Model for Shared Intention and Aired Responsibilities

Thompson (2018) explains qualitative research that intended to explore the value of practicing coaching philosophy and skills with a small number of project managers. Coaching was explained through one day's training and practice, and the participants coached another project manager whom they did not know for just six coaching sessions over 6 months. Interviews covered soft skills used in the coaching sessions and explored whether and how those were applied outside the practice. Despite the minimal coaching practice, there was evidence of behavior change at work. The results for these participants suggested that they adopted a coach-like philosophy that is now expecting more contribution and responsibility from their colleagues: to input ideas to planning, solve problems by themselves, and accept delegation. There was no organizational pressure to act differently; rather, the project managers felt value in their role to apply learned skills. From a personal perspective, the introduction to coaching philosophy and practice seemed to empower them as a leader.

Concerning intention, the project managers suggested that they now wanted to be supportive generally; they intended to listen more to others. Their attention became more focused, and they desired to hear more. They felt that if they appeared to listen well, the other person gave them more information. In some cases, there appeared to be an intention to collaborate more with others, with a willingness to air who was responsible for finding solutions to a team's problems; ideally, the team should work on this first and then the project manager could be called upon for support. There was an intention to delegate to specific individuals in one or two situations, and conversations about delegation were initiated. The soft skills associated with coaching were felt to be helpful. Only in the delegation situation it was felt that a coaching relationship could be initiated; this would be a partnership to develop the individual's capabilities for the delegated responsibilities – these three intentions of supporting, collaborating, and delegating implied different intended relationships with colleagues.

Research participants' soft skills and changed intentions led to a proposal for a soft skills framework shown in Figure 5.1, which aligned with the associated soft skills literature review. A simple way to explain the model is as follows. Imagine you are in a helicopter hovering over a person standing. The model's center represents the mind or head of the person, where they do all their thinking, sensing of feelings and emotion, and the resultant processing to decide behavior. The effective communication layer represents the person's body, which is typically wholly involved in the interpersonal skills of communication and relationship building. Project managers in the research found it impossible to separate self-management, communication, and relationship building, so this layer represents all three skill areas. The reason for choosing effective communication to name this layer is because the outer layer sets an intentional frame for communication; the outcome of the intention can measure effectiveness. The outer intention layer represents the energy field around the body. Even if we cannot explain this energy, we know something exists because we can tell in an instant of meeting someone whether we like them or not. Relationship, too, is an intangible concept, but humans feel connection and criteria such as whether they feel close or distant or how much trust exists. This field is named intention for relationship because the project managers seemed to set different intentions for colleagues, mostly supportive relationships but certain people pursued stronger relationships where others took more responsibility.

Although the model is useful in understanding soft skill lists, its emergent value is perhaps easier to appreciate when two models are placed side by side, as in Figure 5.2. The value is the reminder to recognize that all humans have intentions for their relationships with others. Any specific relationship is dependent on all those involved in it. We all know this and that relationships can change over time. Bratman (1999) suggests that intention is part of conscious thought but can be considered internal rather than a social commitment because we can just "change our mind"(p. 2). Intentions can thus be rather fluid. Little conscious thought may be given when considering the term intention for a relationship; we may subconsciously assume how relationships will work based on our role or societal position. Bratman (2009) talks about shared intention and the dependence of intention on beliefs.

We may be unused to thinking about relationship intentions consciously. However, a lack of consideration of qualities such as the current level of trust, honesty, or engagement could imply risk to any conversation regarding collaborative contribution. The research highlighted that project managers noticed the difference between coaching and their work environment. They then sought to be more supportive mainly through better listening for more engagement generally; this likely did not need much negotiation of the relationship. They did, though, need conversation to encourage

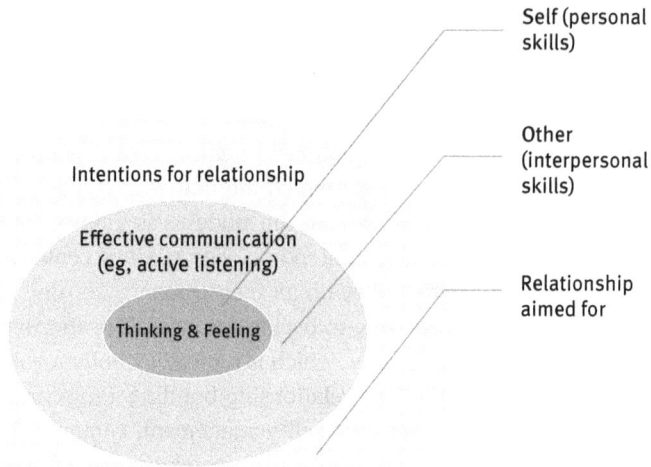

Figure 5.1: Three foci soft skills model from Thompson (2018).

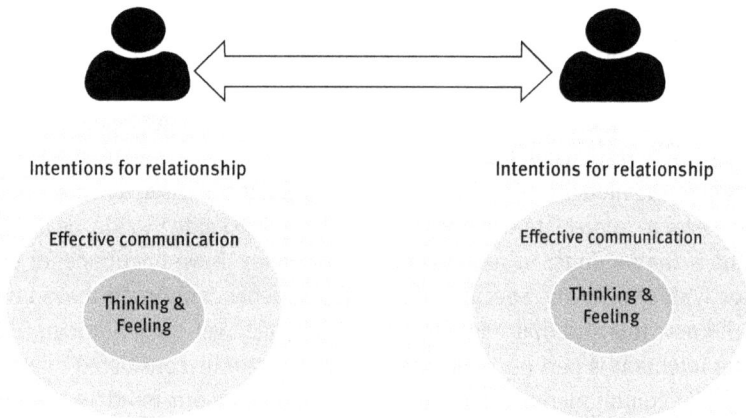

Figure 5.2: Shared intention for the agreed relationship.

others to seek their solutions to problems and in the case of delegation. These conversations may have started with one-sided intentions but needed an appropriate response to share intentions.

The finding that the coaching philosophy seemed to be adopted at work suggests value in experiential learning. Some ideas are not able to be grasped without practical experience. Blasco (2012) relates that students can learn more about PRME through real experience outside of courses. Laasch (2018b) suggests that a learning culture must also be established beyond courses by sharing information from managers' real practice. Mohammed et al. (2019) relate that business schools need to recognize the importance of partnership between students, faculties, and businesses, suggesting a "co-created and shared value framework" (p. 81). This links with giving voice to values (Tams & Gentile, 2020), but philosophy potentially goes beyond just values. Both explore how individuals think and hold subconscious principles. Talking about such topics seems a requirement for shared understanding in collaboration.'

Coaching philosophy is clear about the intended relationship for the coaching partnership. The coaching space is designed to be psychologically safe, exploring trust through discussion of expectations such as confidentiality, openness, honesty, and the opportunity for feedback and boundaries to coaching. This "contracting" support is questioning the ground rules from the start to the end of the relationship; established expectations provide a basis for feedback and re-contracting at any time. A checklist of the Thompson (2018) training can be found in Figure 5.3. This was suggested because such contracting tends to be unusual outside of formal relationships. Managers can use coaching-style conversations rather than formal coaching relationships (Grant, 2017). However, it is emphasized that the research participants felt empowered to have more conversations with colleagues about them trying to solve a problem together than asking for help, and in one-to-one situations about the opportunity for delegation. This sounded very much like the contracting conversation coaches use, even though the content of any checklist for it would be different. Such exploratory conversations are thus an opportunity to negotiate and establish shared intention. (The checklist in Appendix 1 is provided to plan for any conversation regarding responsibilities.)

This section has explored research that showed project managers became empowered to change the intention of relationship to discuss responsibility with colleagues and request more collaborative effort. Such empowerment may be useful to project managers in confidently embracing societal responsibilities in conversation with stakeholders. The experience of real coaching practice seemed influential. Coaching philosophy seems to contribute to changed intention for relationships with others. Supportive behavior and shared intention in conversation can empower others to follow. For responsible leadership development, the needs are to establish a philosophy for engagement, thus intention for relationships, and facilitate discussion of shared intention and responsibility. This assumes such soft skills as listening with focused attention, empathy, and effective questioning.

Coaching Agreement

Act ethically, follow ICF guidelines
Clarify not consulting, not therapy
Refer on to other professionals
Contract – times, fees, location
      – boundaries/others involved (sharing info, learning)
Paperwork – who keeps?
Opt out any time
No interruptions
Non-judgement, confidential
Respectful, honesty, no hidden agendas
Coachee owns the agenda, decisions, path forward
Overall goal – measured?

Figure 5.3: Coaching agreement checklist typed from flipchart example in Thompson (2018).

5.4 Responsible Conversation in Practice: Coaching, Mentoring, Empowering

RPM use this definition of responsible conversation "Partnering with stakeholders in a thought-provoking and creative process that inspires them to maximise their personal and professional responsibility." It deliberately models the ICF (2019) definition of coaching as "Partnering with clients in a thought-provoking and creative process that inspires them to maximise their personal and professional potential" in recognition of a partnering relationship with intentions for the process and participants. It is both the dialogue and the conversation to agree on the partnering dialogue at the outset that the term "responsible conversation" is intended to represent. It is interesting to note that Bachkirova and Borrington (2019) present coaching as an enquiry for learning using the philosophical framework of pragmatism. This highlights how coaching sessions are potentially common to all coaching situations. Coaching definition is elusive because purpose, process, context, and clientele vary across coaching examples.

Coaching philosophy adopts the idea that the coachee is an able, self-determining human responsible for their decision-making. The coachee sets the agenda for the content of a coaching conversation after the potential coaching relationship between coach and coachee has been explored and agreed upon. Thus, the partnership between coach and coachee supports the coachee's thinking to achieve their desired outcomes. A professional coach would normally expect some formality to the coaching relationship with expectations expressed verbally or in written terms and conditions at the outset, and there may be additional informal contracting as the relationship and coaching conversation progresses. This enables shared intention on the coaching process and the outcome of a coaching conversation.

Coach training typically encourages the introductory explanation of what a coaching relationship means and how the conversation is expected to work. This can be important, for example, to clarify expectations around advice that can be expected by the coachee and may not be expected by the coach. Airing expectations allows both parties to share views and establish responsibilities of each partner, presenting opportunities to build trust in the relationship and support feedback on the process. Thompson's (2018) research showed that project managers did recognize that shared intention is needed to collaborate and delegate and that both cases presented conversational opportunities to request more responsibility from some colleagues. The practice of asserting responsibility for personal thinking, goal setting, and decision-making during coaching prepared research participants for a conversation about responsibility. Just as coaching is an example of a responsible conversation, agreement to collaboration and delegation can be.

There are potentially many conversations that need to discuss the responsibilities of both parties; mentoring is another one for which there are many styles. Reverse or upward mentoring, which relates to situations where more senior employees are mentored by those more junior who have specific expertise, is one example that likely needs some clarity about the relationship. Levin (2014) promotes formal or informal mentoring by project managers where success depends on the underpinning relationship. Several PMI chapters offer mentoring programs to support project managers in their work roles. (See examples at pmi.org.uk/prof-development/mentoring, hmi-nl.nl/pmi-nl-mentorship-program, pmisydney.org/professional-development/ mentoring2020.) Gannon and Washington (2019) report on formal schemes generally in the UK after noting a shift from informal to formal. They relate that matching mentors and mentees is a provocative topic with human intervention by a mentoring coordinator considered ideal. Several schemes offer "no-fault divorce" clauses where the relationship does not work despite attempts to match requirements and interests. Thus, the importance of a working relationship is clear; the resultant quality depends on both parties' intentions to engage.

Thompson and Cox (2017) suggested project managers have a patchy understanding and experience of coaching and mentoring, with confusion existing about the meaning of both. One way of clarifying is to consider relationship phenomena such as the direction of knowledge transfer, expertise and power balance expected, the period of support is needed, and the boundaries of discussion. This could cover terms such as reverse mentoring while also allowing customization. Personal involvement in the PMI UK mentoring program that initially sought only to support project managers in their job roles has recognized that different situations demand different relationships. Generally, because the mentor and mentee can be in different organizations, it is recommended that the mentee sets their agenda and makes their own decisions, even though the mentor can share information and experience.

Airing intentions is done at the outset, too, including an exploratory session with potential mentor and mentee for introductions and testing of the relationship. Buddying has also been used for more short-term mutual support.

I initially became interested in coaching through sport and had a sense of personal growth through acting as a coach in an unfamiliar sport. A professional coaching course reinforced this unique opportunity for growth. I felt other project managers could benefit from supporting others in better thinking and acting for themselves. As indicated elsewhere in the book, project managers cannot have equivalent knowledge as all specialists in a project team. However, they need to ensure that risks emerge and are analyzed, which inevitably must involve stakeholder conversations. It has always been clear that project managers must hold the bigger picture yet ensure stakeholders air details about interdependencies. Their ability to hold the space for such dialogue empowers everyone to be responsible for the project. Through mentoring with PMI UK, I have seen how the scheme empowers mentors and mentees to take responsibility for their personal development.

My current research focuses on how coaching practice (being coached and coaching) can better empower people to empower themselves and colleagues outside of the practice. An early finding is that people can empower themselves in certain situations at work but need to be given power in other situations. Considering the simpler situation of students engaging "in-class" discussion, some may not feel empowered to supposedly ask "dumb" questions. This may be relevant to stakeholder relationships for exploratory discussion of social responsibility where an imbalance or lack of knowledge exists for RPM. There is a sense, too, that empowerment evolves. A facilitator may need to set expectations with student learning to encourage those who do not want to display a lack of knowledge to ask specific people questions or give helpful feedback to help engagement and learning. With societal responsibilities, either party may feel psychologically unsafe, so learning to create trust is a requirement so that uncertainties can be aired. This may require leaders to help create a culture for empowerment to speak the truth.

5.5 Responsible Project Manager Leadership Development

This chapter has presented some clear requirements for leadership development: to understand the aims of responsible (vs. irresponsible) leadership, thinking skills that include ethics and philosophy, and soft skills that include the idea of intention for relationship and effective communication. In terms of the development approach, it has been suggested that practice as a coach, possibly as a mentor, can help improve skills. Particularly, there is a need to practice responsible conversation that emphasizes adopting a philosophical stance for partnering in discussing responsibility. The overall aim is to empower project managers to become responsible leaders and empower others to engage with RPM.

RPM and ethics have been addressed elsewhere in this handbook. Traditional leadership development covers many personal and interpersonal skills. This leaves a focus on philosophy and soft skills for responsible leadership here to enable responsible conversation with stakeholders. Philosophy may be challenging but understanding how people hold different perspectives seems justifiable, initiating responsible conversation. Beddewela et al. (2017) suggest that PRME experience shows this because business schools reevaluate their ethos. Though postmodernist beliefs may be increasing, we can all think in traditional and modern ways on different topics. Evolution is continuous, and integral philosophy (Wilber, 2001) may be needed for a responsible world. When two people hold widely different perspectives, common ground between the positions can be necessary. The aim is to practice negotiating responsible conversation that includes psychological safety and trust to search for common ground thus support project managers in learning to achieve this. Coaching philosophy already encompasses responsibility for personal decisions, thus exploring one's intentions, beliefs, and values. Beliefs about reality and truth emerge from our life experiences, affecting what we do and thus our intentions (Dweck, 2017). Dennett (1989) presents a belief as a predictive strategy that adopts an intentional stance. RPM challenges our intentions for societal responsibilities. Supporting project managers to understand their own beliefs and values could help them clarify their intentions for discussions with stakeholders.

It is recommended that the philosophy surrounding empowerment and responsibility is specifically considered. Empowerment theory does exist, but the term "empowerment" can be used in different ways. Conger and Kanugo (1988) describe the use of relational and motivational constructs. The former is about relative power reflecting the net dependence of one actor on another. The latter relates to intrinsic belief or self-efficacy. For responsible conversation, both need to be explained since the aim is to equalize power in discussing societal responsibility to create an environment of possibility for project managers and stakeholders. Conger and Kanugo highlight that empowerment in such situations means enabling and recognizing where powerlessness may occur. Mandlik and Kadirov (2020) suggest that power must be conferred sometimes, and individuals in a group working together can empower each other. Avery (2018), when studying the empowerment of cancer survivors, suggests that despite the traditional view of the term relating to autonomy and control, it may also be a dynamic process between taking and relinquishing control; not all situations are controllable. Empowerment becomes more about "personal growth and a display of fortitude and strength."

Philosophy tends to be assumed in project management (Gauthier & Ika, 2012), and pragmatism may be a reasonable assumption for such a practical subject. However, understanding that philosophy is a search for wisdom in a sea of universal doubt may help people become conscious of their beliefs, and that other person can easily hold different views. Mindset has become a commonly used word for philosophical intention; this often selects the beliefs around one topic: growth (vs. fixed; Dweck, 2017) concerns belief about one's potential in life. Using one word for mindset seems deceptively simple, resulting in a common-sense assumption that adoption will result. Promoting a particular mindset may indeed aspire to impose rather than recognize that people can choose their own beliefs, whether consciously or unconsciously. Distinguishing such mindsets is problematic: for example, the Agile mindset is about adaptability to change, implying a growth mindset. The Agile manifesto aims for the breadth of influence throughout the group and team culture to empower autonomy. A philosophy for a role as a project manager would similarly cover a more comprehensive set of beliefs. Societal responsibility adds a further dimension people may yet be unclear about.

The Agile methodology already focuses on team members' interactions regarding soft skills, though the idea of intention for relationship and measuring effectiveness is not necessarily happening. Rather weight is given to role specification, including mentioning different relationship requirements such as facilitator, teacher, and negotiator. Roles can give an idea of the sorts of relationships that must be managed, but the focus is generally on the role holder and outcomes, not on the relationship, which could be made more explicit. Practice in building and negotiating relationships with stakeholders seems appropriate. Intentions may be hidden due to assumptions, emotional reasons, or political games, but exploring intentions for a relationship can help find common ground. Practice can build confidence to explore assumptions and respect others' positions through better understanding to allow essential collaboration.

Because coaching is a recognized tool in leadership development (CIPD, 2021) and is part of the Agile philosophy, it seems natural to recommend learning to act as a coach and receiving coaching can be helpful. The wide adoption of the discipline of project work (Lundin et al., 2015) suggests that leadership development in organizations may not distinguish between project managers and other personnel. However, it is unclear if project managers are included in such programs because they are confused between mentoring and coaching (Thompson & Cox, 2017). Different contexts help spread misunderstanding (Salter, 2014), so experiencing the philosophy and intentions for collaborative relationships through responsible conversation could provide a more precise focus.

There seems to be a fundamental need to explore and understand the conversation. According to Liddicoat (2021), "a conversation is a way people socialise and develop and sustain their relationships with each other" (p. 1). This author explains conversation analysis that recognizes that participants create order to conversation dynamically. Much more is going on than the linguistic communication that might appear in any transcript; nonverbal communication and context influence the exchanges in many complex ways. Brennan et al. (2010) relate the failure of several common dialogue models to model collaboration well. These authors highlight that nonverbal cues convey participants' intentions to each other, hypothesizing about what a partner will understand and looking for evidence of understanding in response. Kopp and Kramer (2021), in their work on human-agent communication, offer a co-construction communication model that recognizes the mental processing of all participants and aims to include both the "overt communicative interaction as well as the covert mutual understanding and deepening of common knowledge" (p. 5). There is an assumption that no conversation would happen if participants had no common ground. Thus, there must also be an assumption that there is no responsible conversation unless both parties are willing to co-construct a partnership to explore personal and professional responsibility.

Understanding how people develop may also be useful since leadership involves influencing others to change somehow. People may be at different development levels across multiple intelligences in any situation. Projects are often seen as the drivers of change, but humans need to be motivated to change in various ways. Understanding the power of intrinsic motivation rather than extrinsic may be helped by education on self-determination theory (Deci & Ryan, 2012) or similar. Watkins (2013) recommends thinking about performance beyond motivation to the coherence of mind and body; ideally, the body is in an anabolic state, which means a stable, healthy body and positive emotions for effective working or growth. This implies an understanding of mind–body phenomena to support the building of awareness. Appreciation of some of these matters could help motivate project managers to engage stakeholders with more curiosity and focused attention rather than holding assumptions.

These are additional requirements beyond traditional leadership development for project managers personally and their interactions with stakeholders. In extending the leadership development of project managers beyond immediate concerns of project delivery, we must broaden the leader's will to embrace issues connected with societal responsibility. The responsible conversation empowers project managers to have a peer-to-peer dialogue with stakeholders about potential risks for extended project lifecycle responsibilities. While leaders have always been expected to influence others, now project managers must model expectations of RPM and request collaboration from stakeholders. This requires an understanding of empowering others to act with societal wisdom. They will engage in collaborative partnerships like coaching, mentoring, or empowerment approaches to agree on responsibilities relevant to the collaboration. Fundamentally, RPM focuses on the practice of responsible conversation and thus responsible relationships with stakeholders where expectations are discussed.

Appendix 1: Considerations for Planning a Responsible Conversation

1. What is the relationship I would like with the other person for this conversation (e.g., equal partners in this conversation)?
2. What is the ideal relationship for this conversation?
3. What ideally is to change about our relationship, if anything?
4. Assuming the topic is of interest to the other person, what would make the other person want to agree to the relationship I desire for this topic?
5. What intentions do I anticipate the other person will have for our relationship?
6. What is the shared context for the conversation?
7. What shared intentions might we aspire to in this conversation?

What could ground rules for this conversation and relationship be useful to agree on? (For example, honesty, openness, feedback, timing, note-taking, interruptions, space for thinking, timeouts, social environment, technology, and who is responsible for what.)

References

Abdelgaffar, H. A. (2021). A critical investigation of PRME integration practices of the third cycle champion group. *The International Journal of Management Education*, *19*(1), 100457.

Adams, J. (2019). *Intentions matter*. Intentional Creations Cambridge, UK.

Agile. (2021). *Principles behind the Agile Manifesto*. [online] Downloaded 1 Oct 2021 from https://agilemanifesto.org/principles.html

Akkaya, B. (2020). Review of leadership styles in perspective of dynamic capabilities: An empirical research on managers in manufacturing firms. *Yönetim Bilimleri Dergisi*, *18*(36), 389–407.

Al Khajeh, E. H. (2018). Impact of leadership styles on organisational performance. *Journal of Human Resources Management Research*, *2018*, 1–10.

Alcaraz, J., Marcinkowska, M. W., & Thiruvattal, E. (2011). The UN principles for responsible management education: Sharing (and evaluating) information on progress. *Journal of Global Responsibility*, *2*(2), 151–169.

Amaladoss, M. X., & Manohar, H. L. (2013). Communicating corporate social responsibility–A case of CSR communication in emerging economies. *Corporate Social Responsibility and Environmental Management*, *20*(2), 65–80.

Al-Malki, M., & Juan, W. (2018). Leadership styles and job performance: A literature review. *Journal of International Business Research and Marketing*, *3*(3), 40–49.

APM. (2016). *APM competency framework*. [Online] Downloaded 1 Oct 2021 from https://www.apm.org.uk/media/2274/apm-competence-framework.pdf

Avery, J. (2018). A Grounded Theory of Empowerment in Cancer Survivorship and Rehabilitation (Doctoral dissertation, Université d'Ottawa/University of Ottawa).

Bachkirova, T., & Borrington, S. (2019). Old wine in new bottles: Exploring pragmatism as a philosophical framework for the discipline of coaching. *Academy of Management Learning & Education*, *18*(3), 337–360.

Beddewela, E., Warin, C., Hesselden, F., & Coslet, A. (2017). Embedding responsible management education – Staff, student and institutional perspectives. *The International Journal of Management Education*, *15*(2), 263–279.

Blanchard, K. H., Zigarmi, D., & Nelson, R. B. (1993). Situational Leadership® after 25 years: A retrospective. *Journal of Leadership & Organizational Studies*, *1*(1), 21–36.

Bratman, M. E. (1999). *Faces of intention: Selected essays on intention and agency*. Cambridge University Press, Cambridge, UK.

Blasco, M. (2012). Aligning the hidden curriculum of management education with PRME: An inquiry-based framework. Journal of Management Education, 36(3), 364–388.

Bratman, M. E. (2009). Modest sociality and the distinctiveness of intention. *Philosophical Studies*, *144*(1), 149–165.

Brennan, S. E., Galati, A., & Kuhlen, A. K. (2010). Two minds, one dialogue: Coordinating speaking and understanding. In *Psychology of learning and motivation* (Vol. 53, pp. 301–344). Academic Press, Cambridge, USA.

Burchell, J., Murray, A., & Kennedy, S. (2014). Responsible management education in UK business schools: Critically examining the role of the United Nations principles for responsible management education as a driver for change. *Management Learning*, *46*(4), 479–497.

Conger, J. A., & Kanungo, R. N. (1988). The empowerment process: Integrating theory and practice. *Academy of Management Review*, *13*(3), 471–482.

CIPD. (2021) *Management development factsheet*. [Online.] Downloaded from https://www.cipd.co. uk/knowledge/strategy/development/management-factsheet

Clarke, N., D'amato, A., Higgs, M., & Vahidi, R. (2018). *Responsible leadership in projects: Insights into ethical decision making* (Kindle ed.). Project Management Institute, Pennsylvania, USA.

Coleman, S., & MacNicol, D. (2016). *Project leadership*. Routledge, Farnham, UK.

Cornuel, E., & Hommel, U. (2015). Moving beyond the rhetoric of responsible management education. *Journal of Management Development*, *34*(1), 2–15.

Deci, E. L., & Ryan, R. M. (2012). Self-determination theory. In Van Lange, P. A. M., Kruglanski, A. W., & Higgins, E. T. (Eds.), *Handbook of theories of social psychology* (pp. 416–436). Sage Publications Ltd, London UK.

Dennett, D. C. (1989). *The intentional stance*. MIT Press, Cambridge, USA.

de Paula Arruda Filho, N., & Beuter, B. S. P. (2020). Faculty sensitisation and development to enhance responsible management education. *The International Journal of Management Education*, *18*(1), 100359.

De Pree, M. (1989). *Leadership is an art*. New York: Doubleday (Random House Inc), New York.

Doherty, B., Meehan, J., & Richards, A. (2015). The business case and barriers for responsible management education in business schools. *Journal of Management Development*, *34*(1), 34–60.

Drath, W. H. (1998). Approaching the future of leadership development. In McCauley, C. D., Moxley, R. S., & Van Velsor, E. (Eds.), *The center for creative leadership handbook of leadership development* (Vol. 29, pp. 403–432). Jossey-Bass Publishers, San Francisco, USA.

Dweck, C. (2017). *Mindset: Changing the way you think to fulfil your potential*. Robinson, London, UK.

Dymitrow, M., & Ingelhag, K. (2020). *Anatomy of a 21st-century sustainability project: The untold stories*. Gothenburg: Mistra Urban Futures/Chalmers University of Technology.

Eskerod, P., & Huemann, M. (2013). Sustainable development and project stakeholder management: What standards say. *International Journal of Managing Projects in Business* 6(1), 36–50.

Eskerod, P., Huemann, M., & Savage, G. (2015). Project stakeholder management – Past and present. *Project Management Journal, 46*(6), 6–14.

Freeman, R. E., & Phillips, R. A. (2002). Stakeholder theory: A libertarian defense. *Business Ethics Quarterly, 12*(3), 331–349.

Gannon, J. M., & Washington, R. (2019). *Many things to many people: Formal mentoring schemes and their management: A report.* Oxford Brookes University Oxford, UK.

Garvey, B., Stokes, P., & Megginson, D. (2014). *Coaching and mentoring: Theory and practice* (2nd ed.). Sage, London, UK.

Gauthier, J. B., & Ika, L. A. (2012). 'Foundations of project management research: an explicit and six-facet ontological framework', *Project Management Journal, 43*(5), 5–23.

Grant, A. M. (2017). The third 'generation' of workplace coaching: Creating a culture of quality conversations. *Coaching: An International Journal of Theory, Research and Practice, 10*(1), 37–53.

Gustafsson, S., & Hailey, V. H. (2016). Responsible leadership, trust, and the role of human resource management. In Kempster, S., & Carroll, B. (Eds.). (2016). Responsible leadership: Realism and romanticism. (pp. 151–166). Routledge, Abingdon, UK.

ICF. (2019). *Definition of coaching.* [Online] Downloaded in 2019 from https://coachingfederation.org/about.

Kempster, S., & Carroll, B. (Eds.). (2016). *Responsible leadership: Realism and romanticism.* Routledge Abingdon, UK.

Khan, N. U. M., & Haynes, P. (2021). *The role of corporate governance failure in the Grenfell Tower fire.* [online] Downloaded 1Oct2021 from https://www.researchgate.net/profile/Paul-Haynes-2/publication/349467897_The_role_of_corporate_governance_failure_in_the_Grenfell_Tower_fire/links/60fac3561e95fe241a81ad5d/The-role-of-corporate-governance-failure-in-the-Grenfell-Tower-fire.pdf

Khan, Z. A., Nawaz, A., & Khan, I. U. (2016). Leadership theories and styles: A literature review. *Leadership, 16*(1), 1–7.

Klein, C., DeRouin, R. R., & Salas, E. (2006). Uncovering workplace interpersonal skills: A review, framework and research agenda. *International Review of Industrial and Organisational Psychology, 21*, 79–126.

Kopp, S., & Krämer, N. (2021). Revisiting human-agent communication: The importance of joint co-construction and understanding mental states. *Frontiers in Psychology, 12*, 597.

Laasch, O. (2018a). Just old wine in new bottles? Conceptual shifts in the emerging field of responsible management. *Centre for Responsible Management Education Working Papers, 4*(1), 1–13.

Laasch, O. (2018b). Delineating and reconnecting responsible management, learning, and education (RMLE): Towards a social practices perspective on the field. *CRME Working Papers, 4*(5), 1–28.

Levasseur, R. E. (2013). People skills: Developing soft skills – A change management perspective. *Interfaces, 43*(6), 566–571.

Levin, G. (2014). *Key competencies for success in navigating complexity.* Project Management Institute Pennsylvania, USA.

Liddicoat, A. J. (2021). *An introduction to conversation analysis* (3rd (Kindle) ed.). Bloomsbury Academic, London-New York-Oxford-New Delhi-Sydney.

Lozano, R., Barreiro-Gen, M., Lozano, F. J., & Sammalisto, K. (2019). Teaching sustainability in European higher education institutions: Assessing the connections between competences and pedagogical approaches'. *Sustainability, 11*(6), 1602.

Lozano, R., Merrill, M. Y., Sammalisto, K., Ceulemans, K., & Lozano, F. J. (2017). Connecting competences and pedagogical approaches for sustainable development in higher education: A literature review and framework proposal. *Sustainability*, *9*(10), 1889–1903.

Lundin, R. A., Arvidsson, N., Brady, T., Ekstedt, E., Midler, C., & Sydow, J. (2015). *Managing and working in project society*. Cambridge University Press, Cambridge, UK.

Maak, T., & Pless, N. M. (2006). Responsible leadership in a stakeholder society – A relational perspective. *Journal of Business Ethics*, *66*(1), 99–115.

Mandlik, M. A., & Kadirov, D. (2020). Towards a theory of integrated empowerment: A service ecosystems agenda for future. *International Journal of Qualitative Research in Services*, *4*(1), 56–76.

Martins, L. P., & Lazzarin, M. D. L. (2019). *Unmasking irresponsible leadership: Curriculum development in 21st-century management education*. Routledge, Abingdon, UK.

McCauley, C. D., Moxley, R. S., & Van Velsor, E. (Eds.). (1998). *The center for creative leadership handbook of leadership development*. Jossey-Bass Publishers, San Francisco, USA.

Mohamed, A. K., Khadir, S. B., El Jelly, A., & Mansour, I. (2019). StakeholdersPerception and Attitude Based Framework for Developing Responsible Management Education (RME) Program. In Proceedings of International Conference on Social and Education Sciences (pp69–83). ISTES Organization, Monument, USA.

Millar, J., & Koning, J. (2018). From capacity to capability? Rethinking the PRME agenda for inclusive development in management education. *African Journal of Business Ethics*, *12*(1), 22–37.

Molthan-Hill, P., Robinson, Z. P., Hope, A., Dharmasasmita, A., & McManus, E. (2020). Reducing carbon emissions in business through responsible management education: Influence at the micro-, meso-and macro-levels. *The International Journal of Management Education*, *18*(1), 100328.

Pichler, S., & Beenen, G. (2014). Toward the development of a model and a measure of managerial interpersonal skills. In: Riggio, R.E & Tan, S. (Eds.), *Leader interpersonal and influence skills: The soft skills of leadership (11–30)*. Routledge, Hove, UK.

Pless, N. M., & Maak, T. (2011). Responsible leadership: Pathways to the future. In In: Pless, N.M., Maak, T. (eds) *Responsible leadership* (pp. 3–13). Springer, Dordrecht.

PMI. (2017). *Project management job growth and talent gap 2017–2027*. [Online.] Downloaded 1Oct21 from https://www.pmi.org/learning/careers/job-growth

Salter, T. (2014). *Mentor and coach: Disciplinary, interdisciplinary and multidisciplinary approaches*. International Journal of Evidence-Based Coaching & Mentoring, (S8), 1–8.

Scouller, J. (2014). *The three levels of leadership: How to develop your leadership presence, knowhow and skill* (Kindle ed.). Cirencester: Management Books, 2000.

Spillane, J. P. (2006). *Distributed leadership* (Kindle ed.). Jossey-Bass, San Francisco, USA.

Svejvig, P., & Andersen, P. (2015). Rethinking project management: A structured literature review with a critical look at the brave new world. *International Journal of Project Management*, *33*(2), 278–290.

Tams, C., & Gentile, M. C. (2020). Giving voice to values: Responsible management as facilitation of ethical voice. In Laasch, O., Suddaby, R., Freeman, R. E., & Jamali, D. (Eds.). *Research handbook of responsible management* (pp 532–548). Edward Elgar Publishing, Cheltenham, UK.

Thompson, S. (2018). *Coaching for soft-skill development: An action research study with project managers*. [Doctoral dissertation, Oxford Brookes University].

Thompson, S., & Cox, E. (2017). How coaching is used and understood by project managers in organisations. *Project Management Journal*, *48*(5), 64–77.

Uribe, D. F., Ortiz-Marcos, I., & Uruburu, Á. (2018). What is going on with stakeholder theory in project management literature? A symbiotic relationship for sustainability. *Sustainability*, *10*(4), 1300.

Watkins, A. (2013). *Coherence: The secret science of brilliant leadership*. Kogan Page Publishers, London, UK.

Wilber, K. (2001). *A theory of everything: An integral vision for business, politics, science and spirituality*. Shambhala Publications, Boston, USA.

Reinhard Wagner

6 The Ambivalent Role of Professional Bodies for RPM

Context: This chapter is about the role that professional bodies take to advance project management in general, and responsible project management (RPM) in particular, within their respective contexts. It is critical to examine the role that project management associations have played in advancing the profession in general and specifically in RPM.

Characters/entities: Over the past decades, project management associations have contributed to developing project management processes, methods, and tools nationally and internationally through standards and disseminating these standards in the form of qualification and certification programs.

Locations: Examples are drawn from the experience of the German Project Management association.

Research gaps: The focus has been primarily on corporate enterprises, whereas societal issues have been somewhat limited. Due to their interconnectedness with professionals from different fields in society, professional bodies are an ideal breeding ground for RPM. In the chapter, examples are presented on how this development is currently being supported.

Challenges/conflict tensions: Developing pathways for how established professional bodies can support society and orient toward the common good.

Keywords: professional associations, IPMA, PMI

6.1 Introduction

Since the 1960s, project management associations have taken on an increasingly important role in advancing the knowledge necessary for managing projects (Morris, 2013), in spreading the idea that professional management enables projects to be implemented more efficiently, and in qualifying and certifying project personnel under accredited systems (Hodgson & Muzio, 2012). Nowadays, project management associations can be found regionally (e.g., Hong Kong Institute of Project Management), nationally (e.g. German Project Management (GPM) association), as well as internationally (e.g., International Project Management Association (IPMA)), in specific industries (e.g., International Construction Project Management Association) or subject areas (e.g., International Institute of Legal Project

https://doi.org/10.1515/9783110724783-009

Management), whereby the degree of maturity of the professional association varies greatly. For example, the Association for Project Management (APM) has achieved massive recognition by obtaining a Royal Charter (Hodgson et al., 2015). In contrast, project managers and the national association in Germany have not yet received government recognition for what they do in project management (Nicklich et al., 2020).

In the context of responsible project management (RPM), this raises the question of the extent to which project management associations are already contributing to people, society, and nature. In the literature (Muzio et al., 2011) and recent surveys (Wagner et al., 2021), however, criticism is voiced that professional bodies and their work are too much focused on the interests of the economy, partly because there is money to be earned that is so important for them to perform their activities. Moreover, the bodies are rarely interlinked with the relevant societal groups. Therefore, the following section takes a critical view of the professional bodies in the project management domain and their activities. This is followed by an elucidation of what they should do for RPM. Finally, this is exemplified by a wealth of examples. In this context, the bodies have an essential mediating role in making a significant contribution to RPM.

6.2 A Critical View of Professional Bodies

The development of the project management discipline is closely linked to the engineering projects of the defense or aerospace industry following the end of World War II, which involved solving complex problems using models of mathematical computation based on operations research (Morris, 2013). Projects and project management are accepted in many areas of the economy and increasingly in society and are now part of everyday life (Hodgson & Cicmil, 2006).

Professional bodies have supported the dissemination of projects with the development of a body of knowledge (BoK), which describes essential steps of project management from the initiation of a project to its completion from a procedural or a methodological perspective. This can be seen as an attempt by bodies such as the US-based Project Management Institute (PMI) to establish an entry barrier or training prerequisite on the way to professionalizing their field of practice with a description of what is required and to draw the boundaries between members of the project management profession and other professions (Morris et al., 2006).

Project managers offer a service in their organizations and often have to justify what enables them to bring projects successfully to the finish line. Belonging to a professional body and having acquired the knowledge outlined in a specific BoK, and possibly even proving that they have the appropriate certification, gives them a legitimacy that helps their work to be better recognized. However, the orientation of

BoKs is also viewed critically, in particular, that they are summarized in concise books and prepared in a very undifferentiated manner. Above all, it is commented that these books are hardly based on research results that would lend legitimacy (Shepherd & Atkinson, 2011).

Even if other professional bodies have taken different paths in the development of process models, the basic ideas for the management of projects are still represented today in literature, national and international norms and industry-specific standards in such a way or similar to a BoK. In terms of content, today's BoKs are criticized for focusing too much on the execution of projects and addressing far too little attention to their framework conditions, the process of initializing and clarifying objectives, or achieving social integration. This plays an essential role in RPM in particular. With the development of the ISO 21500 series of norms, aspects of sustainability for the management and governance of projects, programs, and portfolios were incorporated. The IPMA member associations decided on a different path in the 1990s (Pannenbäcker, 2001). They opted for a competency-based standard that today, with the IPMA Individual Competence Baseline (IPMA ICB) in its fourth version, defines the competencies for managing projects. This baseline covers three areas of competence: practice competencies, people competencies, and perspective competencies. Aspects of sustainability have also been considered (Silvius, 2017), although the criticism of Shepherd and Atkinson (2011) concerning the lack of scientific foundation also applies to the ICB.

Together with the development of the norms and standards for project management, the professional bodies successfully established and marketed offers for the qualification and certification of project personnel. Together with developing the norms and standards for project management, the professional bodies successfully established and commercialized offerings for qualification and certification. Although the basis for such offerings is a different BoK or competence baseline in each case, it helps the professional bodies to generate revenue to finance other voluntary activities. At the same time, qualification and certification also bring new members so that the associations today reach out to several million project managers globally. Scholarly research on the value of certification for project managers finds a more indirect relationship between certification and performance in projects (Blomquist et al., 2018). However, project managers and their employers benefit from increased self-confidence and professionalism in projects (Farashah et al., 2019). Research also shows that when there is tension over the sustainability of projects, project managers tend to "greenwash" and prefer to stick to the familiar patterns acquired in their qualification or certification (Sabini & Alderman, 2021). Finally, only specialized providers, such as the US-based Green Project Management (GreenPM®), offer training and certification with a clear focus on sustainability.

Another point of criticism regarding project management bodies is their one-sided focus on the world of business. Unlike traditional professions such as doctors or judges, the bodies specializing in project management are not out for closure through credentials. As an emerging profession, they are concerned with marketing their services and thus benefit businesses (Muzio et al., 2011). This may include the promise of greater efficiency through the application of project management, greater effectiveness of project managers through credentials, or generally a more professional appearance of the company through membership in a professional body. The main criticism here is that the professional bodies in project management "would only preach to those already converted" and would completely disregard innovative or even societal fields of application (Wagner et al., 2021). This is reflected in their membership, primarily aimed at individual project managers and corporate members and their linkages across societal groups. As a result, only in a few exceptional cases do the project management bodies support civic or grassroots environmental groups, development aid initiatives, or community projects. For example, the GPM association was actively involved in integrating Syrian refugees from 2015 to 2017 in Germany (Wagner, 2018).

Within the framework of a scientific study using the example of GPM in Germany, it was analyzed how project management associations influence society's projectification (Wagner, 2021). In this context, projectification refers to an increasing prevalence of projects in all areas of society and the changes that accompany this. It became clear that GPM, with its activities, has no significant direct influence on the projectification of society but indirectly via cultural-cognitive and regulative institutions. This is particularly surprising given that both the literature and GPM's strategy have primarily emphasized the importance of normative activities. Thus, GPM has sought to develop norms and standards as a basis for the qualification and certification of project managers and, at the same time, to claim them as the "state of the art" when it comes to project execution. However, this "push" strategy of GPM turns out to be less valuable according to the study, and a "pull" strategy is found to be more advisable. The aim here is to present the image of projects and project management positively in public relations work, highlight exemplary organizations and entrepreneurs, and tell the narrative of successful projects (e.g., in the Project Excellence Awards). The more projects are successfully portrayed as an effective mechanism for overcoming societal challenges, the more they will be accepted and embraced. In the study, the respondents also clearly expressed that GPM as a professional body should do much more for society and help address societal challenges, such as the COVID-19 pandemic and the climate crisis, and be more involved in social initiatives or organizations such as the Red Cross or the United Nations with their 17 Sustainable Development Goals (SDGs).

6.3 Professional Bodies as Advocates for RPM?

RPM requires the support of all those involved in project management and who can influence the mindset and behavior of the stakeholders involved: project managers, specialized trainers, consultants and coaches, exemplary organizations, entrepreneurs, and professional bodies. "In very general terms, this is true of all those who, playing an active role in the expansion and *animation* of networks, act as *mediators* . . . They possess the art of reconciling opposites, and know-how to bring very different people together, and put them in contact" (Boltanski & Chiapello, 2018, p. 115).

Professional bodies attract professionals who want to exchange ideas and experiences and develop themselves. Moderating this exchange and directing the professional exchange toward topical issues is one of the critical tasks of professional bodies. However, practitioners join professional bodies to learn new things, exchange with colleagues and gain recognition in their field of practice through their membership (Hodgson et al., 2015). In their field of responsibility, professionals then take the expertise provided by professional bodies and apply it to their projects. In this way, they become a kind of "lord of the dance" (Scott, 2008) and, in many cases, change the way projects are implemented in a particular setting (Suddaby & Viale, 2011).

Since members of professional bodies do, of course, also bring new requirements from their field of activity into the discussion, professional bodies are "not only key mechanisms for, but also primary targets of institutional change. They act and are acted upon by a myriad of social, economic, technological, political, and legal forces" (Muzio et al., 2013, p. 700). This can be in the setting of new ventures (Auschra et al., 2019), in the establishment of new technologies in a market (Bohn & Braun, 2021), in the context of social enterprises (Bogacz-Wojtanowska & Jalocha, 2016), in the realization of projects in developing countries (Narayanan & Huemann, 2021), or for global institution-building (Manning & von Hagen, 2010). However, this requires professional bodies to address societal issues and groups important to the community, be open to new developments, and continuously evolve. The criticism of the professional bodies expressed in the previous section on the one hand and "shared interpretations and routinized behaviour on the other, are certainly not made for supporting organizational change but for protecting third parties' interest, and, at best, to support the present functioning forms of organizing. They tend to preserve existing forms rather than accommodate for expected or realized change" (Lundin et al., 2015, p. 171). In this context, the question arises whether professional bodies are still attractive and accepted if they do not adapt to the challenges of our time. For example, Generation Z (i.e., those born after 1995) chooses its field of activity based on whether or not that field values societal concerns, sustainability, and responsibility-conscious action.

In general, crowdsourcing, government funding, and project financing increasingly consider sustainability aspects a disadvantage for traditionally oriented bodies. Resistance to projects that violate sustainable solutions triggers opposition from social groups, thus forcing projects to halt or delay and making them more expensive in the long term (McAdam, 2011). These examples indicate that professional bodies are increasingly under pressure to realign themselves, and there are even calls for a "New Project Management" movement that focuses on sustainability and impact while learning from experiences of social projects (Picciotto, 2020). However, this requires a strategic re-focusing of the project management associations and a realignment of their entire portfolio of activities. Therefore, the following aims to present examples of existing practices worldwide or inspire new activities.

6.4 Professional Bodies' Practices in Support of RPM

It is still largely unclear what RPM even means, how it can be realized, and what potential can be realized; as a result, there is still much research to be done. Research is an original task for universities and institutions specialized in it. However, professional bodies can undertake studies and applied research in their field, fund research at universities, or support it through case studies. The PMI, for example, sponsored an extensive research program on the relationship between project management and sustainable development principles (Gareis et al., 2013). Furthermore, the Danish Project Management Association and member of IPMA supports the research initiative "Half Double," a project management methodology that can deliver "Projects in half the time with double the impact" and focus on sustainable development (Rode & Svejvig, 2021). Several national and international professional bodies recognize excellent research work in project management through awards and increasingly consider contributions to sustainability.

We have already referred above to the work of professional bodies concerning the development of norms and standards. The bodies typically define terminology, approaches, processes, methods, and tools appropriate to their context and publish them for application in projects, training and education, and certification. To date, however, there are only a few standards and norms that would directly feed into RPM. Only the US-based not-for-profit organization Green Project Management has released a set of standards for sustainability in project management, such as "The GPM P5 Standard for Sustainability in Project Management v2.0" (GPM, 2019). Although the internationally active project management associations have been involved in the intensive work of the International Organization for Standardization (ISO) for several years, principles or approaches to sustainability have so far only found their way into the standards in a few cases, for example, in ISO 21505 for the governance of projects, programs, and portfolios, where a short section deals with "sustainability and ethics" (ISO, 2017).

Another example of sustainability regarding project personnel competencies can be found in the IPMA ICB 4.0 (IPMA, 2015a). Ethical behavior is critical to professional bodies nowadays, and most of them have published a Code of Conduct that is obligatory for members and serves as a kind of blueprint for the realization of projects in practice, among others, the IPMA Code of Ethics and Professional Conduct (IPMA, 2015b).

The topics may be addressed as essential aspects in the training of the professional bodies, but apart from Green Project Management, which specializes in sustainability, only a few other providers offer specific training and certificates on the market. These include training providers such as the Foundation for European Sustainable Tourism (FEST), which offers a course for Project Management for Sustainable Development (PM4SD), or PM4NGOs, offering a Qualification and Certification aiming at Project Management for Development Professionals (PMD Pro). There are educational offers from some professional bodies that target children, adolescents, secondary school students, and vocational trainees and aim to impart the skills to solve complex tasks through project-based learning. IPMA Poland, for example, works with the youth and provides these future project professionals with a better understanding of what can be achieved through projects and appropriate management. The main aim is to shape a positive attitude and create awareness. With the help of initial pilot applications, it has been possible to spread the initiative among future young project managers, who have also been awarded a Junior Project Manager certificate, and encourage trainers working in the IPMA context to join the project and spread it further. More extensive offerings for students in secondary levels 1 and 2 in Germany and Switzerland are provided by the professional bodies in these countries (Gessler & Uhlig-Schoenian, 2008; Scheuring & Erne, 2013) and include instructional materials for teachers and descriptive guides for students (also in the form of cartoons) that help them to organize projects in day-to-day school life easily and thus prepare for the life in the professional world. In addition, the project management association in Austria (PMA) offers a junior award every year for school or student project teams that have achieved outstanding performance in projects.

Promising is also the Young Crew, established mainly in the context of the IPMA, which has introduced in almost all member states a group of young professionals up to the age of 35 who experience and exchange ideas on projects either from their university or from the first role in their professional life. In an international competition called "PM Championship," the young professionals learn how projects are responsibly brought to the finish line. They celebrate annually the "Global PM Days" and "Global Young Crew Workshop." The IPMA Young crew firmly believes that professionalism is developed by improving competence, responsibility, and accountability.

Many professional bodies have an awards program to recognize excellence in project management. For example, PMI has awards for individuals such as the "Fellow Award" or the "Young Professional Award," projects and Project Management Offices, and academics and researchers. Likewise, IPMA has an award program that offers awards for individuals and projects on an international level based on the IPMA Project Excellence Baseline (PEB), which is also replicated in many of the member associations (see Figure 6.1).

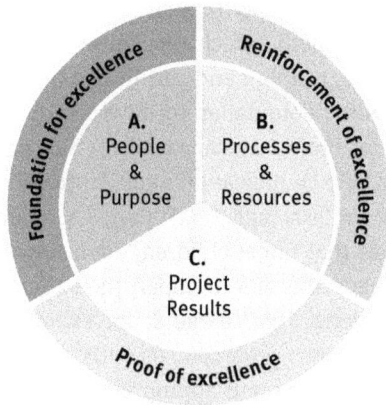

Figure 6.1: Project excellence model (IPMA, 2016).

Excellent projects must demonstrate excellent performance in all project management aspects, including the management of people, purpose, processes, resources and results. Results are only credited as they result from leadership and management processes. Excellent projects apply the approaches and methods of project management in professional and innovative ways, reflecting on their approach, methodologies, and results to learn from them and take actions for improvement when necessary. (IPMA, 2016, p. 44)

Strong emphasis is placed on the sustainability of project execution and outcomes, looking not only for tangible deliverables but also for customer, employee, and other stakeholder satisfaction.

In addition to the Global Project Excellence Awards for projects in various categories, the Achievement Awards of IPMA recognize a Young Project Manager, Project Manager, and Agile Leader of the Year annually. Furthermore, IPMA also honors cultural, volunteer, or not-for-profit delivered projects and projects to achieve SDGs and social benefits for a community, a city, or a region. Awards are used to draw attention to successful projects and those involved in them, encouraging others to follow suit and helping to improve project management in a wide range of areas. Charitable organizations such as Water Air and Food Awards (WAFA) also help shine a light on projects in developing countries where "silent heroes" are implementing successful concepts and practical solutions, attracting imitators only through the spotlight of the award.

Professional bodies mean the exchange of like-minded people who meet regionally or in special interest groups and exchange information on their challenges, experiences, and mutually beneficial development opportunities. For example, the APM in England has more than 13 branches and 14 professional groups publishing papers and reporting on their activities via social media. GPM also has several regional and special interest groups, including one that deals with sustainability in project management. The specialist group aims to establish a competent, well-networked group that bundles and further develops know-how on sustainability in project management. This knowledge will then be available to all interested parties within GPM and beyond for practical implementation.

Professional bodies are relatively underdeveloped when it comes to social or community activities. One positive example is IPMA's "Coaching for Development" initiative. It aspires to help non-profit organizations (NPOs) worldwide in their social development and humanitarian aid projects by providing project management knowledge and experience in coaching (see Figure 6.2). Focus are projects that support one of the United Nations SDGs. The coaches support the beneficiary's project by enabling the project manager. This will have sustainable benefits not only for the project in scope yet also for all future projects of that organization. It is of utmost importance that the coaching approach allows the coached project leaders to find the most fitting solutions for their own culture and context. PMI also offers support for the Social Good, with experienced project managers voluntarily sharing their experience through "PM Philanthropy" to help those in need in society, including but not limited to developing countries.

Figure 6.2: Coaching for development in Nepal.

An inspiring example of responsible action by professional bodies in RPM is the support that GPM volunteers provided in the refugee crisis between 2015 and 2017

(Wagner, 2018, p. 71). More than 1 million refugees from the war zone in Syria reached Germany (Khedjari et al., 2017). Society was quickly at its limit, and the public administration could hardly cope with the situation. As a result, GPM organized language classes for the refugees, assisted them in dealing with the authorities, and drafted a master plan for cities and municipalities that outlined project-based activities for integrating many refugees. This master plan was adopted by the Berlin Senate, among others, and implemented jointly. Finally, GPM also offered project management training with a certificate for refugees to be integrated more quickly into the professional world.

Professional bodies also advocate for RPM by raising awareness through publications, social media, and events. This can be done by disseminating reference books, such as Silvius et al. (2012), periodicals, newsletters, or blog posts. At events at the local, regional, national, or even international level, the topic of RPM is reflected in the form of lectures, workshops, or even seminars. For example, the 31st IPMA World Congress in 2019 in Merida (Mexico) was dedicated to the theme "Integration Sustainability into Project Management" (see Cuevas et al., 2021).

6.5 Conclusion and Outlook

The above highlights both the light and shadow of the work that professional bodies do toward the cause of RPM. On the one hand, they are the natural platform for exchanging ideas and experiences of professionals from different fields of application in project management. On the other hand, the professional bodies concerned with project management are one-sidedly focused on the economy and still do not pay enough attention to society and the concerns of both people and nature. However, the examples listed show that there are many promising initiatives and that already, today, some professional bodies are facing up to their responsibility for the common good. If this were to become more widespread, it would create a dynamic that only benefits RPM. Generation Z also brings new momentum to the cause because, as the grassroots movement of Fridays-for-Future and others prove, adolescents or young adults can mobilize many people within a short period and push politicians to act.

Professional bodies should reconsider their role in society and position themselves strategically for the common good. This will only be successful if they network with all societal groups and inspire them to become members. Otherwise, there is a risk that professional bodies will become irrelevant and no longer be attractive. This works less through a "push" using legal regulations, norms, or standards than through the persuasive power of successful projects, project managers, or activists, whose narrative inspires people to follow suit. All too often, projects also have a negative image due to many negative stories in the media. Here, professional associations can lead by example with their public relations work, awards programs, or commitment. It ultimately takes action or changes programs to move from ambition to fruition.

Professional bodies should also feel called upon to cooperate more, draw from the experiences, and adapt to their settings. Cross-fertilization can occur across national boundaries, between disciplines and professions pursuing RPM. Professional bodies could also jointly engage in initiatives such as "Race to Resilience and Race to Zero" or the "Business Declares" initiative, which aims at raising awareness across business sectors of the need to accelerate action in the context of climate change, biodiversity loss, and social injustices. Anyhow, it is time to take action now, in the sense of a transformation for the benefit of society and nature.

6.6 Reflections

In this chapter, we reflected on the role of professional bodies concerning RPM.
1. Professional bodies play an essential role in RPM; however, they do not actively embrace this role and focus more on activities related to economic interest and less related to the common good.
2. Thanks to a wide range of activities performed by professional bodies, RPM can be framed, advanced, and applied, as evidenced by many real-world examples.
3. Professional bodies should reflect on their significant role for people, society, and nature, closely connect with all critical social groups, and draw from their midst to remain relevant and attractive in the future.

The following questions may help the readers to promote RPM in the context of professional bodies actively:
1. What can I do to help professional bodies better understand and embrace their RPM role?
2. Which practical experiences concerning RPM can I bring to the professional body and thus inspire others to follow suit?
3. How can I pass on what I have learned and experienced during my career in project management to others who have not had the chance for professional training themselves?

References

Auschra, C., Braun, T., Schmidt, T., & Sydow, J. (2019). Patterns of project-based organizing in new venture creation. Projectification of an entrepreneurial ecosystem. *International Journal of Managing Projects in Business*, *12*(1), 48–70.

Blomquist, T., Farashah, A. D., & Thomas, J. (2018). Feeling good, being good and looking good: Motivations for, and benefits from, project management certification. *International Journal of Project Management*, *36*, 498–511.

Bogacz-Wojtanowska, E. & Jalocha, B. (2016). The bright side of the social economy sector's projectification: A study of successful social enterprises. *Project Management Research and Practice*, *3*, 1–20.

Bohn, S. & Braun, T. (2021). Field-configuring projects: How projects shape the public reflection of electric mobility in Germany. *International Journal of Project Management*.

Boltanski, L. & Chiapello, E. (2018). *The new spirit of capitalism*. London: Verso.

Cuevas, R., Bodea, C. N., & Torres-Lima, P. (Eds.). (2021). Research on project, programme and portfolio management. In *Integrating sustainability into project management*. Cham: Springer.

Farashah, A. D., Thomas, J., & Blomquist, T. (2019). Exploring the value of project management certification in selection and recruiting. *International Journal of Project Management*, *37*, 14–26.

Gessler, M. & Uhlig-Schoenian, J. (2008). *Projektmanagement macht schule*. Nürnberg: GPM.

Hodgson, D. & Cicmil, S. (Eds.). (2006). *Making projects critical*. Basingstoke: Palgrave Macmillan.

Hodgson, D. & Muzio, D. (2012). Prospects for professionalism in project management. In Morris, P. W. G., Pinto, J. K., and Söderlund, J. (Eds.), *The oxford handbook of project management* (pp. 107–130). Oxford.

Hodgson, D., Paton, S., & Muzio, D. (2015). Something old, something new?: Competing logics and the hybrid nature of new corporate professions. *British Journal of Management*, *26*, 745–759.

IPMA. (2015a). *IPMA individual competence baseline version 4.0*. Amsterdam: Author.

IPMA. (2015b). *IPMA code of ethics and professional conduct*. Amsterdam: Author.

IPMA. (2016). *IPMA project excellence baseline*. Amsterdam: Author.

ISO. (2017). *ISO 21505 Project, programme and portfolio management – guidance on governance*. Geneva: Author.

Gareis, R., Huemann, M., & Martinuzzi, A. (2013). *Project management & sustainable development principles*. Newtown Square: Project Management Institute.

GPM. (2019). *The GPM P5™ standard for sustainability in project management. Version 2.0*. Novi: Author.

Khedjari, R. H., Xie, L., & Sundareswaran, K. (2017). *Refugees in the large metropolis: Sharing welcome and innovations*. Berlin: EKBNO.

Lundin, R. A., Arvidsson, N., Brady, T., Ekstedt, E., Midler, C., & Sydow, J. (2015). Managing and working in project society. In *Institutional challenges of temporary organizations*. Cambridge: Cambridge University Press.

Manning, S. & von Hagen, O. (2010). Linking local experiments to global standards: How project networks promote global institution-building. *Scandinavian Journal of Management*, *26*, 398–416.

McAdam, D. (2011). Social movements and the growth in opposition to global projects. In Scott, R. W., Levitt, R. E., and Orr, R. J. (Eds.), *Global projects: Institutional and political challenges* (pp. 86–110).

Morris, P. G. W. (2013). *Reconstructing project management*. Chichester: John Wiley & Sons.

Morris, P. G. W., Crawford, L., Hodgson, D., Shepherd, M., & Thomas, J. (2006). Exploring the role of formal bodies of knowledge in defining a profession – The case of project management. *International Journal of Project Management, 24*, 710–721.

Muzio, D., Brock, D. M., & Suddaby, R. (2013). Professions and institutional change: Towards an institutionalist sociology of the professions. *Journal of Management Studies, 50*(5), 699–721.

Muzio, D., Hodgson, D., Faulconbridge, J., Beaverstock, J., & Hall, S. (2011). *Current Sociology, 59* (4), 443–464.

Narayanan, V. K. & Huemann, M. (2021). Engaging the organizational field: The case of project practices in a construction firm to contribute to an emerging economy. *International Journal of Project Management*.

Nicklich, M., Braun, T., & Fortwengel, J. (2020). Forever a profession in the making? The intermediate status of project managers in Germany. *Journal of Professions and Organization, 7*(3), 374–394.

Pannenbäcker, O. (2001). *Kanonisierung, qualifizierung und zertifizierung im projektmanagement.* Frankfurt am Main: Peter Lang Europäischer Verlag der Wissenschaften.

Picciotto, R. (2020). Towards a 'New project management' movement? An international development perspective. *International Journal of Project Management, 38*, 474–485.

Rode, A. L. G. & Svejvig, P. (2021). *Project half double: Mid-term evaluation of phase 3 and consolidation of phase 1, 2 and 3.* Aarhus: Aarhus University.

Sabini, L. & Alderman, N. (2021). The paradoxical profession: Project management and the contradictory nature of sustainable project objectives. *Project Management Journal, 00*(0), 1–15.

Scheuring, H. & Erne, T. (2013). *Projektmanagement macht schule.* Luzern: ZIPP Zentrum Impulse für Projektunterricht und Projektmanagement.

Scott, R. W. (2008). Lords of the dance: Professionals as institutional agents. *Organization Studies, 29*(2), 219–238.

Shepherd, M. & Atkinson, R. (2011). Project management bodies of knowledge; conjectures and refutations. *The Electronic Journal of Business Research Methods, 9*(2), 152–158.

Silvius, G., Schipper, R., Planko, J., van den Bring, J., & Köhler, A. (2012). *Sustainability in project management.* Farnham: Gower.

Silvius, G. (2017). Sustainability as a new school of thought in project management. *Journal of Cleaner Production, 166*, 1479–1493.

Suddaby, R. & Viale, T. (2011). Professionals and field-level change: Institutional work and the professional project. *Current Sociology, 59*(4), 423–442.

Wagner, R. (Ed.). (2018). *IPMA insight No. 1: Realizing smart cities through professional project, programme and portfolio management.* Amsterdam: IPMA.

Wagner, R. (2021). The impact of institutions on the projectification of society. Doctoral dissertation. Maribor: Alma Mater Europaea ECM.

Wagner, R., Huemann, M., & Radujkovic, M. (2021). The influence of project management associations on projectification of society – An institutional perspective. *Project Leadership and Society, 2*, 1–13.

Alexia Nalewaik

7 Responsible Reporting in Project Management

Context: This chapter offers guidance regarding data sources for reports, report audiences, and common challenges in reporting. Key concepts include two-way communication and information-sharing, increasing transparency, fostering openness, and focusing on ethical obligations to stakeholders and stewardship.

Characters/entities: The chapter considers project reporting from the perspective of the responsible project manager to reduce information asymmetry and provide assurance.

Locations: The chapter does not consider a specific geographical location; however, reporting is a required activity on all projects.

Research gaps: There is a need to investigate the underpinnings of responsible reporting, which can be achieved through critical questioning, understanding stakeholders, good governance, and behaving ethically and with professionalism.

Challenges/tensions: This chapter identifies the challenges of a carefully considered approach to crafting project reports to increase the likelihood of identifying and acting on project issues and risks, thus improving project performance.

Keywords: transparency, information asymmetry, responsible reporting, assurance

7.1 Introduction

Reports are a primary mechanism for transmitting information to an intended audience across many situations and disciplines. Reporting occurs everywhere: at various levels within companies, at regular intervals on projects, after a consulting engagement or study, for a particular purpose, and to stakeholders both internal and external. Examples can be found in abundance, from end-of-semester grades to monthly project reports, to annual shareholder accounts of financial status and activity.

Regular reporting is expected on projects; it is an essential and often contractually required communication element across many stakeholders. It is also crucial for governance, legal documentation, and responsible project management.

https://doi.org/10.1515/9783110724783-010

7.2 What Is Reporting?

According to the *Oxford English Dictionary*,[1] "to report (verb)" means to "give a spoken or written account of something that one has observed, heard, done, or investigated." Similarly, a "report (noun)" is "an account given of a particular matter, especially in the form of an official document, after thorough investigation or consideration by an appointed person or body"; also "a spoken or written description of an event or situation, especially one intended for publication or broadcast in the media." The utilization of the word can be traced to the mid-nineteenth century.

Reviewing these definitions yields some insight into the concept:

i. A report is a method of documenting a situation, occurrence, or activity.
ii. The authorship of a document is a matter of significance or appointment.
iii. Written reports tend to be more formal or official than verbal reports.
iv. Reporting is a crucial mechanism of both communication and governance.

What does a report look like? Because reports, as a concept, serve an incredibly variety of purposes, there is no universal standard. However, organizations often develop standardized formats according to purpose. Ultimately, the intended usage of the report and the information contained within determine its content and form. Reports may be qualitative or quantitative, or (most likely) a combination of both, and may supplement the written word with images (graphics and/or photos). They may communicate progress, disseminate information, provide data for decision-making, and/or document and elevate the visibility of problems, risks, and opportunities. The type and quantity of available information will change during the project lifecycle, uncovering new opportunities and risks, and possibly necessitating a revision of the report format. Reports are a required element of accountability and assurance on projects, which become a permanent part of the record, vital in incidence changes and claims.

Responsible project management embraces the notion of communication as critical to perceived project success. This means ensuring constant, appropriate communication with stakeholders to raise awareness of the project and project status and diligent reporting to engage stakeholders, gain support, and reduce power distance.

7.2.1 Stakeholders

The universe of stakeholders on any project includes both internal and external stakeholders, and the list of those stakeholders can be quite extensive if the population is considered beyond just those who are proximate to and active with the project,

---

1 *Oxford English Dictionary* online, https://en.oxforddictionaries.com/definition/assurance. Retrieved 6 December 2018.

have influence, and may affect the project outcome. Every person, entity, or organization with whom the project interacts is a stakeholder, and there will even be additional stakeholders with whom no direct contact is made, extending as far as society-at-large. The term "entity" is used loosely here in that it may also refer to environmental concepts such as land, air, and water. In the digital real-time inter-connected world we live in, projects are constantly under scrutiny from every direction, 24/7/365.

In the context of responsible project management, stakeholders represent the many facets of sustainability (economic, environmental, and social, extending to and through the 17 sustainable development goals of the United Nations[2]). There are layers of stakeholders, like an onion, which is one step further removed from the project. Responsible project management considers projects from societal and sustainability perspectives, which means the list of stakeholders is expanded to include the natural environment and society's future (subsequent generations). The stakeholder population range is intentionally broad in this context.

There is no one-size-fits-all style of the report because there is no one-size-fits-all stakeholder. Stakeholders' own life experiences and perspectives contribute to developing their principles. Their role and relationship to the project, along with their ideas (ideologies, aesthetic preferences, biases, and intentions),[3] define their perspective, expectations, and obligations in the project. Even within the same category of stakeholders, each stakeholder has different motivations, responsibilities, risk tolerance, and definitions of success that define their information requirements. Further embedded within each stakeholder's definition of success is their expectation of value creation. Notions of value will differ between stakeholders, often leading to scenarios where (from the stakeholder's point of view) a project is simultaneously a success and a failure.

The report authors must identify interested stakeholders to whom reports are due, purposely involving a wide range of stakeholders, then ranking them according to the level of influence and interest. Next, the project team needs to create a list of reports and their timing, work with stakeholders to define what success means, and agree on a threshold of information importance and granularity. Understanding and empowering stakeholders are vital to crafting a project report that is meaningful, relevant, timely, comprehensible, and actionable. In turn, well-designed reports encourage information sharing, facilitate collaboration and stakeholder engagement, and promote informed decision-making.

Not all project reports are designed for action by stakeholders; some are purely informational communication of status to interested parties. In such instances, the

2 The 17 Goals. Sustainable Development, Department of Economic and Social Affairs, United Nations. Retrieved 13 February 2022 from https://sdgs.un.org/goals
3 Solomon, Miriam (2012). Socially Responsible Science and the Unity of Values. *Perspectives on Science*, Volume 20, Number 3, Fall 2012, pp. 331–338. Cambridge: MIT Press.

project team should ensure the information contained within is appropriate for the audience, represents the voices, and addresses the concerns of the diverse group of constituents, not just significant stakeholders.

7.3 Reporting and Responsible Project Management

At a minimum, report recipients expect to have confidence that the information in the report is accurate and complete. Report recipients will use information in the report in many ways, not least in informed decision-making and reporting to their constituents.

Responsible project management goes a step further in its reports expectations, embracing management concepts that aim to reduce information asymmetry and provide assurance by collaborating and engaging with stakeholders. For the project team, this means encouraging frequent information-sharing, increasing transparency, fostering openness, and focusing on ethical obligations to stakeholders and stewardship. From a reporting perspective, this means engaging in critical questioning, reducing knowledge gaps, ensuring traceability of report content and reproducible conclusions, conveying information honestly and with impartiality, and reflecting on the potential impacts and consequences of what is reported. It also means confirming appropriate content and ensuring responsiveness to stakeholder concerns about stewardship of all resources, including finance, the environment, and social impacts. All this, considered together, is not a small task.

In project reporting, responsible project management leans toward concepts of responsibility and responsiveness to stakeholders, including ethics and professionalism. This means appropriately designing and managing organizational functions and processes, with (in this context) an end goal of producing useful reports. Poor reporting and good reporting alike have impacts and consequences and responsible project reporting aims not to harm.

The above paragraphs contain various terminology related to stakeholder expectations in reporting, which warrant some further definitions and explanations:
- Meaningful – Useful to the stakeholder for their specific intent and purposes. It does not contain extraneous or unimportant information and does not intentionally or unintentionally obfuscate by burying important information in volumes of less relevant information.
- Relevant – Having practical value appropriate to the report's circumstances, timing, intent, and usage.
- Timely – Received within an appropriate period, such that stakeholder decisions and actions are not hindered. They are related to the prompt collection and undelayed availability of information compiled within the report, meeting stakeholders' deadlines for receipt, assimilation, and distribution.

–   Comprehensible – Written clearly and using language and graphics that are readily understood by the stakeholder, in a format that is easy for them to digest and disseminate. Do not intentionally or unintentionally obfuscate through the use of language.
–   Actionable – Contains sufficient required information, empowering the stakeholder to perform their duties and make decisions to their best abilities.
–   Accurate – Correct in all details to the best of the knowledge and ability of the project team, with project data verified against the data source or multiple sources. Data and conclusions are reliable, traceable, documented, and reproducible.
–   Complete – Comprehensive in that no necessary information is knowingly omitted, and no required data is intentionally or unintentionally delayed.
–   Transparent – Does not conceal information, risks, and opportunities. Documents discuss the mechanisms, data sources, and assumptions used to prepare the report.
–   Honest – Truthful and free of deceit; closely related to accuracy, impartiality, transparency, and completeness.
–   Impartial – Presents information in an unbiased, fair, and just fashion, free from internal or external influence. Do not "choose sides" when discussing issues instead of acknowledging multiple stakeholder perspectives.
–   Critically questioned – Data and conclusions are validated and subjected to appropriate secondary analysis and evaluation. Basic assumptions and evidence are interrogated and reviewed from multiple perspectives, ensuring accurate and reproducible interpretation.

Most of these terms are referred to and elaborated upon in the following section.

7.4 Challenges

There are several obstacles to overcome when trying to satisfy reporting expectations in responsible project management. Some of the challenges are due to the systems used to collect data, and some are due to process, but many are due to human nature.

7.4.1 Data Sources

On a typical project, qualitative and quantitative data are generated from multiple sources, which must be extracted and analyzed and then selected for reporting. Some of these data sources may be more reliable, especially where data handling is necessary to affect appropriate content and format.

Project data is often rife with unintentional errors; data exported from one system and then imported into another may contain mapping errors, and the ubiquitous use of spreadsheets means a high likelihood of incorrect formulas, missing links to other files, hidden columns and rows, and typographical errors made during data entry. Even external data sources require a certain amount of trust, as data received from external sources may be difficult to validate for accuracy.

The ultimate goal is to ensure all data sources contribute to report accuracy, consistency, and comparability, with a source-to-report data path that is as clean and simple as possible, free from human intervention and error. This can be achieved through validation, which checks the completeness of the data and traces it to its source, often requiring the reconciliation of information between multiple systems. Traceability of data to its origin, with assumptions and calculations documented, is an element of transparency.

7.4.2 Timing

Reports take time to prepare, and the availability of (human and system) resources required to produce reports will impact the organization's ability to create timely reports that contain real-time (current) information. Deadlines for specific reports will be tied to the project schedule, driven by milestones, contractual requirements, and meetings. Punctuality in reporting is of utmost importance – information received late means decisions cannot be made or may be made based on incorrect assumptions and unavailable data.

Delays (and, thus, errors) may stem from the time required for manual data entry and report assembly/formatting, lag times for change order and contract approvals, and cutoff dates for reports received from external sources. Some data may become available only after a particular meeting occurs, impacting the timing of all subsequent meetings and reports. When generating reports, the project team may feel constant pressure to keep up while dealing with data that is difficult to extract. One solution to such delays is diagramming and reviewing project processes, literal scheduling of the data-receipt timeline, and a keen eye on data sources (inputs) and anticipated needs for data utilization (outputs), identifying potential obstacles to streamlining the data path. Timely reporting is an element of transparency.

A persistent challenge in the timing of project reports is the problem of always looking backward and reporting what has happened. Responsible project management embraces the anticipation of future scenarios, which means trending and forecasting are essential elements of responsible project reporting. This requires consistency in the content and format of periodic data to ensure apples-to-apples mapping and comparisons.

7.4.3 Language

Every stakeholder's unique combination of education, experience, and environment contributes to the language(s) they use and comprehend. The population of project stakeholders can be very diverse, with stakeholders coming from many different places and organizations. Thus, one step in writing reports requires understanding various stakeholders' grasp of project language and terminology and their preferred language (technical, nontechnical) for communication. It is not uncommon for stakeholders to lack the very words to describe what they need, even though the information exists due to a terminology gap between the stakeholder and the project team. Still, other stakeholders may be unable to visualize a physical project using two-dimensional drawings, which means the project team will need to invest in three-dimensional models to ensure comprehension.

Even once language and terminology have been agreed upon, the potential for miscommunication remains because stakeholder populations are not static during the project's timeframe. People come and go and are then replaced by new people. This means it is not uncommon for stakeholder groups to require retraining in the language used for project reports and may require frequent reintroduction of project concepts, processes, and history. This cycle of stakeholder education can also be seen as an opportunity for developing awareness of risks, opportunities, and long- and short-term project impacts, facilitating learning and sharing between a diverse group of stakeholders.

Stakeholders' failure to grasp project terminology may unintentionally negatively impact the project, leading to misunderstandings that can cause ineffective project design, the potential misuse of data, and the inability to make decisions. For these reasons, reporting and project meetings need to be specifically tailored to their audience with great care. Clear, unobfuscated communication is an element of transparency.

7.4.4 Level of Detail

A common tactic in litigation and audit is to drown the opposition in information and paperwork, wagering that the sheer volume of data cannot be read and absorbed within the available time. It is very effective and, on the receiving end, very frustrating to experience. The same thing occurs inadvertently on projects when well-meaning project team members provide stakeholders and project executives with large amounts of information which is irrelevant to the end user's needs and possibly even contradictory. In such situations, reporting is data-rich but intelligence-poor. When available information becomes burdensome, stakeholders have many potential consequences: confusion, a feeling of being overwhelmed, key facts lost in the details, buried risk, and valuable time lost to sifting and sorting data.

Where a detailed explanation is needed, an executive summary may be used to provide a high-level view of the situation, attached to a more in-depth report.

Similarly, insufficient information also hides risk and may require guesses or assumptions on the part of the stakeholder when making decisions. Effective reporting requires a delicate balance of information, with just enough provided to communicate project status and issues and more available supporting documentation upon request.

7.5 Use of Metrics

A frequently used tool in reporting is the metric, an element (often an input or output) of the project or a quantifiable process, which is then measured, reported periodically, and used as a proxy for progress against a target. Unfortunately, metrics can inspire bad behavior even as they are intended to guide good behavior.

A human reaction to metrics, especially where success is incentivized, is for project team members to focus on achieving their metric goals, even at the expense of other aspects of the project. Metrics can unintentionally create an environment rife with strategic deception instead of functioning as a tool to drive positive outcomes. If the team is scoring well against metrics, but the project is struggling, it is time to reconsider the tools used for project measurement and reporting.

While metrics are a convenient way to communicate the status of a project at-a-glance, they can easily be misunderstood, misused, and misquoted. Metrics alone are not enough; their intent and constitution need to be understood. This means stakeholders need to understand what the metrics are intended to represent, what information (and sources) contribute to their development, and why they are relevant to the project as measures of success. They also need to understand that metrics do not necessarily tell the whole story of the project. Metrics are merely a proxy and a snapshot of project status at a specific time.

7.6 Oh, the Humanity

Project reporting requires confidence in project data, yet it is a hallmark of the human condition that data can be influenced by bias and intentionally or unintentionally misrepresented. Decisions made are not always rational – indeed, they may be predictably irrational. Part of this is simply human error or mistakes made due to missing, incomplete, out of date, or incorrect. The rest finds its roots in psychology and social behavior.

Optimism bias, where reports skew toward the favorable, is particularly prominent in project management – it reflects understatement of risk and a reluctance to admit falling short of expectations. It also reflects wishful (and even irrational) thinking that the situation might be remedied before the next report is due, although a more likely outcome is that small negative changes are temporarily masked, which then must be reported as a bigger (and, to the stakeholder, unexpected) failure. Other types of bias also appear in reporting. Pessimism bias may be used to acquire additional resources (funding and staffing), anchoring bias resists acknowledgment of change, and confirmation bias ignores evidence.

When information is difficult to obtain, or the flow of information seems to slow to a trickle, the project may be experiencing problems. Selective reporting can conceal change and minimize risk, camouflaging warning signs. The information withheld may tell a different story about the project than the skillfully manipulated reports, especially conflict and resistance within the project team. Lack of transparency is ultimately detrimental to project success, preventing early action and mitigation of issues, thus further damaging the project. Key project team members often know the risk of project failure long before it is reported and acted upon.

If selective reporting and/or optimism bias occur frequently enough to impact the project critically, the behavior becomes an ethical problem for the organization. It may be due to individual or group behavior ingrained in the project culture. The issue of ethics in reporting has many facets, among them were concepts of justice, fairness, obligation, and moral hazard.

References

A Manifesto for Responsible Project Management, v2.0. Retrieved December, 2020, https://responsiblepm.com/the-manifesto

Greenwood, M. (2007). Stakeholder engagement: Beyond the myth of corporate responsibility. *Journal of Business Ethics, 74*(4), 315–217.

Oxford English Dictionary online. Retrieved 6 December, 2018, https://en.oxforddictionaries.com/definition/assurance

Smith, J. J., Keil, M., & Depledge, G. (2001). Keeping mum as the project goes under: Toward an explanatory model. *Journal of Management Information Systems, 18*(2), 189–227.

Solomon, M. (2012, Fall). Socially responsible science and the unity of values. *Perspectives on Science, 20*(3), 331–338.

United Nations. *The 17 Goals.* Sustainable Development, Department of Economic and Social Affairs, United Nations. Retrieved 13 February, 2022, from https://sdgs.un.org/goals

Nigel Williams
8 Responsible Project Organizing

Context: Projects located in the UK and an organization that serves the global south. Insights apply to information systems/blockchain projects.

Characters/entities: The chapter discusses NGOs seeking to provide societal value and communities that are impacted by their actions.

Locations: The chapter discusses projects that deliver activities in the UK, Hati, and Peru.

Research gaps: The chapter examines the multiple types of value the project provides and discusses characteristics that distinguish projects from other types of organizing.

Challenges/conflict/tensions: Challenge of reconciling multiple perspectives of organizing and value.

Keywords: blockchain, responsible organizing, temporary organizing, societal value

8.1 Introduction

Extant research in project managers (PM) adopts a temporary organizing perspective or activities defined by specific objectives, and a predetermined endpoint (Lundin & Söderholm, 1995) has also been applied in other disciplines (Sydow & Braun, 2018). In addition to infrastructure and information systems' project perspectives, temporary organizing has been used to examine dynamic phenomena such as inter-organizational supply networks. Temporary organizing also presents organizational learning challenges as actors and processes are not intended to have an ongoing engagement beyond the life of the activity. These domains enable organizational experimentation and deliver innovations (e.g., product development). However, temporary organizing initiatives configured for knowledge creation within contractual and temporal bounds do not quickly transfer tacit learning to other projects or permanent organizations. Researchers have examined the inherent tensions between temporary and permanent organizing that can occur within or across organizations (Lundin et al., 2015). This work has also examined boundary conditions that facilitate temporary and permanent organizing interaction.

Sustainable development seeks to deliver long-term environmental and social value in an equitable manner (Bansal & DesJardine, 2014). This idea is explicitly multidimensional, multitemporal, and dynamic as changes in one domain or at one

https://doi.org/10.1515/9783110724783-011

temporal point will influence others. Post crisis, PMs may be under increasing pressure to deliver societal value (economic and social) benefits as described in the Sustainable Development Goals (SDGs) (Nilsson et al., 2016). SDGs have been integrated into six global transformations (Sachs et al., 2019) aligned with the emerging social value paradigm, which seeks to deliver contextually relevant social benefits by projects (Cicmil & O'Laocha, 2016) in addition to specified outputs (Raiden et al., 2019).

8.2 Past Research

Recent work has identified the impact of project sustainability actions on communities and societies and projects' role in creating and destroying societal value. Country norms can influence societal values. Sponsors and PMs can influence the deployment of societal value activities based on PMs' knowledge, beliefs, and values.

Communities may adopt traditional models such as Ubudehe in Africa (Niringiye & Ayebale, 2012) or directly petition for projects to deliver environmental (climate adaptation or mitigation) or development benefits for targeted stakeholders.

Societal value expectations pose a dilemma for PMs as they go beyond Figure 8.2 to require integration of ethics (doing right behaviors), social (managing enterprises' responsibilities to society), and environmental (managing impact on natural environment) sustainability (Roberts et al., 2020). Country-specific issues such as inequality, identity, and gender norms (Kahneman et al., 1999) also influence the conceptualization, resourcing, and delivery of societal value outcomes, areas that receive little attention in extant PM research. Stakeholders pressure from initiatives such as responsible investing (Shevchenko et al., 2016). While other professions have evaluated their societal value activities and the contribution of educational practices (www.rethinkingeconomics.com), project management has not yet done so.

Therefore, responsible organizing can be defined as how actors organize transformative action toward sustainable outcomes (Langmead & King, 2020). In projects, this will include the coordination of enterprises (public, private, and NGO), project supply chains, networks, programs, and portfolios to provide beneficial outcomes beyond financial value during and after delivery.

Responsible project organizing recognizes that sustainability and social value are not characteristic of a single entity involved in a project but are an emergent property of the exchanges among all entities involved and the environment. This builds on work in responsible management, where responsibility has corporate, individual, and relational dimensions. A distinction can be made between imputability (being responsible for an item or entity) and accountability (based on contract relationships), which implies responsibility and legal obligation (Robinson, 2009).

A PM is responsible, that is, imputable, accountable, and liable for decisions when acting on behalf of stakeholders and shareholders.

Existing definitions for project management focus on the latter two dimensions. This approach minimizes responsibility's moral aspects, which are not necessarily based on defined alternatives but on developing a path through uncertain, ambiguous contexts. Engaging with imputability internalizes the position of indirect stakeholder, recasting responsibility from a contractual obligation to receptive attention to others. This extends responsibility to include responsive and shared meaning and value orientation. Therefore, stakeholders must establish routines of collective actions and emotional ties in empathy, trust, solidarity, and fairness (Rasche et al., 2013). An RO approach also implicitly seeks to address irresponsible social power relations within organizations. This is even more challenging as projects are temporary, and there are multiple perspectives on project organizing: activity, temporal, and relational.

8.3 Activity Perspective

Projects have been viewed as a problem-solving mechanism for organizations and institutions (Grabher, 2002). In this perspective, projects are viewed as conducting a unique task or creating a specific solution for the sponsor. This perspective is not interested in the micro-activities of project actors or the temporal processes of organizing; the people and the relationships between and among them are not critical (Lampel & Meyer, 2008). Projects, programs, and portfolios can range from internal initiatives supported by assigned staff as part of their roles to hybrid ventures that depend on temporary resources such as contract staff and suppliers (Bakker, 2010). The latter can include project networks that can accommodate the delivery of multiple initiatives simultaneously and transfer learning among current and subsequent projects. Each successive category (projects, programs, portfolio, and project network) implies an increased level of complexity, an increasing ambiguity of goals and boundaries. The more recent adoption of projects' environmental and social performance goals has exacerbated this issue as stakeholders will need to agree on which entities (individuals, organizations, and communities) can be considered legitimate actors who can participate in the goal definition process. They then need to jointly agree on measures and acceptable performance thresholds for evaluation. A related view examines how these temporary collections of tasks are embedded within permanent systems, a single organization, or organizational networks (Grabher, 2004).

8.4 Temporal Perspective

Project organizing has also taken a temporal focus that explicitly addresses structural issues such as temporary tasks or temporary allocation of resources. This perspective assumes that individuals and organizational structures or temporary institutions must monitor the input processes, micro-organizing activities, and larger scale emergent outcomes that can be intentional and unintentional (Söderlund, 2011). The organization's activities and individual managers' activities have an explicit time orientation that may align with the project's needs but maybe misaligned with other stakeholders such as the permanent organization (Stjerne et al., 2019). A related issue is that multiple temporalities can exist within a given project setting as there may be times that are relevant to internal actors, and there may be times associated with the meanings assigned to it by other actors (Brookes et al., 2017).

Project deadlines are major transition points that shape both time perception and resource allocation in projects across all entities; they may be seen as external pressure that encourages all participants to defeat a common enemy. As a result, timing norms need to be established in projects, which is a distinct feature of organizing that does not exist in other activities (Sydow & Windeler, 2020). Temporality in projects has also been conceptualized as interaction times where there is active engagement among project participants about project activities compared to project time in which deadlines and schedules drive the entire project activities and the nature of temporal flexibility between contractors and permanent organization members.

The temporal nature of projects may also provide time-based competitive advantages to host permanent organizations via reducing product time to market or capturing a temporal window of opportunity (Whyte, 2019). Temporal organizing raises agency issues where temporary employment, contract work, and temporary assignments from permanent organizations (Manning, 2017). A challenge of this approach is that given the nature of uncertainty in projects and interactions among these diverse actors, some emergent outcomes from projects will necessarily remain unknown and incur unintended consequences. These outcomes can result in unintended consequences, particularly in high dynamism such as agile projects. There may also be a temporal gap in temporary and permanent organizing. Temporary organizations may be formed to respond to urgent needs and identify emergent requirements that institutional structures in permanent organizations have not conceptualized. As a result, a time gap or lag can emerge at the interface between these different organizational types in which responses are negotiated.

8.5 Relational Perspective

The traditional literature on temporary organizations views it as a relational establishment and reconfiguration process. There is an interplay between temporary, permanent, and managerial agencies. The transient temporal contexts allow members to establish temporary audit activities and governance structures to manage them. However, it ignores the complex negotiations that may happen to establish this order. It also ignores the nature of relationships that underpin this order. It also ignores the temporal idiosyncrasies that can exist across project elements. Temporary organizations have also been viewed from a power relationship angle in which organizing is a process of order that emerges from conflicts, and those conflicts may not necessarily be resolved (Phillips-Alonge, 2019). Entities compete, contest, or negotiate for roles, positions, and outcomes and establish collaborative relationships (Suprapto et al., 2015).

Organizations must establish relationships with permanent stakeholders who are either suppliers or customers for project outputs. In other cases, permanent organizations host temporary organizations. Many of the resources within the temporal organization have been assigned by the host on a problem-solving basis to return to the substantive position at the end of the process. A temporal perspective brings in the possibility of evolution where interactions among these project entities, both human and nonhuman or the social structure, can evolve, raising emergence change and complexity issues. These complex temporal relationships and alignments can be suboptimal, resulting in project failure in complex projects. Symbolic resources, norms, and values can also be influenced by these relational interactions (Schultz et al., 2013). This perspective brings the idea of inequality among stakeholders to the fore as stakeholders may have differing capacities to achieve outcomes (Biygautan et al., 2020) via ambiguous relationships with dynamic collaboration and competition, which some partners can exploit at the expense of others (Ninan et al., 2019)

8.6 Combined Perspectives on Responsible Organizing

Responsible organizing requires individual relational and multi-relational interests and their diverse claims, routines, and temporal constraints acknowledged and addressed via organizational actions. This suggests that projects will have to be temporary institutions with a moral character that seeks to address oversight or resources, equity, and justice issues and be temporary organizations. These structures must be accountable via governance mechanisms such as transparency oversight and meaningful mutual consultation. Ethics is critical for emergent institutions as they provide a way for values to be represented and claims from entities that may not hold a financial stake to be addressed as a moral or justice issue. In this way, governance structures, leadership, and control mechanisms align with a single definition of value or shareholder value and address broader value concerns to all stakeholders. While governance practices can support these activities via embedding routines such as guidelines, ethics policies, and structures such as committees and training courses, organizing recognizes the limits of this approach to ensure that the ethos is embedded in individuals carrying out the activities.

One must be careful not to rely solely on externally driven mandates since responsibility has both a formal and an informal component. These areas are critical since formal recognition places stakeholders' essential issues, such as sustainability, on the agenda. However, researchers indicated that practitioners who aim to act sustainably or ethically or responsibly could be silenced within organizations by becoming overlooked or non-noted actors whose role is merely ceremonial and whose position, while formally acknowledged in the organization structure, is informally ignored, marginalized, and excluded from decision-making (Andersen, 2008).

8.7 Responsible Organizing Value Outcomes

Responsible organizing of projects poses a challenge to stakeholders (Roberts et al., 2020). PMs have attempted to deliver outcomes beyond financial value by using frameworks such as the triple bottom line and the more recent SDGs to balance projects' short- and long-term benefits. In addition to the challenges of delivering against multiple criteria, project participants may be distributed temporally and geographically. The term "value" has been defined as a preferred outcome (e.g., benefits) as perceived by project stakeholders. Values are a somewhat broader but related concept that examines the rationale for attitudes, ideology, and beliefs. Since a value component is perceived, values can influence perceptions of value. Early research in project management did not expressly address the concept of value. The later emergence of "modern" project management (i.e., the use of dedicated tools and techniques) introduced the idea of delivering financial value from projects.

An integrated approach to value creation suggests that five types of value or capital are created in projects (https://www.forumforthefuture.org/the-five-capitals). Please see figure 8.1.

8.8 Natural Capital

Natural capital is generally captured in environmental perspectives, which examines the natural resources and the processes that organizations require to perform the physical and service transformations to deliver outcomes. Natural capital also aligns with the UN SDGs in the domains of SDG 6 (clean water and sanitation), SGD 14 (life below water), and SDG 15 (life on land). Therefore, projects influence the natural environment and create or destroy natural capital to generate outcomes for stakeholders. The trend is for project organizations to maintain natural outbound capital to stay within the renewable boundaries of the environment for resources that are themselves renewable and reduce the use of nonrenewable resources (Aarseth et al., 2017). In this approach, organizations attempt to extract maximum value from natural capital while respecting the limits of renewable and nonrenewable resources. For projects, natural capital is considered in frameworks such as the triple bottom line, green and sustainable project management, and deploying tools such as life cycle analysis. More recent use of digitization, such as building information modeling and digital twins, have been used to reduce carbon and water usage in projects (Greif et al., 2020).

8.9 Human Capital

Human capital incorporates the individual's intellectual, physical, and emotional capacity, facilitating beneficial outcomes for stakeholders. Human capital is also captured in SDGs in the areas of SDG 2 (zero hunger), SDG 3 (good health and well-being), and SDG 4 (quality education). It is a crucial driver of organizational value and forms a significant part of the intangibles that underpin such relational properties as brands, intellectual property, and knowledge capital of organizations. While limited effort has been placed in project management to conserve human capital or respect it (Suhonen & Paasivaara, 2011), the increasing trend has been to address the human issue via embedding HR and leadership approaches in project management and to recognize the impact of a project working on issues such as burnout in project teams (Pinto et al., 2016). Projects also contribute human capital to communities via training programs and providing internship experiences for residents (De los Ríos-Carmenado et al., 2015). More recently, the living wage and modern slavery eliminated worker exploitation (Trautrims et al., 2020). In addition to the health of workers and communities, projects contribute to society's overall well-being, improving productivity and emotional well-being. For example, a public transport project can reduce commuting times and increase family time. Human capital also identifies the issues of connection among various types of value. Physical health, emotional health, and mental health have been linked, and these are also related to environmental well-being since polluted environments can disrupt physical and emotional health.

8.10 Social Capital

Social capital examines the relational aspect of value, captured in the SDGs of SDG 5 (gender equality), SDG 10 (reduced inequality), SDG 16 (peach, justice, and social institutions), and SDG 17 (partnerships for the goals). As an explicitly networked phenomenon, projects interact among different stakeholders, including individual organizations, individual members within organizations, NGOs, public sector bodies, private sector bodies, and institutions. From an organization or temporary organizing perspective, social relationships build bridging and bonding social capital, mobilizing other resources to deliver outcomes (Miković et al., 2020). Bridging social capital integrates people from different social groups. Bonding social capital acts to support and reinforce identities. Bonding capital creates loyalty, enabling identity building and providing support for community members that is required (Talbot et al., 2020).

From the community perspective, social capital can provide a license to operate, enabling organizational activities to be considered legitimate or legitimate (Jijelava & Vanclay, 2014). Social capital can also create discrimination, cronyism, and corruption and erect barriers to social and economic inclusion that could increase inequality (Villena et al., 2011). Organizations can foster social capital by building relationships and strengthening the capacity of civic organizations. Social capital can also improve the effectiveness of broader national institutions such as government or health systems. The presence of social capital provides an opportunity for trust-building that enables institutions to engage in complex tasks if they are viewed as legitimate by citizens in a given country or region.

8.11 Manufactured Capital

Manufactured capital perhaps receives the most attention in project management via large-scale initiatives like megaprojects which transform the natural world (Sankaran et al., 2020). It comprises the goods that contribute to the production process but do not become embodied in the output of that process. Manufactured goods are buildings such as the built environment, infrastructure, and technologies created directly by projects and project management. Manufactured capital is captured in SDGs 9 and SDG 11 (sustainable cities and communities), SDG 12 (responsible consumption and production), SDG 7 and SDG 13 (climate action). Nonrenewable resources from the natural environment have driven the recent growth in manufactured capital in the last 200 years.

8.12 Financial Capital

Finally, financial capital is another related asset commonly deployed in projects and project management. Financial capital is captured in the SDG in SDG1 (no poverty) and SDG 8 (decent work and economic growth). It is the traditional way of enterprises. They are evaluated and linked directly to notions of shareholder value. While there are recent initiatives or ideas to move beyond financial capital, other value types are commonly translated into financial terms to determine if they are worth pursuing. For example, environmental initiatives are frequently promoted as value for money where the amount saved in waste or recycling is sold to stakeholders as not just good for the environment but as fiscally responsible (Martens & Carvalho, 2016). There is an increasing movement, especially among the responsible investing community, to ensure that financial values are aligned with and reflect the value of other types of capital (Losse & Geissdoerfer, 2021).

More recently, financial capital has been using an activist manner to drive changes until support initiatives like net-zero, which reduce carbon. Responsible investing initiatives seek to focus financial capital in areas where goods can be done and away from areas such as fossil fuels. The intent is to use the market to drive appropriate change. This includes valuing intangible assets and the metrics applied to producing or measuring the value of natural stocks and floors and the benefits to be derived from social capital. Companies now seek to balance financial and other capital as expressed by initiatives like the triple bottom line. However, critics suggest that the triple bottom line underweights other forms of capital regarding financial capital (Isil & Hernke, 2017). These changes are limited to organizations that damage the natural world, and advertising has been withdrawn from entities that spread misinformation or incite violence.

The Plastic Bank has a target that by 2025, it will be become a billion-dollar company, impacting a billion lives and preventing a billion kilos of plastic from entering the ocean every year.

Plastic Bank seeks to generate economic and social value by building a marketplace for plastic waste in low-income countries. Plastic Bank reduces plastic ocean waste and poverty, enabling the exchange of plastic for money, goods, or blockchain-secured digital tokens. Plastic in developing countries may be improperly discarded due to the lack of formal waste management structures and enters marine ecosystems, causing harm. Plastic Bank addresses this issue by creating a recycling infrastructure and incentivizing participation by paying a Social Plastic® premium for waste material. Plastic Bank also enables local entrepreneurs to create franchises (bank branches). The material collected by the Plastic Bank network is sold at a premium to manufacturers who seek to use ethical products in their supply chain. The Plastic Bank also offers the opportunity for firms to offset their plastic footprint by funding the collection and recycling of an equal amount of social plastic. The organization adapts its approach by country. For example, in Hati, where there are no recycling facilities, plastic

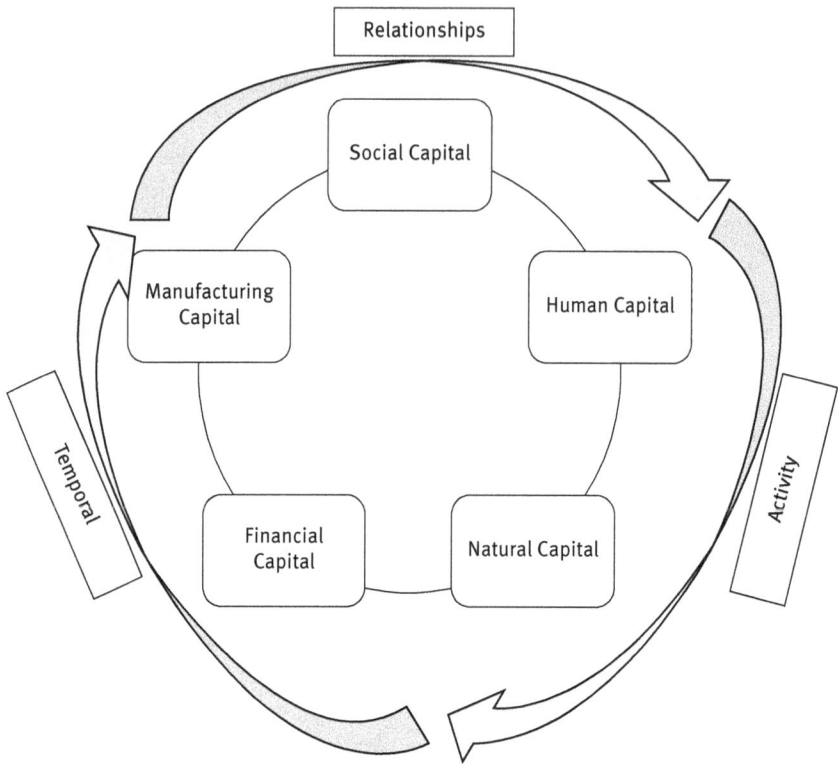

Figure 8.1: Relationships and activities of capital types (author).

banks have created storefronts for collectors to return material. In contrast, the Philippines are a mature market, so the firm worked with a cooperative of shops to create a franchising model. In 2015, the team partnered with IBM to create a blockchain-based management system. This consisted of backend infrastructure and a mobile-based blockchain app that manages payments, stores credit, and validates impact claims by the company. Blockchain is a secure digital ledger that provides a trusted way for peer-to-peer data exchanges in an encrypted manner.

When brands purchase Social Plastic, the revenue is used to fund utility tokens earned by collectors and can be used for purchases or transferred into cash. The process enables individuals with poor banking systems to access financial services such as loans and a secure digital ID. The IBM Hyperledger blockchain enables transparency in financial transactions for many small plastic sales without expensive fees, making the activity less profitable for collectors. The system has been subsequently expanded to use social plastic as a medium of exchange where collectors could purchase products and services by depositing plastic with approved retailers' redemption locations. In addition to financial benefits, the Plastic Bank team trains participants in finance, marketing, and strategy, improving their productivity and building skills deployed elsewhere.

8.13 Plastic Bank's Blockchain

The blockchain project was launched to meet the need for a digital payment and reward program in poor countries with limited infrastructure that was traceable and auditable. While several blockchain projects claim to meet these requirements, organizations were seeking to adopt them to face multiple issues. The first is that specialized technology might be required, which is beyond the ability of Plastic Banks at that time. The second is that the energy requirements may be high to provide the required verification. Finally, a related issue is that there may be transaction delays while verification is done. After an extensive search, the IBM Montpellier blockchain team was engaged by Plastic Bank to build the Hyperledger Fabric blockchain platform, using IBM LinuxONE Servers on IBM Cloud.

This technology approach was selected to meet the requirements of Plastic Bank. A key constraint is that Plastic Bank has few employees, so the system had to provide tracking, auditing, and payment services with minimal manual input. External stakeholders wanted to obtain oversight to ensure that the plastic deposits were valid. This is required for plastic used for customer's production processes, such as Henkel, who required the process to be ethical and needed plastics with specific performance characteristics. The blockchain system needed to capture other verification details such as geographic data from the collector to confirm that the plastic was ocean-bound material.

For auditing, the blockchain system also provided a digital ID that the Plastic Bank team could evaluate the quantity and quality of material collected. This ID was also linked to a digital wallet used for payments. The team also deployed their digital payment token stored in these wallets. For some of the countries Plastic Bank operates, electricity supplies are intermittent. The technology solution needed to work on a mobile phone and provide rapid payments to collectors.

The token was later extended from cash to a larger reward and transactions program. Plastic Bank collectors could obtain discounts from participating vendors and use the tokens to purchase needed products directly without converting them to cash.

This case study presents an overview of the challenges of temporary organizing and its impact on permanent organizing. To support its expansion, the company launched a technology project that conferred time-based advantages (market entry for future expansion) and met the current needs of customers for oversight and payments. In addition to the temporal aspects, specific activities had to be done by the firm, such as information search to scan the existing market for a solution that met the infrastructure and oversight requirements of the firm. The Plastic Bank also had to train its collectors on both the usage and benefits of the system. The firm subsequently extended the token system to incorporate purchases by collectors, increasing its value. Finally, the case demonstrated the relational value of organizing as Plastic Bank had to establish relationships with technology firms, multinational goods producers and vendors in developing countries to deploy the blockchain network (figure 2).

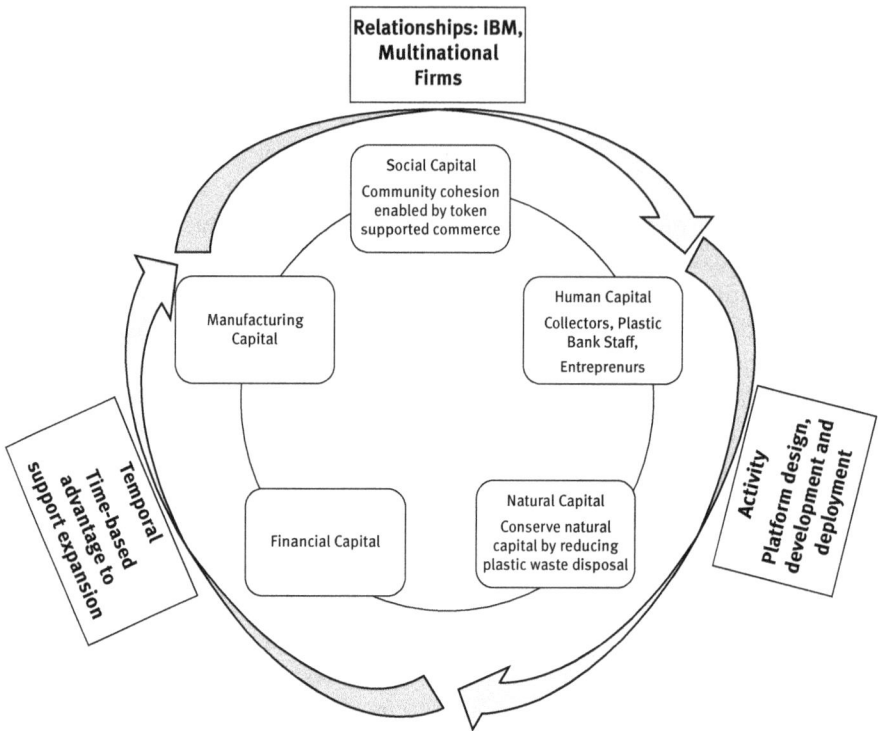

Figure 8.2: Relationships: IBM and multinational firms (author).

8.14 Embedding Responsible Project Organizing

Project control frameworks extend over the entire period, from conceptualization to handover and use. They facilitate performance measurement of activities and outcomes. The former is structured to ensure that temporal and resource constraints are planned and adhered to. For the latter, controls seek to ensure that planned benefits are realized. At the early stage of a project, a business case is created that justifies the overall initiative, intended beneficial outcomes, and alignment with the host organization's needs. To embed responsible organizing into projects, sponsors and organizers will have to create or adapt business cases to incorporate natural, social, and human capital types that may not be represented in current processes. In this way, stakeholders' conceptualization of value types and priorities can then be translated into action via objectives for the project. Since stakeholders' priorities may vary by context, it would be helpful to identify these differing perspectives, tensions, and contradictions among them.

As possible, definable performance metrics for each of these value dimensions should be confirmed at this stage. At the early stage of the project, there may be a high level of uncertainty in the form of ambiguity. These areas must be highlighted and prioritized for clarification as the project progresses. Additional types of uncertainty in the form of variability may be associated with subsequent activities such as estimation, design, and stakeholder priorities. The assumptions made for each type of uncertainty should be documented and monitored throughout the project. Teams can then develop an integrated baseline that identifies sources of data pathways of project data, including relevant individuals and intended targets for project process elements.

Case Study 2: Wabbits
Non-fungible tokens (NFT) are tokens stored on a blockchain used to indicate a reference for an item. NFT differs from cryptocurrency coins as they cannot be exchanged like-for-like, enabling the assignment of a unique identifier for digital assets. The value of their non-fungibility is that they can claim originality to assets by providing proof and history of blockship ownership exchanges. In this way, while digital art could be copied, the NFT can indicate the original owner. This enables the assignment of tradable property rights to assets that could otherwise be infinitely copied. The idea of NFTs began with "Colored Coins" in 2012, which were tokens issued on the Bitcoin blockchain to prove ownership of real-world physical and financial assets. Later, in 2014, the Counterparty protocol enabled the creation of tradable currencies on the Bitcoin blockchain (https://blog.portion.io/the-history-of-nfts-how-they-got-started/). The first art token, "Quantum," was created on May 3, 2014.

In 2016, Counterparty was used to create digital collectables and memes. In 2017, CryptoKitties NFTs, a blockchain-based game with asset creation capabilities, was created on the Ethereum platform. NFTs represent digital assets on blockchain platforms, including finance, data, art, Curios, and Collectibles. For asset owners, NFTs are meant to assure that the owner of a given token is the owner of the asset. NFTs are also intended to indicate that the asset was owned by the original creator of the token (Mackenzie & Bērziņa, 2021). Since they are based on a blockchain, NFTs provide further advantages of selling fractional ownership of assets and providing royalties on resale via smart contracts. The market grew rapidly in 2021 (https://nonfungible.com/blog), and from a project management perspective, NFTs provide an interesting opportunity to examine a context in which formal institutions do not exist.

The case study, Wabbits (https://wabbits.co/), is two lines of 2222 Rabbit NFTs on the Solana blockchain. Wabbit aims to raise awareness and fund ADHD and autism through online communications and revenue.

The creator of Wabbits was initially involved in the trading of NFTs and launched their project in 2022. Unlike most projects designed to gain revenue, the Wabbits NFT

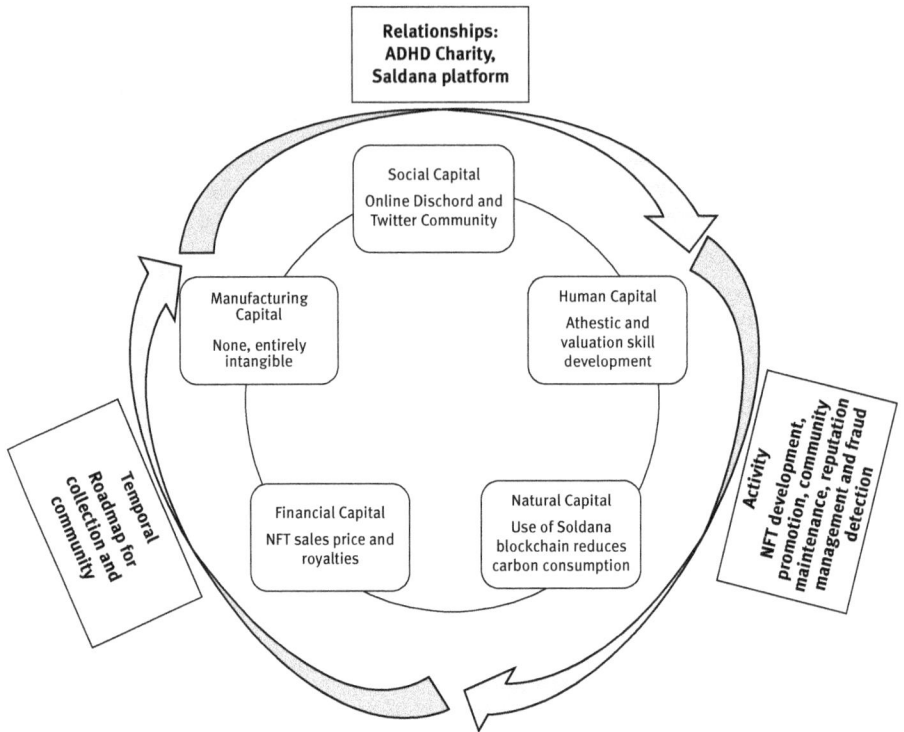

Figure 8.3: The case of Wabbits: relationships and capital types (author).

is linked to a cause that resonated with the online community. The team chose an American charity (CHADD) because most NFT community is American.

The team has the following roadmap:

Phase-1
- Launch the 2222 Wabbits on our site
- Become listed on marketplaces after Launch
- NFT giveaways for community members

Phase-2
- Weekly sweep events
- Weekly use 20% Royalties for periodic sweeps (open for vote)
- Creation of Wabbits DAO

Phase-3
- Donate 30% Royalties to the ADHD charity CHADD each month
- Toon Wabbit airdrops for Wabbit holders

Phase-4
- – Voting in DAO for how to use wallet Royalties moving forward
- – Expand the project under community lead

In 2021, the NFT market grew significantly due to the & lure of higher prices and the symbolic lure of cultural capital (Aluma-Baigent & Perissinotto, 2021). These characteristics have also attracted unethical practices such as generating NFTs for digital assets that the NFT creator does not own. The reliance on online platforms and blockchain governance does not prevent other actions such as impersonation of projects, artists, owners, and artwork. Additional systemic risks may also occur where projects and platforms can be hacked, resulting in the loss of assets. Due to the high level of automated actions in these systems, the temporal horizon for activities can be compressed. As a result, items can be removed and resold multiple times before owners know they are missing.

Organizers may engage in fraud such as rug pulls, where promoters will recruit investors and then abandon the project without delivering the promised items or returning the funds. The Wabbit community has not been immune, and the team has faced challenges from fraudulent individuals who have mimicked their website copied their Discord identity. They have also joined the main Dischord site and posted links to sites that would steal funds from community members. The team has been required to establish communication approaches such as specialized linkages that prove their authenticity so that community members do not fall victim to fraud. As the initiative develops, the team plans additional projects that increase community participation, such as a Digital Autonomous organization that enables input such as voting on future action. This final action can align the NFT team with the potential for a responsible controls framework that assures the community and external parties.

This chapter examines the characteristics of responsibility in a project management context. As stated previously, existing conceptualizations of professional and organizational responsibility overlook moral aspects. In contexts where defined alternatives do not exist, as in the case examples of community care and NFTs, PMs must negotiate a path through these uncertain domains. For both of these examples, PMs had to establish routines of collective actions. In the first case, this was based on stakeholder consultation with beneficiaries; in the second case, the team intends to set up a digital infrastructure to support direct participation in decision-making from the community. The outcomes are multiple types of value for stakeholders.

References

Aarseth, W., Ahola, T., Aaltonen, K., Økland, A., & Andersen, B. (2017). Project sustainability strategies: A systematic literature review. *International Journal of Project Management, 35*(6), 1071–1083.

https://assets.publishing.service.gov.uk/government/uploads/system/uploads/attachment_data/file/642659/hs2_planning_context_report_for_solihull.pdf

Aluma-Baigent, A. (2021). Crypto: Art, Currency, and Capital. Available at: http://hdl.handle.net/10393/42756

Bakker, R. M. (2010). Taking stock of temporary organisational forms: A systematic review and research agenda. *International Journal of Management Reviews, 12*(4), 466–486.

Biygautane, M., Clegg, S., & Al-Yahya, K. (2020). Institutional work and infrastructure public–private partnerships (PPPs): the roles of Religious symbolic work and power in implementing PPP projects. Accounting, Auditing & Accountability Journal, 33(5), 1077–1112.

Brookes, N., Sage, D., Dainty, A., Locatelli, G., & Whyte, J. (2017). An island of constancy in a sea of change: Rethinking project temporalities with long-term megaprojects. *International Journal of Project Management, 35*(7), 1213–1224.

Cicmil, S., & Gaggiotti, H. (2018). Responsible forms of project management education: Theoretical plurality and reflective pedagogies. *International Journal of Project Management, 36*(1), 208–218.

Cicmil, S., & O'Laocha, E. (2016). The logic of projects and the ideal of community development: Social good, participation and the ethics of knowing. *International Journal of Managing Projects in Business, 9*, 546–561. doi:10.1108/IJMPB-09-2015- 0092

Cullen, J. G. (2017). Educating business students about sustainability: A bibliometric review of current trends and research needs. *Journal of Business Ethics, 145*(2), 429–439.

De los Ríos-Carmenado, I. G. N. A. C. I. O., Lopez, F. R., & Garcia, C. P. (2015). Promoting professional project management skills in engineering higher education: Project-based learning (PBL) strategy. *International Journal of Engineering Education, 31*(1), 184–198.

Godemann, J., Haertle, J., Herzig, C., & Moon, J. (2014). United Nations-supported principles for responsible management education: Purpose, progress and prospects. *Journal of Cleaner Production, 62*, 16–23.

Golicic, S. L., & Smith, C. D. (2013). A meta-analysis of environmentally sustainable supply chain management practices and firm performance. *Journal of Supply Chain Management, 49*(2), 78–95.

Grabher, G. (2002). Cool projects, boring institutions: Temporary collaboration in social context. *Regional Studies, 36*(3), 205–214.

Grabher, G. (2004). Learning in projects, remembering in networks? Communality, sociality, and connectivity in project ecologies. European urban and regional studies, 11(2), 103–123.

Greif, T., Stein, N., & Flath, C. M. (2020). Peeking into the void: Digital twins for construction site logistics. *Computers in Industry, 121*, 103264.

Holbrook, M. B. (1999). Introduction to consumer value. *Consumer Value: A Framework for Analysis and Research*, 1–28. London: Routledge.

Imbrogiano, J. P. (2020). Contingency in business sustainability research and the sustainability service industry: A problematisation and research agenda. *Organization & Environment*, 1086026619897532.

Isil, O., & Hernke, M. T. (2017). The triple bottom line: A critical review from a transdisciplinary perspective. *Business Strategy and the Environment, 26*(8), 1235–1251.

Jijelava, D., & Vanclay, F. (2014). Social licence to operate through a gender lens: The challenges of including women's interests in development assistance projects. *Impact Assessment and Project Appraisal, 32*(4), 283–293.

Kahneman, D., Ritov, I., Schkade, D., Sherman, S. J., & Varian, H. R. (1999). Economic preferences or attitude expressions?: An analysis of dollar responses to public issues. In: Fischhoff, B., Manski, C.F. (eds) *Elicitation of preferences* (pp. 203–242). Dordrecht: Springer. https://doi.org/10.1007/978-94-017-1406-8_8

Manning, S. (2017). The rise of project network organisations: Building core teams and flexible partner pools for interorganizational projects. *Research Policy, 46*(8), 1399–1415.

Langmead, K., & King, D. (2020). Realising the critical performative potential of responsible organisational research through participant action research. In *Research handbook of responsible management.* (pp. 700–714). Edward Elgar Publishing.London

Losse, M., & Geissdoerfer, M. (2021). Mapping socially responsible investing: A bibliometric and citation network analysis. *Journal of Cleaner Production,* VOL 296, 126376. https://doi.org/10.1016/j.jclepro.2021.126376

Lundin, R. A., Arvidsson, N., Brady, T., Eksted, E., Midler, C., & Sydow, J. (2015). *Managing and working in project society: Institutional challenges of temporary organisations.* Cambridge: Cambridge University Press.

Lundin, R. A., & Söderholm, A. (1995). A theory of the temporary organisation. *Scandinavian Journal of Management, 11*(4), 437–455.

Mackenzie, S., & Bērziņa, D. (2021). NFTs: Digital things and their criminal lives. *Crime, Media, Culture,* 17416590211039797.

Martens, M. L., & Carvalho, M. M. (2016). The challenge of introducing sustainability into project management function: Multiple-case studies. *Journal of Cleaner Production, 117*, 29–40.

McNamee, S., & Gergen, K. J. (1999) Relational responsibility: Resources for sustainable dialogue. Thousand Oaks, CA: Sage.

Miković, R., Petrović, D., Mihić, M., Obradović, V., & Todorović, M. (2020). The integration of social capital and knowledge management is the key challenge for nonprofit organisations' international development and cooperation projects. *International Journal of Project Management, 38*(8), 515–533.

Nilsson, M., Griggs, D., & Visbeck, M. (2016). Policy: Map the interactions between Sustainable Development Goals. *Nature, 534*(7607), 320–322.

Ninan, J., Mahalingam, A., & Clegg, S. (2019). External stakeholder management strategies and resources in megaprojects: An organisational power perspective. *Project Management Journal, 50*(6), 625–640.

Phillips-Alonge, O. K. (2019). The influence of partnering on the occurrence of construction requirement conflicts and disputes. *International Journal of Construction Management, 19*(4), 291–306.

Pinto, J. K., Patanakul, P., & Pinto, M. B. (2016). Project personnel, job demands, and workplace burnout: The differential effects of job title and project type. *IEEE Transactions on Engineering Management, 63*(1), 91–100.

Raidén, A., Loosemore, M., King, A., & Gorse, C. A. (2019). Social value in construction. London: Routledge.

Rasche, A., De Bakker, F. G., & Moon, J. (2013). Complete and partial organising for corporate social responsibility. *Journal of Business Ethics, 115*(4), 651–663.

Roberts, J., Steinberger, J., Dietz, T., Lamb, W., York, R., Jorgenson, A., . . . Schor, J. (2020). Four agendas for research and policy on emissions mitigation and well-being. *Global Sustainability, 3*, E3. doi:10.1017/sus.2019.25

Robinson, S. (2009). The nature of responsibility in a professional setting. *Journal of Business Ethics, 88*(1), 11–19.

Sachs, J. D., Schmidt-Traub, G., Mazzucato, M., Messner, D., Nakicenovic, N., & Rockström, J. (2019). Six transformations to achieve the sustainable development goals. *Nature Sustainability, 2*(9), 805–814.

Sankaran, S., Müller, R., & Drouin, N. (2020). Creating a 'sustainability sublime to enable megaprojects to meet the United Nations sustainable development goals. *Systems Research and Behavioral Science, 37*(5), 813–826.

Schultz, F., Castelló, I., & Morsing, M. (2013). The construction of corporate social responsibility in network societies: A communication view. *Journal of Business Ethics*, 115(4), 681–692.

Shevchenko, A., Lévesque, M., & Pagell, M.. (2016). Why firms delay reaching true sustainability. *Journal of Management Studies*, 53(5), 911–935.

Söderlund, J. (2011). Pluralism in project management: Navigating the crossroads of specialisation and fragmentation. *International Journal of Management Reviews, 13*(2), 153–176.

Stjerne, I. S., Söderlund, J., & Minbaeva, D. (2019). Crossing times: Temporal boundary-spanning practices in inter-organisational projects. *International Journal of Project Management, 37*(2), 347–365.

Suhonen, M., & Paasivaara, L. (2011). Shared human capital in project management: A systematic review of the literature. *Project Management Journal, 42*(2), 4–16.

Suprapto, M., Bakker, H. L., & Mooi, H. G. (2015). Relational factors in owner-contractor collaboration: The mediating role of teamworking. *International Journal of Project Management, 33*(6), 1347–1363.

Sydow, J., & Braun, T. (2018). Projects as temporary organisations: An agenda for further theorising the interorganizational dimension. *International Journal of Project Management, 36*(1), 4–11.

Sydow, J., & Windeler, A. (2020). Temporary organising and permanent contexts. *Current Sociology, 68*(4), 480–498.

Talbot, J., Poleacovschi, C., Hamideh, S., & Santos-Rivera, C. (2020). Informality in postdisaster reconstruction: The role of social capital in reconstruction management in Post–Hurricane Maria Puerto Rico. *Journal of Management in Engineering, 36*(6), 04020074.

Trautrims, A., Gold, S., Touboulic, A., Emberson, C., & Carter, H. (2021). The UK construction and facilities management sector's response to the Modern Slavery Act: An intra-industry initiative against modern slavery. *Business Strategy & Development*, 4(3), 279–293.

Villena, V. H., Revilla, E., & Choi, T. Y. (2011). The dark side of buyer-supplier relationships: A social capital perspective. *Journal of Operations Management, 29*(6), 561–576.

Whyte, J. (2019). How digital information transforms project delivery models. *Project Management Journal, 50*(2), 177–194.

Nigel Williams and Beverly Pasian

9 Public Health-Care Management

Context: Projects located in Canada, the UK, and the Gambia. Insights are applicable to publicly funded health-care systems.

Characters/entities: The chapter organizational entities drawn from the countries mentioned including government of New Brunswick, NHS, and Gambian Health Charity.

Locations: Canada, the UK, and Gambia. Other countries in the global north and south.

Research gaps: The chapter examines the gap of exploring the delivery of projects as part of an autonomous adaptive system.

Challenges/conflict/tensions: The multilevel impact of context and participants on project management in health care.

Keywords: health care, Canada, the Gambia, UK

9.1 Introduction

At this point of writing, public health is foremost in most of our minds. Before the events of 2020, for most people, public health was an issue to be engaged with for personal, political, or social reasons. Due to the Covid 19 pandemic, obscure discussions on infection rates, personal protective equipment, and health vulnerability are part of the daily discourse and may be embedded in discussions in the future. This chapter examines the responsibilities of project management in public health care. PM in health care has macro-level and meso-level forces shaping responsibilities for the overall contexts. In addition to the specific Project Management (PM) constraints of temporality and precarity, health-care PM has political and research responsibilities. For the former, a long-term orientation is needed as health systems provide long-term care for members of the population as they go through stages of life. This chapter is examined in the context of the health-care systems responding to long-term trends and emergent emergencies.

Health care is a science and technology-oriented domain involving the research-intensive nature of health-care results in new treatments for communicable and noncommunicable diseases and new analytical and delivery approaches. In the latter two areas, digitization, including artificial intelligence (AI) tools, has supported actions such as digitizing records to reduce cost and increase the quality of care. From a systems perspective, health care can be classified as an autonomous,

https://doi.org/10.1515/9783110724783-012

anticipative, and adaptive (AAA) system with the capacity for reconfiguration and self-organization (Collier & Hooker, 1999).

Autonomous adaptive system (AAS) requires integrating components to function across not just spatial but temporal frames. This also posits the presence of an anticipative capability to predict possible future states and ensure that the system is receptive to these changes (Fuchs, 2003). AAS differentiates from other methods such as simple linear systems, systems that can be statistically specified, statistically selected systems near equilibrium (e.g., gases and fluids), and complicated systems such as machines that are decomposable and tractable (Collier, 2006). AAS are complex (a large number of independent pieces of information are required to describe them) and have many interrelationships among parts. Control or management actions in AAS systems act across multiple timescales as identified earlier in Responsible Organizing and require harmonizing of participants' interorganizational and internal activities. AAS also respond selectively and differentially to previously unseen external forces as anticipatory systems. One of these responses is an adaptation that enables modification while preserving the system's purpose, characteristics, and integrity.

Overall, this presents more complex project governance and delivery scenario that influences responsibility as evolving, uncertain, and incompatible stakeholder needs (Loch et al., 2002). Unlike domains such as construction, responsible organizing health projects have additional activities and interactions among the public, private, and not-for-profit entities. These entities can include health and social care provision, infrastructure, funding, basic research, and applied research. This system has distinct relational-temporal characteristics, including subsystems required to respond to long-term patterns of change such as aging trends in countries and emergent crises such as Covid 19. Further, unlike other systems, defining boundaries in health and social care is complicated.

Stakeholders' interests and values evolve, and meeting expectations may result in a fundamental rethinking of members and relationships. As universal providers, national health systems must serve all, including those who may not trust the health service for religious, social, historical, or political reasons (Whyle & Olivier, 2020). Merely balancing stakeholder interests may not be sufficient to provide care as there is no easily definable point of agreement between those who trust the health service and those who do not.

9.2 Macro (Societal Responsibility)

Economic, social, political, and environmental changes, in addition to emerging technologies, generate a complex global health agenda where epidemiological, demographic, and societal characteristics are constantly evolving (Senkubuge et al., 2014). Health and social care providers are tasked with many initiatives to keep pace with service demand, such as introducing new models of working and provision, designing new pathways of care, introducing a broader workforce, making greater use of technology, and encouraging peoples' ability to self-care while also working closely with other teams and organizations (Wright & Durán, 2020). Health-care systems are challenged by fragmentation, duplication, and poor coordination (Goddard & Mason, 2017). Addressing these challenges in some settings has resulted in benefits of prolonged independent living with delayed admission to institutional care, improved quality of life, and enhanced cost-effectiveness (Nolte, 2021).

Global spending on health care is forecast to triple in less than 30 years to $29.72 trillion (Tardieu et al., 2020). A significant amount of this cost change is driven by a globally aging population with a higher likelihood of developing health conditions requiring hospitalization, diagnosis, and treatment. A related component is the cost of health-care administration, which can account for a high percentage of overall costs (Himmelstein et al., 2020). Organizations seek to develop new patient-centralized approaches to minimize the need for hospitalization, new organizational structures to minimize administrative and other costs and digitized systems to improve coordination among health-care participants. These responses require projects in which PMs have to address individual relationships and existing organizational dynamics (Valentijn et al., 2015).

9.3 Meso (Health System)

Building this collective yet dynamic approach across health and social care systems requires systems and structures that acknowledge shared responsibility (Clark & Harley, 2020). To address macro-level challenges, there is a requirement to establish mutually beneficial relationships with clearly defined roles among many stakeholders united by shared values to achieve more considerable outcomes than individual efforts. Existing health-care systems have already utilized shared leadership approaches, delivering various services within different organizational types and involving staff from health and social services (Scott-Young et al., 2019). Coordination can be viewed as a bottom-up, emergent process where entities evolve processes to perform collective actions, including formal protocols, roles, or knowledge sharing practices (Weber & Khademian, 2008). Coordination of health enterprises reduces duplication of services, conserving human and material resources. However, the coordination process can be challenging and confuse outcomes, policy, and authority, resulting in sub-optional project outcomes.

Coordination at the macro-level is even more complicated when health and social care crises occur. These scenarios require a response by entities from multiple disciplines and locations under conditions of high uncertainty (Ansell et al., 2010). Early in the crisis, no single organization has the knowledge, skills, or formal authority to manage the entire response and instead, a network approach is adopted to integrate the efforts of a heterogeneous group of national, international, and community actors (Nolte & Boenigk, 2013). It can be defined as the process of social resource and material interactions among enterprises that seek common health and social care outcomes. Crisis response is complex as project teams are often a mixture of fixed and ad hoc operational partners, which have ambiguous interorganizational dynamics in the project teams.

9.4 The Individual (Micro-Level)

Health care is consumed and provided by individuals. The latter group needs to be aware of cognitive, physical, and other abilities and constraints. The individual perspective has grown in prominence in the last decade, where health systems have adopted patient and public involvement (PPI) approaches (Renedo et al., 2015). PPI provides stakeholders with a voice in health systems, resulting in benefits such as improved health research, services, and legitimacy. From a patient perspective, PPI offers an opportunity to obtain care that respects their values and preferences, which results in increased emotional, cognitive, and behavioral engagement with care. Previous research has identified four approaches to patient involvement: consumer (procurer of services), citizen (influencer of services provider), partner (co-creator of services), and researcher (co-creator of health-care knowledge) (Forbat et al., 2009). In practice, most projects focus on the first mode and not the latter three. These other three dimensions will also need to be considered part of system planning and integration to deliver appropriate care.

9.4.1 Case 1: The Canadian Health-Care System

Meso-level responses to macro-level challenges are unique in the Canadian health-care system and its aging population. Citizens aged 65 and older are Canada's most rapidly growing demographic. There has been a recognition that the hospital-based care-based system has to evolve to incorporate new participants to facilitate home and community-based care. To address the impending aging population crisis, the Canadian health-care system has taken steps to address the project delivery challenges caused by fragmentation, financing, and geography. As shown in Figure 9.1, Canadian health systems have a three-layer structure, where critical medical care is provided free to the population, while layer 2 and layer 3 services may require private funding support. While payment structures are unitary, the actor layer is highly fragmented. Physicians are independent contractors, and participant organizations also have their forms of governance, which can influence how projects are realized.

Geographically, Canada's population distribution requires distributed support or transport, which can be expensive for emergency operations.

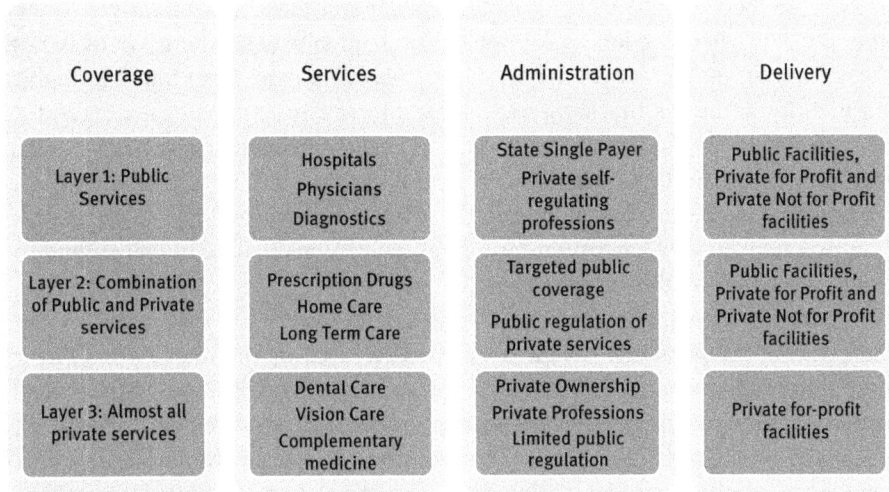

Coverage	Services	Administration	Delivery
Layer 1: Public Services	Hospitals Physicians Diagnostics	State Single Payer Private self-regulating professions	Public Facilities, Private for Profit and Private Not for Profit facilities
Layer 2: Combination of Public and Private services	Prescription Drugs Home Care Long Term Care	Targeted public coverage Public regulation of private services	Public Facilities, Private for Profit and Private Not for Profit facilities
Layer 3: Almost all private services	Dental Care Vision Care Complementary medicine	Private Ownership Private Professions Limited public regulation	Private for-profit facilities

Figure 9.1: Canada's three-tier health-care system (adapted from Martin et al., 2018).

Canada's geographical and administrative context will require multifaceted approaches to not only achieve the required coverage but to address systemic challenges that shape the delivery of care. To address this challenge, provinces have been launching their multi-project initiatives. For example, New Brunswick launched the Healthy Seniors Pilot Program, which aims to support seniors and healthy aging (Government of New Brunswick, 2018). The program was established in 2018 and demonstrated Canada's multilevel governance structure for health. The Social Development and Health department provides oversight at the provisional level, and participant organizations are drawn from public, private, and NGO sectors, including universities. In January 2021, $49.9 million was allocated for the delivery and evaluation costs of 39 projects in the following areas:

- Design physical and social spaces to support independent and healthy living by seniors (seven projects).
- Improve health and social support access to undersupported rural and ethnic communities populations (nine projects).
- Increase physical activity and mental activity to improve quality of life in seniors (six projects).
- Create technology-enhanced health and social support services for seniors and caregivers (five projects).
- Create new care pathways to improve choice and access to health and social support services (12 projects).

Combined, this program explores multiple options to improve the quality of life of seniors by changing the nature, location, and administration of health care. For responsible project management, there is a need for harmonizing the tension that may emerge between the existing health system and these new initiatives. Unlike other projects where the link to societal value creation may be unclear or even negative, these projects can benefit society by improving care. Even failed initiatives can identify pathways that may not be feasible and support the development of subsequent initiatives that can be fruitful. However, embedding the practices that have been trialed in these projects will require managers to negotiate a multilevel funding process, particularly if the outcomes need support from layer 3 private sector providers who may have short-term funding horizons that do not align with the long-term benefits of these projects.

At the meso-level, it is necessary to understand the roles of system participants and position interventions within the context created by the interactions among these roles. A challenge that this program may face will be positioning these interventions within existing providers seeking to deliver integrated care. There may need to be an additional intervention that encourages system awareness and reflection where organizations can rethink their roles in the system and their approaches to managing activities. To incorporate the innovations created by this program, the organization needs to allocate time and resources to ensure alignment between the experimental knowledge creation orientation of academic researchers and the routines of health-care providers. Once established, organizational sharing of knowledge, resources, and technology can influence the activities of system participants, encouraging meso-level evolution.

Challenges in coordinating planned and emergent projects may face interorganizational, organizational, and uncertainty of resources and demand that affect the participation of NGOs in collaborative engagement. A related issue is the increased scope of action by nonstate actors, which create a hybrid, multilevel governance structure. The differing temporal perspectives further complicate this issue among these organizations. Smaller NGOs with project-based funding may seek immediate benefits to continue operations. Larger organizations may seek to develop long-term partnerships that may not provide these immediate returns, making collaboration with smaller firms difficult.

An overlooked area in these adaptation projects is the individual perspective of values. As presented, these projects focus on patients as consumers but not as citizens or partners. These other three dimensions will also need to be considered part of system planning and integration to deliver care.

9.5 Meso-perspective

Beyond project benefits, health projects are evaluated by community and system impact. The shift to multilevel and multistakeholder health-care provision sees an increased role for local communities. Achievement of complex goals such as quality of life is difficult to evaluate at the national level, and the involvement of local community members as recipients and providers is a robust indicator. Further, unlike many other initiatives, project processes work alongside research processes. For health-care projects, outcomes are frequent evidence that can have direct practice and policy impact. Health-care systems also have various organizational structures that vary by function. These organizational structures also need to adapt to meet the demands of collaboration across a landscape that can be dynamic.

9.5.1 Case 2: UK Vaccine Rollout

Founded in 1946, the National Health Service (NHS) provides public health care to all permanent residents free at the point of need. While there is a small and growing private health system, the NHS's universal coverage and free access principles have been maintained from inception (Hardy and Rhodes, 2017). The NHS has adapted to a growing and demographically shifting population via incorporating management and technological innovations. More recently, the NHS was a lead partner in response to the Covid 19 pandemic. In response to the emergent pandemic, the UK Government established a vaccination task force in April 2020 with three goals (Bingham, 2021):
- Ensure access to effective COVID 19 vaccine
- Enable international distribution of Covid 19 vaccines
- Prepare the UK for future pandemics

The vaccine development program had the following main elements:
- Vaccine development: Academic and industry research on possible vaccine approaches, their efficacy, and side effects
- Manufacturing requirements: Materials, transformation processes, and storage processes to ensure production at the required scale
- Contractual documentation: Resource and activity management documentation ensure participants to provide and align required outputs.

The delivery of this program required the alignment of the following stakeholders in the UK medical system:

NGOs: NGOs, including a range of social, religious, and community groups, provided nonmedical volunteers to support the delivery of vaccination services, promoted vaccine adoption in targeted communities, translation services for non-English speakers, and education services to encourage vaccination.

Military: The military provided support staff for vaccination services. They also provided logistics support to ensure that coverage targets were met. These included analysis of vaccination site location to ensure that they were accessible by 96% of the UK population and planning for the subsequent expansion of the vaccination program beyond the initially targeted groups.

Technology: Technology partners enabled vaccines' development, testing, and approval based on new approaches. This included the development of simulations, trials, and evaluations. They also supported the subsequent scale-up to ensure production of the required volume and developed distribution systems to ensure availability to the UK population. This included support for developing the online booking system used by the NHS to serve the UK population.

Universities: Universities provided some basic research for vaccines and behavioral research into receptivity for vaccination. The latter analysis was used to support the development of communication interventions for targeted groups identified as hesitant or mistrusting of vaccines.

Manufacturing: Pharmaceutical manufacturing capacity was developed to ensure the production and distribution of the required amounts of vaccines. In addition to capacity development, the team also worked to identify and resolve national capacity bottlenecks. Since vaccines had specific storage requirements, manufacturers had to develop systems that met these requirements. Figure 9.2 shows the system participants and their interactions.

A budget of £6 billion was initially allocated to support vaccine development and procurement. After establishment in May 2020, the program monitored vaccination development by research labs to identify effective vaccines that could quickly be delivered to the population while meeting safety standards. In August 2020, the program sought to expand domestic manufacturing capacity for promising vaccine technologies to ensure no delivery bottlenecks. In November 2020, Pfizer/BioNTech, Moderna, Oxford, and Astra-Zeneca group confirmed levels of 95% efficacy for their vaccines. Once the UK government approved vaccines in December 2020, the country prioritized delivery to individuals classified as high risk for Covid and frontline health and social care staff (Gov.UK, 2020). In January 2021, the delivery capacity was established to vaccinate 2 million adults per week. To meet this scale, three types of facilities were used:
– 50 large-scale vaccination centers accessed using an online booking service and supported in some locations by volunteers,
– 206 hospitals, and
– 1,200 local centers of GP practice and pharmacies.

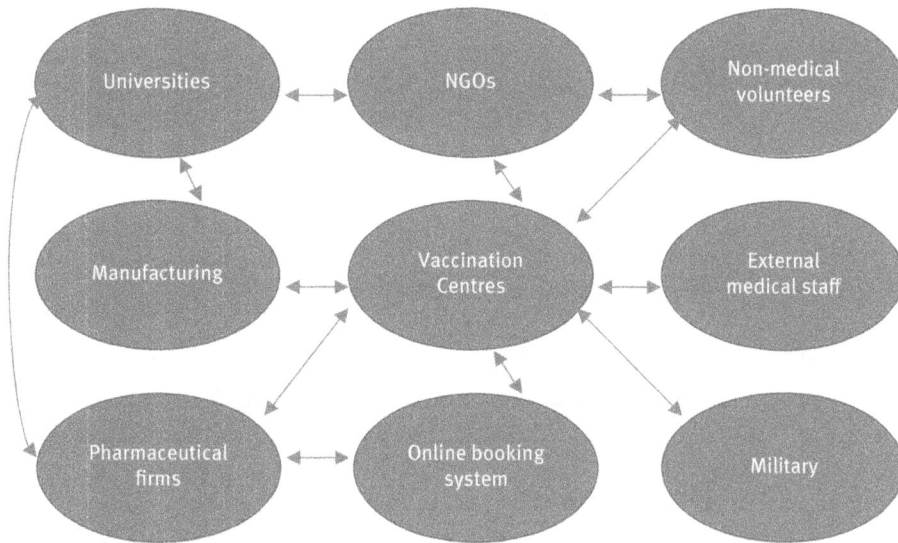

Figure 9.2: System participants in the UK medical system (author).

While the initial goal was to vaccinate all adults by the autumn, the emergence of new variants saw the expansion to all adults in June 2021. Waning efficacy of vaccination required the delivery of booster shots after 6 months for residents, which were initially aimed at older citizens but was subsequently expanded to over 40s in November 2021. To ensure that human resources were available, the NHS recruited staff from within and outside the NHS. External staff included health professionals in NGO services and nonmedical staff such as airline cabin crew. The response exemplifies the multistakeholder characteristics of health systems. The vaccine rollout project demonstrates the structural complexity and uncertainty faced by project managers in health-care systems and crisis management. Structural complexity refers to many distinct and interdependent elements, including NGOs, manufacturing, and the military (Daniel & Daniel, 2018) – responding to structural complexity requires formal planning and control systems to ensure alignment of the multiple components and interdependencies. The management of the vaccine rollout needed a holistic view of the overall system and identifying emerging uncertainties as each component of the vaccination rollout (technological, logistics, and staff) was also changing over time. For the UK, the formation of a vaccination task force and the identification and deployment of systems-level interventions such as removal of manufacturing bottlenecks enabled rapid action.

Since the vaccination program was an emergency response, the project's complexity could not be negotiated, and organizers needed to adapt over time. Many of the options that have been used to reduce complexity in project settings, such as shifting activities (offsite manufacturing in building projects) or simulation, have limited value since crises such as Covid can evolve. The experimental approach that was applied by the Canadian health system to explore the problem space was also not applicable since the nature of uncertainties faced by the team was both variable (probability and impact of issues) and ambiguous (limited information and lack of stakeholder agreement over issues). Over time, new requirements emerged (booster shots), and the team adapted activities to address them.

9.5.2 Case 3: The Gambian Health Support

Frequently, the individual perspective of health care is overlooked. Particularly in small, resource-constrained countries, providing basic health care is a difficult challenge that is not always met. The Gambia public health system has a primary layer (community clinics, 643 posts), secondary (47 health centers), and tertiary (four general hospitals and two specialized hospitals). In addition to the public health system, private organizations, international organizations, and NGOs provide health services. While private health services are expensive, most costs are based on improved customer service, not medical procedures. The system is also supplemented with external assistance from other countries, most notably Cuba, that sends doctors and nurses. The Gambia is also visited by a mobile Cuban hospital ship that visits for 3–4 months and conducts surgeries.

The Gambia Health Care Charity is a project-based organization and international NGO that seeks to meet the overlooked gaps in the public health-care system by providing equipment and staff. The charity consists of UK NHS professionals who seek to combine their local knowledge with what they have learned from the UK and those working in the Gambian system. The project started when founders were sent images via social media about how bad some of the facilities were. The members also get requests for donations and help individually. The team formed a WhatsApp group and held initial discussions to create a charitable entity that grew to 90 members who support the delivery of projects in the Gambia. An executive committee performs decision-making and several subcommittees that support the delivery of specific projects. As a registered charity, the organization has to report to the UK commission on financial and purchasing matters.

The team rarely does formal impact measurement outside of occasional surveys and prefers to do qualitative engagement with hospital managers and other stakeholders such as government ministers. The organization tends to focus on system-level interventions that improve individual well-being that may have been overlooked by other support institutions, which can have a significant impact. For example, workers at a mental health hospital did not have a place to keep their personal belongings, which resulted in the theft of items. While this seems a relatively minor issue, the impact on staff reduced their ability to provide care. The team obtained lockers that improved worker well-being and, ultimately, the performance of the staff. Another project was repairing the roof of a hospital where leaks were causing damage.

The team believes that there is a need to address these issues to resolve the problems and increase dignity for staff and health-care workers. By leaving problems to persist, the team believes that health-care stakeholders get the impression that they are of lesser worth. While citizens are using social media to highlight issues with the system, the responses are reactive.

There is also an economic incentive to engage with these issues as shortages in the hospital system require relatives of patients to buy food and toiletries. The team also performs follow-up to ensure that items are distributed, and project outputs are utilized. The team also uses the connections established via skills transfer to ensure that the items requested are needed. "What we always do before we embark on anything, is to contact the local professionals (the nurses or whoever) and ask. . . okay, what's going on"?

The team recognizes that multiple charities are attempting to assist, ensuring that efforts are not duplicated. The team also has to avoid particular projects since, based on local knowledge, the outcomes are likely failure. For example, the team prefers to replace rather than repair electrical items since replacement is more useful due to the difficulty of obtaining spare parts and skilled personnel.

The network also seeks to improve the well-being of its participants, guiding career support and personal management. In addition to local private providers, residents may also send their family members to nearby Senegal if they can afford it. The country has also recently begun discussing a proposed health insurance scheme met with skepticism since it is not entirely certain what additional services would be obtained from the existing health system.

9.6 Tensions and Paradoxes in Responsible PM in Health Systems

These case studies illustrate the complex context, tensions and paradoxes that influence the delivery of health projects. In both cases, health-care projects are knowledge-intensive and engage stakeholders with differing goals. In addition to the obvious technical challenges of treatment or drug development, both a macro- and a meso-context influence micro-project delivery. At the macro-level, the more prominent trends around the need to provide services to an aging population have increased service expectations as well as expectations of care that have increased over time as treatments have improved life expectancies. Furthermore, quality management systems have ensured consistency of care. Unlike in the past, care recipients are increasingly vocal and will use tools such as social media to highlight issues with care. Expectations due to increased knowledge of new and potential treatments across health systems may increase the external pressures on the health-care service. While we choose to focus only on a single trend (aging) in this chapter, these areas are important and influence project delivery.

A related issue is the multitemporal nature of health-care stakeholders. For example, public sector stakeholders may have long-term orientation, NGOs may have project temporal horizons due to funding, while private stakeholders may have quarterly financial targets. Private sector participants, including publicly traded organizations and independent contractors and private practices, have particular views on their role in health care and different temporal orientations based on financial dictates. Private sector organizations may have to respond to market dictates that happen quarterly. This results in a complex situation because these health-care participants do not share common goals and do not necessarily have the same ideology about how profit relates to public care. Individual concerns may be overlooked or relegated to a customer role in which participants in the health systems are recipients, not co-creators of care.

These negotiations present a tension or paradox that influences project delivery which provides sociotechnical complexity based on the roles of the public versus private stakeholders will not be easily resolved in the short term and will shape how projects are delivered. Geographic fragmentation requires strong systems to capture and transfer learning across projects. Technology, including analytics and AI, has been postulated as a response that suggests increased levels of technology not just in outputs but in project controls. These approaches can incorporate analysis of past project performance to identify areas that might be high cost, variability, or poor delivery. In addition to developing predictive approaches to project management based on the archive of previously completed health projects, they may also support the facility to learn from the multiple ongoing projects in a health-care system to adapt practice or minimize challenges for the future. New projects will be linked to analytical approaches based on digitizing text or learning from video and audio interactions among project teams that can help guide project delivery. The learning process will be new ways of visualizing data and presenting data that can be absorbed by complex stakeholders who do not share similar orientations, such as public-private community stakeholders and religious organizations.

Responsible project managers must navigate these complex dynamics while still meeting long-term goals. For project managers in health-care scenarios, some responsibilities need to be considered, such as governance. Specifically, the interaction among these participants can result in emergent ambiguities where a given stakeholder is unclear on the actions and intent. There is a need to design governance structures that facilitate the input of multiple stakeholders at a participant level who have different goals and at the community level who have different goals, so both internal and external stakeholders have differing and, in some cases, contradictory goals, and governance structures have to be designed appropriately. Further, these structures need to be dynamic because the nature of health and social care is that crises may emerge that require immediate responses in addition to long-term challenges. These influences shape project governance activities and may require the design of project organizing structures that acknowledge these differences and the need for alignment.

In each of the cases, the alignment of organizations was done in a very different manner. The first experimentation was encouraged to allow participants to play to their strengths. To respond to a multifaceted issue such as aging, the organization supported the development of a response using a portfolio approach to fund multiple projects to achieve a common good. In the second case, alignment was done top-down by the overall goal of vaccines in a certain percentage of the population and the state-funded multiple interventions all aligned to that goal. Further, the nature of crises is dynamic and subject to change. For example, with the Covid response, the emergence of new variants required the UK to adapt strategy and hence projects. In the final case, a nonstate actor, the diasporic Gambian charity, aimed at supporting individuals in a health context. The challenge of capturing this learning and transforming it into usable advice in the short term is difficult for most health-care systems. In systems with higher levels of public participation, these approaches may be possible, but more fragmented systems with a much higher level of private participation, such as the US system; therefore, learning from these is far more complex, which will present additional tensions and paradoxes.

References

Ansell, C., Boin, A., & Keller, A. (2010). Managing transboundary crises: Identifying the building blocks of an effective response system. *Journal of Contingencies and Crisis Management, 18*(4), 195–207.

Bingham, K. (2021). The UK Government's Vaccine Taskforce: Strategy for protecting the UK and the world. *The Lancet, 397*(10268), 68–70.

Clark, W. C., & Harley, A. G. (2020). Sustainability science: Toward a synthesis. *Annual Review of Environment and Resources, 45*, 331–386.

Collier, J. (2006, June). Conditions for fully autonomous anticipation. *AIP Conference Proceedings, 839*(1), 282–289. American Institute of Physics.

Collier, J. D., & Hooker, C. A. (1999). Complexly organised dynamical systems. *Open Systems & Information Dynamics, 6*(3), 241–302.

Daniel, P. A., & Daniel, C. (2018). Complexity, uncertainty and mental models: From a paradigm of regulation to a paradigm of emergence in project management. *International Journal of Project Management, 36*(1), 184–197.

Forbat, L., Hubbard, G., & Kearney, N. (2009). Patient and public involvement: Models and muddles. *Journal of Clinical Nursing, 18*(18), 2547–2554.

Fuchs, C. (2003). Structuration theory and self-organisation. *Systemic Practice and Action Research, 16*(2), 133–167.

Goddard, M., & Mason, A. R. (2017). Integrated care: A pill for all ills?. *International Journal of Health Policy and Management, 6*(1), 1.

Gov.UK. (2020). https://www.gov.uk/government/publications/regulatory-approval-of-pfizer-biontech-vaccine-for-covid-19

Government of New Brunswick. (2018). https://www2.gnb.ca/content/gnb/en/news/news_release.2018.06.0822.html

Hardy, B & Rhodes, R 2003, 'Beliefs and institutional change: the UK National Health Service', in Holland, I & Fleming, J (eds), Government reformed: values and new political institutions, Ashgate, Aldershot.

Himmelstein, D. U., Campbell, T., & Woolhandler, S. (2020). Health care administrative costs in the United States and Canada, 2017. *Annals of Internal Medicine, 172*(2), 134–142.

Nolte, E. Evidence supporting integrated care In: Amelung, V, Stein, V, Goodwin, N, Balicer, R, Nolte, E and Suter, E (eds.), Handbook integrated care, 2017; 25–38. Cham: Springer; DOI: 10.1007/978-3-319-56103-5_2

Nolte, E. (2021). Evidence supporting integrated care. In *Handbook integrated care* (pp. 39–52). Cham: Springer.

Nolte, I. M., & Boenigk, S. (2013). A study of ad hoc network performance in disaster response. *Nonprofit and Voluntary Sector Quarterly, 42*(1), 148–173.

Pich, M. T., Loch, C. H., & Meyer, A. D. (2002). On uncertainty, ambiguity, and complexity in project management. *Management Science, 48*(8), 1008–1023.

Martin, D., Miller, A. P., Quesnel-Vallée, A., Caron, N. R., Vissandjée, B., & Marchildon, G. P. (2018). Canada's universal healthcare system: Achieving its potential. *The Lancet, 391*(10131), 1718–1735.

Renedo, A., Marston, C. A., Spyridonidis, D., & Barlow, J. (2015). Patient and public involvement in healthcare quality improvement: How organisations can help patients and professionals to collaborate. *Public Management Review, 17*(1), 17–34.

Scott-Young, C. M., Georgy, M., & Grisinger, A. (2019). Shared leadership in project teams: An integrative multilevel conceptual model and research agenda. *International Journal of Project Management, 37*(4), 565–581.

Senkubuge, F., Modisenyane, M., & Bishaw, T. (2014). Strengthening health systems by health sector reforms. *Global Health Action, 7*(1), 23568.

Tardieu, H., Daly, D., Esteban-Lauzán, J., Hall, J., & Miller, G. (2020). Case study 2: the digital transformation of health-care. In *Deliberately digital* (pp. 237–244). Springer, Cham Switzerland.

Valentijn, P. P., Ruwaard, D., Vrijhoef, H. J. M. et al. Collaboration processes and perceived effectiveness of integrated care projects in primary care: a longitudinal mixed-methods study. BMC Health Serv Res 15, 463 (2015). https://doi.org/10.1186/s12913-015-1125-4

Weber, E. P., & Khademian, A. M. (2008). Wicked problems, knowledge challenges, and collaborative capacity builders in network settings. *Public Administration Review, 68*(2), 334–349.

While, E., & Olivier, J. (2020). Social values and health systems in health policy and systems research: A mixed-method systematic review and evidence map. *Health Policy and Planning, 35*(6), 735–751.

Wright, S., Durán, A. (2020). Business Models and Hospitals. In: Durán, A., Wright, S. (eds) *Understanding Hospitals in Changing Health Systems*. Palgrave Macmillan, Cham. https://doi.org/10.1007/978-3-030-28172-4

Rich Maltzman and Luigi Morsa

10 Lessons Learnt from Irresponsibility in Project Management

Context: This chapter examines the role of a project manager in projects where there is a disconnect between an organization's long-range intent and initiatives driven by short-term outcomes, using two cases that had disastrous results.

Characters and entities: Two companies – one from the aircraft industry and one from the energy industry – provide the backdrop. Regulators, unions, and end customers are also key actors.

Locations: Cases are drawn from a US-based multinational aircraft manufacturer which had crashes in Indonesia and Ethiopia and from a regulated US energy provider which had a major incident in Massachusetts, USA.

Research gaps: The chapter encourages project managers to take on a more significant leadership role in situations where the truth must be spoken to power. Real cases help fill the gap and illustrate the need for this to happen.

Challenges: Two critical tensions are featured: (1) tensions between organizational imperatives and individual responsibility, and (2) tensions between a broad technical orientation versus one focused on specific project outcomes.

Keywords: leadership, outcomes, Boeing, Columbia Gas, responsibility, disaster

10.1 Introduction

Projects are unique (Wiewiora et al., 2009). That simple fact motivates project managers to learn from previous projects. Carole Osterweil wrote a short, compelling article about this, called "How to Walk in Fog" (Osterweil, 2018), which deals with the neuroscience behind managing projects under uncertain conditions.

As project managers – or better yet, as project *leaders* – it is the authors' opinion that we can clear that fog by using lessons learnt from previous projects, which, although not identical, still offer us best practices and areas for improvement. As educators, we have found that case studies expedite learning, so we have chosen case studies to convey this knowledge. This chapter focuses on those "areas for improvement" based on two recent projects with disastrous results that have become notorious.

It is not our intent to blame or single out the organizations or individuals within the organizations we discuss here. We acknowledge that the project managers and organizations we discuss here dealt with significant uncertainty inherent in their

https://doi.org/10.1515/9783110724783-013

industries. Our singular aim here is to highlight the lessons learnt from these disasters to help project managers enhance their level of responsibility and to have them realize that they may have more power than they think in avoiding these disastrous results, even if the results may not be as striking in their projects as the two we have chosen. (Wiewiora et al., 2009) in their research maintain that "One way to ensure effective knowledge transfer across projects is to document and transfer lessons learned beyond the project. Lessons learnt are the key project experiences, which have general business relevance for future projects." We hope that the lessons learnt here will steer project managers toward responsibility and enable them to steer their organizations toward more successful outcomes, even advancing from project managers to project *leaders* focused on *delivering value in its most broad, most durable sense.*

The two project cases we will discuss are Boeing's introduction of the 737 Max aircraft and the Columbia Gas of Massachusetts (CGM) pipeline replacement project in the Merrimack Valley of Massachusetts, USA. These projects are from two different industries with radically different scope, size, complexity, and geography. However, in our opinion, they share essential characteristics in the area of responsibility in project management and, taken together, provide insight and lessons learnt for *all* project managers in any organization.

10.2 Project Case 1: The Launch of the Boeing 737 Max

The Boeing 737 Max aircraft has suffered a significant loss of brand reputation (Light, 2019) due to two recent disasters, namely:
- in October 2018, Lion Air Flight 610 crashed just minutes after taking off from Jakarta, Indonesia, killing 189 people;
- in March 2019, another 737 Max, Ethiopian Airlines Flight 302, crashed minutes after takeoff; all 157 people on board died.

According to the US Federal Government (DeFazio and Larsen, 2020), a software-based system known as the Maneuvering Characteristics Augmentation System (MCAS) erroneously activated the maneuver to prevent the wing's stall[1] and it sent the planes into irrecoverable nose dives. Aside from the significant loss of life and brand reputation, Boeing also made a US \$2.5B "criminal monetary amount"

---

1 A stall is a condition in aerodynamics and aviation such that if the angle of attack increases beyond a certain point, then lift begins to decrease. The angle at which this occurs is called the critical angle of attack.

payment in an agreement with the Government of the United States (US Justice Department, 2021).

It is important to note that this chapter segment is not meant to delve deeply into the *technical* root causes of these two crashes, nor is it meant to attempt to assign responsibility. Instead, it intends to highlight and analyze essential lessons learnt *from a project management point of view*. We recommend that project managers consider applying these lessons inside and outside the aircraft industry. Even though it happened *within* that industry, the authors assert that the lessons can be transposed *across industries*.

Boeing's 737 and Airbus' A320 aircraft families[2] are the two leading players in the massive – and highly profitable – market for narrow-body passenger jets.[3] Together, these two models comprise nearly half of the world's 28,000 commercial airliners (The Boeing Company, 2020; Airbus, 2020), and both manufacturers are locked in a race to make their airplanes cheaper for airlines to operate, especially when it comes to the most significant contributor of cost to the airlines: the fuel (Campbell, 2019). To illustrate this significance, in 2018, the fleet of the world's largest low-cost carrier, Southwest Airlines (consisting of 751 Boeing 737 aircraft), burned 2.1 billion gallons (Southwest media, 2019) of fuel at an average cost of $2.20 per gallon for a total of $4.6 billion. A *1 per cent increase in fuel efficiency* would save $46 million (Campbell, 2019).

On December 1, 2010, Airbus stunned the aviation community. In secret, it had planned and executed a project to produce a more efficient version of the A320 called the A320neo with "neo" having the double meaning of "new" and the acronym "New Engine Option." It would burn about 6% less fuel than Boeing's current 737NG (Campbell, 2019).

Airlines loved the "neo." The following summer, at the 2011 Paris Air Show, the aerospace industry's showcase and sales event, Airbus sold a record-setting 667 A320neos weekly (Airbus press releases, 2011), more orders than the 737s had received in 2010 (Boeing news release, 2011).

In the face of the existential threat from the A320neo, Boeing's executives quickly decided to respond by launching a project to create a fourth-generation 737 called the 737MAX and would do this in record time (Campbell, 2019). The *schedule* became the primary constraint. The authors' opinion is that the project management team failed to look at anything broader (more holistically) than the launch of the 737 Max and limited their view to the launch date.

---

2 Airbus "A320 Family" is meant to include A318/A319/A320/A321, while the "737 MAX family" includes 737 MAX 7, 737 MAX 8, and 737 MAX 9.

3 A narrow-body or single-aisle aircraft is an airliner arranged along a single aisle permitting up to 6-abreast seating in a cabin below 4 m (13 ft) in width. In contrast, a wide-body aircraft is a larger airliner usually configured with multiple aisles and a fuselage diameter of more than 5 m (16 ft), allowing at least 7-abreast seating and often more travel classes.

The project management team was severely constrained – and not only by time. Senior management also required that this new design would not require pilot training. This plays very heavily into the story, as you will see below.

Boeing wanted to use an existing, already-certified mechanical structure – with the "only" changes being the new engines and avionics. This would mean that Boeing could avoid the time-consuming certification process required for a redesigned airplane (Palmer, 2020). The challenge for Boeing was to develop an aircraft that was remarkably more fuel-efficient than the existing Boeing 737 NG. To help accomplish this, Boeing installed larger, more fuel-efficient engines (the LEAP engine) on the 737 Max (Gelles et al., 2019).

The existing engines on the 737 NG aircraft were located under the wings and, in their current configuration, were already positioned relatively low to the ground. As a result, there was not enough ground clearance to simply swap out the old engines and replace them with new, larger, more efficient ones (Vartabedian, 2019). Airbus had existing ground clearance to work with, so Airbus did not encounter the same issue (Figure 10.1). Boeing's solution was to extend the engine up and well in front of the wing (Figure 10.2).

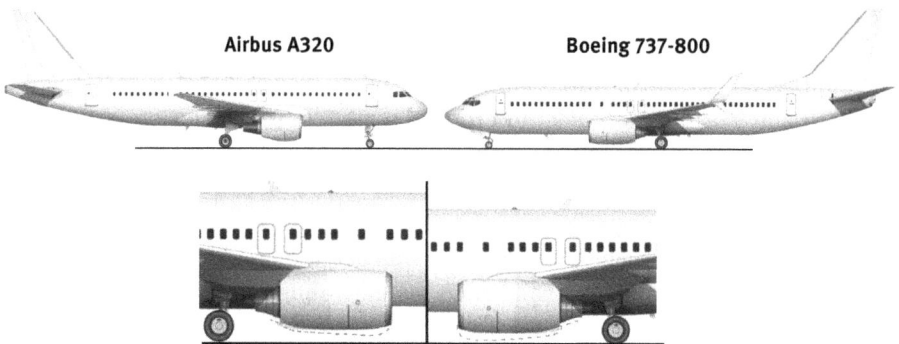

Figure 10.1: Airbus A320 versus Boeing 737-800 – engine location (the dotted line shows a profile of a larger engine and ground clearance).

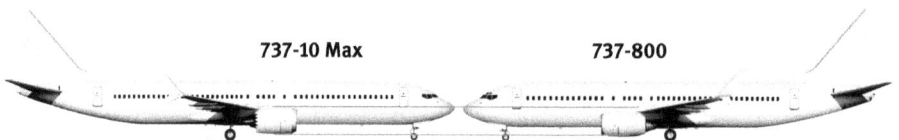

Figure 10.2: Location and height of the new fuel-efficient engine (the LEAP engine) in the Boeing 737 Max in comparison with a former Boeing 737 version.

This new configuration was tested in 2012 using a scale model in Boeing's wind tunnel in Seattle. When the data were analyzed, according to an engineer involved in the testing, there was an issue to address. *Engineers observed a tendency for the plane's nose to pitch upward*, which in some situations could put the aircraft into a "stall" condition (Gates and Baker, 2019). The wing no longer generates the lift force needed to keep the plane airborne – which causes the stall condition. Therefore, to remedy this situation, an automated flight control system named "Maneuvering Characteristics Augmentation System (MCAS)," referred to in the remainder of the chapter as simply the MCAS system was designed and implemented in the 737 Max. The MCAS system processes data provided by an angle-of-attack (AOA) sensor placed at the nose of the plane (Devine and Griffin, 2019). The MCAS system adjusts the angle of the tail stabilizer to counteract the "nose-up tendency" of the new engine configuration (Figure 10.3). In other words, MCAS would automatically *force the plane's nose down* when it determined it to be appropriate. However, if the data provided by the AOA sensor is incorrect, or the MCAS system has a general failure, the nose of the plane could be forced down *inappropriately*, leading to a rapid descent and possible crash *if the pilot does not intervene*. It should be stressed that timely pilot intervention could reverse the rapid descent. This, in turn, requires that the pilots know about MCAS and have to be trained as to how to respond.

Horizontal Tail Maneuver

Figure 10.3: The two vertical contrary arrows or equivalently the upper curved arrow indicate the opposing (clockwise) moment induced by MCAS software – by controlling the horizontal tail position.

In the authors' opinion – and that of investigators (DeFazio and Larsen, 2020), the pilot needs to know that (1) MCAS exists, (2) the purpose of the system, and (3) how to defeat its actions if it has been triggered inappropriately. MCAS is a much less expensive solution – and importantly, a much less time-consuming solution – than extensively modifying the airframe to accommodate the larger engines. This is because such an airframe modification would have required additional (expensive) changes, such as longer landing gear (which might not then fit in the fuselage when retracted) and more wing dihedral (upward bend) (Travis, 2019). Early signs were encouraging. Two years into development, Boeing promised (Boeing news release/statements, 2013) that the 737 Max would be 13% more fuel-efficient than most current efficient single-aisle aeroplanes (including the newest 737s). In 5½ years, the US Federal Aviation Authority (FAA) granted the Max its Amended Type Certification.

The impact of the Boeing 737 Max was immediate. In 2010, the Airbus A320neo was placed on the market with 30 orders; the Boeing 737 Max was also introduced in 2011, and the orders at that time were 1081 and 150 for Airbus A320neo and Boeing 737 Max, respectively, but in 2012 the Boeing 737 Max surpassed its competitor with 908 orders to 378 for Airbus A320neo (The Boeing Company, 2020; Airbus, 2020).

10.2.1 Boeing 737 Max Accidents

In the picture the time us given in UTC, therefore better to write on October 29, 2018, at 6: 20 a.m. local time (Universal Time Coordinated+7)., Lion Air flight 610 took off from Jakarta, Indonesia. But immediately after flight 610 took off, warning signals in the cockpit alerted the pilots that the plane might be stalling. The pilots could determine neither the plane's speed nor altitude, and they told air traffic controllers that they felt the nose of the aircraft was being pulled downward. The aircraft crashed 12 min after takeoff, killing all 189 people aboard (Palmer, 2020). In Figure 10.4 – which shows the elevation overtime (UTC) at the critical timeframes – it is well evident how the pilot struggled against the MCAS before the crash.

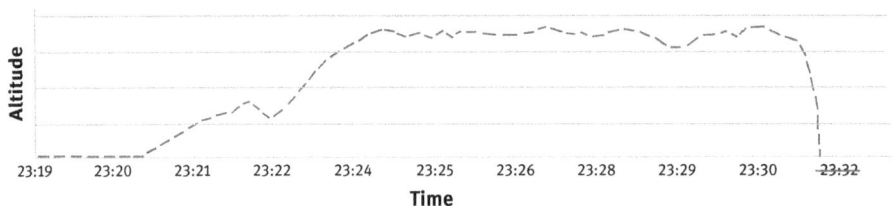

Figure 10.4: Altitude versus time for the last minutes of Lion Air flight 610 *(Komite Nasional Keselamatan Transportasi (K.N.K.T.), Republic of Indonesia (Tjahjono, 2018).*

The same plane, just the day before, had suffered the same issue, but fortunately, a third pilot, who *happened to be on board*, correctly diagnosed the problem and told the crew to cut power to the motor in the trim system that was driving the nose down and save the plane. By contrast, the crew on the flight that crashed the next day did not have this advice and *did not know how to respond* to the malfunction (Levin and Suhartono, 2019).

Within days of the Lion Air crash, Boeing deployed account representatives worldwide to shore up confidence in the Max. They succeeded: Boeing announced new orders from multiple airlines between November 2018 and March 2019 and even managed to talk Lion Air out of canceling its *own* $5 billion order. The Max continued to fly (Campbell, 2019). Then, on March 10, 2019, disaster struck again. ET-AVJ (Flight 302), another 737 Max owned by Ethiopian Airlines, took off from Addis Ababa, Ethiopia, bound for Nairobi, Kenya. Two minutes into the flight, MCAS activated, pitching the nose downward. The pilots soon regained control of the plane, but MCAS started a second time. The aircraft crashed 6 min into the flight, killing all 157 people on board (Palmer, 2020).

On March 13, 2019, the FAA grounded the airplane. Boeing CEO Dennis A.Muilen-burg admitted that MCAS was directly responsible for both crashes and promised that Boeing would fix its broken system. "It's our responsibility to eliminate this risk," he said. "We own it, and we know how to do it" (Campbell, 2019). The authors' opinion is that this is another way of saying that the behavior we must change is in our risk identification and response, improved stakeholder engagement, and the overall leadership role that project leaders should take in selecting and managing projects. We see a broader and longer term view of risk planning, *which includes how pilots would truly be interacting with MCAS in operation,* as critical.

After the second crash, the US House Committee on Transportation and Infrastructure started to conduct a deep investigation that lasted 18 months. A detailed report about the design, development, and certification of the 737 MAX aircraft and related tragic matters was produced (DeFazio and Larsen, 2020). The conclusions made by the Committee were quite serious:

> The MAX crashes were not the result of a singular failure, technical mistake, or mismanaged event. They were the horrific culmination of a series of faulty technical assumptions by Boeing's engineers, a lack of transparency on the part of Boeing's management, and grossly insufficient oversight by the FAA – the pernicious result of regulatory capture on the part of the FAA concerning its responsibilities to perform robust oversight of Boeing and to ensure the safety of the flying public.

The Boeing Company, which stated that it cooperated fully and extensively with the Committee's inquiry since it began in early 2019, hurried to declare the following:

> We have learned many hard lessons as a company from the accidents of Lion Air Flight 610 and Ethiopian Airlines Flight 302 and from the mistakes we have made. As this report recognises, we have made fundamental changes to our company and continue to look for ways to improve. Change is always hard and requires daily commitment, but we are dedicated to doing the work.
> (Boeing Communications, 2020)

Note the recognition by Boeing of the transformative nature of improvements needed. In the authors' opinion, the changes would – in a significant way – manifest themselves in lessons learnt for project managers and project management methods, tools, and artifacts.

The Committee's 238-page report identified five central project-centric themes that affected the design, development, and certification of Boeing's 737 MAX and FAAs oversight. These themes include the following, among others.

10.2.2 Faulty Design and Performance Assumptions

Boeing made fundamentally faulty project assumptions about critical technologies on the 737 MAX, most notably with MCAS. Based on these faulty assumptions, Boeing permitted MCAS – a system designed to automatically push the airplane's nose down in certain conditions – to activate input from a *single AOA sensor.* It also expected that pilots, *who were largely unaware that MCAS even existed*, would be able to recognize and calmly manually mitigate any potential malfunction in a minimal amount of time. Boeing also failed to classify MCAS as a safety-critical system, which attracted greater FAA scrutiny during the certification process.

10.2.2.1 Production Pressures

There was tremendous financial pressure on Boeing and the 737 MAX project to compete with Airbus' new A320neo aircraft. This pressure resulted in extensive efforts to cut costs, maintain the 737 MAX program schedule, and avoid slowing the 737 MAX production line.

10.2.2.2 Culture of Concealment

Boeing withheld crucial information from the FAA, its customers, and 737 MAX pilots in several critical instances. This included concealing the very existence of MCAS from 737 MAX pilots and failing to disclose that the AOA Disagree alert was inoperable on the vast majority of the 737 MAX fleet, despite having been certified as a standard aircraft feature. The AOA Disagree alert is intended to notify the crew if the aircraft's two AOA sensor readings disagree, an event that can occur if one sensor is malfunctioning or providing incorrect AOA data. Boeing concealed this information from both the FAA and pilots and continued to deliver MAX aircraft to its customers, knowing that the AOA disagree alert was inoperable on most of these aircraft. This fits very neatly under the category of open and honest communications – a well-known core attribute of successful and responsible projects (reference: *Responsible Management Handbook*).

Could the project manager have made a difference? In the authors' opinion, yes – if the PM and their team had been aware of the impact of these assumptions about the MCAS technology, and if they had been more willing to "speak truth to power" about the implications of these assumptions being incorrect, these disasters could have been avoided (as discussed in the next section). It is really about the project manager taking on the role of project leader and being in tune with Boeing's higher level mission/vision/values – aware of the critical outcome of the 737 MAX project, but not in "standalone" mode. Instead, the 737 MAX project is one means to a much larger corporate.

10.2.3 Aspects of Responsible Project Management

One can see from the findings that this disaster contains elements much broader than project management. However, it is the opinion of the authors that the project managers could have and should have made a difference. This section presents details about the most critical project management aspects of the 737 Max launch and presents recommendations for project managers.

10.2.3.1 Agile Application

Boeing embraced Agile concepts to reduce cost and schedule risks during 2009. As reported in the Boeing *Frontiers* magazine of February 2009 (Ivanis, 2009) at SeaTac (Seattle, Washington State), engineers from the Material and Process Technology (M&PT) group working for the Boeing 777 program started to use agile development methods to design and implement solutions faster and more efficiently than ever before. Larry Hazlehurst, an engineer at M&PT, declared: "Agile development is a methodology that promotes rapid turnaround, iterations, teamwork, collaboration and process adaptability throughout the life cycle. It works especially well in rapidly changing environments or where requirements are not well-defined."

A critical quality element to a successful agile implementation is connecting the development team to the end-users – directly and early on. In this regard, Hazlehurst declared: "With agile, we get our first iteration done quickly and then keep improving it with the customer's input." Based on the Boeing 737 Max events, there are the symptoms and behaviors of a weak agile adaptation (Flikop, 2019). In other words, the agile approach, which in the case of software development is aimed at better satisfying the end-users requests, should have facilitated the identification of critical failures that could have been encountered during the flight operations. It is reasonable to maintain that *if the software development team had spent more time with the pilots, they would have understood how their users, the pilots, do their work.* They would have elicited User Stories (Atlassian, 2021) such as:

> As a pilot, I want to understand automatic system operations and know-how to defeat them if needed so that I can prevent them from taking inappropriate action.

The authors strongly recommend that readers watch the recent Netflix documentary "Downfall," which thoroughly covers the entire Boeing 737 Max story, and in particular, focuses on the failure of Boeing to involve and inform one set of key users – the pilots – in the design and implementation of MCAS.

The authors' opinion is that how pilots would interface with MCAS would have allowed the project team to make different design decisions, run more realistic tests, create better documentation, and develop training informed by the pilot's current practices. The pilots, clearly primary stakeholders, and users of the plane's hardware and software were not told about the system (Innovel International Inc., 2019). Although beyond the scope of this chapter, it is worth noting that these are key themes from DevOps,[4] bringing customers (pilots in this case) earlier into testing (Harvard Business Review, 2019).

The way Agile was applied was not the reason for the crashes. However, if it had been adopted and managed more effectively, the authors' opinion is that it would have contributed to delivering a better-quality product and would have advised top management more clearly and at an earlier stage about the risk of using MCAS as it was first developed. Different decisions could have been made had the Agile practice taken the pilots' (end-users) input into consideration. The project and program managers play a crucial role to make this happen. Project managers coordinate activities; they have direct contact with employees from multiple "silos" (Figure 10.5), working "horizontally". Above all, they also operate vertically in the corporate pyramid. This should allow and empower them to bring high-impact risks to senior management's attention at an early enough timeframe.

Figure 10.5: Organizational silos.

---

4 A compound of development (Dev) and operations (Ops), DevOps, is the union of people, processes, and technology to provide value to customers continually.

What does DevOps mean for teams? DevOps enables formerly siloed roles – development, IT operations, quality engineering, and security – to coordinate and collaborate to produce better, more reliable products. (Microsoft: https://azure.microsoft.com/en-us/overview/what-is-devops/).

10.2.4 Project Leaders' Unawareness of Technical Issues and Profit's Priority

In a transcribed interview with the US House Committee on Transportation and Infrastructure staff, Michael Teal, who served as Vice President and 737 MAX Chief Project Engineer from August 2011 to March 2017, acknowledged that when he approved the MCAS redesign in March 2016, he was unaware of the following critical technical project attributes:

1. that MCAS operated from a single AOA sensor,
2. that MCAS could activate repeatedly, or
3. Boeing had internal test data showing that one of its test pilots took more than 10 s to react to undesired MCAS activation in a flight simulator and described the results as "catastrophic."

In the interview, Mr. Teal explained that he was "responsible for the requirements, the configuration, the design, the testing, the certification and overseeing any issues in the build process, mainly the engineering work." Nevertheless, while serving in that position, "no employees report[ed] to me. . . . . no engineers directly report[ed] to me," he said. "They all are functionally aligned to the engineering leaders of the company." According to Mr. Teal, the structural engineers reported to the structural engineering Integrated Product Team (IPT) lead. For example, the propulsion experts reported up through the propulsion IPT leader (DeFazio and Larsen, 2020).

The highly "functional" reporting structure organization described by Mr. Teal is quite understandable and familiar. It is also quite common practice that a project leader lacks direct authority over all the company engineers. However, it is essential that the project and engineering leaders, as soon as they are informed about potentially disastrous outcomes, have the culture and encouragement to speak truth to power and escalate such issues. As we discuss above, in most organizations, the program and project managers also operate vertically in the corporate pyramid; therefore, their role is crucial in these cases. They need to balance the business desires expressed by the board that would like to accomplish the program objective and the risks that some technical decisions bring. It is easy to imagine the difficulties encountered when the program objectives have a high business impact, such as the 737 Max, obtaining maximum Level B[5] (non-simulator) pilot training requirements from the FAA. This would have implied that a pilot with a license for the 737 NG could have been easily (16 h or more minor training requirements)

---

5 The FAA may require five distinct levels of pilot "differences training" for new or derivative aircraft. The differences in training requirements increase from "Level A" to "Level E." According to the FAA, "Level B" differences are those differences in systems, controls, and indicators that have only minor procedural differences (DeFazio and Larsen,2020).

authorized to pilot the 737 MAX. As highlighted in the Committee report, *ensuring that there was no need for pilot simulator training* was a fundamental tenet of Boeing's business strategy for marketing the MAX to airlines. It became a constraint for the project team. Therefore, there were tremendous financial incentives to ensure the MAX program met this goal. In this regard, it is interesting to remember that in December 2011, Boeing agreed to pay Southwest Airlines $1 million per MAX airplane that Boeing delivered to Southwest if its pilots could not operate the 737 NG and 737 MAX interchangeably due to any reason. In addition, if the FAA required more than 10 h of pilot training and/or flight simulator training, Boeing would reimburse SWA for any direct training expense exceeding 10 h (DeFazio and Larsen, 2020).

The US House Committee highlighted the importance of a concern for safety over these business needs:

> Boeing has gone from being a great engineering company to a big business focused on financial success. Continuing on the same path it followed with the 737 MAX, where safety was sacrificed to production pressures, exposes the company to potentially repeating those mistakes and additional reputational damage and financial losses.   (DeFazio and Larsen, 2020)

The financial losses in the case of 737 Max have been estimated at $18.7 billion (Isidore, 2020). This does not cover intangibles such as damage to the brand, employee morale, and the loss of human life suffered by hundreds or thousands of families and friends.

10.3 Role of the Project Manager

This case study gave the authors the chance to underscore the importance of the project manager as a critical actor in orienting a company's decision-making. Regardless of the specific organizational structure of a company, a project manager usually can operate not only in the *horizontal* (across functional organizations, but also in the *vertical* direction in the pyramid organizational structure of a company; in a nutshell, we could say that they can "hear from the bottom and report to the top" (see pyramid organizational structure in Figure 10.6). Indeed, the project manager's stakeholders are, at the same time, the technical team leaders and the guys at the top management level. For this reason, once the technical experts highlight some risks in making decisions, the project manager's task is to collect all the needed information/data and bring good arguments in front of the executives.

Usually, the technical experts are safety-oriented, and they run the risk of "desiring" too much precision in their outputs (computations or products). On the other hand, the attitude of the people who make a business decision in a company is to avoid "wasting" precious time to reach a degree of perfection that most of the time is even not required with the risk of losing good market opportunities, to fall

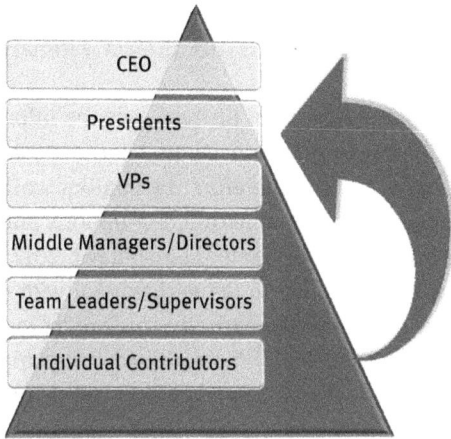

Figure 10.6: Pyramid organizational structure.

behind the competitors. This view is exaggerated for effect, but it is meaningful to understand the different worlds the project manager is immersed in. In any case, the power relationships are not symmetrical because the executives have the last word; therefore, in the case of weighing decisions, such as the level of training required for pilots, it is the task of the project manager to persuade the executives to give more consideration to the points highlighted by technical experts even though these are in contrast with the market opportunities.

To this end, what are the tools available to a project leader in this situation?

The project manager's task is to bring a "good argument" to the senior management or others in authority. It is essential to quantify the risk to provide numbers to do this. In this regard, it is essential to point out that in the case of the aviation industry, Qualitative and Quantitative Methods for Safety Analysis are used, as recommended, for instance, by the Federal Aviation Administration (FAA, 2000). Both methods are included or are "sub-stages" of the so-called risk analysis; a qualitative analysis allows the primary risk sources to be identified, while a quantitative analysis enables the impacts of the risks to be quantified. The output, therefore, is a number obtained most of the time by probabilistic analysis carried out through sophisticated techniques, usually requiring computer software (Norris, 2000). As applied to the project management field, risk elements that concern project management are the following three (Galway, 2004):

– Schedule – will the project be completed within the planned timeframe?
– Cost – will the project be completed within the allocated budget?
– Performance – will the output from the project satisfy the business and technical goals of the project?

These risks should be quantified to enable the project team to develop effective mitigation strategies or include appropriate contingencies in the project estimate (Meyer, 2015).

Once the risk analysis is complete, the risk management process uses the information collected during the risk analysis phase to make decisions (Norris et al., 2000). Each potential decision has a business impact; therefore, estimators work side-by-side with economic or business analysts to determine different options and decide which option supports the organization's strategic goals (El-Mehalawi, 2012). *In the case of the Boeing 737 Max, in retrospect, it is clear to the authors that with a high risk of a catastrophic event, it would have been better to make the trade-off of lost market share by making appropriate changes, such as more thorough and thoughtful training for pilots regarding the MCAS system. In the authors' opinion, there needed to be an improved environment and audience for those concerned about the plane's operation.*

In the end, the project manager has a *strategic* role in synthesizing the work of the technical experts and business analysts and bringing critical issues to the attention of senior management, emphasizing what decisions need to be made and how they connect with the organization's mission, vision, and values – not just the current urgent situation related to (and *limited* to) to the project's financial goals. The crucial role of a project manager as a *leader* and *communicator* is critical here. The authors believe that disasters such as these crashes could have been averted with an increasingly empowered, responsible project leader and communicator. This is further borne out in our second case regarding Columbia Gas of Massachusetts.

10.4 Project Case 2: Columbia Gas of Massachusetts Pipeline Replacement

On September 13, 2018, at approximately 4:00 p.m. EDT, 911 operators, fire stations, and police stations working in the Andover, Lawrence, and North Andover in the Merrimack Valley region of Massachusetts started receiving a flurry of urgent, panicked calls. (WGBH, 2019). The calls ranged from natural gas smells to actual fires and explosions (at least five recorded). The cause: a low-pressure natural gas supply system (0.5 psig 14 in. water column) was overpressurized by at least one order of magnitude. Approximately 8,600 customers were affected. Of these, 131 customers had some type of "extended overpressure event," such as a release of natural gas within their basement (Willey, 2020).

With homes and businesses receiving this highly elevated gas pressure intended for mass distribution, this was a recipe for disaster. Indeed, a young man, Leonel Rondon, died, over 20 people were hospitalized, 50,000 residents (including the author) were evacuated, and at least 130 structures were damaged – from explosions and fires as a direct result of the overpressurization. More than 180 fire departments and over 1,000 law enforcement officers responded to the incident (CNN, 2019).

Figures 10.7 and 10.8, courtesy of *The Lawrence Eagle Tribune Newspaper*, are photographs of the immediate aftermath of the event.

Figure 10.7: Immediate aftermath of the event (courtesy photo by Carl Russo/*The Eagle-Tribune*).

Figure 10.8: Immediate aftermath of the event (courtesy photo by Amanda Sabga/*The Eagle-Tribune*).

Columbia Gas of Massachusetts, a subsidiary of NiSource, Inc. (referred to as CGM for the remainder of this chapter), initiated projects to modernize its distribution system. This is the story behind the project in that program that resulted in the incident. The following set of events led to "overpressurization."

Feeney Brothers Utility Services, an experienced firm that has been subcontracting to utility companies since 1988, had a permit to do work as a subcontractor for CGM to cut into the street in Lawrence, Massachusetts, a 2-foot-wide, 340-foot-long trench. This would complete the main gas tie-ins to help in the overall initiative to replace the century-old iron pipe with new plastic piping. This subcontractor has worked extensively for Columbia Gas and the region's other major natural gas supplier, Eversource. In recent years, gas utilities in Massachusetts have increasingly relied on contractors to carry out projects like this (Penn, 2019).

As part of the project work package, the subcontractor workers removed a section of cast-iron pipe, capped it, and put it aside. The subcontractor is unaware that a gauge that measures gas pressure is attached to the removed pipe section. The subcontractor is doing work directed under a CGM work package and following the work package steps developed by and approved by CGM – but without the on-site presence of anyone from CGM. *There is no mention of the sensor and its importance in the work package*, and the work order was not (as has been done in the past) approved by a professional engineer. In fact, until 4 years before this incident, a technician from CGM's Meter and Regulation Department assigned to the site would have been responsible for monitoring the pressure of the section of the gas main; however, that process was changed (Penn, 2019).

The discarded pipe section – with the attached sensor – *was still measuring gas pressure*. Having been disconnected, it detected a loss of pressure, doing precisely what it was intended to do. It continued to do its job and signal the primary control system to increase the pressure. Regulator valves received the signal and increased the pressure, but the sensor (disconnected) did not see this increase. It saw a *decrease* in pressure. So, it asked for *even more* pressure. The regulator valves responded again to the signal – now opening fully. This caused a high-pressure distribution system that was supposed to be very much a separate system from the residential distribution system to be, in effect, directly connected to the residential system, *raising the pressure on homes and businesses in the area to an order of magnitude over the intended pressure* – for nearly 30 min (NTSB, 2018).

Alarms went off at the NiSource monitoring station in Columbus, Ohio, but the employees and equipment had no way to reduce the pressure remotely; instead, they contacted the Meters and Regulations Group at CGM. The resources at CGM for this response were minimal – there were two inspectors for about 5,000 miles of pipe (Penn, 2019) – to troubleshoot this problem.

While the incident took place, and for several hours, residents of the affected towns, including myself, were uncertain about what was happening around them. Residents became increasingly frustrated in their attempts to find out what to do next for the safety of their families. Neighbors gathered to look for information, which was sparse at first. I experienced this personally, and I was aghast at the lack of responsibility to communicate urgently to residents and business owners. I can say from personal experience that we would have expected that the social media channels of CGM should have been fully dedicated to transparency, explaining what had happened and, more importantly, what action we – the residents and customers of CGM – should take for our safety. It turned out that we *did* need to evacuate the town and found out from the local police – and continued to have almost no advice from CGM. A very realistic readout of what happened during the incident can be found in a four-part podcast series, *"Fire In The Valley,"* produced by Boston public radio station WGBH (WGBH, 2019).

It was nearly 6 months to re-pipe and restored service in the area. The costs – including the injuries and loss of life – are impossible to enumerate. However, CGM did settle a lawsuit for $143M and eventually went bankrupt, with a cost to the parent company NiSource estimated to be over $1B (WBUR, 2020). Columbia Gas of Massachusetts has now been purchased by Eversource (2020) for $1.1B.

10.4.1 Causes as Determined by NTSB Investigation

NTSB investigators learned that (Maltzman, 2021):

> until about four years ago, Columbia Gas required that a technician monitor any gas main revision work which required depressurising the main. The technician – typically from the Meter and Regulation department – would use a gauge to monitor the pressure readings on the impacted main and communicate directly with the crew making the change. If a pressure anomaly occurred, the technician could quickly prevent an over-pressurisation action. Columbia Gas did not explain why this procedure was phased out.

> Although the Columbia Gas monitoring centre in Columbus, Ohio, received high-pressure alarms and reported the event to the Meters and Regulations department two minutes after receiving the first alarm, no technicians were pre-staged or positioned to close valves when the over-pressurisation occurred immediately. Had Columbia Gas adequately performed MOC (Management of Change) and placed personnel at critical points along with the system, Columbia Gas could have immediately addressed the issue and mitigated the event's consequences. Therefore, the NTSB recommends that NiSource apply MOC processes to all changes to identify system threats resulting in a common mode failure. Additionally, the NTSB recommends that NiSource develop and implement control procedures during modifications to gas mains to mitigate the risks identified during MOC operations. Gas main pressures should be continually monitored during these modifications, and assets should be placed at critical locations to shut down the system if abnormal operations are detected immediately.

10.4.2 NTSB Recommendations

In November 2018, the NTSB issued "urgent" safety recommendations (NTSB, 2018). The report contained four recommendations for NiSource, the parent company of Columbia Gas, and one for the state, seeking to eliminate the professional engineer licensure exemption for public utility work and a requirement for a professional engineer's seal on public utility engineering drawings.

The NTSB report recommends NiSource to do the following:

- revise the engineering plan and constructability review process across all subsidiaries;
- review all records and documentation of natural gas systems;
- apply management of change processes to all changes to identify threats that could result in a common mode failure;
- develop and implement control procedures during main gas modifications to mitigate risks.

10.4.3 Aspects of Responsible Project Management

The NTSB recommendations and the lessons learnt literature on this case call for a shift in culture that allows for *devil's advocacy* – an ability to raise an issue with impunity. The "devil's advocate" can be the project manager or a team member. They also call for – in general – a more responsible organizational attitude concerning transparency, including public communications (Maltzman, 2021).

Organizations often need to make tough decisions. Those decisions often involve project processes or policy changes – like the requirement for an on-site CGM supervisor or scaling down inspector teams to skeletal levels, as was done in this case. In the author's opinion, these decisions call for long-term thinking, considering such decisions' social, economic, and ecological effects. The decisions you have read about here may have served CGM for the short term but in the longer term, resulting in death, injuries, damage, and the bankruptcy of their organization.

10.5 Summarizing the Lessons Learned for Project Managers

Although project managers do not necessarily have to be technical experts on all aspects of their project, they *need easy, quick access to a "technical deputy"* (or deputies) that can give them salient facts about crucial project decisions.

Project managers *become project leaders* when they:

- Use a broad, deep, and thoughtful process to identify risks and stakeholders.
- Make themselves *aware of how end-users* (pilots in the Boeing case) and other stakeholders (subcontractors in the Columbia case) *do their work and engage them in the project's planning.*
- Become *highly sensitive to process and policy changes* within their organization and industry and their impact on their projects. For example, if a particular

inspection or training step is decreed "no longer required," understand that yes, this may make the project go more quickly, but the PM should also step back and ask, "what new threats does this change introduce into the project or the project's product or service?"
- Create an environment in which team members can ask helpfully critical questions.

Arm themselves with the proper technical details and *become empowered to "speak truth to power."* This may mean insisting that pilots test the system more thoroughly and ask questions in the Boeing case. "Why are we relying on a single sensor?" "Why is there no mechanism to inform the pilot of the MCAS status better, or to defeat the system if necessary?" In the Columbia case, the project manager may need to ask, "why are there no Columbia Gas personnel on-site to oversee the contractor?" or "why isn't this plan being passed by the Regulator department for validation"?

In most organizations, especially in projects of this size, scope, and importance, the project manager works in more of a matrix organization. This allows them to interact with both technical experts and the top managers, thus making them the best-suited person to take charge of the requests, suggestions, and warnings. It is also their charge, the authors assert, to weigh project outcomes (very little training should be needed) against corporate values (training for pilots is critical in this case for top priority safety reasons).

The project manager must have the capacity to comprehend the impact and context of these warnings, and, above all, the PM needs to excel in the areas of negotiation and persuasion to influence without authority. The quantitative analysis based on experience or the risk scenarios for the future prediction can be of great support to strengthen some arguments.

Finally, the role of the project manager in a global economy with a high level of pressure coming from inside and outside the organization is not only to perform the task of planning, scheduling, and controlling, but to continuously improve processes and highlight risky choices. A project manager can say to themselves that they have done an excellent job only if they can report to high management that they have done due diligence concerning the project's outcome and delivery of value – including safety, impact on the environment, including social aspects of the project's product, and recommend improvements for future projects.

This means that the project manager must cast the vision of the project past the end date of the project, forward – well forward – into the future, when the project's product (a new airplane, a replaced pipeline system, a new coffeemaker, a new house-cleaning service, whatever) is in service. It is not only the time element that should be considered. The project manager (and team) should consider (as above) the project's ecological, social, and economic aspects. By expanding their view – to the long term and the triple bottom line, the project manager does two positive things for their organization. First, they better identify stakeholders and risks because they consider the project's steady state. Secondly, and perhaps more importantly, this expanded viewpoint helps assure that the project's outcome is connected to the organization's mission, vision, and values.

Does this mean that the project manager is responsible for the project's steady state? Doesn't this provide a paradox and create tensions for project managers since they are focused on the project's end date? Indeed, it does. The "tensions project managers experience when addressing sustainable objectives" are real (Sabini and Alderman, 2021). Still, the steady state of the project's outcome should be a consideration that has the advantages listed above.

10.6 The Tensions of Responsible Project Management

As you may have noted in this chapter, some tensions must be productively confronted in projects involving organizational versus individual responsibility and project versus technical responsibility.

10.6.1 Organizational Versus Individual Responsibility

The project management culture, sometimes aided by middle-management incentivization, leads individual project managers to focus only on objectives set out in their project charter, often intentionally or unintentionally being oblivious or blind to the higher level organization's objectives. Those higher level organizational objectives are increasingly linked to the triple bottom line of social, environmental, and economic considerations (Elkington, 1997) or the United Nations Social Development Goals. This bifurcation of drivers "creates a complicated balance of different conflicting objectives" (Sabini and Alderman, 2021). Without the linkage to the higher level objectives, individual project managers' decision-making can falter, resulting in essential project decisions, which are:
– Suboptimized to meet a particular project goal at the expense of missing a larger organizational goal
– Disconnected from the mission, vision, and/or values of the organization
– Rooted in an "us-against-them" philosophy, where often the "us" is the project team (especially a technical project team) and "them" is often a regulatory agency with the good intention of providing social or environmental value

10.6.2 Technical Versus Project Orientation

Technical individuals and teams tend to focus intently on problem-solving. In doing so, they are often not aware of the project or organizational objectives. This can lead to them avoiding safety or sustainability thinking.

Ironically, the *opposite* can occur in some teams, in which the technical contributors are – in some cases – properly obsessed with safety or sustainability issues. There is a tension between "a need to be perfect" (coming from the technical team), and "a need to get the project done" (from the project manager). An example of this is the classic O-ring issue that destroyed the Challenger Space Shuttle in 1986 (McDonald, 2012). McDonald and other engineers wanted the Challenger launch postponed because a critical component of the rocket booster, a rubber "O-ring" gasket, was highly vulnerable to losing its seal at lower temperatures. These gaskets lose effectiveness at temperatures lower than 53 °F. The warnings from the technical team were ignored, the launch took place, and disaster struck 73 s after launch. "Challenger's liftoff occurred at 11:38 that morning. The temperature at the time of the launch was 36 degrees. After the solid rocket motors ignited, a small puff of black smoke was seen near the right solid rocket booster (SRB). Hot gases from the rocket had slipped past the O-rings in two SRB segments" (Stephenson, G., 2021). In the author's opinion, the project manager needs to balance the need to be perfect with the need to get the project done, always considering the broader, more holistic view. In this case, the trade-off (admittedly with hindsight) would favor the crew's safety (to say nothing of the reputation of the US Space Program) over the delay of the launch.

In the cases above, we have also seen that the project manager is unwilling or unable to *process* the sometimes-overwhelming technical details being provided to them and make thoughtful, reasoned, sustainability-oriented decisions. In this author's opinion, this can be remedied with the simple addition of a "technical deputy" for the project manager, whose function is to help transform the technical information into decision-making knowledge so that the project manager can make wiser decisions.

10.6.3 Conclusion

The case examples in this chapter were about projects with disastrous results in which safety became the issue at hand. Disastrous projects were chosen intentionally because there is well-studied, public information available and visible damage (exploded buildings and plane crashes). However, do not make the mistake that this is only about safety. Safety is used as a proxy for holistic, long-term thinking. You can and should apply the same lessons learnt to less obvious, less immediate outcomes, such as impacts on social systems, inclusion, diversity, and the environment. Use these examples to help you and your organization improve your decision-making and elevate your project managers to project leaders.

10.7 Discussion Questions

Think about your organization, industry, or desired area of focus. Can you think of higher quality decisions if holistic, long-term thinking was implemented?

For each, create a table with the short-term benefits, and alongside those, enter the long-term considerations that may make the short-term decisions seem less attractive.

Have there ever been times in which you wanted to – or needed to – speak up about a project or policy decision? If you did, what empowered you to do so? If you did not, what prevented you from doing so? Finally, what would have enabled or encouraged you to raise the issue if not?

Have you seen the tensions we discussed in your organization – tensions between the responsibility of individuals and organizations and the technical and the project manager? How did they resolve or reach some sort of equilibrium?

References and Related Materials

Airbus. *Airbus Orders and Deliveries*. https://Airbus.com, 26 July, 2020.

Airbus press releases. *Airbus with new order record at Paris Air Show 2011*. https://Airbus.com, 23 June, 2011.

Corcoran, Sean (Host). (2019, September 6). WGBH Radio [Audio podcast episodes]. *Fire in the Valley*. https://www.wgbh.org/podcast/wgbh-news-presents-fire-in-the-valley

Levin, A., & Suhartono, H. *Pilot Who Hitched a Ride Saved Lion Air 737 Day Before Deadly Crash*. https://Bloomberg.com, 20 March, 2019.

Andover, M. A. After Action Report. https://www.google.com/url?sa=t&rct=j&q=&esrc=s&source=web&cd=&ved=2ahUKEwjr1f7Yv63uAhW3QzABHXOkBIsQFjAEegQIEBAC&url=https%3A%2F%2Fandoverma.gov%2FDocumentCenter%2FView%2F7038%2FSeptember-2018-Merrimack-Valley-Natural-Gas-Explosion-AAR_MEMA%3FbidId%3D&usg=AOvVaw3skYK9s_QMbI0RiPkbg3h8

Wiewiora, A., Trigunarsyah, B., Murphy, G., Gable, G., & Liang, C. The Impact of Unique Characteristics of Projects and Project-Based Organisations on Knowledge Transfer. Proceedings of the 10th European Conference on Knowledge Management, Academic Publishing Limited, 2009.

Boeing Communications *"Boeing Statement on the House T&I Committee Report on 737 MAX"*, https://boeing.mediaroom.com, 16 September, 2020.

Boeing news release/statements. *Boeing Completes 737 MAX 8 Firm Configuration*. 23 July, 2013.

Boeing news release/statements. *Boeing Hits 2010 Airplane Delivery Target; Achieves Strong Order Bookings*, 6 January, 2011.

Norris, C., Perry, J., & Simon, P. (2000), Buckinghamshire, England. Project risk analysis and management; edited by P. Simon, D. Hillson and K. Newland, published by the Association Of Project Managers.

Isidore, C. *The cost of the Boeing 737 Max crisis: $18.7 billion and counting*. CNN Business, 10 March, 2020.

Palmer, C. *The Boeing 737 Max Saga: Automating Failure*. ScienceDirect Engineering, February 2020.

Competitive Advantage through DevOps: Improving Speed, Quality, and Efficiency in the Digital World, PDF Download available from Harvard Business Review, https://hbr.org/resources/pdfs/comm/google/CompetitiveAdvantageThroughDevOps.pdf

Devine, C., & Griffin, D., Boeing relied on single sensor for 737 Max that had been flagged 216 times to FAA. CNN, 30 April, 2019.

Ivanis, D. *Commercial Airplanes Material and Process Technology engineers use agile development methodology to drive out waste*. Boeing Frontiers magazine, February 2009.

Campbell, D. *The many human errors that brought down the Boeing 737 Max*. https://TheVerge.com, 2 May, 2019.

Gelles, D., Kitroeff, N., Nicas, J., & Ruiz, R. *Boeing Was 'Go, Go, Go' to Beat Airbus With the 737 Max*. New York Times, 23 March, 2019.

Gates, D., & Baker, M. *The inside story of MCAS: How Boeing's 737 MAX system gained power and lost safeguards*. The Seattle Times, 22 June, 2019.

El-Mehalawi, M. E. Project risk analysis to support strategic and project management. Paper presented at PMI® Global Congress 2012 – North America, Vancouver, British Columbia, Canada. Newtown Square, PA: Project Management Institute.

Elkington, J. (1997). *Cannibals with forks: The triple bottom line of twenty-first century business*. Oxford: Capstone.

Flikop, E. *The Risk of Moving to Mature Agile too Fast: a Cautionary Tale*. https://InfosysConsulting.com, 12 June, 2019.

Eversource completes purchase of Columbia Gas of Massachusetts, retrieved from https://www.eversource.com/content/wma/about/news-room/connecticut/newspost?Group=connecticut&Post=eversource-to-acquire-columbia-gas-of-massachusetts-assets-for-1.1-billion

FAA System Safety Handbook, *Chapter 9: Analysis Techniques*. 30 December, 2000.

Fire in the Valley – Podcast – Four episodes.

Galway, L. (2004), Santa Monica, CA. *Quantitative risk analysis for project management: A critical review*. RAND Corporation working paper series. https://www.rand.org/

Travis, G. *How the Boeing 737 Max Disaster Looks to a Software Developer*. IEEE https://Spectrum.com, 18 April, 2019.

https://www.justice.gov/opa/pr/boeing-charged-737-max-fraud-conspiracy-and-agrees-pay-over-25-billion

Innovel International Inc. *How To Avoid Fatal Product Flaws with agile and Scrum? Lessons from Boeing's 737 Max 8 Program*. https://Innovel.net, 16 May, 2019.

Light, L. *Can The Boeing 737 Max Brand Reputation Be Repaired?*. https://Forbes.com, 4 April, 2019.

Maltzman, R. (2021). *Case study for graduate course in project management*. Boston University. Boston, MA.

McDonald, A. J. (2012). *Truth, lies, and O-rings: Inside the space shuttle "Challenger" disaster*. University Of Florida. Gainesville, FL.

Meyer, W. G. Quantifying risk: Measuring the invisible. Paper presented at PMI® Global Congress 2015 – EMEA, London, England. Newtown Square, PA: Project Management Institute.

National Transportation Safety Board, Pipeline Accident Report Overpressurization of Natural Gas
    Distribution System. Explosions and Fires in Merrimack Valley, Massachusetts
    13 September 2018, retrieved from $143 Million Columbia Gas Settlement Gets Final Approval
    From Judge, retrieved from https://www.wbur.org/bostonomix/2020/03/12/143-million-
    columbia-gas-settlement-gets-final-approval-from-judge
Osterweil, C. (2018). How to walk in fog – creating order in an unordered environment. *Developing
    Leaders*. Issue 30, Page 19.
Penn, N. (2019, June 3). "The Day the Town Blew Up", Popular Mechanics, retrieved from
    https://www.popularmechanics.com/technology/infrastructure/a27309627/andover-gas-
    explosion/
DeFazio, P. A. & Larsen, R. *Final Committee Report: Boeing 737 MAX*. The House Committee on
    Transportation and Infrastructure. September 2020.
Vartabedian, R. (2019). How a 50-year-old design came back to haunt Boeing with its troubled 737
    Max jet. *The Los Angeles Times*.
Sabini, L., & Alderman, N. (2021). The paradoxical profession: Project management and the
    contradictory nature of sustainable project objectives. *Project Management Journal*, *52*(4),
    379–393. https://doi.org/10.1177/87569728211007660
Tjahjono, S. Aircraft Accident Investigation Report PT. Lion Mentari Airlines Boeing 737-8 (MAX).
    Komite Nasional Keselamatan Transportasi (KNKT), Republic of Indonesia, 29 October, 2018.
Stephenson, G. (2021.). How weather caused the loss of the Space Shuttle challenger.
    spectrumlocalnews.com. Retrieved June 15, 2022, from https://spectrumlocalnews.com/nc/
    charlotte/weather/2021/01/19/how-weather-caused-the-loss-of-the-space-shuttle-challenger
Southwest media. Southwest Airlines co. 2018 Annual Report to Shareholders. https://investors.
    southwest.com, 25 March, 2019
The Boeing Company. *Boeing 737: Orders and Deliveries (updated monthly)*. https://Boeing.com,
    30 June, 2020.
User Stories, With An Example and a Template, Atlassian, https://www.atlassian.com/agile/
    project-management/user-stories, retrieved 30 Dec, 2021
Video explanation of 737Max Engine changes. [REFERENCE VIDEO https://youtu.be/H2tuKiiznsY]
    (Vox)
Willey, R. (2020). Insights to the Columbia Gas Explosions Lawrence and North Andover,
    MA 13 September 2018. Process Safety Progress. 10.1002/prs.12195.

Greg Usher

11 Responsible Project Management in the Age of Artificial Intelligence

Context: This chapter investigates some potential impacts of artificial intelligence on the profession and practice of project management.

Characters/entities: Due to the expansive and emerging capabilities of artificial intelligence, the profession of project management is the central focus of this chapter.

Locations: The implications of artificial intelligence on our profession are global. No country, company, or practitioner will be immune from the changes this technology will bring.

Research gaps: This chapter challenges project managers to think about the profession of tomorrow. Specifically, what is the future for project management if artificial intelligence can undertake the roles of planning, monitoring, and controlling projects better than humans?

Challenges/conflict/tensions: Artificial intelligence has the potential to impact every project manager on the planet, making it one of the most significant challenges facing our profession in the coming decades. This chapter explores the challenges, conflicts, and tensions our profession may encounter as these technologies become commonplace.

Keywords: AI, creativity, project lifecycles, Industry 4.0

11.1 Introduction

The term "artificial intelligence" will be commonplace to most readers. However, do we understand the potential impacts this technology may have on our profession? This chapter explores what is meant by the term "artificial intelligence" and the impacts these technologies could have on specific tasks in each phase of the project lifecycle.

We then look at some of the challenges, risks, and opportunities these new technologies present to the profession and practice of project management. Finally, this chapter explores responsible project management in the age of artificial intelligence by asking what we should do with this new knowledge.

> We stand on the brink of a technological revolution that will fundamentally alter how we live, work, and relate to one another. In its scale, scope, and complexity, the transformation will be unlike anything humankind has ever experienced before.
>
> Klaus Schwab, Founder and Chairman of the World Economic Forum (2016)

https://doi.org/10.1515/9783110724783-014

The new technical revolution Schwab is describing is the 4th Industrial Revolution, or "Industry 4.0" (Lasi et al., 2014). This revolution, borne out of the digitization age, heralds the rise of smart machines and AI. Nothing in the previous three Industrial Revolutions has prepared humanity for this revolution's impacts. Industry 4.0 is happening now and simultaneously around the globe (Trevelyan, 2018). No country, race, or religion has the advantage, and no industry, sector, or profession will be immune from its impacts.

This revolution is occurring at a phenomenal rate. The breakthroughs and innovations occurring now outpace society's ability to adapt (Wong, 2020). All around the globe, governments, corporations, people, and individuals are racing to understand how these changes will impact legislation, education, ethics, and society in general (Chelvachandran et al., 2020; Rodrigues, 2020). This revolution will redefine the global economic system (Marwala & Hurwitz, 2017) and wealth distribution (Castelluccio, 2019), destroy traditional labor markets, and create new ones (LeVine, 2014). It may even challenge our understanding of what it means to be human (Feuillet, 2019).

The economic impacts of this revolution are staggering. McKinsey Global Institute estimates that AI-related technologies will increase the global GDP by $13 trillion (+16%) within the next decade (Bughin et al., 2018). Up to 30% of jobs across the USA, Germany, and the UK could be made redundant by AI-based technologies by as early as 2030 (PwC, 2018). While deWind (in Trevelyan, 2018) claims that "almost every job where an employee sits in front of a computer screen and either processes or interprets data is at high risk [of being replaced by AI]."

As a profession and a set of competencies, project management will be profoundly affected by Industry 4.0. But are we ready for the changes that this revolution will bring?
- Do we understand the myriad ways in which AI will change us and our role?
- What new opportunities, threats, risks, and benefits will this revolution bring?
- Is our profession one of those AI will annihilate, or will it flourish?
- How should we respond to the tumultuous times ahead?

As challenging and unsettling as these questions are, they are the types of questions that we must answer if we provide responsible project management in the age of AI.

11.2 What Is Artificial Intelligence?

Before answering some of these questions, we need to understand AI. Finding a universally accepted definition of AI is difficult (Paschen et al., 2020). This is because AI is not "one thing." As Figure 11.1 illustrates, AI covers many technologies, from predictive text to artificial neural networks and deep learning (Paschen et al., 2020; Prieto, 2019). However, not all new technology falls into the category of AI. To be classed as AI, a technology must "demonstrate at least some of the following behaviours that are associated with human intelligence: planning, learning, reasoning, problem-solving, knowledge representation, perception . . . and to a lesser extent, social intelligence and creativity" (Heath, 2020). To explain this another way, you engage with advanced computational technology when using Microsoft Excel to quickly calculate large amounts of data. You engage with AI when Google "learns" your search habits and uses predictive text to finish your search requests.

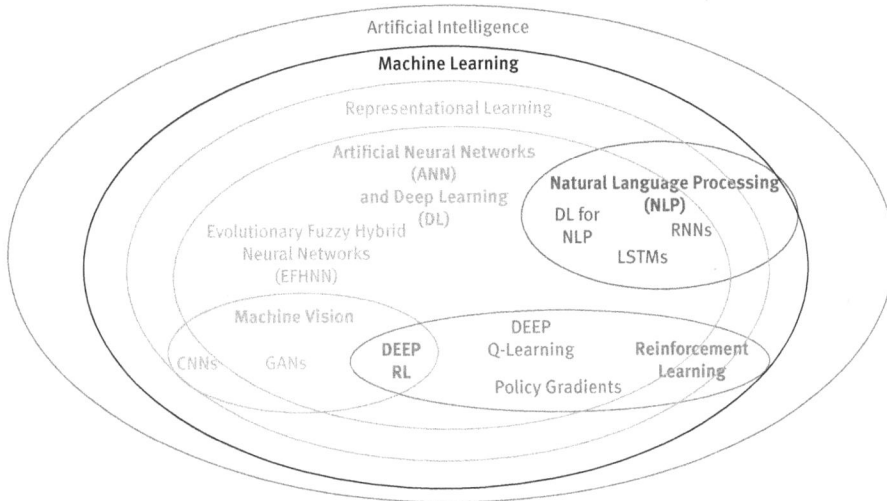

Figure 11.1: Artificial intelligence and its subsets (adapted from Belharet et al., 2020).

Before we can begin a rational discussion regarding AI and its impact on project management, we need to understand two things about AI. First, AI technologies fall along a spectrum. This spectrum ranges from "simple" AI, such as smart home devices, Google maps, and predictive text on your mobile phone, to "'complex" AI, such as artificial neural networks, evolutionary fuzzy hybrid neural networks, and deep machine learning (Davahli, 2020; Patil & Salunkhe, 2020; Woschank et al., 2020). Second, at the time of writing this text, many of us are already, in many cases unconsciously, adopting AI into our daily lives. Furthermore, we have done this for one simple reason – because AI technologies make our lives easier.

11.3 What Is Project Management?

The definitional challenges are not just on the AI side of the equation. Project Management also suffers from its definitional difficulties. As Auth et al. (2019) highlight, "although the basic meaning [of project management] is largely consensual, closer examination opens up a vast and dynamic spectrum of content-related conceptual components . . . such as sub-areas, process models, roles and structures, methods, techniques or types of projects" (p. 28). This diversity remains despite, many years of research and study.

However, like the umbrella definition of AI, project management has also some common ground upon which agreed frameworks can be founded. For example, both ISO21500 and the ANSI/IEEE PMI PMboK agree that all projects have a life-cycle consisting of (i) initiating, (ii) planning, (iii) executing, (iv) monitoring and controlling, and (v) closing (ISO, 2012; Project Management Institute (US), 2017). We can explore how AI can be applied to project management from this common ground.

11.4 The Application of AI in Project Management

Because both AI and project management are far-reaching terms, the specific application of AI to project management will undoubtedly vary significantly for individual practitioners, as will its application in a responsible value chain. To contextualize this discussion, I will discuss the impact of AI on building construction project management (for no other reason other than it is the one I am most familiar with). The following discussion does not aim to explore every potential application of AI in project management. Instead, it provides examples of how AI could be applied in a project's lifecycle.

11.4.1 Initiation

Starting the project begins with an initiation process. The purpose of this process is to define the objectives, stakeholders, and parameters of the project (or project phase); ensure these align with the strategic business objectives; align stakeholder's expectations with the project's planned outcomes; and create a sense of personal engagement with the project for the stakeholders (Gareis, 2013; Kihuga, 2018; Wiegers, 2007). AI can assist project managers in the initiation process in many ways.

In this phase, AI can simplify data collection and improve data analysis. Databases linked through simple algorithms can map the relationship between project elements and stakeholder requirements and highlight potential misalignment or conflict areas. AI programs can identify conflicts between project objectives, stakeholder expectations, and preliminary budgets or schedules.

As the datasets from historical project information expand, the ability of AI software to identify and highlight areas for discussion and resolution grows. With each new project or phase, AI can test new assumptions and requests against previously completed or previously made assumptions.

"Scraper" programs can search previous project databases, current project information, and even related web pages to test the veracity of project assumptions (Chandrika et al., 2020; Haddaway, 2015; Mahto & Singh, 2016). The ability to synthesize data at the project initiation will allow project managers to have data-based discussions with sponsors and stakeholders. Instead of relying on their own past experiences and "gut feelings" to flag potential issues, project managers will be able to draw on empirical data drawn from their own and others' experiences to have meaningful discussions.

When the time comes to draft the project charter document, AI programs will collate the information from the databases and auto-generate documents for the project manager to review and adapt (Aghajani, 2020). With an integrating AI system linking the stakeholder database (i.e., the stakeholder register) via a workflow program, these documents can be issued, authorized, version controlled, and filed with a button (Georgakopoulos et al., 1995; Jayawardana & Jayarathna, 2020).

11.4.2 Planning

Once the project has been defined and authorized to proceed, it moves to the planning phase. Project managers refine and codify the scope, effort, timing, costs, and objectives in this phase. We start creating the documentation that will be the foundation for what the project hopes to achieve during this phase. We create the project management plan components and documents (Project Management Institute (US), 2017). Depending on the project, we might have a team of designers or subject matter experts to create detailed plans, outline quality management parameters and requirements, and identify risks. The purpose of the planning phase is to create a course of action that will assist us to complete the project (or phase) and create a baseline for us to benchmark against through our monitoring and controlling processes. AI will play a significant role in this phase, driven predominantly by the breakthroughs in the Building Information Modeling (BIM) technologies (Eastman et al., 2011; McNamara, 2020) and conversational agents (Bors, 2020).

11.4.2.1 Project Plans and Planning

Using simple workflow processes linked to project databases, AI can develop documentation such as the project management plan, scope management plan, stakeholder management plan, quality, and communication management plans. Using standardized document templates, databases, and data from previous projects, AI will collate information from multiple sources and disciplines and compile these into sophisticated and indexed documents ready for the project manager to review. From the stakeholder register (database), the system can run network planning to identify key decision-makers and "influence-clusters" (Aragonés-Beltrán et al., 2017) to assist the project manager in garnering consensus and/or achieving approval for complex challenges.

11.4.2.2 Scope Management

Conversational agents are AI systems that use natural language processing (NLP), optical gesture, and/or handwriting recognizer to gather information and filter it through a Natural Language Understanding Unit (NLUU) for speech tagging and syntax/sematic (McGreevey et al., 2020). These conversational agents (sometimes referred to as "chatbots") can understand any language and help reduce knowledge gaps. When responding to a human, these conversational agents can use "[text], speech, graphics, virtual gestures of haptic-assisted physical gestures" (Conversational Agent, 2019). Conversational agents will play several roles in the future of project management.

Through these agents, AI will engage with sponsors, stakeholders, and user groups to collect, index, and analyze project requirements. Scope requirements can be refined through the use of AI in collaborative virtual environments, which will allow users and stakeholders to understand, discuss, and "workshop" scope to find a more unified understanding of the objectives, benefits, challenges, and limitations of the project (Churchill et al., 2012). AI will compile and collate these data into standardized scoping documents, such as user requirement briefs, while simultaneously highlighting clashes in requirements, requests, and expectations.

By integrating stakeholder registers and workflows, AI can issue the scoping documents, without human intervention, back to the sponsor, project manager, and stakeholders for review and final approval of scope. Once these decisions have been approved, the systems will utilize this data to create the initial WBS for the project (Iranmanesh & Madadi, 2008).

11.4.2.3 Schedule Management

Breakthroughs in 4D BIM will allow AI to plan all scheduling activities for the project (Tallgren et al., 2020). AI will interpret the data in the BIM to develop multiple options for review and testing. AI will then run scheduling scenarios by constructing the building in the virtual world to test for optimal sequencing (Brito & Ferreira, 2015). This scenario testing will allow AI to identify and define the activities to be completed.

From this, AI will develop the optimal sequencing for these activities, plan the estimated time for these activities, and produce scheduling artifacts such as scheduling documents, milestones, and activities lists (Kim et al., 2013; Park & Cai, 2015). These artifacts can be presented using visualization techniques such as Gantt Charts and Critical Path Methods (CPM) but also other planning techniques such as critical space analysis (CSA), Last Planner Systems (LPS), and Critical Chain Method (CCM) (Baldwin & Bordoli, 2014; Bølviken et al., 2015). Using AI to create these artifacts will allow project managers to be program agnostic. Rather than being trained in one planning method, project managers will prepare schedules in whichever technique or methodology best suits the end-users.

11.4.2.4 Cost Planning

In the planning phase, project managers develop the cost management plans, estimate costs, and determine the budgets. Within this specialized arena, we, once again, find AI having a significant impact. As BIM capability expands into 5D (cost estimation), the ability for AI follows (Ghazaryan, 2019). BIM allows the production of quantity take-offs of materials, but AI completes these take-offs and links them to up-to-date cost information (Solomon Olusola et al., 2016).

But that is not all, as materials are only part of the cost planning equation. There is also an understanding of building standards, availability of supply, labor, plant, and overheads. AI can integrate it all. Using "scrapers" linked to Contractors & Suppliers' databases, AI can prepare preliminary cost estimates either as the BIM develops or at particular milestones in the schedule (Shen & Izza, 2010). These technologies can reduce cost planning time by up to 80% and result in on-site cost savings greater than 10% of the overall construction costs (Nagalingam et al., 2013).

With this information, project managers will be able to test pricing assumptions, confirm funding, and approve the project cost plans (Moses & Hampton, 2017). Databases can be developed to act as assumption logs and change registers, and the interoperability of these "live" lists can be used to flag documents and project plan changes.

11.4.2.5 Quality Management

Quality management incorporates all the processes necessary to ensure that project activities during design, planning, and implementation are effective, efficient, and meet the project objectives. It includes identifying and documenting quality requirements and standards, translating these into executable activities, and monitoring project activities against the stated quality requirements to ensure these are complete, correct, and meet stakeholder expectations (Project Management Institute (US), 2017). AI will be able to manage all of this.

AI can extract, analyze, and prepare intelligent quality management and procurement specifications linked to BIM data. These documents will automatically reference the most up-to-date standards across all technical disciplines. While collating and validating this information, AI will simultaneously prepare the testing regimes and input these into the BIM information to ensure witness and hold points are incorporated into the building schedule.

Drawing from real-time design, AI will assist with the quality control of construction documentation by interpreting visual data, such as construction plans, and using clash-detection technology to ensure that no errors or omissions are contained with the documentation – before it is released into the procurement packages or to the contractors on site (Solomon Olusola et al., 2016).

11.4.2.6 Human Resource Management

Human resource management (HRM) includes all the processes needed to plan, acquire, and utilize the project team within the project management. It also includes tracking team performance, identifying areas for competency improvement, providing feedback to team members, monitoring the actual team utilization against the planned utilization, and taking corrective actions as necessary (Project Management Institute (US), 2017). AI will assist project managers in a range of HRM activities, including hiring, team selection, optimizing resource allocations, and reducing absenteeism.

Using knowledge-based, semantic search engines, AI can actively run candidate searches across web-based job boards to identify new project team members (Bizer et al., 2005). By matching experience, skills, and competencies to current positions available, AI will recommend suitable benefits and remuneration packages to secure the employees.

When linked to Enterprise Resource Platforms (ERPs) and team experience registers, AI will be able to align project requirements, team member availability, competencies, and skills to select the best team members for a project (Auth et al., 2019). Using genetic algorithms, AI will optimize and automate rostering allocations by exploring a wide range of resourcing scenarios across various constraints and variables (Aickelin & Dowsland, 2004; Desai & Joshi, 2010). In addition, AI will re-duce costs and productivity loss by predicting staff turnover and absenteeism (Strohmeier & Piazza, 2015).

11.4.2.7 Communication Management

Communications management is the process project managers use to plan, collect, create, distribute, store, retrieve, control, monitor, and ultimately dispose of project information (Project Management Institute (US), 2017). AI excels in these types of management processes.

Intelligent personal assistants (IPAs) will answer phone calls, create messages, and issue emails (Saad et al., 2017). IPAs will schedule meetings for stakeholders, follow up on action items, and coordinate minute meetings (Han & Yang, 2018). Electronic meeting platforms will allow stakeholders to make anonymous comments or raise concerns without being identified, encouraging creative ideation and challenging assumptions without fear of repercussions (Chen et al., 1994).

"Intelligent Automation" bots will review, analyze, extract, collate, and high-light targeted information from detailed reports at the rate of 2,000 documents an hour and use the relevant information to create agendas, briefing notes, and op-tions papers (Moses & Johantgen, 2018). At the same time, cognitive systems will automatically generate reports and responses to stakeholders (Johnsonbabu, 2017).

Through deep and machine learning, AI will be able to analyze stakeholders' social networks, email communications, and collaborative work platforms and un-derstand their sentiments and feelings toward the project or elements of it (John-sonbabu, 2017). Using augmented transition network parsing, AI will be able to hyper-personalize project information into newsfeeds from the project, to manage stakeholders' concerns and expectations (Candelon et al., 2020).

11.4.2.8 Risk Management

Risk management requires project managers to identify, assess, and control risks. AI will assist with this across the entire project lifecycle.

Through deep and convolutional neural networks, AI will scour online incident reports and risk registers and identify risks that align with the current project's scale, complexity, and type (Krizhevsky et al., 2012). Through feature extraction and object recognition, AI will review BIM data to identify inherent safety issues within the design and automatically correct them or flag them for assessment by a designer (Tallgren et al., 2020). Once construction commences, AI will use image classification and captioning data, activity recognition, object detection and tracking, and wearable sensors to continuously monitor the site and workers to detect poten-tial risks (Akinosho et al., 2020; Wonil et al., 2017; Yan et al., 2017).

A risk assessment will be completed by running real-time Monte Carlo simulations against these data. AI will constantly assess the probability of risks resulting in lost time, additional cost, or injuries (Kokkaew & Wipulanusat, 2014; Rezaie et al., 2007). By comparing these risks to risk registers from similar projects, AI will make data-driven assessment decisions regarding the likelihood and consequences of individual risks and prioritize the risk hierarchy.

Running concurrently with risk identification and assessment, AI can use analytical hierarchy processes (AHP) to propose or directly enact risk mitigation strategies such as adjusted contingencies (Mohamed et al., 2009), deactivation of site-based plant and equipment, safety alerts to individuals at risk through innovative, wearable devices (Wonil et al., 2017). Concurrently, "scrapers" will constantly review new safety codes and legislation and incorporate these into risk registers, designs, and specifications for future reference.

11.4.2.9 Procurement Management

Procurement management has been described as "the processes to purchase or acquire the products, services or results needed from outside the [organisation] to perform the work" (Project Management Institute (US), 2017). Planning, selection, administration, and closing are the four significant procurement processes.

In the procurement planning process, AI will run scenarios on multiple procurement options based on specific criteria such as project type, market capacity, available supplier networks, and even the success or failure of previous procurement processes (Zhen et al., 2018).

Any procurement selection process requires a comparison of submissions against predetermined criteria. This process does not always result in the best outcome for the project because the assessments are skewed by hidden bias, subjectivity, miscommunication, and bureaucracy (Kashiwagi & Byfield, 2002). However, by using multi-criteria decision-making (MCDM) algorithms (Tzeng & Huang, 2011), artificial neural networks (ANN) (Yu et al., 2019), and techniques for order of preference by similarity to ideal solution (TOPSIS) (Junior et al., 2014), AI can remove the bias from the process and recommend the submission that represents the best outcome for the project based entirely on the predetermined criteria (Kashiwagi & Byfield, 2002).

The administration of a procurement process can be time-consuming. But with the growing acceptance of electronic tender submissions, AI will quickly begin to take on the tender administration process. AI will manage the tender administration process when linked with workflow processes, intelligent specifications, and legal databases. Respond to requests for information, prepare addenda, manage submission cut-offs, and ensure probity is maintained.

AI will manage the procurement closing process quickly and smoothly. Acceptance letters, letters of intent, notification of unsuccessful tenders, and issuance of draft contracts are all simple workflow processes. AI will manage this process with a minimum of human interaction.

11.4.2.10 Stakeholder Management

Stakeholder management involves several complex processes: identifying stakeholders, analyzing and managing their needs and expectations, and developing strategies for working with multiple stakeholders (Project Management Institute (US), 2017). The ethical management of stakeholders is foundational to the concept of responsible project management, and once again, AI will manage all of the administrative processes involved.

Stakeholder identification can be completed using advanced search capabilities. AI only needs a minimal number of project stakeholders to start the process. By searching their email contacts and linking this against project metadata, organizational websites, and previous projects, AI can create comprehensive stakeholder registers, including personal and contact details. AI can create detailed, responsive influence maps (Pan et al., 2012).

Collaborative platforms such as Aconex (https://project-management.com/aco nex-software-review/) provide central repositories for all project information and communications – including email traffic. Through these repositories, AI will use sentiment analysis algorithms and NLP to data-mine project communications and identify any dissatisfaction with the project or misalignment between the project progress, outcomes, and stakeholder needs and expectations (Johnsonbabu, 2017).

Using MCDM algorithms, Monte Carlo scenario modeling, and behavioral analysis, AI will undertake a continuous risk analysis of stakeholders, identifying their concerns and hyper-personalizing project communications to allay their concerns highlight how their needs are being incorporated into the project (Caygill n.d.).

11.4.3 Executing

The executing phase includes all the processes necessary to move the project to its completed state as defined in the initiation and planning phases (Alby n.d.). The executing processes are instituted to coordinate resources, manage stakeholders and their expectations, and integrate and successfully perform the activities outlined in the planning documents (Project Management Institute (US), 2017).

AI will develop complex and evolving process modeling for each project (Myers & Berry, 1999). Using a combination of communication, artifact, and activity-based modeling, AI will be able to integrate "information flow requirements, activity decomposition and communication constraints" (Myers & Berry, 1999) to develop the most efficient project workflow. AI will continually adjust these workflows to create optimal outcomes (Huang & Fan, 2003). All manual administrative tasks project managers currently undertake to manage their projects will be replaced with AI technologies (Moses & Johantgen, 2018).

In supply chain management, AI will integrate site monitoring technologies to assess when supplies will be needed and raise purchase orders for the additional supplies (Al-Sinan & Aljaroudi, 2020). Using automated workflows linked to intelligent specifications, intelligent contracts (iContracts), BIM, and "scrapers," AI will be able to review price options on the internet with multiple suppliers, confirm stock levels in distribution centers, select the best value for money, place an order, check bills of lading through smart sensors, RFID, and barcode technologies (Kashiwagi & Byfield, 2002), and confirm receipt and issue payment through blockchain technologies (Lau et al., 2009; McNamara, 2020).

11.4.4 Monitoring and Controlling

The monitoring and controlling processes in project management have two primary functions. Monitoring provides information about the progress of a project by assessing it against planned targets while controlling processes are used to ensure compliance and, if necessary, correct project elements that are not following planned targets, goals, or objectives (Callistus & Clinton, 2018).

The impacts of AI within project management will be felt most in the Monitoring and Controlling Processes Group. As emergent technologies such as BIM (Eastman et al., 2011), iContracts (McNamara, 2020), Blockchain (McNamara & Sepasgozar, 2018), smart sensors (Rossi et al., 2019), site-based bots (Balzan et al., 2020; Saidi et al., 2016), and automated supply chains (Al-Saeed et al., 2020) make their way into the Construction Industry, AI will be there – integrating it all.

AI technologies will be able to assess site progress through cameras, smart sensors, and site-bots (Balzan et al., 2020). Through the Internet of things (IoT), AI will interpret whether the project is ahead or behind the planned schedule by reviewing it against the BIM (Eastman et al., 2011) and taking into account any variables (e.g., inclement weather or extreme temperatures) that the site sensors have recorded.

AI will plan and conduct site inspections using BIM and IoT functionality without human interaction. AI will map flight paths to allow micro-drones fitted with high definition, thermal, and infrared cameras to undertake detailed site inspections. Then, use this data to undertake performance and compliance assessments by linking the site to quality standard databases and intelligent specifications (Solomon Olusola et al., 2016). Where noncompliance is detected, AI will issue the necessary notices under contract without a single human being involved.

AI will complete contract administration functions as per the terms of the iContract (McNamara, 2020). AI will ensure that these iContracts are updated with the latest case law and legal definitions as the courts make new rulings (Betts & Jaep, 2017). AI will also be able to recommend, and in some cases, automatically update, iContracts to ensure they align with this new information or legal precedent (Gervais, 2019).

By integrating these technologies, AI will be able to determine and issue extension of time claims, delay notices, and authorize and complete payments to contractors, sub-contractors, consultants, and suppliers without the need for human interaction (Li et al., 2019; Woodhead et al., 2018).

11.4.5 Closing

The project closing phase is finalizing all the activities associated with the project. This includes ensuring all deliverables are finalized per the project documentation, making sure the project is formally transferred to those who will now take responsibility for it, ensuring that all documentation is signed off and archived, and that project resources are released and reassigned elsewhere (Project Management Institute (US), 2017).

AI will manage this process progressively throughout the project lifecycle. Predetermined workflow processes with firm hold-points will ensure that documentation is systematically signed off and approved by the authorizing parties, then automatically indexed, referenced, and archived.

iContracts will ensure a smooth transfer of assets to the owners and facilities managers (McNamara, 2020) through financial reconciliation, final payments, and asset transfer documentation. In conjunction with building monitoring systems, AI will use iContracts to initiate defects liability processes and automatically generate the required contractual notices (McNamara, 2020; Pillai & Matus, 2021).

To update the BIM, AI will use data collected throughout the building process from IoT, smart sensors, drone imagery, and site wearables (McNamara, 2020). "Scraper" programs will cross-reference intelligent specifications with the latest product technical specifications and embed this information in the construction BIM to seamlessly become the facilities management BIM (Liu et al., 2020).

11.5 Data-Driven Project Management (DPM)

As AI evolves, it will transition from project management assistant to project management peer. Data-driven project management (DPM) envisages human and AI working collaboratively on projects. As Auth et al. (2019) explain, the core idea of DPM is widely accepted, that is, the notion that the more relevant information that is known and can be brought to bear on a problem, the more options can be considered and the more likely the selected alternative will be successful.

A wide range of mathematical and statistical processes can be utilized in DPM to inform decision-making. It is doubtful that most project managers will be experts in earned value management, CPM, CCM, AHP, Program Evaluation and Review Techniques (PERT), Lean Processes (Six Sigma), and Monte Carlo simulations, but AI can. The latest computers can complete quintillion (10^{18}) calculations per second (Wiggers, 2019). AI will run multiple scenarios and find optimal solutions to complex problems; before humans can locate the reports, we need to start thinking about the problem.

11.6 Fiction or Fact?

It might be tempting to think that everything you have just read is pure speculation or science-fiction. However, nothing could be further from the truth. Every technology outlined above is currently available within the project management arena in varying stages of maturity. These technologies are already forming part of the project management suite of tools, and the rate of "techceleration" within the profession is increasing (Prieto, 2019).

A recent study by KPMG (2019) indicated that early adopters in the construction industry are already investing heavily in BIM, drone, virtual reality/augment reality and smart sensors, and the use of AI and machine learning "will become commonplace in the next 5–10 years." Nimmo and Usher (2020) agree with this assessment, and their research suggests that by 2025 more than 75% of the project management "hard skill" processes and as much as 50% of the "soft skill" process will either be done by or involve some form of AI.

In light of this, there can be no doubt that our profession will change dramatically in some ways. However, it is not yet to time "board the lifeboats" and look for a new line of work. As Trevelyan (2018) explains, "in the near term, AI will likely replace tasks rather than jobs [but] it will also create new, higher-value tasks to be undertaken given the power of the new tools." This measured perspective appears to be held by project management practitioners, AI developers, and educators (Nimmo & Usher, 2020).

Over the coming decade, we can expect to see both basic administration tasks (e.g., report generation, register management, scribing, and distribution of meeting minutes) and complex routine tasks (e.g., identification of delay impacts on project schedules, probabilistic risk assessments, and even cost plan management) undertaken by AI. But is this a bad thing? Who among us would not like to see those time-consuming, mind-numbing administration tasks completed by AI? Furthermore, if our time as project professionals is no longer consumed with the mundane and routine, what else could this free us to do?

As project management professionals, the most important discussion for us lies in these questions. Rather than worrying about whether the rise of AI will bring about the demise of our profession, the better response is to focus on what AI cannot do because it is in that space that the future of project management will thrive.

11.7 The Future of Project Management

There can be no doubt that AI has exceeded our ability to perform computational tasks. However, managing projects is not just about "crunching" the numbers. Project management is more than just a science. It is also an art. The key characteristic that will create an insurmountable hurdle for AI in the project management space, at least within the foreseeable future, is people. As Feuillet (2019) eloquently explains, "Projects are for the people, by the people and of the people. Every project starts with a business case – to solve a people problem. Without people, there is no project." Whenever the management of people is involved, AI will always run into its three inherent weaknesses. For all the unique opportunities that AI will bring to our profession, it will always struggle with:
1. perception;
2. creativity; and
3. social skills (Rexford, 2018).

11.7.1 Perception

Harris and Fiske (2015) describe perception as the ability to consider another person's mind spontaneously. Although succinct, this description fails to convey the immensity of perception. Our ability to perceive derives from our self-awareness. It requires the complex and instantaneous assessment of stimuli from multiple senses, such as tactile, visual, and audial cues (Schwiedrzik et al., 2018). These stimuli are then filtered through a nuanced understanding of the social context, which allows us to perceive how another person feels (Barrett et al., 2011). Perception requires understanding and relating to another person's feelings, thoughts, and behavior (Barr, 2011). Our ability to perceive is at the core of being human.

AI cannot understand what it is like to be human. Despite its enormous ability to calculate, collate, and analyze vast amounts of data, AI does not understand all that information. Sure, it can tell you that a project is now forecasting an over-run in time or money, but it cannot feel the anxiety of delay or the panic that comes from the realization that there is not enough money left to finish the project. These emotional responses are the realm of humanity – our blessing and our curse.

AI cannot feel these emotions, so it cannot understand how to contextualize and narrate information so that stakeholders become emotionally comfortable with difficult situations or unexpected events. So as long as people remain the central purpose of projects (Feuillet, 2019), there remains a need for a human agent, such as a project manager, to interpret, explain, and contextualize project information.

11.7.2 Creativity

AI has written symphonies (Barrett & Ward, 2019), painted masterpieces (Conner-Simons, 2020), and displayed highly complex problem-solving skills (Kopec, 2017). Watching AI undertake these activities may lead us to think that AI exhibits creativity, but that is simply not true. Rexford (2018) explains, "machines may behave in ways that seem creative . . . but they are born of exhaustive enumeration and evaluation of underlying data." AI will never have the desire to create. Even the most sophisticated AI system cannot do what a human child can do – find inspiration in their world and use this to create (Barrett & Ward, 2019).

Creativity has been defined as the ability to perform innovative thinking that generates original and valuable products, services, and ideas (Amabile, 2018; Amabile et al., 1996). Creativity requires solving problems and finding and defining them to be solved (Runco, 1994). It is a unique mixture of "inspiring, chaotic idea generation and focused knowledge generation" (vom Brocke & Lippe, 2010).

For an outcome to be considered creative, it must have a radical newness or involve a novel combination of existing elements or solutions (Couger et al., 1993), and it must result in an outcome that is useful and valuable (Amabile et al., 1996). When we consider that projects have been defined as "temporary endeavour was undertaken to create a unique product, service or result" (Project Management Institute (US), 2017), we begin to see the significant role that creativity plays in project management. From the early initiation stages of project definition, problem-finding, and innovative application of project management processes, to the closing phases, problem-finding and solving can still form a large part of our role (vom Brocke & Lippe, 2010).

Isaksen et al. (2010) highlight that creativity requires defining the issues, collecting relevant data, and capitalizing on existing knowledge or generating new knowledge to resolve the issue. At present, AI can only assist project managers with collecting relevant data; it cannot yet define complex project issues or generate new knowledge to resolve them.

11.7.3 Social Skills

As we have already discussed, people are at the heart of all projects, and people are social creatures. We have developed a vast range of verbal and nonverbal methods for communicating with one another, such as language, text, gestures, body language, voice tone, volume and patterns of speech, and even personal appearance (Beauchamp & Anderson, 2010). Social skills are the broad range of skills that we use to describe the way we communicate with other humans (Hargie et al., 1994).

Within the literature, project management-specific social skills are often referred to as "soft skills" and indicate the ability to:
- create and communicate a vision (Matinheikki et al., 2016);
- build trust, inspire and empower teams, and build their culture (Madsen, 2015; Shenhar, 1999);
- discern and manage personal agendas and unspoken expectations (Knox et al., 2017; Usher & Whitty, 2017);
- ability to identify and resolve interpersonal conflicts (Aga et al., 2016);
- make sense of complex issues and communicate these through stories, narrative, text, and visual media so they can be understood by large, divergent groups (Ang, 2018; Johansson-Sköldberg et al., 2013; Weick et al., 2005); and
- identify assumptions and meaningfully collaborate (Brown, 2008; Gaim & Wåhlin, 2016; Liedtka, 2015).

The importance of these soft skills in project management cannot be understated. Recent studies have indicated that a primary contributor to project failure could be the lack of soft-skill competencies in project management professionals (Ling et al., 2009; Muzio et al., 2007). Zuo et al. (2018) describe the quantitative effect of soft skills on project success as "statistically significant" and Goleman et al. (2013) argue that soft skills could be twice as critical as technical skills in achieving success.

Fortunately for us, AI cannot, and may never, accurately replicate project management soft skills. The fundamental reason for this is that soft skills derive from emotional intelligence (Goleman et al., 2013). The successful management of projects will always involve the management of people. The ability to interact and communicate with multiple stakeholders through sensemaking, commitment, teamwork, decision-making, conflict resolution, cultural awareness, and negotiation will always be central (Fisher, 2011; Ruuska & Vartiainen, 2003; Simon, 2006; Thi & Swierczek, 2010).

11.8 A Revolution Brings New Risks

Feuillet (2019) argues that the rise of AI could represent one of the most significant risks the human race has ever encountered. It can simultaneously impact humanity on economic, sociological, philosophical, and technological fronts. Not all these risks can be relegated to the distant future. Some of these risks are upon us now in these early stages of development.

Foremost among them is to understand that humans have created all AI. It is an extension of the programming and specific training provided. The algorithms used by AI to "learn" are designed to replicate, as closely as possible, the way humans think, and this introduces the potential for biases to be incorporated into the AI (Prieto, 2019). As AI begins to make its way into project management, we need to remain cautious of the information it provides us. There will always be the need for a domain specialist (i.e., the project manager) to check the veracity of what is produced. This will require a new level of competency. We will need to learn how to assess AI's final outputs' veracity, despite not fully understanding how that information was arrived at.

Another risk derives from the way AI "thinks." AI deals exclusively with statistical truth, not morally constrained truth (Prieto, 2019). While the outputs from AI can be "true" in the sense of empirical testing, this does not guarantee that the outputs represent an acceptable truth. The importance of morally constrained truth is easily illustrated. One of the greatest threats facing humankind is water scarcity driven by over-population (Fuller & Harhay, 2010; Kummu et al., 2016). Current forecasts indicate that 57% of the global population (over 4 billion people) will face severe water scarcity issues by 2050 (Boretti & Rosa, 2019). From a raw statistical perspective, the solution is simple: kill every second person on the Earth before 2050. As humans, we understand this is not a viable option, but AI does not. As project managers, we need to understand that statistical "truth" does not always represent the right outcome, and there needs to be a human overlay placed on that "truth." We must remember that AI is only a tool. A sophisticated and complex tool that can do things humans cannot, but a tool, nonetheless.

Another risk class to consider is liability risks. AI systems will resolve complicated and complex problems faster than we can. However, what happens if AI provides incorrect information? What if this results in millions of dollars in losses, or worse, injury or death? AI cannot be held accountable in a court of law; it cannot be held legally responsible for its information. So, where does the liability reside? With designers and programmers who wrote the AI? With those who provided the datasets used to train the AI? With the project manager, who implemented the actions? The legal profession is only starting to grapple with these questions (Čerka et al., 2015; Kingston, 2016). Until these issues are resolved, AI represents a risk to project managers.

11.9 What Is Responsible Project Management in the Age of Artificial Intelligence?

Whether we like it or not, AI, in one form or another, will significantly impact our profession within the coming years. It is inevitable. The genie has been let out of the bottle, and there is no way for any of us to put it back in. We must ask ourselves: "What is responsible project management in the age of Artificial Intelligence?"

Our first response should acknowledge that progress is crucial to the development of every profession. Will AI change project management? Absolutely. Will it destroy some of the old ways of managing projects? Without a doubt. But that does not mean the change is bad? It could be argued that this is the price we pay for betterment. One of the most influential economists of the early twentieth century, Joseph Schumpeter, noted that creative destruction is a fundamental tenet of capitalism (Schumpeter, 1942). We must innovate to survive, and in doing so, we must be willing to put behind us anything that holds back our progress.

In light of this, we cannot approach the dawn of Industry 4.0 in a spirit of fear. Fear clouds our judgment, blinds us from seeing opportunities, and impairs the ability to act. Fear in the face of AI serves absolutely no purpose. There is nothing positive to be gained in choosing to fear AI's changes to our profession. However, choosing not to fear something is not the same as acting without caution. Caution is a responsible reaction considering the coming changes. This caution should create a desire to understand better the drivers, barriers, and risks of this new technology.

In terms of drivers, AI potentially reduces time and cost in delivering. This will increase project performance and enhance project benefits, leading to greater stakeholder satisfaction. AI will allow us to gather and review more meaningful data for project managers, increasing our ability to make accurate predictions and forecasts. It will reduce the need to undertake routine administration tasks, focusing on high-level value creation activities, decision-making, and planning (Cubric, 2020; Prieto, 2019).

However, there are many current barriers to AI in the project management arena. There are technical challenges involved with gathering, cleansing, and curating project data so that AI can learn what we do (Bodea et al., 2020). There are prohibitive costs associated with systems implementation and maintenance (Cubric, 2020). The lack of model reusability and concerns over data privacy, security, and digital ethics still need to be addressed (Bodea et al., 2020). Finally, we still have social barriers such as lack of knowledge, fear of job security, increased dependency on non-human agents, and an underlying lack of trust in AI's ability to answer complex questions correctly (Cubric, 2020).

Despite the benefits and opportunities that AI may bring to our profession, it also brings significant risks. Hidden biases and prejudices embedded into AI's design, data collation, and training system (Prieto et al., 2020) can produce skewed or erroneous outcomes. Who is liable when these errors occur? Then there are the social license, ethical and contractual risks to consider (Trevelyan, 2018), all of which must feature in any discussion of responsible project management in the coming decade.

11.10 What Should We Do?

AI will have a place in the future of responsible project management, and it starts now – with us, Acting responsibly in the age of AI requires us to be engaged. We must acknowledge that we have done things over the last seven decades is changing. To maximize the benefit and reduce the risks associated with AI in project management, we must be willing to rethink and redesign our profession (KPMG, 2019). As responsible project managers, we need to be involved and invested in developing the AI that will be deployed. The more input, guidance, data, and training AI developers have regarding our profession, the better technology they will provide us. AI developers need our domain knowledge to design the systems, and they need good quality project data to train the systems.

Finally, we need to ready ourselves for the shift in labor markets that will undoubtedly come. As AI becomes more commonplace, it will challenge the traditional notion of "value" and "value-adding." We should expect outdated pricing models based on "time to complete the job" to be replaced with models that reward the quality of outcome regardless of the time required to achieve it (Balzan et al., 2020; Prieto, 2019). This will require a fundamental shift in the way we view the concept of value and how it is created in and through projects (Usher, 2021). This change will also move away from traditional careers toward more transportable, portfolio careers based on systems experience, not just project experience (Trevelyan, 2018).

References

Adams, H. 2016, A Different Approach to Project Management: The Use of Soft Skills, Harrisburg University, viewed 15 October 2019, <http://digitalcommons.harrisburgu.edu/pmgt_dandt/2>.

Aga, D. A., Noorderhaven, N., & Vallejo, B. (2016). Transformational leadership and project success: The mediating role of team-building. *International Journal of Project Management*, *34*(5), 806–818.

Aghajani, E. (2020). *Software documentation: Automation and challenges*. Università della Svizzera italiana.

Aickelin, U., & Dowsland, K. A. (2004). An indirect genetic algorithm for a nurse-scheduling problem. *Computers & Operations Research*, *31*(5), 761–778.

Akinosho, T. D., Oyedele, L. O., Bilal, M., Ajayi, A. O., Delgado, M. D., Akinade, O. O., & Ahmed, A. A. (2020). Deep learning in the construction industry: A review of present status and future innovations. *Journal of Building Engineering*, 101827.

Al-Saeed, Y., Edwards, D. J., & Scaysbrook, S. (2020). Automating construction manufacturing procedures using BIM digital objects (BDOs). *Construction Innovation*.

Al-Sinan, M. A. & Aljaroudi, Z. (2020). Autonomous Procurement System (APS): Pro forma development. *IEEE*, 1–6.

Alby, T. (n.d.). Executing Processes, viewed 24 January 2021, <https://project-management-knowledge.com/definitions/e/executing-process/>.

Amabile, T. M. (2018). *Creativity in context: Update to the social psychology of creativity.* Routledge.

Amabile, T. M., Conti, R., Coon, H., Lazenby, J., & Herron, M. (1996). Assessing the work environment for creativity. *Academy of Management Journal*, 39(5), 1154–1184.

Ang, C. S. K. (2018). *Multi-stakeholder perspectives of value in project portfolios.* Sydney: UTS.

Aragonés-Beltrán, P., García-Melón, M., & Montesinos-Valera, J. (2017). How to assess stakeholders' influence in project management? A proposal based on the analytic network process. *International Journal of Project Management*, 35(3), 451–462.

Auth, G., Jokisch Pavel, O., & Dürk, C. (2019). Revisiting automated project management in the digital age–a survey of AI approaches. *Online Journal of Applied Knowledge Management (OJAKM)*, 7(1), 27–39.

Baldwin, A., & Bordoli, D. (2014). *Handbook for construction planning and scheduling.* John Wiley & Sons.

Balzan, A., Aparicio, C. C., & Trabucco, D. (2020). Robotics in construction: State-of-art of on-site advanced devices. *International Journal of High-Rise Buildings*, 9(1), 95–104.

Barr, J. J. (2011). The relationship between teachers' empathy and perceptions of school culture. *Educational Studies*, 37(3), 365–369.

Barrett, L. F., Mesquita, B., & Gendron, M. (2011). Context in emotion perception. *Current Directions in Psychological Science*, 20(5), 286–290.

Barrett, M., & Ward, J. (2019). AI can now compose pop music and even symphonies. Here's how composers are joining in., NBC News, viewed 30 January 2020, <https://www.nbcnews.com/mach/science/ai-can-now-compose-pop-music-even-symphonies-here-s-ncna1010931>.

Beauchamp, M. H., & Anderson, V. (2010). SOCIAL: An integrative framework for the development of social skills. *Psychological Bulletin*, 136(1), 39.

Belharet, A., Bharathan, U., Dzingina, B., & Madhavan, N. (2020). Report on the impact of artificial intelligence on project management. *SSRN Electronic Journal*.

Betts, K. D. & Jaep, K. R. (2017). The dawn of fully automated contract drafting: Machine learning breathes new life into a decades-old promise. *Duke Law and Technology Review*, 15, 216.

Bizer, C., Heese, R., Mochol, M., Oldakowski, R., Tolksdorf, R., & Eckstein, R. (2005). The impact of semantic web technologies on job recruitment processes. *Wirtschaftsinformatik, 2005* (Springer), 1367–1381.

Bodea, C.-N., Mitea, C., & Stanciu, O. (2020). Artificial intelligence adoption in project management: Main drivers, barriers and estimated impact. In *Sciendo* (pp. 758–767).

Bølviken, T., Aslesen, S., & Koskela, L. (2015), 'What is a good plan?' IGLC. net.

Boretti, A. & Rosa, L. (2019). Reassessing the projections of the world water development report. *NPJ Clean Water*, 2(1), 15.

Bors, L. (2020). *Oracle digital assistant: A guide to enterprise-grade chatbots* (1st ed.). Berkeley, CA: Apress.

Brito, D. M. & Ferreira, E. A. (2015). Strategies for representation and analyses of 4D modeling applied to construction project management. *Procedia Economics and Finance*, 21, 374–382.

Brown, T. (2008). Design thinking. *Harvard Business Review*, 86(6), 84–92.

Bughin, J., Seong, J., Manyika, J., Chui, M., & Joshi, R. (2018). *Notes from the AI frontier: Modeling the impact of AI on the world economy*. Brussels, San Francisco, Shanghai, Stockholm: McKinsey Global Institute.

Callistus, T. & Clinton, A. (2018). *The role of monitoring and evaluation in construction project management* (pp. 571–582). Springer.

Candelon, F., Reichert, T., Duranton, S., Di Carlo, R. C., & De Bondt, M. (2020). The rise of the AI-powered company in the postcrisis world. *Boston Consulting Group*.

Castelluccio, M. (2019). A new AI social contract. *Strategic Finance, 100*(9), 61–62.

Caygill, S. (n.d.). AI set to impact stakeholder mapping, risk analysis, and more, viewed 04 February 2021, <https://communicateinfluence.com/ai-set-to-impact-stakeholder-mapping-risk-analysis-and-more/>.

Čerka, P., Grigienė, J., & Sirbikytė, G. (2015). Liability for damages caused by artificial intelligence. *Computer Law & Security Review, 31*(3), 376–389.

Chandrika, G. N., Ramasubbareddy, S., Govinda, K., & Swetha, E. (2020). Web scraping for unstructured data over the web. In *Embedded systems and artificial intelligence* (pp. 853–859). Springer.

Chelvachandran, N., Trifuljesko, S., Drobotowicz, K., Kendzierskyj, S., Jahankhani, H., & Shah, Y. (2020). Considerations for the governance of AI and government legislative frameworks. In *Cyber defence in the age of AI, smart societies and augmented humanity* (pp. 57–69). Springer.

Chen, H., Hsu, P., Orwig, R., Hoopes, L., & Nunamaker, J. F. (1994). Automatic concept classification of text from electronic meetings. *Communications of the ACM, 37*(10), 56–74.

Churchill, E. F., Snowdon, D. N., & Munro, A. J. (2012). *Collaborative virtual environments: Digital places and spaces for interaction*. Springer Science & Business Media.

Conner-Simons, A. 2020, Using AI to recreate how artists painted their masterpieces, viewed 30 January 2021, <https://www.csail.mit.edu/news/using-ai-recreate-how-artists-painted-their-masterpieces>.

Conversational Agent. (2019). Deep AI, viewed 26 January 2021, <https://deepai.org/machine-learning-glossary-and-terms/conversational-agent>.

Couger, J. D., Higgins, L. F., & McIntyre, S. C. (1993). (Un) structured creativity in information systems organisations. *MIS Quarterly*, 375–397.

Cubric, M. (2020). Drivers, barriers and social considerations for AI adoption in business and management: A tertiary study. *Technology in Society, 62*, 101257.

Davahli, M. R. (2020). The last state of artificial intelligence in project management. arXiv preprint arXiv:2012.12262.

Desai, V. S. & Joshi, S. (2010). *Application of decision tree technique to analyse construction project data* (pp. 304–313). Springer.

Eastman, C., Teicholz, P., Sacks, R., & Liston, K. (2011). *BIM handbook: A guide to building information modeling for owners, managers, designers, engineers and contractors*. John Wiley & Sons.

Feuillet, T. (2019). Humans and robots: How to create a better future together? *PM World Journal, VIII*(V), 1–30. June 2019.

Fisher, E. (2011). What practitioners consider to be the skills and behaviours of an effective people project manager. *International Journal of Project Management, 29*(8), 994–1002.

Fuller, A. C. & Harhay, M. O. (2010). Population growth, climate change and water scarcity in the southwestern United States. *American Journal of Environmental Sciences, 6*(3), 249.

Gaim, M. & Wåhlin, N. (2016). In search of a creative space: A conceptual framework of synthesising paradoxical tensions. *Scandinavian Journal of Management, 32*(1), 33–44.

Gareis, R. (2013). Re-thinking project initiation and project management by considering principles of sustainable development. In *Sustainability integration for effective project management* (pp. 129–143). IGI Global.

Georgakopoulos, D., Hornick, M., & Sheth, A. (1995). An overview of workflow management: From process modeling to workflow automation infrastructure. *Distributed and Parallel Databases, 3*(2), 119–153.

Gervais, D. J. (2019). 'The machine as author'. *Iowa Law Review, 105*, 2053.

Ghazaryan, M. (2019). 'BIM and cost estimation issues (5D): Case of Armenia', IOP conference series. *Materials Science and Engineering, 698*(2), 22076.

Goleman, D., Boyatzis, R. E., & McKee, A. (2013). *Primal leadership: Unleashing the power of emotional intelligence.* Harvard Business Press.

Haddaway, N. R. (2015). The use of web-scraping software in searching for grey literature. *Grey Journal, 11*(3), 186–190.

Han, S. & Yang, H. (2018). Understanding adoption of intelligent personal assistants. *Industrial Management + Data Systems, 118*(3), 618–636.

Hargie, O., Saunders, C., & Dickson, D. (1994). *Social skills in interpersonal communication.* Psychology Press.

Harris, L. T., & Fiske, S. T. (2015). Dehumanized perception. *Zeitschrift für Psychologie.*

Heath, N. (2020). What is AI? Everything you need to know about Artificial Intelligence: An executive guide to artificial intelligence, from machine learning and general AI to neural networks., viewed 16 January 2021, <https://www.zdnet.com/article/what-is-ai-everything-you-need-to-know-about-artificial-intelligence/>.

Huang, C., & Fan, Y. (2003). Intelligent workflow management: Architecture and technologies. pp. 995–999.

Iranmanesh, H. & Madadi, M. (2008). An Intelligent system framework for generating activity list of a project using WBS mind map and semantic network. *30*, 338–345.

Isaksen, S. G., Dorval, K. B., & Treffinger, D. J. (2010). *Creative approaches to problem-solving: A framework for innovation and change.* Sage Publications.

ISO. (2012). ISO 21500:2012 – Guidance on project management. International Organisation of Standardisation (ISO).

Jayawardana, Y., & Jayarathna, S. (2020). Streaming analytics and workflow automation for DFS. 513–514.

Johansson-Sköldberg, U., Woodilla, J., & Çetinkaya, M. (2013). 'Design thinking: Past, present and possible futures'. *Creativity and Innovation Management, 22*(2), 121–146.

Johnsonbabu, A. (2017). Reinventing the role of Project manager in the Artificial intelligence era. pp. 15–17.

Junior, F. R. L., Osiro, L., & Carpinetti, L. C. R. (2014). A comparison between Fuzzy AHP and Fuzzy TOPSIS methods to supplier selection. *Applied Soft Computing, 21*, 194–209.

Kashiwagi, D. T., & Byfield, R. (2002). Testing of minimization of subjectivity in best value procurement by using artificial intelligence systems in state of Utah procurement. *Journal of Construction Engineering and Management, 128*(6), 496–502.

Kihuga, A. G. (2018). *Project initiation process, monitoring and evaluation team capacity, compliance with legal framework and building projects success: The case of building projects in Roysambu constituency, Nairobi County, Kenya.* University of Nairobi.

Kim, H., Anderson, K., Lee, S., & Hildreth, J. (2013). Generating construction schedules through automatic data extraction using open BIM (building information modeling) technology. *Automation in Construction, 35*, 285–295.

Kingston, J. K. (2016). *Artificial intelligence and legal liability* (pp. 269–279). Springer.

Knox, D., Ellis, M., Speering, R., Asvadurov, S., Brinded, T., & Brown, T. (2017). *The art of project leadership: Delivering the world's largest projects*. Australia: McKinsey Capital Projects and Infrastructure Practice Sydney.

Kokkaew, N., & Wipulanusat, W. (2014). Completion delay risk management: A dynamic risk insurance approach. *KSCE Journal of Civil Engineering*, *18*(6), 1599–1608.

Kopec, D. (2017). *Artificial intelligence and problem solving*. Mercury Learning, Place of publication not identified.

KPMG. (2019). Future Ready Index: Leaders and followers in the engineering & construction industry – Global Construction Survey.

Krizhevsky, A., Sutskever, I., & Hinton, G. E. (2012). Imagenet classification with deep convolutional neural networks. *Advances in Neural Information Processing Systems*, *25*, 1097–1105.

Kummu, M., Guillaume, J. H., de Moel, H., Eisner, S., Flörke, M., Porkka, M., . . . Ward, P. (2016). 'The world's road to water scarcity: Shortage and stress in the twentieth century and pathways towards sustainability. *Scientific Reports*, *6*(1), 1–16.

Lasi, H., Fettke, P., Kemper, H.-G., Feld, T., & Hoffmann, M. (2014). Industry 4.0. *Business & Information Systems Engineering*, *6*(4), 239–242.

Lau, H. C. W., Ho, G. T. S., Tang, C. X. H., & Tse, Y. K. (2009). Development of an information exchange model for supporting logistics operations. *International Journal of Intelligent Systems Technologies and Applications*, *6*(3-4), 215–226.

LeVine, S. (2014). No one is prepared to stop the robot onslaught. So what will we do when it arrives? Quartz, viewed 30 June 2019, <https://qz.com/940977/no-one-is-prepared-to-stop-the-robot-onslaught-so-what-will-we-do-when-it-arrives/>.

Li, J., Greenwood, D., & Kassem, M. (2019). 'Blockchain in the built environment and construction industry: A systematic review, conceptual models and practical use cases'. *Automation in Construction*, *102*, 288–307.

Liedtka, J. (2015). Perspective: Linking design thinking with innovation outcomes through cognitive bias reduction. *Journal of Product Innovation Management*, *32*(6), 925–938.

Ling, F. Y. Y., Pham, V. M. C., & Hoang, T. P. (2009). Strengths, weaknesses, opportunities, and threats for architectural, engineering, and construction firms: Case study of Vietnam. *Journal of Construction Engineering and Management*, *135*(10), 1105–1113.

Liu, H., Abudayyeh, O., & Liou, W. (2020). *BIM-based smart facility management: A review of present research status, challenges, and future needs* (pp. 1087–1095). Reston, VA: American Society of Civil Engineers.

Madsen, S. (2015). *The power of project leadership: 7 keys to help you transform from project manager to project leader*. London, United Kingdom: Kogan Page Limited.

Mahto, D. K. & Singh, L. (2016). A dive into web scraper world. IEEE, pp. 689–693.

Marwala, T. & Hurwitz, E. (2017). *Artificial intelligence and economic theory: Skynet in the market* (Vol. 1). Springer.

Matinheikki, J., Artto, K., Peltokorpi, A., & Rajala, R. (2016). Managing inter-organisational networks for value creation in the front-end of projects. *International Journal of Project Management*, *34*(7), 1226–1241.

McGreevey, J. D., Hanson, C. W., & Koppel, R. (2020). Clinical, legal, and ethical aspects of artificial intelligence–assisted conversational agents in health care. *JAMA: The Journal of the American Medical Association*, *324*(6), 552–553.

McNamara, A. (2020). Automating the chaos: Intelligent construction contracts. In *Smart cities and construction technologies* (pp. 119–138). IntechOpen.

McNamara, A., & Sepasgozar, S. M. (2018). Barriers and drivers of intelligent contract implementation in construction. *Management*, *143*, 02517006.

Mohamed, D., Srour, F., Tabra, W., & Zayed, T. (2009). A prediction model for construction project time contingency, pp. 736–745.

Moses, R. & Johantgen, A. 2018, The Robots are coming – Driving efficiencies in contracting, viewed 28 July 2019, <https://www2.deloitte.com/content/dam/Deloitte/us/Documents/public-sector/us-fed-robots-are-coming.pd>.

Moses, T., & Hampton, G. (2017). Cost certainty: A lead driver for 5D building information modeling implementation. paper presented to the 21st Pacific Association of Quantity Surveyors Congress (PAQS 2017), Vancouver, BC, Canada, July 24th – 25th.

Muzio, E., Fisher, D. J., Thomas, E. R., & Peters, V. (2007). Soft skills quantification (SSQ) FOI project manager competencies. *Project Management Journal*, *38*(2), 30–38.

Myers, K. L., & Berry, P. M. (1999). At the Boundary of Workflow and AI.

Nagalingam, G., Jayasena, H. S., & Ranadewa, K. A. T. O. (2013). Building information modelling and future quantity surveyor's practice in Sri Lankan construction industry. paper presented to The Second World Construction Symposium 2013: Socio-Economic Sustainability in Construction, Colombo, June 14–15.

Nimmo, L., & Usher, G. (2020). Job-ready' project managers: Are Australian Universities preparing manages for the impact of AI, ML and Bots? *Project Management Research and Practice*, *6*, Oct-Dec.

Pan, W., Dong, W., Cebrian, M., Kim, T., Fowler, J. H., & Pentland, A. S. (2012). Modeling dynamical influence in human interaction: Using data to make better inferences about influence within social systems. *IEEE Signal Processing Magazine*, *29*(2), 77–86.

Park, J., & Cai, H. (2015). Automatic construction schedule generation method through BIM model creation. *Computing in Civil Engineering*, *2015*, 620–627.

Paschen, U., Pitt, C., & Kietzmann, J. (2020). Artificial intelligence: Building blocks and an innovation typology. *Business Horizons*, *63*(2), 147–155.

Patil, P. A., & Salunkhe, A. (2020). Comparative analysis of construction cost estimation using artificial neural networks. *Journal of Xidian University*, *14*, 7.

Pillai, V. S., & Matus, K. J. (2021). *Towards a responsible integration of artificial intelligence technology in the construction sector*. Science and Public Policy.

Prieto, B. (2019). Impacts of artificial intelligence on management of large complex projects. *PM World Journal*, *VIII*(V). June 2019.

Prieto, S., de Soto, B. G., & Adán, A. (2020). A methodology to monitor construction progress using autonomous robots. Series A Methodology to Monitor Construction Progress Using Autonomous Robots ISARC.

Project Management Institute (US). (2017). *A guide to the Project Management Body of Knowledge (PMBOK® Guide)* (6th ed.). Newtown Square, Pa: Project Management Institute, Inc.

PwC. (2018). UK Economic Outlook, Price Waterhouse Cooper. viewed 04 March 2019, <https://www.pwc.co.uk/services/economics-policy/insights/uk-economic-outlook.html>.

Rexford, J. (2018). The role of education in AL (and vice versa). interviewed by R. Kirkland, viewed 18 November 2020, <https://www.mckinsey.com/featured-insights/artificial-intelligence/the-role-of-education-in-ai-and-vice-versa>.

Rezaie, K., Amalnik, M. S., Gereie, A., Ostadi, B., & Shakhseniaee, M. (2007). Using extended Monte Carlo simulation method for the improvement of risk management: Consideration of relationships between uncertainties. *Applied Mathematics and Computation*, *190*(2), 1492–1501.

Rodrigues, R. (2020). Legal and human rights issues of AI: Gaps, challenges and vulnerabilities. *Journal of Responsible Technology*, *4*, 100005.

Rossi, A., Vila, Y., Lusiani, F., Barsotti, L., Sani, L., Ceccarelli, P., & Lanzetta, M. (2019). Embedded smart sensor device in construction site machinery. *Computers in Industry*, *108*, 12–20.

Runco, M. A. (1994). *Problem finding, problem-solving, and creativity*. Greenwood Publishing Group.

Ruuska, I., & Vartiainen, I. (2003). Critical project competences–a case study. *Journal of Workplace Learning*.

Saad, U., Afzal, U., El-Issawi, A., & Eid, M. (2017). A model to measure QoE for virtual personal assistant. *Multimedia Tools and Applications*, *76*(10), 12517–12537.

Saidi, K. S., Bock, T., & Georgoulas, C. (2016). Robotics in construction. In *Springer handbook of robotics* (pp. 1493–1520). Springer.

Schumpeter, J. (1942). *Capitalism, socialism and democracy*. New York: Harper, 1975.

Schwab, K. (2016). The Fourth Industrial Revolution: what it means, how to respond., viewed 16 January 2021, <https://www.weforum.org/agenda/2016/01/the-fourth-industrial-revolution-what-it-means-and-how-to-respond/>.

Schwiedrzik, C. M., Melloni, L., & Schurger, A. (2018). Mooney face stimuli for visual perception research. *PloS One*, *13*(7), e0200106–e.

Shen, Z., & Izza, R. (2010). Quantitative evaluation of the BIM-assisted construction detailed cost estimates. *Journal of Information Technology in Construction*, *15*, 234–257.

Shenhar, A. J. (1999). Strategic project management: The new framework. Paper presented to the Portland International Conference on Management of Engineering and Technology (PICMET) Proceedings, Portland, OR.

Simon, L. (2006). Managing creative projects: An empirical synthesis of activities. *International Journal of Project Management*, *24*(2), 116–126.

Solomon Olusola, B., Srinath, P., Lei, Z., & Chika, U. (2016). Stakeholder perceptions on critical success factors for public-private partnership projects in Nigeria. *Built Environment Project and Asset Management*, *6*(1), 74–91.

Strohmeier, S. & Piazza, F. (2015). Artificial intelligence techniques in human resource management – a conceptual exploration. In Kahraman, C. and Onar, S. Ç. (Eds.), *Intelligent techniques in engineering management* (Vol. 87). Springer.

Tallgren, M. V., Roupé, M., Johansson, M., & Bosch-Sijtsema, P. (2020). BIM tool development enhancing collaborative scheduling for pre-construction. *Journal of Information Technology in Construction*, *25*, 374–397.

Thi, C. H., & Swierczek, F. W. (2010). Critical success factors in project management: Implication from Vietnam. *Asia Pacific Business Review*, *16*(4), 567–589.

Trevelyan, L. 2018, rise of the robots: the implications for legal teams, viewed 26 July 2019, <https://www.ibanet.org/Article/NewDetail.aspx?ArticleUid=9bfea263-fa14-4e88-981f-5efa7b58>.

Tzeng, G.-H., & Huang, -J.-J. (2011). *Multiple attribute decision making: Methods and applications*. CRC press.

Usher, G. (2021). *Project management in the twenty-first century*. Springer Nature.

Usher, G. & Whitty, S. J. (2017). Identifying and managing drift-changes. *International Journal of Project Management*, *35*(4), 586–603.

Vom Brocke, J., & Lippe, S. (2010). Towards creativity-aware project management–An initial study on creativity in research projects.

Weick, K. E., Sutcliffe, K. M., & Obstfeld, D. (2005). Organising and the process of sensemaking. *Organization Science*, *16*(4), 409–421.

Wiegers, K. (2007). *Practical project initiation: A handbook with tools*. Microsoft Press.

Wiggers, K. 2019, Intel claims Aurora will be the first US supercomputer to hit 1 exaflop, viewed 06 February 2021, <https://venturebeat.com/2019/03/18/intel-claims-aurora-will-be-the-first-u-s-supercomputer-to-hit-1-exaflop/>.

Wong, A. (2020). The laws and regulation of Ai and autonomous systems. In *Unimagined futures—ICT opportunities and challenges* (pp. 38–54). Springer.

Wonil, L., Seto, E., Lin, K., & Migliaccio, G. (2017). An evaluation of wearable sensors and their placements for analysing construction worker's trunk posture in laboratory conditions. *Applied Ergonomics, 65,* 424–436.

Woodhead, R., Stephenson, P., & Morrey, D. (2018). Digital construction: From point solutions to IoT ecosystem. *Automation in Construction, 93,* 35–46.

Woschank, M., Rauch, E., & Zsifkovits, H. (2020). A review of further directions for artificial intelligence, machine learning, and deep learning in smart logistics'. *Sustainability, 12*(9), 3760.

Yan, X., Li, H., Li, A. R., & Zhang, H. (2017). Wearable IMU-based real-time motion warning system for construction workers' musculoskeletal disorders prevention. *Automation in Construction, 74,* 2–11.

Yu, C., Zou, Z., Shao, Y., & Zhang, F. (2019). An integrated supplier selection approach incorporating decision maker's risk attitude using ANN, AHP and TOPSIS methods. *Kybernetes.*

Zhen, L., Wu, Y., Wang, S., Hu, Y., & Yi, W. (2018). Capacitated closed-loop supply chain network design under uncertainty. *Advanced Engineering Informatics, 38,* 306–315.

Zuo, J., Zhao, X., Nguyen, Q. B. M., Ma, T., & Gao, S. (2018). Soft skills of construction project management professionals and project success factors: A structural equation model. *Engineering, Construction, and Architectural Management, 25*(3), 425–442.

Ganesh Devkar and Shankar Sankaran

12 Responsible Leadership in Megaprojects

Context: Megaprojects are a phenomenon for fulfilling infrastructure requirements and aspirations of citizens of a nation.

Characters/entities: Leaders of project teams working on megaprojects.

Locations: Megaprojects occur worldwide, an example is given from Panama.

Research gaps: Owing to the sheer quantum of resources consumed in megaproject development and its future impact, the delivery of these megaprojects under the aegis of responsible leadership has become a cornerstone. This chapter discusses the four framework levels for responsible leadership in megaprojects: stakeholder relations, operational roles, leadership roles, and character.

Challenges/tensions: This framework provides a roadmap toward imbibing the principles of responsible leadership in megaprojects derived from academic and professional literatures. The framework provides direction for research and professional trajectories to build capacity in the domain of megaproject development.

Keywords: megaprojects, leadership, stakeholder management, operations

12.1 Introduction

The worldwide demand for quality infrastructure has been a never-ending juggernaut. In recent years, megaprojects have become a popular vehicle for delivering much-needed infrastructure (Flyvbjerg, 2014 b). Megaprojects have been broadly described as "large-scale, complex investments that typically cost a billion dollars and up, take many years to develop and build, involve multiple public and private stakeholders, are transformational, and impact millions of people" (Flyvbjerg, 2014 b). Although there is no single definition of the megaproject, they are commonly characterized by the quantum of investment. The differentiation of a project as a megaproject based on investment was highlighted by Flyvbjerg (2016). The US Federal Highway Administration classifies major infrastructure projects costing more than USD 1 billion as megaprojects (Capka, 2004). The definition varies among countries, and projects costing substantially higher (around USD 20 billion) or lower (USD 500 million) than the American figure of USD 1 billion are classified as megaprojects (Flyvbjerg, 2016). Hu, Chan, Le, & Jin (2015) attempted to systematize the definition of megaprojects based on the cost figures by examining megaproject cost–GDP ratios of different countries and regions. Based on this analysis, they arrived at 0.01% as a reasonable criterion for characterizing a project as a megaproject. There are various synonyms for megaprojects,

https://doi.org/10.1515/9783110724783-015

including large engineering projects, complex projects, and large infrastructure projects. Megaprojects are conceived, nurtured, constructed, and operated owing to their symbolic roles (Warrack, 1993) and driven by sublimes (Flyvbjerg, 2014 b). While referring to symbolism, Warrack (1993, p. 2) states that "megaprojects have powerful economic, social, and symbolic roles in the society." In a similar vein, Flyvbjerg (2014) explains four sublimes that drive megaproject development, viz., technological, political, economic, and aesthetics. This symbolism and sublimes have fueled the development of megaprojects across many industries and sectors like airports, seaports, hospitals, health systems, information technology and communication, large-scale signature architecture, dams, wind farms, and logistics. Interestingly, Flyvbjerg (2014 b) propounded the "megaproject paradox" concept, which posits that more and more megaprojects are being built despite the cost and schedule overruns and benefit shortfalls. This indicates that megaprojects will continue to lead the infrastructure development across the globe despite their poor performance measured using conventional project management success criteria.

The characterization of megaprojects is an ever-evolving process. Even though investment figures may be a reasonable attempt at providing a glimpse of what constitutes a megaproject, other dimensions like the social, economic, environmental, and technological footprint could be more promising dimensions for defining megaprojects. The most common features discussed in the literature are size, which refers to a project's physical size or impact, cost in terms of quantum of investments, and timeline or duration referring to contractual milestones or specific timelines for project completion (Love & Ahiaga-Dagbui, 2018). The feature of risk, complexity, and uncertainty have been gaining attention in the recent past (Giezen, 2013; Kardes et al., 2013; Sanderson, 2012; Wang et al., 2020). These characteristics mainly capture the technical and managerial face of megaprojects. However, with the advent of the UN's Sustainable Development Goals (SDGs), the sustainability sublime is expected to elicit more attention in the coming years (Sankaran et al., 2020). This includes focusing on aspects like societal gains, protection of marginalized, environmental protection and ensuring the interests of future generations, societal governance, co-creation of shared value by all stakeholders, and community involvement and benefits (Bornstein, 2010; Ma et al., 2017).

The diverse characteristics of megaprojects mentioned earlier have directed the attention of both academics and practitioners toward more effective planning, procurement, construction, and operation of megaprojects. For a nonspecialist, megaprojects often elicit various engineering, technological, and political feats, as sublimes mentioned by Flyvbjerg (2014 b). Along with these feats, the megaprojects often gain public attention, owing to poor performance on parameters like time and cost overruns. There exist many research articles prominently written by Flyvbjerg (Cantarelli et al., 2010; Flyvbjerg, 2014; Flyvbjerg et al., 2002, 2018), highlighting the failure to complete the megaprojects within time and budget. The poor performance of megaprojects has led to many inquiries at the governmental levels and research studies investigating causes or factors leading to this poor performance.

In recent years, policy discourses and academic debates include the need to revisit the traditional lens of project "success" and "failure" while investigating the performance of a megaproject. This is an important silver lining in megaprojects because megaproject implementation is more often mentioned in poor light. Megaprojects, in essence, are crafted to meet the goals and aspirations of the present and future generations. There is no doubt that these megaprojects have contributed significantly, but the state of art still needs substantial improvement. Rather than branding megaprojects as either failure, which is more often, or success, it may be relevant to conduct a retrospective analysis for identifying "what has been good about the process so far" and "how specifically might we improve this process in the future" (Mossman, 2021; Nanda et al., 2017). This analysis, referred to as plus delta analysis, is a popular technique in lean manufacturing.

The "plus" in state of art of megaproject implementation has been studied in recent literature in terms of characteristics and drivers that make megaprojects successful and redefining measures for megaprojects' success. Turner and Xue (2018, p. 798) developed a new model for the success of megaprojects and have applied this model in case studies of megaprojects. The analysis from this study is interesting and states that "Many of the projects that were finished late and/or overspent, and so would be considered a project management failure by traditional standards (Cooke-Davies, 2002) delivered an asset of value at a time and cost that made it valuable." The authors have also highlighted the examples of case studies wherein the megaprojects provide the general public good. However, these benefits are not measurable regarding financial aspects such as value for money. Along similar lines, Shenhar and Holzmann (2017) analyzed the success of 14 megaprojects on dimensions of efficiency, customer, business/financial, and society. The analysis showed that each mega project was successful in at least one dimension. As these studies indicate the megaprojects are indeed successful or effectively implemented, provided the performance of these projects is measured against a new set of parameters rather than traditional standards, the other research trajectory focused on the secrets of megaprojects' success.

Literature on project management often focuses on success factors and success drivers for a diverse set of projects implemented with contracting models like public–private partnerships, engineering procurement, and construction. Research on megaprojects has been identifying and conceptualizing the success factors by analyzing success, rarely from the traditional lens, which is used to measure the success of projects in general. Shenhar and Holzmann (2017) discussed three distinguishing elements of successful megaprojects – strategic vision, total alignment, and adapting to complexity. Although the studies have more commonly analyzed the dataset of megaprojects from varied sectors, studies focus on megaprojects' success in specific sectors such as the energy sector (Locatelli et al., 2014), events, and exposition (Hu et al., 2015).

Studies have explored the other side of the coin – the poor performance of megaprojects. The most commonly discussed aspect is the time and cost overrun of megaprojects in this domain. Similar to studies focusing on the success of megaprojects, the poor performance of a megaproject is investigated from either a cross-sector overview or sectoral focus. These studies do not stop merely at citing the reasons for the poor performance of megaprojects but also provide remedies and directions to avoid these pitfalls in future megaprojects. For example, the analysis of nuclear power plant projects (NPPs) in France, Germany, and Finland conducted by Locatelli (2018) revealed that a novel complex technology with a complex network of stakeholders results in late and over-budget delivery of the NPPs. Further, Locatelli (2018) advocated remedies like technical standardization and project delivery chain standardization.

Among sector-specific studies, mega transportation projects continue to be under the microscope. One interesting aspect of these studies is crafting the conceptual framework or hypothesis for deciphering the causes and suggesting areas of improvement. The relationship between project ownership and cost performance of transportation megaprojects was investigated by Cantarelli and Flyvbjerg (2015). They showed a lack of evidence for private parties' involvement and better project performance. However, an analysis of the case study project, namely, HSL-South, a high-speed railway line in The Netherlands, showed that the contracting strategy and private financing are better determinants for project performance. In a similar vein, Cantarelli (2010) categorized the explanations for cost overruns in large transportation projects under technical, economic, psychological, and political factors. They proposed that political explanations can be theorized with agency theory while nonpolitical explanations can be understood with various theories like rational choice theory and prospect theory. These research investigations help solve the panacea of time and cost overruns faced by megaprojects. These issues are intertwined with other facets that require a substantial improvement in megaproject management, such as stakeholder management, IT innovation, accountability, and transparency. Hu et al.(2015) have performed a systematic review of megaprojects' literature and showed that the earlier mentioned facets had gained attention in the academic literature. Among these facets, "leadership" has recently gained academic and practitioner literature attention, which was not analyzed much earlier. This chapter posits that this aspect will gain more attention in the coming years and will be a prominent area of future megaproject research.

12.2 Megaprojects' Leadership – Improving the State of the Art of Megaproject Implementation

Megaprojects leadership as an essential ingredient for delivering successful mega-projects was highlighted by Hoover (2019). The paper mentions five leadership success constituents: building trust and communication, cohesion and collaboration among team members, transparent and authentic leadership, creating nimble and autonomous teams, and educated – experienced ownership. A report authored by Nuno Gill and Colm Lundrigan titled "The Leadership and Governance of Megaprojects" is a culmination of insights gained from events organized by the Center for Infrastructure Development (CID) for bringing two communities – management and organization scholars and industry on a common platform (Gil & Lundrigan, 2012). This report states that the "megaproject leadership function is fundamentally different from the megaproject management function" (Gil & Lundrigan, 2012, p. 2). This statement directs attention toward a new research trajectory for megaproject researchers. Often, leadership is deliberated from the viewpoint of project managers or project engineers, which is grounded more in operational roles. At the same time, this report carves out "megaproject leadership" as a distinct area. The leadership traits mentioned in this report are sincerity, empathy, openness, effective communication, and simplification.

There exist other studies focusing on traits in megaproject leaders. Anderson Jr. and Polkinghorn (2008) examined the Woodrow Wilson Bridge. They attributed the successful completion of this megaproject, despite the risk and complexity associated with it, to the following leadership traits: (1) awareness by project leadership of the immense public scrutiny a major infrastructure project can draw; (2) leadership that responds to political and public demands (both previously mentioned); and (3) leadership that employs conflict prevention and management philosophies, tools, and processes efficiently and effectively.

There has been a spate of reports and initiatives by the practitioner community about embracing the concept of "megaproject leaders." The need for shifting focus from technical to people was highlighted in Roth et al. (2016), mentioning key differentiators of future megaproject leaders: strategic mindset, change leadership, communication in all its forms, business acumen, balanced decision-making, and political intelligence. McKinsey released a report titled "The art of project leadership: Delivering the world's largest projects" in 2018. As part of this report, mega-project leaders across the globe were interviewed, which led to the synthesis of four mindsets that define the "art" of project leadership. The megaproject leader necessitates visualization of the megaproject as a business and subsequently provides leadership at this level to deal with various organizational issues. The accountability for project delivery must be created with the project owner by keeping them informed across the project life cycle and, in turn, enabling them to make tough decisions. Mutual trust and joint problem solving should lay the foundation for the contractor–owner relationship. A megaproject leader must trust and enforce appropriate processes and step in resolving challenges that arise in megaprojects.

The above requirements necessitate the reinvention of the traditional concept of "leadership." This reinvention was the focus of a report by the Australian Contractors Association titled "Changing the game: Australian new world of megaprojects" (ACA, 2019), and it mentions "changing the megaproject leaders" is the cornerstone for achieving megaproject success in Australia. The required changes proposed in this report are (1) creation of new leadership models to lead complex social solutions rather than managing complicated technological projects alone, (2) shift in the current form of the centralized project leader to enabling leadership, and (3) development of next generation of leaders by apprenticeship or other mechanisms. A research study by the Association of Project Management highlights the need for a new approach required for gender balance in major projects' leadership. In this context, developing responsible leaders becomes a vital component. This aspect is discussed in greater detail in the chapters of this book that focus on education and responsible leadership.

This academic and professional work has brought the topic of "megaproject leadership" to the forefront. In terms of consolidation of narratives, life stories, and practical insights on megaproject leadership, the recently published book *Megaproject Leaders: Reflections on Personal Life Stories* is a torchbearer and has paved the way for future research in this area (Drouin et al., 2021). There is no doubt that the existing studies have created a fertile ground for further research trajectories. However, an established overarching framework can provide direction to this existing discourse on megaproject leadership. The theme of "responsible leadership" can steer the discourse on leadership in megaprojects.

12.3 Responsible Leadership in the Context of Megaprojects

Marques et al. (2018), who performed a bibliometric review of research in the area, confirm that "responsible leadership is becoming a hot topic both in academia and the business world." They also point out that responsible leadership is distinct from other perspectives on leadership, such as transactional or transformational or ethical leadership, as "it is anchored on the assumption that leaders must balance different (and potentially conflicting) sets of interests." Their analysis of the reviewed articles shows that the interest in responsible leadership increased rapidly between 2006 and 2020 and is showing further growth.

Maak and Pless (2006), who have published extensively on the concept, explain that responsible leadership is concerned with "leadership dynamics in the stakeholder society and includes the ethical perspective – the norms, values and principles" (Pless, 2007, p. 438). They also propose how responsible leaders can engage with their internal and external stakeholders (Maak & Pless, 2006).

- Employees: Leaders can ensure that they have created working conditions that are humane, safe, healthy, and nondiscriminatory. They could also provide equal employment opportunities and strive to enable a good work–life balance.
- Clients and customers: In addition to delivering products and services that customers want, responsible leaders should ensure "safe and not harmful."
- Business partners: Responsible leaders treat their business partners "respectfully and fairly." They would also ensure that their partners adopt the labor standards adhered to by the leader's organization.
- Social and natural environment: Responsible leaders will "assess the impact of their business decisions on the social and natural environment." In addition, they will also arrange to "train their people in sustainable development."
- Shareholders: While taking care of other stakeholders, responsible leaders should also see that their shareholder's interests are protected and "ensure an adequate return" from their investment.

Pless (2007) suggests that while responsible leadership started as a social and moral phenomenon due to scandals such as Enron, Parmalat, and World.com, there is also a positive side "multinational corporations and their leaders have an enormous potential for contributing to the betterment of the world." Pless (2007) focuses on the essential behavior of responsible leaders as intrapsychic drivers or motivational-led systems and moral drivers.

The intrapsychic drivers include a need to explore or experiment, a need for attachment through connectedness, and enjoyment. In contrast, moral and normative drivers consist of a need for justice – "fairness and a moral framework as a basis of human interaction," a need for recognition, and a motivating environment by recognizing others. They demonstrate a sense of care by considering the needs of others, nature and living conditions when working in less developed locations, and keeping future generations in mind.

Pless and Maak (2011) state that there is a growing need for current leadership theories to address the challenges, roles, and responsibilities of leaders in light of social and environmental crises such as the Exxon Valdez spill in Alaska, the Bhopal disaster for Union Carbide, Shell's Brent Spar, and Nigerian failures. Responsible leadership also places new demands in business contexts to meet stakeholder expectations "to take active roles in fostering responsible behaviour, within and outside the organisation" that includes creating responsible cultures and acting as good citizens.

A recent systematic literature review of research into the challenges, outcomes, and practices of responsible leadership (Greige Frangieh & Khayr Yaacoub, 2017) clarifies that it is not viewed in the same way by all. There could be limited economic or shareholder views of responsibility based on the Friedman doctrine (1970). Freeman et al.'s (2004) view on stakeholder theory could be based on which Doh and Quigley (2014) clarify that a responsible leader should consider "shareowners, employees, customers, communities and suppliers" as stakeholders, confirming the views expressed by Maak and Pless (2006).

Greige Frangieh and Khayr Yaacoub (2017) conclude from their systematic review that responsible leadership is still emerging as a leadership theory and needs more empirical evidence to be established. Furthermore, while the theory has led to academic interest, it has not offered any practical solutions for leaders to prioritize stakeholder interests when they conflict. There is a need to discuss "the different kinds of organisational pressures that leaders face in organisations and the means to alleviate these pressures to allow for more responsible behaviour." However, the authors add that literature does provide evidence of positive financial outcomes from responsible leadership, but further research is required to confirm causality.

In summary, the idea of responsible leadership is gaining worldwide attention and is moving beyond just focusing on ethical and moral behavior. Researchers are asking leaders to improve stakeholder relationships and suggest the development of metrics to evaluate the benefits of responsible leadership. It is expected that these metrics could help leaders improve their responsible behavior toward society while also delivering results expected from their business.

12.4 Responsible Leadership and Project Management

The idea of responsible project leadership is also gaining attention with recent research on governance, trust, and ethics in projects (Müller et al., 2013). The PMI has sponsored a study on responsible leadership (Clare et al., 2018). However, the role of project management in sustainability and sustainable development, which is linked to responsible leadership, has been a topic of interest to project management researchers for almost a decade now. A brief review of this literature might be useful at this juncture.

Gauthier and Ika (2012) point out that managing projects may have to change to align closely with sustainable development in the postmodern social world. Morris (2013) urges us to reconstruct project management to consider sustainable development a challenge to project, program, and portfolio management. Morris suggested that project managers play a lead role in advancing sustainability at the IRNOP 2015 conference held at University College London.

It is also interesting to see how project management's key bodies view the field's responsibility toward sustainability. At the International Project Management Association's expert seminar held in Zurich in February 2016, Yvonne Schoper identified the sustainability of projects as one of the important issues that project managers face. Schoper and Gemünden (2016) elaborated further at the seminar that projects' environmental, social, and life cycle aspects need to be considered. They suggested that "The implication of the trend [sustainability] is that it will increase the accountability of organisations contracting a project beyond their risks and benefits towards the risks and benefits of external stakeholders affected by their project. It will transform the role of project management by challenging if they do the 'right things right'. The specific reference to stakeholders aligns with the literature on responsible leadership."

The Project Management Institute's Pulse of the Profession Report 2018 states that sustainable development, climate change, and renewable energy are affecting businesses as a disruptive trend that needs to be dealt with by project management professionals. Silvius and van den Brink (2014) report the Association of Project Management's Vice President Mary McKinlay (2008) stressed that "the further development of project management profession requires project managers to take responsibility for sustainability at the IPMA World Congress." These trends predicted by the key bodies of project management confirm that there is indeed a growing recognition in the profession that sustainable development is a challenge we can no longer ignore.

Some researchers (Silvius et al., 2009; Garies et al., 2009) have also been investigating the role of project management in sustainable development. Marcelino-Sádaba et al. (2015) point out that sustainability has been recognized as a challenge in several constructions, infrastructure, mining, energy, and new product development. Huemann and Silvius (2017) have recently suggested that sustainability could even gain importance by becoming a new school of thought in project management, extending the nine schools proposed by Turner et al. (2010). In a guest editorial of papers published under the title "Projects to create the future: Managing projects meets sustainable development," Huemann and Silvius (2017, p. 1066) emphasize that "project management has a vital role in contributing to the sustainable development of organisations and society, raising the societal responsibility of our profession."

Despite the growing awareness of project management's role in sustainable development, there seems to be no clear guidance on how to go about it (Huemann & Silvius, 2017). Martens and Carvalho (2016) add that "there is a gap between the perception of importance and the actual use of Sustainability in Project Management (SPM) practice." Marcelino-Sádaba et al. (2015) propose that one way to deal with this is to develop sustainability competencies that project managers must acquire. However, addressing environmental sustainability issues is insufficient to demonstrate responsible leadership in projects.

Labuschagne and Brent (2005) argue that, as a project management community, we need to address three goals of sustainable development: social equity, economic efficiency, and environmental performance. They add that we must establish ways to achieve sustainable life cycle management.

One of the issues facing project management regarding sustainable development is the temporary nature of projects. Projects are often bound by time, cost, scope, and quality and are often defined as temporary with a finite end (Jones & Lichtenstein, 2009).

This poses a conundrum as sustainability challenges are rarely time-limited, nor can they be decoupled from the context, nor are they easily predictable. There is also limited research focusing on the wider organizational considerations to carry out sustainable projects by balancing social, environmental, and economic issues in both short- and long-term orientation and local and global contexts (Silvius and van den Brink, 2014). This also makes it difficult to set project goals.

In summary, project management faces a knowing–doing gap in identifying practical ways in which it would have to change to deal with the increased awareness of its societal and environmental responsibilities. Aarseth et al. (2017), who carried out a systematic literature review of project sustainability strategies, highlight the importance of setting strategic sustainability goals and developing sustainability competencies. These can help in the development of responsible leadership in projects. Next, we propose an initial framework for responsible leadership in projects based on the literature reviewed for this chapter.

12.5 Framework for Responsible Leadership in Megaprojects

Based on the role model of responsible leadership proposed by Maak and Pless (2006), there are four levels of responsible leadership in megaprojects – character, leadership role, operational role, and stakeholder connections. These are shown in Figure 12.1.

12.5.1 Stakeholder Relations

a. Customer (end-user, project owner, or sponsor)
b. Governance bodies (board, steering committee, PMO)
c. Project team members
d. Peers (functional managers, other project managers in programs)
e. Suppliers (contractors, suppliers of products and services, labor)
f. Community (if project causes displacement)
g. Family (work–life balance)

h. Fellow citizens (social responsibility)
i. Future generations (environmental responsibility)

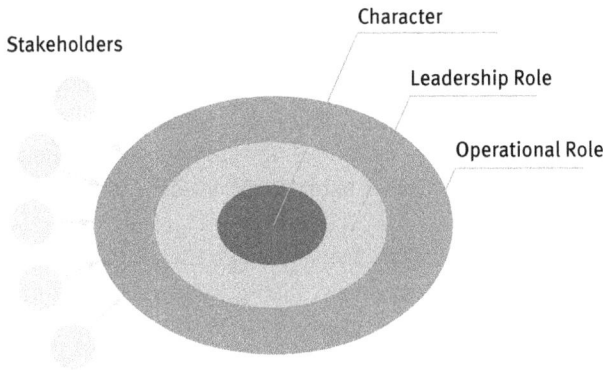

Figure 12.1: Proposed responsible leadership framework for project leaders (adapted for this chapter from Mark & Pless, 2006, p. 107).

12.5.2 Operational Roles

a. Change agent (assist in delivering benefits)
b. Coach (developing team members)
c. Meaning enabler (work across cultures, shared meaning of the project and its goals)
d. Project leader (delivering project, ethical and moral decision-making)

12.5.3 Leadership Roles

a. Visionary (work toward common purpose or goals)
b. Citizen (environmental and social responsibility)
c. Steward (focus on community and society)
d. Servant (sharing power, putting people first)

12.5.4 Character (Ethical and Moral Qualities)

Several roles are not new and are practiced in projects in various ways. Nevertheless, some may be beyond the current scope and understanding of the role of a project leader. In the next section, we discuss literature related to these roles where they already exist.

12.5.5 Stakeholder Relations

Relationships listed under stakeholder relations, points a to e, could be considered expected of a project leader. Relationships f to i are relatively new.

Megaproject delivery is often driven by parameters like time, cost, and quality and is mentioned in supply chain partners' various binding contractual arrangements. Due to this focus, the construction supply chain or megaproject delivery supply chain partners comprising governmental bodies, sponsoring organizations, approval agencies, subcontractors, and project team members have been given preference in the megaproject development. First, the megaproject leader must reinvent the relationships with these stakeholders. Secondly, there is a need to integrate and bring other stakeholders like community, family, fellow citizens, and future generations to the center stage.

The megaproject leader must understand the values and expectations of customer care. These customers can be end-user, sponsors, or project owners. Furthermore, it is necessary to direct these values and expectations in the right direction during the megaproject life cycle. For example, Theurillat and Crevoisier (2013) explained how the involvement of financial actors and their interaction with other actors in the institutional, spatial, and temporal context influences the creation of sustainability in megaprojects.

The governing structure of megaprojects has not attracted much attention in megaproject literature. It is expected that the megaproject leader understands the influencing role played by cultural practices on the governance of this megaproject. In a similar vein, the analysis of intra-organization and inter-organization trust under the conditions of power asymmetry and power-sharing in megaproject governance has been conducted by Deng et al. (2021). These studies draw attention to the increasingly important issue of megaproject governance, and the megaproject leader should be aware of and tuned to these developments.

Although megaprojects are conceived, developed, constructed, and operated by the project owners and sponsors, one cannot deny that these projects are created to serve the ultimate end user – the general public or taxpayer or a specific set of users. The embedment of the megaproject into the surrounding social-cultural milieu is missed by many megaproject leaders, resulting in resistance and value erosion for the facility users and the surrounding community. In large infrastructure projects, this causes displacements, and community relationships assume importance, as communities are often affected adversely during and after the projects are implemented. Stakeholder involvement tools have been proposed in project management literature on appropriate community engagement in megaprojects (El-Gohary et al., 2006). However, in the megaproject literature, the general public or users are often referred to as "external" stakeholders (Di Maddaloni & Davis, 2017; Ninan et al., 2019). The megaproject leader must internalize these "external" stakeholders like users, community, and even future generations to shape and implement megaprojects (Di Maddaloni & Davis, 2017). Neglecting this is a recipe for community resistance (Jordhus-Lier, 2015) and asymmetric legitimacy perception (Witz et al., 2021).

Supply chain management necessitates greater attention due to megaprojects' uncertainty and complexity. With the greater emphasis on social responsibility and environmental protection, there is a call for embracing sustainability in supplier selection in megaprojects (Mahmoudi et al., 2021). The megaproject leader must play a crucial role in green supply chain management with practices like green supplier selection (Liang & Chong, 2019).

Aspects like social and environmental responsibility are relatively new in the context of megaprojects. Hence, direction and leadership by the top echelon of megaprojects are paramount. The relationship between the adoption of megaproject social responsibility and personal psychological traits of top managers, with particular focus on chief executive officer (CEO) narcissism, is discussed in a study by Lin et al. (2018). This study is relevant for megaproject leaders. The requirements are mentioned aptly as "managers should be motivated to think modestly about the relationship of megaprojects with society from a sustainable perspective and be driven to improve their cognition of MSR to promote the megaproject's social responsibility."

Megaproject leaders have to play a transformative role in changing the perceptions of project participants toward Megaproject Environmental Responsibility (MER) practices and their commitment to the environment (Wang et al., 2017). The importance of leadership in this regard is mentioned by Wang et al. (2017) as follows: "leadership has been recognised as one of the most critical factors influencing the emergence of organisational citizenship behaviours for the environment (OCBEs)."

Relationships with family would need more exploration on how project leaders can deal with these stakeholder demands. Although the general management literature has advocated the need for work-life balance both for the manager and their subordinates, this aspect has not been investigated much in a project management situation, even though managing a project can be a stressful experience. A few papers are written about the project manager's role in improving the working conditions in projects to manage stress (Gällstedt, 2003) and the effect of transformational leaders in projects on the stress management of their team members (Keegan & Den Hartog, 2004).

The relationship of projects with the associated stakeholders has been discussed at greater length in the chapters of this book, focusing on responsible project management for communities.

12.5.6 Operational Roles

In operational roles (Item 2 in our framework), the role of the project manager may not generally extend to benefits management. In some instances, the operational part of the project is included in the scope of the megaprojects when the project management organization may also be involved in benefits realization. However, there is an increased realization that project managers should be aware of the benefits of change management after the project is delivered. Benefit management seems to fall under the responsibility of program management (Axelos, 2014). Therefore, project managers would be conscious of the need for benefits management when their project is overseen in a program. The role of the project manager as a coach is becoming relevant in leadership responsibilities (Müller et al., 2018). Pilkienė et al. (2018) and Marrewijk et al. (2016) have described the role of coach and mentor played by the agent, in this case, the US-based CH2M Hill, a global leader in program management and Autoridad del Canal de Panamá (ACP), for the temporary organization of the Panama Canal Expansion Program (PCEP). The term "meaning making" is not commonly used in project management, but "sensemaking" is becoming an important part of complex projects (Alderman et al., 2005). This could create shared meaning across a project. Delivering the project is a basic operational responsibility of a project leader, but doing it ethically and morally is important for responsible leadership (Clarke et al., 2018).

12.5.7 Leadership Roles

In leadership roles, the visionary role has been discussed in project management research on project managers' competencies for success (Müller & Turner, 2010) and the role of a transformational leader (Keegan & Den Hartog, 2004). The roles of citizen and steward are relatively new but will become important as increased importance is placed on the role of project management in the UN SDGs (Aarseth et al., 2017; UN, 2018), even identifying indicators in developing sustainable infrastructure (Fernández-Sánchez & Rodríguez-López, 2010), which is expected in megaprojects (Kwak et al., 2009). Ma et al. (2020) investigated stewardship behavior in a case study project – the South-to-North Water Diversion Project. They reported that the behavior could be identified through psychological, situational, and relational dimensions. Melé (2016) mentions humanistic management as "people-oriented management that seeks profits for human ends." Stewardship sustainability is one of the seven propositions put forth by Melé (2016) on what form of genuine humanism.

Along with other propositions like wholeness, comprehensive knowledge, human dignity, development, common good, and transcendence, the stewardship-sustainability proposition that "recognises the interconnection of the human being with the environment and all living things and promotes a sense of stewardship (Camargo & Vázquez-Maguirre, 2021)" is well connected with megaprojects, owing to social and environmental footprint. Megaproject leaders being in the leadership position have to ingrain a "humanistic/people-oriented approach" in megaproject management. Servant leadership is often associated with a scrum master's role in projects using an agile methodology (Yi, 2011). Avery (2015) proposed servant leadership in projects that use conventional methods to reduce risks when these projects become complex.

12.5.8 Character

Character, ethical, and moral judgment were discussed in responsible leadership in projects by Clarke et al. (2018). These could also fall under authentic leadership, which was discussed by Lloyd-Walker and Walker (2011). From the preceding discussion, we can see that several elements of our proposed framework have been discussed in various ways in the project management literature. However, a comprehensive discussion of responsible leadership is still needed to guide project leaders. The ethical dimension in responsible project management may be expected to take center stage in coming years and have immense research potential. This dimension is discussed in the chapter of this book that focuses on ethical research questions in responsible project management.

12.6 Conclusions

By adopting the character of responsible leadership, megaproject leaders would deliver societal benefits while reducing ecological harm by taking a wider view of stakeholder interests over space and time. This does not mean that they should overlook the economic benefits that megaprojects were conceived to achieve but do so culturally and ecologically responsible ways. This can be achieved through the five dimensions of a responsible leader – awareness, vision, imagination, responsibility, and action (Bettignies, 2014).

Environmental, social, and governance issues are becoming increasingly important to organizations to achieve their long-term goals, and they will also become essential to project organizations. Megaprojects are no exception. The World Economic Forum points out that the investment in megaprojects by the G-20 countries is equivalent to 8% of the global GDP (Alexander, 2015). While such investment may be necessary to meet the demands of a growing population, megaprojects must be carefully managed to be sustainable. The forum felt that rapid growth could cause irreparable social and environmental damage. Drouin et al. (2021) suggest that while mega projects are essential to societies, modern-day megaproject leaders have a great responsibility.

Research trajectories:
- To conduct narrative analysis of life stories of megaproject leaders from the lens of responsible leadership

260 — Ganesh Devkar and Shankar Sankaran

- To analyze the challenges and opportunities faced by megaproject leaders in translating responsible leadership to practice
- To explore interlinks of responsible leadership with relevant theoretical frameworks

References

Aarseth, W., Ahola, T., Aaltonen, K., Økland, A., & Andersen, B. (2017). Project sustainability strategies: A systematic literature review. *International Journal of Project Management, 35*(6), 1071–1083.

ACA. (2019). *Changing the game: How Australia can achieve success in the new world of megaprojects* (pp. 1–35). Sydney: Australian Constructors Association.

Alderman, N., Ivory, C., McLoughlin, I., & Vaughan, R. (2005). Sensemaking is a process within complex service-led projects. *International Journal of Project Management, 23*(5), 380–385.

Alexander, N. (2015). "Is the boom in megaprojects sustainable?" World Economic Forum, Switzerland.

Anderson, L. L., Jr., & Polkinghorn, B. (2008). Managing conflict in construction megaprojects: Leadership and third-party principles. *Conflict Resolution Quarterly, 26*(2), 167–198.

Avery, G. (2015). *Neuroscience and the servant leader: Reducing the risks of complex projects.* PMI® Global Congress 2015-EMEA, London, England, Project Management Institute, Newtown Square, PA.

Axelos. (2014). *Managing successful programmes*. London, Axelos Ltd.

Bettignies, H.-C. d. (2014). *Five dimensions of responsible leadership*. INSEAD, Fontainebleau, France (pp. 1–3).

Bornstein, L. (2010). Megaprojects, city-building and community benefits. *City, Culture and Society, 1*(4), 199–206.

Camargo, B. A., & Vázquez-Maguirre, M. (2021). Humanism, dignity and indigenous justice: The Mayan Train megaproject, Mexico. *Journal of Sustainable Tourism, 29*(2–3), 372–391.

Cantarelli, C. C., & Flyvbjerg, B. (2015). Decision making and major transport infrastructure projects: The role of project ownership. In R. Hickman, M. Givoni, D. Bonilla, & D. Banister (Eds.), *Handbook on transport and development* (pp. 380–393). Cheltenham: Edward Elgar.

Cantarelli, C. C., Flyvbjerg, B., Molin, E. J. E., & Wee, B. (2010). Cost overruns in large-scale transportation infrastructure projects: Explanations and their theoretical embeddedness. *European Journal of Transport and Infrastructure Research, 10*, 1.

Capka, J. R. (2004). *Megaprojects – They are a different breed*. Public Roads, Federal Highway Administration, New Jersey.

Clarke, N., D'Amato, A., Higgs, M., & Vahidi, R. (2018). *Responsible leadership in projects: Insights into ethical decision making*. Project Management Institute, Newtown Square, Pennsylvania.

Cooke-Davies, T. (2002), "The 'real' project success factors", International Journal of Project Management, Vol. 20 No. 3, pp. 185–190. https://doi.org/10.1016/S0263-7863(01)00067-9

Deng, B., Xie, W., Cheng, F., Deng, J., & Long, L. (2021). Complexity relationship between power and trust in hybrid megaproject governance: The structural equation modelling approach. *Complexity, 8814630*, 1–13.

Di Maddaloni, F., & Davis, K. (2017). The influence of local community stakeholders in megaprojects: Rethinking their inclusiveness to improve project performance. *International Journal of Project Management, 35*(8), 1537–1556.

Doh, J. P., & Quigley, N. R. (2014). Responsible leadership and stakeholder management: Influence pathways and organisational outcomes. *Academy of Management Perspectives, 28*(3), 255–274.

Drouin, N., Sankaran, S., Marrewijk, A. v., & Müller, R. (2021). *Megaproject leaders: Reflections on personal life stories* (pp. 338). Cheltenham Glos: Edward Elgar Publishing.

El-Gohary, N. M., Osman, H., & El-Diraby, T. E. (2006). Stakeholder management for public-private partnerships. *International Journal of Project Management, 24*(7), 595–604.

Fernández-Sánchez, G., & Rodríguez-López, F. (2010). A methodology to identify sustainability indicators in construction project management – Application to infrastructure projects in Spain. *Ecological Indicators, 10*(6), 1193–1201.

Flyvbjerg, B. (2014a). *Megaproject Planning and Management: Essential Readings*. Cheltenham and Northampton: Edward Elgar Publishing.

Flyvbjerg, B. (2014b). What you should know about megaprojects and why: An overview. *Project Management Journal, 45*(2), 6–19.

Flyvbjerg, B. (2016). What is a megaproject?. (2016, December 1).

Flyvbjerg, B., Ansar, A., Budzier, A., Buhl, S., Cantarelli, C., Garbuio, M., Glenting, C., Holm, M. S., Lovallo, D., Lunn, D., Molin, E., Rønnest, A., Stewart, A., & van Wee, B. (2018). Five things you should know about cost overrun. *Transportation Research Part A: Policy and Practice, 118*, 174–190.

Flyvbjerg, B., Holm, M. S., & Buhl, S. (2002). Underestimating costs in public works projects: Error or lie?. *Journal of the American Planning Association, 68*(3), 279–295.

Freeman, R. E., Wicks, A. C., & Parmar, B. (2004). Stakeholder theory and "The corporate objective revisited". *Organization Science, 15*(3), 364–369.

Friedman, M. (1970). The social responsibility of business is to increase its profits BT – Corporate ethics and corporate governance. *The New York Times Magazine*, 2–6.

Gareis, R., Huemann, M., & Martinuzzi, R.-A. (2009). Relating sustainable development and project management. IRNOP IX, Berlin.

Gällstedt, M. (2003). Working conditions in projects: Perceptions of stress and motivation among project team members and project managers. *International Journal of Project Management, 21*(6), 449–455.

Gauthier, J.-B., & Ika, L. A. (2012). Foundations of project management research: An explicit and six-facet ontological framework. *Project Management Journal, 43*(5), 5–23.

Giezen, M. (2013). Adaptive and strategic capacity: Navigating megaprojects through uncertainty and complexity. *Environment and Planning. B, Planning & Design, 40*(4), 723–741.

Gil, N., & Lundrigan, C. (2012). *The leadership and governance of megaprojects*. CID Technical Report No. 3/2012, Centre for Infrastructure Development (CID), Manchester Business School, The University of Manchester, Manchester (pp. 1–18).

Greige Frangieh, C., & Khayr Yaacoub, H. (2017). A systematic literature review of responsible leadership. *Journal of Global Responsibility, 8*(2), 281–299.

Hoover, S. (2019). Megaprojects: Five leadership success ingredients. *FMI Quarterly, 3*, 1–8.

Hu, Y., Chan, A. P. C., & Le, Y. (2015). Understanding the determinants of program organization for construction megaproject success: Case study of the Shanghai Expo Construction. *Journal of Management in Engineering, 31*(5), 05014019.

Hu, Y., Chan, A. P. C., Le, Y., & Jin, R.-z (2015). From construction megaproject management to complex project management: Bibliographic analysis. *Journal of Management in Engineering, 31*(4), 04014052.

Huemann, M., & Silvius, G. (2017). Projects to create the future: Managing projects meets sustainable development. *International Journal of Project Management, 35*(6), 1066–1070.

Jones, C., &Lichtenstein, B.B. (2008). "Temporary inter-organizational projects: How temporal and social embeddedness enhance coordination and manage uncertainty," In: S. Cropper, M. Ebers, C. Huxham and P. Smith Ring, Eds., The Oxford Handbook of Inter-Organizational Relations, Oxford University Press, Oxford, pp. 231–255.

Jones, C., & Lichtenstein, B. B. (2009). Temporary inter-organizational projects: How temporal and social embeddedness enhance coordination and manage uncertainty. *The Oxford Handbook of Inter-Organizational Relations (March 2019)* (pp. 1–27).

Jordhus-Lier, D. (2015). Community resistance to megaprojects: The case of the N2 Gateway project in Joe Slovo informal settlement, Cape Town. *Habitat International, 45*, 169–176.

Kardes, I., Ozturk, A., Cavusgil, S. T., & Cavusgil, E. (2013). Managing global megaprojects: Complexity and risk management. *International Business Review, 22*(6), 905–917.

Keegan, A. E., & Den Hartog, D. N. (2004). Transformational leadership in a project-based environment: A comparative study of the leadership styles of project managers and line managers. *International Journal of Project Management, 22*(8), 609–617.

Kwak, Y. H., Chih, Y., & Ibbs, C. W. (2009). Towards a comprehensive understanding of public-private partnerships for infrastructure development. *California Management Review, 51*(2), 51–78.

Labuschagne, C., & Brent, A. C. (2005). Sustainable project life cycle management: The need to integrate life cycles in the manufacturing sector. *International Journal of Project Management, 23*(2), 159–168.

Liang, R., & Chong, H.-Y. (2019). A hybrid group decision model for green supplier selection: A case study of megaprojects. *Engineering, Construction and Architectural Management, 26*(8), 1712–1734.

Lin, H., Sui, Y., Ma, H., Wang, L., & Zeng, S. (2018). CEO narcissism, public concern, and megaproject social responsibility: Moderated mediating examination. *Journal of Management in Engineering, 34*(4), 04018018.

Lloyd-Walker, B., & Walker, D. (2011). Authentic leadership for 21st-century project delivery. *International Journal of Project Management, 29*(4), 383–395.

Locatelli, G. (2018). *Why are megaprojects, including nuclear power plants, delivered overbudget and late? Reasons and remedies.* Report MIT-ANP-TR-172, Center for Advanced Nuclear Energy Systems (CANES), Massachusetts Institute of Technology, Cambridge (pp. 1–28).

Locatelli, G., Littau, P., Brookes, N. J., & Mancini, M. (2014). Project characteristics enabling the success of megaprojects: An empirical investigation in the energy sector. *Procedia – Social and Behavioral Sciences, 119*, 625–634.

Love, P. E. D., & Ahiaga-Dagbui, D. D. (2018). Debunking fake news in a post-truth era: The plausible untruths of cost underestimation in transport infrastructure projects. *Transportation Research Part A: Policy and Practice, 113*, 357–368.

Ma, H., Zeng, S., Lin, H., Chen, H., and Shi, J. J. (2017). The societal governance of megaproject social responsibility. *International Journal of Project Management, 35*(7), 1365–1377.

Ma, T., Wang, Z., Skibniewski, M. J., Ding, J., Wang, G., & He, Q. (2020). Investigating stewardship behavior in megaprojects: An exploratory analysis. *Engineering, construction and architectural management* (ahead-of-print).

Maak, T., & Pless, N. M. (2006). Responsible leadership in a stakeholder society – A relational perspective. *Journal of Business Ethics, 66*(1), 99–115.

Mahmoudi, A., Deng, X., Javed, S. A., & Zhang, N. (2021). Sustainable supplier selection in megaprojects: Grey ordinal priority approach. *Business Strategy and the Environment, 30*(1), 318–339.

Marcelino-Sádaba, S., González-Jaen, L. F., & Pérez-Ezcurdia, A. (2015). Using project management as a way to sustainability. From a comprehensive review to a framework definition. *Journal of Cleaner Production, 99*, 1–16.

Marques, T., Reis, N., & Gomes, J. F. S. (2018). Responsible leadership research: A bibliometric review. *BAR – Brazilian Administration Review, 15*(1), 1–25.

Martens, M. L., & Carvalho, M. M. (2016). Sustainability and success variables in the project management context: An expert panel. *Project Management Journal, 47*(6), 24–43.

Melé, D. (2016). Understanding humanistic management. *Humanistic Management Journal, 1*(1), 33–55.

Morris, P. W. G. (2013). *Reconstructing project management*. John Wiley & Sons. New Jersey, United States.

Mossman, A. (2021). *Using plus/delta for feedback and improving social processes*. <https://leanconstructionblog.com/Using-Plus-Delta-for-Feedback-and-Improving-Social-Processes.html> (July 16, 2021).

Müller, R., Andersen, E. S., Kvalnes, Ø., Shao, J., Sankaran, S., Turner, J. R., Biesenthal, C., Walker, D., & Gudergan, S. (2013). The interrelationship of governance, trust, and ethics in temporary organisations. *Project Management Journal, 44*(4), 26–44.

Müller, R., Sankaran, S., Drouin, N., Vaagaasar, A. L., Bekker, M. C., & Jain, K. (2018). A theory framework for balancing vertical and horizontal leadership in projects. *International Journal of Project Management, 36*(1), 83–94.

Müller, R., & Turner, R. (2010). Leadership competency profiles of successful project managers. *International Journal of Project Management, 28*(5), 437–448.

Nanda, U., K. Rybkowski, Z., Pati, S., & Nejati, A. (2017). A value analysis of lean processes in target value design and integrated project delivery: Stakeholder perception. *HERD: Health Environments Research & Design Journal, 10*(3), 99–115.

Ninan, J., Mahalingam, A., & Clegg, S. (2019). External stakeholder management strategies and resources in megaprojects: An organizational power perspective. *Project Management Journal, 50*(6), 625–640.

Pilkienė, M., Alonderienė, R., Chmieliauskas, A., Šimkonis, S., & Müller, R. (2018). The governance of horizontal leadership in projects. *International Journal of Project Management, 36*(7), 913–924.

Pless, N. M. (2007). Understanding responsible leadership: Role identity and motivational drivers: Tame Anita Roddick, founder of the body shop. *Journal of Business Ethics, 74*(4), 437–456.

Pless, N.M., Maak, T. Responsible leadership: Pathways to the future. Journal of Business Ethics, 98, 3–13 (2011). https://doi.org/10.1007/s10551-011-1114-4

Roth, H., Macaulay, N., Suhonen, S., & Ho, R. (2016). *Megaproject leaders: Shifting the focus from technical to people leaders*. Houston: Russell Reynolds Associates.

Sanderson, J. (2012). Risk, uncertainty and governance in megaprojects: A critical discussion of alternative explanations. *International Journal of Project Management, 30*(4), 432–443.

Sankaran, S., Müller, R., & Drouin, N. (2020). Creating a 'sustainability sublime' to enable megaprojects to meet the United Nations sustainable development goals. *Systems Research and Behavioral Science, 37*(5), 813–826.

Schoper, Y., Gemünden, H. G., & Nguyen, N. N. (2016). *Fifteen future trends for Project Management in 2025*. Future Trends in Project, Programme and Portfolio Management.

Shenhar, A., & Holzmann, V. (2017). The three secrets of megaproject success: Clear strategic vision, total alignment, and adapting to complexity. *Project Management Journal, 48*(6), 29–46.

Silvius, A. J. G., Brink, J., & Köhler, A. (2009). Views on sustainable project management. Human side of projects in modern business. *IPMA Scientific Research Paper Series* (pp. 545–556). Helsinki, Finland.

Silvius, A. J. G., & van den Brink, J. (2014). Taking responsibility: The integration of sustainability and project management. *Advances in project management: Narrated journeys in unchartered territory* (pp. 137–137). Oxfordshire, England.

Theurillat, T., & Crevoisier, O. (2013). The sustainability of a financialised urban megaproject: The case of Sihlcity in Zurich. *International Journal of Urban and Regional Research, 37*(6), 2052–2073.

Turner, J. R., & Xue, Y. (2018). On the success of megaprojects. *International Journal of Managing Projects in Business, 11*(3), 783–805.

Turner, R. J., Huemann, M., Anbari, F. T., & Bredillet, C. N. (2010). *Perspectives on projects*. London: Routledge.

UN. (2018). *The sustainable development goals report 2018* (pp. 1–36). New York, United Nations Publications.

van Marrewijk, A., Ybema, S., Smits, K., Clegg, S., & Pitsis, T. (2016). Clash of the titans: Temporal organizing and collaborative dynamics in the Panama Canal Megaproject. *Organisation Studies, 37*(12), 1745–1769.

Wang, D., Wang, Y., & Lu, Y. (2020). Impact of regulatory focus on uncertainty in megaprojects: Mediating role of trust and control. *Journal of Construction Engineering and Management, 146* (12), 04020142.

Wang, G., He, Q., Meng, X., Locatelli, G., Yu, T., & Yan, X. (2017). Exploring the impact of megaproject environmental responsibility on organisational citizenship behaviors for the environment: A social identity perspective. *International Journal of Project Management, 35*(7), 1402–1414.

Warrack, A. (1993). Megaproject decision making: Lessons and strategies. *Western Centre for Economic Research Information Bulletin, 16*, 1–15.

Witz, P., Stingl, V., Wied, M., & Oehmen, J. (2021). Asymmetric legitimacy perception across megaproject stakeholders: The case of the Fehmarnbelt Fixed Link. *International Journal of Project Management, 39*(4), 377–393.

Yi, L. (2011). *Manager as scrum master*. Proceedings – 2011 Agile Conference, Agile 2011 (pp. 151–153).

Further Readings: Journals

Cao, T., Locatelli, G., Smith, N., & Zhang, L. (2021). A shared leadership framework based on boundary spanners in megaprojects. *International Journal of Managing Projects in Business, 14*(5), 1065–1092. doi: https://doi.org/10.1108/IJMPB-03-2020-0090

Cho, T. S., & Hambrick, D. C. (2006). Attention as the mediator between top management team characteristics and strategic change: The case of airline deregulation. *Organization Science, 17*(4), 453–469. doi: https://doi.org/10.1287/orsc.1060.0192

Chung, J. K. H., Kumaraswamy, M. M., & Palaneeswaran, E. (2009). Improving megaproject briefing through enhanced collaboration with ICT. *Automation in Construction, 18*(7), 966–974. doi: https://doi.org/10.1016/j.autcon.2009.05.001

Control, P. P., Performance, P. M., & Contexts, D. (2008). Project portfolio control and portfolio. *Project Management Journal, 39*, 28–42. doi: https://doi.org/10.1002/pmj. March.

Daniel, E., & Daniel, P. A. (2019). Megaprojects as complex adaptive systems: The Hinkley point C case. *International Journal of Project Management, 37*(8), 1017–1033. https://doi.org/10.1016/j.ijproman.2019.05.001

Drouin, N., van Marrewijk, A., Sankaran, S., & Müller, R. (2021). What is done through the lens of megaproject leaders life stories. *Megaproject Leaders,* 2–11. 2003. doi: https://doi.org/10.4337/9781789902976.00010.

Gil, N., & Pinto, J. K. (2018). Polycentric organising and performance: A contingency model and evidence from megaproject planning in the UK. *Research Policy, 47*(4), 717–734. doi: https://doi.org/10.1016/j.respol.2018.02.001

Haynes, W. (2011). Infrastructure megaproject leadership, management, innovation, and accountability. *Public Works Management and Policy, 16*(3), 193–198. doi: https://doi.org/10.1177/1087724X11410576

Li, M., Ma, Z., & Tang, X. (2021). Owner-dominated building information modeling and lean construction in a megaproject. *Frontiers of Engineering Management, 8*(1), 60–71. doi: https://doi.org/10.1007/s42524-019-0042-3

Liu, H., Yu, Y., Sun, Y., & Yan, X. (2021). A system dynamic approach for simulation of a knowledge transfer model of heterogeneous senders in megaproject innovation. *Engineering, Construction and Architectural Management, 28*(3), 681–705. doi: https://doi.org/10.1108/ECAM-01-2020-0077

Liu, J., & Ma, G. (2020). Study on incentive and supervision mechanisms of technological innovation in megaprojects based on the principal-agent theory. *Engineering, Construction and Architectural Management, 28*(6), 1593–1614. doi: https://doi.org/10.1108/ECAM-03-2020-0163

Liu, J., & Ma, G. (2021). Study on incentive and supervision mechanisms of technological innovation in megaprojects based on the principal-agent theory. *Engineering, Construction and Architectural Management, 28*(6), 1593–1614. doi: https://doi.org/10.1108/ECAM-03-2020-0163

Locatelli, G., Mancini, M., & Ishimwe, A. (2014). How can system engineering improve supplier management in megaprojects? *Procedia – Social and Behavioral Sciences, 119,* 510–518. doi: https://doi.org/10.1016/j.sbspro.2014.03.057

Ma, T., Ding, J., Wang, Z., & Skibniewski, M. J. (2020). Governing government-project owner relationships in water megaprojects: A concession game analysis on allocation of control rights. *Water Resources Management, 34*(13), 4003–4018. doi: https://doi.org/10.1007/s11269-020-02627-z

Oliomogbe, G. O., & Smith, N. J. (2012). Value in megaprojects. *Organisation, Technology & Management in Construction: An International Journal, 4*(3), 617–624. doi: https://doi.org/10.5592/otmcj.2012.3.5

Qiu, Y., Chen, H., Sheng, Z., & Cheng, S. (2019). Governance of institutional complexity in megaproject organisations. *International Journal of Project Management, 37*(3), 425–443. https://doi.org/10.1016/j.ijproman.2019.02.001

Rampersad, H. K. (2001). The TQM Magazine Emerald Article: A visionary management model Perspectives A visionary management model. *Group, 13*(2001), 211–223.

Sergeeva, N., & Zanello, C. (2018). Championing and promoting innovation in UK megaprojects. *International Journal of Project Management, 36*(8), 1068–1081. https://doi.org/10.1016/j.ijproman.2018.09.002

Turner, M., Lingard, H., & Francis, V. (2009). Work-life balance: An exploratory study of supports and barriers in a construction project. *International Journal of Managing Projects in Business, 2*(1), 94–111. doi: https://doi.org/10.1108/17538370910930536

van Marrewijk, A. (2007). Managing project culture: The case of Environ Megaproject. *International Journal of Project Management, 25*(3), 290–299. https://doi.org/10.1016/j.ijproman.2006.11.004

Van Marrewijk, A., & Smits, K. (2016). Cultural practices of governance in the Panama Canal Expansion Megaproject. *International Journal of Project Management, 34*(3), 533–544. doi: https://doi.org/10.1016/j.ijproman.2015.07.004

van Wyk, C. (2016). Facilitative Leader and Leadership development during a megaproject implementation phase: A case study. *PM World Journal, V*(VII), 1–12.

Wang, G., Locatelli, G., Wan, J., Li, Y., & Le, Y. (2021). Governing behavioral integration of top management team in megaprojects: A social capital perspective. *International Journal of Project Management, 39*(4), 365–376. doi: https://doi.org/10.1016/j.ijproman.2020.11.005

Wells, J. (2010). Responsible leadership. In *Peace and Prosperity through World Trade*. https://doi.org/10.1017/CBO9780511723285.053.

Westley, F., & Mintzberg, H. (1989). Visionary management and strategic leadership. *Strategic Management Journal, 10*, 17–32, 1989.

Williams, N. L., Ferdinand, N., & Pasian, B. (2015). Online stakeholder interactions in the early stage of a megaproject. *Project Management Journal, 46*(6), 92–110. doi: https://doi.org/10.1002/pmj.21548

Guangdong Wu, Cong Liu, Xianbo Zhao, Jian Zuo & Junwei Zheng (2022) Effects of fairness perceptions on conflicts and project performance in Chinese megaprojects, International Journal of Construction Management, 22:5, 832–848, DOI:10.1080/15623599.2019.1652952

Yang, D., He, Q., Cui, Q., & Hsu, S.-C. (2018). Organisational Citizenship Behavior in Construction Megaprojects. *Journal of Management in Engineering, 34*(4), 04018017. doi: https://doi.org/10.1061/(ASCE)me.1943-5479.0000614

Zhai, L., Xin, Y., & Cheng, C. (2009). Understanding the value of project management from a stakeholder's perspective: Case study of mega-project management. *Project Management Journal, 40*(1), 99–109. doi: https://doi.org/10.1002/pmj.20099

Zhu, J., Hertogh, M., Zhang, J., Shi, Q., & Sheng, Z. (2020). Incentive mechanisms in mega project-risk management considering owner and insurance company as principals. *Journal of Construction Engineering and Management, 146*(10), 04020120. doi: https://doi.org/10.1061/(ASCE)co.1943-7862.0001915

Zidane, Y. J.-T., Johansen, A., & Ekambaram, A. (2015). Project evaluation holistic framework – Application on megaproject case. *Procedia Computer Science, 64*, 409–416. https://doi.org/10.1016/j.procs.2015.08.532

Vladimir Obradović and Marija Todorović

13 Responsible Value Chain

Context: This chapter underlines project value and indicates how existing concepts and approaches can be combined or extended to meet responsible project management principles.

Characters/entities: This chapter aims to provide a mutual understanding of project responsibility through a project value chain framework. The presented framework is not just focused on the project level but also at the organizational level or even local or national context, depending on the project purpose.

Locations: This chapter is oriented on a project as a critical entity without limitations to industry, geographical locations, organization, or individuals.

Research gaps: Accelerated technological development, globalization, world population growth, and increased resource consumption make a project environment more and more complex. Nevertheless, each project strives to create value as a mechanism to reach business and social goals.

Challenges/tensions: The challenge of understanding the organizational factors that create values for responsible behavior and implementing mechanisms that can provide responsible project value chain implementation.

Keywords: project value, value management, stakeholder alignment, globalization

13.1 Introduction

Theory and practice are evolving. Industries are growing, technologies are developing, the limitless market, and many organizations have become networked. Still, each project aims to create value as a mechanism to reach business and social goals. This chapter aims to underline the project value, value management, and project value chain and reflect the key drivers of project value creation in a post-industrial society.[1] The above provides the need to develop a responsible value chain that will consider stakeholders, sustainability, and ethics as the main dimensions of responsible management. The chapter indicates how existing concepts and approaches can be combined or extended to meet responsible project management principles. A

---

1 This chapter is a result of the Project International Research Programme 2020–2030 on Capabilities for delivering projects in the context of societal development (CaProSoc) – Alma Mater Europaea (AME) Serbian Project Management Association – IPMA Serbia.

https://doi.org/10.1515/9783110724783-016

responsible project value chain framework is being proposed to provide a mutual understanding of the responsibility of projects. The expected benefits of this framework are to enhance project results, gain new knowledge, leverage the advantages of new technologies, find innovative solutions, network with stakeholders, support the community, and help to deal with environmental issues and to provide more value for interested parties.

13.2 Project Value Chain

Michael Porter introduced the value chain concept. This approach was developed in the mid-1980s and is analyzing organizational activities that create value – does the organization has strengths or weaknesses in these areas. Value chain analysis is a tool aimed at helping organizations understand how better to integrate internal activities (Nishiguchi, 1994). The value definition and value chain analysis have also evolved through the years. The scholars' effort led to the concept of Creating Shared Value (CSV), introduced in the Harvard Business Review in 2011 (Porter & Kramer, 2011). This concept is that companies should move beyond meeting customer needs to address societal needs. The authors stated that the market is not defined by economic needs only but the social (including environmental) needs. The authors state that companies can impact social issues via their products and services by discovering new market groups, for example, vulnerable groups, and companies can find new expanding opportunities and create shared value.

The second way is to innovate through the value chain. Since all organizations are using resources (various natural resources such as energy water), they can rethink the way they supply and use the option to bring benefits to suppliers and the community. From the perspective of energy usage and other resource usages, procurement, transportation, distribution channels, support services, infrastructure, and human resource management can be innovated to create shared value. The third option to create value is to enhance the business environment, focusing on the local cluster development (Porter & Kramer, 2011).

Porter's value chain initial model allows us to understand the organization's value chain, presenting the project context and environment. The project value chain can be grounded on the same logic. Creating the value chain summarizes the structure and offers a simplified view of a value chain incorporating the key elements that reflect the value creation process.

13.3 Project Value Management Perspectives

13.3.1 Project Value

The value in the broader context is the measure of satisfaction of needs. The value is relative and can be perceived differently by different parties (European Standard 12973–2000, 2000). Value creation helps organizations maintain their position on the market, and a significant number of papers deal with value management, benefits, success, and performances.

Considering projects, there is a consensus between authors that the project's values should not be viewed from the project's product's perspective only (Lepak, 2007; Vrečko & Lebe, 2013; Toljaga-Nikolić et al., 2020). The project's impact after the results are achieved and provide change. Therefore, the overall project management process, results, and impact should be evaluated in value. Laursen and Svejvig (2016) have summarized the key concepts within project value creation: strategy, value, project, output, outcome/change, benefit, and value creation. It can be concluded that the project value definition is a very complex and multidimensional term.

13.3.2 Value Management: Stages and Perspectives

Lalevée et al. (2020) analyze project management through value management's perspective to manage a project sustainably. Value management is a proactive, solution-seeking process, used to enhance the project's value managing project from its initiation to the operational use" (Hayles et al., 2010). "a structured means for achieving better business decisions; which can be supported by all stakeholders . . . " (BSI, 2000).

Value management should provide project managers with the choice in dealing with the ambiguity of stakeholders' needs and the complexity of a changing environment, financial, environmental, and social requirements. Value management can be a framework for a more responsible project management process. Value management includes several stages:

- stakeholder identification, focusing on different stakeholders (Lalevée et al., 2020; Lazar, 2014). In the project management context, stakeholders are owners, individuals, and other organizations interested in the organization's or project's actions (Martinsuo & Geraldi, 2020).
- Needs analysis of their needs and expectations, focusing on conflicted interest and their perception of value. Different groups of stakeholders can have

separate, even contradictory, expectations. For example, the investor may have financial interest above others, and the local government could use green technological solutions. This phase also introduces the social value or any value that presents responsible management (Lalevée et al., 2020). Thiry (2014) explains the system analysis, gap analysis, and the agreement on expected benefits (critical success factors and key performance indicators) as *sensemaking*.

- It was finding a solution that should align different viewpoints, clear, and understandable to all the interested parties (Lalevée et al., 2020; Martinsuo & Geraldi, 2020). What is also important is to analyze the influence of one value on another, for example, if increasing the value X will cause an increase or decrease in Value Y. Thiry (2014) explained this through the ideation stage to generate creative alternatives to be innovative. Values should be aligned with the project's objectives to ensure that project delivery will provide results to meet stakeholder value.
- Establishing or elaboration phase means creating viable options to enable the decision-making process based on their contribution – expected benefits and feasibility. Feasibility analysis includes an investor's eligibility, market analysis, technical requirements, human resource requirements, cost estimation, financial assessment, and the capability to meet deadlines. This phase should include quantitive and qualitative benefits, tangible and can be monetized, and intangible (Boadway, 2006).
- What has also been recognized in the literature is that stakeholders can appear in different project phases and have a different impact on these phases (Angus et al., 2005). Competing stakeholders' expectations and multiple ways of influence are crucial for the decision-making process. As mentioned above, it is necessary to align the values.
- Value delivery adds value to consumed resources and beneficiaries in terms of quality, time, and technical performance (Browning, 2014).
- Project benefits realization consists of an evaluation and business implementation. The most popular project management approaches and methodologies recognize the benefits realized through the project business implementation phase since the project results need to be in use after the project is closed, and this phase is crucial for the project value evaluation. Following project handover, measurements will then not be continued by the project team but by an entity within the organization where the project is implemented or beneficiaries (Open PM2, PRINCE2, PMI), usually is the organizational unit (e.g., Project Managemen Office) responsible for the benefits realization (Mochal & Krasnoff, 2013).

Value management initiation is the agreement on expected benefits to be delivered, followed by the value delivery process's program. Then follow project initiation, planning, execution, monitoring, and closing. After the project is completed, the next phase is the project business implementation. Based on the success of the project's business implementation (development of new capabilities and creation of value), it depends on evaluating the value produced. Value management should enable decision-makers to take necessary action to deliver results that will fulfil stakeholder expectations.

The above is more of a generic view, but it is inevitable to focus more on agile management in a dynamic environment. If they are not in ICT, many projects rely on technology, the internet, research, or innovation. The traditional approach to project management argues that stakeholders' needs should be defined at the beginning of the project, while agile management contends that the project team should learn stakeholders' values. It is not easy to estimate costs for software projects, and it is suggested to assess value in terms of benefits. One of the most frequently used agile methodologies is Scrum. Scrum methodology includes user stories; therefore, user stories can estimate the values as user stories (Dingsøyr & Lassenius, 2016). This could help balance product values in a product backlog.

To stay competitive in the market, companies move toward continuous value delivery. They need to build their capacity to quickly use data about customer behavior in innovative ways. Considering IT projects, for example, software development projects, the literature emphasizes continuous integration, which means constant integration. Continuous delivery aims at constantly keeping the software in a releasable state and includes faster feedback and empowerment (Humble & Farley, 2010). Agility requires constant reconsideration of the values identified at the beginning of the project and customer feedback during the project. Obradović et al. (2018) analyze the projects' complementary sustainability and agility. The main conclusion is that implementing any new concept requires the maturity of a company to accept the change, that sustainability and agility are complementary concepts, and that agility helps project managers deal with environmental and social constraints.

Project management is spread to many different industries, and besides construction, production, and other areas, project management is more and more applicable in creative industries. The definition of the value to be produced. Creative projects are related to creative industries and culture and are present in the construction industry (building design, architecture solution) in the automotive industry (design, advanced innovations). Value management in those projects requires a specific framework. Gillier et al. (2015) state that creative projects constantly generate enormous scope and variety of unknown concepts to provide robust design capabilities to explore the familiar unknown. In a typical value management process, the project value should be monitored regarding set goals, deliverables, and values approved by stakeholders. On creative projects, the monitoring is performed, but the expected final result is unknown. The value management is not to minimize uncertainties and ambiguities but preserve these areas and is oriented to discover new knowledge investment in the unknown by preserving areas of uncertainties and ambiguities during the project creating "common unknown" as missing knowledge, creating new concepts. One of the value management principles in a creative project is that the targeted values are changeable and can be renewed during the project.

13.3.3 Integrating and Monitoring Project Values

Many authors consider the Earned Value Method a project management concept to manage the value of work performed during a project. Earned Value Method is focused on tracking cost, schedule, and scope. By using parameters Budgeted Costs of Work Scheduled, Budgeted Costs of Work Performed, and Actual Costs of Work Performed, it is possible to calculate Cost Variance (CV), Schedule Variance (SV), Cost Performance Index (CPI), and Schedule Performance Index (SPI). Based on the context of nowadays projects (e.g., projects in the green building field, irrigation systems, social problems, wireless networks, and new technologies), the cost is not calculated based on material and human resources costs but on the energy consumption (Dwaikat & Ali, 2016) or water consumption (Du et al., 2017), where Earned Value is provided in terms of irrigation. Memarzadeh & Golparvar-Fard (2012) introduce the metrics Budgeted Carbon Footprint (CF) of the Work Performed, Budgeted CF of the Work Scheduled, and the Actual CF of the Work Performed.

Based on these examples, Koke and Moehler (2019) advocate revising these fundamental EVM indicators, introducing Earned Green Value Method.
- $CV^{®}$ Net Green Value = EGV – Actual Costs (AC).
- $SV^{®}$ Variance of Green Value = EGV – Planned Green Value (PGV).
- Cost Performance Index $(CPI)^{®}$ Cost of Green Value = EGV/AC.
- $SPI^{®}$ Rate of Green Value = EGV/PGV.

The implementation of this concept starts with the project's scope definition. Maltzman and Shirley (2012) explain that value creation (in this case, sustainability values) should be introduced at the earliest phase of the project, even in the business case.

The second proposed step uses Work Breakdown Structure (WBS) to define values and indicators. P5™ Standard for sustainability in project management (GPM, 2019) promotes applying a Sustainability management plan to the project. The sustainability management plan includes clear sustainability objectives. The next step in the project management process is the scope and project structure definition. Koke and Moehler (2019) stated that sustainability values should be introduced in scope definition and WBS structure, providing examples of the projects with indicators on the lowest WBS level. A sustainability management plan can be developed along with other project plans.

One of the crucial steps in introducing sustainability values is incorporating defined indicators and targets in the cost and schedule plan. This practically means that plans should include direct and indirect costs. The main reason for that is the long-term orientation of the project and the value delivery, primarily when the values are related to the environment and social protection. Environmental and social impacts are usually difficult to quantify and monetize. There are several approaches to calculating an economic value of qualitative cost and benefits, and one that is most commonly used is cost-benefit analysis. Cost-benefit analysis is a method that offers a broader and more detailed analysis of benefits for citizens and society in general (Greenberg & Robins, 2008). One of the most general concepts in financial evaluation and quantification of intangible benefits – typical of social protection services – is Willingness To Pay (WTP), based on the theory of well-being. WTP is the maximum price a consumer is willing to pay for a product or service, for example, the price a consumer would pay for enhanced transport security or data security, improved quality of life, and social activities (Horowitz & McConnell, 2002). For the business is particularly important to quantify each variable until the link to profit is clear (Epstein & Buhovac, 2014).

Koke and Moehler (2019) stated that measuring the project progress could show that the actual cost is above the planned costs; still, this can be the result of an investment in recyclable materials or additional work to achieve sustainable performance and provide at the end of the project, a great success. If the project was introduced in the earliest phase, it was implemented in the project scope, objectives, and plans (as stated above).

Using the Earned value method's logic, all the measures we can use to forecast future performance, be more adaptive to change, and resilient to different circumstances.

13.4 Trends in the Project Management Environment

The need to digitize the entire value chain to create competitive advantages is caused by Industry 4.0. Moreover, it has significant policy support from the European Commission and different member states. The development of technology brings other chances for development and improvement and numerous requirements for adaptation, especially for the teams working on the project. Today's modernization of jobs brought by Industry 4.0 requires fundamental changes concerning how organizations are set up. In developed countries, where smart technologies have an exceptional application, and their development is promoted, testing the work of hybrid teams is being done – which should carry out a wide range of activities, consisting of humans and robots (Shehadeh et al., 2017; Schwartz et al., 2016).

However, this transition opens concerns regarding social aspects such as security, human rights, and employees' rights (Gutiérrez & Ezponda, 2019). We cannot neglect the changes in the education system, the orientation of responsible learning, the long-life learning concept, the second-life concept, and the trend of online learning with available online learning platforms, audio and video materials, and podcasts by the leading social network.

The constant concern for society is environmental protection. Scarce resources disturbance of flora and fauna present the triggers to be more responsible in everyday business activities (Amade, 2020). One of the key economic concepts nowadays is a circular economy (CE). CE is perceived as a model that regenerates itself, producing and consuming goods through closed-loop material flows (Garcia-Muiña et al., 2018). CE business models can be classified based on the following criteria: regenerate (energy recovery, circular supplies, sustainable product location); share (product lease, maintaining ad repair, upgrading); optimize (assets management, waste management; produce on-demand); loop (recycling, resource recovering); virtualize (dematerialized services); exchange (new technologies) (Lewandowski, 2016).

Industry 4.0. has a business but also political and international institutions support, initiatives such as the sustainable development goals (UN Sustainable Development Summit), human rights, education for democratic citizenship (European Council), inclusion, and integration (European Commission). In addition to development in different areas, the world faces regional conflicts and global crises (Otegi-Olaso et al., 2019).

All these have been recognized in the literature and practice. Therefore, twenty-first century requires more responsible business practices (Palazzo & Wentland, 2011), including sustainability, responsible education (Ostojić et al., 2020), behavior in a sustainable manner, effective governance, responsible innovations, transparency, decision-making, and responsible connection to the world (security, digital technologies, GDPR) (Palazzo & Wentland, 2011).

13.5 Responsible Project Value Chain

13.5.1 Project Value Chain

Based on the project mentioned above environment, project value chain management can be challenging. Projects are mainly implemented within the existing organization, and besides, the external environment has the organizational environment and internal stakeholders. Therefore, from the project point of view, the value chain can present a network of individuals and/or legal entities that buy from or deliver to, providing the project's product to the customer/beneficiary. The number of interested parties has increased and the demand of society and the environment.

Lazar (2014) is strongly relating the value chain with stakeholders. The author emphasized the relation between project value and measurement of the results. The critical project value chain activities are:
- Mapping of stakeholders – project stakeholder identification.
- Stakeholder categorization – mapping their interest, influence, and intent.
- The expression of the stakeholder's expectations – identification of the expectations regarding project objectives

- Identifying needs – identifying conflicting interests from different parties could arise from, for example, lack of information and knowledge, the diverse interests of stakeholders related to new technologies, environment protection, social issues, and green solution. The next step is to create a balance on which expectations must be accomplished and the second priority.
- Formalizing objectives – prioritizing needs, including a relevant element in the project objectives.
- Defining functions – functional analysis of the project to determine which functions need to be performed to meet project objectives and create value.
- Construction critical success factors and key performance indicators – defining how to measure project results and objectives and defining key performance indicators.

13.5.2 The Need to Manage the Project Value Chain Responsibly

Through back to project management theory development, it can be seen that each evolving step and new approach aims to face existing challenges. For example, the Agile project management approach has been developed to avoid rework, increase the percentage of completed projects successfully, and manage change. Further, to meet the needs of a community, adjusting the management approach to projects characteristics such as project purpose, number of beneficiaries, number of stakeholders, project impact and donors, the European Commission launched an Open Project Management Methodology – Open PM2. This methodology is dedicated to EU institutions and the public sector (European Commission, 2018). Green Project Management Institute presented GPM P5™ Standard for sustainability in project management (GPM, 2019). Therefore, one logical continuity is to discuss the concept that can contribute to different parties' needs and interests in the project value chain.

13.5.3 Responsible Project Management Domains and Principles

Being responsible means directing projects focusing on the project's impact (Thompson & Williams, 2018). Certain scholars even state that the use of the word "responsible" along with the "management" is a pleonasm; still, the responsible project value chain is not a preference but a must (Laasch, 2018).

Under the terms of responsibility, generating value assumes that projects are managed sustainably, are focused on the value for stakeholders, and are not performing any unethical behavior (Laasch & Conaway, 2015; Laasch et al., 2020).

Ethical behavior is the translation of values into actions. Organizational and individual values and the organizational climate are the key drivers of ethical behavior in a project. Gadeken (2008) emphasizes the project leader's role to take action for ethical alignment of organizational culture, core ethical values, project culture, project team practices, policies, and steps to create a proper climate. The project leader has a role in communicating vital ethical values to team members and creating policies that will provide the necessary support to deal with ethical issues. One of the recognized challenges in project management is an ethical dilemma in value delivery, such as value for the client or society, value for a few people versus value for many (Drevland et al., 2017). Core instruments that could be used are a code of ethics, audits, and training. Moreover, key ethical issues are corruption, human rights, and discrimination (Laasch, 2020).

Creating value for stakeholders presents the domain of responsible management. As explained above, the project value chain can be seen through stakeholder mapping, analyzing of interest, and needs to balance their needs and create value. Core management instruments to be used are stakeholder assessment and engagement. Key ethical issues are related to clients, community, partners, and employees (Laasch, 2020)

Sustainable project management involves planning, monitoring, and controlling projects considering environmental, economic, and social aspects (people, planet, profit). One of the mechanisms that enable sustainable management is life-cycle management. Sustainability in project management refers to all project results, processes, and resources used. Key issues related to sustainability are decent work, human rights, community and customers, consuming natural resources (water, energy), business cases, business agility, and economic prosperity (GPM, 2019).

Responsible Project Management includes eight principles (Thompson & Williams, 2018):

1. Purpose – understand the intention and expected contribution of the project from a different perspective.
2. Awareness – analyze the project impact, arising issues, or implications that would be unrevealed without the project.
3. Curiosity – understand possible conflicts and ethical issues.
4. Uncertainty – embrace change and be more resilient and plan to meet uncertainty.
5. Anticipation – facilitate the evaluation of different options to provide more efficient decision making.
6. Creativity – find opportunities and, for innovation, support imagination.
7. Stewardship – manage stakeholder experience and the usage of natural resources.
8. Balance – make a proper balance between short-term and long-term project objectives and consider the dimensions of people, planet, and profit.

13.5.4 Integrating Responsibility in the Project Value Chain: A Framework

To balance short-term and long-term project objectives and sustainably manage, a project manager needs to deal with many challenges. Most of the challenges are related to the project initiation phase, such as analysis of project benefits, the conflicted interest of stakeholders, especially related to green technologies and investment in dealing with social and environmental issues, and lack of reference point to measure sustainable alternatives (Agarval & Kalmar, 2015). As the way for reaching project goals, project strategy is crucial for successfully integrating responsibility into project initiatives (Todorović & Obradović, 2018). Therefore, we can discuss how responsible management principles could be integrated into the project's value chain.

Based on the concept mentioned above of Value management and CSV, we can conclude that projects can create value through innovation in the project value chain.

Principles: 1. *Purpose*, 2. *Awareness*, 7. *Stewardship*, and 8. *Balance* is mainly presented in the Value management concept and could be implemented through activities in the value chain developed by Lazar (2014): Mapping of stakeholders; stakeholder categorization; the expression of the stakeholder's expectations and identifying needs. To deal with trends in the project environment and to enable responsibility, the innovation recommended in the literature is to:

13.6 Align Stakeholder Values

Different stakeholders can have different knowledge, information, interests, and consequently different needs and expectations. Identifying and analyzing expectations is necessary to balance them to define values for the project. Further, it is necessary to deal with conflicting interests (if any) and especially analyze a mutual impact of the specified values – if reaching one value will defeat other values or decrease or positively impact additional value(s) (Lalevée et al., 2020; Thiry, 2014; Martinsuo & Geraldi, 2020). A responsible project value chain should include ethical values and decision-making, and ethical environment, and trust in the project (Kitcher, 2011). Therefore, balancing different values and aligning them with project objectives should include the value that describes ethical behavior. Project values should include long-term and short-term values and express quantitative and qualitative benefits concerning the wider environment (Boadway, 2006). This phase could help select one alternative or create an innovative solution (e.g., using the advantages of new technologies). This can support principles: 1. *Purpose*; 2. *Awareness*; 7. *Stewardship*; 8. *Balance*.

13.7 Revise Values During the Project

Project literature and examples from practice and contemporary trends have shown us how important it is to be agile and build resilience. Concerning IT projects and creative projects (that can be applied in many sectors of society), the value definition at the beginning of the project is not enough, especially because some stakeholders can appear in different project stages. Values should be revised during the project based on the client feedback, user experience, and response to environmental and social issues (Dingsøyr & Lassenius, 2016; Humble & Farley, 2010; Gillier et al., 2015). The fact that is crucial here is that an agile approach aims to help the system come with changes and contribute to incorporating additional project management elements (Obradović et al., 2018). Using stakeholder feedback and user stories to reconsider and revise values during the project will support agility and provide resilience and support thrust building on the project (between key stakeholders) (Smyth et al., 2010). This can support principle 3. Curiosity and principle 4. *Uncertainty* of responsible project management.

13.8 Consider Responsible Sourcing

Sourcing includes people with proper knowledge and skills, products, and services. Responsibility can be seen in the social and economic aspects of the project and the community (Laasch & Conaway, 2015). In line with this, procurement from the local suppliers is promoted in sustainable project management (GPM, 2019) and Porter's CSV concept (Porter & Kramer, 2019). Further, significant environmental protection can be achieved (minimizing footprint and fuel consumption). This could improve the application of principle 8 – *balance*, especially in people, planet, and profit orientation. Reaching local knowledge can target principles 3. *Curiosity* and 5. *Creativity* (where the communication and stakeholder management approach can be adjusted to the specific project and the community and provide better mutual understanding, gather new knowledge, and create new solutions).

13.9 Measure and Review

Measurement is included in the proposed project value chain Lazar (2014) proposed. Still, if we consider that the value chain should be created to illustrate the project's value, the recommendation is to develop KPIs and monitor the project's value delivery. Measuring project performances using KPIs can improve the integration of principle 4. *Uncertainty* and principle 5. *Anticipation*. Measuring should be oriented not only on project objectives and expected results but also on changes, revealing new innovative solutions and creating knowledge to impact the ecosystem. Traditional monitoring methods can be extended to involve new values to be measured to be responsible to people, the planet, and profit (Koke & Moehler, 2019; Dwaikat & Ali, 2016; Du et al., 2017). Measuring progress and reporting can provide a baseline for decision-making to improve project resilience and readiness to change. According to Laasch (2020), an audit is one of the critical mechanisms for ethical behavior and transparency in the project.

Based on the project value chain presented by Lazar (2014), value management stages, the concept of CSVs, and responsible project management principles in Figure 13.1 are shown in the Responsible project value chain framework, aimed to provide a mutual understanding of the responsibility on projects. This framework's expected benefits are enhancing project results, gaining new knowledge, leveraging the advantages of new technologies, finding innovative solutions, networking with stakeholders, supporting the community, dealing with environmental issues, and providing more value for interested parties.

13.10 Conclusion

This chapter indicates how existing concepts and approaches can be combined or extended to meet responsible project management principles. Being responsible means changing the way we think about a project. Even though responsibility is becoming mainstream, not everyone accepts responsible value creation as a natural part of the project management discipline. Through the research provided in the software industry, Boehm and Turner (2005) defined three main barriers to implementing new methodologies: development process conflicts, business process conflicts, and people conflicts. This chapter is oriented on the value chain process development, which steps to take to address responsibility using project management processes, concepts, and approaches to meet project sustainability, reach value for the stakeholders, and achieve ethical behavior.

The core element of creating a responsible value chain is to create a culture and climate that values responsibility not just on the project level but also at the organizational level. It is closely connected with the organizational culture and behavior, organizational strategy, and long-term orientation. Future research could be oriented toward the organizational factors that create the culture and values for responsible behavior and the implementation of mechanisms that can provide responsible project value chain implementation and people conflicts.

Revise values during the project

Stakeholders appearance through project stages analysis
Client feedback and user experience analysis
Response to environmental and social issues

Value alignment	Project definition	Project delivery	Measuring & Review	Benefits realisation
Stakeholder identification Stakeholder needs and interest analysis Long-term and short-term values Balance stakeholders values (conflicted interests, mutual impact of identified values, appearance of stakeholders in different project phases) Ethical values introduction (ethical decision-making) Different viewpoints innovative solutions	Establishing phase-feasibility analysis, Project tangible and intangible benefits analysis and monetisation project objective definition Project scope definition Critical success factor definition Responsible sourcing initiation (project staff, product and services)	Value delivering process definition - project initiation, planning, execution, monitoring and closing, Functions needed to be Performed to meet project objectives and create value.	Measurement system definition (measure ment process, tools (eg. EVM) Key performance indiators definition (KPIs_ People, planet and profit KPS introduction	Project evaluation Business implementation process definition Beneficiaries analysis Responsibility on business implementation defined Impact analysis

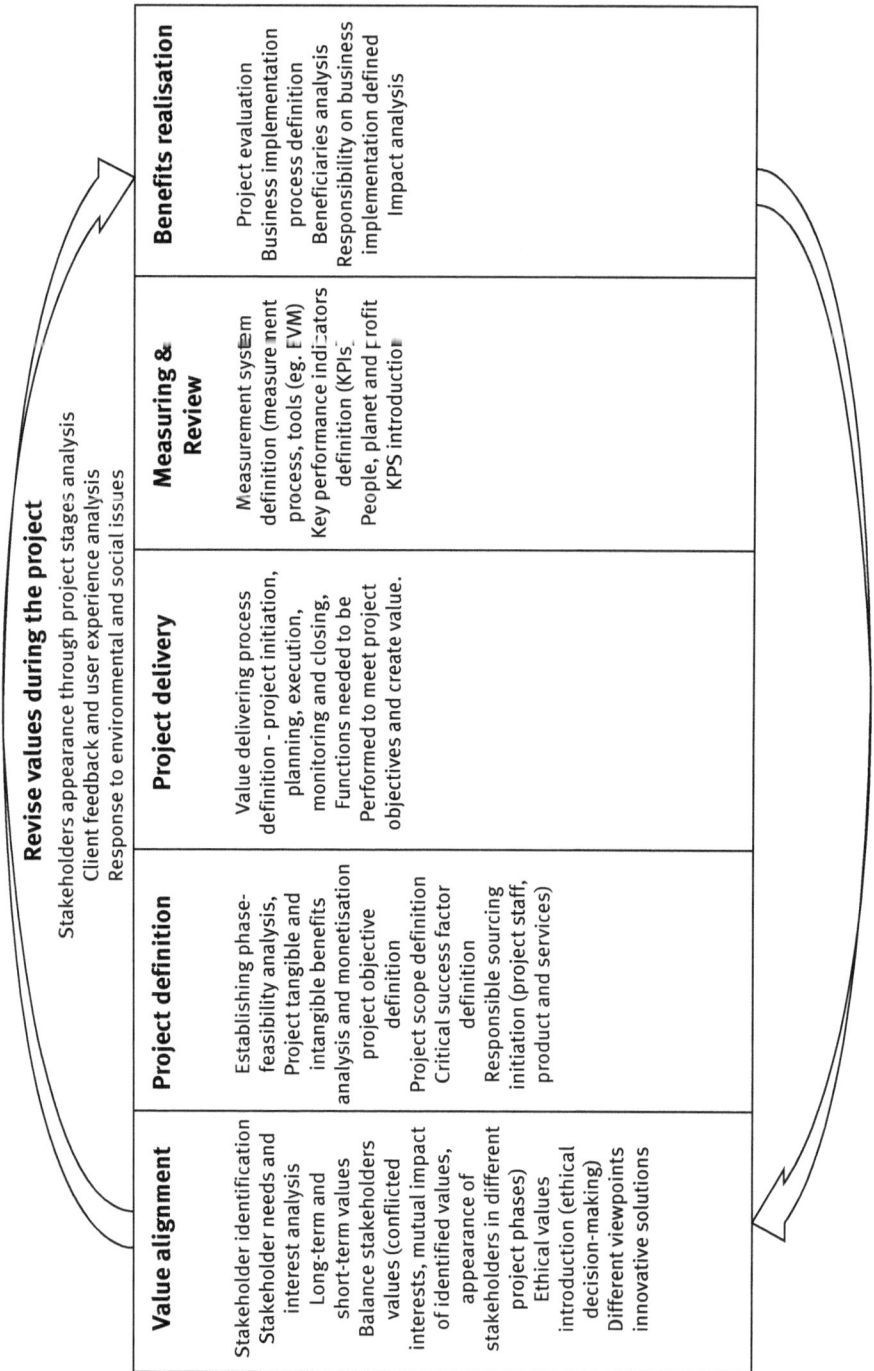

Figure 13.1: Responsible project value chain framework (author).

References

Agarval, R. S., & Kalmar, T. (2015). *Sustainability in project management – Eight principles in practice.* Umeå School of Business and Economics, Sweden, 2015.

Amade, B., Adeyomo, A. A., Ogbonna, A. C., Okore, O. L., & Okwara, I. D. (2020). Barriers to green supply chain management (GSCM) adoption on construction projects. *European Project Management Journal, 10*(2), 41–50.

Angus, G. Y., Flett, P. D., & Bowers, J. A. (2005). Developing a value-centred proposal for assessing project success. *International Journal of Project Management, 23*(6), 428–436.

British Standard Institute (BSI). (2000). *BS EN 12973:2000: Value management.* London: BSI.

Boadway, R. (2006). Principles of cost-benefit analysis. *Public Policy Review, 2*(1), 1–44.

Boehm, B., & Turner, R. (2005). Management challenges to implementing agile processes in traditional development organisations. *IEEE Software, 22*(5), 30–39.

Browning, T. R. (2014). A quantitative framework for managing project value, risk, and opportunity. *IEEE Transactions on Engineering Management, 61*(4), 583–598.

Carboni, J., & Gonzalez, M. (2013). Aligning projects to the united nations global compact and the global reporting initiative: Monitoring the impact of project processes and products on people, the planet, and profitability. *PM World Journal, 2.*

Dingsøyr, T., & Lassenius, C. (2016). Emerging themes in agile software development: Introduction to the special section on continuous value delivery. *Information and Software Technology, 77,* 56–60.

Drevland, F., Lohne, J., & Klakegg, O. J. (2017). Ethical dilemmas in value delivery: Theoretical conditions. In 25th Annual Conference of the International Group for Lean Construction, Vol. 1, 145–152.

Du, S., Kang, S., Li, F., & Du, T. (2017). Water use efficiency is improved by alternate partial root-zone irrigation of apple in arid northwest China. *Agricultural Water Management, 179,* 184–192. ISSN 0378-3774. https://doi.org/10.1016/j.agwat.2016.05.011.

Dwarka, L., & Ali, K., 2016. Measuring the actual energy cost performance of green buildings: A test of the earned value management approach. Energies 9, 188 European Standard 12973-2000, 2000. Value Management.

European Commission. (2018). Open Project Management Methodology – PM2.

Epstein, M. J., & Buhovac, A. R. (2014). *Making sustainability work: Best practices in managing and measuring corporate social, environmental, and economic impacts.* Berrett-Koehler Publishers.

Gadeken, O. C. (2008). *Ethics for project managers: It's not [i.e. not] just a set of rules.* Paper Presented at PMI® Global Congress 2008 – North America, Denver, CO. Newtown Square, PA: Project Management Institute.

Garcia-Muiña, F. E., González-Sánchez, R., Ferrari, A. M., & Settembre-Blundo, D. (2018). The paradigms of Industry 4.0 and circular economy as enabling drivers for the competitiveness of businesses and territories: The case of an Italian ceramic tiles manufacturing company. *Social Sciences, 7*(12), 255.

Gillier, T., Hooge, S., & Piat, G. (2015). Framing value management for creative projects: An expansive perspective. *International Journal of Project Management, 33*(4), 947–960.

Green Project Management. (2019). *The GPM P5 standard for sustainability in project management, Version 2.* USA. https://greenprojectmanagement.org/the-p5-standard

Greenberg, H., & Robins, K. (2008). Incorporating nonmarket time into benefit-cost analyses of social programs: An application to the self-sufficiency project. *Journal of Public Economics, 92*(3), 766–794.

Gutiérrez, R. T., & Ezponda, J. E. (2019). Technorati and the need of a responsible industry 4.0. In *Handbook of research on industrial advancement in scientific knowledge*. Hershey PA: IGI Global, Information Science Reference.

Hayles, C., Graham, M., & Fong, P. S. (2010). Value management for sustainable decision making. *Proceedings of the Institution of Civil Engineers-Municipal Engineer, 163*(1), 43–50. Thomas Telford Ltd.

Humble, J., & Farley, D. (2010). *Continuous delivery: reliable software releases through build, test, and deployment automation*. Pearson Education.

Horowitz, J., & McConnell, K. (2002). A review of WTA /WTP studies. *Journal of Environmental Economics and Management, 44*(3), 426–447.

Jugdev, K., & Müller, R. (2005). A retrospective look at our evolving understanding of project success. *Project Management Journal, 36*(4), 19–31.

Koke, B., & Moehler, R. C. (2019). Earned green value management for project management: A systematic review. *Journal of Cleaner Production, 230*, 180–197.

Laasch, O. (2018). Just old wine in new bottles? Conceptual shifts in the emerging field of responsible management. *Centre for Responsible Management Education Working Papers, 4*(1), 135–147.

Laasch, O., & Conaway, R. (2015). *Principles of responsible management: Glocal sustainability, responsibility, ethics*.

Laasch, O., Suddaby, R., Freeman, R. E., & Jamali, D. (2020). Mapping the emerging field of responsible management: Domains, spheres, themes, and future research. In *Research handbook of responsible management*. Edward Elgar Publishing. https://www.e-elgar.com/shop/gbp/research-handbook-of-responsible-management-9781788971959.html

Lazar, O. (2014). *Delivering benefits: The who, the what and the how!* Paper Presented at PMI® Global Congress 2014 – EMEA, Dubai, United Arab Emirates. Newtown Square, PA: Project Management Institute.

Lewandowski, M. (2016). Designing the business models for circular economy – Towards the conceptual framework. *Sustainability; 8*(1), 43. https://doi.org/10.3390/su8010043

Lalevée, A., Troussier, N., Blanco, É., & Berlioz, M. (2020). The interest of an evolution of value management methodology in complex technical projects for improving project management. *Procedia CIRP, 90*, 411–415.

Laursen, M., & Svejvig, P. (2016). Taking stock of project value creation: A structured literature review with future directions for research and practice. *International Journal of Project Management, 34*(4), 736–747.

Lepak, D. P., Smith, K. G., & Taylor, M. S. (2007). Value creation and value capture: A multilevel perspective. *Academy of Management Review, 32*(1), 180–194.

Kitcher, P. (2011). *The ethical project*. Harvard University Press.

Mochal, T., & Krasnoff, A. (2013). GreenPM®: The Basic Principles for Applying an Environmental Dimension to Project Management. 1, 121–139. DOI: 10.4018/978-1-4666-4852-4.ch007.

Maltzman, R., & Shirley, D. (2010). *Green project management*. CRC Press. https://www.routledge.com/Green-Project-Management/Maltzman-Shirley/p/book/9781439830017

Martinsuo, M., & Geraldi, J. (2020). Management of project portfolios: Relationships of project portfolios with their contexts. *International Journal of Project Management, 38*(7), 441–453.

Nishiguchi, T. (1994). *Strategic Industrial Sourcing: The Japanese Advantage. illustrated*. Oxford University Press. 318. ISBN: 0195071093, 9780195071092.

Mochal, T. & Krasnoff, A.. (2013). GreenPM®: The Basic Principles for Applying an Environmental Dimension to Project Management. 1. 121–139.10.4018/978-1-4666-4852-4.ch007.

Obradović, V., Todorović, M., & Bushuyev, S. (2018). Sustainability and agility in project management: Contradictory or complementary? In Conference on Computer Science and Information Technologies. Cham: Springer, 522–532.

Otegi-Olaso, J. R., López-Robles, J. R., & Gamboa-Rosales, N. K. (2019). *Responsible project management to face urgent world crises and regional conflicts*. Birzeit, Palestine: Birzeit University-Project Management.

Ostojić, B., Berić, I., Pavlović, K., & Pećić, M. (2020). Management education and sustainable development projects. *European Project Management Journal, 10*(1), 69–77.

Palazzo, G., & Wentland, M. (2011). *Responsible management practices for the twenty-first century*. Université de Lausanne. Ecole des hautes études commerciales. Pearson. Published by Pearson Education France 2011 - 1 vol. (VI-208 p.).

Porter, M., & Kramer, M. (2011). The Big Idea: Creating Shared Value. How to Reinvent Capitalism—and Unleash a Wave of Innovation and Growth. *Harvard Business Review, 89*, 62–77.

Porter, M. E., & Kramer, M. R. (2019). Creating shared value. In *Managing sustainable business*. Dordrecht: Springer, 323–346.

Schwartz, T., Feld, M., Bürckert, C., Dimitrov, S., Folz, J., Hutter, D., Hevesi, P., Kiefer, B., Krieger, H., Lüth, C., Mronga, D., Pirkl, G., Röfer, T., Spieldenner, T., Wirkus, M., Zinnikus, I., & Straube, S. (2016). Hybrid Teams of Humans, Robots, and Virtual Agents in a Production Setting. 2016 12th International Conference on Intelligent Environments (IE), 234–237.

Shaoqing Du, Shaozhong Kang, Fusheng Li, Taisheng Du, Water use efficiency is improved by alternate partial root-zone irrigation of apple in arid northwest China, Agricultural Water Management, 179, 2017, 184–192, ISSN 0378-3774, https://doi.org/10.1016/j.agwat.2016.05.011.

Shehadeh, M. A., Schroeder, S., Richert, A., & Jeschke, S. (2017). Hybrid teams of industry 4.0: A workplace considering robots as key players. In IEEE International Conference on Systems, Man, and Cybernetics (SMC). Banff, AB, 2017, 1208–1213.

Smyth, H., Gustafsson, M., & Ganskau, E. (2010). The value of trust in project business. *International Journal of Project Management, 28*(2), 117–129.

Thiry, M. (2014). Strategic value management. In Paper presented at PMI® Global Congress 2014 – EMEA, Dubai, United Arab Emirates. Newtown Square, PA: Project Management Institute.

Thompson, K. M., & Williams, N. (2018). A Guide to Responsible Project Management. Bournemouth University. http://responsiblepm.com/

Toljaga-Nikolić, D., Todorović, M., Dobrota, M., Obradović, T., & Obradović, V. (2020). Project management and sustainability: Playing trick or treat with the planet. *Sustainability, 12*(20), 8619.

Todorović, M., & Obradović, V. (2018). Sustainability in project management: A project manager perspective, published in Sustainable growth and development in small open economies, Editors Isidora Ljumović, Andrea Éltető, Institute of World Economics, Centre for Economic and Regional Studies of the Hungarian Academy of Sciences, ISBN 978-963-301-664-0 (e-book), ISBN 978-963-301-663-3, 88–106.

Toshihiro Nishiguchi, Strategic Industrial Sourcing: The Japanese Advantage illustrated Oxford University Press, 1994 0195071093, 9780195071092 318 pages

Vrečko, I., & Lebe, S. S. (2013). Project management supports (requisitely) holistic: Socially responsible action in business systems. *Systemic Practice and Action Research, 26*(6), 561–569.

Section 3: **Responsible Communities**

Early work in sustainability builds on the notion of community stewardship that seeks to protect the environment from exploitation for the long-term benefit of residents (Caradonna, 2014). These early contributions identified the interdependence between economic growth, consumption, and well-being along with potential trade-offs among these domains (Lumley & Armstrong, 2004). An aspect of this research that is of particular interest to project management is the tension between capitalist and alternative economic organizing approaches (Arndt, 1987).The former argues that economic growth provides community well-being while others argue against the importance of growth as a goal. For project managers, a shift in economic approach will influence the type of projects that are prioritized and supported by local regions.

This section explores the tensions that emerge between project-driven development and community well-being. The chapter on climate change outlines these arguments at a macro level. The project profession, despite its scale, has only recently begun to acknowledge its responsibility for a societal transformation to address climate change. Project Management journals have published few articles to date on this subject, and this chapter synthesizes the current discourse. It identifies the systems, perspectives, and actors that influence climate action and the implications for the project profession seeking to engage with responsibility.

The chapter from John Lannon examines the role and responsibility of projects in organized civil society action. Drawing on the author's experiences working in the international development sector and a nationally based service delivery and advocacy NGO, the chapter is an important contribution to the literature on project organizing in differing community environments. The chapter explores the tension between project-based organizing which enables delivery of outcomes but can constrain the ability for NGOs to build capacity to facilitate longer-term development. José Ramón Otegi-Olaso, Leticia Fuentes-Ardeo, and José Ricardo López-Robles also explore the responsibility of Project Organizing to address humanitarian issues. The chapter examines the case of a nonprofit association dedicated to feeding people in refugee camps. Like Dr. Lannon's chapter, the authors examine the tensions between the need to deliver beneficial outcomes while meeting the requirements of external stakeholders who may hold different perspectives.

Ghasan Al Mamari examines the contextual nature of project management and the challenges in ensuring that the voice of the community is not lost in the drive for development. Oman is seeking to diversify its oil-based economy through multiple venues, including tourism developments. With the tourism industry, however, comes the debate about its positive and negative impacts in multiple areas, including the protection of culture. Nantangopan and Gamlath explore the challenge of developing governance frameworks in an overlooked context, post-conflict countries. While over 50 countries worldwide fit this category, little work has examined how governance frameworks have been adapted to ensure community cohesion in these delicate societies.

https://doi.org/10.1515/9783110724783-017

References and Further Reading

Arndt, H. W. (1987). *Economic development: The history of an idea*. Chicago: University of Chicago Press.

Caradonna, J. L. (2014). *Sustainability: A history*. Oxford University Press. https://oxford.university pressscholarship.com/view/10.1093/oso/9780199372409.001.0001/isbn-9780199372409

Lumley, S., & Armstrong, P. (2004). Some of the nineteenth century origins of the sustainability concept. *Environment Development and Sustainability, 6*(3), 367–378.

Purvis, B., Mao, Y., & Robinson, D. (2019). Three pillars of sustainability: In search of conceptual origins. *Sustainability Science, 14*, 681–695. doi:https://doi.org/10.1007/s11625-018-0627-5

WCED. (1987). *Our common future, World Commission on Environment and Development*. Oxford: Oxford University Press.

Ghasan Almaamari

14 Responsible Project Management for Communities Protection of Culture

Context: Projects drive the change in every sector, but this change must be managed well to ensure long-term success. Although the tourism industry is one of the principal project commissioners, research linking tourism and PM is limited.

Characters/entities: Define stakeholders and differentiate between stakeholders' management and engagement.

Locations: Oman is the case study of this chapter, as it is paving its way toward diversifying its oil-based economy through multiple venues, including tourism developments. Oman has planned tourism growth to protect the local communities and culture, which can be challenging and may not yield the predicted results.

Research gap: The need to examine the responsibility of PM for the protection of culture in different phases of a project life cycle. There is a need to explore the role of PM in realizing tourism projects that can impact culture.

Challenges/conflict/tension: With the tourism industry growth comes the debate about its positive and negative impacts in multiple areas, including the protection of culture. It is a dilemma where governments strive to manage the expectations of business, society, and the environment.

Keywords: cultural protection, tourism, Oman

14.1 Introduction

"For centuries, Oman had been a powerful centre of travel and trade. This is a strong basis for modern tourism. Today, the opportunity exists for Oman's tourism sector to grow into a powerful engine of economic diversification, cultural expression, and social development" (OTS, 2016).

Most research linking project management and culture focuses on the organization's culture and enhancing performance and success (Suda, 2007). However, protecting the culture outside the organization has not had much attention. This is because project management has focused on the process and techniques targeted for the project management phase, which is temporary by definition, whereas protection of culture is a long-term outcome of executing projects. The responsible project management (RPM) concept has newly emerged, and its effect can be extended to include the life cycle of the project rather than the project execution phase only. In addition,

https://doi.org/10.1515/9783110724783-018

as the project life cycle changes, the stakeholder's roles and responsibilities change, which makes the RPM responsibility change as well. This chapter will review the different definitions of projects that influence and focus on projects' long-term aspects. Then it will discuss the stakeholder's role within project management and how their role changes over the life cycle of projects.

The chapter will bring tourism, signifying one of the leading project commissioners worldwide and its different impacts, including culture. The case of Oman tourism will demonstrate how culture could be protected throughout the project life cycle phases using RPM principles. Although Oman is selected to be the case study, the principles of protecting the culture can be applied to other states as well as every country has a unique culture that it wants to preserve.

14.2 Project Management Growth

Project management is growing in terms of academic contribution and practice. The development of the PM discipline led to its expansion, with more organizations becoming keen to use project management tools and techniques to help achieve their strategies (Bredillet, 2005; Vlahov et al., 2019), and it is estimated that around 30% of the world economy is project-based (Turner, 2010). Humans have undertaken project-type work for centuries to facilitate their life (Kloppenborg & Opfer 2002; Morris & Geraldi 2011; Morris, 2013). Earlier projects were executed based on intuition, and people found ways toward improving project performance, but they did not have proper PM tools and techniques (Lientz & Rea 2007, p. 44). Projects were instead taken as particular endeavors for nation-building or act of war, for example, and were led by specific persons who were called rulers or generals and not project managers (Weaver, 2006). Scholars are uncertain about the beginning of the PM discipline as there is a lack of research in this area except for a handful of studies (Söderlund & Lenfle, 2013). It is argued that understanding the history of the discipline can help apprehend the basis of its knowledge base and hence improve it (Morris, 2013).

Nevertheless, scholars argue that the development of modern PM research originated from operational management research (Bredillet, 2007a; Weaver, 2007; Morris & Geraldi, 2011). The initial research had led to the development of several techniques that established the discipline in the 1950s (Söderlund, 2002; Morris, 2013; Pasian, 2016). Earlier methods that were targeting the management of time to schedule different project activities can be observed in the literature of the 1950s and 1960s (Söderlund, 2002; Morris & Geraldi, 2011). The discipline began primarily in the defence, engineering, and construction industries and eventually expanded to other sectors (Kapsali, 2011; Archibald, 2017). With the establishment of the field, related professional and academic organizations started, such as specific discipline journals and conferences (Söderlund, 2002). The majority of the scholars who established PM organizations had either a scheduling background aiming to optimize the time or a cost engineering background working to optimize the cost (Weaver, 2007). Therefore, the initial PM research was classified as either optimization research dealing with techniques and tools or critical success factor research focusing on factors that help in the success of projects (Packendorff, 1995; Söderlund, 2002). PM has been viewed more as operational rather than strategic (Jugdev & Thomas, 2002), and the success of projects was measured in operational terms such as budget and time (Killen et al., 2012).

A broader expansion of PM research has led to the emergence of several PM schools of thought, extending the PM research to a new horizon (Söderlund, 2011; Bredillet, 2015; Turner, 2018). Weaver (2007) argues that the development of PM tools, the growth of the PM science, and the PM profession are signs of the development of modern PM.

The growth of PM within the last seven decades has attracted its applications in several industries (Morris, 2013; Lebe & Vrecko, 2014; Bredillet, 2015; Samset & Volden, 2016; PMI, 2017). This expansion has led PM to be adaptive and responsive to complex issues that face different realities and contexts (Morris & Geraldi 2011). More researchers have called for pluralistic viewpoints for the PM to cater for this expansion (Cooke-Davies et al., 2007; Leybourne, 2007; Söderlund, 2011). The project definition and concepts play a crucial role in further developing the field.

So, what is a project and what is project management? Zwikael and Meredith (2018) argue the importance of defining project terminologies if PM research and theory develop further. Having clear and comprehensive definitions for projects and PM enhances the development of appropriate tools and techniques (Zwikael & Smyrk, 2012), which will help to achieve RPM.

It is essential to define what the project is and what does it include. Most definitions of the project focus on the short-term project deliverables instead of realizing the project-intended benefits (Ashurst et al., 2008). Consequently, the efficiency of the process becomes a more important criterion than the effectiveness of the investment and the realization of benefits (Zwikael & Smyrk, 2012; Morris, 2013). This aligns with the classical project life cycle phases that consist of four stages: starting the project, organizing and preparing, carrying out the work and closing the project (PMI, 2017). This life cycle presents the project until the delivery stage and neglects the long-term effects that projects usually produce (Eduardo Yamasaki Sato & de Freitas Chagas Jr, 2014).

Project Management Institute PMI (2017, p. 4) defined a project as a "temporary endeavour undertaken to create a unique product, service or result." This definition focuses mainly on the deliverables or short-term outputs of the project and neglects the longer-term impacts. However, PMI does recognize the long-term deliverables of the project "projects are temporary, but their deliverables may exist beyond the end of the project" (PMI, 2017).

Other attempts were made to modify the project definition to expand beyond delivering the output, which was observed in literature where Turner (2010) introduced the term "beneficial change" to the description. Zwikael and Smyrk (2012) defined the project as "a unique process intended to achieve target outcomes." These definitions have extended the focus of project performance evaluation beyond PM success. Hence, projects shall be understood as vehicles to achieve goals rather than merely delivering outputs (Tillmann et al., 2012). Deguire (2012) argues that benefits realization is not usually within the project manager's authority and beyond his scope.

The expansion of the project definition brings about benefits, outcomes, and outputs and the necessity to distinguish between their definitions to design appropriate success evaluation criteria (Nogeste & Walker, 2005). As per Zwikael and Smyrk (2012), the outputs are the products from the project, the outcomes are the "measurable end-effect that arises when stakeholders realise the outputs from a project," and the benefits are the "flow of value" from utilizing the outcomes. Xue et al. (2013) gave a similar definition, with benefits defined as the "ultimate desired impacts of the project." For example, for a built tourism project, the output would be the buildings and related facilities, the outcomes would be the utilization of the resort by guests and flow of revenue, and the benefits would be improving the quality of life for the community, improving the country tourism infrastructure, and developing a successful brand image. It is evident that unless outputs are realized, outcomes or benefits cannot be realized (Zwikael & Smyrk, 2015). In addition, despite the common belief that benefits realization may be linked to program levels, there is a rising agreement in academia that even projects not part of a program have benefits to realize (Samset & Volden, 2016). Within the phases of projects, decisions are taken that influence each phase's performance, and there comes the importance of RPM, an emerging area in project management research and practice.

14.3 Responsible Project Management

Many efforts have been carried out to define responsible management. It has multiple definitions and covers a broader range of topics, as summarized by Carroll et al. (2020). Although there is criticism over the lack of a common, unified concept for responsible management, the absence of a unified definition suggests that it is essential to recognize the development of a new field of inquiry (Cullen, 2020). On the other hand, RPM has recently emerged, which focuses mainly on PM. Like responsible management, RPM can be defined in different ways; however, for this book, RPM is defined as "the actions of people involved in the management of projects who seek to deliver societal value (environmental and social) ethically but who may not have formally delegated organisational accountability and authority as part of their roles." So, RPM involves actions of stakeholders that can have different impacts. These actions and their impact determine the success of projects where various stakeholders use different criteria to evaluate project performance.

The actions could be taken throughout the phases of the projects and should be linked in the chain where the actions may be interconnected. These actions start from strategy development for projects, leading to feasibility studies to the close-out and benefits realization stage. Different stakeholders could plan, decide, influence, and execute these actions. The stakeholders in project management literature have been examined, and the term has been expanded to stakeholder engagement and management for stakeholders rather than the traditional stakeholder management. This chapter will focus on the project's impact on the culture, where the tourism project's context will be used to demonstrate it.

14.4 Stakeholder's Roles

Stakeholder roles in projects have grown significantly, as demonstrated in project management literature. The stakeholders' management concept originated from the theories of strategic management in Freeman's book in 1984, where he emphasized the stakeholder view of the organization (Eskerod et al., 2015). Freeman (2010) defined the stakeholders as groups or individuals who can affect or are affected by the organization. Stakeholder Management processes involve identifying stakeholders, analyzing their expectations and impact on the project, and developing strategies for engaging stakeholders (Aragonés-Beltrán et al., 2017). The concept was adapted in different contexts and industries, including PM and tourism. Stakeholder management in PM is considered one of the essential elements of projects (Littau et al., 2010). Cleland and Ireland (2006) defined project stakeholders as

> persons or groups that have, or claim, ownership, rights, or interests in a project and its activities: past, present or future.

Stakeholder theory considers a project as a network of complex interdependent and dynamic relationships with a wide range of stakeholders that can affect each other (Teo & Loosemore, 2017). As per Eskerod et al. (2015), the significance of stakeholders in PM literature stems from reasons such as their financial and non-financial role in projects, establishing success evaluation criteria, and the negative or positive impact of the outcomes. Managing stakeholders effectively and nurturing the relationships helps achieve organizational objectives (Littau et al., 2015; Baumfield, 2016), which are as important as the organizational broader responsibility to society (Teo & Loosemore, 2017). As per Freeman, responsible for the stakeholders within the organization and extends to stakeholders that impact their lives (Carroll et al., 2020). This is crucial where RPM actions could affect the wider society.

The concept of stakeholder management has evolved from managing stakeholders to managing stakeholders and stakeholder engagement. Management of stakeholders is talking and informing them while management for stakeholders is creating continuous communication channels with them to explain how the project can meet their expectations, and at the same time, the project wins their support (Eskerod & Huemann, 2016). Stakeholder engagement is similar to management for stakeholders (Turner, 2018), where the project should engage with the stakeholders via marketing the idea to them, demonstrating that its benefits are valuable and getting their acceptance of the project (Turner & Lecoeuvre, 2017). The early steps of the stakeholder engagement process are to identify stakeholders and their interests and predict their potential responses (Turner, 2014). It is similar to the market segmentation principle (Kotler et al., 2016), where communication should be tailored to the requirement of each stakeholder (Turner, 2014). Turner (2018) argue that in most cases, engagement with or management for stakeholders is appropriate, but occasionally "of" is appropriate.

Scholars have come up with different classification typologies to understand how to manage stakeholders effectively, which is challenging given the dynamic nature of projects (Loosemore & Phua, 2010). Gibson (2000) divided project stakeholders into two groups based on their connection to the project: internal and external stakeholders. According to their role in the projects, Cleland and Ireland (2006, p. 174) classified stakeholders into primary and secondary. The primary stakeholders have a contractual relationship with the project, such as owners, suppliers, investors, and local authorities. In contrast, the secondary stakeholders are not regularly engaged in the project, and they may not be essential to project success, such as media, community, and special interest groups (Cleland & Ireland, 2006). Littau et al. (2015) categorized stakeholders based on dimensions of power, interest, and six categories with different management strategies, as shown in Table 14.1.

Table 14.1: Littaue et al. (2015) classification of project stakeholders.

Stakeholder type	Management strategy
Acquaintances	Keep them informed with conduct only communication style
Sleeping giants	Sleeping till other negative actors awake them for considering their claims. Managers should engage with them to get their support for the project.
Irritants	Interested in social and environmental issues. Need to get clear and transparent communication.
Friends	Project managers should use them as confidants.

Table 14.1 (continued)

Stakeholder type	Management strategy
Saboteurs	Power is obtained from other stakeholders like the Media or Governments. The project manager can either provide feedback to their claims using clear and transparent communication or, in some cases, managers should gain other players' support to reduce their power.
Saviours	These are vital players to the project manager, and it is essential to keep on their side.

PM literature identifies typical project stakeholders, including investors, suppliers, customers, users, authorities, neighbors, and media (Turner & Zolin, 2012). Therefore, it is imperative to identify and manage all related stakeholders to ensure successful projects (Cleland & Ireland, 2006) and their interest, which varies with time (Turner, 2010; McLeod et al., 2012). The involvement and interest of stakeholders in a project varies with time as not all stakeholders need to be involved at all phases of the project (McLeod et al., 2012; Zwikael & Smyrk, 2012; Elbaz & Spang, 2018).

This gains more importance when it comes to managing stakeholders outside the organizations. As specified in Table 14.1, sleeping giants and irritants stakeholders are crucial for the success of the projects and interested in managing social and environmental issues. If the project starts to have any negative impact, that will irritate specific stakeholders and wake them up, harming the overall project results. The criteria stakeholders use to evaluate the results and effectiveness of the project of any RPM actions differ with stakeholders and the time of project evaluation.

Turner and Zolin's (2012) model claimed that stakeholders could simultaneously judge the performance at all project stages. However, their evaluation criteria differ depending on the phase of the project, that is, completion, months, or years after. The public or the community, the main stakeholders concerned with the impact on the culture, evaluates the projects throughout the project phases. The project evaluation includes assessing the actions taken as a part of RPM measures. These actions are part of the project and affect the overall project performance criteria and perceptions of success by the different stakeholders. One of the contexts involving multiple stakeholders and project impact that can last for a long time is tourism-related projects. Tourism projects can have both positive and negative impacts on multi-dimensions, and RPM actions greatly influence the evaluation of these projects. Diedrich et al. (2009) argue that assessing and understanding these impacts on communities is essential to maintaining the long-term success of tourism developments.

14.5 Tourism Impact and Culture

Although tourism is a significant project commissioner, there is a lack of research on PM and tourism. A search in databases of the terms "tourism project management" does not return any literature. However, tourism projects are an essential element of countries' development as tourism is becoming one of the main components of GDP in many countries. Nevertheless, what is meant by tourism and what is its impact?

Literature reveals that several definitions for tourism have been proposed that vary according to their technical aspects and whether they are used for statistical purposes or conceptual elements to convey the function of tourism (Sharpley & Telfer 2015, p. 6). For this research, the UK Tourism Society definition is going to be used as it encompasses both aspects.

> Tourism is the temporary short-term movement of people to destinations outside the places where they normally live and work and their activities during their stay at these places; it includes movement for all purposes as well as day visits or excursions.
>
> (Sharpley & Telfer 2015, p. 6)

Tourism is of significant economic and social prominence (Wall & Mathieson 2006, p. 1). With the tempting potential impact of tourism on long-run economic development, governments invest in developing their destination to attract tourists (Alhowaish, 2016). Governments have developed policies to enhance the sector, enabling international companies to invest (Uysal et al., 2012) and develop new tourist attractions (Gil-Lafuente & Barcellos Paula, 2013). However, despite the positive perceptions of the impacts of tourism, there are also concerns that tourism can negatively impact the quality of life of the local community (Andereck et al., 2005; Nunkoo, 2017). There is substantial literature about the different effects of tourism on the economy, the environment, the society, and the culture, with researchers reporting both positive and negative impacts in each category (Wall & Mathieson, 2006; Kim et al., 2013; Zhu et al., 2017; Liu & Li, 2018). It is argued that the tourism impact gets exaggerated for different reasons (Pratt & Tolkach, 2018), so it is challenging to have a realistic understanding of the impacts. This may be due to the other variables that influence the interpretations of the tourism impact, such as demography, education level and gender, distance from the tourism development, and stage of tourism development (Liu & Li, 2018). Responsible tourism has been discussed thoroughly, leading to the increasing literature on sustainable tourism (Kirppendorf, 1987). There are multiple research perspectives on responsible tourism, such as whether studies focus on production or consumption, ethical beliefs impact, and corporate social responsibility, examining relations between host-guests or worker-employers, individual and group responsibilities, and political influences on tourism (Bramwell et al., 2008).

Tourism impacts on culture can be positive or negative, determining how different stakeholders view these impacts. Tourism can revitalize cultures to attract tourists and learn about different cultures (Wang et al., 2006; Liu & Li, 2018). On the other hand, tourism can disturb traditional cultural structures and behavioral patterns. Local culture may disappear, diminishing the small-town charm (Chase et al., 2012; Frent, 2016). Nevertheless, what is culture, and how is it defined? Akkuş et al. (2017) claim that it has proven impossible to define what culture is, but the most dominant definition of culture is a set of standard meaning systems translated into values. Some of the cultural values are captured by the World Values Survey (Inglehart-Welzel, 2020), as indicated in Figure 14.1.

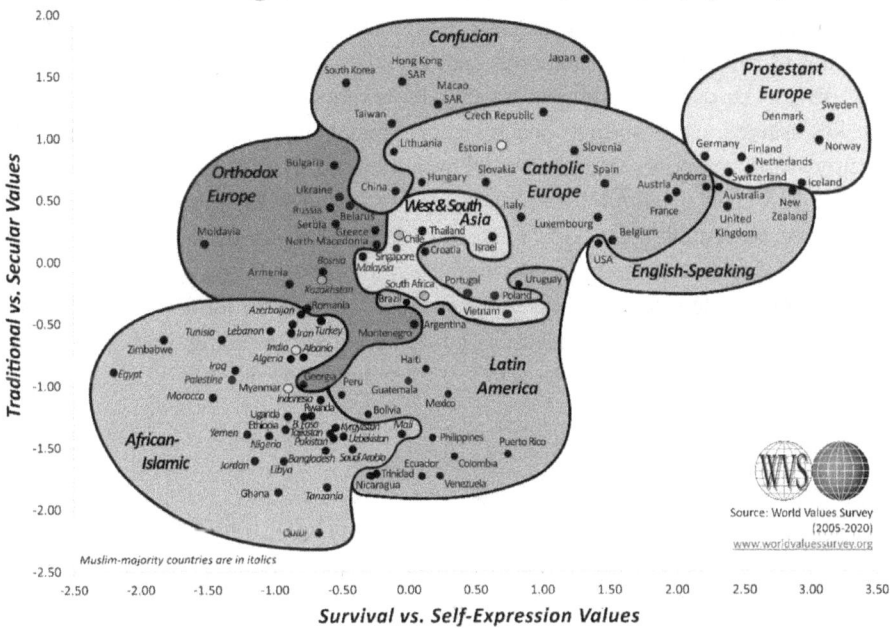

Figure 14.1: Inglehart-Welzel World Cultural Map (2020).

There is no right or wrong culture but values and meanings to each society regarding cultures. People have pride in their culture and practices that have developed over the years and usually are keen to keep them and stick to them. They form a sense of pride and belonging that has developed over the years. Although values and culture change, the change happens slowly and over a long period. As stated above, projects being generally new and non-routine tend to disturb reality, and tourism-related projects have multiple impacts. In addition, it is common in tourism that projects are designed to attract foreign tourists and be similar to their culture, which has a long-term impact on the host community's culture. The chapter will not elaborate on cultural changes but instead focus on how the RPM could protect the cultures. This can happen at different levels of project life cycles and with the responsible actions of different stakeholders. If we take the project life cycle, the protection of culture should be a chain of actions throughout the life cycle of the projects. It should start from the overall strategy, which is reflected in projects selection and execution. Stakeholders' involvement must be practised at all project phases. The case of Oman will demonstrate how RPM principles can be applied to protect the culture in tourism projects.

14.6 Case of Oman

Oman, officially the Sultanate of Oman, is an Arab country located in the southeast of the Arabian Peninsula, bordering Yemen, UAE, and Saudi Arabia. The country has a total area of 309,500 square kilometres, making it larger than the UK area. Oman has a very diverse landscape varying from "Wadis (valleys), mountains, caves, deserts, beaches, islands, water springs, beach lagoons, and canyons" (Henderson, 2014). The country's land comprises roughly 82% of desert and dry riverbeds, 15% of mountains, and 3% of a coastal plain (MoNE, 2009). The coastline spans more than 3000 kilometres over the Arabian Sea, Gulf of Oman, and the Arabian Gulf. Figure 14.2 shows the map of Oman demonstrating the long coastline and different topographies. The country's diverse landscape offers challenges and activities for tourists, such as scuba diving, skydiving, camping, cruises, mountain climbing, trekking, golf, kitesurfing, camel riding, and watching whales, birds, turtles, and dolphins (Oukil et al., 2016).

Figure 14.2: Map of Oman.

Oman was selected as the case of this research as it has recently developed a tourism strategy 2016–2040 and has plans for the tourism sector to improve its contribution to GDP to diversify the oil-dependent economy. With its unique nature, attractions, culture, and history, Oman attracts a niche tourism market with mainly high spending tourists (OTS, 2016). Oman is in the African-Islamic quadrant, with traditional and survival values as crucial elements of its culture. It plans to develop high-end tourism infrastructure and accommodations to achieve its policy objectives. Hence resorts were selected to be the majority of the new developments to capitalize on the country's unique features.

Until the late 1990s, Oman has still considered a closed country to tourism (Winkler, 2007); it opened up relatively late compared to its neighboring states. Tourism is not perceived positively by people; there is widespread fear of its negative impacts. Although naturally welcoming guests and hospitable, the people in Oman are conservative regarding cultural sensitivity. They are concerned with anything that could influence the culture negatively. In many cases, tourists are advised to respect the local norms regarding dress codes and other behaviors that can have long-term impacts on the culture and society.

Culture protection played an essential element in the strategy development for Oman tourism, where it has emphasized the importance that local culture plays for the future of the sector. "Tourism will bring additional economic prosperity, benefit the people of Oman and enhance its nature and culture" (OTS, 2016). The strategy aims to "Strengthen Oman's identity and brand by enhancing the national culture and heritage" (OTS, 2016). It is designed to strengthen the culture rather than compromise it (2016). On the other hand, tourism can negatively impact the country, making tourism jobs not culturally acceptable and negative perceptions about them (Bontenbal & Aziz, 2013). Tourism resorts aim to attract foreign tourists where they provide certain activities and food to cater to tourists-taste even if they are against the local culture or religion. Having to serve culturally unacceptable products can harm the attractiveness of employment at such resorts from local employees, the majority of Muslims may create an adverse result for the policy developers (Bontenbal & Aziz, 2013).

Decisions are usually made top-down with a minimal public consultancy with the country's monarchy government system. When it comes to tourism, most of the Integrated Tourism Complexes (ICTs) that already exist in Oman have been awarded without the involvement of the local community (Hamza et al., 2017). Unlike other industries, tourism depends highly on communities, and their acceptance of the projects plays a high role in the overall success. Therefore, most of the ICTs in Oman were criticized widely for lacking the community's involvement, forcing the government to take an alternative approach. In my PhD research, one of the interviews participants from the Ministry of Tourism has claimed that due to a lack of public consultation, the Ministry had to cancel some projects and, in some cases, pay penalties to contractors (Almaamari, 2020). This could have been avoided had the government engaged with the stakeholders at the early stages, which is now gaining more importance.

14.6.1 RPM in the Protection of Culture in Oman

As mentioned elsewhere in this book (Governance, Policy and Politics), Drouin & Turner (2022)) suggest that there are four levels of governance in project-based organizations where different decisions are taken:
- Project governance; operational decisions
- Governance of projects; tactical decisions
- Governance at the board level; strategic decisions
- Governmentality, which is at the policy level, policy decisions

These four levels of governance and decisions points coincide with the project's life cycle stages. The policy level is what the government identify as the overall framework. As per Priemus (2010) project stages, every project starts with a problem or needs analysis that develops an appropriate strategy to address it. The strategy then transforms into a functional program of requirements. These requirements get elaborated further in a multi-dimensional aspect: technical, practical, economical, social, and environmental. This leads to developing the project scope that is ready for execution. Then the execution phase starts through to the project's finish with all contingencies that may happen. The final stage is the operation of the stage to realize the outcomes and benefits of the project.

Applying this concept to the protection of culture in tourism projects requires that responsible stakeholders take decisions at all the different stages of the project development. An example case of Oman tourism projects will be analyzed to demonstrate how decisions taken at different stages can help the overall protection of culture.

14.6.2 Protection of Culture: Policy and Strategic Decisions

The Oman tourism policy 2040 had mentioned that it aims to strengthen and protect the culture. This was the basis for the overall approach to target niche tourism that capitalizes on existing strengths. The strategy states:

> Oman's strategy is not aimed at chasing mass tourists; it is designed instead to invite fewer premium visitors who will spend more time and bring greater benefits with minimum negative impacts on culture and the environment. Oman's tourism will:

- be high-touch rather than high-tech;
- be authentic rather than artificial;
- strengthen Omani culture rather than compromise it;
- be a source of pride;
- be experienced by the world as an enlightened treasure (OTS, 2016).

These measures highlight the importance of protecting the culture at the highest level, which determines the roadmap for the sector. They guide the selection process for the type of projects to be developed, their design, and their long-term impact. The protection of culture must be managed during the execution phase of tourism development. However, the approach taken to implement the strategy may differ depending on the government–public relationship. With the Oman top-down system, the government usually works as custodian of the strategy and assigns projects that are deemed fit.

14.6.3 Protection of Culture: Tactical Decisions

Although it can be considered a temporary phase, the execution of projects can impact society and culture with results lasting for the long term. After the investors tender their project scope and select appropriate contractors, the investors' role is to adhere to the local culture and values. This is especially important when the contractors are international companies that may not know the local norms. Although the project's overall duration may be small compared to the expected lifetime of the project, it takes years to execute many tourism projects. These execution years can harm the local culture, impacting the overall results. Therefore, contractors must be selected carefully and aware of the local cultures and norms.

In addition, issues can arise during the execution phase, linked to stakeholders' engagement and expectations. For example, one of the ITC projects took place on a beach in a village near Muscat. People were very excited about the project, especially as it has been over the media with many promises of improvement. The community, however, had not been consulted about the project before the awarding. Although the community was happy about the project's potential, they did not see any benefits while the execution occurred. They expected minimum services such as paved roads to their village or support providing infrastructure for telecom or other services, but that did not happen. They were also expecting more benefits during the execution phase, such as employment, social support, and SME support. However, the project contractor did the minimum requirement for roads that served their project, neglecting the village. In addition, they were not interested in providing other support or services. The community tried to raise the issue to the contractors and the investors, but no feedback was received. Eventually, they raised to the governor, and they only received promises. This has caused the community to take a step that has been rarely practised in the monarchy government, which is protesting. The community gathered and closed the road to the project and did not allow the construction work to continue. This has raised the flag with the authorities and made them intervene and take action. The Ministry tried to resolve the problem between the two parties, the community and their benefits, and the investors and the promises. Since the community issue was not emphasized enough to the investors and the contractors, it was hard to ask them to provide benefits that had not been accounted for. Eventually, the project continued with some settlement between the two parties.

This issue has negatively impacted the relationship between the project team and the community, which has both short and long-term impacts. It has increased the hostility toward the project and transformed the community's excitement to resist the project. They felt that the project had occupied more than half of their village area that their next generations would otherwise use. This transformation of feeling within the community can be extended beyond the execution phase, and during the operation, tourists and visitors will flow through the area. The community will not welcome them as the norm and culture.

14.6.4 Protection of Culture: Operation Decisions

The final stage of Priemus's (2010) life cycle is the operation and realization of the outcomes and benefits of the project. This is an essential item in the chain of protecting the culture as it involves different stakeholders and lasts for a long time. The selection of the operator is crucial in preserving the culture. Many operators, especially the international ones, may have their own culture and values to bring in the projects. These values could contradict with county's culture. This is especially true in many developing countries where tourism projects are designed to attract the guest culture even if that means losing of own culture. With Oman having its unique culture, there is a cultural difference compared to western countries. This is a concern for communities, as any tourism project by default means a foreign culture to Oman. This was especially true in the past when most projects were designed for foreigners.

The community perception that tourism projects may not fit the Oman culture. Locals link it to bad habits like alcohol bars, clubs, gambling, and Omani culture. One of the participants in my research said, "one area is our perception in Oman that resorts are usually associated with a bad reputation, especially in remote communities. It brings the issues of alcohol and women; our nature is that we are still a conservative community which is not a negative thing, maybe the opposite. However, it is imperative when developing the project to clarify the idea to the society" (Almaamri, 2020).

This creates a cultural problem and society as many local people reject working in such an environment because it is culturally and religiously unacceptable. For example, as Muslims believe that the religion forbids alcohol, it is also believed that the provision of alcohol is forbidden. It stems from the fact that people need to promote good deeds and eliminate the bad ones. A study conducted by Bontenbal and Aziz (2013) revealed that many Omani college students avoid working in the tourism sector, especially hotels, as society perceives it negatively. The tourism sector is one of the most promising sectors in the country, with the strategy predicting up to 500,000 jobs by 2040. However, many dry hotels that do not serve alcohol cater to locals' expectations. Therefore, it is vital to discuss these when selecting the operators. It should also involve the relevant stakeholders, including the local communities, as the project would impact them.

14.7 Conclusion

Projects and project management are dynamic, and their application has expanded to several industries. With the expansion, the definition and boundaries of the project have grown as well. RPM calls for actions to be taken by projects to protect or limit the negative impacts of external such as social, environmental, and cultural. The application of RPM principles increases the awareness of the project management team about what needs to be done aside from the specific financial and strategic project goals.

Cultures are values and meanings developed by communities over the years, and in many cases, projects, especially tourism-related, disturb these cultures. RPM has a significant role in protecting the cultures, and different stakeholders can do this at the various stages of the project life cycle. The Oman approach to protecting culture starts with an overall country strategy for the tourism projects reflected in the developed projects. Then the project management team has a role in ensuring the protection of the culture by ensuring that the project team and contractors are educated and informed about the place-specific norms and values. The final and ongoing operations and benefits realization stage is essential in protecting the culture.

References

Akkuş, B., Postmes, T., & Stroebe, K. (2017). Community collectivism: A social dynamic approach to conceptualising culture. *PLoS One, 12*(9), e0185725.

Akadiri, S. S., Akadiri, A. C., & Alola, U. V. (2019). Is there growth impact of tourism? Evidence from selected small island states. *Current Issues in Tourism, 22*(12), 1480–1498.

Alhowaish, A. J. S. (2016). Is tourism development a Sustainability economic growth strategy in the long run? Evidence from GCC countries. *8*(7), 605.

Al Maamari, G. (2020). Multiple stakeholders' perception of the long-term success of project: a critical study of Oman tourism resort projects (Doctoral dissertation, Bournemouth University).

Andereck, K. L., Valentine, K. M., Knopf, R. C., & Vogt, C. A. (2005). Residents' perceptions of community tourism impacts. *Annals of Tourism Research, 32*(4), 1056–1076.

Aragonés-Beltrán, P., García-Melón, M., & Montesinos-Valera, J. (2017). How to assess stakeholders' influence in project management? A proposal based on the analytic network process. *International Journal of Project Management*, *35*(3), 451–462.

Archibald, R. D. (2017). Five decades of modern project management: Where it came from–where it's going. *PM World Journal*, VI(2), 2nd edition.

Ashurst, C., Doherty, N. F., & Peppard, J. J. (2008). Improving the impact of IT development projects: The benefits realisation capability model. *European Journal of Information Systems*, *17*(4), 352–370.

Baumfield, V. S. (2016). Stakeholder theory from a management perspective: Bridging the shareholder/stakeholder divide'(2016). *Australian Journal of Corporate Law*, *31*, 187.

Bontenbal, M., & Aziz, H. (2013). Oman's tourism industry: Student career perceptions and attitudes. *Journal of Arabian Studies*, *3*(2), 232–248.

Bramwell, B., Lane, B., McCabe, S., Mosedale, J., & Scarles, C. (2008). Research perspectives on responsible tourism.

Bredillet, C. (2005). Understanding the very nature of project management: A praxiological approach. Project Management Institute (PMI) Research Conference.

Bredillet, C. N. (2007a). Exploring research in project management: Nine schools of project management research (Part 1). Project management journal. *38*(1), 3–4.

Bredillet, C., 2015. Finding a way in Broceliande Forest: the magic domain of project management research. Designs, methods and practices for research in project management, Gower Publishing, Wey Court East, UK, pp.43–55.

Carroll, A. B., Adler, N. J., Mintzberg, H., Cooren, F., Suddaby, R., Freeman, R. E., & Laasch, O. (2020). What is responsible management? A conceptual potluck. In *Research handbook of responsible management*. Edward Elgar Publishing.

Chase, L. C., Amsden, B., & Phillips, R. G. (2012). Stakeholder engagement in tourism planning and development. In Handbook of Tourism and Quality-of-Life Research (pp. 475–490). Springer, Dordrecht.

Cleland, D. L., & Ireland, L. R. (2006). *Project management*. New York, NY: McGraw-Hill Professional.

Cooke-Davies, T., Cicmil, S., Crawford, L., & Richardson, K. (2007). We're not in Kansas anymore, Toto: Mapping the strange landscape of complexity theory and its relationship to project management. *Project Management Journal*, *38*(2), 50–61.

Cullen, J. G. (2020). Varieties of responsible management learning: A review, typology and research agenda. *Journal of Business Ethics*, *162*(4), 759–773. Deguire, M., (2012). In the eyes of the beholder. Paper presented at PMI® Global Congress 2012 – .

Drouin, N. and Turner, J. R. 2022. The Elgar Advanced Introduction to Megaprojects. Cheltenham: Edward.

Diedrich, A., & García-Buades, E. (2009). Local perceptions of tourism as indicators of destination decline. Tourism Management, 30(4), 512–521.

Eduardo Yamasaki Sato, C., & de Freitas Chagas, M. Jr. (2014). When do megaprojects start and finish? Redefining project lead time for megaproject success. *International Journal of Managing Projects in Business*, *7*(4), 624–637.

Elbaz, A., & Spang, K. (2018). Mapping the success dimensions of the infrastructure projects in Germany. International Project Management Association Research Conference 2017, Sydney: NSW: UTS ePRESS.

Eskerod, P., & Ang, K. (2017). Stakeholder value constructs in megaprojects: A long-term assessment case study. *48*(6), 60–75.

Eskerod, P., & Huemann, M. (2016). *Rethink! project stakeholder management*. Project Management Institute.

Eskerod, P., Huemann, M., & Savage, G. (2015). Project stakeholder management – Past and present. *Project Management Journal, Newtown Square, 46*(6), 6–14.

Freeman, R. E. (2010). *Strategic management: A stakeholder approach.* Cambridge university press. New York, NY.

Frent, C. J. (2016). An overview on the negative impacts of tourism. *Revista de turism-studii si cercetari in turism, 22,* 245–257.

Gibson, K. (2000). The moral basis of stakeholder theory. *Journal of Business Ethics, 26*(3), 245–257.

Gil-Lafuente, A. M., & Barcellos Paula, L. (2013). Algorithm applied in the identification of stakeholders. *Kybernetes, 42*(5), 674–685.

Hamza, J., Atif, T., Albusaidi, Y., Albalushi, M., Baoein, M., Abu Shaiba, M., . . . AlSaqri, S. (2017). Full impact of integrated tourism complexes in the Sultante of Oman. Study by Sultan Qaboos University, College of literature and social science, Department of Tourism and the Ministry of Tourism. Unpublished.

Henderson, J. C. (2015). The development of tourist destinations in the Gulf: Oman and Qatar compared. Tourism Planning & Development, 12(3), 350–361.

Jafari, J., & Scott, N. (2014). Muslim world and its tourisms. Annals of Tourism Research, 44, 1–19.

Jugdev, K., & Thomas, J. (2002). Student paper award winner: project management maturity models: The silver bullets of competitive advantage?. *Project Management Journal, 33*(4), 4–14.

Kapsali, M. (2011). Systems thinking in innovation project management: A match that works. *International Journal of Project Management, 29*(4), 396–407.

Killen, C. P., Jugdev, K., Drouin, N., & Petit, Y. J. I. (2012). Advancing project and portfolio management research: Applying strategic management theories. *International Journal of Project Managementx, 30*(5), 525–538.

Kim, K., Uysal, M., & Sirgy, M. J. (2013). How does tourism in a community impact the quality of life of community residents? *Tourism Management, 36,* 527–540.

Kloppenborg, T. J., & Opfer, W. A. (2002). The current state of project management research: Trends, Interpretations, and predictions. *Project Management Journal, 33*(2), 5–18.

Krippendorf, J. (1987). Ecological approach to tourism marketing. Tourism Management, 8(2), 174–176.

Kotler, P., Keller, K. L., Armstrong, G., Armstrong, G., & Keller, K. J. E. P. E. L. (2016). *Marketing management* (15th global ed.), England: Pearson.

Lebe, S., & Vrecko, I. (2014). Kybernetes. Systemic integration of holistic project-and hospitality management. *43*(3/4), 363–376.

Lewis, J. P. J. E. (2000). *The project manager's desk reference: A comprehensive guide to project planning, scheduling.* Systems, Boston: McGraw-Hill.

Leybourne, S. A. (2007). The changing bias of project management research: A consideration of the literatures and an application of extant theory. *Project Management Journal, 38*(1), 61–73.

Lientz, B., & Rea, K. (2007). *Project management for the twenty-first century.* London: Routledge.

Littau, P., Dunović, I. B., Pau, L.-F., Mancini, M., Dieguez, A. I., Medina-Lopez, C., . . . Nahod, -M.-M. (2015). Managing Stakeholders in Megaprojects-The MS Working Group Report.

Littau, P., Jujagiri, N. J., & Adlbrecht, G. (2010). 25 years of stakeholder theory in project management literature (1984–2009). *Project Management Journal, 41*(4), 17–29.

Liu, X., & Li, J. J. (2018). Host perceptions of tourism impact and stage of destination development in a developing country. *Sustainability, 10*(7), 2300.

Loosemore, M., & Phua, F. (2010). *Responsible corporate strategy in construction and engineering: Doing the right thing?* London: Taylor & Francis.

McLeod, L., Doolin, B., & MacDonell, S. G. (2012). A perspective-based understanding of project success. *Project Management Journal, 43*(5), 68–86.

MoNE. (2009). *Ministry of national economy 2009, statistical year book* (Vol. 37th). Muscat, Oman: Information and Publication Center.

Morris, P. W. (2013). *Reconstructing project management.* Chichester, West Sussex: John Wiley & Sons.

Morris, P. W., & Geraldi, J. (2011). Managing the institutional context for projects. *Project Management Journal, 42*(6), 20–32.

Nogeste, K., & Walker, D. H. (2005). Project outcomes and outputs: Making the intangible tangible. *Measuring Business Excellence, 9*(4), 55–68.

Nunkoo, R., & Gursoy, D. (2017). Political trust and residents' support for alternative and mass tourism: An improved structural model. *Tourism Geographies, 19*(3), 318–339.

OTS. (2016). Oman Tourism Strategy The Ministry of Tourism: Oman. Available at https://omantourism.gov.om/wps/wcm/connect/mot/4bd8ab5a-f376-44b0-94f0-812a31bd0b99/ENGLIGH+EXECUTIVE+SUMMARY+.pdf?MOD=AJPERES&CONVERT_TO=url&CAC HEID=4bd8ab5a-f376-44b0-94f0-812a31bd0b99.

Oukil, A., Channouf, N., & Al-Zaidi, A. (2016). Performance evaluation of the hotel industry in an emerging tourism destination: The case of Oman. *Journal of Hospitality and Tourism Management, 29*, 60–68.

Packendorff, J. (1995). Inquiring into the temporary organisation: New directions for project management research. *Scandinavian Journal of Management, 11*(4), 319–333.

Pasian, B. (2016). *Moving from 'Hunches' to an interesting research topic: Defining the research topic. designs, methods and practices for research of project management* (pp. 159–172). London: Routledge.

PMI, A. J. N. S., Pennsylvania USA: Project Management Institute Inc. (2017). A Guide to the Project Management Body of Knowledge (PMBOK® Guide), 6th Edition. ProQuest Ebook Central, http://ebookcentral.proquest.com/lib/bournemouth-ebooks/detail.action?docID=5180849. Created from Bournemouth-ebooks on 2019- 06-2708:34: 36.

Pratt, S., & Tolkach, D. (2018). The politics of tourism statistics. *International Journal of Tourism Research, 20*(3), 299–307.

Priemus, H. (2010). Megaprojects: Dealing with pitfalls. *European Planning Studies, 18*(7), 1023–1039.

Samset, K., & Volden, G. H. (2016). International journal of project management, Front-end definition of projects: Ten paradoxes and some reflections regarding project management and project governance. *34*(2), 297–313.

Sharpley, R., & Telfer, D. J. (2015). *Tourism and development in the developing world.* London: Routledge.

Söderlund, J. (2002). On the development of project management research: Schools of thought and critique. *International Journal of Project Management, 6*(1), 20–31.

Söderlund, J. (2011). Pluralism in project management: Navigating the crossroads of specialisation and fragmentation. *International Journal of Management Reviews, 13*(2), 153–176.

Söderlund, J., & Lenfle, S. (2013). *Making project history: Revisiting the past, creating the future.* Elsevier.

Suda, L. V. (2007). The meaning and importance of culture for project success. Paper presented at PMI® Global Congress 2007 – EMEA, Budapest, Hungary. Newtown Square, PA: Project Management Institute.

Teo, M. M., & Loosemore, M. (2017). Understanding community protest from a project management perspective: A relationship-based approach. *International Journal of Project Management, 35*(8), 1444–1458.

The Inglehart-Welzel World Cultural Map – World Values Survey 7. (2020). [Provisional version]. Source: http://www.worldvaluessurvey.org/

Tillmann, P., Tzortzopoulos, P., Sapountzis, S., Formoso, C., & Kagioglou, M. (2012). A case study on benefits realisation and its contributions for achieving project outcomes.

Turner, J. R. (2010). The handbook of project-based management: Leading strategic change in organisations. McGraw-Hill, New York, NY.

Turner, J. R. (2018). The management of the project-based organisation: A personal reflection. International Journal of Project Management, 36(1), 231–240.

Turner, J. R. (2014). *The Handbook of project-based management* (4th ed.). New York, NY: McGraw-Hill.

Turner, J., & Lecoeuvre, L. (2017). Marketing by, for and of the project: Project marketing by three types of organisations. *International Journal of Managing Projects in Business*, 10(4), 841–855.

Turner, R., & Zolin, R. (2012). Project management journal, Forecasting success on large projects: Developing reliable scales to predict multiple perspectives by multiple stakeholders over multiple time frames. 43(5), 87–99.

Uysal, M., Perdue, R., & Sirgy, M. J. (2012). *Handbook of tourism and quality-of-life research: Enhancing the lives of tourists and residents of host communities*. London: Springer Science & Business Media.

Vlahov, R. D., Vrecko, I., & Petje, R. (2019). Maturity models and success in project management–review of the literature. Economic and Social Development (Book of Proceedings), 42nd International Scientific Conference on Economic and Social Development (pp. 225).

Wall, G., & Mathieson, A. (2006). *Tourism: Change, impacts, and opportunities*. Essex: Pearson Education.

Wang, S., Fu, -Y.-Y., Cecil, A. K., & Avgoustis, S. H. (2006). Residents' perceptions of cultural tourism and quality of life-A longitudinal approach. *Tourism Today Tourism Today*, 6, 47–61.

Weaver, P. (2006). A brief history of project management. APM Project, 19(11), pp 1–4.

Weaver, P. (2007, April). The origins of modern project management. In Fourth annual PMI college of scheduling conference (pp. 15 18).

Winkler, O. (2007). The birth of Oman's tourism industry. *Tourism: An International Interdisciplinary Journal*, 55(2), 221–234.

Xue, Y., Turner, J. R., Lecoeuvre, L., & Anbari, F. (2013). Using results-based monitoring and evaluation to deliver results on key infrastructure projects in China. *Global Business Perspectives*, 1(2), 85–105.

Zhu, H., Liu, J., Wei, Z., Li, W., & Wang, L. J. S. (2017). Residents' attitudes towards sustainable tourism development in a historical-cultural village: Influence of perceived impacts, Sense of Place and Tourism Development Potential. 9(1), 61.

Zwikael, O., & Meredith, J. (2018). International Journal of Operations & Production Management, Who's who in the project zoo? The ten core project roles. 38(2), 474–492.

Zwikael, O., & Smyrk, J. (2012). A general framework for gauging the performance of initiatives to enhance organisational value. *British Journal of Management*, 23, S6–S22.

Zwikael, O., & Smyrk, J. (2015). Project governance: Balancing control and trust in dealing with risk. *International Journal of Project Management*, 33(4), 852–862.

José Ramón Otegi-Olaso, Leticia Fuentes-Ardeo,
and José Ricardo López-Robles

15 Project Management in Humanitarian Aid Organizations: The Case of Nongovernmental Start-Ups

Context: Humanitarian projects are initiated when crises occur due to accidents or war, and these crises cause suffering in part or all of the local population. The humanitarian projects aim to bring relief to the victims of the accidents.

Characters/entities: The chapter examines nongovernmental organizations (NGOs), donors, and beneficiaries. The management of projects developed by NNGOS follows a set of procedures around specific methodologies. One of the most extended is the logical framework. It serves for the daily management of projects and the justification to the donors.

Location: The chapter examines cases in the Basque country.

Research gaps: Questions have been raised about the degree of Responsible behavior by NGOs and their level of use of standard project management best practices. This chapter tries to answer by studying the case of a nonprofit association dedicated to feeding people in refugee camps in Greece.

Challenges/conflict/tensions: The challenge to respond to the needs of stakeholders while still providing oversight and planning using project management tools and techniques.

Keywords: humanitarian projects, NGOs, Greece, case study

15.1 Humanitarian Aid Projects

Projects represent a significant part of the gross domestic product of any country (Schoper et al., 2018). Besides, they are the vectors of change.

Responsible project management emerges as a modern positioning of project management professionals and academics who understand the relevance of projects to bring change into all aspects of life (Laasch et al., 2020). The competence to manage projects cannot be limited to processes and knowledge areas; it needs to incorporate long-term and broad scope approaches. The principles outlined in the RPM manifesto show practitioners' importance to sustainability principles (Beckmann et al., 2020).

https://doi.org/10.1515/9783110724783-019

Organizational literature on responsible management predominantly focuses on how for-profit corporations may adopt responsible principles in their operations. Literature is plenty with recommendations on how the organization establishes procedures for staff to behave ethically, and specific management positions are created: Corporate social responsibility manager. On the other side, responsible management explicitly focuses on the individual (Laasch, 2018) whenever he or she is on the organizational ladder.

Humanitarian projects are initiated when crises occur due to accidents or war, and these crises cause suffering in part or all of the local population. The humanitarian projects aim to bring relief to the victims of the accidents. As a rule, these projects do not aim to correct the causes of the problems. However, in some cases, they do have the sensitization of society in general and governments as one of their objectives.

Most humanitarian aid projects are coordinated and managed by NGOs. Some NGOs are backed by international organizations, such as United Nations (OCHA,[1] UNHCR[2]). Others were created by philanthropists (Red Cross), professionals (Médecins Sans Frontières), religious orders (OXFAM), etc. Volunteer donors fund all NGOs.

OCHA calculates that, in the world, more than 130 million people need humanitarian aid. Out of those, 70 million are displaced, some of them recognized as refugees by UNHCR, and others as asylum seekers.

In the case of the refugee crisis, by supplying essential goods and services, they try to preserve or give back the dignity that the people lose in the refugee camps (Donalson & Walsh, 2015). The work of these NGOs is mainly developed through projects and by volunteers.

Different types of humanitarian organizations exist. Large and small, backed by institutions or individuals, influential individuals, or civil society. It is not difficult to understand that their management and projects will vary depending on these characteristics.

The management of projects developed by NGOs follows a set of procedures around specific methodologies. One of the most extended is the Logical Framework. It serves for the daily management of projects and the justification to the donors.

In the case of humanitarian organizations, responsibility as a main driving force is taken for granted. However, some look like large profit corporations, requiring considerable budgets to operate their administration. The effectiveness of the Aid budget is questioned. And there have been cases where the principles have been compromised: corruption, in the filed misbehavior. This creates mistrust on the part of volunteers and funding parties.

This is probably the reason why a specific type of organization has appeared. They are created by a small group of people – the founders – who share a concern

---

1 OCHA: United Nations Office for the Coordination of Humanitarian Affairs.
2 UNHCR: United Nations High Commissioner for Refugees.

about the individual responsible for the well-being of others. The founders know each other from participating in activities unrelated to the humanitarian issue. They are doctors, engineers, sportspeople, and so on. One day, they realize that they can help others with the competencies they share. And they become involved.

Lack of confidence in the behavior of large NGOs moves them to join resources and create their association. This process has produced the apparition of small NGOs organized by the civil society around concrete, specific ideas: fleeting boats for saving migrants from drowning, feeding refugees, and so on. These NGOs try to fill the gap left by governments and incumbent NGOs. They resemble start-ups.

In these organizations, responsibility is the motor and is embedded into its culture. But they need to balance visionary leadership with frequently nonexisting management capabilities (Stid & Bradach, 2009).

In this chapter, we try to discover the influence of responsibility on the structure of project-based humanitarian organizations. Following classification by (Geraldi & Jonas, 2017), we could locate the research in the crossing between Level 1 (Individual/ Team) and Type 2 (practical with a focus on interpretation and understanding in social interactions).

This chapter studies civil society nonprofit organizations' start-ups (NGO-SU)-organized projects. Participants in those project teams share values and objectives but may not have experience managing projects or formally delegating organizational accountability and authority as part of their roles.

15.2 Methodology

The research project has followed a grounded theory approach (Strauss, 1997). At the start of the project, a basic literature review was performed: areas of interest in literature were looked for. With the results, a brainstorming session was run to understand how project management guides could help improve the performance of the humanitarian projects. In parallel, a Desk exploration of the NGO sector in the Basque Country was done. And an interview was held with a local expert, a professor who is publicly known to be involved with the work of NGOs.

These activities brought light to the issue and focused on the research objective. A second brainstorming session shifted the research objectives: from trying to help the NGO to trying to learn from their development. A local NGO-SU which collaborates in international humanitarian projects was selected as case study (Yin, 2011).

This was analyzed based on publicly available information: in press releases and on their web page. New questions appeared, which had to be solved through in-depth interviews with participants in the NGO. Starting to know the organization and their management just with the published information helped the research team access the information without any subjective filter. There were several information sources as the interview is in the press, collaborations with artists in the organization of events to collect money that has been recorded and their publications on their website and social networks.

Once the aim and outputs of the organization were identified, the second step was more oriented to learn how the internal process was produced. The organization would manage the resources to achieve their objectives, manage the number of volunteers taking part, and maintain all this work for so many years as it started as a punctual collaboration. Interviews collected all this information, and the first challenge was to access the internal working group. There were several contacts via social networks, and on their website, the answer was received, and one time the communication channel was established, all the communication and information was easily shared.

Another option could have been, contacting the organization without previous in-depth research regarding the project and its management. However, the in-depth interviews will probably be less productive as much accessible information will be required to be shared or explained during their interviews, or probably more interviews will be required.

During the interviews, the research team, it was identified the portfolio and program management that is implicitly performed in the organization management. As this terminology is not often used in the organization's daily activities for them, it was not an easy activity to map their work with this project management task. While interviewing, it is crucial to identify these ideas (e.g., portfolio management). Some organizations are probably not even aware of the use of the project management concepts and theories that have naturally been included in their organization.

An additional aspect of taking into account interviews is that even a structured interview is highly recommended to collect more specific information. It is also essential to leave a place and time for spontaneous communication and to listen to anecdotes, as on some occasions during this not "structured" speech, there is much implicit information that helps the interviewer understand the organization's management.

With the idea of saving time and space for spontaneous comments, the interview was structured in general sections with specific inter-related questions; that is a key aspect to help the interviewed person give specific information and join ideas from one answer to others.

The chapter shows the relevant information extracted from that case. Based on the information found, the assessment of how they fit within the responsible PM philosophy was elaborated.

A new literature review was conducted, the organizational structure of the case study was modeled, and the Braid model was produced. The research project ends up with more questions than answers.

15.3 Associated Research

First, to understand the relevance of concepts in the humanitarian topic, the bibliometric literature review was pursued to identify the evolution of the concepts with project management.

Based on the first review of the scientific production and state of the art, it was decided to take as a source from the Scopus database. In this respect, the raw data has been retrieved using the following advanced query: TITLE-ABS-KEY ("humanitarian project" OR "development project" OR "project management") AND TITLE-ABS-KEY ("humanit*" OR "refuge*" OR "environmental disas*" OR "emergency reli*" OR "catastrophe*" OR "nongover*" OR "ngo" OR "development aid*" OR "disast* manage*" OR "emigrat*" OR "immigra*" OR "international cooper*"). Finally, this search was refined, limiting the results to articles, proceedings, and reviews published in English from 1985 to 2020.

This search retrieved 761 publications from 1985 to 2020 (Figure 15.1). Once this was done, all publication abstracts were downloaded and reviewed.

Considering the results of the figure, the publications and citations have been increasing year by year from 1985 to 2020, which reveals the growing interest in this knowledge field. The most productive authors, organizations, countries, and sources are presented in Table 15.1.

On the other hand, using Scimat, a bibliometric analysis software, the main research themes have been identified and classified into four classes according to their relevance. To that end, the research themes identified have been set out in a strategic diagram. It is a two-dimension map separated into four different areas by their relevance, where the research lines (themes) are shown as a sphere: (i) The upper-right quadrant: motor themes (themes within this quadrant are relevant to structure and develop the research field); (ii) upper-left quadrant: highly developed and isolated themes (themes within this area are significant but do not have enough importance to be considered more than a very specialized or peripheral activity for the big data research field); (iii) lower-left quadrant: emerging or declining themes (the research lines within this quadrant are weak, but this weakness can be understood as emerging or disappearing themes); (iv) lower-right quadrant: basic and transversal themes (themes included in this are not developed enough but could be relevant for the knowledge area). The spheres are proportional to the number of documents related to each research theme, with the number of citations in parentheses.

From 1985 to 2020, 16 themes related to the knowledge field analyzed could be identified and arranged (see Figure 15.2). Nine themes are considered key due to their contribution to the field growth (motor themes and basic and transversal themes): sustainable development, local participation, decision-making process, research-and-development management, biodiversity, aid effectiveness, international cooperation, developing country, and emigration and immigration.

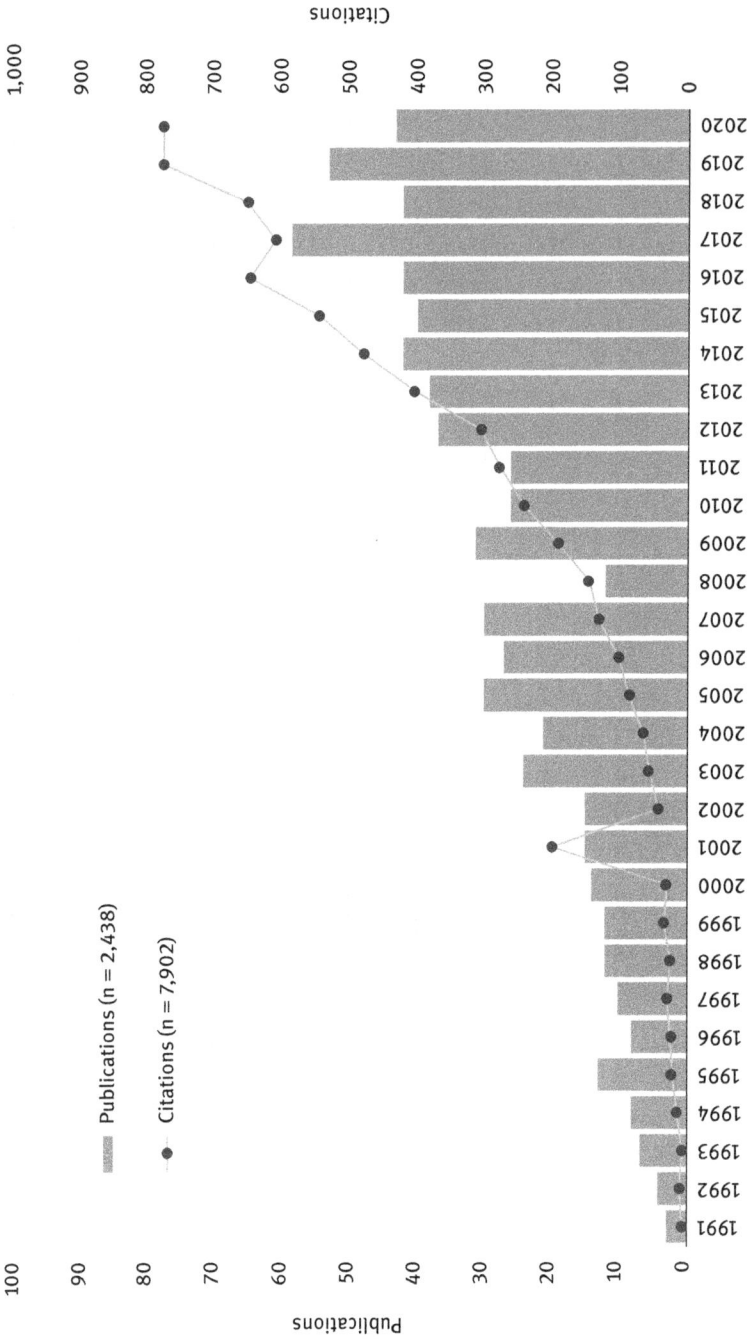

Figure 15.1: Distribution of publications and citations from 1985 to 2020 (authors).

Table 15.1: Several publications were retrieved from 1985 to 2020 by authors, organizations, countries, and sources (authors).

Category	Publications
Author(s)	(4) Ellis, H.J.C.; Parks, B.C. (3) Alikberova, A.R.; Golini, R.; Landoni, P.; O'Reilly, K. (2) Ahlborg, H.; Ahmad, M.M.; Al-Nammari, F.; Alfnes, F.; Altinbilek, H.D.; Amadei, B.; Bachke, M.E.; Bachmann, J.; Baruah, B.; Bawole, J.N.; Bloom, J.D.; Burdge, D.; Burdick, W.P.; Clements, P.; Daou, A.; De Lanerolle, T.R.; Giessen, L.; Gow, D.D.; Hardoy, J.; Hens, L.; Hislop, G.W.; Hollenbach, P.; Kirkby, J.; Kock, T.; Kurosaki, T.; Metzger, L.; Morelli, R.A.; Murakami, M.; O'Keefe, P.; Oyedele, L.; Poole, A.H.; Rahman, M.S.; Scholte, P.; Shava, E.; Thomas, E.; Tierney, M.J.; Tsopanakis, G.; Turnock, D.; Urpelainen, J.; Venkatraja, B.; Wik, M.; Wilson, G.; Wilson, P.C.; Xi, J.; von Meding, J.
Organization(s)	(8) Columbia University in the City of New York; The World Bank, USA (7) University of Washington, Seattle (6) University of Cape Town; The University of Manchester; The Australian National University; Texas A&M University; University of Oxford (5) Göteborgs Universitet; KU Leuven; University of Michigan, Ann Arbor; Universiteit Gent
County(ies)	(230) The United States (98) The United Kingdom (50) Australia (36) Canada (32) The Netherlands
Source(s)	(43) *Development in Practice* (17) *World Development* (13) *Sustainability Switzerland* (11) *Journal of International Development* (9) *Forum for Development Studies*; *International Journal of Water Resources Development*

Finally, analyzing the results from the scientific literature review, the following topics appeared as relevant for the project: aid effectiveness, decision-making process, and emigration and immigration.

The literature review results created the need to understand how NGOs deliver value. The second goal was to identify PM tools and techniques that could help their performance. To do it, the analysis of a Case was determined.

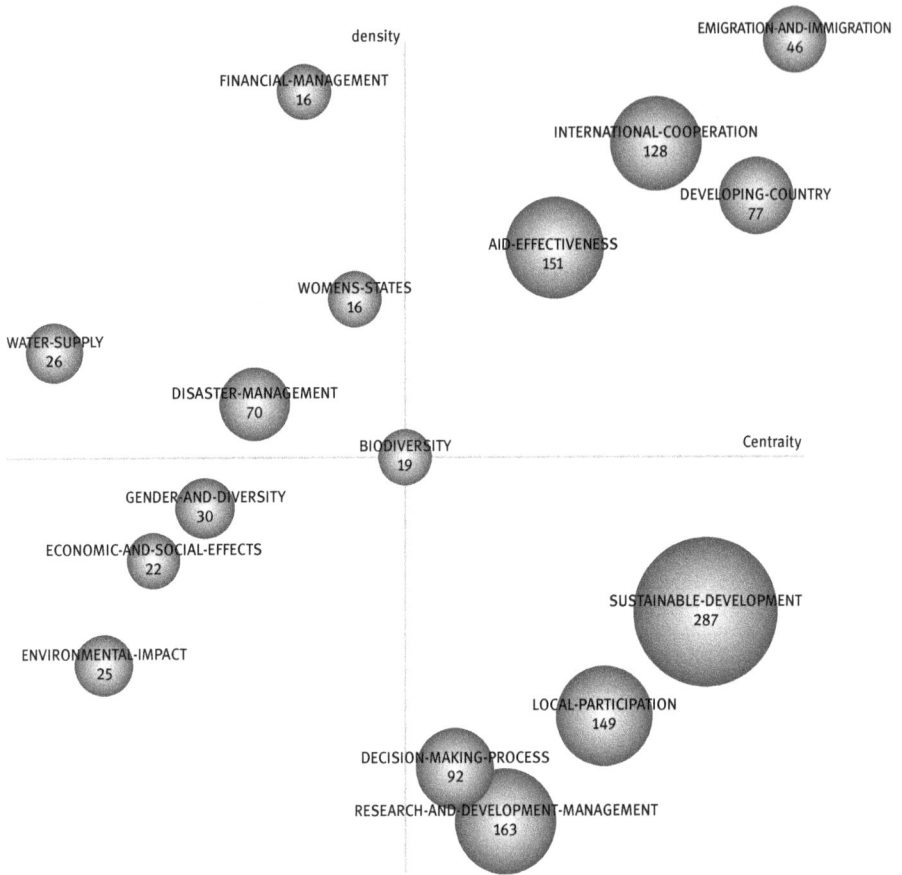

Figure 15.2: Density versus centrality diagram (authors).

15.4 Preparation of Case Study Analysis

The research team decided to center the study of ONGs in the Basque Country due to the easiness of data collection because the authors reside and where there is a significant NGO activity. In Basque County, there is a coordinating office (Coordinadora de ONGD Euskadi, 2020) with 79 NGO groups from different sectors. Thirty of them are registered under the Humanitarian and Emergency Relief epigraph. The list comprises large, among them OXFAM or UNRWA,[3] and small ones. Besides, other NGOs are not members of the coordinating office but show activity in the press.

---

3 UNRWA: United Nations relief and works agency for Palestine refugees in the Near East.

In the interview with the local expert, some ideas flourished:

- NGOs behave very differently depending on their size, belonging to a larger organization, or the management staff's professionalism.
- Management of NGOs is becoming professionalized, with staff experienced in fundraising and project justification. Although some tools are implemented, project management does not follow PM guides, that is, logical framework.
- The official NGOs may participate in public funding programs. They must be registered and must submit accountancy ledgers.
- In the region, those officialized NGOs coexist with several nonofficialized ones. The most important reason for their existence is their unwillingness to become part of the establishment.

The research team decided to select Case Study 1 with the following criteria:

- Providing relief within the refugee crisis in Europe.
- An organization not a member of the coordinating agency.
- Nonaffiliated to a larger organization.
- Active in the field for at least 5 years.
- Publicly known. The information is available in the press or on the Internet.

A questionnaire was designed to document the information about the NGO, with the questions in Table 15.2.

Table 15.2: Content of the questionnaire for the information search and the interviews (source: The authors).

Content	Questions
Description	Type of organization: Management team, full-time volunteers, part-time volunteers, etc.
	Size of the organization over time: number of staff, yearly budget, etc.
Motivations	Which was the goal of the NGO at its creation?
	Did they participate with other stakeholders in the definition of the goals?
	Has it evolved?
	How do members participate: volunteers? Some volunteers and some paid ones?
	Are there measures for ensuring (including measuring) the engagement of volunteers both before joining and at the camp?
Performance	Which were the objectives at the beginning?
	Have they evolved? For example, evolution from relief providing only to society sensibilization to denounce.Coordination with other NGOs and/or local government
	Have the objectives been met? Numbers?
	Do they have feedback from refugees or other stakeholders?

Table 15.2 (continued)

Content	Questions
Use of PM tools and techniques	Is there PM knowledge among the founders? And among the management now?
	Do they act as a project-based organization, i.e., each campaign is a project or is it more like a standard operation? How many "projects" in a year? In total?
	Do they follow standard PM processes: initiation, planning, etc.?
	Do they follow standard PM tools: project chapter and scope definition, scheduling, risk assessment, etc.?
	How do they coordinate among internal teams? Is there a General Manager or Coordinator?
	Do they think that some (PM or other) tool could help them reach their objectives?
	Coordination with other entities: Basque organizations, local organizations, Basque and Greek governments, and other NGOs.

After review, Zaporeak (Flavours, in the Basque language) (Zaporeak, 2020) was selected for the Case Study, a small NGO born in San Sebastian, which provides "dignified.[4] Food" in the refugee camps in Greece (Chios, Moria, Lesbos, etc.). More information can be found on the YouTube channel managed by their own: Link to the YouTube channel.

The selected case represents the opposite extreme to large incumbent corporations. It can be considered a start-up.

15.5 Description of the Case Study

Once it was decided that Zaporeak was the selected case study, it began a phase of research to collect as much information as possible. On the one side, we focused on the information published online: on their website, YouTube channels and their Social Network, mainly on Twitter (.Zaporeak's profile on Twitter).

Some publications let us know the output of their project; for instance, it was an excellent opportunity to watch interviews with the volunteers who have taken part in the cooperation in the field (Interview with a volunteer) and access more information about their daily activity. This phase helped the research team know more about the project, but the genuine interest was oriented to the internal process needed to get all these results.

---

4 In the Refugee crisis literature, "dignity" appears as one of the rights to be guaranteed for every people.

To help the reader understand Zaporeak, we have added a small summary to define the organization being analyzed. While reading the following section, it will be interesting for the reader to have a reflexive reading and think of an organization with similar characteristics: the similar size that is organized by projects is based mainly on volunteers to develop their work, etc. It is not so relevant to be oriented to the same aim; in this case, the refugees project, but it is more important to focus on managing their project. This could help the reader or students reflect on similar organizations they can access or learn from.

15.5.1 Zaporeak, from Creation to Nowadays

The project was started in 2015 to collaborate with the volunteers that were helping the refugees in Greece. It was formed by seven friends who coordinated a small team to visit Chios (Greek Island, which receives refugees from Turkey) to identify their real needs. The figure 15.3 shows the temporal evolution of the organization focusing on the type of management that is needed on each stage.

After this first meeting with reality, they realized that the real need in Greece was the refugees. They decided to use their experience in cooking to feed the refugees that were in transit. These seven founders got in touch with Basque local firms and individuals to collect all the needed resources. The beginnings were difficult as they needed to start the kitchen's workflow, merging the food donations from the Basque Country and the other supplies from the local providers.

When we, as researchers, started diving into all this information, it was a great surprise, as Zaporeak has started as a small friends' project (seven people) to help and collaborate with the refugees in real need.

They focused on their expertise and realized collaborating with their cooking to face this challenge. However, they included a global and local perspective in the way they acted, as they were receiving donations from the Basque Country but also considered the importance of buying locally, not only for the importance of accessing fresh food and fruit but also for positively impacting to the small marketplaces that were in the surroundings.

The first purpose was to give 700 meals daily, but as the number of refugees increased, Zaporeak had to optimize their kitchen workflow to reach 2000 meals each day. Greek authorities did not allow them to enter the camp; thus, they had to prepare the meals outside, and other authorized volunteers did the delivery.

Zaporeak was doing a great job, and the communication of their performance generated engagement from the Basque Community; the donations and help they received were increasing. Besides, they received many Basque people volunteering. Many volunteers were on the list to go to the refugee camp and help collect resources in the Basque Country. A positive spiral emerged.

During the development of this chapter, we have commented with family and colleagues, and many people already know Zaporeak and their actions, the significant communication actions that have not been massive or very oppressive. On the contrary, Zaporeak has been working small and well. The impact has arrived with time and long-term work.

Until 2019, the organization was formed exclusively by volunteers without an explicit structure. Autonomous teams were created ad hoc to answer to needs.

Unfortunately, not all stakeholders are welcoming, and the volunteers and their equipment have suffered threats and direct violence from xenophobe extremists. The two worst incidents happened in August 2016, when the kitchen was salvaged, and in March 2020, the van was attacked, and two volunteers were physically assaulted.

Nonetheless, Zaporeak has continued with its task, and the incidents served to enlarge its image in the face of society. As we have mentioned before, Basque society knows Zaporeak and their work, and there is an admiration sensation regarding the work they are performing.

In 2019, coordination errors surged due to the dimension and lack of formalized structure. A technical office was formed by three people in San Sebastian: a coordinator, a treasurer, a communication responsible, and one coordinator in Greece. The project's founders formed a "Chief Executive Board" that is involved in the crucial decisions of Zaporeak to maintain the essence of the initial project.

Once the coordination was "professionalized," there was space for integrating other challenges to the project. For example, they reduced the amount of single-use plastic used in food delivery.

In another project, they started substituting the plastic bag used for delivering food with bags netted with fishing nets recovered from the Mediterranean and the Atlantic coasts; a team of webbing volunteers manufactured them.

These projects that consider the sustainability aspect are an example of how Zaporeak is going ahead with the definition of their aims, and they are not just focusing on the feeding objective. They are also including new improvements in the way they are working, so they also try to improve the processes involved in their project.

Collaborations with other NGOs in the campsite were also reinforced: with a clinic, they identified the most vulnerable refugees, and with a nutritionist, they identified the most suitable menu depending on their situation and the year season.

2020 was undoubtedly the most challenging year for the project as borders were closed due to COVID-19. The volunteers from the Basque Country were not allowed to travel, and collaborating and working with the refugees was a pivotal element to face the uncertainty of the situation and continue providing food. The capacity to adapt to the circumstances has been one of the main characteristics of the organization throughout the time they have been working on the camp.

One of the axes of their work has been to dignify the food. From the beginning, they delivered hot food. Refugees' curiosity and feedback drive them to adapt the cooking style to the flavors, species, and textures appreciated by the beneficiaries. In 2020, they built a bakery to make pita bread.

2015/2016	2017/2018	2019	2020	2021

| Small group of friends aim to feed volunteers and finally switch to feed refugees | At the beginning the aim was to give 700 meals/day but they improved their resources to get 2000 meals/day.

Basque volunteers travelling there to collaborate. | Lots of collaboration with others NGOs to established a better meal distribution system and identification of the most vulnerable habitants.

Sustainability dimension integration reducing the plastic delivery and the environmental impact. | Closure of the borders due to COVID-19.

Volunteers and workers from the camp to collaborate in the kitchen.

New delegations around the Basque Country organising activities.

Construction of a bakery to be self-sufficient. | New challenges:

To give periodically "Food-box" to all the refugees camp population (mora than 7000 people).

Maintain the 2000 meals/day rate.

Improve sustainability dimension in the new tasks.

Search of new donation collaborations. |

Small management needed	Management Challenge	High level of coordination	Teams working coordinated	New management challenges

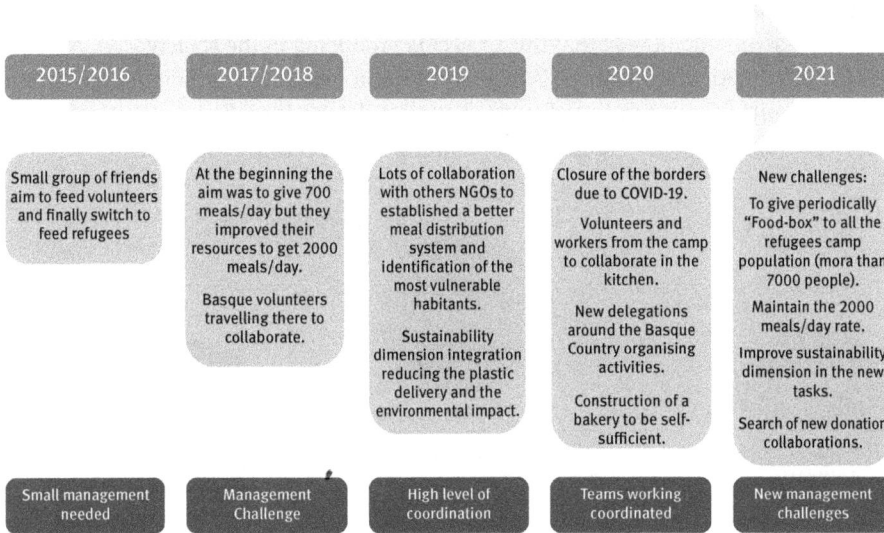

Figure 15.3: Evolution of the Zaporeak project (authors).

For facing the following challenges, Zaporeak needs to focus on new projects, and apart from the bakery, they need to update the van they use for food delivery. They have started a crowdfunding action collaborating with a Basque foundation (Crowdfunding action information).

Zaporeak does not give much importance to the efficiency of their activities; they are concerned with the well-being of the beneficiaries, and their major goal is to find ways to improve it. You do not reach them by analyzing or measuring but by acting and reflecting on the results.

15.5.2 The Organizational Structure of Zaporeak

Regarding project organization, Zaporeak is organized around autonomous teams with different roles: those cooking in the camps, communication, and donation seeking teams in the Basque Country, etc. Ideas, resources, and needs flow among the teams. There is little need for centralized coordination.

The kitchen in the refugee camp of Moria has the resources, volunteers, and help to cook 2000 meals a day. Meanwhile, in San Sebastian, seven retired volunteers analyze the following steps and look for donations and collaborations. Ideas spontaneously appear from artists willing to organize concerts. There is a list of more than 700 volunteers in reserve.

As researchers, we have identified the number of volunteers in reserve as a quantitative reference that can be used to measure the Zaporeak organization status, as the fact of having so many people waiting to take part in your actions can be a reference to measure the interest that this project is producing in the society.

In 2019–2020, volunteers in Bilbao and Vitoria (two other principal cities in the Basque Country) have requested to open project delegations. These delegations operate autonomously (see Figure 15.4), planning and executing functions.

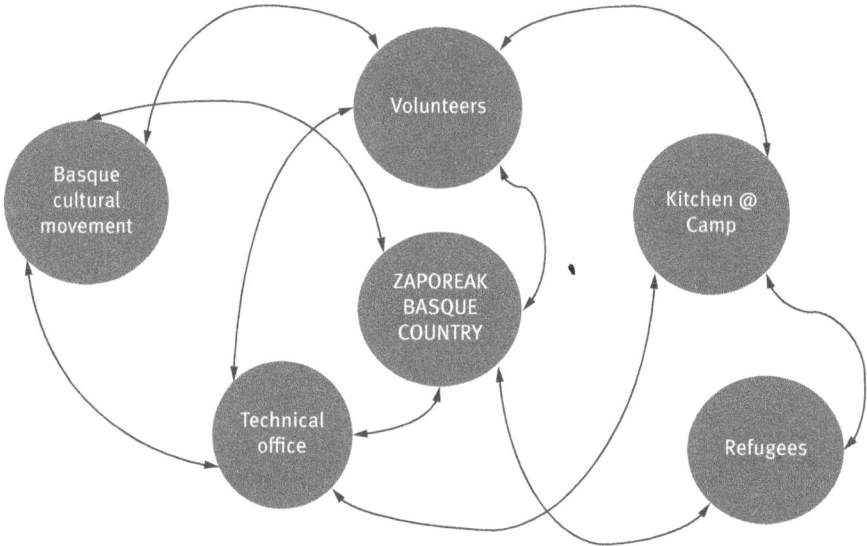

Figure 15.4: Collaboration network of autonomous teams (authors).

15.5.3 Management for Stakeholders: The Threads Fortify Each Other

Another relevant aspect of this type of project is the close management of stakeholders. In Zaporeak, four relevant groups of stakeholders have been identified: the refugees, the government, the society, and the volunteers. While the organization's starting point was to provide relief to the refugees, this soon converted into only one of the four goals or threads that now fortify the project. In Table 15.3 has been listed the goals and the types of stakeholders for this project

The stakeholder operational model of Zaporeak may be represented by a four-thread braid, where strands intertwine. Each of the threads is fed and strengthened by the results of the others. For each stakeholder, a goal or thread has been identified. Figure 15.5 represents the intertwining.

STAKEHOLDERS   GOAL / THREAD

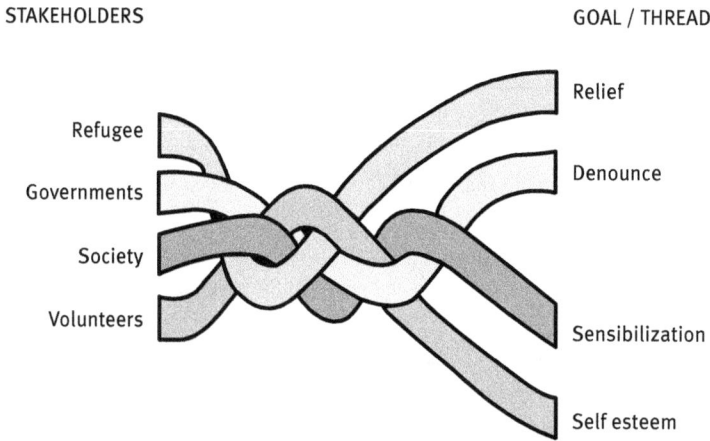

Figure 15.5: Intertwining of threads to conform to the Zaporeak project model (authors).

Table 15.3: List of goals and types of stakeholders for the Zaporeak project (authors).

Goal/thread	Type of stakeholder
Relief	Refugee
Denounce	Governments
Sensibilization	Society
Self-esteem	Volunteers

15.6 Responsibility of NGO Start-Ups

To assess the degree of responsibility, we take the ten principles of the RPM Manifesto as a framework. Observing the assessment table (see Table 15.4), we deduce that this NGO behaves quite responsibly with clear improvement areas. From the point of view of formal management skills, they represent the opposite extreme of large corporations. But they lack a component that is a must: Transparency.

Organizational mainstream literature focuses on "traditional" organizations (hierarchical, profit-oriented, etc.), and research projects describe methodologies, tools, and techniques which can be considered Best Practices. When these are disseminated, for example, in Bodies of Knowledge or Guides, they cover the whole spectrum of organizations.

More and more, we find organizations that are separate from the "traditional" paradigms: Nonprofit organizations pervade different sectors; horizontally structured firms become successful (i.e. the multinational bus manufacturing firm Irizar), nonprofit (i.e. Greenpeace), and nonhierarchical (i.e. Zaporeak).

Table 15.4: Assessment of commitment to Responsible Project Management Manifesto in the case of the Zaporeak project (source: The authors).

Purpose	The goal is to provide decent food to refugees, preserving their dignity. Zaporeak understands the constraints and involves other NGOs.	✓
Awareness	Food is purchased in the proximity of the camps. Sea waste is used to generate new carrying bags.	✓
Engagement	Engagement is at the heart of the project. Volunteers learn from the feedback from beneficiaries. Refugees participate in the preparation of food.	✓
Curiosity	The initial project was to cook for the volunteers. It has evolved into cooking for the refugees and adapting the food to their taste.	✓
Uncertainty	Crude reality (fire, attack, overcrowding, etc.) forces the project to evolve continuously.	✓
Anticipation	Needs are so extreme that opportunities appear everywhere. Also, do risks.	✓
Creativity	Is there room for reflexivity in the project? Do the participants analyze the results?	?
Transparency	The information provided on the webpage does not include performance reports. Budget, funding, resources, etc. are not shown.	☹
Stewardship	The organization is more influenced by the local (Basque) community than suppliers or funders.	✓
Balance	The project delivers, but it is not guaranteed that they manage efficiently.	?

When trying to export "best practices," the incumbent paradigm cannot avoid reflecting on its mindset, and it is observed that the mindset affects the selection of fundamental organizational characteristics: structure, relationship with stakeholders, communication, etc.

There has been done a comparison between the main characteristics of the goals, strategies and stakeholders in the case of a normal for-profit organisation and NGO Start-up and it has been summarize in the Table 15.5. An extended criticism of Humanitarian Aid is the degree of efficiency of the projects (Clements, 2020). However, it is not easy to evaluate their impact objectively. Even evaluations based on Development Assistance Committee (DAC) criteria (relevance, effectiveness, efficiency, impact, and sustainability) are arguable (Clements, 2020). But the increased administrative burden is "naturally" opposed by founders and volunteers (Stid & Bradach, 2009).

Logical framework methodology is an explicit exponent of this. The objective of the Logframe is to help participants obtain the results expected from the project (and to inform the donors). There is no room to address responsibility principles such as Curiosity, Participation, and Purpose.

Table 15.5: Comparison between "normal" and NGO start-ups' behavior (source: The authors).

	"Normal" for-profit organization	NGO start-up
Goal	Maximize profit	Provide relief
The setting of values and ethics	They are defined well after the organization has been up and running.	Founders build the organization as an answer to their values and ethics.
Strategy	Top-down definition	Fluid strategy. Opportunistic.
Coordination	The management team follows strategy and coordinates the portfolios and programs.	Specialist teams (in the field, communication, fundraising, etc.) operate autonomously and coordinate as needed.
Power	Shareholders	Active volunteers
Relationship with stakeholders	Follows strategy	Nonorganized
Evaluation	Standard business reporting	Subjective assessment
Communication focus	Improve reputation	Raise awareness
Origin of new projects	Search opportunities	Active listening (to the beneficiaries)

15.6.1 The Networked Organization of Volunteers in Autonomous Teams

One of the main outputs of the study has been that we may focus on and learn from projects which do not follow the incumbent organizational paradigm. There is a highly motivated group of people working in autonomous teams in this case. They have been delivering for more than six years and each year with new challenges.

The organizational model has been identified as autonomous systems working in "free" collaboration. It looks like a neuronal network. Each neuron team has its aim. It has its fundamental challenge and organizes itself considering its own needs but simultaneously monitors the other teams' needs and opportunities. But the interdependency makes it compulsory a close collaboration between teams for global success.

Figure 15.6 models the interconnection between each of the components of the team. There is a close relation and much communication between the people within a team, but there is also a connection between elements in other teams. There is no figure of the coordinator in any of the teams when communication is lived as essential.

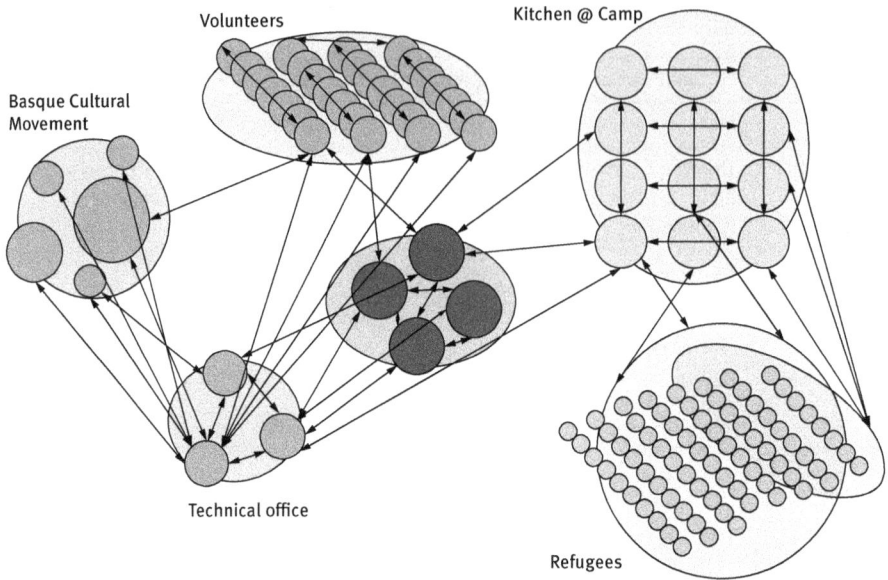

Figure 15.6: Neuronal network communication between autonomous teams (authors).

The question arises: How can PM guides help these new types of organizations? PM is about improving the management of the iron triangle or its evolutions. It focuses more on efficiency than on efficacy.

NGO start-ups may be successful without following standard organizational structures. The passion and leadership of the founders and coordinators help them overcome obstacles. Nevertheless, literature shows that Aid Effectiveness is also to be considered. To fulfil the responsible Project Management Manifesto, organizations such as Zaporeak should include a fifth thread addressing effectiveness. NGO start-up's managers and volunteers could and should use proven tools to ensure the levels of transparency and accountability that society demands.

References

Beckmann, M., Schlategger, S., & Landrum, N. E. (2020). Sustainability management from a responsible management perspective. In Laasch, O., Suddaby, R., Freeman, E., & Jamali, D. (Eds.), *The research handbook of responsible management* (pp. 122–137). Elgar: London.

Clements, P. (2020). Improving learning and accountability in foreign aid. *World Development*.

Coordinadora de ONGD Euskadi. (2020). *Coordinadora de ONGD Euskadi*. Accessed December 27, 2020, http://www.ongdeuskadi.org

Donalson, T., & Walsh, J. P. (2015). Toward a theory of business. *Research in Organizational Behaviour, 35*, 181–207.

Geraldi, J., & Jonas, S. (2017). Project studies: What it is, where it is going. *International Journal of Project Management*.

Laasch, O. (2018). Just old wine in new bottles? Conceptual shifts in the emerging field of responsible management. *CRME Working Papers, 4*(1).

Laasch, O., Roy Suddaby, R., Freeman, E., & Jamali, D. (2020). Mapping the emerging field of responsible management: Domains, spheres, themes, and future research. In Laasch, O., Roy Suddaby, R., Freeman, E., & Jamali, D. (Eds.), *Research handbook of responsible management* (pp. 2–38). London: Edward Elgar.

Strauss, A., & Corbin, J. M. (1997). *Grounded theory in practice. Sage*.

Schoper, Y.-G., Wald, A., Ingason, H. T., & Fridgeirsson, T. V. (2018). Projectification in Western economies: A comparative study of Germany, Norway and Iceland. *International Journal of Project Management, 36*(1), 71–82.

Stid, D., & Bradach, J. (2009). How visionary nonprofits leaders are learning to enhance management capabilities. *Strategy & Leadership*.

UNHCR. (2021). http://www.unhcr.org. Accessed January 17, 2021, http://www.unhcr.org

United Nations Office for the coordination of Humanitarian Affairs (OCHA). (2021). http://www.unocha.org. Accessed January 17, 2021, http://www.unocha.org

Yin, R. K. (2011). *Applications of case study research*. London: Sage Publications Ltd.

Zaporeak. (2020). *Zaporeak*. Accessed December 27, 2020, http://www.zaporeak.eus

John Lannon

16 Responsible Project Management: Hunger and Poverty Alleviation

Context: This chapter looks at the role of projects in organized civil society action and reflects on what responsible project management means in non-governmental organizations (NGOs) working in this space.

Characters/entities: It draws on the author's experiences working in the international development sector and a nationally based service delivery and advocacy NGO.

Locations: The reflections are relevant to efforts to achieve positive social change and enhance the quality of life of communities anywhere.

Research gaps: It addresses the dearth of literature on project organizing in environments where principles underpin community development and human rights-based approaches, including empowerment and participation, are paramount.

Challenges/conflicts/tensions: For NGOs, acting responsibly means being responsive to the needs of communities. Project-based organizing is their primary means of operation, but without close attention to other rationalities underpinning their raison d'etre, this can restrict the potential to achieve their long-term objectives for communities.

Keywords: NGOs, civil society, poverty alleviation, international development, case study

16.1 Introduction

In its broadest sense, civil society consists of all the organizations, formally constituted or otherwise, in the space between family, the State, and the market. These include schools and universities, the media, professional associations, churches, cultural institutions, and social movements. They are an essential source of information for both citizens and government. They monitor government policies and actions, hold the government accountable, engage in advocacy, and offer alternative policies for the government, the private sector, and other institutions. Services are delivered (especially to the underserved), and they defend citizen rights while working to change and uphold social norms and behaviors (Ingram, 2020).

While there has been a resurgence of the concept of civil society in political theory and practice, since the 1980s, it has been criticized as vague, empirically broad, and ideologically stretched (Chandhoke, 2003; Howell & Pearce, 2002). Others see

https://doi.org/10.1515/9783110724783-020

it as having been shaped to serve the goal of better governance, including demo-cratic.reform, at the expense of a deeper understanding of the relationships be-tween social formations, the associations that represent them, and the State. As such, the inclusion of organizations under the umbrella of civil society largely de-pends on whether or not they contribute to better governance or stand in their way (Kasfir, 1998).

In the development sector, civil society has been seen as the solution to the endur-ing "problem" of development and democratic change, with donors devoting large amounts of assistance to civil society projects worldwide (Van Rooy, 2013). The number of such projects continues to increase almost daily, with a large amount of the funding going to one particular form of civil society organization, the nongovernmental organi-zation (NGO). Seen through the lens of neoliberalism, NGOs are a valuable means for achieving the agenda of donor organizations, be they state, multilateral agencies, or philanthropic (Mohanty, 2002). Bodies like the Council of Europe see NGOs as a valu-able representative of civil society, making "an essential contribution to the realisation and development of democratic societies, in particular through the promotion of public awareness and the participatory involvement of citizens in the res publica" (Council of Europe, 2002). And while the concept of civil society has been critiqued as purely func-tional to the reproduction of capitalist or any other hegemony, Cohen and Arato (1994) suggest that the norms and organizational principles of modern civil society nonethe-less constitute the condition that makes possible the self-organization, influence, and voice of all groups.

The imprecisely defined NGO world is quite heterogeneous, with variations in vital organizational attributes, the types of activities that NGOs engage in, and their level of operation. They range from small, informal pressure groups comprised a small number of people (usually voluntary) and attracting small funding levels, to large, professional, bureaucratic agencies with multi-million-dollar budgets. They are active in various fields related to social transformation and improving quality of life, most notably development, humanitarian assistance, human rights, and the environment. Some operate at the local or community level, others at the national level, and some internationally.

NGOs' relationships with governments range from cooperation to adversity, with some providing market-based solutions to a broad set of policy problems and others acting as vehicles for progressive change (Srinivas, 2009). Take the area of trade liberalization, for example. There are some NGOs that operate as the "connec-tive tissue" that helps bridge the gap between the World Trade Organization (WTO) and the distant constituents they are meant to serve, thereby ensuring that the for-mer's actions are perceived as responsive and fair (Esty, 1998). Others present a dif-ferent perspective to governments in international trade debates. They seek to broaden the base of information and thinking upon which decisions are made, thus improving the quality, authoritativeness, and perceived fairness of the policy choices and judg-ments emanating from the WTO. Furthermore, as Srinivas (2009) put it, some NGOs can be described as representing the grassroots, while others see themselves in more of a helping role for policymakers.

As a means of organizing, projects and projectification are becoming increasingly crucial for NGOs, with donors preferring to package their support for organized activities in response to proposals to achieve specific outcomes. Public and private bodies offer resources to develop NGOs' projects, but the funding tends to be smaller than the NGOs' demands, thus creating competition between them (Lacruz & Cunha, 2018). As a result, NGOs professionalize their management processes and put governance structures in place according to donor expectations. Indeed, despite their independence from the government, many NGOs rely heavily on state funding to function. This "NGO-ization" of grassroots civil society movements (Alvarez, 2009; Ghosh, 2009; Meyers, 2016; Polanska, 2020) sees them as co-opted by outside actors through formalization and professionalization processes that significantly alter the ethos and thrust of the movement. This potentially makes the associations less representative and less responsive to the needs of the communities they represent.

When donors fund projects, they require assurances that their money is being spent wisely to achieve the intended outcomes and have the desired impact (Cicmil & O'Laocha, 2016). But for NGOs that rely on many small donations rather than a small number of large donations, projects do not come with the same expectations or overheads or indeed oversight. There is less demand for efficiency, and donations are made based on trust instead of clear expressions of outputs and outcomes. In these situations, NGOs have more flexibility when choosing how best to use their funds. The downside is that without some form of governance, they may struggle to use their resources in the most impactful way.

This chapter looks at the meaning of responsible project management in what NGOs do or should be doing. Managing projects with conscious attention to their intended and unintended outcomes and impact (Thompson & Williams, 2018) should come naturally to organizations whose raison d'etre is to achieve positive societal change. However, the project manager's capacity to manage responsibly is often constrained by the environment where projects occur. Drawing on my experience in the international development sector and supported by the experience of working with a national-based service delivery and advocacy NGO, I explore some of these constraints and provide pointers for approaches to project delivery that are likely to lead to sustainable outcomes and results.

16.2 The Projectification of Development

Over the decades, official funders in the development sector have preferred to fund projects, hoping to push international NGOs (INGOs) active in the sector to rationalize procedures, demonstrate effectiveness, and slash overhead (Cooley & Ron, 2002).

From an economic perspective, donor thinking was that they and the development "beneficiaries" could expect more output from the NGOs if the less efficient organizations were squeezed out of international development activities (Nunnenkamp et al., 2013). In 2003, Glaeser (2003) described NGO financing as a "donation market" (p. 15), with movements similar to those on stock exchanges. He described how public and private organizations offered resources to develop NGOs' projects, usually by examining proposals submitted to public notices. As such, funds are likely to be smaller than NGOs' demands, they create competition. NGOs attempted to professionalize their management processes to deal with this situation, using various means to make project management more efficient.

While this situation still prevails across much of the development sector, the 1980s saw a shift from funding projects to a program-based approach. This was in response to calls for the project design process to become a longer-term effort to build local coalitions and mobilize local resources (Honadle & Rosengard, 1983; Ika, 2012; Lannon & Walsh, 2020). For many INGOs active in the sector, there was also a shift away from the traditional donor-recipient model to a partnership approach involving local NGOs and communities. This was to make development more effective and sustainable.

Partnerships are intended to build collaborative relationships between entities working toward shared objectives through a mutually agreed division of labor (World Bank, 1998). This is underpinned by a commitment to trust, transparency, accountability, reciprocity, and respect (Contu & Girei, 2014; Lannon & Walsh, 2020; Schaaf, 2015). The working relationship must evolve through mutual learning, voluntary participation, and mutually agreed-upon goals. In other words, the efforts of all those involved, including communities and government authorities, need to be sustainable.

The link between sustainability and sustainable development is also essential. The former is often thought of as a long-term goal (i.e., a more sustainable world), while the latter refers to the many processes and pathways to achieve it (UNESCO, 2012). The 1987 Bruntland Commission Report described sustainable development as "development that meets the needs of the present without compromising the ability of future generations to meet their own needs" (United Nations General Assembly, 1987). Its four dimensions, society, environment, culture, and economy, are seen as intertwined and must be balanced to improve quality of life. A flourishing society, for example, relies on a healthy environment to provide food and resources as well as safe drinking water and clean air (del Mercado & Uribe, 2013). This is encapsulated in the 17 Sustainable Development Goals (SDGs), a universal call to end poverty, protect the planet, and ensure everyone enjoys peace and prosperity by 2030. They recognize that action in one area will affect others' outcomes and that development must balance social, economic, and environmental sustainability.

Nowadays, development is seen through the lenses of project cycles, program stages, and logical frameworks. Local NGOs are close to the reality of what happens on the ground and can identify with the tendency of communities to employ rationalities other than those the intervention model was based on. The latter favor a more nuanced, context-sensitive engagement than the knowledge-driven change processes that dominate the sector (King et al., 2016; Porter, 2003). Kontinen (2016) characterizes this as a dichotomy between two "vocabularies of practice": project management and community. There are other vocabularies, too, like bureaucracy which emphasizes rules and well-defined positions, and enterprise, which prioritizes knowledge that can be marketed (e.g., to attract donors). There are also vocabularies of friendship, in which actual knowledge is seen as emerging from human encounters and trust between collaborators; of faith, where knowledge of the "right" conduct provides guidance for what gets done; and of science which is seen as the knowledge that exists "out there" in academia and elsewhere. The latter typically draws on rigorous research but is not always relevant in the field (Kontinen, 2016).

Responsible project management aimed at achieving the SDGs must avoid donor-led selectivity and reductionist approaches that result in project management crowding out other perspectives on affecting change. However, development these days has come to be managed in terms of "performative efficiency" (Racz & Parker, 2020, p. 688). By adopting project management practices, supervisors and staff in local NGOs can efficiently mobilize all the resources at their disposal toward designing and implementing sustainable interventions and thus guarantee the on-going support of their benefactors (Batti, 2015). The problem is that they risk trading their knowledge of what is best for the community, in terms of both process and outcomes, for a reified form of efficiency that is privileged within the sector. NGOs may have to choose between two different approaches to their work, one rooted in the technical instrumentality of traditional project management and another with a more ethically driven focus on social good (Cicmil & O'Laocha, 2014). The NGO sector in Bangladesh is an interesting example of how this has played out in practice over the last few decades (Lewis, 2015). Its growth during the 1990s coincided with the discovery of NGOs by the wider development industry and the increased availability of funding. Many NGOs expanded and professionalized their operations, while others, including some key organizations, went out of operation. This revealed an overall lack of sustainability and a vulnerability to patron-client structures. More recently, there has been a marketization and hybridization of the NGO sector (Heitzmann, 2010), with most organizations becoming small contracting organizations. While many NGOs in Bangladesh do essential and valuable work, their quality and sustainability vary (Lewis, 2015), and most lack the dramatic organizational histories that characterized many influential NGOs active in the 1990s.

The imitation of market mechanisms in the development sector aims to increase transparency in assessing costs and results (Heitzmann, 2010). Nevertheless, even though the importance of approaches embedded in local contexts, negotiated and delivered by local actors, has been demonstrated (Faustino & Booth, 2014), competition for funding drives the formulation of programs that are primarily responsive to donor demands and expectations. Tools like results-based management and the logical framework that provide a standard project management approach have become the "discursive technologies of governance" of international development (Kerr, 2008). However, they also become a donor requirement that diverts time, energy, and resources away from doing development work (Hatton & Schroeder, 2007; Lannon & Walsh, 2019).

Critical management studies proponents argue that so long as the market is the dominant mechanism for allocating resources in our societies, community and government influences are forced into a subordinate role (Adler et al., 2007). Even though many in the field see any attempt at making management more humanistic or responsive as a futile exercise, as it does not fundamentally transform the underlying dynamics of managerial control (Racz & Parker, 2020), it still offers us a means to consider how to make development project and program management more responsible.

Working within the well-intentioned but prescriptive development domain, individual program and project managers can each act responsibly to deliver on their goals and achieve the desired outcomes as best they can. However, their role is characterized by a tension between learning to shape program activities on the one hand and reporting on intended projects and program outcomes on the other (Lannon & Walsh, 2020). Tensions in the micro contexts in which highly localized action takes place are connected to tensions in the macro (institutional) context where broad commonalities of action are formed. These inter-related tensions can be best understood as a conflict between co-existing recursive and adaptive tendencies at the individual actor, program, and institutional levels. The epistemological divides between the vocabularies of development practice are often reflected in attempts to reconcile global expertise and local knowledge that are less than successful.

The institutional tendency toward projects and programs constituted in pre-defined program cycles and stages presents a recursiveness problem for the individual manager, obscuring how practice adapts. It is also likely to ignore that communities may employ rationalities other than those the intervention model was based on to achieve their desired outcomes. Therefore, responsible project management must look beyond how to make individual project managers responsible and question the responsibility of development and its institutions. The constraints on the agency of individual project managers leave them caught in an ongoing struggle between doing what is expected by donors and policymakers and taking their lead from the communities that are supposed to benefit from their interventions. In other words, the problem is project-based organizing and not the project managers.

16.3 A Community Development Approach

In examining the relationship between project-based organizing and initiatives seen as international development or aid, Cicmil and O'Laocha (2016) used the notion of community development to represent the nature and critical intentions commonly assumed. They characterize it as "inherently a responsible calling" (p.548) and highlight the contradictions of the developmentalism-projectification double-act. The delivery of pre-defined goals is at odds with engagement in participatory knowing of what is optimal in terms of benefit or impact. Community development is about bringing people together to take action on what is important to them. Using planned and participatory efforts to improve quality of life takes a holistic approach grounded in principles of empowerment, human rights, inclusion, social justice, self-determination, and collective action (Kenny, 2007; Phillips & Pittman, 2014). The planned efforts begin with community organizing and move on to visioning, planning, implementation, and evaluation. Different approaches can be taken, ranging from needs-based to asset-based (Nel, 2018), but community development is likely to be a time-consuming and challenging process as the community works to develop a vision of its future.

There are three approaches to problem-solving in communities: service, advocacy, and mobilizing (Green & Haines, 2015). The first two do not involve the community, with service focusing on addressing individuals' problems (such as poverty) and advocacy involving people or organizations speaking for the community. On the other hand, mobilizing gets community members to take direct action. Traditionally, the focus is on identifying problems and needs, but in recent times, greater emphasis is being placed on the community's strengths, assets, and capabilities. The intention of both is to enhance the quality of life of community members in becoming sustainable, but the underlying assumptions, attitudes, motivations, methods, and techniques of the approaches differ (Nel, 2018). For example, with asset-based community development (ABCD), communities drive the process by identifying and mobilizing existing but often unrecognized assets. ABCD approaches to development understand that meaningful and lasting community change always comes from within. Local community members are the experts and the key agents of change (Nel, 2018; Yeneabat & Butterfield, 2012).

Many organizations active in community development also take a human rights-based approach (HRBA) to what they do. This focuses on the conscious and systematic enhancement of human rights in all aspects of project and program development and implementation. It is normatively based on international human rights standards and promotes and protects human rights. An HRBA is about empowering people to know and claim their rights while increasing the ability and accountability of individuals and institutions responsible for respecting, protecting, and fulfilling rights. It puts the people most affected at the center of any policy or process for change and has two objectives: the first is to empower rights holders to claim and exercise their rights; the second is to strengthen the capacity of duty bearers who have obligations to respect, protect, promote, and fulfil human rights. Rightsholders can be individuals or social groups with particular entitlements, while duty bearers can be state or non-state actors.

When implementing an HRBA to health, Silberhorn (2015) noted that in order to achieve sustainable impacts, human rights need to be integrated from the outset of project planning, and measurable indicators for human rights need to be included within the monitoring and evaluation frameworks. The approach should give people opportunities to participate in shaping the decisions that impact their human rights, and these rights need to be respected in both the processes and the outcomes of a project. From a human rights perspective, participatory processes are based on "active, free and meaningful participation as established in the United Nations Declaration on the Right to Development." People affected by a project (the rights holders) should always have the potential to influence project decisions and contribute to achieving outcomes that protect and fulfil their rights. In the context of development, an HRBA means that development programs must be based on the use of legal mechanisms and a clear articulation of the duty bearer's responsibilities as well as principles of equality, non-discrimination, and universality – for example, universal access to health care (Broberg & Sano, 2018). There must also be a strong emphasis on the engagement of assistance recipients in development projects.

Indeed, responsible project management should always include the assessment of a project's human rights impact. In their work on project-induced displacement and resettlement of people Van der Ploeg & Vanclay (2017), note that when project sponsors have obtained legal rights over land, either by government grant or market acquisition, displaced families and communities have human rights that must be fully respected and fulfilled by project proponents and contractors.

Development organizations that take an HRBA attribute lack of adequate services or poverty to unequal power relations and see them as violations of rights. A rights-based approach is an effective tool for challenging those unequal power relations. It also provides a means to tackle discrimination, another dimension of power relationships that previous development paradigms did little to recognize or address (Cornwall & Nyamu-Musembi, 2004). Community development also seeks to achieve an equal distribution of power. The formal and informal means through which people participate and influence decisions and actions are seen as crucial to challenging the power inequalities between groups that lead to a lack of access to services (Beck & Purcell, 2020). However, the problem with project organizing is that the identification and definition of needs and responses are likely to be shaped more by the expectations and parameters of donors than by the community. Cicmil and O'Laocha (2016) talk about delivering pre-defined goals versus the engagement in participatory knowing of what good or benefit might mean in a given locality, and project-based structuring versus the idea of participatory action and social change. Seeing communities as beneficiaries of such projects rather than rights holders and participants does little to challenge the unequal power relations that lead to the need for interventions in the first place.

16.4 Case Study

Nowadays, States are increasingly outsourcing service delivery to NGOs, with the latter taking a more active role in health, education, socio-economic improvement, and other areas. Service projects and programs often address specific problems one at a time but do not examine or challenge the root causes of those problems (Green & Haines, 2015). Furthermore, the project-based nature of the funding can often fail to deliver much-needed services to communities that are often vulnerable and powerless to advocate on their behalf.

Working with an Irish-based migrant support and human rights organization, I experienced first-hand how this impacts an NGO's capacity to affect social change. Operating with a staff count of 11 (part-time and full-time) plus volunteers, the organization provides legal support, advice, and information for asylum seekers, refugees, and migrants across various areas, including immigration, international protection, and human trafficking. Core functions like senior management salaries, communications, operational costs, and fundraising are primarily covered through general donations, typically 15% to 20% of the overall annual budget. The rest of the organization's income is project-specific, with provisions made in some cases for overhead and management costs. Project proposals typically include salary and project costs, although funding is only available for the latter in many cases. Nonetheless, the NGO is fortunate to have project funding from a philanthropic organization primarily used to cover salaries (17% of the overall budget). In this case, the "project" is the operation of the organization's advice and information center for 3 years.

In the middle of 2021, the organization had 25 active projects. These ranged from a 2-year government-funded refugee resettlement initiative with clearly defined targets for the number of families to be supported and the services provided to a series of events promoting integration and celebrating diversity. The first covered salaries, overheads, and project costs, whereas the funding available for the second covered project cost only. The latter highlights the problematic nature of project-based funding; to achieve the desired outcomes and impact, the organization must draw on resources essential to its longer-term viability and sustainability.

A project to examine and respond to the difficulties asylum seekers and refugees face in getting access to decent work produced some interesting evaluation results. As outlined elsewhere in this book, decent work is a multidimensional concept concerned with the availability of employment in conditions of freedom, equity, security, and human dignity. As such, it has a particular resonance with discussing responsible management. Nonetheless, the evaluation concluded that the short-term nature of funding for NGO-run employment support programs, combined with the relatively few evaluations of the services (linked to the nature of the funding provided), means there has been little opportunity to learn from and build on work done to achieve suitable and sustainable employment opportunities for the target community. In this respect, the transformation of NGOs into project-oriented extensions of the State falls short when addressing inequalities and exclusion. This presents a question for NGOs: to what extent they should seek and accept project funding if they know they may not be able to leverage the new knowledge they create throughout the project? In these situations, how can the responsible project manager look beyond the short-term objectives and find ways for sustainability and project management to sit comfortably together?

As Racz and Parker (2020) put it, part of the answer lies in need for sustainability, ethics, and responsibility to be a collectivized, not an individualized concept. For the organization I worked with, their organizational commitment to a human rights rights-based approach also provided opportunities to deliver on the commitment to holding the State to account. This provides them with a framework within which wider involvement in decision-making over the resources and institutions that affect people's lives is possible. For the individual project manager, ensuring a focus on a participation right from the start shifts the frame from assessment of the needs of beneficiaries to recognition of rights and responsibilities. Legitimate action should always flow from a desire to shift the power balance and not be focused exclusively on delivering pre-determined short-term outcomes.

16.5 Responsibility and Fundraising

As noted already, the NGO-ization of civil society leaves it susceptible to co-option by outside actors in ways that may alter the ethos and thrust of a movement for social change. Nonetheless, NGOs have become an essential component of efforts to progress sustainability-related issues like climate change and human rights. The same is true in humanitarian aid delivery, as outlined in another chapter in this book. In some cases, they operate on a small scale to either deliver services (in effect, outsourcing by the government), advocate on behalf of communities, or work with communities to affect change. Acting responsibly should come naturally to them, particularly if they are responsive to the communities they represent. But while a project manager can take responsibility for developing awareness among stakeholders of the consequences of a project's activities and outcomes, the decision to commit time and resources to a project must first be made in line with a responsible organizational strategy. NGOs must pay salaries; hence, one of such organizations' oft-cited critiques is that they always act for their survival. The ideal is that they can secure sufficient unrestricted funding to align what they do with their theory of change, but the reality is that they must make their case, often in a competitive environment, for funding from a small set of donors. Delivering value "without preference to stakeholders representing environmental, social and financial interests" (Thompson & Williams, 2018, p. 20) becomes more challenging under these circumstances.

Undoubtedly, emphasizing accountability for the funds they receive improves NGO effectiveness and performance, increases their credibility, and builds donors' trust in them (Amagoh, 2015). However, excessive focus on donor accountability can restrict the organization's capacity to learn and adapt (Lannon & Walsh, 2020). This must be balanced with the need for flexible planning that responds to the needs and expectations of all stakeholders. To achieve this, the must coordinate and prioritize resources across projects while ensuring that resources are efficiently managed and that work methods demonstrate a commitment to ethical values and beliefs. So too is committing to the principles of participation and empowerment that underpin HRBA. Indeed, when it comes to determining what an organization will do and how it will do it, these will go a long way toward ensuring meaningful listening and learning.

16.6 Final Thoughts

For Thompson and Williams (2018), managing projects responsibly facilitates sustainable change rather than simply delivering outcomes prescribed by a project sponsor. They emphasize the importance of connection, engagement, and participation for learning to occur. These are consistent with a human rights-based or community development approach, but while the flexibility of project organizations can be an advantage, the need to constantly adjust to the expectations of new funding streams, i.e. projects, means, in effect, that there is much unfinished business.

Projects intended to contribute to improvements in the capacities and development of communities must take their lead from the lived experiences of the people intended to benefit from them. Communities know that projects are not quick fixes for entrenched social problems. But with clear, uncomplicated structures, good governance, careful design, and meaningful monitoring and evaluation, they can achieve positive changes. The process by which outcomes are achieved, like the community working out new ways to open pathways to employment, or even better, creating their own employment opportunities, can only be determined by the community themselves, supported by people who bring helpful skill sets and resources. If managers feel responsible for all of their interest groups, the likelihood of them not behaving irresponsibly is reduced (Armstrong, 1977). With this in mind, the responsible project/program manager's job is to listen, assist with planning, monitor, ensure the agreed goals are being achieved; and always be ready to learn and adapt.

Responsible management, including associated constructs of managerial responsibility, sustainability, and ethics, is to some extent a characteristic of managers and their environment, but equally, it is a process whereby managers learn to become more responsible (Laasch & Moosmayer, 2015). This should be the natural inclination for managers working to achieve positive social change, but the reality is that project imperatives sometimes cause them to lose sight of the long-term objectives. Therefore, aligning project management practices with what NGOs want to achieve in terms of sustainable change is an area that requires particular attention. Plenty of attention is given to developing a responsible learning mindset that enables business and management students to develop long-term multi-stakeholder perspectives when looking for solutions (Sunley & Leith, 2017). However, people in NGO settings may not have had the opportunity to avail themselves of these formal education opportunities. And even if they did, management classes are likely to leave agents of social change still searching for the right balance between the competing rationalities inherent in their work. The only meaningful way to overcome this is for organizations to provide space and time for reflection and learning. Despite the constraints imposed by the dominant ways of working, there are always opportunities to act more responsibly. For civil society organizations to achieve their objectives, these must be embraced.

Racz and Parker (2020) said that responsible management must move from an explicit focus on agents, managers, and agencies to responsible organizations, discourses, and contexts. If funders, particularly State funders, exert too much control or influence over a civil society organization, or if it becomes consumed by vocabularies of practice that reinforce the power dynamics behind the need for change, it should look again at what it is doing, how it is doing it, and why.

References

Adler, P. S., Forbes, L. C., & Willmott, H. (2007). Critical management studies. *Academy of Management Annals, 1*(1), 119–179.

Alvarez, S. E. (2009). Beyond NGO-ization?: Reflections from Latin America. *Development, 52*(2), 175–184.

Amagoh, F. (2015). Improving the credibility and effectiveness of non-governmental organisations. *Progress in Development Studies, 15*(3), 221–239.

Armstrong, J. S. (1977). Social irresponsibility in management. *Journal of Business Research, 5*(3), 185–213.

Batti, R. C. (2015). Development project management within local NGOs: 10 recommendations to meet 10 challenges. *Global Business and Organizational Excellence, 34*(5), 21–29.

Beck, D. & Purcell, R. (2020). Community Development for Social Change: Routledge.

Broberg, M. & Sano, H.-O. (2018). Strengths and weaknesses in a human rights-based approach to international development—an analysis of a rights-based approach to development assistance based on practical experiences. *The International Journal of Human Rights, 22*(5), 664–680.

Chandhoke, N. (2003). A critique of the notion of civil society as the 'third sphere'. *Does Civil Society Matter*, 27–58.

Cicmil, S. & O'Laocha, E. (2014). Responsible management of projects in the context of international development: A critical overview of governance, leadership and power. In Paper presented at the Delivering Social Good: Managing Projects in the Non-Profit Sector. 20/21 October 2014, Limerick, Ireland.

Cicmil, S. & O'Laocha, E. (2016). The logic of projects and the ideal of community development: Social good, participation and the ethics of knowing. *International Journal of Managing Projects in Business*, 9(3), 546–561. doi:10.1108/IJMPB-09-2015-0092

Cohen, J. L. & Arato, A. (1994). *Civil Society and Political Theory*. MIT press.

Contu, A. & Girei, E. (2014). NGOs management and the value of 'partnerships' for equality in international development: What's in a name?. *Human Relations*, 67(2), 205–232.

Cooley, A. & Ron, J. (2002). The NGO scramble: Organisational insecurity and the political economy of transnational action. *International Security*, 27(1), 5–39.

Cornwall, A. & Nyamu-Musembi, C. (2004). What is the "Rights-based approach" all about? Perspectives from international development agencies? Institute for Development Studies, Working Paper(234).

Council of Europe. (2002). Fundamental Principles on the Status of Non-governmental Organisations in Europe and explanatory memorandum. Retrieved from http://www.coe.int/t/dghl/standardsetting/cdcj/ONG/Fundamental%20Principles%20E.pdf.

Del Mercado, R. V. & Uribe, R. (2013). Fostering sustainability through watershed-based education. *Journal of Sustainability Education*, 5.

Faustino, J. & Booth, D. (2014). Development entrepreneurship: How donors and leaders can foster institutional change. Working Politically in Practice Series.

Ghosh, B. (2009). NGOs, civil society and social reconstruction in contemporary India. *Journal of Developing Societies*, 25(2), 229–252.

Glaeser, E. L. (2003). Introduction to" The Governance of Not-for-Profit Organisations". In *The Governance of Not-for-Profit Organisations*, University of Chicago Press, 1–44.

Green, G. P. & Haines, A. (2015). Asset building & community development: Sage publications.

Hatton, M. J. & Schroeder, K. (2007). Results-based management: Friend or foe?. *Development in Practice*, 17(3), 426–432.

Heitzmann, K. (2010). Poverty relief in a mixed economy: theory of and evidence for the (changing) role of public and non-profit actors in coping with income poverty: Peter Lang.

Honadle, G. H. & Rosengard, J. K. (1983). Putting 'projectized' development in perspective. *Public Administration and Development*, 3(4), 299–305.

Howell, J. & Pearce, J. (2002). *Civil Society & Development: A Critical Exploration*. Lynne Rienner Publishers.

Ika, L. (2012). Project management for development in Africa: Why projects are failing and what can be done about it. *Project Management Journal*, 43(4), 27–41.

Ingram, G. (2020). Civil society: An essential ingredient of development. Retrieved from

Kasfir, N. (1998). The conventional notion of civil society: A critique. *Commonwealth & Comparative Politics*, 36(2), 1–20. doi:10.1080/14662049808447765

Kenny, S. (2007). Reconstruction in Aceh: Building whose capacity?. *Community Development Journal*, 42(2), 206–221.

Kerr, R. (2008). International development and the new public management: Projects and log frames as discursive technologies of governance. In Dar, S. and Cooke, B. (Eds.), *The New Development Management*, London & New York: Zed Books, 91–110.

King, S., Kontinen, T., Narayanaswamy, L., & Hayman, R. (2016). Introduction: Why do NGOs need to negotiate knowledge? In Hayman, R., King, S., Kontinen, T., and Narayanaswamy, L. (Eds.),

Negotiating Knowledge: Evidence and Experience in Development NGOs. Rugby, UK: Practical Action Publishing Ltd, 1–14.

Kontinen, T. (2016). What sense does it make? Vocabularies of practice and knowledge creation in a development NGO. In Hayman, R., King, S., Kontinen, T., and Narayanaswamy, L. (Eds.), *Negotiating Knowledge: Evidence and Experience in Development NGOs*, Practical Action Publishing Ltd, 29–45.

Lacruz, A. & Cunha, E. (2018). Project management office in non-governmental organisations: An ex post facto study. *Revista de Gestão, 25*(2), 212–227. doi:10.1108/REGE-03-2018-033

Lannon, J. & Walsh, J. N. (2019). Paradoxes and partnerships: A study of knowledge exploration and exploitation in international development programmes. *Journal of Knowledge Management*.

Lannon, J. & Walsh, J. N. (2020). Project facilitation as an active response to tensions in international development programmes. *International Journal of Project Management, 38*(8), 486–499.

Laasch, O. & Moosmayer, D. (2015). *Responsible Management Competences: Building a Portfolio for Professional Competence*. Academy of Management Annual Meeting Anaheim.

Lewis, D. (2015). Non-governmental organisations and civil society. Routledge.

Meyers, S. (2016). NGO-Ization and human rights law: The CRPD's civil society mandate. *Laws, 5*(2), 21.

Mohanty, R. (2002). Civil society and NGOs. *The Indian Journal of Political Science*, 213–232.

Nel, H. (2018). A comparison between the asset-oriented and needs-based community development approaches in terms of systems changes. *Practice, 30*(1), 33–52.

Nunnenkamp, P., Öhler, H., & Schwörer, T. (2013). US based NGOs in international development: Financial and economic determinants of survival. *World Development, 46*, 45–65.

Phillips, R. & Pittman, R. (2014). An introduction to community development: Routledge.

Polanska, D. V. (2020). Going against institutionalisation: New forms of urban activism in Poland. *Journal of Urban Affairs, 42*(2), 176–187.

Porter, G. (2003). NGOs and poverty reduction in a globalising world: Perspectives from Ghana. *Progress in Development Studies, 3*(2), 131–145.

Racz, M. & Parker, S. (2020). Critically responsible management: Agonistic answers to antagonistic questions. In Laasch, O., Jamali, D., Freeman, E., and Suddaby, R. (Eds.), *Research Handbook of Responsible Management*. Edward Elgar Publishing, 686–699.

Schaaf, R. (2015). The rhetoric and reality of partnerships for international development. *Geography Compass, 9*(2), 68–80.

Silberhorn, T. (2015). Germany's experience in supporting and implementing human rights-based approaches to health, plus challenges and successes in demonstrating impact on health outcomes. *Health and Human Rights Journal, 17*, 21.

Sunley, R. & Leigh, J. (Eds.). (2017). *Educating for Responsible Management: Putting Theory into Practice*. Routledge.

Thompson, K. M. & Williams, N. L. (2018). A Guide to Responsible Project Management. Retrieved from https://sustainabilitypractitioners.org/wp-content/uploads/2018/12/rpm_web_booklet.pdf

UNESCO. (2012). Education for Sustainable Development. In *Sourcebook*. Paris: UNESCO.

United Nations General Assembly. (1987). Report of the world commission on environment and development: Our common future. Retrieved from Oslo: Norway.

Van der Ploeg, L. & Vanclay, F. (2017). A human rights-based approach to project induced displacement and resettlement. *Impact Assessment and Project Appraisal, 35*(1), 34–52.

Van Rooy, A. (2013). Civil society and the aid industry: Routledge.

World Bank. (1998). Partnership for Development: Proposed Actions for the World Bank. SecM98-421, May 28, 1998.

Yeneabat, M. & Butterfield, A. K. (2012). "We Can't Eat a Road:" asset-based community development and the gedam sefer community partnership in Ethiopia. *Journal of Community Practice, 20*(1–2), 134–153.

Gamlath, G. R. M. and Yogarajah Nanthagopan

17 Project Governance in a Post-Conflict Setting

Context: This chapter summarizes the importance of the project governance concept in a post-conflict setting. Focusing on the theoretical and empirical understandings, the chapter also draws attention to the crucial intervention in the project governance framework through a post-conflict environment in the theme of sustainable post-conflict project governance. It uses a broad perspective to understand project governance roots better and look at how the framework is constructed and the rationalized value-added focus of the project governance perspective.

Characters/entities: The government of Sri Lanka

Locations: Sri Lanka, which is a post-conflict country setting.

Research gap: Authors explore the methodological implications of responsive project governance in research. It concludes with Sri Lankan case studies and lessons, emphasizing the essence of governance to achieve optimal project financial and physical performance and fulfill stakeholders' expectations.

Challenges: There is a need to examine how project governance enables delivery in different communities and post-conflict situations.

Keywords: project governance, conflict settings, Sri Lanka

17.1 Introduction

Project governance (PG) is an overall framework that oversees a project to run smoothly on budget with timely deliveries and beneficiaries' satisfaction. For public sector projects, the goal of PG is to attract resources and can have the following elements (Brunet, 2018):
- Documented decision-making process for project stages and phases
- Formal process for analysis to support decision-making
- Codification of project management resources, time and cost processes

According to Drouin and Turner (2022), based on OECD's definition of corporate governance, it defined that governance is the structure that includes the objectives that we need to achieve at the organizational level through means of attainments through a well-determined monitoring mechanism. The governance structure includes the areas of the organization's stakeholders' roles, responsibilities, rights, and relationships. The

https://doi.org/10.1515/9783110724783-021

stakeholders include the management, owners, employees, suppliers, customers, and the local community. The management, owners, employees, and suppliers are internal stakeholders, whereas customers and the local community are external stakeholders.

To apply the above contextual parameters and guidelines, the organizations are to use a way forward for implementing the governance to plan, implement, and monitor the organizational decision-making through a stepping paradigm; operational, tactical, strategic, and policy decisions. In this perspective, governance is also a conceptual framework covering four specific themes: transparency, accountability, responsibility, and fairness (Derakhshan et al., 2019; Millstein et al., 1998; Müller et al., 2014, 2016). The thematic determination of good governance describes how organizations verify the orderly, fair, transparent, ethical, societal, and accountable organizational outcome as a team spirit and commitment of all stakeholders.

In the light of the outcome of governance (Derakhshan et al., 2019; Millstein et al., 1998), project governance is an interrelated context that supports administering and regularizing the implementation of all aspects of projects. This is meant to verify, achieve project performance, create value for all internal and external stakeholders, create ethical behavior, create transparency, define accountability, and define stakeholders' rights and responsibilities. So, project governance is an essential tool to produce specific outcomes/deliverables, which can be measured in realistic and time-bound nature. The success of PG is finally concentrated as a co-sign to strengthen the good governance of organizational governance and the governance of the whole country.

Post-conflict countries have the additional challenge of civil wars, terrorism, riots, and ethnic conflicts. Due to these issues, huge physical and societal damages have happened to society. For these instances, the countries implement the rebuilding activities within the existing project governance frameworks. However, there can be a gap in implementing projects and the achievements of project deliverables due to the smooth resettlements and reconstructions of the projects in conflict-affected areas governed by the existing mechanisms. Consequently, project governance is necessary for a post-conflict setting for public sector projects.

17.2 Project Governance and Performance

According to the findings of Brunet (2018), several theories are used to examine the relationship between project governance practices and performance. The "Theory of Constraints," founded by Goldratt (1990), emphasizes that project management needs to identify the project constraints that can limit the project performance, and efforts are to give direct approaches to solving the constraints such as cost overruns due to poor budgeting and corruption. In addition, the theory of constraints is a systematic way to identify constraints that hinder project success to effect the changes to move them. This is a logical purview that specific steps can be combined with cause-effect, experience, and intuition to gain knowledge, and it assists organizations and projects in achieving their goals by providing a mechanism to gain better control of their initiatives. Further, this theory is a mechanism to minimize the constraints that can reduce the quality and quantity of the products and services delivered. Henceforth, this theory emphasizes the utmost need to find what gaps or lapses have been identified to be mitigated as the first put print.

The management theory of project management, introduced by Koskela and Howell (2002), comprises three subtheories: planning theory, execution theory, and control theory. First, the planning theory says that planning acts as an organizing event that management uses to assemble all the necessary resources (money, materials, mechanisms, methods, manpower) for carrying out the work defined in the project. Then, the project execution asserts managerially to dispatch the tasks to workstations with a proper communication channel emphasizing that conveys the operatives understanding of the instructions passed with enabling tasks to be executed as it is envisaged in the plan. After that, control theory verifies that the project is to be effectively and scientifically governed to confirm the fulfillment of project deliverables. These subtheories under this theory emphasized integrating these theories into practice in project implementation. These three subtheoretical project processes are conceptual to be linked as; project planning at the managerial level, controlling processes like monitoring and evaluation, and implementing or executing projects. A project-driven organization or project should utilize all resources effectively and efficiently to achieve the project performance as it is the successive end as per the management thought.

Another theory was introduced by Kylie (2013) as "Social Information Processing Theory." Strong communication bonds can be formed through the very few clues that individuals can get from online communications, where email correspondences sometimes happen more often than in-person conversations. In these instances, project managers should concentrate more on passing their verbal and written views despite the lack of social context. This theory, therefore, emphasizes the importance of this bridge to prolong the survival of project design to the objective end with performance and success. In addition, communication accommodation theory emphasizes the need to change communication approaches and use those that suit a particular group or team to help collect all the required information from the project groups for better performance.

Even though project managers must determine the availability of needed project resources before the planning so that the planning process can be done and the implementation and control processes can be done, according to the legal-based management perspective, each project implementation process should be logically and strategically designed with the project governance perspective. Therefore, the above theories encountered that the essence of project governance exists with adhering to a common effective structural framework. The following section provides the rationale for the project's governance that justifies the thematic view of governance.

17.2.1 The Project Governance Rationale

In the beginning, the project management theories are founded primarily on North American research. Western-oriented project management techniques are straightforward procedures that anyone can learn and implement. However, there are considerable cross-cultural problems in using the approach in non-Western countries. Countries in the global south seek resources, and project management capability enables them to attract support from funders to achieve development aspirations. However, most projects in developing countries fail or are delayed due to various barriers, according to reports from the IMF (2014); World Bank (2015). The use of project governance practices has been a powerful tool to improve project performance in meeting the time, cost, quality, scope, impact, stakeholders, satisfaction and beneficiaries' satisfaction, and ultimately contributing to the fulfillment of the country's economic and development needs through the successful delivery of all business or development projects.

Existing research that has been published in academic journals focuses on the public sector in European, North American countries, Australia or New Zealand, and other developing countries. There is also little literature about project governance practices in post-conflict countries identifying different barriers and delays in achieving project outcomes. A few of the barriers are improper shortcomings from project initiation and planning, lengthy administrative structure, lengthy approval procedures, procurement delays, change of orders, flawed cost estimations, lack of proactive coordination and communication, lack of skilled technical staff and laborers, and delays on fund disbursements (Nanthagopan & Williams, 2021).

Project governing mechanisms should align with the requirements of project funding institutions and government authorities. For countries, it is a justifiable legal framework that enables countries to maximally utilize the project resources in a timely, accurate and reliable manner. Project governing also ensures that the project deliverables are transparent and accountable aggregately to society. Then, all the project stakeholders are satisfied with the performance of their responsibilities as stipulated to be governed, and the project deliverables are injustice with good governance. The intended outcome is that economic value is added to society and the nation.

In post-conflict countries, project implementation to fulfill the livelihood requirements and accelerate regional development is a requirement for rebuilding, rehabilitation, and reconstruction of affected areas of particular countries. Therefore, a proven considerable effect on the contextual development of a responsible project governance mechanism in a post-conflict setting will increase transparency and accountability in the field. The concept of project governance with the integration of the post-conflict environment, which highlights the essence of taking a global perspective of the project-driven approach, is explained in the next section.

17.3 Post-Conflict Scenario

Many conflict-affected or affecting countries have severe damage to the economy, requiring efforts have been taken to improve the livelihood of people and auxiliary products and services provided by the public sector. Major and megaprojects are required to rebuild infrastructure and develop new sustainable industrial systems in post-conflict country environments. The current dissemination of knowledge and exposure has limited applicability in post-conflict countries with institutional constraints on project delivery such as a lack of trained personnel, a lack of project governance structure, legal systems, and a slow post-recovery process in place for the conflict-affected people, which results in poor project performance or project failure.

17.3.1 Contextual Definition of Term "Post-Conflict"

As defined in the terminology post-war by United Nations Development Programme and Chr. Michelson Institute, Bergen Seminar series (2004) clarifies that terminology is important at the outset. It was noted that the term "post-conflict" is misleading, not only because conflict is an inherent element in all societies, but because violence often continues in societies after a peace settlement has been accepted. Whether politically motivated or manifested, it would be violence, mainly as a significant problem to good governance in a broad sense. In some countries, it is estimated that the number of violent deaths in the first five years after the peace agreement was about the same as the annual average during the war (Pearce, 1999).

Combining a violent reality with the nonviolent implications of the language used by the international aid agencies can produce serious misrepresentations in recognizing problems and expectations of solutions. For instance, would agencies that operate in a "post-conflict society" and within "post-conflict programs" readily special projects designed to reduce violence? Programmatic emphasis on "the rule of law" captures only a small dimension of the violence problem. This defining emphasis on post-conflict conceptualization is in line with the theoretical and empirical findings by Brunet (2018); Derakhshan et al. (2019); Joslin and Muller (2016); Maddaloni and Davis (2017); Muzawar et al. (2017); Zeng et al. (2014); and Zeng et al. (2017). These findings direct the phenomenal path for the appropriate, flexible and reflective governance and characterize it across different organizational and project layers.

In the project governance scenario, the projects view well-planned mechanisms and structures in line with the set of local and global statutory and professional standards to cover formalities and put forward for project implementation. However, there is still much to be uncovered in the interplay among these layers, particularly the projects that record their failure or are behind schedule during the periods under review. Project governance can identify the gap between different processes, procedures, and avenues for exploring and understanding the most appropriate and pre-requisite structural model.

17.3.2 Project Governance and Post-Conflict Scenarios

After emphasizing the linkage between project governance and post-conflict scenario, analytical tools must also account for the dynamic nature of financial and physical resources and post-conflict situations. Changing circumstances are unavoidable, and analysis must be future-oriented. The project deliverable should always align with the project governance frameworks to rebuild, resettle, and rehabilitate all conflict-affected areas' economic, social, and community stances through a project-based strategy. In a post-conflict situation, many forces can have an impact on the resource base: the restart of economic development; return of conflict-affected and internally displaced persons who need the basic human requirements; (1) shelter; (2) population growth; and (3) resource consumption resulting from rehabilitation, reconstruction, and development work. In analyzing the social, political, economic, and ecological contexts, these trends must be addressed so those contextual development scenarios can be developed to identify and avoid potentially conflicting or mutually amplifying negative trends. Nevertheless, after a significant conflict, at least a generation is necessary for reconciliation and the social contract. Thus, analytical tools need to support efforts to visualize the range of ways in which the environment may be significantly altered during a post-conflict transition.

For instance, a resource abundant at the end of a violent conflict may become critically scarce a decade or two later. If tensions between former warring parties are not resolved, such a change may transform a formerly trivial resource dispute into an activation for conflict. Integrating conflict-sensitive adaptation into post-conflict work will be critical in this context. That is why the project proponents and stakeholders should emphasize project governance to eliminate the drawbacks and difficulties in resettling the conflict-affected mode to rebuilding nature in a post-conflict scenario. Finally, it would be a screen up sketch to see the reality of a conflict-affected environment and turn to the fulfillment of societal needs through a formal administrative context.

Integrating the challenge of an energetically changing environment will require a scenario-based approach that includes realistic projections of these changes and how they may affect society in the future. It is imperative to explore, outline, and understand the likely shape of the world post-conflict reconstruction. Actively integrating stakeholders into such a process is crucial and can improve their ownership and awareness of environmental concerns. To create and predetermine the following activities: (1) goal setting: develop an overall framework of goals to be achieved in a post-conflict transition process, (2) decision-making: provide points of orientation for policy formulation and strategy development for an uncertain future, and (3) communicating: promote an exchange of ideas, disseminate information, and shed light on priorities and trends, the whole related parties in the project management process from the beginning to end should adopt an overall optimal project governance mechanism and perform the real achievement and success of project deliverables thereby confirming the fulfillments of conflict-affected communities sustainably complying the said governance within the pre-specified framework for post-conflict setting.

17.3.3 Project Governance in a Post-Conflict Perspective

According to the internal and external project governance viewpoints, authors Brunet (2018), Derakshan et al. (2019), Musavir et al. (2017), and Zeng et al. (2017) emphasized the need to consider the nature of interorganizational relationships between participating in a project in the governance structure used to govern their collaborations. From the internal point of view, the internal project governance overlooks that the project's governance structure should be aligned with both internal and external possibilities. To a certain extent, these are on organizational capabilities and regulatory practices. Though, the projects are implemented to fulfill the societal requirements according to periodic pillars as emphasized by Brunet (2018); Maddaloni and Davis (2017). In this instance, the external project governance emphasizes that project-based organizations' interest is to ensure the executing efficiency of a project linking with the organizational strategy through a common organizational relationship. There is a growing demand indicating that the project managers should demonstrate the value of their projects to the project-driven organizations with integrated support, which helps implement an organizational strategy through projects, thereby maximizing organizational returns from public investments as emphasized by PMI (2016).

Organizations use projects to manage customized, one-off events across various functions (Davis, 2017). Project management is an essential operational tool and process to effectively and efficiently manage resources, tasks and activities, and associated timelines to achieve the specific project objectives and fulfill the common societal needs. Comparatively, public sector projects are actively implemented rather than private sector projects to accelerate the distribution of socio-economic, environmental, cultural, health, educational, and political benefits to the people as much as the government needs. Athukorala et al. (2017) and Maddaloni and Davis (2017) emphasized that the project performance has seen little improvement in recent years, and their inability to meet basic targets of cost, time, and benefits realization is well documented. In addition, an organizational strategy frequently fails to achieve desired results and performs poorly in terms of benefits and public support due to its impact on people, places and wastage of public resources (Joslin & Muller, 2016). Therefore, the importance of project governance to the project success in projects is needed to demonstrate and sustain the transparency and accountability of public money through the general treasury of governments as per the contributions by Joslin and Muller (2016); Maddaloni and Davis (2017).

As Brunet (2018) reiterated, surprisingly, the concept of post-conflict scenario is in the concentration of project management, project governance as practice project management has a recognized important object of any inquiry, of what is performed by different role players and stakeholders having to manage the projects. Concurrently, Joslin and muller (2016) viewed that the projects successfully require achieving the project's financial and nonfinancial performance, thereby fulfilling the societal needs and beneficiaries' expectations in a project governance mechanism and fulfilling the expectations especially reciprocated from the projects in a post-conflict environment. Therefore, integrative mechanism for project-based organizations and individual projects, especially in the post-conflict environment's rehabilitation, reconstruction, and rebuilding process. Global international humanitarian organizations, the governments of post-conflict countries, and the public must facilitate and maintain efficient and effective socio-economic project governance linking the post-conflict sensitive approach. This creates shared and sustainable value for the community and society throughout the projects as per their lifecycle confirming the project performance by adopting different project governance practices with frameworks at a front-end decision-making phase in surviving project sustainability and the maximum utilization of project resources (Zeng et al., 2017). According to the thematic nature of project governance in a post-conflict setting, the following framework exhibits the context which relates to the project governance in the project performance.

17.4 Responsible Project Governance Framework for Post-Conflict Project Implementation

Responsible project management is an adherent collaborative practice in implementing the projects to fulfill communities' needs in the global scenario. Different project governance viewpoints (Brunet, 2018; Derakshan et al., 2019) emphasize a need to consider the nature of interorganizational relationships between participating in a project in the governance structure used to govern their collaborations. Internal project governance oversees that the project's project governance structure should be aligned with both internal and external possibilities. To a certain extent, these are on organizational capabilities and regulatory practices. Though, the projects are implemented to fulfill the societal requirements according to periodic pillars. In this instance, the external project governance emphasizes that the interest of project-based organizations is to ensure the executing efficiency of a project linking with the organizational strategy through a common organizational relationship. There is a growing demand indicating that the project managers should demonstrate the value of their projects to the project-driven organizations with integrated support, which helps implement an organizational strategy through projects, thereby maximizing organizational returns from public investments as emphasized by (PMI, 2016).

In the project governance scenario, the performance of a project can be divided in terms of financial performance and nonfinancial performance. Generally, projects concentrate on utilizing funds under the purview of governance structure, complying with the predetermined rules and regulations, directions and stipulated professionally accepted local and international set of concepts and standards. The financial performance is measured in terms of revenue and cost. After granting or allocating a certain amount of allocations, the budget is prepared based on the action plan with the targets. Then, the project administrators utilize the funds according to the stipulated activities to implement every project activity to achieve the set objectives based on the abovementioned three perceived project governance practices under the aforesaid (Department of Project Management and Monitoring, 2020).

Nonfinancial performance is in the sense that it is highly concentrated on the physical performance of a project. It comprises the subsections such as timely achievement, project scope, project quality, beneficiaries' satisfaction, stakeholders' satisfaction, project impact, and project sustainability (Nanthagopan et al., 2019). However, the implementation of projects is in the process of having done all these assessments based on the monetary and funding perspectives, where the project governance is conceptualized. Ultimately, the authorities or stakeholders may satisfy with the utilization of project funds, and consequently, other progress themes are in performativity in terms of financial utilization. The project aims to achieve the physical targets of all subsections; this nonfinancial performance assesses the project efficiency and output, which are derived from the project operations from the short term to the long run. In this case, this is to specify that all variables of nonfinancial performance are assessed based on the incremental value added based on the financial allocation or public fund provisions made from the annual budget passed annually by the same project stakeholders and/or project-driven organization (Project Management Institute (USA), Colombo Chapter, 2021). Therefore, financial performance evaluation is a parallel assessment with the nonfinancial performance of public sector projects as stipulated within the governance framework.

Organizations use projects to manage customized, one-off events across various functions (Davis, 2017). Project management is an essential operational tool and process to effectively and efficiently manage resources, tasks and activities, and associated timelines to achieve the specific project objectives and fulfill the common societal needs. The public sector is actively implementing projects to accelerate the distribution of socio-economic, environmental, cultural, health, educational, and political benefits; however, their inability to meet basic cost, time, and benefits realization targets is well documented (Maddaloni & Davis, 2017). Flyvbjerg (2014); emphasized that project performance has seen little improvement in recent years. In addition, an organizational strategy frequently fails to achieve desired results and performs poorly in terms of benefits and public support due to their impact on people, places, and wastage of public resources. Therefore, the importance of project governance to the project success in projects is needed to demonstrate and sustain the transparency and accountability of public money through the general treasury of governments as per the contributions by Joslin and Muller (2016); Maddaloni and Davis (2017); Samset and Volden (2015).

Concurrently, Joslin and Muller (2016) and Zeng et al. (2014) viewed that the projects successfully require achieving the project financial and nonfinancial performance, thereby fulfilling the societal needs and beneficiaries' expectations in a project governance mechanism and fulfilling the expectations especially reciprocated from the projects in a post-conflict environment. Therefore, an integrative mechanism is needed for project-based organizations and individual projects, especially in the post-conflict environment's rehabilitation, reconstruction, and rebuilding process. This scenario is surprisingly linked with responsible project governance, which would fulfill the particular project aspirations as per the societal/beneficiary/stakeholding consent. Global international humanitarian organizations, the governments of post-conflict countries, and the public are essentially is required to facilitate and maintain efficient and effective socio-economic project governance linking post-conflict sensitive approach, thus creating shared and sustainable value for the community and society throughout the projects as per their lifecycle confirming the project performance adopting different project governance practices with frameworks at a front-end decision-making phase in surviving of project sustainability along with the maximum utilization of project resources (Samset and Volden, 2015; Zeng et al., 2017).

Brunet (2018), Derakshan et al. (2019), Leung and Fong (2011), and Nanthagopan et al. (2016) have elaborated that project governance practices are to be selected to be practiced according to the country, regional, or project background. Then a specific project governance framework is to be prepared to implement and oversee the project process emphasizing the achievement of project performance at an optimal level to comply with the fulfillment of societal needs and expectations in a responsible global governing scenario and practice/applications. After completing the whole process, the project is to be sustained with aiming a sustainable post-conflict governance concept with a responsive project management paradigm. That is why the governors and administrators must emphasize and concentrate on strategic project governance. They have to be reshaped on successful integration and adoption of the ideas of economic logic into the responsive project governance in a post-conflict setting. Therefore, the project management can be concerned with the strategic management assessing the effectiveness of project governance practices to financial and nonfinancial performance of projects through a substantial framework as to why and how the specified approach competes to project governance in a post-conflict setting, as emphasized in need to pursue collaborative project governance approaches in order to minimize future conflicts in the case of project implementation, achievement of project objectives, verifying the real project deliverables, and fulfillment of stakeholders expectations in the modern global project management and governance perspectives.

Figure 17.1 shows the two aspects of project performance to be assessed affecting the use of PG practices. From the above-discussed dimensional viewpoints, project governance is an ideal standardized platform to address the connectivity

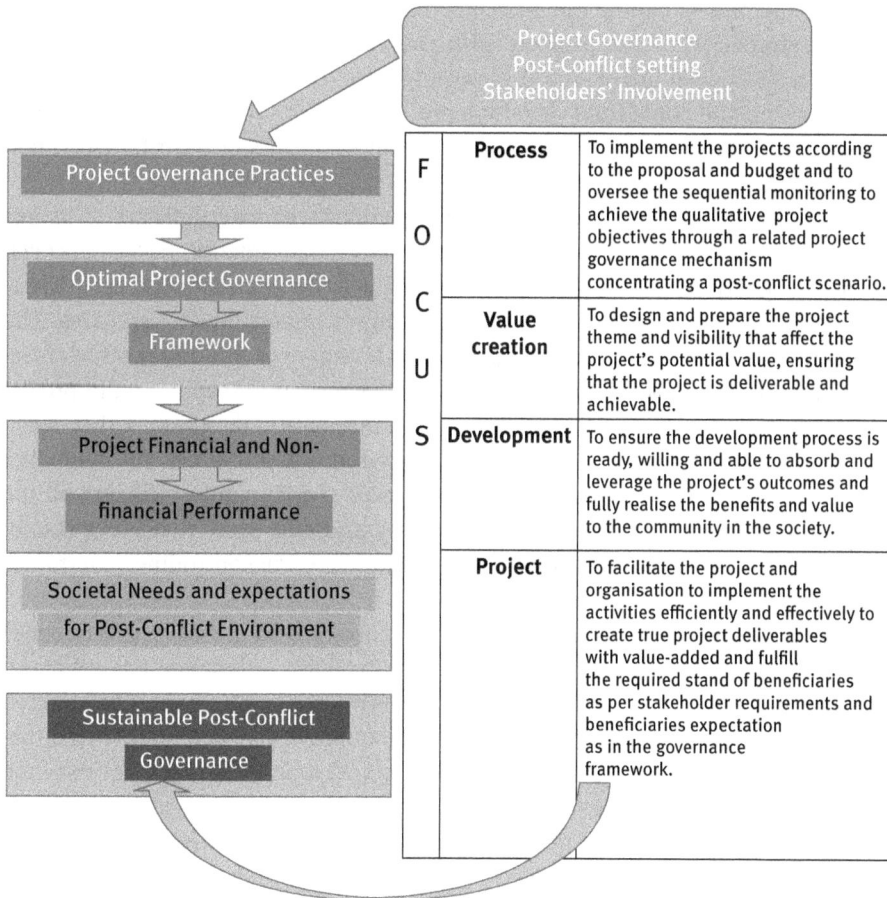

Figure 17.1: Responsible post-conflict project governance framework for project implementation (authors).

of responsive mapping strategy to achieve economic and social objectives through project-oriented scenarios. PG mechanisms should be in place to achieve the expected objectives. It would be an inevitable and justifiable legal framework that governs a debatable path to maximally utilize the project resources in a timely, accurate, and reliable manner and ensure that the project deliverables are transparent and accountable aggregately to society and the country's nation. Then, all the project stakeholders are satisfied with the performance of their responsibilities as stipulated to be governed. Simultaneously, the project governance mechanism is considered an approach for avoiding gaps among project stakeholders and minimizing the risks associated with the project implementation. The economic value is added to the society and the nation within a contextual framework as governed. Therefore, a conceptualization for project governance in practice to unfold a knowledge articulation process of an institutional project governance structure to each specific project aiming the reflection and gaining deeper insights on the successful completion of the projects with the achievement of project objectives through a sharpened document of governing practices. Thus, a proven considerable effect on the contextual development of a project governance mechanism will increase transparency and accountability in the field and contribute to a better performance of the projects globally.

In such a way, there has been a major vacuum for stronger linkages to project management, responsible project management, project governance, post-conflict setting sustainability, and social value/economic value in the global environment. Therefore, project governance in a post-conflict setting is interesting for each area. The incorporation of globally accepted professional practices and illustrative cross-sectional opportunities on how project governance is addressed to obtain project success and verify the optimal project performance within the post-conflict sensitive approach. According to the above dimensional expressions, the following project governance framework sets the framework, which guides utilizing all the financial and nonfinancial resources efficiently and effectively to achieve the set objectives and produce project deliverables through a firm controlling governance mechanism.

Especially the challenge and focus in the current field of business economics are attaining and sustaining competitiveness in today's dynamic environment. Based on this contextual theme, the project governance practices must be selected to be practised according to the country, region, or project background. Then a specific project governance framework is to be prepared to implement and oversee the project process emphasizing the achievement of project performance at an optimal level to comply with societal needs and expectations. After completing the whole process, the project is to be sustained with aiming a sustainable post-conflict governance concept. Research in strategic management has successfully integrated and adopted some of the ideas of economic logic into the field. So, the project management can be concerned with the strategic management assessing the effectiveness of project governance practices to financial and nonfinancial performance of projects through this framework as to why and how the specified approach competes to project management in a post-conflict setting.

Project governance in a post-conflict setting is always to be integrated with project management diversity, innovation, ethical research context, project management education, capacity building of skilled and genuine transformation from traditional perspective, and adaptation of responsible management framework beyond the traditional perspective. After this contextual integration, the responsible management into the project management perspective would be a ladder to make contemporary designs for researching and overseeing nature for verifying optimal progress than normal. Therefore, this framework is purely competed of adopting and applying the above approach with complying the empirical findings by Derakshan et al. (2019), Brunet (2018), Maddaloni and Davis (2017), Musavir et al. (2017), and Zeng et al. (2017). Therefore, this confirmatory theoretical Project Governance Model would be ideal for implementing the projects in the post-conflict project areas and many kinds of projects implementing with verifying the achievement of the financial and nonfinancial performance of the projects.

17.4.1 Case: Project Governance in Sri Lanka

The rehabilitation, reconstruction, and resettlement of social and economic infrastructure in a post-conflict environment in Sri Lanka are still complex; Sri Lanka has faced a thirty-year civil war in the northern and eastern regions. However, the civil war ended in 2019, and now there is a civil, administrative system. Nevertheless, the adverse impact of the civil war was undergone all over the island. This is a long-debated issue in the development process of the country. In addition to war creating large-scale human suffering, generating refugees, displacing populations, engendering psychological distress, obliterating infrastructure, and transforming the economy, in post-conflict situations, deepening chaos and disorder can be found at the highest social, economic, and political levels; serious developmental challenges remain insufficiently addressed.

A challenge for Sri Lanka and all other post-conflict countries is repairing war-damaged infrastructure to reactivate the local economy. In this connection, the Sri Lankan government has concentrated on how the development process handles in the northern and eastern regions occasionally linked with other provinces. The government concentrates on various issues and problems in fulfilling the aims of the development process. Planning and implementing reconstruction projects in areas affected by conflict have proven to be far more challenging than expected, and practitioners, aid agencies, and government responses are regarded as inadequate. For example, in a post-conflict country like Sri Lanka, the government, in collaboration with other international development organizations and missions (monetary and infrastructure facilities), is implementing projects; however, the sources of the Department of Project Management and Monitoring (2019), Ministry of Finance and Planning (2019), and World Bank (2018) expressed in their reports that there are some particular issues on poor project performance or behind schedule beyond the existing governing structure in place.

The changing political, economic, and social factors in Sri Lanka after the war in 2009 have significantly influenced the limited adoption of a project management methodology in development and reconstruction projects. The findings from the exploratory study aimed to improve understanding of the planning, pre-designing, and implementation of infrastructure projects through a well-defined project governance framework in this post-conflict setting in Sri Lanka. Therefore, there is a major vacuum for a need to promote a better understanding of how projects are undertaken at all levels of the organization and describe processes, procedures, and tools used to apply projects. Furthermore, it was found that structuring, normalizing, and facilitating deficiencies with the practising strategy exist, and there are some contradictions in applying the governmental statutory tools and applications. Also, it was identified poor quality of planning and implementation of rehabilitation, reconstruction, and resettlement projects in an environment of complexity, change, and uncertainty.

Finally, the Sri Lankan government identified to introduce and prepare a sustainable project governance framework linking an exploratory post-conflict sensitive approach to community involvement and other stakeholder participation in project identification, planning, and implementation. Infrastructure projects implemented in Sri Lanka and this framework would benefit from developing a common framework for designing development projects and programs more likely to achieve socio-economic development outcomes for post-conflict society in Sri Lanka.

The country's stakeholders are monitoring these projects to identify the causes and effects of the conflict-sensitive environment, how those affect the post-conflict environment in any country, what, why, and how those would be assessed, and how to prepare the structural models for reshaping and adopting into the resistance to change and how it can be best suited for the acceleration of the development process through strategically balancing the affected communities aspirations and stakeholders' expectations. The following useful links and documents are the stories that the researchers, policymakers, and other interested parties can explore and understand the project governance in a post-conflict setting in the Sri Lankan context.

Sri Lanka is a third-world developing country, and there are some issues to be considered in project governance. According to Sri Lankan studies (Christine, 2006; Ramasamy, 2020) and government sources (Department of Project Management and Monitoring, 2019), it was found that Sri Lankans bribe public officials and politicians for reasons such as to receive a service entitled to, to avoid a problem with the authorities that provide various services, and to speed up things. Different public institutions have been implementing development and infrastructure development projects, and benefits have been delivered to society under financial and physical support from national and international funding agencies. In this case, such institutions and agencies adopt different legitimate systems based on the mutual consents which are agreed upon. In the event of being considered, the stakeholders of all such projects implement project control mechanisms and standards/parameters to ensure the nation's qualitative project outcomes. Even though there are project governance-related issues that can be seen. The main reasons are bribery and corruption, political interference during project implementation, formulating and drafting delays, communication delays, procurement delays, lack of proper mechanisms for pre-arrangement of project resources, and social and cultural nonequalities.

These reasons described above affect negatively showing good performance in projects, so it is visualized that there are some gaps between the lack of good governance and optimal project performance (Department of Project Management and Monitoring, 2019). It could be argued that project governance measures induced by the principal-agent framework appear to help maintain good project governance rather than reporting and punishing corrupt behavior, political leaders, and citizens. Any anti-corruption effort without genuine political will and commitment that can be unsuccessful will fail, as in the case of Sri Lanka (Ramasamy, 2020). Considering these drawbacks, foreign countries and international donor-funding organizations have emphasized introducing good governance mechanisms for the public sector development projects all over the island. At this point, Sri Lanka is compulsorily agreed in a position to agree and monitor interdependent good project governance verifying sustainable project deliverables for all stakeholders and ultimately for a country's concern (Kalegama, 2011). It is more positively agreed to cover the good governance practice for the development work in the post-conflict affected areas in Sri Lanka. Due to these changes, the project implementation of all geographical areas, including post-conflict affected areas, is in a considerable quality standard up to a certain extent. However, some projects also show low performance (Ministry of Finance and Planning, 2019).

This book chapter explored contemporary governance mechanisms and post-conflict settings in Sri Lanka. As Sri Lankans, we need administrative, policy, and legal reforms, and institutional changes will improve governance quality, strong political, governmental, and bureaucratic commitment, system stability, and institutional revolutions can be ensured. Furthermore, the community expects quality benefits by implementing development projects through a good administrative and governance mechanism. Even if we are in a conflicting environment or not, the project proponents, stakeholders, and administrators are in an equal concentrating purview to ensure quality service to the whole society. In this connection, different projects were implemented by the project-driven organizations in Sri Lanka with the financial and physical grants provided by the international funding agencies and foreign countries under the considerably adopted governance mechanisms. This process is still being implemented mostly in conflict-affected areas and other districts in the country.

Table 17.1: Useful links and documents on the project governance in a post-conflict setting in the Sri Lankan context.

No.	Title	Access link	Year of publication	Publisher
01.	Post-war reconstruction in Sri Lanka: reconstruction and development of the socio-economic sectors	https://www.researchgate.net/ publication/305468887_Post_ War_Reconstruction_in_Sri_ Lanka_Reconstruction_and_De velopment_of_the_SocioEco nomic_Sectors/link/ 578fc1a908ae64311c0c75da/ download	2016	Research Gate
02.	Resettlement of conflict-induced IDPs in Northern Sri Lanka: Political economy of state policy and practice	https://securelivelihoods.org/ wp-content/uploads/Resettle ment_of-conflict_induced_ IDPs_in_northern_Sri-Lanka. pdf	2014	Secure Livelihoods Research Consortium
03.	Good Practices and Lessons Learned in Post-Conflict Reconstruction in Sri Lanka	https://www.fukuoka.unhabi tat.org/docs/publications/pdf/ habitat_newsletter/Good_prac tices_and_lessons_learned_ Final003.pdf	2017	United Nations Human Settlements Programme
04.	Introducing Organic Home Gar dening to families in Sri Lan ka's Northern Province.	https://www.fukuoka.unhabi tat.org/projects/sri_lanka/pdf/ Organic_Home_Gardenng.pdf	2016	UN-Habitat – Asia & Pacific Region
05.	Constructing Cost-effective, Demonstration Houses in Sri Lanka's Northern Province	https://www.fukuoka.unhabi tat.org/projects/voices/sri_ lanka/pdf/Demonstration_ house_case_study_Ms.Kar thiyayini_UN_Habitat_Sri_ Lanka.pdf	2015	UN-Habitat – Asia & Pacific Region
06.	Reconstruction of the Vivekananda Preschool in Kilinochchi District	https://unhabitat.lk/news/im proving-living-conditions-through-housing-news/build ing-a-brighter-tomorrow-recon struction-of-the-vivekananda-preschool-in-kilinochchi-district/	2010	UN-Habitat – Asia & Pacific Region
07.	Re-Greening the North: UN-Habitat Promotes Tree Planting in Kilinochchi, Mullaitivu, Mannar and Jaffna Districts	https://www.fukuoka.unhabi tat.org/projects/voices/sri_ lanka/pdf/Tree_Planting_in_ the_North240615_24June.pdf	2015	UN-Habitat – Asia & Pacific Region

Table 17.1 (continued)

No.	Title	Access link	Year of publication	Publisher
08.	Improving Accessibility in Villages in Batticaloa District	https://www.fukuoka.unhabitat.org/projects/voices/sri_lanka/pdf/Case_Study_2_Eralukulam_Batticaloa_240615.pdf	2013	UN-Habitat – Asia & Pacific Region
09.	New Community Centre for Illupadichchenai Residents in Batticaloa District	https://www.fukuoka.unhabitat.org/projects/voices/sri_lanka/pdf/Case_study_1_Batticaloa_community_centre_Phase2_240615.pdf		UN-Habitat – Asia & Pacific Region
10.	Providing Fresh Water to Weligahakandiya Residents in Batticaloa District	https://www.fukuoka.unhabitat.org/projects/voices/sri_lanka/pdf/Sri_Lanka_2_Community_well_for_Weligahakandiya_Batticaloa_0415.pdf	2014	UN-Habitat – Asia & Pacific Region
11.	Building Environmentally-Friendly Houses in the North of Sri Lanka	https://www.fukuoka.unhabitat.org/projects/sri_lanka/pdf/Housing_Phase_2_case_study_Model_House_Mannar_district.pdf	2014	UN-Habitat – Asia & Pacific Region
12.	Improving Living Conditions in Returnee Areas of Sri Lanka through Housing (video)	http://unhabitat.lk/p14video1.html	2015	UN-Habitat – Asia & Pacific Region
13.	Water for Life: Providing Fresh Water to School Children in Mannar	https://www.fukuoka.unhabitat.org/projects/sri_lanka/pdf/Phase_2_Mannar_Mini_Water_Supply_Scheme.pdf	2015	UN-Habitat – Asia & Pacific Region
14.	Empowering Women to Rebuild Homes in the Conflict-Affected Northern Province	https://www.fukuoka.unhabitat.org/projects/voices/sri_lanka/pdf/Housing_Phase_2_case_study_Caroline_Nirmala_Mullaitivu.pdf	2015	UN-Habitat – Asia & Pacific Region
15.	Empowering Female-Headed Homeowners to Reconstruct their Damaged Homes	https://www.fukuoka.unhabitat.org/projects/voices/sri_lanka/pdf/CaseP14-5.pdf	2015	UN-Habitat – Asia & Pacific Region
16.	Building Blocks for a Brighter Tomorrow	https://www.fukuoka.unhabitat.org/projects/voices/sri_lanka/pdf/CaseP14-4.pdf	2015	UN-Habitat – Asia & Pacific Region

Table 17.1 (continued)

No.	Title	Access link	Year of publication	Publisher
17.	A New Beginning for Returnee Families in the North of Sri Lanka	https://www.fukuoka.unhabitat.org/projects/voices/sri_lanka/pdf/CaseP14-3.pdf	2015	UN-Habitat – Asia & Pacific Region
18.	Workshop on Incremental Housing	https://www.fukuoka.unhabitat.org/projects/voices/sri_lanka/pdf/Workshop_on_Incremental%20Housing_1114.pdf	2014	UN-Habitat – Asia & Pacific Region
19.	European Union Delegation Visits UN-Habitat Housing Beneficiaries in Batticaloa District, Sri Lanka	https://www.fukuoka.unhabitat.org/projects/voices/sri_lanka/pdf/European_Union_Visits_UN-H_locations_in_Batticaloa.pdf	2014	UN-Habitat – Asia & Pacific Region
20.	UN-Habitat Provides Training on Innovative Construction Techniques for Artisans and CBO Members from Mannar District	https://www.fukuoka.unhabitat.org/projects/voices/sri_lanka/pdf/training_on_Innovative_Construction_0514.pdf	2014	UN-Habitat – Asia & Pacific Region
21.	Rebuilding Homes in Conflict-Affected Mullaitivu District	https://www.fukuoka.unhabitat.org/projects/voices/sri_lanka/pdf/Case_study_2_Iranapali_Mullaitivu_April_17_2014.pdf	2015	UN-Habitat – Asia & Pacific Region
22.	Reconstructing Conflict Damaged Homes in the East of Sri Lanka	https://www.fukuoka.unhabitat.org/projects/voices/sri_lanka/pdf/CaseP16_1.pdf	2015	UN-Habitat – Asia & Pacific Region
23.	Building a Foundation for the Future: Ambassador of the European Union Visits Housing Beneficiaries in the North of Sri Lanka	https://www.fukuoka.unhabitat.org/info/news/20131106_en.html	2013	UN-Habitat – Asia & Pacific Region
24.	European Union Parliamentarians Visit Housing Beneficiaries in Sri Lanka's Northern Province	https://www.fukuoka.unhabitat.org/info/news/20130806_en.html	2013	UN-Habitat – Asia & Pacific Region
25.	Australian Members of Parliament Visit Housing Project in Killinochchi District	https://www.fukuoka.unhabitat.org/info/news/20130216_en.html	2013	UN-Habitat – Asia & Pacific Region

Table 17.1 (continued)

No.	Title	Access link	Year of publication	Publisher
26.	Housing Support for Four Thousand Families in the North and East with Funding from the European Union, Australian and Swiss Governments	https://www.fukuoka.unhabi tat.org/info/news/201301_en. html	2013	UN-Habitat – Asia & Pacific Region
27.	European Union Launches Housing Project for Returnee Families in Batticaloa District	https://www.fukuoka.unhabi tat.org/projects/voices/sri_ lanka/detail07_en.html	2013	UN-Habitat – Asia & Pacific Region
28.	Catalytic Support to Peacebuilding in Sri Lanka	https://www.fukuoka.unhabi tat.org/projects/sri_lanka/de tail32_en.html	Weblink retrieved on Sep. 2021	UN-Habitat – Asia & Pacific Region
29.	Preparation of the Resettlement Plan (RP) for Households Affected by the Rehabilitation of the Kelani Valley (KV) Railway Line in Sri Lanka (Phase I)	https://www.fukuoka.unhabi tat.org/projects/sri_lanka/de tail31_en.html	Weblink retrieved on Sep. 2021	UN-Habitat – Asia & Pacific Region
30.	Emergency Shelter Relief for Flood and Landslide Affected Households in Kalutara and Galle Districts of Sri Lanka	https://www.fukuoka.unhabi tat.org/projects/sri_lanka/de tail30_en.html	Weblink retrieved on Sep. 2021	UN-Habitat – Asia & Pacific Region
31.	The State of Sri Lankan Cities Report	https://www.fukuoka.unhabi tat.org/projects/sri_lanka/de tail29_en.html	Weblink retrieved on Sep. 2021	UN-Habitat – Asia & Pacific Region
32.	Human Development Initiative through Empowerment and Settlement Improvement in the Plantation Settlements in Sri Lanka	https://www.fukuoka.unhabi tat.org/projects/sri_lanka/de tail28_en.html	Weblink retrieved on Sep. 2021	UN-Habitat – Asia & Pacific Region
33.	Indian Housing Project in Central and Uva Provinces	https://www.fukuoka.unhabi tat.org/projects/sri_lanka/de tail27_en.html	Weblink retrieved on Sep. 2021	UN-Habitat – Asia & Pacific Region

Table 17.1 (continued)

No.	Title	Access link	Year of publication	Publisher
34.	Emergency Shelter Relief for Flood Affected Families in Colombo and Gampaha Districts in Western Province, Sri Lanka (Completed)	https://www.fukuoka.unhabitat.org/projects/sri_lanka/detail26_en.html	Weblink retrieved on Sep. 2021	UN-Habitat – Asia & Pacific Region
35.	Sustainable Resettlement through Community-Driven Improvement of the Learning Environment in Mannar District, Sri Lanka	https://www.fukuoka.unhabitat.org/projects/sri_lanka/detail25_en.html	Weblink retrieved on Sep. 2021	UN-Habitat – Asia & Pacific Region
36.	Support My School: Supporting Schools in Northern Sri Lanka with Access to Water and Sanitation Facilities (Completed)	https://www.fukuoka.unhabitat.org/projects/sri_lanka/detail24_en.html	Weblink retrieved on Sep. 2021	UN-Habitat – Asia & Pacific Region
37.	Project for Rehabilitation of Community Infrastructure, Improvement of Livelihoods and Empowerment of Women in the Northern and Eastern Provinces (RCI) (Completed)	https://www.fukuoka.unhabitat.org/projects/sri_lanka/detail23_en.html	Weblink retrieved on Sep. 2021	UN-Habitat – Asia & Pacific Region
38.	Rainwater Harvesting in a Water Scarce Small Village in Northern Sri Lanka (Completed)	https://www.fukuoka.unhabitat.org/projects/sri_lanka/detail22_en.html	Weblink retrieved on Sep. 2021	UN-Habitat – Asia & Pacific Region
39.	Climate Resilient Action Plans for Coastal Urban Areas (Completed)	https://www.fukuoka.unhabitat.org/projects/sri_lanka/detail21_en.html	Weblink retrieved on Sep. 2021	UN-Habitat – Asia & Pacific Region
40.	Disaster Resilient City Development Strategies for Sri Lankan Cities (Completed)	https://www.fukuoka.unhabitat.org/projects/sri_lanka/detail20_en.html	Weblink retrieved on Sep. 2021	UN-Habitat – Asia & Pacific Region
41.	Disaster Resilient City Development Strategies for Four Cities in the Northern and Eastern Provinces of Sri Lanka (Phase II) (Completed)	https://www.fukuoka.unhabitat.org/projects/sri_lanka/detail19_en.html	Weblink retrieved on Sep. 2021	UN-Habitat – Asia & Pacific Region

Table 17.1 (continued)

No.	Title	Access link	Year of publication	Publisher
42.	Rehabilitation of Community Infrastructure and Facilities in the Conflict-Affected Areas in Northern Province of Sri Lanka (Completed)	https://www.fukuoka.unhabitat.org/projects/sri_lanka/detail18_en.html	Weblink retrieved on Sep. 2021	UN-Habitat – Asia & Pacific Region
43.	Improving Living Conditions in Returnee Areas of Sri Lanka through Housing (Completed)	https://www.fukuoka.unhabitat.org/projects/sri_lanka/detail16_en.html	Weblink retrieved on Sep. 2021	UN-Habitat – Asia & Pacific Region
44.	Indian Housing Project (Completed)	https://www.fukuoka.unhabitat.org/projects/sri_lanka/detail17_en.html	Weblink retrieved on Sep. 2021	UN-Habitat – Asia & Pacific Region
45.	Support to Conflict Affected People through Housing (Completed)	https://www.fukuoka.unhabitat.org/projects/sri_lanka/detail15_en.html	Weblink retrieved on Sep. 2021	UN-Habitat – Asia & Pacific Region
46.	Shelter Support to Conflict-affected IDPs in the North of Sri Lanka (Completed)	https://www.fukuoka.unhabitat.org/projects/sri_lanka/detail14_en.html	Weblink retrieved on Sep. 2021	UN-Habitat – Asia & Pacific Region
47.	Jaffna Tsunami Recovery and Reconstruction Project (Completed)	https://www.fukuoka.unhabitat.org/projects/sri_lanka/detail13_en.html	Weblink retrieved on Sep. 2021	UN-Habitat – Asia & Pacific Region
48.	Community Recovery and Reconstruction Partnership to Support the People's Process of Rebuilding (Completed)	https://www.fukuoka.unhabitat.org/projects/sri_lanka/detail12_en.html	Weblink retrieved on Sep. 2021	UN-Habitat – Asia & Pacific Region
49.	Reconstruction of Fish Market in Galle (Completed)	https://www.fukuoka.unhabitat.org/projects/sri_lanka/detail11_en.html	Weblink retrieved on Sep. 2021	UN-Habitat – Asia & Pacific Region
50.	Rebuilding Community Infrastructure and Shelter in Tsunami-Affected Areas (Completed)	https://www.fukuoka.unhabitat.org/projects/sri_lanka/detail10_en.html	Weblink retrieved on Sep. 2021	UN-Habitat – Asia & Pacific Region

Table 17.1 (continued)

No.	Title	Access link	Year of publication	Publisher
51.	Luna Lake Environment Improvement and Community Development Project (Completed)	https://www.fukuoka.unhabitat.org/projects/sri_lanka/detail09_en.html	Weblink retrieved on Sep. 2021	UN-Habitat – Asia & Pacific Region
52.	Pro-Poor Partnerships for Participatory Settlement Upgrading (Completed)	https://www.fukuoka.unhabitat.org/projects/sri_lanka/detail08_en.html	Weblink retrieved on Sep. 2021	UN-Habitat – Asia & Pacific Region
53.	Support to the Urbanization Framework	https://www.fukuoka.unhabitat.org/projects/sri_lanka/detail06_en.html	Weblink retrieved on Sep. 2021	UN-Habitat – Asia & Pacific Region
54.	Post Disaster Housing Coordination Project (Completed)	https://www.fukuoka.unhabitat.org/projects/sri_lanka/detail05_en.html	Weblink retrieved on Sep. 2021	UN-Habitat – Asia & Pacific Region
55.	Sustainable Cities Programme (Completed)	https://www.fukuoka.unhabitat.org/projects/sri_lanka/detail04_en.html	Weblink retrieved on Sep. 2021	UN-Habitat – Asia & Pacific Region
56.	Urban Governance Support Project (UGSP) (Completed)	https://www.fukuoka.unhabitat.org/projects/sri_lanka/detail03_en.html	Weblink retrieved on Sep. 2021	UN-Habitat – Asia & Pacific Region
57.	Rebuilding Communities in North-East Sri Lanka (Completed)	https://www.fukuoka.unhabitat.org/projects/sri_lanka/detail02_en.html	Weblink retrieved on Sep. 2021	UN-Habitat – Asia & Pacific Region
58.	Urban Poverty Reduction Strategy – Colombo (Completed)	https://www.fukuoka.unhabitat.org/projects/sri_lanka/detail01_en.html	Weblink retrieved on Sep. 2021	UN-Habitat – Asia & Pacific Region

Source: UN-Habitat websites: retrieved on September 2021. Research Gate, Secure Livelihoods Research Consortium, Un Habitat Asia & Pacific Region, and United Nations Human Settlements Programme websites: Retrieved on September 2021

17.5 Summary

The project governance framework provides an overseeing direction for the project owners' administrators and other stakeholders to run a project smoothly within the budget for the performance of timely deliveries and beneficiaries' satisfaction. Connectively, this process verifies concentrating the maximum utilization of financial and physical resources to achieve the optimal project performance as aforesaid and linking common development objectives in the contemporary post-conflict setting to devastate the backward of project performance.

The theoretical findings on the theme of project governance in a post-conflict setting emphasized that the planning, execution, and control of either process or a system or a project are the important halts of their path so that the project performance can be attained and the project success can be achieved. The project managers must intend to determine what kind of overseeing is needed for scrutinizing project operation to the overall project performance in pre- and post-conflict sensitive situations in local and international settings. So, each project implementation process should be logically and strategically designed with the project governance perspective in compliance with the structured legitimate managerial perspective. In the spirit of the project governance literature concentrating on the post-conflict setting, it was encountered that the essence of project governance exists with adhering to a common effective structural framework identified as the "Responsible Post-Conflict Project Governance Framework." Further, it was emphasized that the project proponents, governors, stakeholders, experts, and administrators should professionally and ethically adhere to and disseminate their efforts to design and implement the projects according to the post-conflict setting as most countries were affected and/or have been affected by the different types of civil and war conflicts. Therefore, the project governance is an utmost need to adhere to and use to attain the project success with high quality and satisfy all the stakeholders.

Parallel, a concentration on the governance in a post-conflict setting is commendable to be discussed in making a pointing device from this chapter emerged from understanding the nature of project governance practices and how it will contribute to the post-conflict project management scenario in practice. Moreover, the project proponents, stakeholders, and policymakers should strategically concentrate and resist changing and adapting the contextual post-conflict scenario to fulfill the societal requirements to build sustainable project governance throughout the above-specified framework within a post-conflict setting.

This section sought to identify the success factors required to design and develop workable sustainability governance frameworks of infrastructure delivery systems in a post-conflict context. It is clear that project governance practices foster the inclusion of project deliverables complying with sustainable development goals through the undertaken projects but lack the proper monitoring and control for achieving the desired outcomes. Evidence from the various kinds of past research, studies, and discussion forums highlights the continuous flow of operations as usual by project team members to measure the success of projects based on time, cost, and quality. At the same time, they pay diminutive attention to sustainable development as a parameter for project success. Moreover, project-driven organizations or project administrators do not have the complete subsystems to properly plan for achieving sustainable development in all development or business projects.

Sustainable development deliverables seem to be missed right from the commencement of the projects; secondly, the outcomes are only measured after the projects are completed. In such a way, a relative project governance mechanism provides an opportunity to measure the outcome of sustainable development deliverables in the entire project life cycle. Factors relating to the project success identified from the findings include a detailed definition of the project outlined right from the beginning with all project stakeholders present. Then, the early involvement of the project stakeholders proved to be imperative for project success as specified. Sustainable development as an outcome is proving to be complicated for project teams to implement due to the continuous project management success factors being the only measurement of the performance of systems.

A proper policy/strategy on sustainable development is imperative to communicate with all stakeholders of the project delivery systems to cascade that to the implementation phases of the projects. A clear and concise communication pathway is the key to achieving sustainable deliverables on infrastructure delivery systems. Accordingly, the geo-political/context-based variables/features identified in the study can influence the conceptualization and/or design of effective sustainability governance implementation frameworks in developing countries and the nature of project success in infrastructure delivery systems. Finally, this section concludes that we still have time to adjust to the sustainable human development approach based on sustainable development goals (SDGs) that would be the most powerful tool to enrich the country. With a deeper understanding and the concrete philosophical dimensions of SDGs, the essence of a predetermined and specified governance framework is a must to prepare in a global context to fulfill the communal aspirations commonly concentrated for post-conflict-affected/not affected people in the world.

Analysis of post-conflict situations will be further complicated by climate change, which is likely to significantly alter regional and local environments and redraw political, economic, and social maps. Research studies on project governance and project implementation under the post-conflict scenario suggest this process is accelerating beyond what was conceivable only a few years ago, foretelling significant impacts in just a few decades. The goal of limiting global warming to 2 °C above preindustrial levels will require reductions of global greenhouse gas emissions of 80% and beyond, implying a radical and massive change from current modes of economic development and management of natural resources, particularly against the background of growing global population and resource demand.

The world is now facing a fourth industrial revolution. Based on the digital revolution of the second half of the twentieth century, rapid technological innovations in several fields are coming together to bring about transformational changes worldwide. These changes are happening very fast, affecting almost every industry in every country. The current global epidemic has accelerated the pace of these changes. To link with conceptual context, the countries, the respective governments, project-driven institutions, and project administrators involved in all fields must consider the changes in this important evolution. Those who concentrate on this perspective must adapt rapidly to the global turmoil and transformation. As per the top-level experts' iterations, we are still lagging. Our whole development structure needs to adapt quickly to modern methods with extremely adaptable possibilities, even amid rapidly changing conditions, which will help them find better enhancements in the future. After linking the said relationship between sustainable development and project governance in a post-conflict environment, it would be beneficial to explore, understand, and adopt project governance to make a perceptual adaptation with minimizing the adverse effects (if any) in implementing the best option on post-conflict sensitivity.

References

Athukorala, P., Ginting, E., Hill, H., & Kumar, U. (2017). Sri Lankan economy: Chartering a new course. Publication of Asian Development Bank, ISBN 978-92-9257-973-9 (Print), 978-92-9257-974-6 (e-ISBN). http://dx.doi.org/10.22617/TCS178786-2

Brunet, M. (2018). Governance-as-practice for major public infrastructure projects: A case of multilevel project governing. *International Journal of Project Management*. http://doi.org/10.1016/j.ijproman.2018.02.007

Christine, B. (2006). Good governance and conflict transformation in Sri Lanka; a political analysis of people's perceptions of institutions at the local level and the challenges of decentralised governance, PhD dissertation, Political Science Department of the South Asia Institute, Heidelberg University.

Davis, K. (2017). An empirical investigation into different stakeholder groups perception of project success. *International Journal of Project Management*, 35, 604–617. http://dx.doi.org/10.2016/j.ijproman.2017.02.004

Department of Project Management and Monitoring. (2020). Annual Report.

Department of Project Management and Monitoring. (2019). Annual Report.

Derakhshan, R., Mancini, M., & Turner, J. R. (2019). Project governance and stakeholders: A literature review. *International Journal of Project Management*, 1, 98–116.

Drouin, N., & Turner, R. (2022). Advanced Introduction to Megaprojects. Edward Elgar Publishing Ltd.

Flyvbjerg, B. (2014). What you should know about megaprojects and why: An overview, project. *Project Management Journal*, 45(2). 10.1002/pmj.21409

Maddaloni, F. D. & Davis, K. (2017). 'Project manager's perception of the local communities' stakeholder in megaprojects. An empirical investigation in the UK. *International Journal of Project Management*. http://doi.org/10.1016/j.ijproman.2017.11.003

Millstein, I., & MacAvoy, P. (1998). The active board of directors and performance of the large publicly traded corporation. Columbia Law Rev. 98 (5), 1283–1322.

Goldratt, E. M. (1990). *What is this thing called the theory of constraints?*. Croton-on-Hudson, NY: North River Press.

Governance in post-conflict situations. UNDP Background Paper for Working Group Discussions, United Nations Development Programme & Chr. Michaelson Institute, Bergen Seminar Series, Bergen, Norway, 5–7, May (2004).

International Monetary Fund, Performance Report. (2014).

Joslin, R. & Muller, R. (2016). The relationship between project governance and project success. *International Journal of Project Management, 34*, 613–626. http://dx.doi.org/j.ijproman.2016.02.008

Kalegama, S. (2011). *Presentation on socio-economic challenges of post-conflict reconstruction in Sri Lanka*. Colombo, Sri Lanka: Institute of Policy Studies.

Koskela, L. & Howell, G. (2002). The underlying theory of project management is obsolete. Proceedings of the PMI Research Conference, 2002. pp. 293–302.

Kylie, P. (2013). Communication Theories applied on Project Management. Project Management Articles, updated February 2022. Retrieved from https://project-management.com/communication-theories-applied-on-project-management/

Leung, J. K. L. & Fong, P. (2011). The power of stories in the construction industry: Lessons from other domains. *Vine, 41*(4), 466–482. 10.1108/03055721111188548

Ministry of Finance and Planning, Annual Report. (2019).

Musawir, A. ul, Serra, C.E.M., Zwikael, O. and Ali, I. (2017). Project governance, benefit management, and project success: Towards a framework for supporting organizational strategy implementation. *International Journal of Project Management*, 35(8), pp.1658–1672. doi:10.1016/j.ijproman.2017.07.007.

Müller, M.F., Dralle, D.N., and Thompson, S.E. (2014): Analytical model for flow duration curves in seasonally dry climates. *Water Resources Research 50(7)*: 5510–5531. http://dx.doi.org/10.1002/2014WR015301 DOI: 10.1002/2014WR015301

Muller, R., Zhai, L., Wang, A, & Shao, J. (2016). A Framework for governance of projects: Governmentality, governance structure and projectification. International Journal of Project Management, 34, 957–969, doi: http://dx.doi.org/10.1016/j.ijproman.2016.05.002

Nanthagopan, Y. & Williams, N. L. (2021). Project managing in post-conflict environments: An exploration of the resource profiles of Sri Lankan non-governmental organisations involved in development projects. *International Journal of Managing Projects in Business, vol. ahead-of-print*(No. ahead-of-print). https://doi.org/10.1108/IJMPB-05-2020-0179

Nanthagopan, Y., Williams, N. L., & Thompson, K. (2019). Levels and interconnections of project success in development projects by non-governmental organisations (NGOs). *International Journal of Managing Projects in Business, 12*(1). 10.1108/IJMPB-04-2018-0085

Nanthagopan, Y., Williams, N. L., & Page, S. (2016). Understanding the nature of project management capacity in Sri Lankan non-governmental organisations (NGOs): A resource-based perspective. *International Journal of Project Management, 34*(8), 1608–1624. 10.1016/j.ijproman.2016.09.003

Pearce, R. D. (1999). Decentralized R&D and strategic competitiveness: Globalised approaches to generation and use of technology in multinational enterprises (MNEs). *Research Policy, 28*(issue 2-3), 157–178.

Project Management Institute, United States of America, Performance Report. (2016).

Project Management Institute, United States of America, Colombo Chapter, Performance Report. (2021).

Ramasamy, R. (2020). Governance and administration in Sri Lanka: Trends, tensions, and prospects. *Public Administration and Policy: An Asia-Pacific Journal*, *23*(2), 187–198. https://doi.org/10.1108/PAP-03-2020-0020

Samset, K. & Volden, G. H. (2015). Front-end definition of projects: Ten paradoxes and some reflections regarding project management and project governance. *International Journal of Project Management*, *34*(2). 10.1016/j.ijproman.2015.01.014

World Bank, Annual Report. (2018).

World Bank, Annual Report. (2015).

Zeng, S., Hanyang, M., Lin, H., Chen, H., & Shi, J. J. (2017). The social governance of megaproject social responsibility. *International Journal of Project Management*. http://dx.doi.org/10.1016/j.ijproman.2017.01.012

Zeng, S., Ma, H. Y., Lin, H., Zeng, R. C., & Tam, V. W. Y. (2014). Social responsibility of major infrastructure projects in China. *International Journal of Project Management*. http://dx.doi.org/10.1016/j.ijproman.2014.07.007

Nigel Williams and Beverly Pasian

18 Why Isn't the Climate Changing Our Research?

Context: This chapter examines the issues that impact the project profession's engagement with climate change.

Characters: The chapter identifies public, private, and nonprofit movements involved in the development and enacting of climate action.

Location: A UK project that incorporates carbon reduction approaches is examined.

Research gaps: Climate change has received little attention in project management.

Challenges: Differing philosophical positions imply entirely different paths of development with attendant impacts on communities.

Keywords: climate change, project management risks

18.1 Missing the Climate in PM Research

Unlike many other domains of management, project management places uncertainty at its core. The need to address uncertainty is embedded in PM in ambiguities where outcomes are unknown and variability where the extent is unknown. In the context of climate impacts, the risk is used to address the ambiguity and variability of negative impacts of climate hazards on individuals, economies, community quality of life, ecosystems, and infrastructure. In defining climate impacts, one must consider the exposure (the presence of entities in locations that may be adversely affected) and vulnerabil- ity (the susceptibility to harm and lack of resilience). Despite the scale, recency, and frequency of climate impacts, it is curious that the academic literature on Project Management has paid scant attention. An examination of the Climate Change Keyword in Scopus in August 2021 reveals that it has been used 20 times in "Impact Assessment and Project Appraisal," 9 times in "Automation in Construction," 6 times in "Construction Management and Economics," 5 times in the "International Journal of Project Management," 3 times in "Construction Innovation," and 2 times in the "Journal of Construction Engineering and Management." Earlier, Morris (2017) discussed climate change as a future challenge and Abdi, Taghipour, and Khamooshi (2018) presented a methodology for evaluating greenhouse gasses from projects. The international journal of project management (Ika et al., 2020) identified climate change as a global challenge. It is instructive to

https://doi.org/10.1515/9783110724783-022

note that the Morris article has only been cited five times to date, and only one of those citations is from an established project management journal.

Outside of Project Management, Field and Barros (2014) presented iterative risk management approaches to help regions identify climate critical risks and the temporal order of adaptation over time, always known as adaptation pathways. Outside of projects, the financial industry has launched initiatives on Task Force on Climate-related Financial Disclosures (TCFD, 2017) and the Network for Greening the Financial System (NGFS, 2019).

18.2 Climate Change Indicators and Impacts

It is important to note that these changes are already visible and are attributable to human activity (Hobbie and Grimm, 2020). These include the following increases:
– Greenhouse gas concentrations
– Global surface temperatures over land
– Precipitation overland
– Melting of glaciers
– Ocean acidification
– Surface ocean temperatures
– Mean sea level
– Droughts

Due to geographical and infrastructural differences, climate impacts are not uniform and should be considered in context (Sitas et al., 2021). These impacts include:
(a) Sea-level rise and coastal storms: The global consensus is that rising sea levels and coastal storms may be more intense. While there is no ambiguity about this risk, there is some debate on variability, with projections of 1.5-degree warming of 0.3 m and 2-degree warming of 1.3 m by 2100 (Hayhoe et al., 2018). As a result, many residents and infrastructure are exposed to inundation, storm surge, flooding, erosion, and salt-water intrusion. Storms can also damage ecological and technological infrastructure.
(b) Extreme heat: Global temperature is projected to increase by a minimum of 1.5 by 2050, which can increase by 50% further in cities due to the urban heat island (UHI) effect (Spinoni et al., 2021). At high temperatures, productivity and physical health are affected in humans and other living organisms, which increase the risk of death from heating in older or infirm individuals. There is an impact on infrastructure as a significant amount of electricity is required for cooling.

(c) River flooding: Shifting rainfall patterns result in higher precipitation levels in a shorter period, overwhelming traditional protective infrastructure.
(d) Fires: Fires are also exacerbated by climate change due to the increased length of the growing season in some forested areas, along with insects that create deadwood. Fires have increased in frequency and intensity, directly threatening settlements, destroying agriculture, and exposing residents to air pollution.
    – Climate change mitigation
    – Climate change adaptation

18.3 Climate Adaptation

Climate adaptation is actions responding to climate change's current or future negative impacts. Adaptation decisions include an evaluation of timing, extent, types of adaptation and outcomes (e.g., altered exposure, altered sensitivity, altered adaptive capacity) within context variables that define the space for action, including the attributes of the climatic and nonclimatic stimuli, institutions, resources, and involved actors (Moser, 2009). The process of adaptation can follow a rational decision-making process which includes understanding the problem (detection, information gathering, and determining if further action is necessary), planning adaptation actions (development, evaluation, and selection of options), and managing the implementation of the selected option (implement, monitoring and evaluation). While this process is presented as deterministic, the members are part of a complex, evolving system in which the entities may change over time. For example, the actors incorporate community and corporate stakeholders, the socio-technical context of action, and the specific location in which these adaptation activities are required. The environmental changes resulting from climate change will only spur action if the actors change their paradigms and influence political and social institutions that provide capacity and legitimacy for action. Even though there may be physical manifestations of climate change, actors and institutions determine if these signals are detected or interpreted as a rationale for action (Noble, 2014). If such a rationale is provided, projects are formulated to deliver protective physical infrastructural, technological advances to create new products or services and social actions to reduce vulnerabilities.

18.4 Climate Mitigation

In contrast to adaptation, mitigation seeks to stabilize or reduce the amount of greenhouse gas concentrations. These approaches include avoiding, reducing, or removing emissions via natural or technological means. These include several actions:

1) Generation and distribution of renewable energy
2) Energy efficiency improvement
3) Low carbon mobility
4) Use of low carbon materials
5) Carbon capture and utilization
6) Carbon capture and storage
7) Enhancing natural carbon sinks

While renewable energy has made good progress in this area, progress has been slow in most other domains. The complex transformations of supply chains requiring changes to technologies, practices, organizations, financial incentives, and regulations are slow.

18.5 Climate Governance Perspectives and Projects

There are multiple discourses on climate change (Jaworska, 2018). This makes the challenge of reducing carbon emissions by projects greater as there is a need to align socio-technical systems, which may have been calcified via investments in suppliers or technological systems. Since projects may employ extended supply chains in multiple locations, it may be challenging to incorporate carbon-reducing innovations to meet windows of opportunity for change created by shifts in public priorities since they may not be applicable in every location. While exogenous shocks such as climate-induced natural disasters can also trigger rapid shifts in public opinion, these may be country-specific as impacts can vary by country (Palm et al., 2017). For example, low-lying countries may be more concerned about sea-level rises and coastal storms, while heavily forested countries may be more concerned about fires.

18.5.1 Green Growth

The emerging discourse on project management and addressing climate change has embraced the paradigm of economic growth through climate actions. This idea has come out from the OECD United Nations development program and the World Bank; the OECD published reports about the idea of green growth (Hickel and Kallis, 2020). These organizations have defined green growth as the decoupling of the relationship between material growth, carbon growth, and economic growth. The central idea is to facilitate economic growth with as minimal material and energy use as possible (Tarabusi and Guarini, 2018). In this way, green growth supports human well-being and national incomes, which are desirable outcomes for citizens while still saving the environment by reducing carbon emissions, which will reduce threats to society. This concept of decoupling supports such activities as the substitution of fossil fuels for sustainably generated sources and the reduction in the use of harmful materials in construction which are cited as approaches that provide economic and social well-being but not at the same level of environmental costs, as in other areas.

Green growth has been associated with the political philosophy of neoliberalism, where market-based approaches are prioritized, individual responsibility is highlighted, and the role of the state, including the local community, is minimized. This approach has an economic focus on free-market capitalism, which has the stated goal of maximizing shareholder value. The state's role is to protect free-market exchange, and social issues are only meaningful when they affect market exchange. Ecological modernization is a related view where advocates believe that the existing market/state governance systems can deliver green growth. At the national and international level, integrated assessment models attempt a systems-based approach of modeling multiple uncertain scenarios to represent possible futures based on different types of environmental action or inaction. Financial instruments are then used to assign value to environmental resources and climate impacts, which provide the rationale to adopt new processes, practices, and technologies facilitated by appropriate state institutions. Ecological modernization seeks to these values (protect the environment) into a form of competitive advantage for organizations.

The idea of green growth has been challenged while some countries have shown that relative decoupling (improved economic growth rates, but at a lower rate of material energy usage), absolute decoupling is not possible for most countries (Vaden et al., 2021). Green growth approaches have been criticized as overly reliant on assumptions that direct institutions toward technological solutions and financial instruments such as taxes. From a responsibility perspective, they tend to ignore complex, socio-political systems-level uncertainties arising from the number and configuration of participants. A related issue beyond the content of models is the researchers themselves, where research is primarily performed by groups from western countries, ignoring the global south. This is a particular oversight since the countries most likely to be impacted by climate change are less responsible for carbon emissions.

Further, carbon decoupling may not occur as carbon-intensive activities have been shifted to other countries, and the outputs are then imported into the global north from the global south. Another challenge that needs to be considered is when the coupling is expected to occur. As some theorists argue, some aspects of current activity need to be scaled back so that they will disrupt social well-being.

They preserve existing socio-industrial political systems and the specter of future technologies such as carbon capture or legal frameworks such as carbon trading lock-in symbolic signaling (Røttereng, 2018) over actual implementation. The latter issue is complex as establishing a technology such as carbon capture and storage (CCU) intended to remove emissions at the source will require creating a supply chain at the local and international levels. This chain will need an institutional framework that develops technology, manages risk, and incentives support from local communities where this infrastructure will be located. Few countries have developed the framework required for the large-scale deployment of these technologies to date. Of critical importance is obtaining public consensus for CCU projects since the infrastructure required (pipelines) is significantly disruptive to communities and raises safety concerns. The policy discussions over mitigation vs. adaptation in a green growth perspective are more pertinent to project management. Specifically, which stakeholder is responsible for taking action, the need for transformative change, the capacity to be accomplished, who pays, how to pay, and who benefits from these actions (McKie, 2019). The following case study illustrates PM from a green growth perspective.

18.5.2 Project Overview (Activities and Timeline)

HS2 is a new high-speed rail megaproject designed to reduce motor vehicle usage and increase coverage and capacity to 30 million people in the UK. As part of this project, a new interchange station will be built in Solihull, the first railway station to be awarded BREEAM "outstanding" certification. The station aims to be an environmentally friendly, net-zero operational station. Four platforms will be built at the station and two central high-speed through lines capable of carrying up to 2,100 passengers per hour in each direction. The scope also incorporates cycle storage for 176 bicycles with additional room for expansion. An automated people moving system will connect Solihull station with Birmingham Airport and be built as part of the station. The station is designed to have a 120-year lifespan requiring the planners to incorporate the potential impact of social and environmental changes as part of the design. The timeline for the project is as follows:
- 2017: Royal assent granted for the project
- 2018: Meet the team consultation events with the community
- 2018: Public events to share scheme design
- 2019: Public events presubmission
- 2019: Formal approval sought for project design
- 2019: Initial construction
- 2026: Project completion
- 2146: Station end of life and possible decommissioning

18.5.3 Natural Capital

The design seeks to minimize nonrenewable resource usage by using life cycle assessment reporting to minimize embodied carbon in materials. For example, the use of timber provided a carbon saving of 400 tons versus steel. The delivery process will also incorporate elements off-site and modularization to minimize material wastage, reducing embodied carbon. Natural capital will also be preserved in operation via renewable energy sources for electricity and natural lighting where available. The design also minimizes water use in operation via the capture and reuse of rainwater. Beyond conservation, the project seeks to encourage regeneration by creating natural habitats in the space around the station to improve biodiversity.

18.5.4 Social and Human Capital

The team worked with the client and 12 different local stakeholder organizations to co-create the design. In addition to sustainability, the design was aimed at creating social capital. The design celebrated community identity by embedding the region's historical character in the station's overall design and the surrounding landscape. Governance and assurance were provided via an independent design panel of stakeholders who held regular design review sessions. The team also held 15 events and a survey to obtain feedback on the design from Birmingham and Solihull residents. The team also engaged with the Solihull Metropolitan Borough Council and its Urban Growth Company. To ensure compliance with local regulations, there were meetings with statutory bodies such as Historic England and the Environment Agency and aligning plans with transport authorities, including Network Rail and Transport for West Midlands, the NEC and Birmingham Airport.

18.5.5 Green Growth and the Integration of Value Types

In addition to the impact during construction, the project seeks to catalyze human and social capital development by creating new jobs from commercial space and new homes. This project creates value outcomes for communities and the environment beyond the traditional manufactured capital (station output) and financial capital.

The case describes how a "green growth" perspective can drive project activities, timeline, value, and relationships. At the early stage of the project, stakeholder perspectives were considered and integrated. These perspectives were translated into beneficial outcomes via project design and delivery. The case also highlights the linkages between value types as improving the biodiversity of the local area (natural capital) increases the area's desirability to community residents (social capital).

18.5.6 Degrowth

Degrowth is based on the concept that it is impossible to decouple economic growth, material growth, and carbon emissions (Victor, 2012). As a result, the protection of society from other climate change impacts, therefore, requires a reduction in material usage and energy consumption. The approach embraces the discourse of climate science which has emerged from the interdisciplinary community examining atmospheric and geographic phenomena. Climate science presents interdisciplinary research evidence to support the claim that the planet's recent warming is man-made (Pihl et al., 2021). This community also clearly states that humanity needs to act as the risks to current societies are severe and may be impossible to mitigate if urgent, radical action is taken to reduce carbon and methane emissions.

Degrowth also incorporates a climate justice discourse by focusing on maximizing well-being for all societies while reducing material growth, which requires entirely new production and consumption systems (Dick, 2021). The need to respond to climate change has exposed international and interregional deficiencies which can inhibit climate action. Countries in the global south face disproportionately higher impacts from flooding, storms, droughts, and higher temperatures, contributing to smaller carbon emissions. As a collective, these countries also have a lower level of negotiating power to set international rules, norms, and regulations. For example, none of the global reserve currencies is from the global south. These countries are generally subject to international regulation without a significant say in how these rules are made. The result can reduce the impetus for drastic action since countries with a greater degree of creating the present scenario are less impacted by the outcomes. Given its control over international regulatory schemes, it is less likely to seek drastic action that impacts its citizens (Okereke and Coventry, 2016). Further, even within wealthy countries, lower-income individuals mostly feel harm, and higher-income individuals can secure personal protection against climate-induced disasters such as flooding (De Koning and Filatova, 2020). Some of these individuals may even lobby against climate action if new taxes or levies challenge their wealth to pay for climate protection.

A climate justice perspective requires radical changes to national and international governance to reduce carbon and methane emissions in an equitable manner that does not harm communities requiring economic development. Climate justice explicitly requires increased state action as these advocates believe that enterprises will not self-organize and deliver equitable solutions. In this way, degrowth embraces multiple discourses, including the need for the global south to improve the well-being of its societies.

18.5.7 Growth

Degrowth has always been criticized as antigrowth, which is not politically feasible. An emerging position alongside green growth and degrowth is the idea of "agrowth" or agnosticism about growth (van den Bergh, 2018). In agrowth, organizations and individuals are not pro or anti-growth but critically evaluate the role of growth in societal well-being. In other words, it takes a precautionary approach to identify the possible risks of growth and not treat growth as a primary goal. One of the benefits of agrowth is that it provides an opportunity to search for policies that improve well-being that may not necessarily require growth (Gerber, J.F. and Raina, R.S., 2018). Agrowth also allows for the possibility that while decoupling may not be entirely possible today, it may be possible in the future.

In an agrowth society, periods of high, low, or even negative growth can occur once environmental sustainability is prioritized and societal welfare (Jakob et al., 2020). Agrowth is associated with ecolocalism, which takes a place-based approach to mobilize citizens to implement adaptation and mitigation actions (Ganesh and Zoller, 2014). Ecolocalism explicitly incorporates the idea of the quality of life for residents in specific locations and suggests that since each area has different characteristics and benefits, the solutions suggested by ecomodernization may not be applicable everywhere. Rather than global solutions such as CCS, ecolocalism focuses on local stewardship of nature, residents' health, and self-reliance. In ecolocalism, the geographical and economic definitions vary from previous conceptualizations. For geography, this domain focuses on the community and local natural environment. For economy, the definition incorporates place-specific formal, informal, and non-market actors, including volunteering (Hines, 2013). Ecolocalism also incorporates the five capitals framework (identified in the "Responsible Organising" chapter) and integrates the idea that these capitals are symbiotic and each type depends on the other. While ecolocalism does not reject technology, the emphasis is on smaller scale approaches that minimize material and energy use. Ecolocalization also seeks to address consumption at the local level to shift preferences away from signaling and maximization toward the quality of life. The focus is on needs rather than wants by prioritizing the consumption of local items.

Outside of all of these approaches are perspectives that reject the concept of climate change. Climate contrarians challenge climate science and the need to act (Odenbaugh, 2012). In addition to public opposition, there are intellectual debates over the nature of climate responses. This opposition is rooted in political attacks based on climate skepticism. Direct opposition to the reality of climate challenge or the supporting science has been well documented but is waning in the current societal discourse. Another approach seeks to ensure that others enact their responsibilities before a given country can act so that heavier polluters can pay their fair share and that no country has a financial advantage over the other (Dunlap and McCright, 2011). The cost of climate adaptation and mitigation is a burden that reduces their ability to meet their communities' health, infrastructure, and social needs. There is a specter of job losses for countries involved in mineral extraction, large-scale agriculture, or export-oriented carbon-intensive production (for example, steel). Recently, communities need to adapt to the possibility of societal collapse. Sometimes combined with doomism, this area suggests that the actions taken would not prevent climate catastrophe. These responses have been criticized as removing the agency to address the climate emergency.

18.6 Climate Change Actors

There are many actors involved in addressing climate change, and it would be helpful to classify or present them at a high level for subsequent discussions (Costoya, 2007). Geographical scale: international organizations (e.g., Intergovernmental Commission on Climate Change); national (UK Net Zero Commission); and regional organizations (Zero Carbon Dorset). Organization types: public sector, private sector, nongovernmental organizations, social movements, networks (extinction rebellion), plateaus, and online collective identity. The former three are formally structured enterprises. These latter three are segmented (composed of multiple groups) and polycentric (many different leaders) (Smith and Christie, 2021). Table 18.1 summarizes.

Nongovernmental organizations are defined as formalized, structured initiatives. NGOs have formal legal and financial ties to national and transnational structures. These ties are also required as part of legitimization which proves that these organizations have formal operational capability and transparency via formal accountability mechanisms such as elections, a board of directors, monitoring, standards and codes of conduct, certifications, ratings, and reporting (Bendell and Unies, 2006). They may be granted the right to engage with multinational organizations as a critical stakeholder and influence rules and frameworks.

Social movements may share the beneficial intent of NGOs but have entirely different structural characteristics. They do not have formal relationships and use shared experiences, emotive language and symbols to attract support. Unlike NGOs that develop partnerships, social movements stress direct action or mobilization to resolve their perceived problems. Also, unlike NGOs, social movements may fragment without formal structures due to lack of formal structures. Membership in social movements is not formal and is based on emotional, social, and identity relationships. Resource exchange in movements is noneconomic, and these initiatives share or exchange without financial mechanisms. Social movements also do not seek to legitimize public or private entities and may attract support by positioning themselves in opposition to these enterprises. Governance is done by assemblies or other forms of participatory accountability.

Networks are internet-enabled collectives of NGOs who combine their efforts to resolve the inherent constraints of operating within institutional frameworks. By linking NGOs into an extended entity, they provide flexibility and resource sharing to achieve a more significant, shared goal via direct actions. The combination of NGOs establishes a collective identity that provides the space to apply pluralistic, multiperspective approaches to resolve societal challenges.

Table 18.1: Categories of climate change actors.

Category	Structural characteristics	Formulation of the Problem	Modus operandi	Tensions	Conception of society	Examples
Public	Institutionalized and rationalized organization	Specialized, technical discourse	Monitoring, campaigns, lobbying and project development	Inter- and intragovernment policy requirements	State support of citizen's activities	UK Committee on Climate Change
Private	Institutionalized and rationalized organization	Specialized, technical, discourse	Monitoring, campaigns, lobbying and project development	Market returns vs. societal value	The market facilitates consumption and production activities	Allianz Group (Climate change insurance products)
NGO	Institutionalized and rationalized organization	Specialized, technical, discourse	Monitoring, campaigns, lobbying and project development	Alignment with state/ market system	Third sector	Practical Action
Social Movement	Pre institutional and amorphous social relations	The emotional and symbolic discourse	Direct action	Fragmentation of movement	Third sector	https://www. leave-it-in-the-ground.org/
Network	Flexible and decentralized systems of organizations	Technical discourse	Campaigns and lobbying	Network goals are misaligned with individual participants.	Third sector	Green alliance of the UK
Plateau	Global social movement actors	Combination of The technical and symbolic discourse	Group framing of common problems	Plateau goals are misaligned with individual participants and network goals.	International/Global society	Extinction Rebellion

(continued)

Table 18.1 (continued)

Category	Structural characteristics	Formulation of the Problem	Modus operandi	Tensions	Conception of society	Examples
Online Collective Identity	No geography	The emotional and online symbolic discourse	Online Campaigns, platform construction and organizing capability development	Fragmentation, subidentity formation, counter identity formation	International/ Global society and individual identity subgroupings	Fridays for Future

Plateaus apply the internet approach to facilitate action at multiple levels and develop exchange and governance systems. Plateaus can originate from the intense networking among participants at protest events. Social relationships may be reconfigured, and the rapid, temporally bounded exchange provides the opportunities to generate the reconfiguration of networks and the creation of new, informational network ties which facilitate subsequent knowledge exchange. Plateaus also create new spaces for interaction and create new networks, interpretative schemes, and resource exchange (Chesters and Welsh, 2005).

Collective identities have been formed in virtual spaces, driving mobilizing around issues more recently. Unlike networks and movements, these identities do not have fixed ideologies and are built on an emotional connection to a virtual community (Nasrin and Fisher, 2021). Ubiquitous online connections have facilitated the growth of these identities by validating the views of individuals and allowing for a wide range of participation types. A common form of signaling these identities is hashtags, which can create decentralized information-sharing spaces on online platforms (Abul-Fottouh and Fetner, 2018). They facilitate the creation of communities that can drive subsequent activism, including online signaling of support or opposition and offline mobilization. These online identities may enter into internal conflicts about representation and competition with offline movements.

18.6.1 Individual Perspective

The individual perspective seeks to examine the values and resources of citizens. The values speak to environmental consciousness, a given individual experience, knowledge and the capability to engage in activities and activism. Personal worldviews can also change due to changing personal circumstances, such as the experience of a climate event as closer threats are perceived as more relevant, which will change a given's uncertainty evaluation approach. This improved understanding may drive subsequent effects, including emotional responses, increased information search, and reflection on self-efficacy regarding these risks (Yang et al., 2014).

These changes do not go unopposed, and scholars from the humanities have attempted to identify the political and behavioral ideals embedded in current energy usage patterns (Jones, 2019). Since existing social and economic systems are built around the characteristics of fossil fuel energy, the transition requires citizens in countries to change their conceptualization of energy. This has far-reaching consequences for lifestyles beyond comfort to affect entertainment, well-being, and education.

These domains can include:

- Affect and values: Responsible attitudes toward carbon and material consumption. Values are reflected in a moral orientation that encourages active participation in environmental protection.
- Ecological systems knowledge: Understanding of the interdependence of natural and social systems
- Environmentally responsible behaviors: Perception of creating positive change and adopting environmentally responsible personal and professional activities.

18.7 Responsible PM and Climate Change

Climate change presents several tensions for project management responsibility. At the highest level, the philosophical perspective adopted by national and international bodies may place a more significant or lower emphasis on economic development. In this macro domain, tensions may exist among growth/degrowth/agrowth perspectives. This may result in country-level preferences for technological development (growth) instead of social development (degrowth), influencing the delivery of certain types of projects, say built environment by region. At the meso level, the actors involved may advocate for varying philosophies and influence individual values. Formally recognized enterprises and movements may lobby formally for their perspectives, while virtual identities may prefer disruptive forms of activism. Finally, the beliefs and perceptions may shape the extent of personal and group action at the individual level.

As climate change and its impacts have become an increasingly urgent public priority, a national and international societal consensus is required to achieve policies that are perceived as equitable and will not be reversed by successive political administrations (Winkler et al., 2018). The profession of project management is still defining its role and function in responding to climate change. It is important to note that society has transitioned from other energy types before beginning with biomass to coal to petrochemicals, and the current mix incorporates renewables.

One of the barriers to this transition, as in previous occasions, lies in the path of dependency built in the current society regarding the central rule of fossil fuels. Beyond industrial production of goods and services, the current energy configuration provides infrastructure for leisure, life, and livelihood. While project management has presented initial research, it is generally confined to green growth perspectives. For example, research on construction projects has identified that the alignment of innovations such as Digital Twins, new materials, off-site manufacturing, and analytics can significantly reduce waste and hence the carbon footprint of projects. This approach, however, may constrain development to options that sustain the existing material and carbon consumption patterns while simultaneously marginalizing other

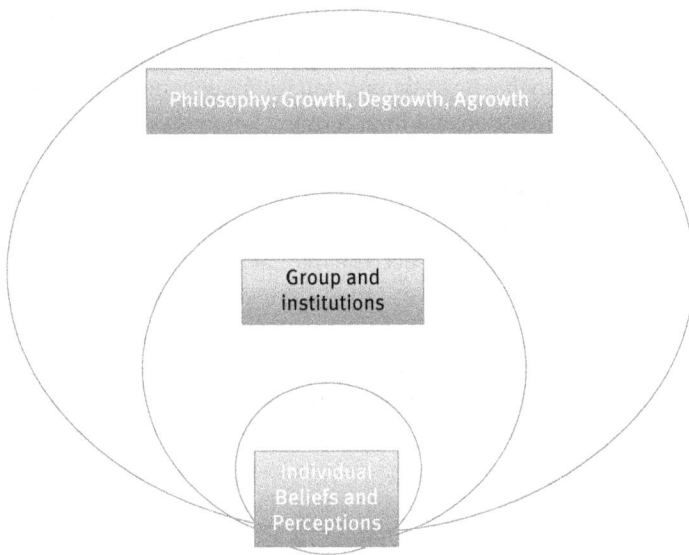

Figure 18.1: Levels of tension for responsible climate change (authors).

approaches to addressing the needs that require project delivery (Levidow and Raman, 2020).

Our current approaches to energy transitions are undermined by framing a revolution as an evolution. Both proponents and detractors see the promises as hollow because it is instinctively understood that society from society and energy transitions will require significant changes in culture, society, and politics (Paterson, 2020). The fissures opened by the climate emergency can destroy the social capital required for coordinated action. At the national and international level, a challenge to societal transformation is the embedded narratives of carbon-based development. These social representations or imaginaries may underpin the reluctance to transform societal systems. They are embedded in work patterns, leisure, and scholarship to the point where they constrain future visions to incremental improvements that mimic carbon-intensive lifestyles with substitute products and offsets where they are not available (Bridge and Gailing, 2020).

Little research has been allocated to identifying how we will build the necessary political coalitions that combine business citizens of communities and international governments to meet the grand challenge of climate change-related issues. Climate change is inherently into discipline and has interconnected impacts. Researchers tend to work within disciplinary boundaries. There is, therefore, an opportunity for project management as a discipline to integrate disparate stakeholders to provide a framework by which actors can address challenges.

These changes suggest a change in activities and how projects are perceived for projects. As discussed in responsible organizing, projects have an activity, relationship, and temporal domain. A related perspective is that project management supports the realization of socio-technical imaginaries, defined as the collectively held view of future social and economic life attainable by designing and fulfilling nation-specific scientific and technological projects (Jasanoff and Kim, 2009).

A less examined domain explores how Projects can act as a space to align disparate stakeholders. This can happen directly in projects or as test cases/living labs for other technologies. Projects can provide examples that support the development of legitimacy in communities. They can also act as experimental spaces where new approaches can be attempted by businesses or other stakeholders, which can then be adopted or scaled elsewhere.

Project management may have a role to play in building this consensus. There is a need to bridge the macro and the micro to respond to the overwhelming challenge of climate change. While project management has a role in delivering socio-technical imaginaries, project management plays a role in conceptualizing features to ensure that communities that might be marginalized are embedded as part of formal processes.

References

Abul-Fottouh, D., & Fetner, T. (2018). Solidarity or schism: Ideological congruence and the Twitter networks of Egyptian activists. *Mobilisation: An International Quarterly, 23*(1), 23–44.

Bendell, J., & Unies, N. (2006). *Debating NGO accountability*. NGLS.

Bickerstaff, K., & Walker, G. (2002). Risk, responsibility, and blame: An analysis of vocabularies of motive in air-pollution(ing) discourses. *Environment and Planning A, 34*(12), 2175–2192. https://doi.org/10.1068/a3521

Bridge, G., & Gailing, L. (2020). New energy spaces: Towards a geographical political economy of energy transition. *Environment and Planning A: Economy and Space, 52*(6), 1037–1050.

Bohr, J. (2016). The 'climatism' cartel: Why climate change deniers oppose market-based mitigation policy. *Environmental Politics, 25*(5), 812–830. https://doi.org/10.1080/09644016.2016.1156106

Chesters, G. & Welsh, I. (2005). Complexity and social movement (s) process and emergence in planetary action systems. *Theory, Culture & Society, 22*(5), 187–211.

Costoya, M. M. (2007). *Toward a typology of civil society actors: The case of the movement to change international trade rules and barriers*. Geneva: United Nations Research Institute for Social Development.

De Koning, K., & Filatova, T. (2020). Repetitive floods intensify outmigration and climate gentrification in coastal cities. *Environmental Research Letters, 15*(3), 034008.

Dick M. Global recovery requires degrowth, not ever increasing GDP BMJ 2021; 375 :n2657 doi:10.1136/bmj.n2657

Dunlap, R. E., & McCright, A. M. (2011). Organised climate change denial. *The Oxford Handbook of Climate Change and Society, 1*, 144–160.

Ganesh, S., & Zoller, H. (2014). Organising transition: Principles and tensions in eco-localism. In *The routledge companion to alternative organisation* (pp. 260–274). Routledge.

Gerber, J. F., & Raina, R. S. (2018). Post-growth in the global south? Some reflections from India and Bhutan. *Ecological Economics, 150*, 353–358.

Hayhoe, K., Wuebbles, D. J., Easterling, D. R., Fahey, D. W., Doherty, S., Kossin, J. P., . . .
  Wehner, M. F. (2018). Our Changing Climate. Impacts, Risks, and Adaptation in the United
  States: The Fourth National Climate Assessment, Volume II.
Hickel, J., & Kallis, G. (2020). Is green growth possible?. *New Political Economy*, *25*(4), 469–486.
Hines, C. (2013). *Localisation: A global manifesto*. Routledge.
Hobbie, S. E., & Grimm, N. B. (2020). Nature-based approaches to managing climate change
  impacts in cities. *Philosophical Transactions of the Royal Society B*, *375*(1794), 20190124.
Ika, L. A., Söderlund, J., Munro, L. T., & Landoni, P. (2020). Cross-learning between project
  management and international development: Analysis and research agenda. *International
  Journal of Project Management*, *38*(8), 548–558.
IPCC, 2014: Climate Change 2014: Impacts, Adaptation, and Vulnerability. Part A: Global and
  Sectoral Aspects. Contribution of Working Group II to the Fifth Assessment Report of the
  Intergovernmental Panel on Climate Change [Field, C.B., V.R. Barros, D.J. Dokken, K.J. Mach,
  M.D. Mastrandrea, T.E. Bilir, M. Chatterjee, K.L. Ebi, Y.O. Estrada, R.C. Genova, B. Girma, E.S.
  Kissel, A.N. Levy, S. MacCracken, P.R. Mastrandrea, and L.L.White (eds.)]. Cambridge
  University Press, Cambridge, United Kingdom and New York, NY, USA, 1132 pp.
Jacques, P. J., & Knox, C. C. (2016). Hurricanes and hegemony: A qualitative analysis of micro-level
  climate change denial discourses. *Environmental Politics*, *25*(5), 831–852. https://doi.org/10.
  1080/09644016.2016.1189233
Jakob, M., Lamb, W. F., Steckel, J. C., Flachsland, C., & Edenhofer, O. (2020). Understanding
  different perspectives on economic growth and climate policy. *Wiley Interdisciplinary Reviews:
  Climate Change*, *11*(6), e677.
Jasanoff, S., & Kim, S.-H. (2009). Containing the Atom: Sociotechnical Imaginaries and Nuclear
  Power in the United States and South Korea. Minerva, *47*(2), 119–146. http://www.jstor.org/
  stable/41821489
Jaworska, S. (2018). Change but no climate change: Discourses of climate change in corporate
  social responsibility reporting in the oil industry. *International Journal of Business
  Communication*, *55*(2), 194–219.
Jones, J. L. (2019). Beyond oil: The emergence of the energy humanities. *Resilience: A Journal of the
  Environmental Humanities*, *6*(2), 155–163.
Kim, Gowoon., Vaswani, Rahul., Kang, Wanmo., Nam, Miri & Lee, Dowon. (2017). Enhancing
  Ecoliteracy through Traditional Ecological Knowledge in Proverbs. Sustainability. 9. 1182.
  10.3390/su9071182.
Levidow, L., & Raman, S. (2020). Socio-technical imaginaries of low-carbon waste-energy futures:
  UK techno-market fixes displacing public accountability. *Social Studies of Science*, *50*(4),
  609–641.
McKie, R. E. (2019). Climate change counter movement neutralization techniques: A typology to
  examine the climate change counter movement. *Sociological Inquiry*, *89*(2), 288–316.
  https://doi.org/10.1111/soin.12246
Morris, P. W. (2013). *Reconstructing project management*. John Wiley & Sons.
Morris, P. W. (2017). *Climate change and what the project management profession should be doing
  about it: A UK perspective*. Association for Project Management.
Moser, S. C. (2009). Costly knowledge–unaffordable denial: The politics of public understanding
  and engagement on climate change. *The Politics of Climate Change: A Survey*, *1*, 293–302.
Nasrin, S., & Fisher, D. R. (2021). Understanding collective identity in virtual spaces: A study of the
  youth climate movement. *American Behavioral Scientist*, 00027642211056257.
Noble, I., Huq, S., Anokhin, Y., Carmin, J., Goudou, D., Lansigan, F., . . . Villamizar, A. (2014).
  Adaptation needs and options (Chapter 14). In Field, C., Barros, V. R., Mastrandrea, M. D.,
  et al. (Eds.), *Climate change 2014: Impacts, adaptation and vulnerability. Contribution of*

working group II to the fifth assessment report of the intergovernmental panel on climate change. Cambridge: Cambridge University Press, 2014. 10.1017/CBO9781107415379.019.

Odenbaugh, J. (2012). 'Consensus, Climate, and Contrarians.' In The Environmental: Philosphy, Science, and Ethics, edited by W.P. Kabasenche, M. O'Rourke, adn M.H. Slater, 137–150. Boston: MIT Press.

Okereke, C., & Coventry, P. (2016). Climate justice and the international regime: Before, during, and after Paris. *Wiley Interdisciplinary Reviews: Climate Change*, *7*(6), 834–851.

Palm, R., Lewis, G. B., & Feng, B. (2017). What causes people to change their opinion about climate change?. *Annals of the American Association of Geographers*, *107*(4), 883–896.

Paterson, M. (2020). Climate change and international political economy: Between collapse and transformation. *Review of International Political Economy*, *28*(2), 394–405.

Pihl, E., Alfredsson, E., Bengtsson, M., Bowen, K. J., Broto, V. C., Chou, K. T., Cleugh, H., Ebi, K., Edwards, C. M., Fisher, E., & Friedlingstein, P. (2021). Ten new insights in climate science 2020–a horizon scan. *Global Sustainability*, *4*. https://doi.org/10.1017/sus.2021.2

Rao, A., Sandler, J., Kelleher, D., & Miller, C. (2015). *Gender at work: Theory and practice for 21st-century organisations*. Routledge.

Røttereng, J.-K.S. The comparative politics of climate change mitigation measures: who promotes carbon sinks and why? Global Environ. Polit., 18 (1), 52–75.

Simmons, D. (1995). *The NAAEE standards project: Papers on the development of environmental education standards*. North American Association for Environmental Education, PO Box 400, Troy, OH 45373.

Sitas, N., Selomane, O., Hamann, M., & Gajjar, S. P. S. (2021). Towards equitable urban resilience in the Global South within a context of planning and management. In *Urban ecology in the Global South* (pp. 325–345). Cham: Springer.

Smith, S. R., & Christie, I. (2021). Knowledge integration in the politics and policy of rapid transitions to net zero carbon: A typology and mapping method for climate actors in the UK. *Sustainability*, *13*(2), 662.

Spinoni, J., Barbosa, P., Füssel, H. M., McCormick, N., Vogt, J. V., & Dosio, A. (2021). Global population-weighted degree-day projections for a combination of climate and socio-economic scenarios. *International Journal of Climatology*, *41*(11), 5447–5464.

Tarabusi, E. C., & Guarini, G. (2018). An axiomatic approach to decoupling indicators for green growth. *Ecological Indicators*, *84*, 515–524.

Vaden, T., Lähde, V., Majava, A., Järvensivu, P., Toivanen, T., & Eronen, J. T. (2021). Raising the bar: On the type, size and timeline of a 'successful' decoupling. *Environmental Politics*, *30*(3), 462–476.

van den Bergh, J. (2018). Agrowth instead of anti-and pro-growth: Less polarisation, more support for sustainability/climate policies. *Journal of Population and Sustainability*, *3*(1), 53–73.

Victor, P. A. (2012). Growth, degrowth and climate change: A scenario analysis. *Ecological Economics*, *84*, 206–212.

Wilber, K. (1997). An integral theory of consciousness. *Journal of Consciousness Studies*, *4*(1), 71–92.

Winkler, H., Höhne, N., Cunliffe, G., Kuramochi, T., April, A., & de Villafranca Casas, M. J. (2018). Countries start to explain how their climate contributions are fair: More rigour needed. *International Environmental Agreements: Politics, Law and Economics*, *18*(1), 99–115.

Yang, Z. J., Rickard, L. N., Harrison, T. M., & Seo, M. (2014). Applying the risk information seeking and processing model to examine support for climate change mitigation policy. *Science Communication*, *36*(3), 296–324.

Section 4: **Responsible Research and Education**

Projects are epistemologically challenging domains as they are uncertain with ambiguous spatial and temporal boundaries. As an emerging profession, project management is still in the process of defining its academic domain. There are increasing calls for diversity of knowledge created by project management researchers from academia and industry. This is complemented by a need to develop new researchers and practitioners which goes beyond the creation of knowledge to examine the learning processes in the classroom and beyond. Both of these needs are brought together in the emerging requirements to generate responsible research which seeks to maximize the societal value created from research in an inclusive and ethical manner (Fitjar et al., 2019).

The opening contribution by Dr. Vahlidi directly addresses the issue of conducting research in a responsible manner. Her chapter examines the nature of knowledge production along with the ethical challenges that can emerge in the project management domain. By focusing on the overlooked area of research questions, the chapter identifies how knowledge creation by project management research can be guided toward beneficial impacts. Dr. Thompson's contribution discusses the need to PM learning to embed values, not just skills. Her chapter identifies the tension between stakeholder and shareholder perspectives of responsibility. The former indicates the need to enhance the social and environmental settings in which our projects are embedded. The latter requires PMs to deliver items on time and within financial constraints. The chapter outlines the requirement to develop mindsets in learners that facilitate the optimization of value for a wider range of stakeholders. The responsibility of PM educators is further explored in the work by Ferdinand, Daly, and Williams. While PM education is aimed at delivering technical and management knowledge, existing approaches may reinforce negative impacts from projects. Further, little attention is paid to learning that takes place outside of formalized settings including the workplace. This chapter reviews the content and delivery approaches that can be used to support the development of responsible project managers in academia and practice.

Reference

Fitjar, R. D., Benneworth, P., & Asheim, B. T. (2019). Towards regional responsible research and innovation? Integrating RRI and RIS3 in European innovation policy. *Science and Public Policy,* *46*(5), 772–783.

https://doi.org/10.1515/9783110724783-023

Ramesh Vahidi

19 Ethical Research Questions in Responsible Project Management

Context: This chapter presents an overview of the responsibilities for project management researchers for ethical research design.

Characters/entities/locations: The chapter focuses on researchers in academia and industry.

Research gaps: The chapter identifies the lack of attention to the crucial impacts of responsibly formulated research questions in responsible conduct of project management research as a multidisciplinary field, in academic and non-academic research settings and education. It also identifies the changing focus of project management research from mathematical modeling to a broader range of contributions.

Challenges/conflict/tensions: The chapter identifies tensions among the requirements for responsible research, impact, and research relevance.

Keywords: ethics, research questions, research relevance

19.1 What Are "Research Questions?"

"Research questions" (RQs) are commonly known for their pivotal role in directing the researcher's efforts throughout research (Miles et al., 2014). They help set the foundations for defining the aim, objectives, and scope, and guide the literature review (Punch, 2006).

The quality of research is closely linked to having well-defined RQs (Huemann and Martinsuo, 2020). They force the researcher to "consider that most basic issues" (Bryman, 2012, p. 10). RQs comprise 21% of the examiners' questions in PhD viva voce (Trafford and Lesham, 2008).

Bryman defines a research question (RQ) as "a question that provides an explicit statement of what it is the researcher wants to know about" – "what is it about your area of interest that you want to know?" (Bryman, 2012, pp. 9, 10). An RQ signifies the "facets of inquiry" (Miles et al., 2014) and helps to structure and organize research by "showing its purpose" (Punch, 2006). Creswell (2014) refers to RQs as means of narrowing down the "purpose statement" of research.

In daily conversations, we loosely use the terms question, problem, or issue interchangeably to refer to an interrogation or asking for information when facing uncertainties or unknowns (Merriam Webster, n.d.). The terms research questions and research problems (RPs) are also used interchangeably in some literature (Punch,

https://doi.org/10.1515/9783110724783-024

2006). While others focus on either phrase as the main facet or starting point of research, and some draw a very sharp line between their concepts, Punch (2006) raises a different argument.

He relates the use of the phrases to the nature of the exploration in research, i.e., whether and how far it is (could be) *preplanned* (e.g., focusing on a clearly defined problem to find an intervention) or requires an *unfolding* process (e.g., exploring an unexplored area) as it proceeds (Punch, 2006). Their distinctions could be more clearly seen in qualitative and quantitative research, as illustrated in Figure 19.1 (Punch, 2006, p. 37).

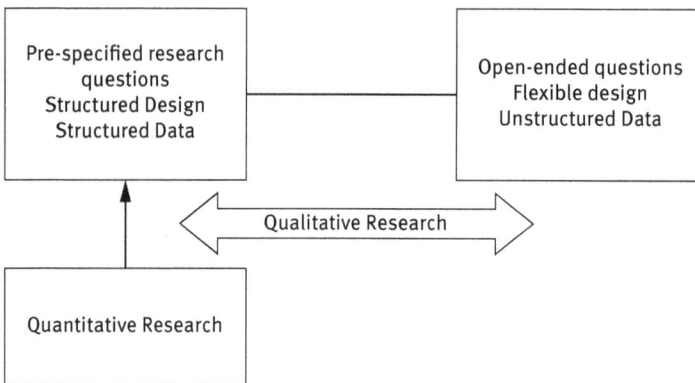

Figure 19.1: Research questions and research types (adapted from Punch (2006)).

Which category of research we belong to is where it fits in the continuum rather than which end of the spectrum. The researchers' awareness of the positioning of their research is essential. It directly affects their proposal, the contract (if there is one), and the clear communication of what the funders and other stakeholders could expect from the research scope, outcome, limitations, resources, and required efforts.

This chapter targets research in general (qualitative, quantitative, and mixed methods), and it considers interchangeable use of the RQs or RPs, assuming that ethical issues could relate to both. It also uses RQs as a general term to refer to the *research queries*, either in *research questions* or *hypotheses* or their combination, as in mixed-methods research; with the similar assumption that responsible research and ethical implications could be related to any research, regardless of its strategy, approach, or methods.

19.1.1 Types of "Research Questions"

Creswell (2014) classifies RQs as *qualitative, quantitative, or hypothesis*, depending on the nature of the research. He breaks down qualitative questions into *"central questions*" or "*associated subquestions*". Central questions should be broad enough (as broad as they could within the research scope) to avoid limiting the "views of the participants" (Creswell, 2014, p. 139). According to the author, formulating such questions would be one of the challenges of quantitative researchers who enter a qualitative query as the quantitative RQs narrow down the query to a few particular variables. He argues that, in contrast, qualitative researchers seek "the general, complex, set of factors surrounding the central phenomenon and present the broad, varied perspectives or meanings that the participants hold" (Creswell, 2014, p. 140).

Quantitative questions, on the other hand, enquire about the "relationships among the variables," while the hypotheses are "predictions the researcher makes about the expected outcomes of relationships among variables" (Creswell, 2014, p. 143) within a quantitative or mixed study.

Miles et al. (2014) classify RQs as *general* vs. *particular and descriptive* vs. *exploratory*.

Punch (2014) also refers to *general* and *specific* research questions based on their level of abstraction. General questions aim at directing the research at the highest level of abstraction (so it could not be answered straight away). Specific questions link the general RQs to data collection and are more specific and answerable. Distinguishing and identifying these types of questions seem to be one of the main challenges of a novice researcher (Punch, 2014).

19.1.2 Where/When of Defining "Research Questions"

Responsibility and ethics in research are broad areas, covering all elements of research, including RQs. Exploring the RQs' positions and how and how far they could affect research could narrow these discussions down to the responsibility and ethics concerning RQs, the main aims of the chapter.

Punch's (2014) simplified illustrations of the research process, position RQs at the junction between pre-empirical and empirical stages. It should be noted that the author clarifies that the RQs could be updated and amended at any point, especially in the case of non-preplanned research, as the researcher learns through a process of learning and discovery and should be open to adjustments accordingly (Punch, 2014). The simplified figures do not demonstrate the feedback loop and the required adjustments in the research practice.

Bryman (2012, p. 11) perceives RQs as *crucial* in guiding the literature review, methodology design, data collection (what and from whom), data analysis and writing-up, and keeping the researcher on track, focused on purpose and right to the point. However, he puts the RQs in a more strategic position right at the beginning of the research (Figure 19.2). The RQs could be selected among a broader set of potential RQ questions, narrowing it down to the researcher's interest (Bryman, 2012).

RQs, according to Miles et al. (2014, p. 25), "may precede, follow, or happen concurrently with the development of a conceptual framework" or at the beginning or later on (Figure 19.2).

Regardless of where and when the researcher formulates the RQs, it is commonly agreed that the questions might be updated by adjusting, narrowing down, or improving as the researcher unfolds the new areas (Bryman, 2012; Miles et al., 2014; Punch, 2014). These reflect the researcher's learning and/or unlearning due to the exploration.

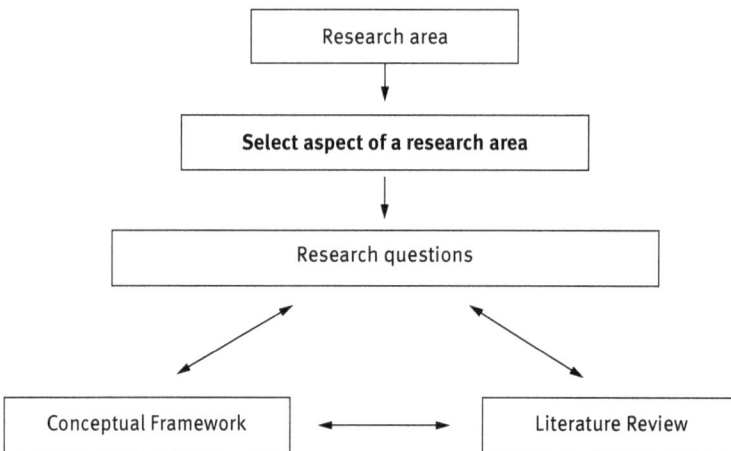

Figure 19.2: Relationships of research questions to a conceptual framework (adapted from Bryman (2012) and Miles et al. (2014)).

Looking at research as a project, RQs could play various roles in the conceptualization and definition of a project, which will affect the subsequent phases of the project. They could set the research aim, objectives, scope, and review of certain literature. RQs derived from the literature will directly determine the research design, scope, and required empirical study type.

Overall, these demonstrate the impact of a responsibly formulated RQ and its potential ethical implications if formulated otherwise.

19.2 Ethical Research and Its Questions

Attention to "ethics" in research has significantly grown in recent years/decades (Bryman, 2012). While it is widely stated that both qualitative and quantitative research could have ethical implications, it generally seems that qualitative research is perceived to be more prone to ethical complications (e.g., see Iphofen and Tolich,

2018). Bryman (2012) links this to the growth in qual research and an intention to avoid scandalous research, following a few such instances in the mid-1900s.

Reviewing various sources, such arguments typically refer to qualitative data collection, particularly involving human participants and their analysis. So, the literature's dominant thinking of identifying, compliance, and preventing ethical issues focuses on conducting a *designed* and *planned* work. In PM terms, assessing and predicting potential ethical issues of *implementation* (empirical study) and *termination* (writing up and reporting). Their focus has mainly been on the most *tangible*, *known*, and *measurable* ethical issues in the design of the empirical study and data collection. What is being rarely discussed (in-depth) is how the RQs *conceptually* and *implicitly* could impact the whole direction of research and the ethical conduct of its empirical study. It has even been less noted in conceptual research that eventually becomes fundamental to other types of research.

Focusing on RQs in conceptualizing, setting the research fundamentals and designing research, this chapter argues the *commonly perceived* significant differences between the ethical risks of qual and quantitative research. As discussed in the rest of the chapter, various causes could lead to ethical issues even before the actual data collection. For example, the hypothesis might not have been drawn responsibly. Hence, even if the data collection and analysis complied with the ethical rules and regulations, they might have been fundamentally misleading, fraudulent, and insufficient.

To prevent and identify potential ethical issues, more and more organizations see research as *the* critical element of their businesses to define ethics policies, regulations, codes of conduct, or principles. Compatibility with these would usually be checked by a relevant committee (or groups, teams, or the like) who reviews the initial proposals (Korenman, n.d.).

Research proposals are typically expected to identify the areas of the research plan with potential ethical implications (e.g., data collection and storage or reporting the findings) and their relevant risks (e.g., breach of anonymity, unauthorized access to the collected data, causing discomfort for the participants and data leakage). The proposals are also expected to clarify the impact of such risks and the researchers' elimination or mitigation plans (e.g., not having vulnerable participants, using consent forms, and storing data in a secure place), among other potential details.

Assuming an ethics approval would guarantee zero ethical challenges during the actual research is far from the reality. Research, as a project, faces uncertainties, ambiguity, and complex situations unknown to the researcher at the outset. In an ideal world, the research in the process will be reviewed and audited throughout and/or in regular intervals further to the initial ethics approval. However, unless the research is exceptionally sensitive and/or resources are available, monitoring and auditing do not regularly occur during the research process unless necessary. Inevitably, they remain the continuous *responsibility* of the researchers.

Identifying the specific ethical implications of RQs (especially those in the PM context that will be discussed later) is difficult for non-experts to set comprehensive and all-inclusive ethics regulations related to such aspects or predict potential scenarios. This again highlights the significance of responsibility-taking as an inherent characteristic and earned competency of a competent researcher.

Organizations typically follow the codes of conduct or ethics principles extracted from those developed by their professional associations or regulators, with a level of adjustment to their particular requirements. Associations could be national (e.g., British Educational Research Association, 2022) and/or international (e.g., World Health Organization, 2022). They regularly regulate and publish ethics principles or codes of conduct to benefit societies, organizations, researchers, and research participants.

Some organizations provide ethics training for researchers at the start of their careers. Nichols-Casebolt (2012, p. 1) argues that "Promoting the responsible conduct of research needs to be an ongoing process, not a one-time educational activity." So, to ensure their continued compliance, some provide such training regularly or in intervals. However, the author raises a further argument: "It is also clear that knowledge about the responsible conduct of research does not mean that everyone will act responsibly. Understanding regulations, policies, and practices are necessary, but not sufficient, for assuring ethical behavior." (Nichols-Casebolt, 2012, p. 1)

One major shortcoming of codes of conduct, rules and regulations, and their training is their inability to predict all the scenarios a researcher might face. Some of these will become ethical or moral dilemmas. Deciding on such situations requires self-reflection, retrospective reflection and questioning the fundamentals of the query; the fundamentals that might have potentially led to the situation and/or were being led by external factors or pressures. As Clarke et al. (2018) posit, facing moral dilemmas, project professionals (in this case, the researchers) would go through a complex and recurring sense-making process as the situation unfolds.

19.3 Responsible Research as a "Shared Responsibility"

Before delving into *what* it takes to define responsible research questions and *how* this section disputes whether such discussions only should be known by and fall within the remit of academic researchers. This provides the context for deciding whether you would benefit from or need to know about responsible research queries or RQs if you assume yourself as being a PM practitioner or educator, or trainer rather than a "researcher."

Close relationships among the three facets of research, education, and practice (REP) in project management (Figure 19.3) strengthen the foundations of the field. These could ensure the profession's continued relevance, adaptability, and growth. A healthy and sound balance of efforts in each facet could help PM professionals learn from the past, thrive in the present, and equip themselves for the future.

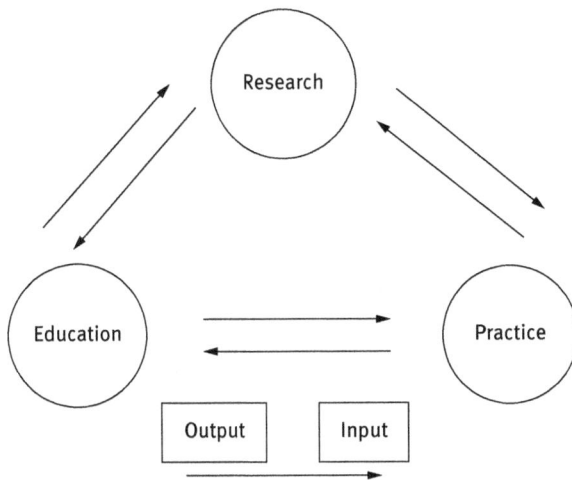

Figure 19.3: Research education and practice (author).

On the one hand, "Research" in this equation tries to systematically understand the past and the current status of the practice; identify its challenges, gaps, and opportunities; and develop (and/or contribute to) resolutions and new ways of thinking and/or working. On the other hand, research informs "education". It acquaints and equips generations of professionals with the invaluable legacies of the discipline and tools for adapting to its future. It could accelerate the passing of the actual knowledge by examining it and, where/as possible, extending it to the broader "practice", outside and beyond a particular industry, situation, or context.

Data, information, and knowledge are circulated among the REP's facets as inputs or outputs, in various forms and for different reasons. Research's pivotal role in this cycle inevitably brings in "responsibilities" and "accountabilities". The cycle of research–education–practice could work effectively and efficiently when each facet *trusts* the inputs from the other two and generates outputs that could be *trusted* by the two; i.e., each facet commits to developing the input with due diligence to ensure its quality, relevance and intention for the *other* facets as much as it does for *itself*. Hence, any broken link among these or deficiency will affect the REP's balance and the other facets' performance and effectiveness.

It is essential to note that the facets, besides their commonalities, have their own particular and distinctive duties, expertise, languages, resources, and methods. They are not supposed to duplicate, replicate, interfere, or monitor others. Reviews in research audits in practice and moderation or quality assurance in education all have to deal with the quality of their results or outputs (i.e., the input to others), but each has its processes. Any deficiency of the inputs/outputs could lead to duplication, rework, and waste of resources within the cycle. The worst-case scenarios (e.g., a researcher's misconduct in collecting data from practice or a practitioner has engineered data fed into research) might result in irreparable relationships and mistrust, causing long-lasting damage to the collaborative spirits.

These are the cases when wrongdoing on each side has become *known, tangible,* and *visible.* For example, there might be a revealed breach of confidentiality during data collection or discovered misinterpretation in the final report during a research project sponsored by industry.

Nonetheless, the *unknown, intangible,* and *invisible* deficiencies could have more profound and fundamental consequences, especially in the long run. The consequences would be proportionate to the significance and scope of the research besides the extent its results are used in or referred to in other areas.

The poor and faulty foundations set by irresponsibly done research could be trusted and used for further field development by other researchers or organizations. Depending on the research scale and sensitivity, these cascading effects could undetectably damage professionalism, stakeholders, the broader societies, and even generations. Examples could be malpractice in research on the design or feasibility of developing a new product/system for public health or fighting climate change or infrastructure facilities.

Histories of different scientific fields show that faulty or fraudulent research would eventually become known by other researchers (e.g., Bryman, 2012; Iphofen and Tolich, 2018). The tangible and intangible nonmonetary and monetary consequences of repairing and rebuilding faulty foundations could be extremely high.

Expectedly, fundamental changes could also face strong resistance from those who had already trusted, invested in and adopted the foundations of their long-established works. Instances could be educators, training organizations or researchers in PM who had set their materials and assumptions based on the old schools of thought (Turner et al., 2010). The scale of such changes for some organizations could easily show the cost of valuable resources wasted. Worse than the costs would be the change in the mindset of those who had put all their faith in such results and adopted them religiously in their education, practice, or research. As PM professionals, we are familiar with the popularity and ease of accepting and implementing change projects!

Hence, the following sections highlight and reinforce the *shared responsibilities* among the REP toward developing and pursuing responsible research queries.

19.4 Nature of the RQs and Their Ethical Impacts

As discussed before, an overall review of the research ethics in classical research methodology sources indicates that their focus has been on the empirical study and afterward. These are when the research design is implemented, e.g., data collection, data storage, analysis, and reporting. In such discussions, the core idea of ethics usually revolves around preserving anonymity and confidentiality and avoiding bias and falsification.

The ethics of data collection pays attention to questions directly used in the "collection of data" (e.g., in interviews or surveys). Such questions are detailed and usually provide enough grounds for an ethics reviewer to predict their ethical implications in advance. There are also sensitivities around selecting the sample and population (e.g., whether the participants are from vulnerable groups or within the acceptable age range or how they would psychologically react to the questions). Data collection questions and sample/population specifications could typically be detailed enough for the ethics reviewers (even from a different discipline) to identify the potential ethical issues or risks (unless the research is too complex, specialized, and/or exceptionally sensitive).

However, predicting their potential ethical risks and issues would be challenging, if always possible, when it comes to research questions. RQs set the overall direction of the research and closely inform the fundamentals of data collection. Unlike data collection questions, they are very general and defined at the very early stages of research. Therefore, similar to projects' conception or definition phases, we are making the most significant decisions (i.e., formulating RQs) with the least information (Gardiner, 2005). Consequently, the nature of the ethical issues related to RQs could differ and have much wider consequences. Nonetheless, these would be hard to note early on due to their subtlety and potential intangible impacts.

A reviewer might also need excellent technical knowledge, besides the contextual and situational knowledge of the field and its research, to understand and predict the ethical risks. They sometimes need to read between the lines of the research proposal, design, or overall plan. In project management, in particular, a good knowledge of the traditional and contemporary PM, besides a deep appreciation of the multidisciplinary and multifaceted nature of the field, could make remarkable differences. For example, what Tuner et al. (2010) refer to as the schools of thought, could be one of the means for a reviewer to judge the relevance, prevalence and validity of a research's overall direction being led by or led to its RQs.

Exploring the potential ethical implications of RQs could highlight the areas in which those involved in research need to be more mindful of lapses or slippages. The areas in which the researchers and their partners need to act (even) more responsibly and have identified the responsible or accountable party in advance. The critical point is prediction and prevention, *as far as possible*.

19.5 Potential Ethical Issues and Responsibilities Related to RQs

No matter where in the research process RQs are formulated, a few primary attributes could generally help with their evaluation and potential for ethical implications. The main attributes related to the general PM research will be discussed: *impact* and *relevance*.

Before discussing these in the context of RQs, the following four key points would be worth considering.

First, these are called attributes in this text for ease of reference and consistency, though other authors might have referred to them differently. *Second,* same as many other concepts in research, they are defined differently by different authors and in various contexts, though they have some core concepts in common. We will focus on such concepts. *Third,* the attributes are not mutually exclusive. They often overlap, e.g., the impact of research might be affected closely by its relevance or bias. To enhance clarity, the attempt here is to cover the core ideas as transparent as possible rather than all the mutual relations among the attributes. *Fourth,* more notably, the attributes are dominantly defined for research as a whole. This implies that research-related literature rarely has focused on how these are or could explicitly and directly be related to RQs, to the best of the author's knowledge. The attempt has been made to keep the discussions within the scope of the chapter (i.e., focus on RQs).

Responsible research makes sense when it is looked at as an isolated entity as much as when it is considered a means besides and in collaboration with education and practice for the PM field to thrive. Accordingly, while the following sections emphasize research and research questions, where appropriate, the discussions address education and practice as the parties who inevitably "share the responsibility."

Hopefully, these will provide a balanced and multiperspective overview of how PM needs to look at the trio (REP) to develop research queries responsibly and ethically. This will also help with providing a more comprehensive and inclusive picture.

Some organizations and individual PM professionals, not known as *research-active institutes* or *academic researchers,* often take on investigative works (e.g., surveys) or publish sources about various topics related to the profession. Examples are whitepapers, results of annual surveys to show the current status of the profession, prediction of the future trends in PM leadership or technologies or examination of the popularity/effectiveness of a particular PM methodology in practice.

These are not necessarily developed academically or referred to as research publications. However, due to the valuable nature of their collected data (and their usually massive participants), many academic research publications use them as trusted input sources. They use such data to support, supplement, or justify their research queries, e.g., Karanja and Malone (2021) use PMI's annual reports (e.g., from 2015 to 2020) and other sources on the growth in the number of PM professionals, etc. The wider PM community (i.e., students, trainers, or educators) has also been using the sources in training and educational settings as teaching and reading materials, sometimes introducing them as research in the academic sense.

Hence, creating such data sources has become more and more popular due to their widespread use and publicity. The increased collaboration has also facilitated this joint efforts and events among the academia and practice (e.g., wider circulation and promotion of the call for participation, promotion of membership and events of organizations by PM academics, some academics supporting the research governance of the nonacademic organizations, etc.).

With the above background on the interrelations between the REP, the following sections provide definitions and elements related to *impact*; *relevance*; *neutrality, impartiality*, or *bias* attributes. Sections discuss how they could be related to (ir) responsible formulation of RQs. These will suggest the areas in a research project and its process that could potentially have the highest risks for ethical implications or complications, hence, the most significant opportunities for avoiding or mitigating the risks.

It should be noted that the text is not exhaustive or *normative* but *descriptive* and *perspectives* (in the sense the terms were defined by Kleindorfer et al., 1993). Arguably, ethical issues could take many forms are, inevitably value-laden, context- and situation-based (Clarke et al., 2018).

Using the specific definitions based on Kleindorfer et al. (1993): is not *normative* as it does (could) not provide fixed checklists and procedures to predict and prevent predefined ethical situations. It is *descriptive* as it explores what and why might have ethical implications evidenced by relevant sources. It is *prescriptive*, as much as it could be, within the scope of this text. This implies that it could enhance, help and provide grounds for informing and training the researchers on acknowledging and avoiding the RQs' ethical implications.

The above clarifications imply that the readers need to reflect on whether, which, when, for who, and how the descriptions might become related to their specific research and the conditions governing it.

19.5.1 Responsible RQs for "Research Impact"

The commitment to Corporate Social Responsibility (CSR) is being more widely discussed nowadays and is gradually becoming mandatory or highly expected from corporations. Along the same lines, "research impact" (RI), as a manifestation of CSR in organizations with research as the cornerstone of their activities, is gradually gaining momentum (see Reed, 2018).

A very general definition of "research impact" refers to research's social and economic benefits (Reed, 2018). UKRI provides a more comprehensive and inclusive definition of RI as "an effect on, change or benefit to the economy, society, culture, public policy or services, health, the environment or quality of life, beyond academia" (UKRI, n.d.).[1]

---

1 https://re.ukri.org/research/ref-impact/

For this section, RI in PM is defined as formulating research questions or queries; their answers positively impact the PM community and the societies that are ultimately supposed to benefit from their projects. This means formulating *RQs* with *their impacts* to direct the research design and its empirical study toward providing long-lasting and beneficial impacts. Otherwise, the research outcomes could have an impact (as any research has!) but perhaps (more) on the researchers' promotion and personal agenda or their organizations' reputation in the academic society (e.g., Glick et al., 2018) or increased chances for financial benefits (future funding), and so on.

Reviewing some of the popular research methodology textbooks reveals that "research impact" does not appear as a standalone topic (e.g., Bryman, 2012; Creswell, 2014; Miles et al., 2014), if discussed at all (even subtly). Of course, they suggest RQs should target filling the gaps through the research, though not necessarily emphasizing the gaps that benefit the wider society or could be considered the *social responsibility* of the researchers and their institutes. Reed (2018) asserts: "But we have been trained to do research, not how to generate impact." Indeed, we have learned more to focus on doing *things right* than doing *the right things*.

Lack of impact in academic research has been heavily debated in various sources, mainly referring to the gap between the research outcome and the industry's actual practices and requirements. The shortage has been criticized by the practitioners and the academic community itself. Glick et al. (2018) argue the research with no or limited impact as a "moral dilemma," as it is sourced by stakeholders that expect a return of investment and positive effects on their relevant societies.

An example of academic research in PM with their impact criticized are the complex numerical models developed for PM by non-PM researchers, dominantly published in non-PM journals. This was well-disputed by Williams (2003), followed by others. These are still popular in non-PM publications, while the leading PM journals have distanced themselves from those approaches (see, Huemann and Martinsuo, 2020; Martinsuo and Huemann, 2020; Müller and Klein, 2018, 2019; Klein and Müller, 2021).

19.5.2 Impact of Academic vs. Nonacademic Research

The open and extensive critical discussions on the lack of impact have mainly focused on *academic* research. Such a heavy focus has overshadowed the same issues (though in different forms) in the publications by nonacademic establishments. As was discussed in the previous section, some works conducted in nonacademic settings are used as inputs to academic research. It seems it is taken for granted that if data is generated in a nonacademic setting, it is fully relevant to the actual practice, as many of them claim, no matter what.

So, the many criticisms of research impact seem to make absolute judgments and universal generalizations as they implicitly assume there are only two types of research. One dominantly lacks impact, and the other (perhaps being impactful) but rarely appreciated or named.

Now the question is, should we put all or most of the research in general and in particular on PM under one dominant category and ignore the studies in the last few decades that have changed our perceptions of projects and had informed (implicitly or explicitly) the PM practices?

Much of this research had been based on a wide range of empirical studies. They have helped shift the narrow focus on the project triangle of time, cost, and quality to many other factors and conditions affecting projects and their management, including stakeholder management and its external environment. They provided the foundations for some of the more recent studies in the areas that informed and/or built on practice and have enabled them to move beyond the delimiting Triangle (especially after the "rethinking project management" since 2005 – see Maylor, 2010; Turner et al., 2010, for more).

So, it could be argued that seeking responsible RQs should be a matter of concern in *any PM research*, i.e., done by academics or nonacademics (potentially used as input to the academics). The responsible outcome of PM research or studies should aim at the type of benefits addressed by the UKRI (n.d.) to ultimately benefit the societies while beneficial to PM REP itself as part of the society.

There seems to be shared consent that ongoing pressures due to competition, limited funds, objective individual and organizational performance measures, and so on in academia have been contributing to low impact but highly ranked research (e.g., Comstock, 2013; Reed, 2018, Iphofen and Tolich, 2018; RRBM, 2020; to name a few). These conditions, exacerbated by other personal and/or organizational motivations, could easily lead to research questions with limited impact. Now, are the situations of narrow or specific purpose RQs only limited to academic research?

It could be argued that other forms of motivation could inform or drive nonacademic research or studies (as described earlier) widely publicized in professional networks. These popular sources could be reports on a specific methodology or technology's popularity or skill set trends in an industry or profession. They are defined, designed, conducted, and reported by the relevant companies or institutes outside of the academic settings (e.g., some published by known consultancies).

Academic reports are normally expected to do comparisons/contrasts to provide a balanced view in the literature review (at least in principle), but this is not necessarily a standard practice in nonacademia. Such reports widely *generalize* their results or findings to the broader PM context, so they seem impactful and could/would be used by the rest of the PM community to inform their training and/or direct their future practices. However, the question would be whether the initial drive was good for the "society" and the "whole profession" (including their competitors) or (understandably/expectedly) for the company's strategies and offered services/products.

If it were for society and the profession, one would expect that such studies reflect on the disadvantages, potential drawbacks, or barriers in the widespread adoption of their designated technology or trend (as much as on their advantages). Another legitimate expectation could be a thorough comparison and contrast with other technologies or trends identified by their competitors (as quite often there are reports on similar subjects but with varying outcomes). Now, the question is how far and how many nonacademic publications would provide such balanced views for the sake of society and go through such scrutiny before being used in practice and even by academics.

Aiming at a broad impact beyond the personal and organizational benefits could often mean swimming against the tide if not supported by or initiated by the organization itself. This applies to academia or industry. The evaluation criteria for the researchers' achievements typically target measurable and tangible outcomes (such as the number of publications in high-rank journals or the growth in sales of a specific tech product or membership). Hence, these services promote fulfilling the requirements and interests of specific stakeholders.

These initially highlight the contextual and organizational factors that provide an environment for RI and support or promote it in principles and practice. On the other hand, we need researchers that could and are willing to swim against that tide by conducting queries that create impact but might not be (at least in the short term) acknowledged or (at least materialistically) rewarded. They should have a powerful sense of responsibility for the profession and the society to drive them to go beyond the norms and the accepted memes of performance criteria.

These lead us to the significant contribution of education, as part of the REP, in increasing impactful research. Educators have the power to develop research capable of raising responsible RQs. Education could develop researchers and practitioners open to asking critical, fundamental questions and having the wider community's interests in mind and heart. Hence, the educational institutes should create environments that *encourage and support* pursuing such research boldly and enthusiastically. Like education providers (higher education institutes), training providers could aim to develop PM professionals who understand the responsibilities in this context should they become involved in studies in their careers.

In summary, promoting research investigating responsible RQs is a collective and interconnected effort among the REP. These are shared responsibilities at many different levels and in many forms. Impact coming only from the academic side but not learned, embraced, and informed by practice will not be compelling enough and potentially will lack enough impact. Also, if the impactful research is not disseminated or does not inform education to promote more impactful *thinking and capacities*, it will only have partial and interim effects.

19.5.3 Responsible RQs for "Research Relevance"

Relevance does not usually appear as a standalone topic in general research methodology literature (e.g., Punch, 2006; Creswell, 2014; Miles et al., 2014), though it has been occasionally addressed as a matter of concern. Bryman (2012) refers to *relevance* as one of the potential criteria in evaluating research, defining it as ". . . importance of a topic within its substantive field or the contribution it makes to the literature on that field" (Hammersley, 1992a, cited in Bryman, 2012, p. 49).

Generally, relevance could be discussed in two areas, i.e., relevance to actual *practice* or relevance to *theories*. The former is already well-positioned within the research impact (the starting point of assessing impact) debates. Nonetheless, the latter seems taken for granted or is loosely addressed in the literature by only mentioning the necessity of drawing from the literature related to the field of study. In a traditional scientific field's research, the relevance to theories would reasonably be easy to reckon. In science, there are well-established theories and their counterarguments. Hence, this might be why relatedness does not appear as a primary concern in the traditional Research literature.

19.5.4 Relevance in PM

The case is different in project management. So, following the previous argument on the interrelations among REP, this section will focus more on the relatedness of RQs to the PM literature (or theories, as some would argue). Once more, the concept of shared responsibility will inevitably be highlighted.

PM is evolving fast (Uchitpe et al., 2016) and is highly multidisciplinary (Padalkar and Gopinath, 2016). Numerous in-depth philosophical discussions over PM epistemology, ontology, and related issues have shed light on PM's actual nature, theories and theory building (Svejvig, 2021). Examples of key studies are the early studies by Turner et al. (2010) that envisaged nine schools of thought to capture the diversity of perspectives in PM. Geraldi and Söderlund (2018) extend PM studies to various levels of analysis and project types. Hence, while the field has benefited from such multiplicities, it has been highly challenged by the ongoing fundamental debates on its "theory or theories."

Undeniably, fragmentation over the definition and even theories (Müller and Klein, 2018) are parts of the PM characteristics. Yet, another fact is that the PM sources are increasingly opening up to the works of scholars from other disciplines, looking for new areas of exploration (Maylor et al., 2018; Padalkar and Gopinath, 2016). These suggest (more than) enough sources of potential confusion on whether and how far a research query is pertinent to PM. So, discussing *relevance* in PM is highly relevant, if not essential.

Project management and operations management (OM) have their very origins in operations research (OR) in the 1940s–50s (Turner et al., 2010; Maylor, 2010), where extensive mathematical modeling developed as their initial tools (Williams, 2002, 2003). With the increase of PM applications in various businesses and industries and the complexity of projects, the field started to grow apart from OR and distinguished itself from OM (Williams, 2003; Maylor, 2010; Turner et al., 2010). Each has developed their research and literature through different lenses (Vahidi, 2016).

Comparing papers in PM journals with many others published in other journals will demonstrate the level of disparity among their focal points, worldviews, designs, and consequently their queries or RQs as inferred from Martinsuo and Huemann (2020), among others.

Interestingly, many papers in non-PM journals still follow the original perspectives on PM and projects, with only little twists in their models rather than concepts (William, 2002; Vahidi, 2016). These have been the sources of confusion seen in PM research and education offered by the faculties of various disciplines. The practice has also been affected by some project management systems' heavy focus on evaluating success and performance based on measured factors and tight controls.

Such disparities have not been unnoticed by the editors and reviewers. The editors of the most influential PM journals have addressed the lack of relevance to the practice and the advancements of the PM theories (see editorials: Martinso and Huemann, 2020; Huemann and Martinsuo, 2020; Müller and Klein, 2018, 2019). The editors explicitly point out many authors' unfamiliarity with the extant PM literature, and IJPM explicitly excludes "purely mathematical modeling or operations research pieces" papers (IJPM, 2022, p.1[2]). Both journals repeatedly emphasize "relevance" besides rigor as their initial criteria for paper acceptance (Huemann and Martinsuo, 2020; Müller and Klein, 2018).

Huemann and Martinsuo (2020), the IJPM editors, emphasize the combinations of "rigour and relevance" as one of the starting points of excellence in the research design and its resulting publication. Referring to Huff (2009, cited in Huemann and Martinsuo, 2020), the editors stipulate: "Irrespective of the mode of enquiry or methods used, the excellence starts when the research is set up for a relevant research question, and a suitable research design is chosen, with rigour in the application of the methods and the analysis (Huff, 2009)." (Huemann and Martinsuo, 2020, p. 311)

Hence, RQs, sources, and assumptions could be the first means of discovering a PM paper's relevance (or otherwise). Of course, some papers might need a deep dive to explore the *extent of their relevance* as being very high-level questions, and RQs might not always say it all. Deviation from the related practice and/or relevant

---

2 https://www.elsevier.com/journals/international-journal-of-project-management/0263-7863/guide-for-authors

body of knowledge could also happen in the later stages or be reflected in other aspects and elements of a research.

Relevance could be closely related to the nonacademic studies on PM (as mentioned, these are often referred to in academic research or educational material). Any researcher has specific areas of expertise. Similarly, a practitioner is familiar with certain types of projects, industries, methodologies, or a range of these based on their career paths and experiences.

Hence, any study conducted by the practice of PM could also benefit from awareness and exploration of new or further developments in PM by other practices and/or in academia. Many academic research projects conduct empirical studies that could enrich the studies in practice (e.g., literature on project success or leadership competencies). Many industries have also done studies that could inform the management of projects out of their industry. These will prevent reinventing the wheel and increase their studies' relevance to benefit the whole PM profession.

Traditionally, it is expected that the initiative for relevance should come from the academia's side. However, emphasizing the impact factor in academia and the increasing collaboration between PM practitioners, professional bodies, and academics, the initiative should be mutual and promoted. Such mutual commitments to maintaining relevance could ensure responsible directions from the PM research and studies.

Finally, the impact of relevance in PM education is quite relevant. While the relevance of education to practice has been frequently addressed (quite often criticized), relevance to contemporary theories has been less emphasized. PM educational and training programs focus on a narrow set of PM theories, and some only on scheduling and budgeting. Such narrow use of contemporary and extended views on PM limits the students' capabilities as future or soon-to-be researchers or PM professionals. Consequently, they would not be able to or would find it challenging to relate their explorations to the relevant and extant literature and practices. The cycle will continue as some will eventually become trainers or educators unable or unwilling to go beyond their acquired knowledge. Hence, the share of PM educators and trainers in developing academic and industry professionals who are aware of and courageous enough (or not) to raise and explore relevant questions would be significant and not to be for granted or forgotten.

References

British Educational Research Association (BERA) (2022). All Publications. Available at: https://www.bera.ac.uk/resources/all-publications/resources-for-researchers (Accessed: 25 June 2022).

Bryman, A. (2012). *Social research methods* (4th ed.). Oxford: Oxford University Press.

Clarke, N., Higgs, M. J., D'Amato, A., & Vahidi, R. (2018). *Responsible leadership in projects: Insights into ethical decision making.* Pennsylvania: Project Management Institute. Inc.

Comstock, G. (2013). *Research ethics: A philosophical guide to the responsible conduct of research*. Published by. Cambridge University Press. © Cambridge University Press 2013.

Creswell, J. W. (2014). *Research design: Qualitative, quantitative and mixed methods approaches* (4th ed.). Thousand Oaks, CA: Sage.

Gardiner, P. (2005). *Project management: A strategic planning approach*. Basingstoke: Palgrave Macmillan.

Geraldi, J., & Söderlund, J. (2018). Project studies: What it is, where it is going. *International Journal of Project Management, 36*, 55–70.

Glick, W., Tsui, A., & Davis, G. (2018). The moral dilemma of business research. BizEd AACSB International, 2 May. https://bized.aacsb.edu/articles/2018/05/the-moral-dilemma-of-businessresearch accessed 9/25/2021.

Huemann, M., & Martinsuo, M. (2020). Editorial: Is the international journal of project management the right choice for publishing your excellent research?. *International Journal of Project Management, 38*(5), 310–312.

IJPM International Journal of Project Management (2022), Guide for Authors. Available at: https://www.elsevier.com/journals/international-journal-of-project-management/0263-7863/guide-for-authors (Accessed: 25 June 2022).

Iphofen, R., & Tolich, M. (Eds.) (2018). *The SAGE handbook of qualitative research ethics*. SAGE Publications.

Klein, G. and Müller, R. (2021) Processes, Methods, Tools, Techniques, and Management Science for Project Management Journal. Project Management Journal, *52*(5) 1–3. doi: 10. 1177/ 8756 9728 2110 37774.

Karanja, E. and Malone, L.C. (2021). The role of industry and academia partnership in improving project management curriculum and competencies. Journal of Economic and Administrative Sciences, Vol. ahead-of-print No. ahead-of-print. https://doi.org/10.1108/JEAS-12-2020-0200.

Kleindorfer, Kunreuther & Schoemaker (1993). *Decision sciences: an integrative perspective*. Cambridge: Cambridge University Press.

Korenman, S. G. (n.d.). Teaching the responsible conduct of research in humans (RCRH). Retrieved from https://ori.hhs.gov/education/products/ucla/default.html

Martinsuo, M., & Huemann, M. (2020). The basics of writing a paper for the International Journal of Project Management. *International Journal of Project Management, 38*(6), 340–342.

Maylor, H. (2010). *Project management* (4th ed.). Harlow: Financial Times Prentice Hall.

Maylor, H., Meredith, J. R., Söderlund, J., & Browning, T. (2018). Old theories, new contexts: Extending operations management theories to projects. *International Journal of Operations and Production Management, 38*(6), 1274–1288. https://doi.org/10.1108/IJOPM-06-2018-781

Merriam-Webster. (n.d.) Question. https://www.merriam-webster.com/dictionary/question#otherwords

Miles, M. B., Huberman, A. M., & Saldaña., J. (2014). *Qualitative data analysis: A methods sourcebook* (3rd ed.). Los Angeles; London: SAGE.

Morris, P. W. G., & Hough, G. H. (1987). *The anatomy of major projects – a study of the reality of project management*. Chichester: John Wiley and Sons Ltd.

Morris, P. W. G. (2013). *Reconstructing project management*. Somerset: John Wiley and Sons.

Müller, R., & Klein, G. (2018). What constitutes a contemporary contribution to project management journal®?. *Project Management Journal, 49*(5), 3–4.doi:10.1177/8756972818791650.

Müller, R., & Klein, G. (2019). Qualitative research submissions to project management journal. *Project Management Journal, 50*(1), 3–5.

Nichols-Casebolt, A. (2012). *Research integrity and responsible conduct of research*. New York, NY: Oxford University Press.

Padalkar, M., & Gopinath, S. (2016). Six decades of project management research: Thematic trends and future opportunities. *International Journal of Project Management, 34*(2016), 1305–1321.

Punch, K. F. (2006). *Developing effective research proposals*. (2nd ed. 2014). London: Sage.Punch.

Reed, M. (2018). *The research impact handbook*. Huntly, Aberdeenshire: Fast Track Impact.

RRBM Responsible Research in Business and Management (2020) Position paper – a vision of responsible research in business and management: Striving for Useful and credible knowledge 1, revised 8 April 2020. Original publication date: 22 November 2017 Copyright 2017: Community for Responsible Research in Business and Management.

Shenhar, A., Pinto, J., Winch, G., & Huemann, M. (2018). Reflections on Rodney Turner's impact and the future of the field: An interview with Aaron Shenhar, Jeffrey Pinto and Graham Winch. *International Journal of Project Management*. https://doi.org/10.1016/j.ijproman.2017.09.004.

Svejvig, P. (2021). A Meta-theoretical framework for theory building in project management. *International Journal of Project Management, 39*, 849–872.

Trafford, V., & Leshem, S. (2008). *Stepping stones to achieving your doctorate: Focusing on your viva from the start*. Berkshire: McGraw-Hill.

Turner, R., Huemann, M., Anbari, F., & Bredillet, C. (2010). *Perspectives on projects*. Oxon: Routledge.

Uchitpe, M., Uddin, S., & Crawford, L. (2016). Predicting the future of project management research. *Procedia – Social and Behavioral Sciences, 226*, 27–34.

Vahidi, R. (2016). Research on contemporary project management through an engineering lens: Challenges and opportunities. *SKEMA Business School EDEN Doctoral Seminar*, August 22–24, 2016.

Vahidi, R. (2018). Educating responsible leaders: Managing a project or business as usual? *PRME Regional Chapter UK and Ireland, 5th Annual Conference*. Queen Mary, University of London, 25th –27th June 2018.

Vahidi, R. (2018). Educating responsible leaders: Do they actually get the opportunities for becoming responsible? *PRME Regional Chapter UK and Ireland, 5th Annual Conference*. Queen Mary University, London, 25th–27th, June 2018.

Williams, T. (2002). *Modelling complex projects*. West Sussex: John Wiley and Sons.

Williams, T. (2003). The contribution of mathematical modelling to the practice of project management. *IMA Journal of Management Mathematics, 14*, 3–30.

World Health Organization (WHO) (2022). Ensuring ethical standards and procedures for research with human beings. Available at: https://www.who.int/activities/ensuring-ethical-standards-and-procedures-for-research-with-human-beings (Accessed: 25 June 2022).

Karen Thompson
20 Competencies for Responsible Project Management

Context: The individual context of learners in formal and informal education settings

Characters/entities: Workshop participants recruited from the RPM network

Locations: Online/UK, insights may be applicable in other parts of the developed world

Research gaps: Gaps in competency frameworks; the need to develop mindset (attributes/values) and provide opportunities for contextual PM learning

Challenges/conflict/tensions: Challenges of classroom limitations; conflict between emphasis on PM as short-term delivery vs. long-term sustainability

Keywords: competencies, education, learning, classroom

20.1 Introduction

Project management drives change around the world and yet is largely invisible. Responsibility challenges project professionals to ensure that people and the natural environment are not harmed and, preferably, are enhanced by project activities. The scale and urgency of the challenge are unprecedented. Nevertheless, the pressure to deliver outputs on time and within budget often eclipses sustainability issues, both in practice and in developing learners' competencies. In this chapter, I argue that a new mindset is required for responsible project management. Project professionals must develop the capabilities to facilitate new understandings and emergent practices among diverse stakeholders to optimize value for all parties. Project management competence frameworks are compared with an integrative portfolio for responsible management competence, and gaps are identified. Taking a practical turn, communication practices in project management are explored as an example of interpreting project practices. Finally, a case study offers an example of techniques for developing a new mindset for responsible project management.

In 1991, Laszlo (1991, p. 69) argued, "Projects impact on a given social environment. They bring benefits if their objectives coincide with wider trends in that environment" and highlighted new challenges and opportunities for (project) managers of a transition into a new kind of society. Responsibility has become a trend in modern society but has yet to become mainstream in the management of projects. The relevance of responsibility in general management is emphasized by Drucker (2001), who stated:

https://doi.org/10.1515/9783110724783-025

"Responsibility for social impacts is a management responsibility – not because it is a social responsibility, but because it is a business responsibility." He elaborated that "managers must convert society's needs into opportunities for profitable business" (Drucker, 2001), and projects can be seen as how organizations change to meet society's needs. There is a growing body of knowledge about making mainstream management responsible. Three distinct but interrelated domains are defined – sustainability, responsibility and ethics (SRE) – and must be integrated into all elements of management practice (Laasch and Conaway, 2015). Sustainability refers to triple bottom line optimization, responsibility denotes embracing stakeholder value optimization, and ethics is concerned with ethical decision making and creating moral excellence (Laasch and Conaway, 2015). For project management, sustainability has been emphasized concerning the product or output of a project and the impact of executing the project. Responsibility and ethics are enacted through the project management process. Thompson and Williams (2022) interpreted responsibility for project management by optimizing stakeholder value rather than the traditional focus on delivering products for shareholders.

Roles, agency, and behaviors required to optimize value for all stakeholders suggest that new competencies are required to support a shift from adopting methods and tools toward facilitating new understandings and emergent practice (Thompson and Williams, 2022). Responsible project management changes what project management is and does. New competencies are required to support practices that optimize value for all stakeholders, and this chapter begins by discussing the requirements for responsible project management and develops the idea of a new mindset for responsible project management. In the second section, project management competence frameworks are compared with competence identified for responsible management and gaps are identified.

Today, every organization, public and private, operate in an environment of continual and sometimes disruptive change (Nieto-Rodriguez, 2021). Laszlo (1991) highlighted a need for project objectives to be aligned with trends in the social environment. Doing so increasingly involves incorporating a more extensive range of stakeholders, including the environment, local and remote communities, and broader society (Sabini and Silvius, 2022). Better connection between a project and the social context within which activity occurs has never been more critical for success, and new approaches are required. In the third section, communication practices in project management are explored in-depth as an example of interpreting project practices for responsibility. A socially constructed perspective of projects explores how project management communication practices can incorporate organizational learning, thereby better connecting a project with its external environment.

Finally, an integrative case study of an online workshop for developing some aspects of a new mindset for responsible project management. Techniques are included for developing new competencies of system thinking, anticipatory skills, and context-specific learning.

20.2 Responsible Management of Projects

Responsibility changes what project management is and does (Thompson and Williams, 2022). Following Laasch and Conaway (2015), who proposed change designed to ensure that mainstream management contributes to developing solutions rather than exacerbating problems, Thompson and Williams (2022) argue that project management needs to do more.

The notion of responsibility challenges project professionals to ensure that people and the natural environment are not harmed and, ideally, are enhanced by the activities undertaken as part of the project and those involved in operation after the project ends. Recent warnings of disruption to economic systems likely to occur from climate change and related human impacts, such as resource conflict, forced migration, and social injustice, highlight the scale and urgency of the challenge. The number of projects is increasing, but Nieto-Rodriguez (2021) argues that project management has somehow stayed in the past. He is critical of project managers who focus too much on inputs and outputs rather than outcomes and value and lack concern for what happens before and after the project (Nieto-Rodriguez, 2021).

Responsible management proposes change to all aspects of management practice. Laasch and Conaway (2015) indicate that the three domains of sustainability, responsibility and ethics (SRE) provide a distinct perspective but are interrelated with some overlap. Development of theory in mainstream management tends to assume permanency in the organization, and literature on responsible management is no different. Projects are usually distinguished from business-as-usual by a temporary organization and an imperative for action (Ludin and Söderholm, 1995). Accordingly, Thompson and Williams (2022) argue that project management requires special attention. In brief, the three domains can be interpreted in the project context as follows.

Sustainability, as optimization of the triple bottom line, has been widely interpreted for project management, and the focus is typically on the project output and resources used during the project process. Interpretations of the triple bottom line are often based on Bruntland's (1987) definition of sustainable development. This has been criticized for suggesting that trade-offs are possible; between the environment, society, and economy and between the short- and long term. Thompson and Williams (2022) explain that optimization of the triple bottom line in project management needs to recognize the dependencies between the pillars of sustainable development and the short and long term. Further, they suggest that notions of sustainability challenge conventional perspectives of success in project management.

Time, cost, and quality are frequently used as measures of project success are measured. A focus on these three metrics tends to drive project decision-making favoring economic considerations viewed within the life of a project, i.e., a short-term perspective. Economic imperatives often eclipse considerations of the environment and interests of broader society, and trade-offs can be illusory (Thompson and

Williams, 2022). For example, activism can interrupt, delay, or cause a project to be terminated if organizations are seen to be disregarding environmental concerns. Project Management success is the project manager's focus and is typically measured in cost, time, and quality. Project success refers to the project outcomes, often from the perspective of stakeholders and incorporates the performance of the project deliverables. Project success might be the focus of a program or portfolio manager. Business value and the delivery of benefits are often considered the project sponsor's responsibility. The future potential may contribute to business value but may not be straightforward to assess and difficult to anticipate. Sustainability might be considered within the scope of future potential but may not be recognized within project management. The definition of sustainable development offered by Rimanoczy (2019) may be more useful in project management than Bruntland (1987). Rimanoczy (2019) defined sustainable development as "development that restores the resources used, reshapes the needs, does more for more, with less" and provides a starting point for interpreting and embedding responsibility into project management (Thompson and Williams, 2022). Another way of conceptualizing sustainability in project management is to consider sustainability as a foundation for project success, as illustrated in Figure 20.1.

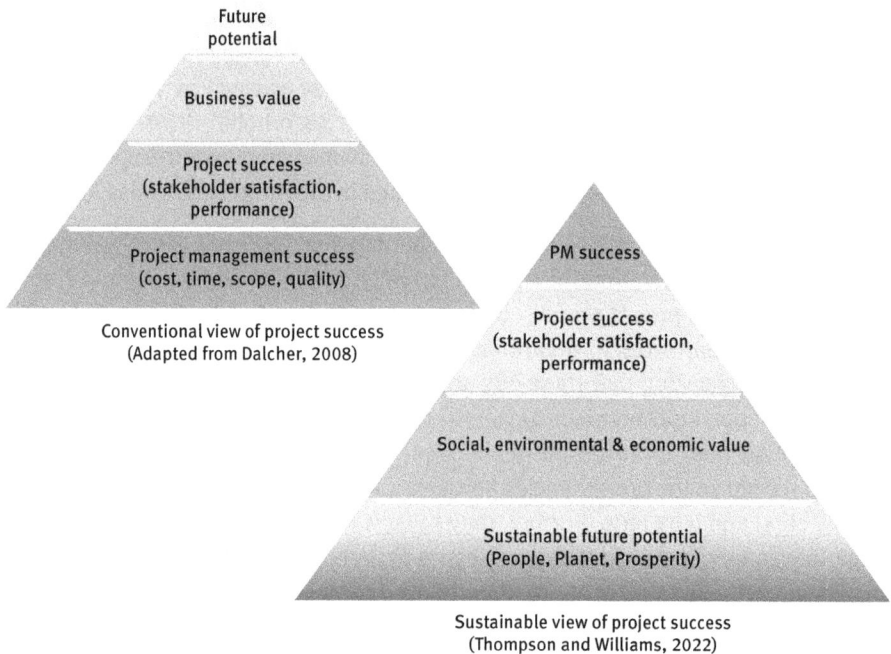

Future
potential

Business value

Project success
(stakeholder satisfaction,
performance)

Project management success
(cost, time, scope, quality)

Conventional view of project success
(Adapted from Dalcher, 2008)

PM success

Project success
(stakeholder satisfaction,
performance)

Social, environmental & economic value

Sustainable future potential
(People, Planet, Prosperity)

Sustainable view of project success
(Thompson and Williams, 2022)

Figure 20.1: Perspectives on project success.

Responsibility is summarized by Laasch and Conaway (2015) as overall stakeholder value optimization instead of a narrow focus on maximizing shareholder value. Integrating responsibility into project management challenges conventional approaches to project management by introducing new requirements to:

- Explore medium, long term, and undefined effects of proposed project actions.
- Incorporate a larger range of stakeholders, including the environment, local and remote communities, and wider society.
- Embrace complexity, for example arising from conflicting interests, rather than dismissing or simplifying it (as traditional methods do) (Sabini and Silvius, 2022).

Thompson and Williams (2022) explore the implications of optimizing stakeholder value for elements of project management and across the life of a project. Focus on the end of a project can constrain thinking about responsibility and sustainability. Locating a project within the context of the medium- and long term can be enabled by using an extended or sustainable project life cycle may be useful, as shown in Figures 20.2 and 20.3.

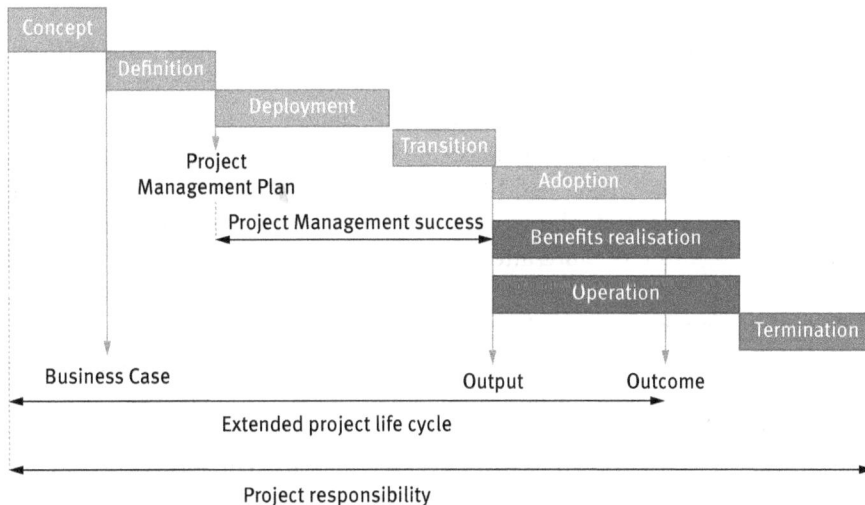

Figure 20.2: Extended project life cycle (adapted from APM, 2019; Thompson and Williams, 2022).

Addressing these new requirements emphasizes interaction between the project and its external environment, bringing communication practices to the fore. Communication practices will be explored later in this chapter in a practical turn.

Ethics is described by Laasch and Conaway (2015, p. 26) as "decisions in management must be morally desirable in both process and outcome. Management practice must embrace ethical decision making and create moral excellence." Ethics in project management is typically addressed by codes of conduct developed by professional

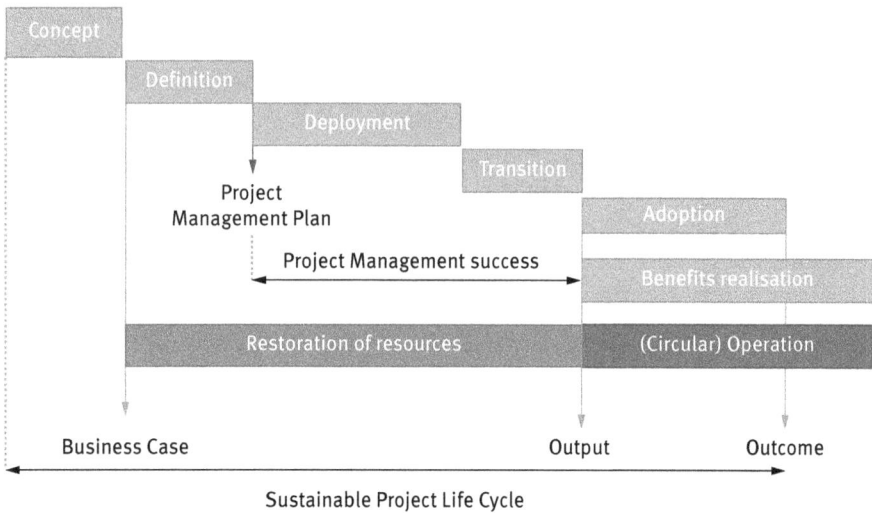

Figure 20.3: Sustainable project life cycle (Thompson and Williams, 2022).

bodies and published separately from bodies of knowledge and other standards. The ethical codes of conduct emphasize compliance with legislation and standards rather than moral excellence. Connections are made with morals; for example, APM (2021) indicate "ethics, compliance and professionalism encompass working consistently in a moral, legal and socially responsible manner," and PMI (2021, p. 21) states that "a code of ethics is related to morals." Further work is needed to integrate ethics into and more attention is required than can be given in this chapter.

Today, concern over climate change and social injustice means that all organizations' environmental, social, and economic impacts, including projects, are under scrutiny. Responsible management can be at the center of a virtuous circle of change, moving toward responsible business (Laasch and Conaway, 2015). Projects as the engines of change emphasize the role of project professionals in driving businesses and society forward. Many of the requirements of responsible project management echo the earlier call for project management to shift from focusing on products toward creating value to recognizing complexity and interactions at the project boundary. There have also been calls for education and learning to develop reflective practitioners who can adapt to change rather than trained technicians (Winter et al., 2006). Laasch and Conaway (2015) argue that responsible management requires a set of attributes, beliefs, skills, and knowledge that is "in many cases, radically different from the set held by a traditional manager" (Laasch and Conaway, 2015). Thompson and Williams (2022) argue that project management is a case.

20.3 A Mindset for Responsible Project Management

Traditional project management emphasizes adopting methods and tools matched by an instrumental mindset. There have been calls to develop practitioners who can learn, operate, and adapt to complex environments rather than practitioners who follow detailed procedures and techniques (Winter et al., 2006). Aspects of project management that involve social interactions, such as stakeholder engagement and leadership, have been the subject of much attention in recent years and calls to develop new capabilities among practitioners continue. For example, a steady stream of project failures related to unsatisfied stakeholders continues to be reported (Dalcher, 2016).

Competencies for responsible management identified by Laasch and Conaway (2015) are subdivided into four groups: knowledge, action, interaction, and self-competencies. Laasch and Moosmayer (2015) build on the four groups to define an integrative portfolio for responsible management competence. The portfolio distinguishes between knowledge and analysis as intellectual capabilities, and the self is subdivided into character and self-adaptation, making six groups, as shown in Table 20.1. Laasch and Conaway (2015, p. 37) compare the set of competencies required for traditional and responsible management and, although they indicate they are radically different, indicate the "two competence sets are often complementary and contain no major contradictions." Some of the analysis and action competencies for responsible management might readily be considered competence for project management, such as initiating action and effecting change.

Understanding of project management competency is fragmented and changing. A review of literature on project management competency by de Rezende and Blackwell (2019) identified 81 competencies in 11 dimensions: influencing skills, communication skills, team working skills, emotional skills, contextual skills, management skills, cognitive skills, professionalism, knowledge and experience, project management knowledge, and personal skills and attributes. The 81 competencies can be mapped onto five out of six of the groups identified by Laasch and Moosmayer (2015), and no competencies are correlated with self-adaptation, as shown in Table 20.2.

In 2021, the Association for Project Management (APM) updated its competency framework to identify knowledge and application in 29 categories and organized it into four groups: setting up for success, preparing for change, people and behaviors, and planning and managing deployment. In all groups, competency is expressed as knowledge and application. These 29 competencies can be mapped onto five out of six of the groups identified by Laasch and Moosmayer (2015), and again no competencies are correlated with self-adaptation.

Table 20.1: Mainstream vs. responsible management competence.

Competence group	Mainstream management competencies (Laasch and Conaway, 2015)	Responsible management competencies (Laasch and Conaway, 2015)	Integrative competence portfolio (Laasch and Moosmayer, 2015)
Knowledge (know)	Technical knowledge and proficiency in a specialized field	Sustainability Responsibility Ethics RM tools	Declarative knowledge Procedural knowledge Knowledge acquisition Knowledge handing
Analysis (think)			System thinking Dealing with complexity Temporal thinking Strategic thinking Creative thinking Decision making Moral reasoning Critical thinking Analyzing social relationships
Action (do)	Conceptual and diagnostic	Systems thinking Interdisciplinary work SRE decision-making	Good behavior and integrity Initiating action Sustaining action Dealing with issues Effecting change Managing SRE Mainstream management skills
Social (interaction/ relate)	Political (exerting influence) Communication Leadership Delegation	Stakeholder networking and communication Change agency skills (leadership) Critical skills	Group skills and collaboration Dealing with social complexity Dealing with dissent Communication Building and maintaining relationships Leadership

Table 20.1 (continued)

Competence group	Mainstream management competencies (Laasch and Conaway, 2015)	Responsible management competencies (Laasch and Conaway, 2015)	Integrative competence portfolio (Laasch and Moosmayer, 2015)
Character (self)	Toughness Efficiency Effectiveness Loyalty (to a company)	Meta-perspective Empathy Embracing attitude Problem awareness Sense of urgency	Sentiments and states of mind Motivations and aspirations Values Attitudes and consciousness Character traits
Self-adaptation (become)		Self-perception (especially about power)	Self-image Introspection Self-control Self-direction Personal development

Also, in 2021, the Project Management Institute (PMI) moved away from specifying the knowledge required by project managers to an approach based on a system for value delivery and 12 principles: stewardship, team, stakeholders, value, systems thinking, leadership, tailoring, quality, complexity, risk, adaptability and resilience, and change. The 12 principles have been compared with the competencies for responsible management, as shown in Table 20.2. No correlation is explicitly identified in the knowledge group, but technical knowledge is required to underpin all principles. As above, no principles seem to be correlated with self-adaptation.

Concluding an analysis of competencies, no project management competencies are currently recognized in the category of a self-adaptation group. Further, not all of the competencies for responsible management can be identified in the current frameworks for project management. Both these findings suggest opportunities for further analysis, research, and development.

In the next section, communication practices in project management are considered in-depth to understand how a project might better connect with its environment.

Table 20.2: Comparison of competencies for (responsible) project management.

Sustainability, responsibility, ethics competency portfolio (Laasch and Moosmayer, 2015)	PM competency framework (deRezende and Blackwell, 2019)	PM principles (PMI, 2021)	APM competency framework (APM, 2021)
1. Knowledge (to know)			
– Declarative knowledge – Procedural knowledge – Knowledge acquisition – Knowledge handling	Knowledge and experience (50–53) PM knowledge (54–71)	(Implicit)	Setting up for success (6) Preparing for change (6) Planning and managing deployment (11)
2. Analysis (to think)			
– Systems thinking – Dealing with complexity – Temporal thinking – Strategic thinking – Creative thinking – Decision making – Moral reasoning – Critical thinking – Analyzing social relationships	Contextual skills (30–34) Cognitive skills (40–47)	(4) Focus on value (5) Recognize, evaluate, and respond to system interactions (7) Tailor based on context	Setting up for success (6) Preparing for change (6) Planning and managing deployment (11)
3. Action (to do)			
– Good behavior and integrity – Initiating action – Sustaining action – Dealing with issues – Effecting change – Managing sustainability, responsibility, ethics – Mainstream management skills	Management skills (35–39) Professionalism – ethics (48) Professionalism – accountability (49)	(6) Demonstrate leadership behaviors (8) Build quality into processes and deliverables (9) Navigate complexity (10) Optimize risk responses (12) Enable change to achieve the envisioned future state	Setting up for success (6) Preparing for change (6) Planning and managing deployment (11)

Table 20.2 (continued)

Sustainability, responsibility, ethics competency portfolio (Laasch and Moosmayer, 2015)	PM competency framework (deRezende and Blackwell, 2019)	PM principles (PMI, 2021)	APM competency framework (APM, 2021)
4. **Interaction** (to relate)			
– Group skills and collaboration – Dealing with social complexity – Dealing with dissent – Communication – Building and maintaining relationships – Leadership	Influencing skills (1–6) Communication skills (7–16) Team working skills (17–23)	(2) Create a collaborative project team environment (3) Effectively engage with stakeholders	People and behaviors (6)
5. **Character** (to be)			
– Sentiments and states of mind – Motivations and aspirations – Values – Attitudes and consciousness – Character traits	Emotional skills (24–29) Personal skills and attributes (72–81)	(1) Be a diligent, respectful, and caring steward (11) Embrace adaptability and resiliency	None
6. **Self-adaptation** (to become)			
– Self-image – Introspection – Self-control – Self-direction – Personal development	None	None	None

20.4 Communication in Project Management

Communication is a critical element of project management. Effective communication in project management is well-recognized, but practices tend to be deterministic, focused on internal requirements, and fail to reflect the complexity of human interaction (Thompson, 2017). Traditional project management practices, including communication, tend to assume a model of an action-orientated process that transforms inputs into outputs. A basic input-output model of project management (Figure 20.4) assumes a project behaves like a static, simple control system that Boulding (1956) classified as level three complexities.

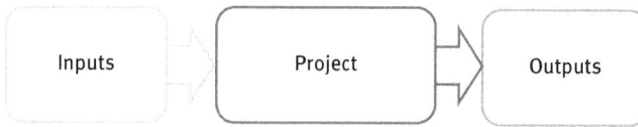

Figure 20.4: Traditional project management as an action process.

In contrast, recognizing a project as socially constructed and operating as a complex open system corresponds with Boulding's (1956) eighth level of complexity, with significant implications for communication between the project and its external environment. Both traditional and agile approaches to project management often rely on defining a clear boundary between a project and the external environment to manage scope and control change. Once defined, an unintended consequence of the project boundary can be that the project becomes decoupled from its external environment (Williams, 2005).

Responsible management of a project requires communication practices that ensure the project is well-aligned with the external environment at the beginning and continues to remain connected as the project progresses. As external change occurs, a project needs to seek out and interpret new knowledge and then adapt appropriately. Thompson (2017) used organizational learning theory to understand the requirements for communication that could connect a project to its environment, enabling a project to detect a change and respond appropriately.

Organizational learning requires an interpretation system involving three stages – scanning, interpreting, and learning – with feedback required between the stages (Daft and Weick, 1984), as shown in Figure 20.5. Viewing a project as an interpretation system shows how a project can connect with its external environment. When the learning process is added to the input-output model, the resulting model shows how a project can better connect with its environment, as illustrated in Figure 20.6. The resulting model combines learning and action, suggesting that these activities are inextricably linked in practice, but more research is required to support this assertion.

Research on communication in project management has shown a lack of good communication beyond the boundary of the project team (Partington, 1997) and internal communication with the project team members, formed for project implementation, rather than customers and external organizations, is emphasized (Müller, 2003). However, interactions between a system and its environment are almost universally significant for all disciplines (Boulding, 1956).

The influence of enterprise environmental factors on communications is recognized in a limited way in the professional literature. Prescribed practices emphasize internal communication and dissemination of project information. For example, Project Management Institute (2021) emphasizes communication "about the project" and how such information will be "administered and disseminated." There is

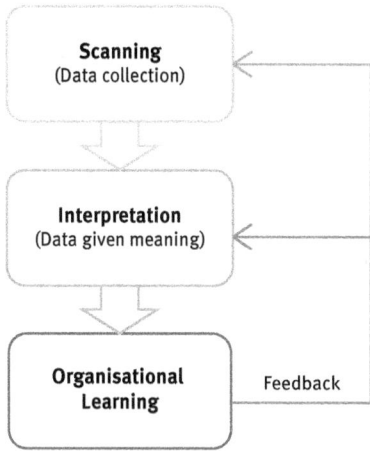

Figure 20.5: Three stages for organizational learning (Daft and Weick, 1984).

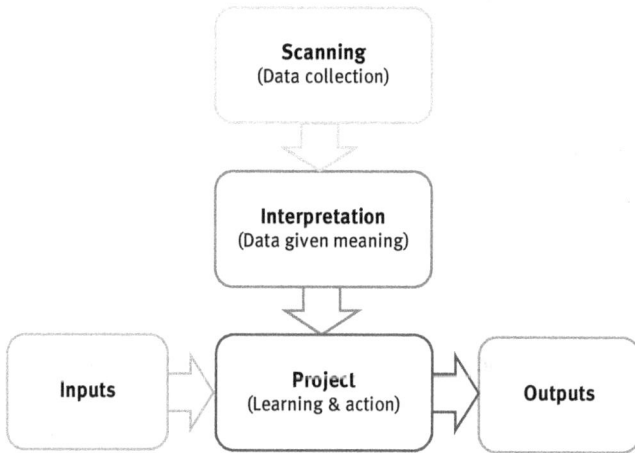

Figure 20.6: Project learning process (Thompson, 2017).

little attention to collecting and understanding how the external environment changes over the project's life, how new factors influencing a project might be identified, new interests uncovered, or how a project might respond to new influences as work progresses.

Connecting a project to its environment creates new requirements for project communication. Three new types of project communication are required for actively seeking out and responding to external knowledge – scanning, interpreting, and learning. Thompson (2017) conceptualized project communication as three layers, or zones, of project communication, as shown in Figure 20.7. Boundaries between the layers are shown as broken lines to illustrate the requirement for data to flow freely across the boundaries – in both directions. For organizational learning to occur, data, information, and knowledge must flow *inward* from the external environment toward the project activities and *outward* into the external environment from the project itself. Feedback in both directions is essential for organizational learning.

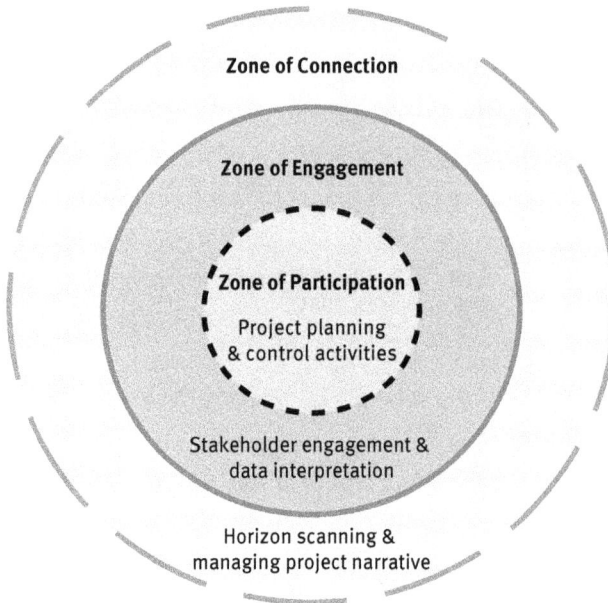

Figure 20.7: Three zones of project communication (Thompson, 2017).

Conventional project management practices tend not to address how new knowledge is developed and managed or how changes in project interests can be identified and understood. In this way, widely prescribed communications practices tend to inhibit identifying, understanding, and responding to external changes and, as a result, lead to a disconnect between the project and its environment.

A project needs to develop an awareness of new influences or changes in factors that could affect the project or its outcomes. Different interpretations are developed by organizations that actively intrude into the environment to search for data from organizations that behave passively (Daft and Weick, 1984). As a temporary organization, a project may not be well connected to the data collection processes within the surrounding organizations and typically relies on stakeholders to communicate new knowledge or changes in influential factors as and when such information becomes available. Accordingly, developing effective connections between a project and its external environment will involve new communication practices, requiring new competencies. The new requirements for practices and competencies are discussed in this section for each type in turn.

Connection emphasizes scanning for and data collection relating to external trends, influences, opportunities, threats, and changes. Traditionally, attention is given mainly to disseminating project information outward rather than actively seeking new information from the external environment. External identified data is usually filtered for relevance to the project before seeking out new interpretations that may affect the project in unexpected ways. For example, opportunities outside the predefined project boundary may be dismissed before new opportunities for a different approach to the project can be assessed. New practices and competencies are required that involve being much more open to new possibilities than would be usual when managing a project.

The second aspect of connection that can be critical for the project concerns the stories told about the project in the external world. Project narratives can develop in ways that are not directly informed by the project activities and can take on a life independent of the project, but never-the-less can determine success, cause delay, change, or even result in complete cancellation of the project. Project professionals need to actively intrude into the external environment and influence narratives about the project more than in project management.

In today's highly connected global society, a different approach is required for presenting project information to the external world. Simply making information available and leaving external actors and the wider public to make their interpretations is no longer adequate. Support for a project is not automatic or widespread. Left to their own devices, people will raise objections and are more likely to express their feelings when opposed to a project than to provide support. Therefore, the narrative about a project needs to be actively managed through activities that might more commonly be thought of as public relations. Social media can be beneficial for connecting with the environment, obtaining external and disseminating project information. Taking project information to the (virtual) places that stakeholders use as part of their day-to-day lives can be more effective than expecting external stakeholders to come to project locations such as a specific project website (Thompson, 2017).

Engagement refers to the communication activities concerned with interpreting external information and "winning hearts and minds" (Cadle and Yeates, 2008). They also suggest that consideration of subjective realities is required in project communication, and they highlight that inward communication across the project boundary is required to gather feedback and surface resistance. Communication activities for engagement need to encourage and support involvement with the project. Surfacing different perspectives and seeking to understand external data in context are crucial. Facilitation skills are required to ensure all voices are heard, diverse views are respected, and the challenges of balancing the requirements over the short-, medium-, and long term are explored.

Participation incorporates communication about project activities and learning. In conventional project management, communication is focused on directing and controlling project action. There has been increasing recognition that projects emerge under external influences (e.g., Williams, 2005). Broader conceptualizations imply projects are "not always pre-defined, but permeable, contestable and open to renegotiation throughout" (Winter et al., 2006). Communication practices need to reflect a shift from rigidly following a plan to enabling the project to emerge as new knowledge develops and adapts as external change is uncovered. Communication practices need to enable innovation and support the development of tacit knowledge among those participating in project activities, leading to earlier recognition of issues and new opportunities. Value and benefit have multiple meanings linked to different purposes and perspectives (Winter et al., 2006). Accordingly, learning can be encouraged by providing opportunities for sharing understandings and perspectives.

In conclusion, communication practices are at the forefront of transforming project management for responsibility. Better connection between a project and its external environment is likely to understand the project context better, leading to improved problem solving and project decision making (Dalcher, 2016). Communication practices, both internal and external, are at the heart of managing projects responsibly. Thompson and Williams (2022) argue that a new mindset is needed to meet requirements for engaging diverse stakeholders, exploring undefined and long-term project impacts, and embracing complexity. In this chapter, some limitations of competency frameworks have been briefly discussed, and further research is identified. A case study of an online workshop on systems thinking is shared to finish.

20.5 Case Study

This case study discusses a workshop delivered online on International Project Management Day in 2021. 2021 was declared the International Year of Responsible Project Management (IYRPM) because, in many societies, reaching 21 is considered the start of adult life. In many places worldwide, young people complete their first undergraduate degree and take up formal roles in industry or wider society. The United Nation's priority for 2021 was "making peace with nature," emphasizing reducing greenhouse emissions to ensure the planet remains habitable for humans. The director-general of the UN declared that 2021 was when the international agreements required to achieve the targets for carbon reduction must be secured. For all these reasons, 2021 was considered an appropriate time for project management to assume its responsibilities to society. For more information on IYRPM, see https://www.responsiblepm.com/2021 and https://www.ipma.world/2021-is-international-year-of-responsible-project-management/

In 2021, the world was also in the grip of the Covid-19 pandemic, with many restrictions in place that prevented normal social interactions. It was anticipated that declaring 2021 as IYRPM would help spotlight project management and the opportunities for responsibly managed projects to contribute to the post-disaster recovery phase, accelerate progress toward achieving the UN's sustainable development goals, and build resilience for the future. In many countries, including the UK, classrooms were largely empty with online education. Taking education online provided opportunities to facilitate collaboration among an international audience, using various social media tools to encourage and capture discussion among learners. The opportunity was to use the new educational environment to explore threshold concepts in project management (Williams, 2022) with participants in an online workshop on system thinking for responsible project management.

Workshop aims and objectives were defined as follows. The aim is to explore how responsible project professionals can use systems thinking to help manage complexity and uncertainty in projects. The concepts of a sustainable project life cycle and adaptive pathways will be introduced to think differently about projects and their management. By the end of the event, a participant was expected to be able to:
a) Understand how to incorporate diverse stakeholder perspectives into a project.
b) Appreciate how to uncover undefined medium- and long-term effects of proposed project actions, including identifying new risks and opportunities.
c) Evaluate their practice for steps to incorporate complexity and identify support requirements.

Participants were recruited using the RPM Network, and there were twelve volunteer learners, comprising four project management educators and eight project practitioners, most of whom operate at the project level rather than programs or portfolios. Three groups of four were formed with a combination of educators and practitioners. Two facilitators managed the workshop using Zoom software for online video interaction, with survey software (Mentimeter) used for "before" and "after" surveys to assess the workshop's impact. In addition, all learners were given access to interactive, visual software (Padlet) to capture group discussions and provide a repository for the learning materials.

The workshop schedule was designed to ensure a high level of activity for the learners, with minimal time spent listening to presentations. The duration of the workshop was limited by the time we felt volunteers would spend online, and this was set at approximately 2 h for the main event. Additional time was allocated at the beginning and end for informal discussion and networking because feedback from professionals in the past suggests that this is desirable, and often insufficient time is available for such interaction.

For each activity, the instructions were explained to learners at the start of the scheduled time, and the details were available via Padlet. A choice of real project scenarios was suggested, and links were provided for learners to learn more about the project. All projects were winners of the EarthShot Prize launched in London for 2021, and each received £1 million in prize money to develop project. The workshop learners were directed to take the perspective of a project consultant, recruited to advise on managing the project to maximize the beneficial impacts from the time of the award to the end of the decade. In this way, learning would be relatable and authentic. The EarthShot Prize will be awarded in each of the next 10 years. Information about the projects will be made publicly available, and the projects, along with future winners, will provide learning opportunities for project professionals and educators over the next decade and beyond.

https://earthshotprize.org/london-2021/the-earthshot-prize-winners-finalists/

Details of the workshop schedule and activities are reproduced in Table 20.3.

Table 20.3: Workshop schedule.

Elapsed time	Activity	No. of facilitators
00:00–00:15	Informal discussion, networking and "before" survey	2 One to welcome people One monitor/respond to chat
00:15–00:20	Introductions and welcome	2 One to deliver the introduction One to welcome late arrivals
00:20–00:30	Part 1 – Introduction to systems thinking and sustainable project life cycle	2 One to deliver the presentation One to monitor chat for questions
00:30–00:55	Group activity A (25 min) Choose a project scenario. Use systems thinking to analyze the chosen scenario. Key questions: – What are the key features of the project as a system? – What is the purpose of the project from different perspectives? – What are the social and environmental elements of the project? Post key findings on Padlet.	3 One In each group

Table 20.3 (continued)

Elapsed time	Activity	No. of facilitators
00:55–01:15	Group activity B (20 min) Choose a future scenario. For the chosen project scenario and future state: – Identify future impacts of project actions. – Identify new risks and opportunities in a future state. – Review risks and opportunities for novelty, specificity, and diversity. Post key findings on Padlet	3 One In Each group
01:15–01:25	Break	1 To Monitor activity
01:25–01:45	Feedback and discussion	2 One to review Padlet and lead the discussion One To monitor chat for questions
01:45–02:00	Part 2 – Introduction to adaptive pathways	2 One To Deliver The Presentation One To monitor chat for questions
02:00–02:10	Individual activity (10 min) Review own practice – Identify actions to be taken to embrace complexity – Identify support/personal development needs. Post action plan on Padlet	1 To monitor activity/questions
02:10–02:15	Feedback and summary	2 One to review Padlet and lead a discussion One to monitor chat for questions
02:15–02:30	Informal discussion, networking and "after" survey	1 To monitor activity/answer questions

For the second group activity, a choice of future states was indicated, and a brief description of each was provided. Again, real work events were used to inform the material and, in this case, use a range of different potential outcomes from the COP26 conference that was running in the UK at the time of the workshop. Learners were briefed on how to assess their list of risks and opportunities for novelty, specificity, and diversity that were derived from the work of Geden et al. (2019) on assessing anticipatory thinking. On reflection, this workshop aspect could have been the subject of a separate workshop.

In conclusion, the workshop provided learners with an opportunity to use systems and anticipatory thinking to explore a project scenario. Discussing perspectives with others enabled ideas to be interrogated, leading to deeper understanding. By developing individual action plans toward the end of the workshop, participants were encouraged to incorporate learning into their practice. The practitioners identified some examples of opportunities to improve processes within their organizations.

References

APM. (2019). *Association for project management body of knowledge* (7th ed.). Buckinghamshire: APM.

APM. (2021). APM competence framework. Available online: Competence Framework | APM.

Boulding, K. (1956 Apr 1956). General systems theory: The skeleton of science. *Management Science, 2*(3). Available online http://panarchy.org/boulding/systems.1956.html.

Bruntland, H. (1987). Report of the World Commission on Environment and Development. Available online: 1987: Brundtland Report (admin.ch).

Cadle, J. & Yeates, D. (2008). *Project management for information systems* (5th ed.). Essex, UK: Pearson.

Cicmil, S. & Hodgson, D. (2006). New possibilities for project management theory: A critical engagement. *Project Management Journal, 37*(3), 111–122.

Cicmil, S., Williams, T., Thomas, J., & Hodgson, D. (2006). Rethinking project management: Researching the actuality of projects. *International Journal of Project Management, 24*, 675–686.

Dalcher, D. (2016). Rethinking project practice: Emerging insights from a series of books for practitioners. *International Journal of Managing Projects in Business, 9*(Issue 4), 798–821.

Dalcher, D. (2009). Software project success: Moving beyond failure Upgrade. *CEPIS Journal, X*(4).

De Rezende, L. B. & Blackwell, P. (2019). Project management competency framework. *Iberoamerican Journal of Project Management, 10*(1), 34–59.

De Wit, A. (1988). Measurement of project success. *Project Management, 6*(3), 164–170.

Daft, Richard & Weick, Karl. (1984). Toward A Model of Organizations As Interpretation Systems. The Academy of Management Review. 9. 10.2307/258441.

Drucker, P. (2001). *The essential drucker* (pp. 55). New York: Harper Collins.

Eskerod, P. & Huemann, M. (2013). Sustainable development and stakeholder management: What standards say. *International Journal of Managing Project in Business, 6*(1), 36–50.

Floricel, S., Bonneau, C., Aubry, M., & Sergi, V. (2014). Extending project management research: Insights from social theories. *International Journal of Project Management, 32*, 1091–1107.

Geden, M., Smith, A., Campbell, J., Spain, R., Amos-Binks, A., Mott, B., . . . Lester, J. (2019). Construction and validation of an anticipatory thinking assessment. *Frontiers in Psychology*. 11 December 2019. Available online: https://www.frontiersin.org/articles/10.3389/fpsyg. 2019.02749/full

Kassel, K., Rimanoczy, I., & Mitchell, S. F. (2018). A sustainability mindset model for management education. In *Developing a sustainability mindset in management education* (pp. 3–37). Routledge.

Laasch, O. & Conaway, R. (2015). *Principles of responsible management: Global sustainability, responsibility, ethics*. Mason: Cengage.

Laasch, O. & Moosmayer, D. C. (2015). Responsible management learning: Reflecting on the role and use of paradigms in sustainability, responsibility, ethics research. CRME Working Paper 2.

Laszlo, E. (1991). Responsible (project) management in an unstable world. *Project Management, 9*(2).

Ludin, R. A. & Söderholm, A. (1995). A Theory of the temporary organisation. *Scandinavian Journal of Management, It*(4), 437–455.

Morris, P. W. G. (2013). *Deconstructing project management*. Chichester: Wiley-Blackwell eBook.

Müller, R. (2003). Determinants for external communications of IT project managers. *International Journal of Project Management, 21*, 345–354.

Nieto-Rodriguez, A. (2021). The project economy has arrived. *Harvard Business Review*. Nov-Dec 2021.

Partington, D. (1997). *Management processes in projects of organisational change: Case studies from four industries*. UK: Cranfield University.

Project Management Institute. (2021). *A guide to the project management body of knowledge 7th ed and the ANSI standard for project management*. Newton Square: Project Management Institute, Inc.

Sabini, L. & Silvius, G. (2022). Embracing complexity in sustainable project management. In *Research handbook on complex project organizing*. Published by: Edward Elgar.

Thompson, K. M. (2017). A framework for using social media in the practice of project management. PhD Thesis: Bournemouth University.

Thompson, K. M. (2022). Digital disruption: How the use of social media can improve project management. In Ninan, J. (ed.), *Social media for project management*. Taylor and Francis: CRC Press.

Thompson, K. M. & Williams, N. L. (2022). Responsibility as a new school in project management. In Silvius, G. and Huemann, M. (eds), *Research handbook on sustainable project management*. Published by: Edward Elgar.

Winter, M., Smith, C., Morris, P., & Cicmil, S. (2006). Directions for future research in project management: The main findings of a UK government-funded research network. *International Journal of Project Management, 24*, 638–649.

Williams, T. (2005) "Assessing and moving on from the dominant project management discourse in the light of project overruns," in IEEE Transactions on Engineering Management, 52(4), 497–508. doi: 10.1109/TEM.2005.856572.

Herbert Daly, Nicole Ferdinand, Karen Thompson,
and Nigel Williams

21 Responsible Forms of Project Management Education

Context: Individual context of learners in formal education or workplace

Characters/entities: University of Wolverhampton, IBM, University of Portsmouth, University of Bournemouth

Locations: The UK and case insights may apply to similar western countries

Research gaps: The need for values-based education, the hidden curriculum in PM

Challenges/conflict/tensions: The challenge of developing a new PM curriculum to create new types of students

Keywords: education, curriculum, values, systems thinking, case study

21.1 The Responsibility of PM Educators

Project management education aims at providing technical knowledge, management knowledge, and bounded experiences. These aims are embedded in PM education by teaching certain content, pedagogical approaches (for example, a live project), and specific delivery modes. General management education has been criticized for being irrelevant and focusing on shareholders over stakeholders (Pfeffer, 2009). This scenario is reinforced as poor management practices (for example, the ruthless search for competitive advantage) have been supported by management theories which are outcomes of partial explanations of reality (Ghoshal, 2005). As explained elsewhere, academic publishing incentives encourage the development of defendable, not relevant, theories, which can reduce the complexity of the business environment. The result of education based on these principles may either reinforce values in students that prioritize profits over society, or create cognitive dissonance among students with different values. The limits of PM's technocratic perspective can be seen in ethics, social responsibility, and sustainability. These domains do not support the generation of definitive answers but rather present paradoxes, ambiguities, uncertainty, and a lack of empirical data from projects in these areas. Integrating this topic of sustainability requires incorporating multiple disciplines that are generally not associated with project management: psychological, social, organizational, ecological, and policy. PM students also need to understand that "good" may not be the same as "right" or permissible or legal.

https://doi.org/10.1515/9783110724783-026

21.2 The Hidden Curriculum in PM Education

The transition toward responsibility in PM cannot be performed by solely adding content on social responsibility and sustainability. It requires a systemic change of the formal curriculum (e.g., course organization, delivery, assessment), interpersonal interactions, and educational governance (Blasco, 2012). Dewey (1963) created the term "collateral learning" to identify how schools shape the mindsets and habits of students beyond learning objectives. The later idea of a "hidden curriculum" (HC) was coined by Phillip Jackson (1968) to show how social norms and values are transferred to students. These include physical structures, processes such as timetables and learning schedules, socialization rituals, extracurricular activities such as associations and clubs, rules of conduct, assessment, interaction, endorsers and the composition of boards of governors, incentives and sanctions, teachers' delivery of the curriculum, curricular content (including skills, knowledge, theories and models taught and omitted), students' characteristics and reception of learning, and unintended outcomes of learning (Sambell and McDowell, 1998). Since they are implicit, these norms may remain unchallenged by educational stakeholders (Cotton et al., 2013). Participants may experience the HC differently as teachers may reinforce an HC and be unaware. Students may use the HC to gain an advantage over others, including teachers (Baker et al., 2008). The outcome can be behaviors and attitudes that are the opposite of what is intended (Giroux and Penna, 1979). By implicitly supporting particular values and delegitimizing others, business schools create individuals to serve shareholders and not stakeholders.

Biases of organizations and academic disciplines, such as the dominance of western perspectives, communicate the priority types of skills and knowledge that are preferred. Traditional PM education, where there is an overemphasis on tools and techniques drawn from the optimization paradigm, results in limited critical thinking, ethical engagement, and self-reflection. This results in PMs applying pseudo-scientific research (that cannot be falsified or replicated) in decision-making. PMs may have a simplified abstraction of reality and a false perspective that serves organizational and shareholder perspectives over stakeholders. For example, case studies in PM are typically from the perspective of a senior PM and not from a novice or a stakeholder. Similarly, a lack of coverage of institutional and other more expansive frameworks more comprehensive embed stakeholders' views (for example, protestors) as irresponsible or oppositional (for example, NIMBY – not in my backyard) that need to be overcome or bypassed to achieve project outcomes (Van der Horst, 2007).

21.3 PM Educators' Responsibility for Values

More recent work has identified sustainability mindsets, the individual or collectively shared values, beliefs, paradigms, and preferences (Kassel et al., 2018). In management teaching of sustainability, there is an emphasis on facts and statistics to present rational, logical arguments that can be debated, confirmed, or discarded. However, these approaches may, ironically, reduce action by students as sustainability becomes perceived as a corporate capacity and not a personal imperative (Gifford, 2011). Sustainability mindsets, therefore, attempt to incorporate personal meanings and values, a domain that also includes self-awareness. Research seeking to change mindsets from current practices toward approaches that increase social and environmental value encourages ecoliteracy and ecojustice to connect personally with individuals (Kim et al., 2017). Learners develop a cognitive and emotional bond that encourages beneficial action by understanding the ecological basis for economic success. Learners also gain self-awareness, appreciation of alternative perspectives, and language for concepts that may be difficult to articulate. These domains include scientific understanding of social and environmental processes, understanding of connections between social and environmental processes and connecting environmental knowledge to existing knowledge in order to create shared meanings. The sustainability mindset indicator integrates these perspectives (Rimanoczy, 2020).

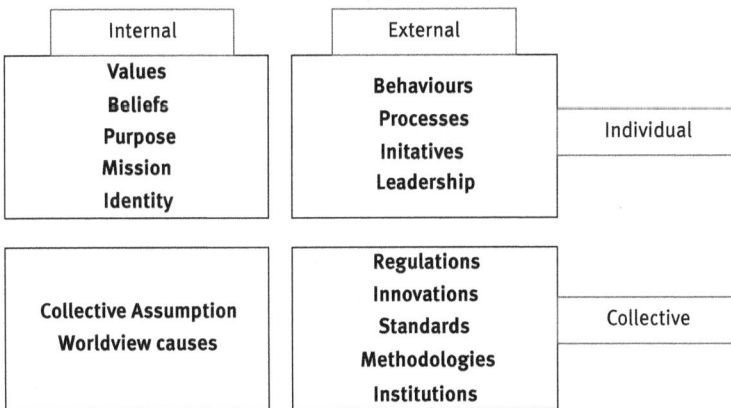

Figure 21.1: Sustainability mindset indicators (adapted from Wilber, 2005).

Regarding sustainability, most PM learning efforts focus on the external aspects, such as the need for new materials and processes, not on the required mindsets and behaviors. Similarly, a significant level of attention is paid to formal regulations, benchmarks, and measures such as the SDGs, which are visible and serve a signaling role for individuals and institutions. Educating responsible project managers requires educators to go beyond explanation to encourage students to reflect on societal needs and the role projects play in exacerbating societal issues or contributing to solutions. PM education should encourage the development of reflective practitioners, which requires the engagement with values that prioritize long-term benefits to stakeholders (Nonaka and Takeuchi, 2011). This suggests that PM educators need to broaden students' perspectives beyond technical domains to improve students' communication, facilitation, and judgment skills. Research suggests that managerial behavior is defined by implicit biases from the host discipline embedded in discipline-specific and organizational self-referential mental frameworks (Giacalone and Promislo, 2013).

While most project managers do not work in the policy domain, they need to appreciate their activities' social, economic, and environmental impacts. Further, unlike the triple bottom line approach (doing good to do well), the individual or citizen perspective on responsible management seeks to encourage behavior based on transformed mindsets, not organizational returns (Anninos and Chytiris, 2012).

Educators can encourage these outcomes by ensuring that values are demonstrated and developed as much as technical competencies. While PM societies have recently made efforts to create and embed ethical frameworks, this work needs to go beyond compliance, moral philosophy and corporate social responsibility. For projects, learning needs to incorporate a deep understanding of the role of projects in realizing the ambitions of funders and shaping societies (Wines, 2008). Since responsible management focuses on the individual, frameworks, codes, rules, and principles can support, but learners need to develop awareness of their own role in shaping project decisions and actions.

21.4 Responsible Project Management Beyond the Classroom

Educational scholarship tends to focus on classroom-based learning. However, knowledge can be acquired at work in broader industry learning networks. Work characteristics such as team-based assessments can be simulated in classroom settings. However, project management requires situation and domain-specific competencies that can only be developed via practice. Table 21.1 summarizes the differences between formal and workplace education.

However, the distinction between work and classroom learning is increasingly becoming blurred with such initiatives as apprenticeships in the UK and workplace project units in the UK and elsewhere (Daly, 2017). In these activities, knowledge can be acquired while conducting work processes such as participation in group activities or receiving feedback on outputs created. Learning can also occur through workplace linked knowledge exchange such as coaching, shadowing or industry conferences. In both scenarios, differing learning approaches can be applied.

Table 21.1: Educational differences: Formal and workplace.

Learning informal education	Learning in the workplace
Intentional (+unintentional)	Unintentional (+intentional)
Structured with formal curriculum, evaluation processes and competency standards	Usually, no formal curriculum or learning outcomes
Mostly uncontextualized	Contextual
Focused on mental activities with a limited tool or process usage	Focused on tool use and mental activities
Produces explicit knowledge and generalized skills	Produces implicit and tacit knowledge and situation-specific competences
Emphasis on teaching and content of teaching	Emphasis on work and experiences based on the learner as a worker
Separation of knowledge and skills	Competences are treated holistically, with no distinction between knowledge and skills.

(Adapted from Tynjälä, 2013)

21.4.1 Experiential Learning

Kolb (Kolb and Kolb, 2005) defined "learning" as "the process whereby knowledge is created through the transformation of experience." Four points were identified at which learning can be initiated:
1) assimilating (abstract conceptualization transformed by reflective observation)
2) converging (abstract conceptualization transformed by active experimentation)
3) accommodating (concrete experience transformed by active experimentation)
4) diverging (concrete experience transformed by reflective observation).

The first can be created in a classroom by the interaction between instructor and student and peer to peer interaction. The others are derived from experiential learning philosophical perspectives, including pragmatist, critical praxis, and embodied (phenomenological) perspectives (Roberts, 2008).

21.4.2 Pragmatist Approach

Pragmatist approaches are commonly used in experiential learning and include field-based learning such as internships, placements, service learning initiatives, and other forms of field-based learning. These are aimed either to understand the project activities of enterprises involved in sustainable activities or to provide

Table 21.2: Approaches to experiential learning (adapted from Roberts, 2008).

Approach to experiential learning	Learning boundary transcended	Example in PM education (classroom)	Example in PM education (workplace)
Pragmatist	Between the classroom and the "real world."	Students working on PM sites, PM internships	Academic guest speaker at workplace explaining a theoretical concept
Critical Praxis	Social structures	Critical praxis among PM faculty with experiences of differing perspectives	Peer discussion, mentoring or coaching with employees with differing perspectives.
Embodied	The situation of one's corporeality	Volunteering in a community affected by a project	

consulting assistance to host companies responding to societal needs. Pragmatist approaches begin with cognitively acquired information from academic research concepts and principles. This cognitive knowledge is then examined via interaction with stakeholders who support learners in applying, internalizing or debating concepts. In this approach, the barriers separating structured classroom learning from "real world" experiences are removed to create a learning space that facilitates interaction with relevant others (Kickul et al., 2010). There are challenges with this approach as students may not be prepared for a critical assessment of their participation and impacts, particularly in terms of issues related to guiding values and ethics to be reflected in their work. Academic knowledge and training may not prepare students to question potentially inaccurate and deleterious assumptions about sustainability (environmental and social) models and ethical practices and how these could be reflected in their work. Pragmatist approaches tend to understand social relations through relatively conventional and dominant perspectives, often assuming relatively deterministic harmonious processes and outcomes among different stakeholders (win-win).

21.4.3 Critical Praxis Approach

The critical perspective identifies structural or systemic factors through which specific individuals suffer social inequality (Roberts, 2008). Through reflection, learners with direct experience develop a critical consciousness about their experience and then engage in a subsequent dialogue with those without experience to act on their world and transform it. Critical praxis approaches cross social structure boundaries, not classroom boundaries. Many business students might have limited experience with inequality or climate-related disruption, so it may be challenging to implement this approach in the classroom (Paton et al., 2012). However, international academics and students with these experiences could dialogue to support these debates. These areas could include recognizing how conventional project management models and educational approaches are often inconsistent with the realities of implementing sustainability in projects. An example may be the focus on project management success (time, cost, and quality), a temporal frame that ignores wider project success that could incorporate aspects of societal value. Reflection among educators is also required to identify how dominant project management perspectives often legitimize both the power relations among various countries (via domination of publications from western, developed countries) and the social order reflected in these power relations (Ly, 2020).

21.4.4 Embodied Approach

Experiential learning approaches begin with experiences that can invoke deeply affecting emotional responses. Individuals can integrate these emotions into their understanding of critical social issues, which can help direct learners' subsequent behavior toward positive ends (Kolb, 1984). Embodied approaches are distinguished from the previous two by their initial focus on emotional learning when individuals experience different contexts outside their life norms. In this way, they open themselves to new learning through emotional responses to novel situations. This approach often involves removing self from daily life to connect with climate-related disruption, poverty, or inequality. Concrete visceral and emotional learning serves in the development of empathy and the enactment of care toward other human beings, including those who might typically be seen as different from us or distant from us. Therefore, the greater the level of caring knowledge developed through emotional responses to diverse human experiences, and the greater our level of caring imagination about how fellow human beings might also suffer in similar situations, the more able individuals are to exhibit social forms of caring that are responsive to the suffering or needs of others. Embodied approaches to experiential learning might also evoke negative emotions such as anxiety, which can constrain learning if not managed carefully. Carefully applied, however, project managers can enhance their sensitivity toward and understanding of those experiencing poverty and other social issues.

In other approaches, learners are exposed to narratives about the experiences of various individuals living with climate disruption, poverty and inequality. Learners can reflect on the content to develop a nuanced understanding of these issues and critically appraise others' perspectives on these issues. The knowledge gained from exposure to these narratives is limited, and learners should not assume that they fully understand these differing perspectives (Lehtonen et al., 2019).

21.5 Threshold Concepts in PM Education

In many disciplines, it has been proposed that there are threshold concepts that have particular characteristics (Meyer & Land, 2003). These concepts provide new knowledge to the learner and transform mindsets or paradigms and act to recreate, reconfigure and transform an individual learner's identity within a given academic discipline. Threshold concepts have been applied in several educational domains such as social sciences, engineering, medical and economic professions. Threshold concepts have five characteristics. The first is that they are transformative. In other words, they change the personal or professional views in a given academic domain, such as project management. They are irreversible; once knowledge is acquired, it cannot be removed, reversed, ignored or forgotten. Once a threshold has been crossed, the academic learner can no longer return to a previous lower, simpler state. They are integrative. They enable the creation of new associations among existing knowledge in a given academic domain. They are bounded; in other words, they set limits or boundaries. Concepts may also identify relationships among other threshold concepts. It is best to conceptualize them as a knowledge network of concepts that link theory and practice. Last but not least, threshold concepts are troublesome; there are tensions and paradoxes. For learners, they may even seem counter-intuitive.

To have a transformative impact, threshold concepts need to be linked to provide learners with an overview of the knowledge domain (Wright and Gilmore, 2012), showing not just concepts but the relationships among them. In this way, learners can develop an organizing schema of concepts, connections, and relationships that support the development of disciplinary thought (Barradell and Kennedy-Jones, 2015). For project management, we have identified these concepts as systems thinking, anticipatory thinking, and uncertainty thinking.

21.5.1 Systems Thinking

Systems thinking encourages examining projects as a whole and not just as discrete units of processes and activities. This approach examines the dynamics of systems behavioral change, the overall structure and relationships among systems elements, collaboration and interactions among elements and the external environment and the emergence of new behaviors from the interaction. It is seen as an exemplary threshold concept as it provides a new perspective on domains such as project management, changing the learner's understanding. Systems thinking encourages learning from a holistic perspective which can complement reductionist learning in other course domains. Systems thinking models scenarios as interconnected, nested, and connected sociotechnical entities where outcomes are not easily predictable by analyzing the individual actions of these entities. Systems can exist at multiple scales (micro and macro) and domains (social, resource, information) with components, interdependencies, interactions and purpose or logic. The perspective provides approaches to examine complex problems, including sensemaking, terms and methodologies.

For projects, systems thinking supports engagement with sustainability, social value, and ethics, influencing multiple dimensions in projects. Project learners can move from examining project activities as individual components and projects as isolated phenomena to considering the structure and intra- and interproject-environment connections. A systems perspective can provide project management students to develop:

The ability to recognize system-level properties that result from dynamic interactions among human, nonhuman and social systems and how they affect the relationships among individuals, groups, projects(programs or portfolios), organizations, communities, and environments.

1. Identify unintended consequences produced by changes made to a project system.
2. The ability to identify feedback loops and "stocks and flows" within a project, program, or portfolio.
3. The ability to identify subsystems (e.g., individuals, social networks, organizations, geographical environments and social communities) within overall systems.
4. Assess the strengths and weaknesses of applying the systems approach to project management.

In existing project management learning, students are generally encouraged to define projects using decomposition approaches and a linear temporal approach in which ideas are generated and evaluated and, either using a deterministic or an incremental approach, developed into final products. However, sustainability and social value create issues of both boundary specification (which entities should be considered) and complexity.

Projects can have structural complexity, that is, several interdependent elements, including human and nonhuman resources (Geraldi et al., 2019). The former gives rise to socio-political complexity where project managers must harmonize different stakeholder perspectives and where a project is required to unite different interests, agendas, or opinions. An application known as soft systems methodology (SSM) has been applied to understand the evolving nature of stakeholders in complex projects (Aramo-Immonen and Vanharanta, 2009). SSM also applies tools to support sensemaking, such as the "rich picture," which enables the examination of a problem from the perspective of multiple stakeholders, which can support the later requirements management process (Niu et al., 2011).

Under these conditions, students need to understand issues holistically to identify systems, subsystems, participating entities, and their relationships (Checkland, 1999). Students also appreciate the challenges of integrating systems, which is critical for understanding how collaboration may occur across different organizations required to enact sustainability. Systems thinking acknowledges that decisions must be made without perfect access to information, with time constraints and cognitive constraints (biases). Systems thinking also enables students to appreciate causality, from simple associations to understanding complex counterfactual (what if) relationships. Finally, students gain an appreciation of the limits of models and frameworks. Too often, time models such as schedules are treated as definitive when they can be incomplete. Recognition of these limitations can be valuable for students to apply theory to practice. For project management and sustainability, learners can engage with the nature and interconnections among environmental, industrial and societal systems (Fiksel, 2012).

21.5.2 Anticipatory Thinking

Anticipatory thinking is the cognitive process that an individual may use when preparing for the future (Geden et al., 2019). Individuals may deliberately consider a range of possible futures and the pathway to achieving them. Anticipatory thinking can be distinguished from prediction as it seeks to identify indicators that could lead to possible futures and not future events or variable states. Anticipatory thinking has three forms: prospective branching, backcasting, and retrospective branching (Figure 21.1). Prospective branching involves envisioning the future states of a given system and identifying qualitative and quantitative indicators for these future states. Backcasting involves analyzing a single future system state and working backward to identify qualitative and quantitative indicators of activities that could lead to that future system state. Finally, retrospective branching identifies unknown past system states and their development pathways that would lead to the current system state (Geden et al., 2019. Examples of these forms of anticipatory thinking are presented in Figure 21.2.

Prospective Branching	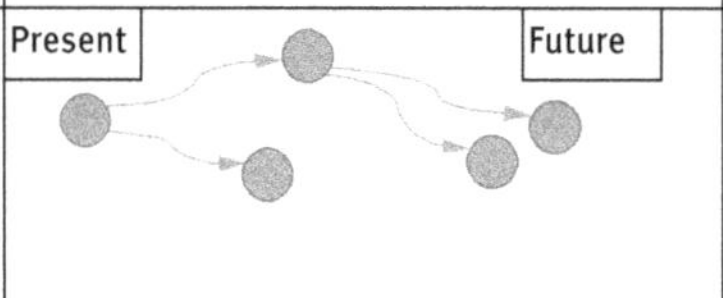 Present · · · Future	Anticipating labour availability for the construction stage of a project
Backcasting	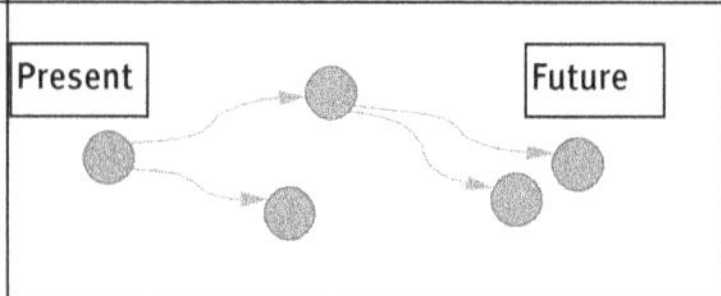 Present · · · Future	Anticipating paths to implement information systems in an organisation
Retrospective Branching	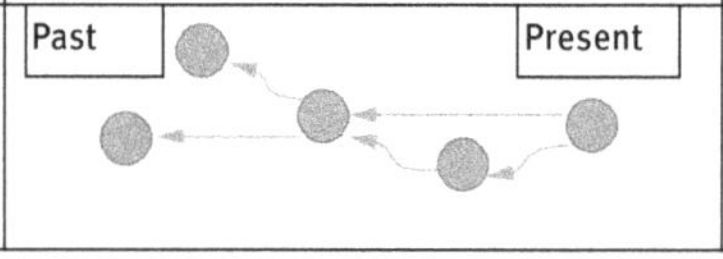 Past · · · Present	Identifying indicators of project delays for lessons learnt.

Figure 21.2: Forms of anticipatory thinking (adapted from Geden et al., 2019).

Anticipatory thinking requires recognizing a situation based on cues obtained from experience, extrapolation to a range of future or past system states, and constructing an imagined system based on the available evidence (McLennan et al., 2009). Identifying anticipatory thinking is difficult as the process does not produce visible outputs. The process, however, can complement systems thinking efforts by encouraging engagement with temporal patterns of activity, which are valuable for projects.

21.5.3 Uncertainty Thinking

Projects, program and portfolio participants, and stakeholders experience significant uncertainty (variability and ambiguity) throughout their duration (Ward and Chapman, 2003). Ambiguity may be highest at the early stage of the project, while variability may be associated with estimation, design, and stakeholder priorities. Specifically, there may be variability associated with estimates which could be related to

- Lack of clear requirements
- Nature of assumptions underpinning estimates
- Biases of estimators
- Novelty of activity
- Complexity of activity
- The possible occurrence of events, circumstances and circumstances
- Impact of unknown knowns and "unknown unknowns."

Uncertainty also has a relational dimension as the interaction of multiple stakeholders in a complex project system can result in emergent uncertainties that influence project characteristics:

- Relationships among stakeholders
- Objectives
- Priorities
- Perceptions of roles and responsibilities

An uncertainty approach encourages learners to go beyond the risk management focus on threats to identify sources of variability and ambiguity. This approach will identify these domains as well as processes of clarification as well as response. This encourages a response based on systems theory and anticipatory thinking in which possible futures based on the resolution of uncertainty are imagined, and the path to these futures is understood. A related issue would be identifying possible variability of metrics encouraging learners to report unitary metrics and the probability distribution associated with the estimate.

21.6 Case Study

This case is based on a research project exploring the competencies and behaviors required for responsible project management (e.g., threshold concepts, dispositions, skills, perspectives, and social practices) and how scenario-based online learning can be developed. An abductive approach was used to design educational events with a project scenario. Participants were project management students, educators, and project professionals recruited using the responsible project management (RPM) network.

By the end of each event, a participant was expected to be able to:

A. Understand the economic impact on a project of decisions made during the initiation and design phase of the business case
B. Analyze the social impact of a project on communities and broader society during the build and implementation phases
C. Appreciate the environmental impact on natural resources and biodiversity locally and remotely, and demonstrate awareness of social-ecological integrity

21.6.1 Scenario Background

The objective of this scenario is to explore the use of LSP to help us understand the underlying assumptions we make when planning an IT project that requires a responsible and sustainable approach, with particular emphasis on **systems thinking**. Collaborative, physical activity systems like LSP help visualize individual decision-making, internal arguments and decisions, set priorities and ground our decisions on particular foundations, among other things. Visualization techniques can also help identify thought processes, share them with others and collaborate on refining, adapting, or changing approaches.

The project brief concerned the fictitious creation of a virtual reality (VR) experience that simulates how Stonehenge may have appeared circa 2200 BCE. Stonehenge is a sensitive site for a range of reasons explored in brief, and such a project would call for collaboration with a range of stakeholders, some with quite different views.

21.6.2 Scenario Context

Stonehenge is part of the "Stonehenge, Avebury and Associated Sites" UNESCO World Heritage Site. It is located in Wiltshire in southern England, OS Grid Ref SU 123 422. The site of Stonehenge itself is owned and managed by English Heritage (EH), while the surrounding land and other monuments such as The Cursus, Woodhenge, and many Bronze Age burial mounds are owned by the National Trust (NT). The visitor center is approximately 1.5 miles away from Stonehenge, and visitors can access the stones by walking or taking a free shuttle bus from the Stonehenge Visitor Centre (SVC). The SVC is owned and run by EH.

The site attracts approximately 1.3 million visitors per year, many overseas on guided tours, especially in the summer.

We see at Stonehenge today what remains of the last phase of a monument that changed significantly over approximately 800 years. It began as a cemetery site consisting of 56 chalk pits that contained cremation burials. The bluestones were brought from the Preseli Mountains in South Wales, but their precise location at Stonehenge is still unclear. Over several hundred years, the stones were moved to form different arrangements, until around 2500 BCE, the large sarsen stones were brought from the Marlborough Downs, and the configuration of Stonehenge we see today was constructed over subsequent years.

The learners formed part of a team commissioned to design and create a VR simulation of Stonehenge as it is understood to have looked circa 2200 BCE. There is no way to precisely tell Stonehenge looked at any particular time in the past, so the simulation aimed to create a plausible model that can help visitors have a sensory experience of elements of the monument that is not possible today. This experience will include standing inside the completed outer circle, getting a feel for the size and arrangement of the trilithons (the five large three-stone arrangements in the center), and walking around the broader ritual landscape in which Stonehenge is situated. The VR simulation will include part of the broader landscape, an essential context for visitors to virtual Stonehenge. English Heritage wants to create an online, remotely accessible VR experience for this exercise. They have five specific target audiences in mind, viz:

1. Potential visitors to Stonehenge from anywhere in the world. The VR experience would act as a primer to inform visitors about the monument and the ritual landscape in which it is situated, enabling them to get the most from their physical visit.
2. Visitors who have already been to Stonehenge and want to explore its history further and/or had insufficient time to explore the surrounding landscape when they visited, for example.
3. For example, people would like to visit Stonehenge but cannot due to disability, caring responsibility, distance, or cost.
4. As an educational experience for school, college, and university students
5. Groups who consider Stonehenge a sacred/spiritual site wish to experience how it may have felt to be there in the distant past.

Their specific role was the responsibility for managing the project, and the exercise they were involved in was the scoping exercise that occurs at the beginning of a project such as this, with a particular emphasis on systems thinking. Their task was to model one of the systems that would need to be considered when scoping such a simulation using Lego Serious Play (LSP), paying particular attention to issues from an RPM perspective. These systems could include:

1. The system to involve stakeholders and interested parties in the scoping exercise
2. A model of the VR simulation as a system, including hardware and potential users and how they interact
3. The system to incorporate sustainability (e.g., energy usage, lifespan models) and environmental issues in the scoping exercise

Their task was to develop an outline scope for such a simulation, paying particular attention to issues that they could anticipate may arise from an RPM perspective, such as:

- the natural environment
- effects on visitor behavior
- societal inclusion/exclusion, e.g., access to IT equipment
- educational value
- how people are physically represented by their avatars

The participants were divided into two teams, approximately five members. One of those teams will work on systems thinking using LSP, and one will work on anticipatory thinking using Ketso Connect.

Table 21.3: Specific timings for the LSP team.

Timing (length of time)	Activities
09:00–09:30	Introduction in a plenary room: – Participant and tutor introductions – Discussion of RPM: benefits to people, planet, and prosperity over short-, medium-, and long term – Introduce extended and sustainable life cycles (each group to choose which they use) – Recap of the scenario being used for this event
09:30–10:00	Breakout into teams to discuss how to approach the first exercise: – Decide on the system your team will be working on – Recap the meaning of systems thinking for this event – Discuss the approach to Exercise 1 and ensure all team members are clear about the task.

Table 21.3 (continued)

Timing (length of time)	Activities
10:00–11:00	Team participants build models offline: – Individual team members go offline and create their first model
11:00–11:15	Coffee break
11:15–12:30	The team meets online to share individual models and form a first-team view.
12:30–13:15	Lunch
13:15–14:00	LSP group presents to Ketso group and vice versa
14:00–14:15	The team meets to discuss how your thinking has been affected by the Ketso team's discussion and plan your approach to Exercise 2.
14:15–15:00	Team participants build models offline: – Individual team members go offline and create their second model
15:00–15:15	Tea break
15:15–16:15	The team meets online to share individual models and form a second team view
16:15–16:45	Plenary to share Lego summaries and Ketso summaries of work for the day
16:45–17:00	Round-up and finish.

For participants, involvement in the workshop provided an opportunity to visualize systems that supported sensemaking. By exchanging perspectives with another group, participants could incorporate ideas that supported them in refining and explaining their concepts. All participants also met to discuss how the activity influenced their overall thinking about sustainability.

The transformation of PM education to embrace real-world systems should emphasize the development of values and shareholder and stakeholder value. From a pedagogy perspective, this suggests the adoption of pedagogical approaches such as active learning, progressive inquiry and developing a perspective for PM education based on the unique characteristics of project management as well as the societal priorities of the context in which they are embedded, collaborating with other domains seeking to address grand societal challenges. These approaches can include experiential learning perspectives like the approach presented in this case study. The second case study presents how learners can co-create outputs using a critical praxis approach that goes beyond changing perspectives to address societal needs.

21.6.3 Case Study 2 Critical Praxis Approach

This project was a submission to the 2020 IBM Call for Code global challenge run in partnership with the Clinton Global Initiative. The team's project Lupe was designed to support the logistics of food distribution during Covid lockdowns. The blockchain system aimed to integrate residents, commercial providers, and third sector organizations. *During the 2020 lockdowns due to the Covid-19 pandemic,* food bank usage in the UK increased by 81% due to increased job losses. The Lupe platform was designed to connect community food stakeholders as a point of contact during the pandemic to meet this challenge.

Lupe utilizes blockchain technology to help reduce the information asymmetries that can exist with community food distribution. The system was designed to help participants identify food that would be wasted if not used quickly and share that information with those in need. Community organizations can then signal their interest via the system and obtain the necessary food items.

The application utilized the blockchain to demonstrate the potential of this technology for providing community solutions that address social issues. Blockchains have been used for verification in commercial product supply chains such as those managed by large retailers. In a blockchain system, stakeholders share all transactions on a shared ledger which provides witnessing and verifying transactions. For food, these transactions can ensure that the origins, composition and quality standards for the item were met.

IBM's Hyperledger software which provides data access to authorized participants was utilized to create the transaction management infrastructure for obtaining food. The benefit of the blockchain in this area is that it provides traceability into the ownership and participants in food transfers. Participants who were entering supplies were also able to add additional metadata to support decision-making, such as expiry dates, so that food with a limited shelf life could be used quickly.

User stories were created for businesses, charities, and individuals and the initial functionality was driven by their requirements. Users were provided with the ability to create, read, update, search, and order entries. Community commercials, individuals, and charity participants would be able to upload information about food items including quantities, ingredients (including allergens), and location. Lupe provided the functionality for businesses to automatically transfer food items that could not be sold in time to community organizations.

Once the application was created, it entered was then further developed using an agile project management approach. The team worked with industry partners to test the system and obtain feedback. Each deployment was seen as an interaction, and feedback was obtained via quantitative feedback surveys given to key community food industry stakeholders who worked in customer-facing and logistics roles.

The feedback indicated that sharing the community's food resources between businesses that were open and those that were closed was beneficial. Stakeholder feedback also indicated a demand for a community food-sharing solution that could reduce food waste while addressing the needs of residents. Participants found the application to be user friendly and the ability to search by local area was also helpful as the UK shifted from national to localized lockdowns.

Commercial providers found that the application could enhance their relationship with local charities, helping them meet their responsibilities to the local community. By automating the process of sharing excess food, Lupe provided the potential to increase food donations by commercial organizations. Finally, the local community use of blockchain reduced the delays that can happen in larger systems. Future Lupe systems can be deployed as small localized instances, reducing latency and benefiting from community cohesion since many participants would be familiar with each other.

This project provided the opportunity for students to demonstrate technical skills and gain empathy and insight into structural social issues in the community. For the former, the students created a blockchain app that integrated user research (qualitative and quantitative), programming skills, and project management skills to deploy and iterate. For the latter, the students gained an appreciation of community issues which included the need for a simple app to reach community members without digital skills. The application, Lupe also demonstrated the potential for an emerging technology (blockchain) to facilitate the development of community social capital, creating new relationships between commercial food providers, charities, and individuals. In this way, the technology facilities the enactment of community responsibility and demonstrates the potential for projects to create beneficial outcomes for stakeholders.

21.7 Building Blocks of Principles Based Responsible Project Management Education

The examples illustrate approaches that educators have used to engage learners with responsibility. Project management practice has been encoded by professional bodies in formal bodies of knowledge since the 1960s. These formal documents still exert a strong influence on practice and qualifications in the field today. Accordingly, project management education tends to be based on knowledge-driven and competencies expressed in terms of knowledge and its application. In contrast, Responsible Management literature proposes a competence portfolio comprising six types of competence – knowledge, analysis, action, social interactions, character, and self-adaptation (Laasch and Moosmayer, 2015). In this way, sustainability challenges conventional approaches to education that are based on the notion of knowledge transfer. The sustainability mindset incorporates all six types of competence in twelve principles that are grouped into four dimensions – ecological worldview, systems perspective, spiritual intelligence and emotional intelligence (Kassel et al, 2018). Moving away from emphasis on declarative knowledge, PMI recently specified a system for value delivery and twelve principles as the standard for project management (PMI, 2021). Bringing principles to the fore provides an opportunity to redefine education in ways that develop the individual rather than simply transfer knowledge.

Action reflection learning (ARL) was originally developed in the 1970s and has been coded as a framework for educators. Key features of ARL adopted for responsible management education (Rimanoczy, 2020) that are relevant for PM education include:

- Social learning using activities that encourage learners to identify their tacit knowledge and connect with the knowledge of others
- Self-awareness and reflection
- Systems perspective that emphasizes interconnectedness throughout
- Paradigm change that challenge assumptions and mental models
- Integrative activities that combine physical, emotional, intellectual, and spiritual dimensions.

A principles-based framework for responsible management education might be developed using the principles from sustainability mindset and PMI, as shown in Table 21.4

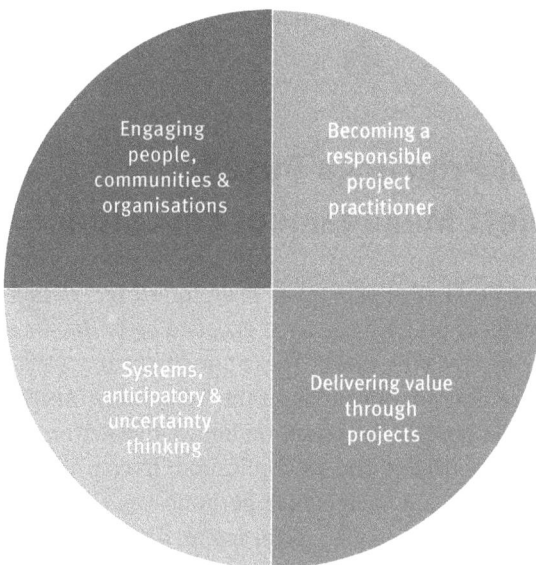

Figure 21.3: Principles of responsible project practitioners.

Table 21.4: Principle-based PM summary (authors).

	RPM Principles	**Sustainability mindset principles**	**Project management institute principles**
Becoming a responsible project practitioner	Awareness Curiosity Stewardship	My contribution Reflection Self-awareness Mindfulness	Stewardship Adaptability and resilience
Delivering value through projects	Purpose Creativity Balance	Purpose Long-term thinking Creative innovation	Value Leadership Tailoring Quality Change
Systems, anticipatory and uncertainty thinking	Awareness Uncertainty Anticipation	Ecoliteracy Both + and thinking Flow in cycles Oneness with nature	Systems thinking Complexity Risk
Engaging people, communities, and organizations	Engagement Transparency	Interconnection	Team Stakeholders

An RPM curriculum that incorporates principles of responsible management would include the perspectives described earlier environmental sustainability, social sustainability, and business ethics education (Laasch and Moosmayer, 2015). This also suggests that a large-scale rethinking of project management courses is required. Table 21.3 presents how the content from the RPM handbook could be used to support such a curriculum. It adopts the building block approach created by the "Rethinking Economics" group (www. Rethinking Economics.com) to identify concepts that can be incorporated into existing courses or standalone units in their own right, along with supporting chapters from the RPM handbook.

Table 21.5: Building blocks RPM education (authors).

Building block	Description	Sustainability	Social sustainability	Ethics	RPM handbook chapter
Project value and values	Origins and development of the field Understanding the rationale for projects, the beneficial and negative outcomes, and the process of starting a project	Basics of environmental sustainability in projects. Identifying potential environmental impacts and assessment criteria for project conceptualization, business cases	Basics of social sustainability in projects Identifying potential social impacts and assessment criteria for business case	Identify the basics of societal responsibility for PMs	Morality and spirituality, climate change, and intro to RPM Responsible value chain Responsible organizing
Project frameworks and project cycles	Understanding the path of development of project initiatives. Understanding the major paradigms of project management	Identify how differing approaches (agile/incremental/planned) may incorporate environmental sustainability.	Identify how differing approaches (agile/incremental/planned) may incorporate social sustainability.	Identify ethical influences on project governance	Responsible value chain. project governance
Project controls	Understanding systems for defining, monitoring and reporting project activities	Identify how environmental sustainability impacts can be monitored in project controls.	Identify how social value impacts can be monitored in project controls.		Responsible organizing
Project people (group perspectives)	Personal perspectives, understanding and leading the stakeholders, shareholders, and participants in projects	Stakeholder inclusion for environmental sustainability	Stakeholder inclusion for social value/sustainability	Understand personal values of yourself and others	Responsible leadership, morality and spirituality

Project outputs and outcomes	Understanding the benefits realization process, outputs and outcomes of projects along with the short- and long-term effects	Identify short and long-term environmental benefits from projects	Identify short and long-term social benefits from projects, stakeholder collaboration for benefits realization	Identifying potential ethical concerns and dilemmas with project outputs and outcomes	Responsible Value chain
Project societal systems	Understanding so projects impacts on societal systems	Understanding.	Understanding project impacts on the community of place and community of interest	Sensitivity to social challenges of projects	Project governance
Project narratives and communication	Understanding the interactions and processes of information exchange in projects			Ethics and transparency in communication	Project communications
Project uncertainty	Understanding the nature of ambiguities and uncertainties in projects				Responsible PM organizing
Project learning, analysis and evaluation	Understanding ethical approaches for project analysis and learning from project initiatives and project participants	Approaches for identifying and analyzing environmental impact information	Approaches for identifying and analyzing social impact information	Ethics of research and evaluation	Responsible competency development
Project innovation and Transformation	Change management projects, organizational development projects, major and megaprojects (society level change)			Ethics and change management initiatives	Responsible leadership

References

Anninos, L. N., & Chytiris, L. S. (2012). The sustainable management vision for excellence: Implications for business education. *International Journal of Quality and Service Sciences*.

Aramo-Immonen, H., & Vanharanta, H. (2009). Project management: The task of holistic systems thinking. *Human Factors and Ergonomics in Manufacturing & Service Industries, 19*(6), 582–600.

Baker, R., Walonoski, J., Heffernan, N., Roll, I., Corbett, A., & Koedinger, K. (2008). Why students engage in "gaming the system" behavior in interactive learning environments. *Journal of Interactive Learning Research, 19*(2), 185–224.

Barradell, S., & Kennedy-Jones, M. (2015). Threshold concepts, student learning and curriculum: Making connections between theory and practice. *Innovations in Education and Teaching International, 52*(5), 536–545.

Blasco, M. (2012). Aligning the hidden curriculum of management education with PRME: An inquiry-based framework. *Journal of Management Education, 36*(3), 364–388.

Checkland, P. 1999. Soft systems methodology: a 30-year retrospective. Chichester, UK: Wiley.

Checkland, P. (2000). Soft systems methodology: A thirty-year retrospective. *Systems Research and Behavioral Science, 17*(S1), S11–S58.

Cotton, D., Winter, J., & Bailey, I. (2013). Researching the hidden curriculum: Intentional and unintended messages. *Journal of Geography in Higher Education, 37*(2), 192–203.

Daly, P. (2017). Business apprenticeship: A viable business model in management education. *Journal of Management Development*.

Dewey, J. (1963). *Experience and Education*. New York: Macmillan.

Fiksel, J. (2012). A systems view of sustainability: The triple value model. *Environmental Development, 2*, 138–141.

Geden, M., Smith, A., Campbell, J., Spain, R., Amos-Binks, A., Mott, B., . . . Lester, J. (2019). Construction and validation of an anticipatory thinking assessment. *Frontiers in Psychology, 10*, 2749.

Geraldi, J., Oehmen, J., Thuesen, C., & Ruiz, P. P. (2019). Organisation and Systems Theory Toolset. In *Evolving Toolbox for Complex Project Management* (pp. 133–151). Auerbach Publications.

Ghoshal, S. (2005). Bad management theories are destroying good management practices. *Academy of Management Learning & Education, 4*(1), 75–91.

Giacalone, R. A., & Promislo, M. D. (2013). Broken when entering: The stigmatisation of goodness and business ethics education. *Academy of Management Learning & Education, 12*(1), 86–101.

Gifford, R. (2011). The dragons of inaction: Psychological barriers that limit climate change mitigation and adaptation. *American Psychologist, 66*(4), 290.

Giroux, H. A., & Penna, A. N. (1979). Social education in the classroom: The dynamics of the hidden curriculum. *Theory & Research in Social Education, 7*(1), 21–42.

Jackson, P. (1968). *Life in Classrooms*. New York: Holt, Rinehart 8c Winston, Inc.

Kassel, K., Rimanoczy, I., & Mitchell, S. F. (2018). A sustainability mindset model for management education. In *Developing a Sustainability Mindset in Management Education* (pp. 3–37). Routledge.

Kickul, J., Griffiths, M., & Bacq, S. (2010). The boundary-less classroom: Extending social innovation and impact learning to the field. *Journal of Small Business and Enterprise Development*.

Kim, G., Vaswani, R. T., Kang, W., Nam, M., & Lee, D. (2017). Enhancing ecoliteracy through traditional ecological knowledge in proverbs. *Sustainability, 9*(7), 1182.

Klein, G., Snowdon, D., & Pin, C. L. (2007) Anticipatory thinking. In Mosier, K., & Fischer, U. (eds) *Proceedings of the Eighth International NDM Conference*. Pacific Grove, CA, June 2007.

Kolb, D. A. (1984). *Experiential Learning: Experience as the Source of Learning and Development*. Englewood Cliffs, NJ: Prentice-Hall, Inc.

Kolb, A. Y., & Kolb, D. A. (2005). Learning styles and learning spaces: Enhancing experiential learning in higher education. *Academy of Management Learning & Education*, 4(2), 193–212.

Laasch, O., & Moosmayer, D. C. (2015). Responsible management learning: Reflecting on the role and use of paradigms in sustainability, responsibility, ethics research. CRME Working Papers, 1(1), 1–35.

Lehtonen, A., Salonen, A. O., & Cantell, H. (2019). Climate change education: A new approach for a world of wicked problems. In *Sustainability, Human Well-being, and the Future of Education* (pp. 339–374). Cham: Palgrave Macmillan.

Ly, N. B. (2020). Cultural influences on leadership: Western-dominated leadership and non-western conceptualisations of leadership. *Sociology and Anthropology*, 8(1), 1–12.

McLennan, J., Elliot, G., & Holgate, A. (2009). Anticipatory thinking and managing complex tasks: Wildfire fighting safety and effectiveness. In Proceedings of the Industrial & Organisational Psychology Conference (pp. 90–95).

Meyer, J., & Land, R. (2003). *Threshold Concepts and Troublesome Knowledge: Linkages to Ways of Thinking and Practising within the Disciplines* (pp. 412–424). Edinburgh: University of Edinburgh.

Niu, N., Lopez, A. Y., & Cheng, J. R. (2011). Using soft systems methodology to improve requirements practices: An exploratory case study. *IET Software*, 5(6), 487–495.

Nonaka, I., & Takeuchi, H. (2011). The wise leader. *Harvard Business Review*, 89(5), 58–67.

Paton, B., Harris-Boundy, J., & Melhus, P. (2012). Integrating global poverty into mainstream business classrooms. *Journal of Teaching in International Business*, 23(1), 4–23.

Pfeffer, J. (2009). Renaissance and renewal in management studies: Relevance regained. *European Management Review*, 6(3), 141–148.

Rimanoczy, I. (2020). The Sustainability Mindset Principles: A Guide to Develop a Mindset for a Better World (1st ed.). Routledge. London https://doi.org/10.4324/9781003095637

Roberts, J. (2008). From experience to neo-experiential education: Variations on a theme. *Journal of Experiential Education*, 31(1), 19–35.

Sambell, K., & McDowell, L. (1998). The construction of the hidden curriculum: Messages and meanings in the assessment of student learning. *Assessment & Evaluation in Higher Education*, 23(4), 391–402.

Tynjälä, P. (2013). Toward a 3-P model of workplace learning: A literature review. *Vocations and Learning*, 6(1), 11–36.

Van der Horst, D. (2007). NIMBY or not? Exploring the relevance of location and the politics of voiced opinions in renewable energy siting controversies. *Energy Policy*, 35(5), 2705–2714.

Ward, S., & Chapman, C. (2003). Transforming project risk management into project uncertainty management. *International Journal of Project Management*, 21(2), 97–105.

Wilber, K. (2005). Introduction to integral theory and practice. *AQAL: Journal of Integral Theory and Practice*, 1(1), 2–38.

Wines, W. A. (2008). Seven pillars of business ethics: Toward a comprehensive framework. *Journal of Business Ethics*, 79(4), 483–499.

Wright, A. L., & Gilmore, A. (2012). Threshold concepts and conceptions: Student learning in introductory management courses. *Journal of Management Education*, 36(5), 614–635.

List of Figures

https://doi.org/10.1515/9783110724783-027

List of Tables

https://doi.org/10.1515/9783110724783-028

Index

https://doi.org/10.1515/9783110724783-029

www.ingramcontent.com/pod-product-compliance
Lightning Source LLC
Chambersburg PA
CBHW072008230326
41598CB00082B/6850